Guide to IFPS®

Guide to IFPS®

(Interactive Financial Planning System)

Second Edition

PAUL GRAY

Claremont Graduate School

McGraw-Hill Book Company

New York St. Louis San Francisco Auckland Bogotá Hamburg London Madrid Mexico Milan Montreal New Delhi Panama Paris São Paulo Singapore Sydney Tokyo Toronto

GUIDE TO IFPS (INTERACTIVE FINANCIAL PLANNING SYSTEM)
INTERNATIONAL EDITION

1 2 3 4 5 6 7 8 9 9 0 SEPFCP 8 9 4 3 2 1 0 9

The editors were Gerald A. Gleason and Joseph F. Murphy.

Library of Congress Cataloging-in-Publication Data
Gray, Paul. (date)
Guide to IFPS (Interactive Financial Planning System)
Rev. ed. of: Student guide to IFPS (Interactive Financial Planning System). 1983.
Bibliography: p.
Includes index.
1. IFPS (Computer system) I. Gray, Paul, 1930 —
Student guide to IFPS (Interactive Financial Planning System) II. Title.
HG4012.5.G7 1987 658.1'5'02855329 86-21514
ISBN 0-07-024394-8

When ordering this title use ISBN 0-07-100519-6

Printed in Singapore.

CONTENTS

PREFACE

The Interactive Financial Planning System (abbreviated IFPS) was originally developed in the early 1970's by Dr. Gerald R. Wagner (at that time a professor at The University of Texas at Austin) and his students. Its original impetus came from the desire to model risk in a way which could easily be understood by executives. The implementation which resulted proved to be a general purpose financial planning language that is particularly "user friendly." In the years since then, IFPS has been developed further and marketed by EXECUCOM Systems Corporation of Austin, Texas, and has been widely adopted in both industry and universities.

The purpose of this book is to provide a way for both students and professionals to learn the IFPS language. The book is intended for both the beginner and the experienced user. The beginner can learn the language by following the text and its many examples step by step. The more experienced user will find many new uses for the capabilities of the language.

In writing this book we have assumed that the reader has access to IFPS at a computer terminal. We also assume that the reader is either a student or a professional in business, engineering, economics, computer science, information science, or related field (or is currently working in some area of business). We have tried to make the book accessible even to the novice with no prior computer experience by starting with the elementary operations of getting on and off the computer. The examples shown use ordinary English names (such as INVESTMENT, SALES, INCOME) rather than abstract symbols. Mathematical concepts are explained as they are needed.

This book is an outgrowth of using IFPS at Southern Methodist University and at The Claremont Graduate School. When IFPS is introduced (rather than a conventional programming language such as BASIC), students learn much more quickly and easily and use IFPS directly in their work. The dissemination of the language through the University becomes student-driven; that is, the students start using IFPS in many of their classes and faculty begin learning the language to keep up with their students.

IFPS Versions

This book is based on release 2.0 of IFPS/PLUS. This release combines Release 10.0 of IFPS and IFPS/DIMENSION. The information in the book should be fully compatible with later versions as they are issued. The book can also be used with implementations of Release 10.0 or later that do not incorporate DIMENSION and with implementations on some minicomputers that provide a subset of IFPS that does not have the simulation capabilities discussed in Chapter V.

A number of mainframe software packages compatible with these releases of IFPS are available. The packages include:

- IFPS/SENTRY for data entry in a form directly compatible with IFPS.
- IFPS/DATASPAN for converting data bases in arbitrary format to a form directly usable by IFPS.

- IFPS/GRAPHICS for presenting IFPS results on color graphics displays.
- IFPS/OPTIMUM for finding optimal solutions of IPFS models by linear, non-linear, or integer programming.

The microcomputer versions of IFPS are called IFPS/PERSONAL for MS-DOS machines and MINDSIGHT for Apple MacIntosh. These versions are quite similar to the mainframe version discussed in this book. In the case of IFPS/PERSONAL, data communications software is provided on both the mainframe and the microcomputer to allow translation of the models from one form to the other and for transmission between mainframe and microcomputer.

Finally, IFPS/DIRECTOR is a microcomputer software product that allows the microcomputer to act as a particularly user-friendly interface to the mainframe.

Organization of This Book

CHAPTER I. This chapter introduces the basic ideas of modeling and decision support systems. These ideas are fundamental to understanding the IFPS modeling language. The discussion includes the reasons for using models, their advantages, and the pitfalls to be avoided in modeling. The chapter concludes with a description of the features of IFPS, particularly those that distinguish it from conventional computer languages.

CHAPTERS II THROUGH V. The purpose of these four chapters is to serve as a text from which to learn successively more and more about IFPS.

Chapter II is the starting point for the novice. It focuses on creating simple models. It shows how to obtain IFPS at a terminal, how to write a very simple model, and how to use elementary commands for manipulating the model and obtaining output. This chapter contains three models of increasing complexity. Each model is described step by step, including the statement of the problem, explanation of the model, and presentation of the results. The simple models of Chapter II appear again in later chapters in expanded form and are used to illustrate more advanced concepts. The chapter concludes with a discussion of the extensive HELP commands available on-line in IFPS to assit in case of difficulty.

Chapter III focuses on the capabilities built into IFPS for supporting decision making. It shows how to ask questions of models (What if...? How sensitive...? If my goal is...?) that help to clarify their implications. The chapter also describes the financial, depreciation, amortization, statistical, and mathematical functions available.

The purpose of Chapter IV is to introduce the features of IFPS that allow communication within the organization. In particular, Chapter IV discusses the graphical presentation of results, the use of data files for dealing with data-driven problems, the creation of output in whatever format is used within the organization, and the consolidation of the results of two or more models. Chapter IV also describes advanced calculational, command, and editing features available in IFPS.

Chapter V explains how to model uncertainty and perform risk analysis. Included is a discussion of the rationale for assessing risk by simulation and the use of fixed-time-interval simulation in general. The chapter shows how to generate scenarios and how to run a statistically significant number of iterations and obtain output statistics. The chapter includes three example simulations; other simulations are included in later chapters.

Chapters II through V serve as an introductory text on IFPS. You, the reader, can work your way through the material sequentially to learn the fundamentals of the language. As you use the language and become experienced in it, you will find it useful to turn to the features designed for the "professional user". These features are covered in Chapters IX and X (see below).

CHAPTER VI THROUGH VIII. The purpose of these chapters is to illustrate the wide range of applications for which IFPS can be used. The applications have been taken, respectively, from three fields:

- finance
- statistics
- operations management.

Each chapter is keyed to the typical course required of MBA students. In fact, the problems discussed are based on standard texts; however, the chapters are self-contained so that they can be followed without consulting these specific texts.

The emphasis in these three chapters is on formulating the application as an IFPS model. Therefore, the models presented involve only a small amount of data and do not use advanced formatting and report features. With the exception of a few sections describing simulations, these chapters can be read immediately after Chapters II and III. THus, access is provided to applications early in the study of IFPS. Chapters VI, VII, and VIII are independent of one another and can be read in any order.

CHAPTER IX. This chapter introduces seven features designed for the power user, that is, the individual who either has gained considerable experience with IFPS and is ready to use the more sophisticated tools in the language or the individual with substantial computer background. Among the features discussed are Command Files and MICRO expressions. Command files allow you to automate many of the command sequences usually performed manually and to create menus that can be used by those who know nothing about IFPS. Micro expressions provide a way of writing generic models and reports that you can custom tailor at the time you use them so that they apply to the specific data and situation you are considering

CHAPTER X. This concluding chapter deals with two major capabilites of IFPS: Universal Consolidation and data base management.

Universal consolidation allows you to analyze all or parts of your business even if the business has complex organizational structure and each unit and group in the organization maintains separate records that need to be combined to achieve managerial control.

A relational data base is provided in many implementations of IFPS. Called IFPS/DIMENSION, this data base provides a multidimensional data base management system. It allows you store data from model output directly into a data base and to use data from the data base in your model. It also provides a query capability which permits simple retrieval of information.

APPENDICES. The appendices contain referfence information that is useful in working with IFPS. Specifically:

- Appendix I contains a listing of the output of various HELP commands available in IFPS.

- Appendix II contains a listing of all the commands available in IFPS. Not all the commands arecovered in this book. Section numbers are indicated for those commands which are discussed in the text. This appendix serves as a reference guide.
- Appendix III lists the "reserved" words in IFPS. these words have specific meanings in IFPS and there are restrictions on how and where they can be used.
- Appendix IV contains a list of twenty of the most frequently encountered IFPS error messages and explains their meaning.
- Appendix V describes the various OPTION commands available in IFPS.
- Appendix VI describes the steps needed to automatically translate IFPS models available on a mainframe to the format needed for IFPS/PERSONAL. It also lists the differences between IFPS on a mainframe and IFPS/Personal.

Additions and Features of the Second Edition

This second edition is an expansion and update of the first edition. It follows the same plan but adds two significant new chapters (Chapters IX and X) that deal with the powerful features that have been incorporated into IFPS in recent years, including Command Files, Micros, Universal Consolidation, and the relational data base. Major expansions have also been made in Chapters III and IV to include improvements and changes that have occurred since the first edition. Chapter VI on applications in finance has been updated to reflect the second, rather than the first edition of Brealey and Myers *Principles of Corporate Finance.* The material in Chapter VIII was revised extensively so that it uses a more recent text, Schroeder's *Operations Management,* as its foundation.

Acknowledgments

This book had as its beginnings a small directed study in the summer of l981 by Kevin L. Roper. Roper prepared a 10-page report that described how to obtain IFPS and use it on the computer at Southern Methodist University. He created the Simple IFPS model of Chapter II to illustrate how the language can be used.

As this book evolved, a number of my former colleagues at SMU, including J. Aronofsky, J. Aronson, R.S. Barr, C.B. Barry, J. Collings, D.A. Goodman, R. Helgason, T.E. Perkins, M.G. Sobol, and M. VanBreda, read the draft of the book, commented on it, and used it in their classes.

I am particularly grateful to the editorial help I received. In particular, Professor Martin K. Starr of Columbia University (who reviewed the first edition with great care and his comments helped shape it), and Dr. W.O. Cain and David Clark at EXECUCOM. Catherine Clark served as copy editor and assured consistency of style, format, and notation throughout.

Finally, a word of appreciation to my wife, Muriel, who spent many an evening listening to my word processor as this manuscript was written.

Paul Gray
Claremont Graduate School

CHAPTER I
INTRODUCTION

1.1 What This Book is About

1.1.1 Financial Planning Languages
1.1.2 The Approach Used

1.2 Modeling

1.2.1 The Nature of Models
1.2.2 Example: The Value of a Savings Account
1.2.3 Example: Market Models
1.2.4 Steps in Model Building
1.2.5 Some Pitfalls and How to Avoid Them

1.3 Decision Support Systems (DSS)

1.3.1 The Decision Process
1.3.2 Characteristics of Decision Support Systems
1.3.3 Situations in Which a Decision Support System is Useful
1.3.4 The Role of Assumptions in Decision Support Systems
1.3.5 Typical Uses of Decision Support Systems
1.3.6 Group Decision Making

1.4 Overview of IFPS

1.4.1 Basic Features of IFPS
1.4.2 What Occurs in an Interactive IFPS Session
1.4.3 The Structure of IFPS

CHAPTER I
INTRODUCTION

1.1 WHAT THIS BOOK IS ABOUT

This book is about an important new invention in methodology. For over 40 years, major strides have been made in the development of new computer-based technology as the computer has become pervasive in business, industry, science, and even the home. We have all become accustomed to the continual outpouring of innovation in technological devices. However, the pace of change in the ways we communicate with computers has been much slower. FORTRAN was developed over 25 years ago and, although ingenious refinements have been made since then, the basic way of telling the computer what to do, that is, computer programming, has remained relatively unchanged since then. A large software profession developed to fill an ever-increasing need for specialists who have programming skills. The net effect was that until recently executives had to rely on others if they wanted to communicate with the computer and obtain its power for answering important business questions. The rapid development of financial planning languages had a major impact in that these languages allowed a change in the way executives work. Specifically, these languages ALLOW EXECUTIVES TO BUILD MODELS WITHOUT INTERMEDIARIES.

1.1.1 Financial Planning Languages

If you think about this change in executive work patterns for a minute, you will see how truly remarkable it is. Computers have previously required individuals either to develop programming skills or to hire professionals who would do the programming for them. With only a handful of exceptions, executives used programmers and other intermediaries to communicate with the computer because of the large amount of time, effort, and special skill required to obtain needed answers. Financial planning languages, however, allow business professionals to sit down at a terminal and rapidly create models that support their decision making process.

The Interactive Financial Planning System (IFPS) described in this book is one of a number of planning languages developed in recent years. These languages provide a new way for managers, analysts, and staff to work directly with the computer. No longer is the language of the computer seemingly reserved for high priests (that is, professional programmers) with specialized knowledge. Rather, the financial planning languages provide a simple, natural language way of communicating with the computer. Furthermore, most of these languages are interactive. That is, they allow you to sit at the terminal and obtain essentially instant feedback. Thus, new models can be created and "what if?" questions can be asked, with answers obtained quickly and at low cost. With these characteristics, financial planning languages have enlarged the number and scope of the alternatives that executives can consider in arriving at a particular decision. In short, the quality of decision making has been improved.

Although called financial planning languages because of the original reason for their development, these languages turn out to be much broader than their name implies. They can be used in creating models in a wide variety of applications in business, in science and engineering, in mathematics and statistics, and many other disciplines. In this book, you will find chapters using IFPS for problems in finance, in statistics, and in operations management. These chapters merely hint at the range of applicability. As you read them and use their results, your imagination should be stirred and you will find innovative new ways to use financial planning languages. Remember that you now need no longer depend on others for formulating and solving your problems on the computer. You have obtained a new freedom.

1.1.2 The Approach Used

This book is really divided into four parts. This introductory chapter is the first part. It describes the role of models and the underlying ideas of decision support systems, both of which are fundamental to understanding what IFPS is about. The second part (Chapters II through V) teaches you the technical aspects of IFPS. It introduces you to the basics and then leads you through successively more advanced capabilities. The third part (Chapters VI through VIII) is devoted to applications of IFPS. The final part (Chapters IX and X) introduces advanced topics for the professional user, including Command Files, Universal Consolidation, and IFPS/DIMENSION, the relational database.

Throughout this book we show you complete IFPS models and their solutions. You will find over 100 different models, ranging from simple ones involving only a few lines to illustrate specific features of the language to much more complex ones that illustrate approaches to problems found in real life. We also include exercises throughout the text which are designed to extend your knowledge and to give you "hands on" experience in using IFPS. These exercises are not difficult; they build on what you see in the text. You will find that if you sit down at a terminal and solve the exercises as you proceed through the text, you will learn IFPS more quickly and will retain the concepts.

This book covers the essentials of IFPS. It is based on Release 10.0 of IFPS. As its title implies, it is an introduction. If you master it you will be proficient in IFPS. However, it does not cover every feature available in the language. If you want to find out about these additional features or want additional information beyond what is in this book, you should consult the *IFPS USER'S MANUAL*, published by EXECUCOM Systems Corporation, P.O. Box 9442 Capital of Texas Highway, North, Austin, TX ., 78759.

1.2 MODELING

1.2.1 The Nature of Models

Most of your education and much of what you do on the job involves using models. Whether you are considering the financial status of a firm by studying its balance sheets, the value of goods in terms of money, the appropriate size of an order to replenish inventory, the appropriate competitive bid to make on a new oil lease, or the flow of goods from factory to customers, you tend to work with an abstraction of the process, that is, a model.

Models are abstractions of systems. They can be regarded as substitutes for the real system which capture the essence, but not necessarily all of the detail, of the real system.

The advantage of a model is that it is usually possible to experiment with a model more quickly, at lower cost, and with less risk than to experiment with the real system. From the point of view of decision making, a model allows the consequences of alternative proposals and the anticipated effects of different contingencies to be evaluated.

Like all abstractions, models involve a large number of assumptions -- assumptions about the nature of the environment in which the system works, about the operating characteristics of its components, and about the way people behave. These assumptions must be fully understood and should be continually reevaluated. For example, it is possible to wind up producing an Edsel by assuming that consumer tastes will be the same three to five years from now as they are today.

The models considered in this book are quantitative. We may write such a model as a set of relations that represent the behavior of all or part of real systems under a variety of environmental conditions. The type of model needed to solve a problem will depend on the question to be resolved. In some cases, answers could be obtained from a "back of the envelope" calculation. In other cases, a large, logically consistent set of relations is required. In still other cases, mathematical or probability representation is needed. As models grow larger, a computer is needed to keep track of the relations and to perform the computations.

Models can be characterized in terms of a continuum of:

complexity:	from one variable to many
degree of uncertainty:	from deterministic to probabilistic
time:	from static to dynamic.

There are eight combinations, which are represented by the eight corners of Figure 1-1. (If you think about it, Figure 1-1 is itself a model.) Corner 1 represents the simplest situation, a deterministic model that involves only one variable, and does not involve time. For example,

TOTAL COST = UNIT COST * NUMBER OF UNITS

is a static, deterministic, one variable model (where unit cost is a given constant), that belongs at Corner 1. As we move away from Corner 1 to Corners 2, 3, or 5, we are still dealing with only one variable but either time or uncertainty or both are introduced. The following are examples of these one-variable problems:

Corner		
2	Deterministic, dynamic	Present value of a savings account
3	Probabilistic, static	Sales this month
5	Probabilistic, dynamic	Price of a share of stock

Corner 4 is the first place where complexity in the form of more than one variable comes in. Corner 4 corresponds to situations which can be modeled by simultaneous equations in many variables. The complexity of many variables is compounded if consideration either of time or uncertainty is added to the model. The most difficult problems and, unfortunately, the ones encountered most frequently in real business decision making, are the ones at Corner 8; that is, problems with many variables, much uncertainty, and rapid variation with time. Although you can often solve problems at Corner 1 and at a few corners adjacent to Corner 1 with relatively simple models, those at Corner 8 require the deepest understanding of the problem and the most sophisticated models.

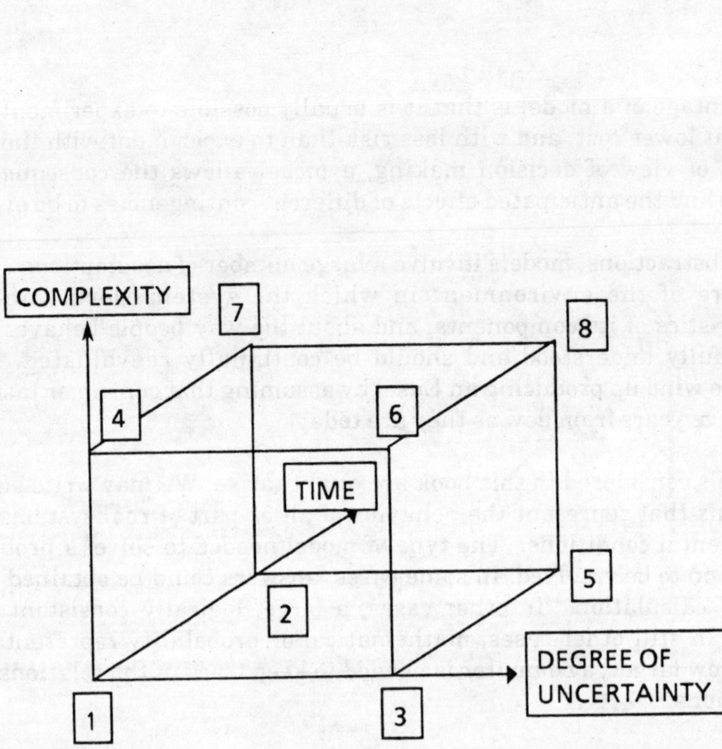

FIGURE 1-1. THE PROBLEM SPACE

Very often, a particular problem will best be solved by using a hierarchy of models, ranging from great aggregation to extreme detail. Many times the degree of detail depends on the level within the organization; the further up the organization, the greater the aggregation. The choice of model detail is important; too much aggregation can result in losing a detail that is critical, whereas attempting to model everything results in high costs and overwhelming amounts of data that hinder rather than help decision making.

Typically, as you work on a problem, your models of the situation proceed from coarse to medium to fine detail. This sequence is consistent with the amount you know about the problem as time progresses. As shown in Figure 1-2, when beginning a major project, because you know relatively little about the problem, your model will be relatively simple and have very little detail in it. Furthermore, your level of uncertainty will be greatest. If the uncertainties in the results based on the simple model are tolerable, you may stop at the initial level. In most cases, however, you will refine your models. For example, in a corporate financial model you may begin by considering only a few of the major product lines and aggregating the rest. As time goes on, you will typically increase the level of detail about company operations. You may also move from a deterministic, accounting model to a probabilistic forecasting model. If, however, the primary purpose of the model is to estimate total revenue of the firm for next year, you may find that an aggregated model is sufficient for your purpose.

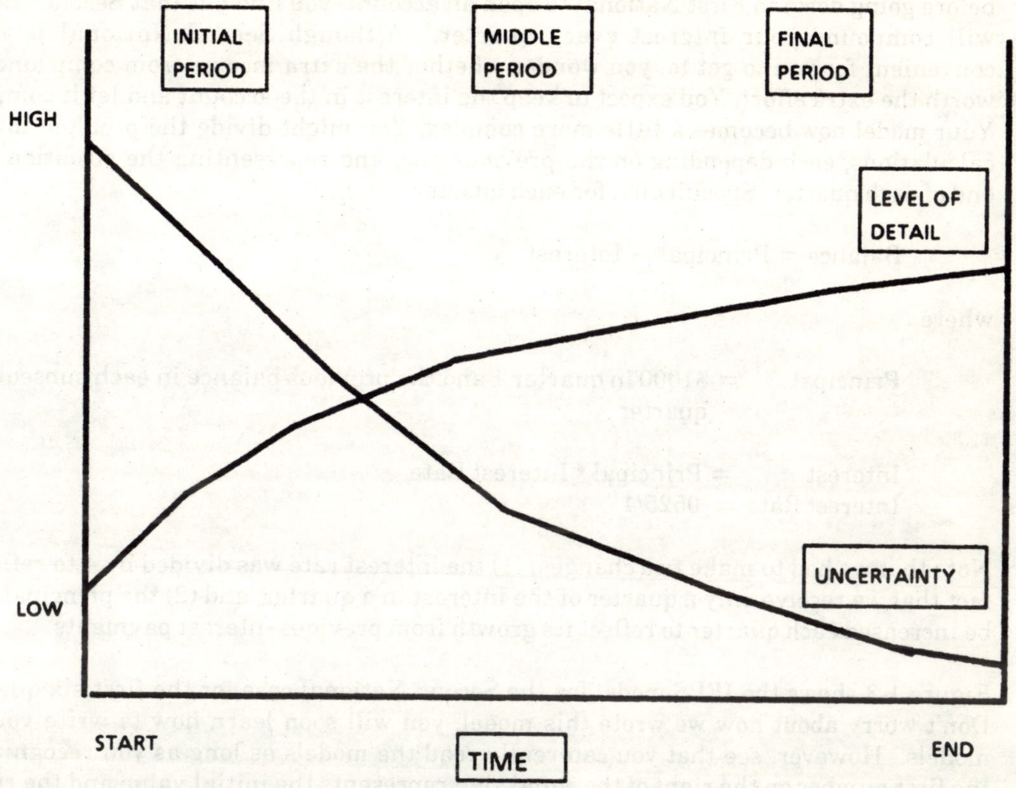

FIGURE 1-2. PROGRESS IN UNDERSTANDING THE PROBLEM

The level of aggregation that can be accepted is a critical choice that you make when you model. Although there is a natural tendency to want to model everything immediately, such an approach is highly risky. Evolving from a coarse model to a fine model is usually much wiser.

1.2.2 EXAMPLE: The Value of a Savings Account

As a simple example of modeling consider the options you might face in deciding on selecting a bank for your checking account. Suppose you expect to keep a minimum balance of $1000 over the next year. First National offers 5.25% simple annual interest on the minimum balance for the year. The model for this situation is:

Balance = Principal + Interest

where:

Principal	**=**	**1000**
Interest Rate	**=**	**0.0525**
Interest	**=**	**Principal * Interest Rate**

This is a model you can solve in your head. The 5.25% interest rate results in a payment of $52.50 on $1000 and your balance at the end of the year will be $1052.50. However, before going down to First National to open an account, you find out that Second National will compound your interest every quarter. Although Second National is not as convenient for you to get to, you wonder whether the extra income from compounding is worth the extra effort. You expect to keep the interest in the account and let it compound. Your model now becomes a little more complex. You might divide the problem into four calculations, each depending on the previous one, and representing the situation at the end of each quarter. Specifically, for each quarter:

Balance = Principal + Interest

where

Principal = $1000 in quarter 1 and the previous balance in each subsequent quarter

Interest = Principal * Interest Rate
Interest Rate = .0525/4

Note that we had to make two changes: (1) the interest rate was divided by 4 to reflect the fact that we receive only a quarter of the interest in a quarter, and (2) the principal had to be increased each quarter to reflect its growth from previous interest payments.

Figure 1-3 shows the IFPS model for the Second National case for the first six quarters . Don't worry about how we wrote this model, you will soon learn how to write your own models. However, see that you can really read the models as long as you recognize that the first number on the right of the equal sign represents the initial value and the relation shows how the numbers build up. You should be able to hand check the results shown.

```
MODEL SECONDNATL  VERSION OF  12/30/82  15:53
10 COLUMNS 1-6
20 BALANCE=PRINCIPAL + INTEREST
30 PRINCIPAL = 1000,PREVIOUS BALANCE
40 INTEREST = PRINCIPAL*INTEREST RATE
50 INTEREST RATE =0.0525/4

END OF MODEL
? solve
MODEL SECONDNATL VERSION OF 12/30/82  15:53 -- 6 COLUMNS 4 VARIABLES
ENTER SOLVE OPTIONS
? all
                          1      2      3      4      5      6

BALANCE                1013   1026   1040   1054   1067   1081
PRINCIPAL              1000   1013   1026   1040   1054   1067
INTEREST              13.13  13.30  13.47  13.65  13.83  14.01
INTEREST RATE         .0131  .0131  .0131  .0131  .0131  .0131
```

FIGURE 1-3. SIMPLE INTEREST MODEL IN IFPS

Real life becomes more complicated as new alternatives are presented to you involving different rates or different interest payment rules (e.g., daily compounding, average rather than minimum balance). You can respond to these situations by building your own model and then asking "what if? " questions that reflect the changes in the marketplace.

1.2.3 EXAMPLE: Market Models

If you took economics in college, you may recall that in the simplest model of the market for a commodity, it is assumed that:

1. As the price decreases, the demand for the commodity will increase.

2. As the price increases, the supply of the commodity available will increase.

3. The supply will equal the demand.

We can represent this model in terms of the following relations:

DEMAND = A - B*PRICE (1-1)

SUPPLY = C + D*PRICE (1-2)

SUPPLY = DEMAND (1-3)

where A, B, C, and D are constants. These three relations form the market model. For this model to match the assumptions, the constants B and D must be positive so that supply goes up and demand goes down as price increases. Furthermore, A must be positive so that if price becomes high enough, the demand goes to 0. Figure 1-4 shows the results for this model for the following values of the constants:

A = 500, B=1000, C = -40, D=800

When supply equals demand, the equilibrium price can be shown to be:

PRICE = (A - C) / (B + D),

which for our example values implies that the equilibrimprice is 30 cents. At this price, according to equations (1-1) and (1-2), supply and demand are 200.

If you think about it, this model is at Corner 4 in Figure 1-1.

EXERCISE: Substitute the values of A, B, C, and D into Equations 1-1 and 1-2 and check that equilibrium occurs at 200 units.

This simple model has several interesting characteristics:

1. It represents a situation in quantitative terms.

2. It contains major assumptions that have to be justified.

3. It neglects the effects of time.

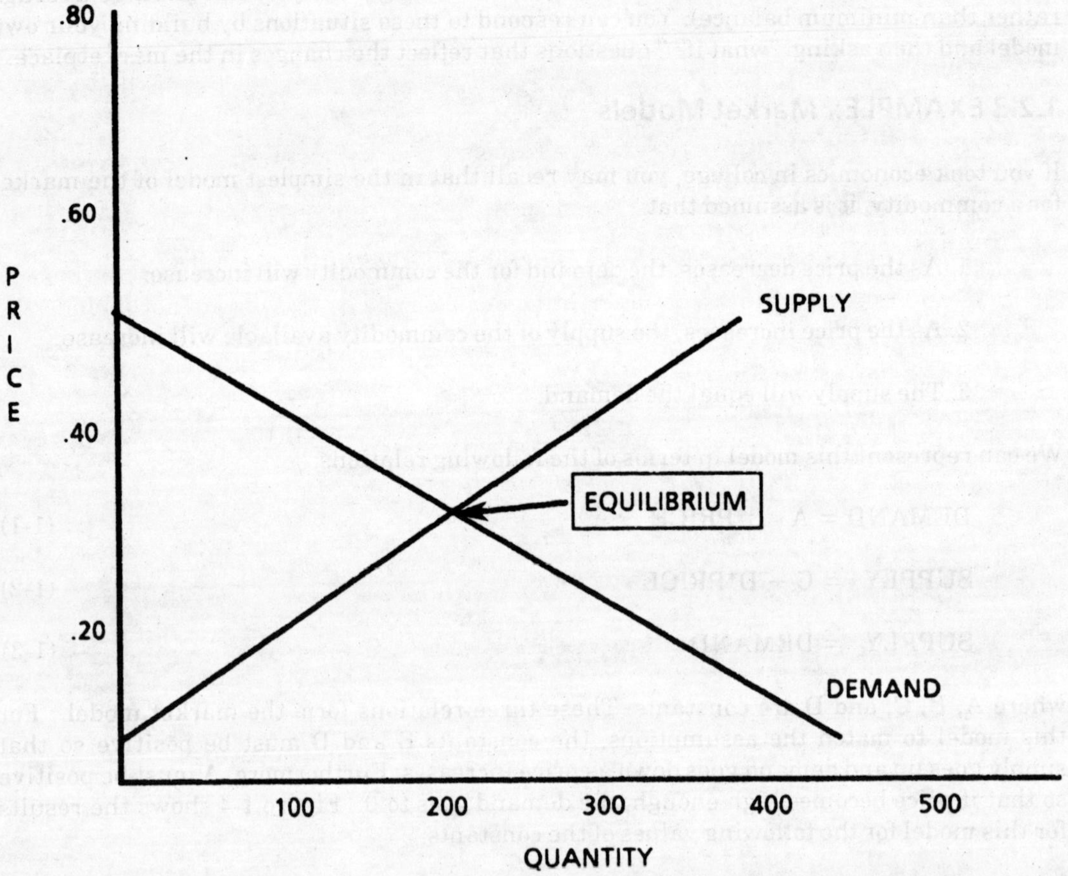

FIG. 1-4. SUPPLY-DEMAND RELATIONS; LINEAR CASE

A more realistic model would recognize that in real markets, information lags the current situation. That is, if we move from Corner 4 to Corner 7 of Figure 1-1. Additional realism is introduced if it is assumed that the supply produced in a given period is based on the price in the previous period. Agricultural markets, for example, might be thought to behave in this way with a period of one year. To introduce this change, we would modify our assumptions about the supply. Specifically,

DEMAND = A − B*PRICE (1-4)

SUPPLY = C + D*(PREVIOUS PRICE) (1-5)

PRICE = (A − C − D*PREVIOUS PRICE) / B (1-6)

where PREVIOUS PRICE is the price one period ago. Note that these equations assume that the market is cleared; that is, the price in the marketplace each period is adjusted so that the demand just equals the supply produced.

Is the model given by Equations (1-4) through (1-6) a satisfactory model? Although it represents how we feel about prices intuitively, it fails to be complete on important issues. For example, it neglects the possibility that producers may base their current production on more historical data than just the last period. It assumes that all production and sales occur in the same period; thereby neglecting the possibility that merchants who maintain inventory will come into the market. Although there are situations where inventory cannot be retained for future sale (e.g., seats in an airplane that just took off) such situations are the exception rather than the rule. These two factors can be taken into account in a more complex version of the model.

In judging the model, recognize that it is a descriptive model. As such it can serve as an aid in decision making. However, descriptive models such as this one do not include the capability for finding the best solution (under the assumptions) for use by the decision maker.

1.2.4 Steps in Model Building

Model building is an iterative process. You typically begin with a very simple model. Then, as your understanding of the system increases, you refine the model and introduce increasing sophistication into it. Even though you may back-track and redo parts or all of the model several times, there is a well-defined progression of steps that are followed. These steps are:

1. Formulate the problem
2. Define the environment
3. Identify the relevant variables
4. Build the model
5. Solve the model

In many respect, formulating the problem is the most difficult part of the job. You have to be clear in your own mind as to what decisions are to be made. Often the problem that is stated by management is not necessarily the problem that needs to be solved. The management science literature abounds with examples in which management asked for one thing and the real problem turned out to be something else. You want to make sure that you do not produce a solution for which there is no problem.

An important way of thinking about problem formulation is to analyze the decisions to be made. What alternatives are available and what choices have to be made? Your model should be such that it can be used to evaluate the alternatives and support the decision process. We will discuss the concept of decision support further in Section 1.3.

Having defined the problem to be solved in terms of the decisions to be made, you must next distinguish between what constitutes the system to be modeled and what constitutes the system's external environment. Particular elements may be within the system for some decisions and outside the system for others. For example, the prime interest rate is part of the environment for a bank; for the Federal Reserve it is a basic decision to be made. The environment affects the system in ways that are usually uncontrollable and can be thought of as belonging to nature; in other words, the effects of the environment are exogenous. Typical factors that are in the environment for a firm are the general state of the economy, interest rates, raw material costs, the law, governmental regulations, social forces, and consumer tastes. In many cases, the principal use of a model is to examine contingencies that can result from changes in the environment (e.g., How do I change my capital construction plans if the interest rate goes up by three points? Goes down by three points? What happens if my industry is deregulated?). Typically, such studies of environmental effects involve building a model based on assumptions about what are the most likely outcomes and then running analyses in which one or more exogenous factors are changed. Such analyses are referred to as sensitivity analyses.

In some models, the interactions between the system and the environment must be taken into account. For example, if you change your pricing structure you may affect the competitive environment. Competitors, after all, are not devoted to your well being. As a result, your actions may cause them to respond in some way (i.e., change the environment) and your model must be sufficiently flexible so that you can determine what to do, depending on their response.

Parsimony is a basic principle of modeling. That is, a model should include only those things that are important to the decision to be made. Although a particular situation may involve many variables, only a few of them affect the outcome, and even fewer are under your control. The more variables that are included in the model, the more data need to be obtained and the greater the complexity of the model. Identifying which variables are relevant to the decision ensures that the model includes the elements that are needed but excludes peripheral considerations. To understand the waiting lines in a business, for example, the rate at which customers arrive and the time required to serve them are relevant variables; however, customer heights or their shoe sizes are usually irrelevant.

What variables are relevant also depends on the level of the organization at which the model is to be used. At the lowest levels, only a few variables are important because only a few can be controlled at that level of the organization. The production supervisor can affect schedules and can attempt to reduce cost; however, product prices, product design, and delivery dates are normally out of the production supervisor's control. For the decision maker higher up in the organization, many more variables are controllable. The more complex the decision the greater the possible dimensionality of the model. In terms of Figure 1-1, we move from Corner 1 to Corner 8 as we move up the organizational ladder. Not only does the number of potentially relevant variables increase, but the variables become more heterogenous. That is, at low levels in the organization you may be able to express everything in terms of a single, easily measured unit, such as cost. At higher levels, complex trade-offs among cost, risk, image, and other factors are involved. The problem is further complicated by the increasing aggregation of details that occurs as you move up the organizational hierarchy (see Section 1.2.1). Fortunately, in most practical management situations only a few variables are considered relevant for a given organizational level. It is part of the modeler's job to build the model to focus on these variables.

You are now ready to build the model. The model building process usually goes through the steps shown in Figure 1-5 a number of times. The real world is, of course, given. The modeler begins by establishing the objectives of the model in terms of the decision to be made and then builds the initial model. This initial model may or may not be satisfactory. The only way to tell is to use the model to predict what happens under different input conditions. Here judgments have to be made. Does the model "match" the real world? Are the objectives established for the model met? In many cases, the match is not exact because of the simplifying assumptions made. The question really is whether the model is sufficiently close to reality to permit decision making. If the model does not match reality adequately or meet the objectives, the model must be revised and the process repeated.

The sequence of building, testing, and revising the model are the essence of the iterative process that is model building. As they are repeated, the belief in the validity of the model improves until you are ready to implement the model and use it to solve the problem at hand.

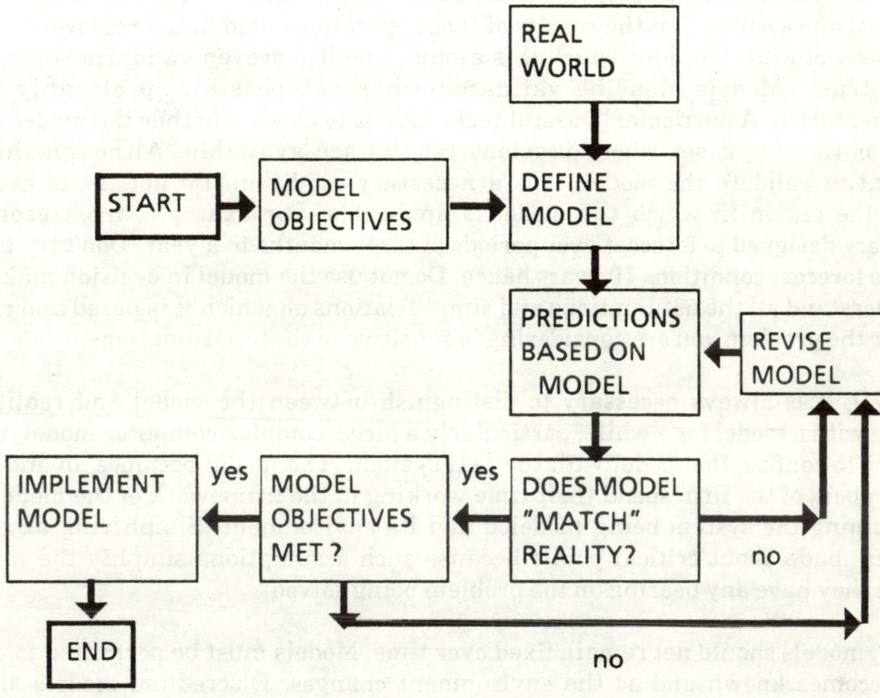

FIGURE 1-5. THE MODEL BUILDING PROCESS

If you observe the following three principles in building the model, your job will be made easier:

1. *Relevance*. The model should only include those elements that affect the decision to be made. If, in modeling profitability, the objective is to compare the effects of different financing methods, the hiring practices of the firm need not be modeled explicitly.

2. *Accuracy*. The accuracy required for input data depends on the decision to be made. Since in most cases, obtaining increased data accuracy implies increased cost, you should try to work with the minimum level of data accuracy that you need to make a decision.

3. *Aggregation*. Aggregation involves grouping a number of individual quantities into a larger quantity. For example, it may be perfectly adequate in a particular model to consider explicitly the seven products that constitute 85% of your sales and to lump the remainder into a product labeled "other".

1.2.5 Some Pitfalls and How to Avoid Them

Modeling is fraught with many pitfalls. In this section, we describe some of these pitfalls and discuss what can be done to avoid them.

FIRST, no model ever perfectly matches what happens in reality. The standard technique is to formulate a model, operate on the model (e.g., with sensitivity and "what if?" questions) and assume that the results of these operations hold in the real world. There is a vast body of experience for which this assumption has proven valid. However, it is not always true! Models must be validated wherever possible, preferably through experimentation. A particularly useful technique is to check whether the model is true in simple or limiting cases where previous results are available. Although this is not sufficient to validate the model, it is a necessary condition. Do not try to extrapolate beyond the region in which the model is applicable. For example, most econometric models are designed to forecast over periods of three months to a year. Don't try to run the model to forecast conditions 10 years hence. Do not use the model in decision making until you understand all the assumptions and simplifications on which it is based and can check whether the problem you are considering is sensitive to these assumptions.

SECOND, it is always necessary to distinguish between the model and reality. After working with a model for a while, particularly a large complex computer model, there is a tendency to confuse the model with the real system. The model becomes an end in itself, and members of the firm spend their time working in the framework of the model instead of examining the system being modeled and its environment. Simplifying assumptions are often made about critical points because such assumptions simplify the model, not because they have any bearing on the problem being solved.

THIRD, models should not remain fixed over time. Models must be permitted to evolve as more becomes known and as the environment changes. Discredited models should be buried quietly, no matter how much effort and pride went into developing them. As new information becomes available that conflicts with the present model, use it to modify and improve the model.

FOURTH, to be useful, a model must serve practical purposes, rather than be an exercise in academic elegance. The point of a model is to help you understand problems and reach decisions. The purpose of technology and nomenclature in a model should be to enhance insight and to facilitate computation, not to impress or confuse. Introducing elegant names for simple ideas (e.g., waste management costs for janitorial) neither solves nor illuminates the problem.

FIFTH, models should not be a substitute for thinking. Too often, results are taken at face value. After all, the numbers came out of the computer. Remember, the fundamental value of the model is to clarify and lay bare the implications of the underlying assumptions that are often implicit rather than explicit.

FINALLY, models should not attempt to over-quantify. Some things cannot really be reduced to numbers. They are externals that should be handled qualitatively. For example, attempts to attach an absolute monetary value to loss of life or loss of wilderness area are generally not accepted by decision makers or by the public at large.

1.3 DECISION SUPPORT SYSTEMS (DSS)

IFPS and other planning languages are a key element of modern decision support systems. In this section we present a brief introduction to such systems that highlights some of the key points. In reading this section recognize that IFPS provides a way of creating the models that managers can use directly to support their decisions; that is, IFPS is a basic building block for a variety of decision support systems. If you would like to know more, consult the references given in the notes at the end of this chapter.

1.3.1 The Decision Process

The general structure of decision processes is shown in Figure 1-6.

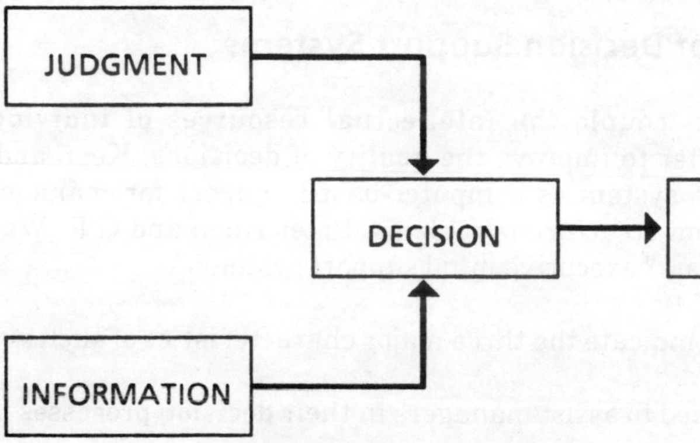

FIGURE 1-6. MAJOR ELEMENTS OF DECISION PROCESS

A decision involves combining information and judgment into a course of action and then implementing that action. The way in which this sequence occurs for a particular decision maker depends on the style of the individual. Peter Keen and Michael Scott-Morton[1] define five styles of decision making.

- The Rational Manager
- Satisficing
- Organizational Procedures
- Political
- Individual Differences

Rational managers attempt to be informed decision makers. They continually look at alternatives and seek to find the best possible alternative for the criterion or criteria that they have set. Typically they try to find the maximum profit or minimum cost solution to problems. Such managers use optimizing methods wherever possible. Few such managers are believed to exist in practice.

In the satisficing approach, optimal solutions to the problem are not required. Rather, the search is for "good enough" answers. The solution methods are typically heuristic (i.e., approximate methods that are known to give good results most of the time). For a manager using the satisficing approach, the role of the decision support system is to improve existing solutions.

The manager concerned with organizational procedures uses the company's standard procedures to reach decisions. The rules of such an organization are precisely laid down and the manager feels that following these rules is the most important aspect of their job. Here, a decision support system tries to find ways of improving the procedures.

In political decision making, the manager tries to reconcile the views and objectives of the different organizational subunits. The decision process involves bargaining between the units, with the decision maker acting as referee.

In the individual differences approach, each decision maker is seen as unique. Support is provided to each manager so that he or she can make best use of their own personal strategies and abilities. It is this view which is *central* to decision support systems.

1.3.2 Characteristics of Decision Support Systems

Decision support systems couple the intellectual resources of individuals with the capabilities of the computer to improve the quality of decisions. Keen and Scott-Morton define a decision support system as computer-based support for management decision makers who deal with semi-structured problems. Peter Keen and G.R. Wagner [2] refer to decision support systems as " executive mind support systems".

The foregoing definitions indicate the three major characteristics of such systems:

1. They are designed to assist managers in their decision processes in semi-structured tasks.

2. They support, rather than replace, managerial judgment.

3. Their objective is to improve the effectiveness of the decisions in solving problems, not the efficiency with which decisions are made.

An important concept here is that of a "semi-structured" task. Tasks can be divided into structured, semi - structured , and unstructured. In a structured task, the procedures for obtaining correct answers are known. In a sense the manager is not needed at all. Whether the problem involves rules for reordering inventory or using linear programming for managing a refinery or deciding on plant location, the objectives are of the simple profit maximum or cost minimum variety and the manager can use the support of clerical, data processing, or management science people and models. In an unstructured task, human intuition is still the basis for decision making. Typical unstructured tasks include selecting the cover of the annual report, hiring a subordinate, or choosing a set of research and development projects for next year. The semi-structured tasks fall in between and involve a combination of both structure and intuition. Keen and Scott-Morton give such examples as trading bonds, setting marketing budgets for consumer products, and performing capital acquisition analysis. Here a decision support system can improve the quality of the information on which the decision is based by providing not only single solutions of models but also providing a range of "what if?", sensitivity, and risk analysis that allows the manager to understand better the nature of the problem and the range of options available.

It is important to recognize that decision support systems (DSS) are different, both quantitatively and qualitatively, from management information systems (MIS) and from management science (MS) models. Table 1-1 compares these three approaches.

TABLE 1-1
COMPARISON OF MIS, MS, AND DSS

MANAGEMENT INFORMATION SYSTEMS	MANAGEMENT SCIENCE MODELS	DECISION SUPPORT SYSTEMS
Structured Tasks	Structured Tasks	Semi-Structured Tasks
Higher Efficiency	Better Solutions	Higher Effectiveness
Provides Reports, Accessto Data	Provides Recommendations on Optimal Decisions/Actions	Provides a Supportive Tool to the Manager

Decision support systems attempt to provide higher effectiveness and deal with semi-structured tasks. Management information systems provide reports and access to data; too often they provide so much information in reports that the reports are never used. They also provide access to data through various retrieval systems including inquiry systems and data base management systems. Their focus is on the past, that is, on what happened and on what was true. They involve record keeping, transaction processing, and business reporting. One of their main objectives is to present information in a consistent manner. Management science models provide recommendations on the optimal action once there is agreement on the assumptions and on the objective to be optimized.

Both management information systems and management science models tend to be slow, with emphasis on large computational efforts that often are not on-line. Both management information systems and management science models can be, and are, key elements of a decision support system. However, they do not by themselves constitute a decision support system. Decision support systems focus on the present and the future and emphasize flexibility and ad hoc utilization. Their main role is to expedite the processes by which people make decisions about the future and communicate those decisions through the organization.

1.3.3 Situations in Which a Decision Support System is Useful

Decision support systems are designed to be used for complex problems that involve large masses of data and which often involve the expenditure of large sums of money. Because of the size of the problem, manipulation of the data base and extensive computations are needed to solve the problem. There are time pressures for reaching a decision; the problem is so urgent that it is not feasible to set a study team to work for six months or a year. Judgment is needed to:

- Recognize or decide what are the objectives
- Create alternatives
- Choose a solution.

In most situations, much of the argument will be around the assumptions (see Section 1.3.4).Once the assumptions are agreed upon, finding a solution becomes a much more straightforward task.

The level of support provided by a decision support system can range from providing access to facts to providing useful models for the manager. Typical levels of support in increasing order of complexity are:

1. Access to facts for information retrieval

Usually based on a data base management system that allows on-line inquiries to be made for specific items.

2. Pattern Recognition Capability in Data Retrieval

Inquiry systems that aggregate information.

3. Simple computations, comparisons, projections

Operations are performed on the data that allow individuals to assess the implications of the assumptions.

4. Useful models for the manager

Here the manager is provided with models and their solutions. He or she can interrogate each model and investigate the implications of changes in assumptions about the external environment (e.g., anticipated sales, price of raw materials).

1.3.4 The Role of Assumptions in Decision Support Systems

In building a model for the manager that represents the elements of a business decision, you make a number of assumptions about the nature of the present and the nature of the future. You make choices as to what are the important variables, what present and past data are applicable, and how the variables are related to one another. You also make assumptions about the effects of time. More interesting, as Keen and Wagner point out, your assumptions encode your beliefs, hopes, and dreams about the future, your fears about what the future may bring, and your habits of thought from the past on how the world works. The role of a decision support system is to allow the decision maker to deal with assumptions. The sequence of steps that is gone through involves:

- externalizing
- understanding
- challenging
- exploring
- communicating
- believing
- owning

the assumptions of the models. Once the assumptions are believed and owned by the decision maker, the actual decision is, in most cases, relatively straightforward.

1.3.5 Typical Uses of Decision Support Systems

Decision support systems have been used in a large number of industries and for a variety of purposes. Various surveys of such systems have appeared. The following are typical of the types of applications found.

- Financial planning models. Here cash flows, returns, budgets, and similar information are produced. A financial planning language such as IFPS is used.
- Market models. Analyses are provided of advertising effectiveness, marketing strategy, product planning, and price decisions.
- Distribution and location models. These models support branch location, work force staffing, and transportation decisions.
- Portfolio management systems. These systems are designed to assist investment decision makers in institutions (e.g., bank trust departments, pension funds) in selecting a portfolio mix.
- Geodata analysis systems. Graphical systems to show map and map-like information for city planning, police beat design, and school district boundary setting.

Other applications reported in the literature include corporate planning, insurance underwriting, budgeting and planning, to name just a few.

EXERCISE: Go to your company or college library and find a description of a decision support system. Prepare a short summary of the article. Indicate the decisions supported, the nature of the assumptions, the models used, and the perceived change in effectiveness from using the system. (Look up Decision Support Systems or DSS in the annual index of journals such as DATAMATION and the MIS Quarterly. Many books on Decision Support Systems also contain case studies.)

1.3.6 Group Decision Making

In most organizations, major decisions involve consultation and agreement among many people. The concept of a single decision maker implicit in what we have discussed thus far is a simplification. If the organization as a whole is not behind a particular decision, it becomes difficult to implement even if it is the correct course of action. Thus, decision making is a group process. Typically, one or more meetings are held that involve both the proposers of a project and the people who will have to implement the decision. You can think of such a meeting as a group of people sitting together around a conference table and holding a discussion. (With modern technology, however, other alternatives such as electronic mail, computer conferences, video conferences, and computer-aided decision rooms can be used for meetings.)

Consider the typical characteristics of such a meeting:

1. The meeting involves the joint activity of a group of five to 25 people who are of near-equal status in the organization. One person may, however, be in charge.

2. The activity as well as its outputs are intellectual in nature.

3. The product depends in an essential way on the judgmental contribution of the participants.

4. The meeting may begin with a formal presentation by a staff or line group outlining the problem, listing the alternative solutions considered, and presenting recommendations.

5. A discussion follows in which the participants ask questions, suggest new alternatives, and present viewpoints based on their own interests. (For example, marketing wants many products, finance wants small inventories, and production wants long production runs.) The discussion often involves bargaining and negotiation among the participants.

6. At the end of the meeting, a decision is (or is not) taken. If reached, the decision may be by vote or it may be by edict from the senior person present. If the decision goes against the concensus around the table, the manager who takes the decision knows that he or she will have a difficult time implementing it.

Although the research and implementation of decision support systems has focused on the single decision maker, many such systems can be used to support group decisions. By making the decision support system available on-line during the meeting, a richer set of "what if?" questions can be answered and a broader set of assumptions explored. The meeting need not degenerate into discussions based on the memories and biases of the people present. In the group meeting setting, the decision support system provides a way of making the implications of the assumptions available to all the participants. For example, if the outputs of an IFPS model are used as the basis for the discussion, then as various alternatives are proposed the implications of these alternatives can be explored by using the model and displaying the results to all the participants.

1.4 OVERVIEW OF IFPS

1.4.1 Basic Features of IFPS

IFPS provides you with a complete modeling language. Its versatility is based on the many built-in features it contains. In this section we describe some of the major features available to you.

NATURAL LANGUAGE. You write the relations in your IFPS model in the same form as you think about them or talk about them. For example, you might write:

```
VARIABLE COST = VOLUME * UNIT COST
```

or

```
TOTAL INVENTORY COST = HOLDING COST + ORDER COST +
                       SHORTAGE COST - SALVAGE COST
```

That is, you can refer to variables in the model by the same names you use in everyday speech in English or any other language. This natural language capability makes it possible for you easily to communicate assumed values and relationships.

NO ORDER RESTRICTIONS. You can write ideas down in the order in which they occur to you or in the order in which you are used to thinking about them. In conventional computer languages such as BASIC or FORTRAN order is important. The computer will interpret the following example differently in IFPS or BASIC or FORTRAN

```
INVENTORY COST      = HOLDING COST + ORDER COST
ORDER COST          = 200
HOLDING COST        = 1000
```

IFPS will compute the inventory cost as being 1200. On the other hand, writing the same information in that order in BASIC or FORTRAN would result in the computer telling you that the inventory cost was either 0 or undefined, depending on which computer you used. In short, IFPS takes care of putting the statements in the correct order for you. The only thing you have to do is make sure that every variable (such as HOLDING COST) which appears on the right of an equal sign is also defined once on the left of an equal sign.

The technical term for such a language is "non-procedural". You will find many arguments in the literature, pro and con, about "procedural" languages such as BASIC or FORTRAN versus "non-procedural" languages. There are advantages and disadvantages to both. The advantages of non-procedural languages are user friendliness and ease of use; the cost is the larger computer memory required to solve a given problem.

SPREAD SHEET SOLUTION. In IFPS you write a series of lines (called a "model") that describe your problem and IFPS creates a spread sheet (or, if you prefer a more technical term, a matrix) for you. The following is a simple IFPS model and its spread sheet output:

Model:

```
10 COLUMNS 1983-1986
20 SALES =1000,1100,1200,1300
30 COST OF GOODS = .8* SALES
40 PROFIT = SALES -COST OF GOODS
```

Output:

	1983	1984	1985	1986
SALES	1000	1100	1200	1300
COST OF GOODS	800	880	960	1040
PROFIT	200	220	240	260

Note how easy it is to read the model. You will see that you first specify the column headings you want (Line 10) and that these are then printed out on top of the spread sheet. The next three lines of the model specify the row names on the left hand side of the equal sign. The calculations are defined on the right-hand side and can be specified either as numerical values (e.g., Line 20 for SALES) or as relationships (e.g., for COST OF GOODS and PROFIT). You receive a neat printout in spread sheet format automatically.

WHAT IF. IFPS's strength as a decision support tool comes from its built in "what if?" capabilities. Given a set of assumptions, there is always the need to explore what happens should conditions change. What if sales are, say, double those estimated? What if they are half? The what if feature allows you to explore what happens when one or a combination of assumptions changes. IFPS also allows you to perform sensitivity analysis on individual variables. For example, you can ask for a the effect on NET PROFIT AFTER TAX and CASH if the SELLING PRICE varies from −5% to +15% in steps of 5%.

GOAL SEEKING. Often management will set a goal and your problem is to determine what has to be done to meet this goal. For example, you may have a goal of NET PROFIT AFTER TAX = 60000 and you want to find the VOLUME needed to achieve this goal.

CONSOLIDATION. Most firms have cost centers and many have multiple branches. A commonly encountered requirement is to consolidate two or more individual reports into a single report in a standard company format. IFPS contains commands which make such consolidations simple. It also has the needed data file handling and report generating capabilities to deal with the large volume of data and the formatting required.

RISK ANALYSIS. The future is uncertain. Although we can make plans and forecasts based on our best estimates and we can explore the effects of specific changes from a model's assumptions through "what if?" and sensitivity analyses, these approaches do not weigh the risks explicitly. For example, we can perform sensitivity analyses for sales decreasing by 20% and by 40%. However, in interpreting the meaning of the results we have to be careful to weigh the likelihood of a 20% decrease occurring in a different way from that of a 40% decrease. In risk analyses, the probabilities of outcomes are included explicitly. IFPS allows you to perform risk analyses by providing a Monte Carlo (i.e., simulation) capability. You specify probability distributions for variables that are uncertain and then tell IFPS to solve the model a large number of times. For each solution, IFPS picks a value at random from each probability distribution, giving a different scenario. IFPS then provides you with statistics (mean, variance, distribution) on the outcomes. (The use of IFPS for risk analysis is discussed in detail in Chapter V.)

BUILT-IN FUNCTIONS. IFPS contains a large number of financial, statistical, and mathematical functions that perform standard calculations for you. For example, financial functions include net present value, internal rate of return, amortization, and a number of depreciation options. Forecasting functions allow you to obtain moving averages, trend extrapolation, and regression analysis. (Each of the functions and their meaning are discussed in Chapter III.)

PREVIOUS and FUTURE. At any point in your IFPS model you can refer to events that happened in previous time periods or will happen in future time periods. For example, you might say:

```
SALES = 1000, PREVIOUS SALES * 1.06
```

to model an initial value of 1000 followed by a 6% growth in sales from period to period, or you might say:

```
ESTIMATED TAX PAYMENT = .2 * FUTURE PROFIT
```

Note that here the estimated tax payment depends on the value of a different variable, namely profit, that will occur in the future. PREVIOUS and FUTURE are powerful tools because they allow you to use data from throughout the spread sheet.

REPORTS AND DATA FILES. To make IFPS useful as a management tool for large-scale problems, it contains built-in capabilities for creating reports and data files. By specifying a report format, you can obtain output in any format you desire in addition to the spread sheet format provided automatically. Furthermore, by creating data files you can use the same IFPS model with a variety of inputs. The data file feature is particularly useful when you have several products or groups in an organization and want to process data about them in a uniform way.

1.4.2 What Occurs in an Interactive IFPS Session

When you sit down at a terminal to use IFPS, you are one of many time-sharing users of a computer. The typical sequence of steps that you follow are illustrated in Figure 1-7.

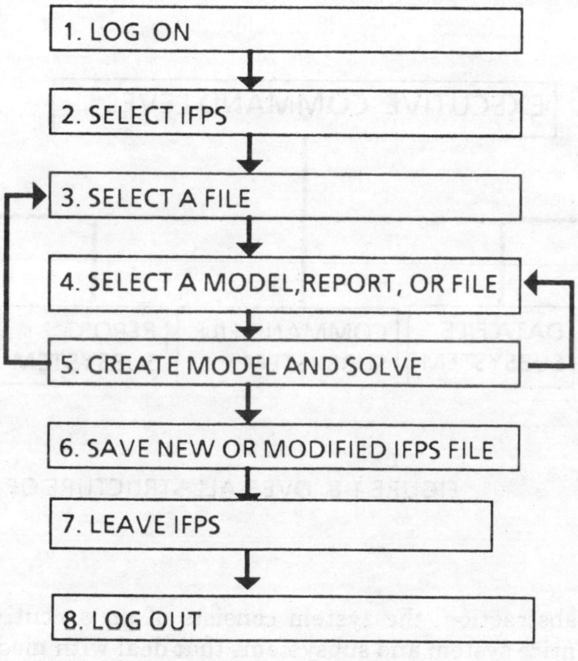

FIGURE 1-7 TYPICAL SEQUENCE OF STEPS DURING AN IFPS SESSION

You begin by telling the computer who you are. This is called logging on. Typically, logging on involves typing your computer number and your computer password. (Step 1). You then tell the computer you want IFPS. Usually, this requires only typing the letters IFPS (Step 2). Because IFPS works with files stored in the computer's memory that contain the models and report formats that you create, you have to tell IFPS which file you want (Step 3) and then which model, report, or data file you want within the file that you selected (Step 4). At this point you can create, solve, modify, or delete (Step 5). Typically you move between Steps 4 and 5 many times during a session. Occasionally, you may go from Step 5 back to Step 3 if you keep several files. Once you have finished your work, you tell IFPS that you are done and IFPS asks you whether or not you want to save the new or modified file that you have created (Steps 6). Finally, when you are finished with your work (Step 7), you log out from your computer by following the standard procedure for your machine (Step 8).

1.4.3 The Structure of IFPS

The purpose of this section is to explain briefly how IFPS is organized internally. This section will be principally of interest to you if you are a computer professional or computer science student who wants to know how the system works. You can safely turn to Chapter II and know that you have not missed anything required to understand the rest of this book. Once you have become proficient at creating and solving IFPS models, you will find it helpful to come back to this section to obtain a deeper understanding of how IFPS works.

The over-all structure of IFPS is shown in Figure 1-8.

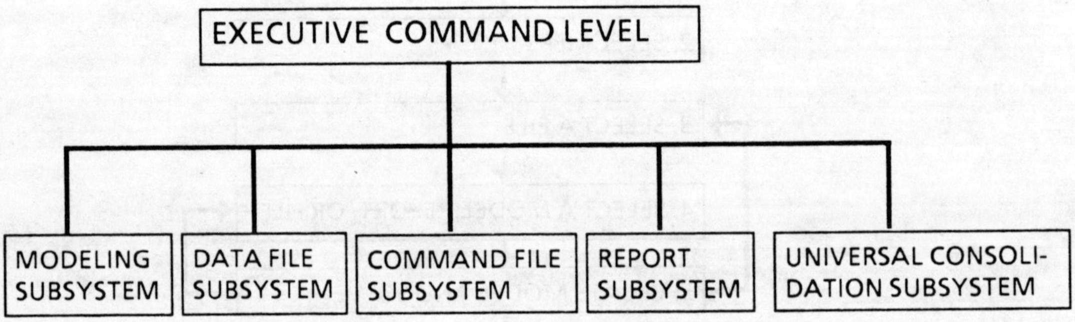

FIGURE 1-8. OVER-ALL STRUCTURE OF IFPS

At this level of abstraction, the system consists of an executive command level that coordinates the entire system and subsystems that deal with models, data files, command files, reports, etc. The descriptions in the following paragraphs provide more detailed views of the executive level and the five subsystems.

EXECUTIVE COMMAND LEVEL: When you enter IFPS you start at the top level, the executive command level. The role of the executive command level is to control the sequence of events that occur. At this level, you have access to

- file manipulation
- execution control
- subsystem selection

File manipulation commands allow you to create files, select which files you want to work on, and to manipulate information within the file in terms of listing, copying, deleting, merging, consolidating, referencing, and selecting specific models and reports. Execution control refers mostly to features that assist in running IFPS. The most often used execution control is the RECORD feature that allows you to obtain a paper copy of an interactive session if you are working at a video terminal that only presents data on a screen. As its name implies, subsystem selection lets you pick a subsystem to work on and to move from one subsystem to another.

MODELING SUBSYSTEM. The modeling subsystem is the core of IFPS. In this subsystem you create new models and edit existing models. You can examine alternative assumptions and build scenarios of what would happen if these assumptions are true. That is, you perform "what if?" and various other forms of sensitivity analyses. You can introduce uncertainty to evaluate the effects of risk. This subsystem also produces the results of solving the model. You can choose automatic spread sheet output, a formal report based on formats set up in the report subsystem, graphical output, or output to a data file for future use. Unless otherwise specified, IFPS provides you with spread sheet output. Finally, this subsystem allows you to consolidate and combine models and their solutions so that you can integrate information from various sources. (Chapters II-V).

REPORT SUBSYSTEM. The report subsystem is used to create and edit report formats. These formats are used in conjunction with models when you want output in other than the automatic spread sheet output. A report format can be saved and used over and over to provide reports in a desired form, for example, in balance sheets or income statements. (Chapter IV)

DATA FILE SUBSYSTEM . The data file subsystem is used to create, edit, and maintain data files for use in the model subsystem. By separating data files from models, you gain flexibility. You can, if you so choose, use one data file with several models or use the same model with several data files. You do not have to have a separate data file to create and solve a model. However, as your IFPS skills increase, you may begin creating more complex models that use large amounts of data. Here the data file subsystem will become of use to you. (Chapter IV and Chapter IX)

COMMAND FILE SUBSYSTEM. This subsystem allows you to create sequences of commands that can be called with a single command. (Chapter IX)

DATA BASE SUBSYSTEM. In combination with the Relation and Query Subsystems, the Data Base Subsystem provides the capabilities of IFPS/DIMENSION. This subsystem is used to create the relational database. (Chapter X).

RELATION SUBSYSTEM. The relation subsystem contains the actual relations used in the data base.

QUERY SUBSYSTEM. The Query Subsystem is associated with the IFPS /DIMENSION database and allows retrieval of information according to the user's needs.

NOTES

[1]Keen, Peter G. W. and Michael S. Scott-Morton, *Decision Support Systems, An Organizational Perspective*. Addison-Wesley Publishing Company (Reading,MA) 1978.

[2]Keen, Peter G. W. and G. R. Wagner, "DSS: An Executive Mind Suppport System", *DATAMATION* (November 1979), pp. 117-122.

CHAPTER II
BASIC ELEMENTS OF IFPS

2.1 How to Obtain IFPS at Your Terminal and Begin Work

2.1.1 Logging On
2.1.2 Making IFPS Available to You
2.1.3 Entering into IFPS for the First Time
2.1.4 Entering IFPS When Your Already Have a File

2.2 Creating and Solving a Simple IFPS Model

2.2.1 A Simple IFPS Model
2.2.2 What Your Type at the Terminal (Use of AUTO for Line Numbers)
2.2.3 Listing Your Program (The LIST Command)
2.2.4 The SAVE Command
2.2.5 Obtaining Answers (The Use of SOLVE)
2.2.6 Keeping the Answers from Rolling off the Screen (SCREENSIZE)

2.3 Multiple Models (The MODEL, FILE, and CATALOG Commands)

2.4 How to Get Out of IPFS (The QUIT Command)

2.5 Correcting Mistakes (The Edit Commands)

2.5.1 Misspellings While Typing
2.5.2 Error in a Completed Line
2.5.3 Using the C Edit Command
2.5.4 Retyping a Line
2.5.5 Deleting a Line
2.5.6 Inserting a Line
2.5.7 Obtaining a Listing of a Single Line
2.5.8 Obtaining a Listing of a Portion of the Model

2.6 Obtaining a Listing at the Line Printer (The RECORD Command)

2.7 The New Product Model--An Example

2.8 Some Principles and Rules in Writing Your Model

2.8.1 COLUMNS Statement
2.8.2 Headings and Blank Lines
2.8.3 The = Sign and Defining Variables
2.8.4 Arithmetic Operations
2.8.5 PREVIOUS and FUTURE
2.8.6 FOR
2.8.7 PERIODS
2.8.8 MATRIX

2.9 Example--ProForma Profit and Loss Statement

2.10 What to Do if You Need Help (The IFPS HELP Commands)

CHAPTER II
BASIC ELEMENTS OF IFPS

This chapter provides the basic information you will need to get started in using IFPS. We will show you how to obtain IFPS at your terminal, enter a model, and leave IFPS. It also shows you how to make corrections in the model and how to obtain a listing on the line printer.

This chapter contains three example models of increasing complexity. Be sure to read and follow these models line by line. They will be referred to frequently throughout the book and will be modified from time to time to illustrate additional concepts.

Finally, the chapter contains two sections you will want to come back to from time to time:

- Some principles and rules in writing your model (Section 2.8).
- What to do if all else fails (the HELP command) (Section 2.10).

2.1 HOW TO OBTAIN IFPS AT YOUR TERMINAL AND BEGIN WORK

Once you have obtained a user number and password for the computer on which you will use IFPS, you can sit down at a terminal and begin work. As its name implies, IFPS is an interactive system. You can use either a video screen terminal (also called a CRT or cathode ray tube), or a personal computer connected through a modem to your mainframe. You will find CRTs generally respond more quickly because they are connected directly whereas microcomputers give you the advantage of providing paper copy that serves as a permanent record if you have a printer attached. If you are working on a video screen, you can also obtain a permanent copy by using the RECORD command (see Section 2.6).

2.1.1 Logging On

The first step in approaching the computer is to log on. You begin by turning the power on and then following the log-on procedures that apply to your computer. Typically these procedures involve the following steps:

1. You tell the computer you want service. This may involve hitting the carriage return or new line key on your terminal.

2. The computer responds by prompting you and asking you for your user number and password.

3. The computer will tell you it is ready for you to begin work.

The foregoing is a very general statement of what happens at most facilities. If you are used to logging on, use the procedure you always use. There is nothing special associated with IFPS. If you have never logged on before or don't recall the details, ask someone to help you -- your instructor if you are a student or someone who works with the computer at your firm. We have left the next few lines blank so that you can write down the log-on procedure here in this guide for easy reference. Another easy way of remembering this information is to paste a copy of a log-on sequence that worked in the space below.

LOG ON PROCEDURES FOR MY COMPUTER

2.1.2 Making IFPS Available To You

Once you have logged on, you ask the computer to make IFPS available to you. This is usually a very simple step. In most cases it only involves typing the letters IFPS. As with logging on, the specific things you have to do depend on the computer installation you use. Use the space on the opposite page to note down what you need to do when you ask the computer to make IFPS available to you.

STEPS NEEDED TO MAKE IFPS AVAILABLE ON MY COMPUTER

2.1.3 Entering Into IFPS for the First Time

In this section we describe what happens the first time you create an IFPS file. The next section describes the sequence of steps to follow if you have already saved an IFPS file and want to work on it again.

Figure 2-1 shows the typical sequence of steps that you follow to begin creating an IFPS model in a new file. You type the words that appear in lower case; the computer gives you the rest. You must press the RETURN key (called New Line on some terminals) after you reach the end of your input. The computer does not respond until you have pressed the RETURN key because it does not know that you are finished giving it an instruction.

```
$ifps
IFPS/Plus 2.0
INTERACTIVE FINANCIAL PLANNING SYSTEM
ENTER NAME OF FILE CONTAINING MODELS AND REPORTS
? sample
FILE SAMPLE NOT FOUND - NEW FILE WILL BE CREATED
READY FOR EXECUTIVE COMMAND
? model gray
BEGIN ENTERING NEW MODEL
```

FIGURE 2-1. SEQUENCE OF STEPS TO OBTAIN IFPS FOR THE FIRST TIME

1. You begin when the computer gives you its standard prompt.In Figure 2-1, the prompt is a $. Other computers may use different symbols such as a ? or a >. When you ask for IFPS in rersponse to the prompt, the computer types two lines. The first line tells you that you have obtained IFPS and gives you the version number (in this case, Plus 2.0). The second line asks you to enter a file name. Your IFPS models will be kept in a permanent file in your private library. Since

you may have many files each with a different name, IFPS needs to know which file to use.

> *IMPORTANT NOTE:* From here on, whenever IFPS types a "?" it is asking you to type something in response. Press the RETURN key after you type your response. Do NOT start typing until the "?" appears because the computer may not understand you.

2. After the question mark, pick a name for your file. Type the name and remember it if you want to use the file again. Choose a name that is different from all existing ones in your private library. The file name should be no longer than the maximum allowed by your computer (e.g., seven letters on some computers and eight letters on others) and have the appropriate format (usually the first character must be a letter of the alphabet). In Figure 2-1, we have assigned the name SAMPLE to the file.

3. Since you are creating a new file, the computer tells you that it can't find the name you just typed and that it will create a new file for you. It then tells you that it is ready for an executive command. Executive commands are instructions to IFPS to do something right now rather than adding to or changing the model you are creating.

4. The *first* executive command that you give the computer is that you want to create a model. To do so, type the word MODEL followed by a space and the name of your choice. In Figure 2-1, GRAY is the model name. Like the file name, you must follow the rules that apply to your computer. For most computers, names that are up to eight characters long with the first character a letter of the alphabet and with no blanks inside the name are acceptable. (These restrictions may be different on your computer.) The model name can be the same or different from the file name. You can keep several models in a file. If you do, each model in the file must have a unique name.

You are now ready to create your IFPS model. Section 2.2 illustrates a simple IFPS model.

2.1.4 Entering IFPS When You Already Have a File

The previous section described the steps to follow when you want to create your first file (or any new file). In this section we describe what you do if you already have a file and want to work on it. For example, you may want to change one of the models, or run a model with different input values, or add new models to the file. Figure 2-2 illustrates the typical sequence followed.

```
$ ifps
IFPS/Plus 2.0
INTERACTIVE FINANCIAL PLANNING SYSTEM
ENTER NAME OF FILE CONTAINING MODELS AND REPORTS
? sample
FILE SAMPLE PROCESSED
READY FOR EXECUTIVE COMMAND
? model gray
READY FOR EDIT, LAST LINE IS 90
```

FIGURE 2-2. OBTAINING AN EXISTING IFPS MODE

1. After the first question mark, type the name of the file you want to work on. If you ask for an existing file, for example SAMPLE which you created earlier, the computer will tell you that the file has been processed and that the computer is ready to receive an executive command.

If you can't remember the file name you have used, you can have the computer help jog your memory by asking it to list a catalog or directory of your private library. You must ask for this catalog before you ask for IFPS. To obtain a catalog you typically ask for CATALOG, or a CATLIST, or a DIRECTORY. Again, this is a system-dependent feature, and what you have to do depends on the computer. Jot down here the way in which you obtain a catalog of file names on your machine.

PROCEDURE FOR OBTAINING A CATALOG OF MY FILES

If seeing the catalog of your files does not jog your memory sufficiently for you to know which file you want, you will have to retrieve each of your files and list them until you find the one you want.

2. Once you have obtained a file, you can find out what is in it. Just as you can obtain a catalog of names of the files in your private library, you can obtain a catalog of the names of the models in your IFPS file. To do so type CATALOG after you are in IFPS. CATALOG gives you the names of all models and reports stored within an IFPS file. (Once you have created a few models, try CATALOG and see what it does.) The IFPS CATALOG command is discussed further in Section 2.3.

3. If you want to retrieve an existing model or create a new model within the file, type the word MODEL followed by the model's name. For an existing model, IFPS responds by giving you the last line number in the model and telling you that the model is ready to be edited.

2.2 CREATING AND SOLVING A SIMPLE IFPS MODEL

Once you have logged on, obtained IFPS, and told the computer you want to create a model, you are ready to begin work. In this section we present a simple problem, its corresponding IFPS model, and the procedure followed to create and solve the model.

2.2.1 A Simple IFPS Model

THE PROBLEM. A new product is to be introduced. Assuming all dollar values in units of thousands, sales are expected to be 100 during the first year and to grow at a 25% annual rate, compounded. Expenses will start at 75 in the first year and will increase by 25 in each succeeding year up to Year 5, after which they will remain fixed.

Management is interested in determining the net income (that is, sales minus expenses) and will use two ratios:

- expenses/sales
- net income/sales

as measures of effectiveness to decide whether to undertake production. The product is expected to be obsolete after six years with no salvage value.

THE IFPS MODEL. The IFPS model that represents the problem is shown in Figure 2-3.

```
MODEL GRAY  VERSION OF  02/06/82  16:01
10 COLUMNS 1-6
20 SALES = 100,PREVIOUS SALES *1.25
30 EXPENSES = 75,100,125,150,175
40 NET INCOME = SALES -EXPENSES
50 *
60 *                                RATIO ANALYSIS
70 *PERCENT OF SALES
80 EXPENSE RATIO = EXPENSES/SALES
90 NET INCOME RATIO = NET INCOME/SALES
END OF MODEL
```

FIGURE 2-3. THE SIMPLE NEW PRODUCT MODEL

DETAILED EXPLANATION OF THE IFPS MODEL SHOWN IN FIGURE 2-3.

line 10 The first instruction tells IFPS how many periods are of interest. The word COLUMNS followed by a definition of the column names is typed. Note that 1-6 implies headings 1, 2, 3, 4, 5, 6. If you had wanted to use years, you would have typed 1981-1986. Unless told otherwise, the computer assumes each period is a year when computing net present value or using other routines involving discounting.

line 20 This line specifies the sales in each period. The first number indicates the initial sales of 100. Sales in subsequent periods are obtained by multiplying the sales in the previous period by 1.25 to reflect the 25% growth. The reserved word PREVIOUS is used.

line 30 This line demonstrates how data can be entered directly as input. Note that only five values are shown. The computer will use the last value (175) for each period beyond the last one.

line 40 This line computes net income as the difference between sales and expenses.

lines 50-70 The * at the beginning of each line tells the computer that what follows is a comment and should be printed verbatim. A line with only an * on it results in a blank line, a convenient way of creating white space in your output to make the output more readable. If information is included after the *, the information will be printed in the same location on the printout. Here the heading RATIO ANALYSIS is neatly centered on the printout.

lines 80-90 These lines compute the ratios requested by management.

Several important points are worth noting about this model.

1. Each instruction is preceded by a line number. IFPS uses line numbers as a simple way of organizing and keeping track of things. Line numbers also allow you to make changes and corrections in the model if needed. It is usually good practice to write your model initially with large, regular intervals between line numbers so that you can insert material later. IFPS organizes information in line number sequence for you. We will talk more about line numbers in 2.2.2.

2. The first line of your model must tell IFPS how many columns you want. If you fail to do this, IFPS assumes your model deals with only one period and your output will only show one column.

__NOTE:__ This assertion is not exact. A COLUMNS statement must appear before the first variable is defined or mentioned. It is a wise procedure to put the COLUMNS statement first.

3. All the instructions that follow the COLUMNS line could have been written in any order. For example, it would have been perfectly reasonable to write:

```
20 NET INCOME = SALES - EXPENSES
30 NET INCOME RATIO = NET INCOME/SALES
40 EXPENSE RATIO = EXPENSES/SALES
50 *
60 *INPUT DATA
70 *
80 SALES = 100,PREVIOUS SALES * 1.25
90 EXPENSES = 75,100,125,150,175
```

In this case we put the calculations first and then provide the input data for the calculations. Most other computer languages with which you might be familiar (such as BASIC or FORTRAN) are "procedural." That is, they require the value of every quantity or variable to be defined before it is used in computation. Because

IFPS is "non-procedural", you can write relations down in any order, as long as you define each variable once on the left-hand side (i.e., on the left of the equal sign).

An advantage of the non-procedural approach is that it lets you organize information in the way you think about it or in the way the user of the output thinks about it. Thus, you can use the format of IFPS output as a way of communicating ideas to others.

4. IFPS makes its computations one column at a time. Therefore when you write

NET INCOME = SALES - EXPENSES

IFPS looks up the value of sales in column 1 and the value of expenses in column 1 and takes the difference of these two values. It then repeats this procedure for each subsequent column.

5. In Line 20 we use the reserved word PREVIOUS. IFPS contains a number of reserved words that have special meanings and are used for specific purposes. Reserved words cannot be used as variable names, model names, or file names. (See Appendix III for a list of reserved words.) PREVIOUS is a particularly powerful way of describing relations because it allows you to use information from earlier time periods. When you write PREVIOUS, IFPS uses the value one column to the left, that is, one period ago. As we will discuss later, you can write PREVIOUS 2 for values 2 periods ago, PREVIOUS 3 for values 3 periods ago, and so on. Even more remarkable is the reserved work FUTURE which allows you to use the value of a variable in the next period (one column to the right). PREVIOUS and FUTURE are discussed further in Section 2.8.5.

2.2.2 What You Type At the Terminal (Use of AUTO For Line Numbers)

The neat printout shown in Figure 2-3 was obtained by asking the computer to list the typed input shown in Figure 2-4. We will show you how to obtain a listing in the next subsection.

Note that by typing AUTO 10 10 the computer prompts you with line numbers starting at 10 and increasing by 10. The executive command AUTO is a request for line number prompting. If you type only AUTO, the computer will give you line numbers starting with 1 and increasing by 1. If you type AUTO 10 the computer will give you line numbers starting with 10 and increasing by 1 (i.e., 10, 11, 12,...). The first number after AUTO tells the computer where to start line numbering and the second number tells it how much to increment line numbers. Thus, AUTO 10 10 starts at line number 10 and increases in steps of 10.

```
? AUTO 10 10
10 ? COLUMNS  1-6
20 ? SALES = 100,PREVIOUS SALES * 1.25
30 ? EXPENSES = 75,100,125,150,175
40 ? NET INCOME = SALES - EXPENSES
50 ? *
60 ? *                                    RATIO ANALYSIS
70 ? * PERCENT OF SALES
80 ? EXPENSE RATIO = EXPENSES/SALES
90 ? NET INCOME RATIO = NET INCOME/SALES
100 ? END
READY FOR EDIT
```

FIGURE 2-4. TYPING THE INPUT FOR THE SIMPLE NEW PRODUCT MODEL

If you do not ask for AUTO, you can either type in your own line numbers or let IFPS do it for you. If you let IFPS assign line numbers, it starts out by assigning line 1 and increasing by 1. In this case, line numbers are not shown when you type your model but do show up whenever you list it. Try this approach and see whether you like it or not.

If you use AUTO, you type END OF MODEL (or simply END) as the last line. Typing END results in IFPS going back to a question mark as a prompt instead of putting line numbers in for you if you are using the AUTO feature. (Alternate ways of stopping the appearance of line numbers are to type LIST or SOLVE. The meaning and use of LIST and SOLVE are described below).

2.2.3 Listing Your Program (The LIST Command)

It is usually good practice to issue the command LIST after you have entered your model. The result will be a neat typing of the form shown in Figure 2-3. At this point, review your model to make sure it is exactly as you intended it to be. If you find mistakes or want to make changes, follow the editing procedures outlines in Section 2.5.

2.2.4 The SAVE Command

When you have completed the model and it is satisfactory to you, you may want to save it. Typing SAVE in response to a question mark replaces the version of the model stored in your file by the current version. For a new model, SAVE adds the model you wrote to your file. Using SAVE periodically guards against losing the work you have done if your computer happens to go down. At the end of an interactive session, if you have created or changed any models and not yet saved them, IFPS will ask you whether or not you want them saved. You should answer YES to that question. Otherwise, you will have to repeat your work.

2.2.5 Obtaining Answers (The Use of SOLVE)

Once you are satisfied that your model is correct, you will want to obtain answers. To do so, you type SOLVE in response to a question mark. The computer tells you the name of the model, when you created it, and how many columns and variables it contains. If you have made any errors, IFPS will tell you which lines need correcting. Follow the procedures outlined in Section 2.5 to make these corrections and then try SOLVE again.

> **<u>WARNING.</u> Be sure to make at least one correction asked for before you try to SOLVE again. Otherwise, IFPS will assume all variables with errors are undefined, will set them to zero, and will give you answers on that basis. This can lead to strange results.**

If you program is correct, as is the case in Figures 2-3 and 2-4, the computer asks you:

```
ENTER SOLVE OPTIONS
```

The simplest answer is to type ALL. (We discuss other solve options in Section 4.1.) The computer will then print out the names and values of all variables for all periods. In other words, it gives you a complete response.

Figure 2-5 shows the results of SOLVE and ALL for our simple new product problem.

```
MODEL GRAY   VERSION OF   02/06/82  16:01 -- 6 COLUMNS 5 VARIABLES
ENTER SOLVE OPTIONS
? all

                                1        2       3       4       5       6

SALES                         100      125   156.3   195.3   244.1   305.2
EXPENSES                       75      100     125     150     175     175
NET INCOME                     25       25   31.25   45.31   69.14   130.2
                                     RATIO ANALYSIS
PERCENT OF SALES
EXPENSE RATIO               .7500    .8000   .8000   .7680   .7168   .5734
NET INCOME RATIO            .2500    .2000   .2000   .2320   .2832   .4266
```

FIGURE 2-5. SOLVING THE SIMPLE NEW PRODUCT MODEL

Go over Figures 2-3 and 2-5 together to make sure you understand how each number in Figure 2-5 is generated from the model in Figure 2-3. For example, in column 1, sales and expenses are input values. Net income is computed by subtracting expenses of 75 from sales of 100. The expense ratio of .7500 is obtained by taking the ration of expenses to sales, that is 75/100. Similarly, net income ration is the result of dividing net income of 25 by sales of 100. When IFPS moves to column 2, sales are 1.25 times the sales in the previous column (i.e., column 1) or 125. Expenses of 100 are an input value and net income is again the difference between sales in the column (125) and expenses of 100. The ratios in column 2 are computed on the same basis as those in column 1, but using the values in column 2. Thus, IFPS divides 100 by 125 to obtain an expense ratio of .8000 and divides 25 by 125 to obtain a net income ratio of .2000. You should continue this process until you are sure you understand how each number in Figure 2-5 was obtained. This form of hand checking for consistency is a valuable technique for verifying the model to make sure that it computes values in the way that you want them computed.

2.2.6 Keeping the Answers from Rolling off the Screen (SCREENSIZE)

If you have a long model or a model solution, you will find that, unless you give a SCREENSIZE command, the lines will roll by faster than you can read them. This phenomenon is called "scrolling." It is terribly annoying and it can be avoided if you type:

```
SCREENSIZE 23
```

in response to a ?. The number after SCREENSIZE refers to the number of lines to be shown at a time. If you have a 24-line screen, 23 is the right number, since one line will be used by IFPS to tell you to PRESS ENTER TO GO TO NEXT PAGE. In general, the number should be one less than the number of lines on your screen.

2.3 MULTIPLE MODELS (The MODEL, FILE, and CATALOG Commands)

When you are finished with creating and solving one model, you may want to start a new problem that requires a new model. To create a new model, you simply type, in response to a question mark:

```
MODEL newname
```

where "newname" refers to the fact that you want to give the new model you create a different name than existing models within that file. The computer responds just as it did when you first started with:

```
BEGIN ENTERING NEW MODEL
```

When you are finished with this model, you will have two models, each with its own unique name in the same IFPS file. You can put as many models in a file as there is space within a file in your computer. For reasons of computer efficiency, it is generally good practice to keep each file small, with only a few models in it. You will find it advantageous to put models that refer to a particular topic (e.g. financial forecasts, market analysis, production analysis, statistical results) in a separate file.

If you want to retrieve a model that is in a file other than the one you are working on, you first have to tell the computer that you need to retrieve that file. You type:

```
FILE
```

The computer first asks you whether you want to save the changes you made in the file you are currently working on. You must respond either YES or NO. The computer then asks you for the name of the file you want. You can give it either the name of an existing file or a new file name. If you give it an existing file name, you can ask for any model in that file; if you give it a new file name it will tell you that a new file has been created.

If you are working with a particular file and do not know what models are contained in it, you can ask for a catalog of that file by typing:

```
CATALOG
```

The computer will come back with a list of the names of the models and reports within your file and will tell you how many lines each contains.

Figure 2-6 shows a simple dialog with the computer that illustrates the MODEL, FILE, and CATALOG commands.

```
? model amort
BEGIN ENTERING NEW MODEL
? file
SAVE UPDATED M&R FILE SAMPLE (YES OR NO)
? yes
MODELS AND REPORTS SAVED ON FILE SAMPLE
ENTER MODELS AND REPORTS FILE NAME
? study
FILE STUDY PROCESSED
? catalog
NAME        TYPE     NUM
SURTN       MODEL    6
SIMPLE      MODEL    9
FORECASTO   REPORT   8
ACRS        MODEL    8
MOVAVG      MODEL    5
SIMPLE1     MODEL    9
```

FIGURE 2-6. RESPONSES TO MODEL,FILE, AND CATALOG COMMAND

2.4 HOW TO GET OUT OF IFPS (The QUIT Command)

After you have completed work on one or more IFPS models, you will usually want to leave IFPS. To do so, in response to a question mark, type:

```
QUIT
```

If you type QUIT, the computer responds by asking you whether you want to save the changes you made in your file during your session at the terminal. Specifically, if your file name happens to be SAMPLE, IFPS will prompt you with:

```
SAVE UPDATED M&R FILE SAMPLE(YES OR NO)
?
```

If you type YES, it updates the IFPS file in your private library (i.e., the permanent file space assigned to you on your computer). Thus, in our example, we had a file SAMPLE. If you type YES, the version of SAMPLE in your private library is changed to reflect the changes you made during your interactive session at the terminal. If you type NO, the original version in your private library is left untouched. Except for any printout you may have obtained, you lose all record of what you did.

Once you have left IFPS, you are still connected to the computer. You can either leave the computer by logging off (using the appropriate logging off word for your machine, such as BYE, LOGOUT, LOGOFF, etc.) or you can go on and do something else at the computer. You could even decide to call IFPS again and begin working on other IFPS models. A typical dialog for getting out of IFPS and logging out is shown in Figure 2-7.. What happens on your computer may be somewhat different since logging off procedures vary from machine to machine.

```
?QUIT
SAVE UPDATED M&R FILE STUDY (YES OR NO)
?YES

MODELS AND REPORTS SAVED ON FILE STUDY
18 SBUS USED
IFPS.
```

FIGURE 2-7. TYPICAL SEQUENCE FOR GETTING OUT OF IFPS

Use the space below to describe how to log off your computer.

PROCEDURE FOR LOGGING OFF FROM MY COMPUTER

2.5 CORRECTING MISTAKES (The Edit Commands)

Even the best of us make mistakes in writing a model. If you do, all is not lost. IFPS has a few simple editing commands that let you correct your mistakes.

You will find that your mistakes are of two kinds:

1. Mechanical mistakes such as typing errors.

2. Substantive mistakes where you give incorrect instructions.

The mechanical mistakes are easier to find because IFPS tells you about them through messages either at the time you make the mistake or at the time you try to SOLVE. Substantive mistakes typically involve errors in logic. They show up as strange and unusual numbers in the output.

2.5.1 Misspellings While Typing

If you spot a spelling mistake while typing a line (and before pressing the return key), you can correct it right then and there. On simple terminals and on DECWRITERS, press the "CONTROL" key and the letter "H" simultaneously. Each time you do this, the computer backspaces one letter and erases that letter. On more sophisticated terminals you may have a backspace available to you. If so, use the backspace key. In either case, go back to the beginning of the error and then type in the correct spelling.

For example, you type:

```
20? PRFOIT
```

and suddenly realize you transposed the F and the O. You backspace using "CONTROL" and "H" all the way to the F and type:

```
OFIT
```

and then continue with the rest of your statement.

> *IMPORTANT NOTE:* On most terminals, you must retype everything you backspaced over since it has been *erased* in the computer. It may still show on your paper copy or on your video screen, but it is not there in memory.

2.5.2 Error in a Completed Line

If you find your error after you have typed the line and pressed the carriage return, you have two choices. You can:

1. Correct the part of the line that was wrong using the C edit command (see Section 2.5.3 below), or

2. Retype the entire line.

You may find it easier to make your corrections *after* you have typed in the complete model rather than while you are in the AUTO MODE. However, if you give editing commands while in the AUTO mode, you will stay in the AUTO mode.

2.5.3 Using The C Edit Command

The sequence for the C edit command is:

line numberC/error/correction/

In place of " line number" type the number of the line containing the error. Do *not* put a space between the line number and the C. Use slash marks to indicate the start and end of the error and the end of the correction. (You may use a : or a " instead of a /.)

You *must* repeat the error exactly as it was made, with *no* spaces other than those in the incorrect or corrected text. For example, if you had typed:

```
30 ? COST = B44
```

and wanted to change the B to a 9, you would type:

```
30C/B/9/
```

and the computer would respond:

```
30 COST = 944
```

That is, the computer will show you the effect of making the correction.

The following are some important notes about the C edit command:

1. When you use the C edit command, the computer scans the indicated line number from left to right until it finds the letter combination that you said was in error. It then replaces the erroneous information with the correction. Thus, if the same letter combination appears twice, it will change the first one. For example, if you had typed:

```
40 PROFIT = OFRTUNE
```

and then had instructed the computer:

```
40C/OF/FO/
```

the computer would respond:

```
40 PRFOIT = OFRTUNE
```

To avoid this problem, it usually pays to include a few letters on one side or the other of the error; for example, you would have been safe if you had typed:

```
40C/OFRT/FORT/
```

2. You can have more letters in the error than in the correction and vice versa. For example

```
50C/PROFITT/PROFIT/
```

works fine.

3. If you have several errors in a line, you can either retype the line number and the whole line or use the C edit command for each error. For example:

```
60 PROIFT = OFRTUNE
```

would be corrected either by:

```
60 PROFIT = FORTUNE
```

or by the sequence:

```
60C/OIF/OFI/
60C/OFR/FOR/
```

2.5.4 Retyping A Line

If you have a lot of errors in a line, or the line is short, you may just want to retype the whole line. As we just demonstrated above, you simply type the line number followed by the correct form of the line. This procedure replaces the incorrect version.

2.5.5 Deleting A Line

If you have a line you want to delete, simply type the line number followed by D, with no space in between. For example, if you want to delete the line:

```
40 PROFIT = FORTUNE
```

you type:

```
40D
```

and the line is gone.

2.5.6 Inserting A Line

If you forgot a line you can insert it at the proper place by choosing an unused line number. For example, if you want to insert a line between 30 and 40 in the Simple New Product Model of Figure 2-4, you might type:

```
35 INTEREST EXPENSE = 10,0
```

IFPS will insert the line in its proper place automatically for you. Line numbers can have up to two decimal places. For example, if you want to insert a line between Lines 16 and 17, you can choose 16.5.

2.5.7 Obtaining A Listing Of A Single Line

If you want to check out a single line, you can have it listed just by typing the line number. For example, if you are working on the Simple New Product Model (Figure 2-4) and want to see Line 40, you type:

```
40
```

and the computer responds:

```
40 NET INCOME = SALES - EXPENSES
```

NOTE: This differs from languages such as BASIC where typing a line number with nothing after it erases the line.

2.5.8 Obtaining a Listing of A Portion of the Model

If you want to list a part of the model you are currently working on (more than a single line but not the whole model), you simply type the first and last line number you want, separated by commas. For example, if you want to see Lines 10 through 40, you type

10,40

IFPS responds by showing Lines 10 through 40 inclusive. The comma is required between the two numbers.

2.6 OBTAINING A LISTING AT THE LINE PRINTER (The RECORD Command)

If you are working on a video terminal rather than a terminal which gives you printed output, you may still want a permanent record of what you are doing. If you are a student you need "hard copy" to hand in to your professor; if you are a professional, you will want records for your permanent files and as a way of communicating results to your co-workers or as an audit trail.

You can obtain "hard copy" by using the following three steps:

1. Once you have entered IFPS and given a file name, you use the executive command.

```
RECORD
```

By typing RECORD, you are telling IFPS that you want the computer to store the complete history of your session at the terminal from this point forward. Such a record will be kept until either you type:

```
NORECORD
```

which turns the RECORD feature off or until you have completed your session by typing QUIT.

2. Choose a file name. After you have given the QUIT command, IFPS will check whether you created a RECORD file. If you did, IFPS will ask you:

```
ENTER FILE NAME FOR RECORD FILE (OR NO)
```

The dialog is shown in Figure 2-8. You can choose any valid file name and assign it to your RECORD file.

```
?QUIT
ENTER FILE NAME FOR  RECORD (OR NO)
?RECORD
1 SBUS USED
IFPS.
```

FIGURE 2-8. TYPICAL SEQUENCE FOR GETTING OUT OF IFPS WHEN USING A RECORD COMMAND

WARNING. The file name for RECORD should be different from any other file name in your private library.

Note that you can reuse a RECORD file already in your library. What you want to avoid doing is destroying material in existing files that is important to you. If you do not heed this warning, you erase the file with the same name and substitute the RECORD file for it.

SUGGESTION: Use the word RECORD for your file name. In this way you will always remember where the file is and not wipe out a file you wanted to keep. It will also help your computer center (and your company's budget) to erase (DELETE, PURGE, or KILL command, depending on the facility) the RECORD file after you have obtained hard copy .

3. Print Your RECORD File. Providing a file name causes the computer to copy your session into your private library. You can print the contents of this file by the standard procedure used at your computer facility to obtain listings of files.

PROCEDURE FOR OBTAINING A LISTING OF MY RECORD FILE

2.7 THE NEW PRODUCT MODEL -- AN EXAMPLE

Throughout this chapter we have used the simple IFPS model of Section 2.2 as an example. We are now ready to formulate a more complex model. In this example, consider the problem faced by a manufacturer trying to decide whether or not to produce or market a new product. The product is a novelty item which is expected to have a market over the next two years, but its future beyond that is uncertain. Management therefore wants to base its decision on the next two years.

The following information has been gathered about this product. (The numbers have been simplified to make them easier to follow.)

1. Anticipated market	8000 units in the first quarter, 3% market growth per quarter thereafter.
2. Market share	15% in first quarter, growing linearly by 1/2% per quarter thereafter.
3. Unit sales price to dealers	\$2.50 during Year 1, \$2.75 during Year 2.
4. Unit production cost	\$1.25 during Year 1, \$1.35 during Year 2.
5. Overhead	80% of production cost.
6. Initial investment	\$2500.
7. Discount rate	15%.

These conditions imply an optimistic forecast of the company's position in a growing market. Some changes are expected to occur after a year, specifically cost inflation (of material, labor, etc.) will raise expenses; however, it is anticipated that these cost increases can be passed along to the customer because the product will be established.

Management wants to use two measures of effectiveness, the present value of the cash flows and the internal rate of return associated with the venture. Figure 2-9 shows the IFPS model for solving this problem.

> <u>NOTE:</u> READ the model carefully. Then read the explanation of each line. Make sure you understand each line, what it says and what it does. Once you have mastered this model, you will have come a long way toward understanding IFPS.

To help you follow the model we show each line and the rationale behind it.

10 COLUMNS 1-8

> The column headings are defined first. This model contains 8 columns representing the 8 quarters during the two-year time horizon.

20*
30* NEW PRODUCT MODEL
40*

> These lines begin with an asterisk. They are comments and will be reproduced exactly as shown. It is good practice to put a title on a model so that you can identify it later and know what it does.

50 SALES = MARKET * MARKET SHARE

> Defines sales as the product of market and market share. We can write this relation even though we have not yet defined MARKET and MARKET SHARE. This is perfectly all right, as long as we define these quantities later in the model.

```
MODEL PRODUCT   VERSION OF   10/11/82   12:27
10 COLUMNS 1-8
20 *
30 *                 NEW PRODUCT MODEL
40 *
50 SALES   =MARKET*MARKET SHARE
60 MARKET=8000,PREVIOUS MARKET*1.03
70 MARKET SHARE =0.15,PREVIOUS MARKET SHARE +0.005
80 GROSS REVENUE = SALES   *  PRICE
90 PRICE=2.50 FOR 4, 2.75
100 OPERATING EXPENSE = (PRODUCTION COST + OVERHEAD) * SALES
110 PRODUCTION COST= 1.25 FOR 4,1.35
120 OVERHEAD=PRODUCTION COST*0.80
130 NET REVENUE = GROSS REVENUE - OPERATING EXPENSE
140 INVESTMENT = 2500, 0
150 *
160 NET PRESENT VALUE = NPVC(NET REVENUE,DISCOUNT RATE,INVESTMENT)
170 INTERNAL RATE OF RETURN = IRR(NET REVENUE,INVESTMENT)
180 *
190 DISCOUNT RATE = 0.15
200 PERIODS 4
END OF MODEL
```

FIGURE 2-9. THE NEW PRODUCT MODEL
(This Figure Continued on The Next Page)

```
? solve
MODEL PRODUCT  VERSION OF  10/11/82  12:27 -- 8 COLUMNS 13 VARIABLES
ENTER SOLVE OPTIONS
? all
                                1       2       3       4       5       6

          NEW PRODUCT MODEL

SALES                        1200    1277    1358    1442    1531    1623
MARKET                       8000    8240    8487    8742    9004    9274
MARKET SHARE                .1500   .1550   .1600   .1650   .1700   .1750
GROSS REVENUE                3000    3193    3395    3606    4209    4463
PRICE                       2.500   2.500   2.500   2.500   2.750   2.750
OPERATING EXPENSE            2700    2874    3055    3245    3720    3944
PRODUCTION COST             1.250   1.250   1.250   1.250   1.350   1.350
OVERHEAD                        1       1       1       1   1.080   1.080
NET REVENUE                   300   319.3   339.5   360.6   489.8   519.4
INVESTMENT                   2500       0       0       0       0       0

NET PRESENT VALUE           -2210   -1913   -1607   -1293    -882  -460.8
INTERNAL RATE OF RET

DISCOUNT RATE               .1500   .1500   .1500   .1500   .1500   .1500
                                7       8

          NEW PRODUCT MODEL

SALES                        1719    1820
MARKET                       9552    9839
MARKET SHARE                .1800   .1850
GROSS REVENUE                4728    5006
PRICE                       2.750   2.750
OPERATING EXPENSE            4178    4423
PRODUCTION COST             1.350   1.350
OVERHEAD                    1.080   1.080
NET REVENUE                 550.2   582.5
INVESTMENT                      0       0

NET PRESENT VALUE          -30.01   410.4
INTERNAL RATE OF RET        .1372   .3056

DISCOUNT RATE               .1500   .1500
```

FIGURE 2-9. THE NEW PRODUCT MODEL
(Continued)

60 MARKET = 8000,PREVIOUS MARKET * 1.03

The market is 8000 in the first quarter. In each succeeding quarter it grows by 3% over the previous quarter.

70 MARKET SHARE = 0.15, PREVIOUS MARKET SHARE + 0.005

The market share starts at 15%, and increases by half a percent (to 15.5, 16, 16.5, 17.....) in each succeeding quarter.

80 GROSS REVENUE = SALES * PRICE

Gross revenue is defined in terms of price and sales.

90 PRICE = 2.50 FOR 4, 2.75

Sales were defined in Line 50, but price was not. Here we use the FOR construct. When we write:

```
2.50 FOR 4
```

we are telling IFPS to use the value 2.50 for four periods. The value of 2.75 applies to the fifth period and all periods thereafter.

100 OPERATING EXPENSE = (PRODUCTION COST + OVERHEAD)* SALES

Having defined revenues, we next look at operating expenses. These are proportional to sales and depend on the production cost and the associated overhead.

110 PRODUCTION COST = 1.25 FOR 4, 1.35

This line has the same format as Line 90.

120 OVERHEAD = PRODUCTION COST *0.80

The overhead is a fixed percentage of the production cost.

130 NET REVENUE = GROSS REVENUE − OPERATING EXPENSE

The net revenue represents cash inflows from the venture.

140 INVESTMENT = 2500,0

The investment is made in Period 1. The way IFPS works, if you specify a single number or expression it applies to all periods. If you want a different value in Period 2, you type a comma and follow it with the Period 2 value. IFPS uses values one at a time until it reaches the last one. It then uses the last value for all subsequent periods. In our example, we invest in Period 1 only. Therefore, the form 2500,0 *must* be used to make sure that no other investments are assumed.

160 NET PRESENT VALUE = NPVC(NET REVENUE,DISCOUNT RATE, INVESTMENT)

NPVC is one of many built-in functions in IFPS. (These functions are discussed in detail in Sections 3.2.1 and 6.2.) The format requires specifying cash inflows, then the interest rate, and finally the cash outflows. IFPS will compute the net present value each period, based on all cash flows through that period. Thus, in Figure 2-9, we see the net present value increasing as time passes and additional revenue is generated.

170 INTERNAL RATE OF RETURN = IRR(NET REVENUE,INVESTMENT)

IRR, like NPVC, is a built-in function. It prints out results only if the internal rate of return is positive. (See Section 3.2.1 for a more detailed discussion of IRR.)

190 DISCOUNT RATE = 0.15

We record the input data value here. It is usually good practice to put constants and other input data at the end of the model. Many sensitivity analyses involve varying these inputs.

200 PERIODS 4

The PERIODS statement is needed if the model does not represent one-year intervals and when built-in financial functions (such as NPVC and IRR) are being used. The PERIODS statement automatically converts the data from annual to the specified number of periods per year. Note that the word PERIODS is followed by a space and then the number of periods per year.

Figure 2-9 also shows the results of solving the model. You will see that we left Lines 150 and 180 blank so that the measures of effectiveness, net present value and internal rate of return, are highlighted. The results show that the net present value is greater than zero and the internal rate of return is greater than the 15% rate used as a hurdle rate by the company.

EXERCISE: Log on to your computer. Create an IFPS file and enter the model shown in Figure 2-9. Solve the model. Make sure you receive the same answers as are shown in Figure 2-9. Use the AUTO command to enter the model and the various editing commands to correct any mistakes you may make. Be sure to LIST the model to obtain neat printout. When you are finished, use the QUIT command to leave the computer. If you use a video screen to do your work, use RECORD and then obtain a hard copy printout when you are done. Save this model in your private library. You will be asked to do additional exercises using this model in later chapters.

2.8 SOME PRINCIPLES AND RULES IN WRITING YOUR MODEL

The Simple IFPS Model of Section 2.2 and the New Product Model of Figure 2-9 illustrate various principles and rules for creating IFPS models. This section summarizes these principles and rules.

2.8.1 COLUMNS Statement

The number of rows (i.e., the vertical dimension) in the IFPS output matrix is defined by the number of equations in your model. The horizontal dimension of the matrix is defined by the COLUMNS statement.

> *NOTE:* The COLUMNS statement *must* appear before any statement with an equal (=) sign in it.

The COLUMNS statement not only defines the number of columns but also the title of each column. If you type COLUMNS 1-8, as in Figure 2-9, you are defining 8 columns starting in column 1. If you had wanted to label the columns in Figure 2-9 QTR1 and so on, you would have typed:

```
10 COLUMNS QTR1,QTR2,QTR3,QTR4,QTR5,QTR6,QTR7,QTR8.
```

You cannot say QTR1-QTR8. On the other hand, you do not have to start at 1; for example, 1983-1988 defines a matrix having 6 columns starting with the heading 1983.

If you do not include a COLUMNS statement, IFPS assumes you want only one column.

2.8.2 Headings And Blank Lines

It is good practice to include a heading or label at the beginning of a model (and often within a model) so that the reader of the output can quickly learn what problem is being solved. In Figure 2-9, Lines 20 through 40 create such a heading. Similarly, you can use blank lines to separate different parts of the model, such as calculations, results, and input data. We have done so in Figure 2-9 by including blanks in Lines 150 and 180.

2.8.3 The = Sign And Defining Variables

Each line of an IFPS model consists of a single variable name on the left side of the equal sign followed by a definition of the variable to the right of the equal sign. For example,

```
SALES = MARKET * MARKET SHARE
```

The only constraint is that each variable to the right of the equal sign must be defined somewhere in the model (or in an IFPS data file being used with the model.) Based on this definition, IFPS evaluates sales each period by taking the size of the market and the size of the market share in the same period and multiplying them together.

If only a single definition is given, it is assumed to be true for all columns and the value of the variable is computed in the same way. If the variable is defined differently in each column, then commas are used to separate these definitions. For example:

```
SALES = 8000,8500,8700,9000
```

results in different values in columns 1, 2, 3, and 4. If the model is defined for more columns than there are data, the last value defined (in our example, 9000) is used for the additional columns. You will have seen by now that you can use numeric values, variable names, built-in functions, and combinations of these on the right side of the equal sign to define the variable.

2.8.4 Arithmetic Operations

IFPS uses +, −, *, and / for addition, subtraction, multiplication, and division. There is a hierarchy of operations. That is, multiplication and division are performed before addition and subtraction. Operations are performed left to right. If there is ambiguity in your mind as to which order will be followed, use parentheses. Operations within parentheses are performed first. For example,

```
X =  3+4/5-2*2
```

results in a value of −0.2 since 4/5 is computed first, 2*2 is computed next and then 3 + 0.8 − 4 lead to the result. If you had intended (3+4) to be divided by (5−2*2) you would have to write:

```
X =  (3+4)/(5-2*2)
```

to obtain the value 7.

2.8.5 PREVIOUS and FUTURE

PREVIOUS and FUTURE are "reserved" words with specific meanings. IFPS has a number of such words (listed in Appendix III) which you cannot use as the name of a variable.

PREVIOUS and FUTURE are particularly powerful instructions because they allow you to refer to values in other columns of the output matrix. PREVIOUS refers to the column to the left and FUTURE to the right. If you use PREVIOUS in column 1, IFPS takes the PREVIOUS value to be 0; similarly if you use FUTURE in the last column, it takes the FUTURE value to be 0. You can also refer to values more than one column away. For example, PREVIOUS 4 refers to a value four columns ago. For example, the statement

```
SEASONALITY FACTOR = 1.1,1.03,0.96,0.91,PREVIOUS 4
```

allows you to define the seasonality factors for the four quarters of the first year and then to use the same factors for all subsequent years. If you are referring to a previous value in the same row, that is for the same variable, you do not need to specify the variable name (but it does no harm if you do). If you want to refer to a PREVIOUS or FUTURE value of another variable, you must give its name. For example, you might write:

```
CASH RECEIVED = CASH SALES + PREVIOUS CREDIT SALES
```

2.8.6 FOR

If you want to repeat a value for several periods, you use FOR. Thus,

```
PRICE = 2.75 FOR 4, 3.00
```

is the same as using 2.75, 2.75, 2.75, 2.75, 3.00 in defining price.

2.8.7 PERIODS

As explained in the previous section, PERIODS allows you to model situations that are quarterly or monthly and to state interest rate in annual terms. The form used is PERIODS followed by a space and a number, where the number can be any integer from 1 to 13. PERIODS is needed only if built-in financial functions (Section 3.2) are being used.

2.8.8 MATRIX

Although you have not yet seen MATRIX as an example, we will be using it at several points in this book. MATRIX is a way of referring to a specific location in the model. One way of thinking about an IFPS model is that it creates a two-dimensional array of numbers, what mathematicians usually call a matrix. The numbers in the matrix (in our case, the IFPS model) can be referred to by their location in terms of the row and the column in which they appear. You can use row names and column names in the reference. For example,

```
MATRIX(REVENUE,6)
```

2.9 EXAMPLE -- A PRO FORMA PROFIT AND LOSS STATEMENT

Budget planning usually involves creation of a pro forma profit and loss statement for an upcoming period of time. In this example, we consider a manufacturing organization, let's call it ACME Company, that produces a single product. We want to create a profit and loss statement for the next twelve months based on assumptions about the anticipated nature of the business. We will first present the assumptions made by the budget planners and then show the IFPS model of the profit and loss statement for the 12-month period that embodies these assumptions.

For ease of following the IFPS model, these are the assumptions:

1. ACME sells one product at a price of $1000/unit. The price will remain fixed for the next year.

2. Sales will average 2500 units per month. However, past experience indicates that there is a seasonality factor. The historical seasonal indices are as follows:

JAN	FEB	MAR	APR	MAY	JUN
0.43	0.61	0.73	0.85	0.94	1.05

JUL	AUG	SEP	OCT	NOV	DEC
1.74	1.89	1.52	1.09	0.66	0.49

3. Cost of production involves material and labor costs. Material costs are $430/unit and are expected to start increasing at a rate of 0.3% per month starting in June. Direct labor costs are $150/unit. Renegotiation of the union contract is expected to increase direct labor costs by 10%/unit in June and remain constant thereafter.

4. The inventory at the start of the year will be 2300 units. The value of the inventory at the start of the year is 1.334M. Production will be constant at 2500 units/month.

5. The following operating expenses are anticipated:

- Advertising expenses will be $26,875 in the first month and 2.5% of the previous month's gross sales, in dollars, thereafter.
- Commissions are 5% of gross sales. They are paid in the month in which the sale takes place.
- Salaries for indirect labor are $70,000/month. A raise of 7% is scheduled for July.
- Payroll and social security taxes are 9.5% of indirect labor.
- The company has a lease on its warehouse and factory that runs through the end of next year. The cost of the lease is $65,000/month.
- The company has a $200,000 note that is not due until after the end of next year. The interest on the note is 1.25% /month (i.e., 15%/year) payable each month. It is a balloon-payment note, with no principal due during the year.
- Depreciation on existing equipment and facilities will be $50,000 in January and will decline at 2%/month, compounded, thereafter.

6. The company expects its tax rate to be 46%.

The IFPS model is shown in Figure 2-10. Note that Lines 10 through 420 define the profit and loss statement. Additional input data and the calculation of quantities derived from the input data follow at the bottom of the model. In this way, either a conventional profit and loss statement can be obtained by displying only Lines 10 through 420 and the assumptions of the model can be shown explicitly by displaying Lines 470 through 610. It is possible to print out only a portion of a model by using the SOLVE options. Specifically, rather than specifying ALL when asked the solve option, you enter :

```
? L10 THRU L420
```

This form tells IFPS that you want all lines from 10 through 420 printed out and no others. Section 4.1 contains further discussion of the SOLVE options.

Read over the model shown in Figure 2-10 line by line and go over the corresponding results in the solution. You will see that the model is set up in the general form of a conventional pro forma profit and loss statement. Each quantity is defined in terms of its accounting relations. For example, GROSS SALES in Line 60 is obtained by multiplying unit price and monthly sales. IFPS finds the value of unit price in Line 470 where it is given as an input. The monthly sales have been computed in Line 510 by multiplying the average sales by the seasonal index.

```
MODEL PROFITLOSS  VERSION OF  01/07/83  11:25
10 COLUMNS 1-12
20 *
30 *                       PROFIT AND LOSS STATEMENT FOR ACME COMPANY
40 *                       ------------------------------------------
50 *
60 GROSS SALES = UNIT PRICE * MONTHLY SALES
70 *
80 *COST OF GOODS SOLD
90 *-----------------
100 *
110 BEGINNING INVENTORY =1334000,PREVIOUS ENDING INVENTORY VALUE
120 *
130 *COST OF MANUFACTURING
140 *---------------------
150 *
160 MATERIAL COST =UNIT MATERIAL COST *PRODUCTION
170 DIRECT LABOR = UNIT LABOR COST*PRODUCTION
180 COST OF MANUFACTURING = MATERIAL COST + DIRECT LABOR
190 *
200 TOTAL INVENTORY VALUE = BEGINNING INVENTORY'
201 + COST OF MANUFACTURING
210 ENDING INVENTORY VALUE = TOTAL INVENTORY VALUE '
211 - COST OF GOODS SOLD
220 COST OF GOODS SOLD = MONTHLY SALES * AVERAGE INVENTORY COST
230 *
240 GROSS PROFIT ON SALES =GROSS SALES - COST OF GOODS SOLD
250 *
260 *OPERATING EXPENSES
270 *------------------
280 *
290 ADVERTISING=26875, .025*PREVIOUS GROSS SALES
300 COMMISSIONS =.05*GROSS SALES
310 SALARIES =70000 FOR 6, PREVIOUS *1.07,PREVIOUS
320 PAYROLL TAXES =.095*SALARIES
330 LEASES =65000
340 NOTE INTEREST = .0125*200000
350 DEPRECIATION=50000,PREVIOUS*.98
360 *
370 TOTAL OPERATING EXPENSE = SUM(L290 THRU L350)
380 NET PROFIT BEFORE TAX =GROSS PROFIT ON SALES -'
381 TOTAL OPERATING EXPENSE
```

FIGURE 2-10. PRO FORMA PROFIT AND LOSS STATEMENT

(This Figure is Continued on the Next Page)

```
390 *
400 INCOME TAX = .46*NET PROFIT BEFORE TAX
410 *
420 NET PROFIT =NET PROFIT BEFORE TAX -INCOME TAX
430 *
440 *INPUT DATA
450 *----------
460 *
470 UNIT PRICE=1000
480 AVERAGE SALES = 2500
490 UNIT MATERIAL COST = 430 FOR 5,PREVIOUS*1.003
500 PRODUCTION = 2500
510 MONTHLY SALES = AVERAGE SALES * SEASONAL INDEX
520 UNIT LABOR COST = 150 FOR 5, 150*1.1
530 SEASONAL INDEX = .43,.61,.73,.85,.94,1.05,1.74,1.89,'
531 1.52,1.09,.66,.49
540 *
550 *QUANTITIES DERIVED FROM INPUT DATA
560 *--------------------------------
570 *
580 STARTING INVENTORY=2300,PREVIOUS STARTING INVENTORY+'
590 PREVIOUS PRODUCTION - PREVIOUS MONTHLY SALES
600 AVERAGE INVENTORY COST = (BEGINNING INVENTORY  +'
610 COST OF MANUFACTURING)/(STARTING INVENTORY + PRODUCTION)
END OF MODEL
```

a. Model

FIGURE 2-10. PRO FORMA PROFIT AND LOSS STATEMENT
(This Figure Is Continued on the Next Page)

```
? solve
MODEL PROFITLOSS   VERSION OF   01/07/83   11:25 -- 12 COLUMNS 29
VARIABLES
ENTER SOLVE OPTIONS
? L10 thru L420

                           1       2       3       4       5       6

                         PROFIT AND LOSS STATEMENT FOR ACME COMPANY
                         ------------------------------------------

GROSS SALES          1075000 1525000 1825000 2125000 2350000 2625000

COST OF GOODS SOLD
------------------

BEGINNING INVENTORY  1334000 2160500 2726000 3117500 3335000 3422000

COST OF MANUFACTURING
---------------------

MATERIAL COST        1075000 1075000 1075000 1075000 1075000 1078225
DIRECT LABOR          375000  375000  375000  375000  375000  412500
COST OF MANUFACTURIN 1450000 1450000 1450000 1450000 1450000 1490725

TOTAL INVENTORY VALU 2784000 3610500 4176000 4567500 4785000 4912725
ENDING INVENTORY VAL 2160500 2726000 3117500 3335000 3422000 3377498
COST OF GOODS SOLD    623500  884500 1058500 1232500 1363000 1535227

GROSS PROFIT ON SALE  451500  640500  766500  892500  987000 1089773

OPERATING EXPENSES
------------------

ADVERTISING            26875   26875   38125   45625   53125   58750
COMMISSIONS            53750   76250   91250  106250  117500  131250
SALARIES               70000   70000   70000   70000   70000   70000
PAYROLL TAXES           6650    6650    6650    6650    6650    6650
LEASES                 65000   65000   65000   65000   65000   65000
NOTE INTEREST           2500    2500    2500    2500    2500    2500
DEPRECIATION           50000   49000   48020   47060   46118   45196

TOTAL OPERATING EXPE  274775  296275  321545  343085  360893  379346
NET PROFIT BEFORE TAX 176725  344225  444955  549415  626107  710427

INCOME TAX             81294  158344  204679  252731  288009  326797

NET PROFIT             95432  185882  240276  296684  338098  383631
```

FIGURE 2-10. PRO FORMA PROFIT AND LOSS STATEMENT
(This Figure is Continued on the Next Page)

```
                              7       8       9      10      11      12

                         PROFIT AND LOSS STATEMENT FOR ACME COMPANY
                         ------------------------------------------

GROSS SALES           4350000 4725000 3800000 2725000 1650000 1225000

COST OF GOODS SOLD
------------------

BEGINNING INVENTORY   3377498 2310631 1007521  238855  105156  617740

COST OF MANUFACTURING
---------------------

MATERIAL COST         1081460 1084704 1087958 1091222 1094496 1097779
DIRECT LABOR           412500  412500  412500  412500  412500  412500
COST OF MANUFACTURIN  1493960 1497204 1500458 1503722 1506996 1510279

TOTAL INVENTORY VALU  4871458 3807835 2507979 1742577 1612151 2128019
ENDING INVENTORY VAL  2310631 1007521  238855  105156  617740 1388495
COST OF GOODS SOLD    2560827 2800315 2269124 1637422  994411  739524

GROSS PROFIT ON SALE  1789173 1924685 1530876 1087578  655589  485476

OPERATING EXPENSES
------------------

ADVERTISING             65625  108750  118125   95000   68125   41250
COMMISSIONS            217500  236250  190000  136250   82500   61250
SALARIES                74900   74900   74900   74900   74900   74900
PAYROLL TAXES            7116    7116    7116    7116    7116    7116
LEASES                  65000   65000   65000   65000   65000   65000
NOTE INTEREST            2500    2500    2500    2500    2500    2500
DEPRECIATION            44292   43406   42538   41687   40854   40037

TOTAL OPERATING EXPE   476933  537922  500179  422453  340994  292052
NET PROFIT BEFORE TAX1312240 1386764 1030698  665125  314595  193423

INCOME TAX             603631  637911  474121  305958  144714   88975

NET PROFIT             708610  748852  556577  359168  169881  104449
```

b. Results

FIGURE 2-10. PRO FORMA PROFIT AND LOSS STATEMENT
(This Figure is Continued on the Next Page))

```
ENTER SOLVE OPTIONS
? 1420 thru 1610

                             1       2       3       4       5       6

INPUT DATA
----------

UNIT PRICE                1000    1000    1000    1000    1000    1000
AVERAGE SALES             2500    2500    2500    2500    2500    2500
UNIT MATERIAL COST         430     430     430     430     430   431.3
PRODUCTION                2500    2500    2500    2500    2500    2500
MONTHLY SALES             1075    1525    1825    2125    2350    2625
UNIT LABOR COST            150     150     150     150     150     165
SEASONAL INDEX           .4300   .6100   .7300   .8500   .9400   1.050

QUANTITIES DERIVED FROM INPUT DATA
----------------------------------

STARTING INVENTORY        2300    3725    4700    5375    5750    5900
AVERAGE INVENTORY CO       580     580     580     580     580   584.8

                             7       8       9      10      11      12
INPUT DATA
----------

UNIT PRICE                1000    1000    1000    1000    1000    1000
AVERAGE SALES             2500    2500    2500    2500    2500    2500
UNIT MATERIAL COST       432.6   433.9   435.2   436.5   437.8   439.1
PRODUCTION                2500    2500    2500    2500    2500    2500
MONTHLY SALES             4350    4725    3800    2725    1650    1225
UNIT LABOR COST            165     165     165     165     165     165
SEASONAL INDEX           1.740   1.890   1.520   1.090   .6600   .4900

QUANTITIES DERIVED FROM INPUT DATA
----------------------------------

STARTING INVENTORY        5775    3925    1700     400     175    1025
AVERAGE INVENTORY CO     588.7   592.7   597.1   600.9   602.7   603.7
```

c. Input Data

FIGURE 2-10 PRO FORMA PROFIT AND LOSS STATEMENT
(Continued)

> *NOTE:* Seasonal index, like all index numbers, refers to the value relative to some standard; in this case, the ratio of sales in a given month to the average sales. For more about index numbers, see Section 7.7.

The rest of the model is straightforward. The only policy question you have to decide is how to compute the cost of goods sold. Since production is the same every month (2500 units) but sales fluctuate, some months you will produce more than you sell and put the extra goods in inventory while in others you will be using up inventory to satisfy demand. If the cost of production were the same from month to month there would be no problem; however, costs are rising. In a typical month, the goods in inventory cost the company less than the goods produced that month. The following are three ways of dealing with this situation:

1. *Current cost.* Assume that all goods sold were produced that month. In the month when you use the inventory, you will be charging yourself more than the actual production cost and your profit will be reduced. (This is a last-in, first-out type of policy.)

2. *Average cost.* Since the items are identical, you can't tell whether you sold an item from inventory or from production. Therefore, average the cost of beginning inventory and the cost of production to determine the average cost per unit sold.

3. *First in, first out.* Sell the oldest units first. Since these units were produced at the lowest cost, cost decreases and profit increases. However, this approach neglects the replacement cost of the units.

We have chosen the average cost approach in Figure 2-10. The average inventory cost is computed in Line 600 from the relation:

$$AVERAGE\ INVENTORY\ COST = \frac{BEGINNING\ INVENTORY\ + COST\ OF\ MFG}{STARTING\ INVENTORY + PRODUCTION}$$

where the numerator represents the cost of the previous inventory plus the cost of manufacturing, and the denominator adds the number of units produced to the number of units in the starting inventory.

EXERCISE: Put the model in Figure 2-10 on your computer. Modify the calculation of the cost of goods sold so that it assumes current cost rather than average cost and determine the effect on the total profit for the year.

EXERCISE: Print out only Lines 10 through 420 to obtain a pro forma profit and loss statement. You will see that the result is almost, but not quite, in the form commonly used for such statements. We will modify Figure 2-10 in Chapter IV (which deals with customizing output) to obtain the commonly accepted format.

2.10 WHAT TO DO IF YOU NEED HELP (The IFPS HELP Commands)

Despite your newly found skill in IFPS and the information available in this book, you may find yourself in a situation in which IFPS does not do what you want it to do or you cannot understand what is happening. Rather than having to give vent to your frustration, you can use the extensive HELP commands available in IFPS.

The simplest way to ask for HELP, is simply type HELP in response to a ? When you do, the following message appears:

```
? help

HELP COMMAND
FORM(S)
 (1)    HELP
 (2)    HELP HELP
 (3)    HELP WHERE
 (4)    HELP CONTENTS
 (5)    HELP *
 (6)    HELP KEYWORD
USAGE
      "HELP" AND "HELP HELP" PROVIDE THIS MESSAGE TELLING HOW TO
      USE THE HELP COMMAND.
      "HELP WHERE" IDENTIFIES WHICH SUBSYSTEM THE USER IS CURRENTLY
      IN, ALONG WITH  THE  CURRENTLY  ACTIVE  FILE,  AND  SPECIFIC
      MODEL, REPORT,  OR STRUCTURE, AS APPROPRIATE.
      "HELP CONTENTS" PRODUCES A TABLE OF CONTENTS OUTLINING MAJOR
      CATEGORIES WITHIN IFPS.  INSTRUCTIONS ARE ALSO GIVEN FOR A
      SUBSEQUENT HELP COMMAND FOR EACH CATEGORY, TO LIST ALL
      CORRESPONDING KEYWORDS FOR WHICH HELP IS AVAILABLE.
      "HELP *" PRINTS A LIST OF ALL KEYWORDS AVAILABLE WITH THE HELP
      COMMAND.
      "HELP KEYWORD" PRINTS THE HELP MESSAGE FOR THE SPECIFIED
      KEYWORD,VALID FROM ANY LEVEL OF IFPS.  CONTROL WILL REMAIN AT
      THE LEVEL WHERE HELP WAS ENTERED.

READY FOR MODELING LANGUAGE COMMAND
```

FIGURE 2-11. RESULT OF HELP and HELP HELP

As you can see, HELP (or HELP HELP) only gives you an index to the HELP commands. HELP WHERE tells you where you are inside IFPS. For example, if you are in a file named SAMPLE and are working on a model named GRAY you would see the sequence in Figure 2-12.

```
?help where
SUBSYSTEM: MODELING
MODEL NAME: GRAY
MODEL AND REPORTS FILE NAME: SAMPLE
READY FOR MODELING LANGUAGE COMMAND
```

FIGURE 2-12. THE HELP WHERE COMMAND

HELP CONTENTS, shown in Figure 2-13, gives you a list of the major categories within IFPS that are available to you. You can obtain a list of the keywords in each category by typing HELP followed by the name of the category; for example, HELP MODS provides you with a list of all the modeling language commands. One way of thinking about HELP CONTENTS is that it is a cross-index of the keywords by which help is obtained (see below).

```
? help contents

CONTENTS OF HELP FILE
THE IFPS  HELP  FILE  IS  ORGANIZED  INTO  THE  CATEGORIES SHOWN
BELOW. FOR A LISTING OF THE COMMANDS/OPTIONS IN ANY CATEGORY, ENTER
HELP CATEGORY WHERE  "CATEGORY" IS THE KEYWORD IDENTIFIER SHOWN TO
THE LEFT OF  THE  DESIRED CATEGORY (FOR INSTANCE, HELP REL8).

       UC        UNIVERSAL CONSOLIDATION
       REL8      OTHER RELEASE 8.0 COMMANDS/OPTIONS
       SROPTS    SOLVE/REPORT OPTIONS
       EXECS     EXECUTIVE LEVEL COMMANDS
       MODS      MODELING LANGUAGE COMMANDS
       CMDS      COMMAND FILE COMMANDS
       DATA      DATAFILE SUBSYSTEM COMMANDS; STORE/STORENT OPTIONS
       FUNCS     IFPS FUNCTIONS & SUBROUTINES
       STMTS     SPECIAL MODELING STATEMENTS
       SYS       SYSTEM-DEPENDENT CHARACTERISTICS & SPECIAL HELPS
       DB        DATABASE SUBSYSTEM
       REL       RELATION SUBSYSTEM
       QRY       QUERY SUBSYSTEM
```

FIGURE 2-13. RESULT OF HELP CONTENTS

HELP * provides you with a list of all the keywords available within the HELP command. This is a table of contents and is shown in Appendix I, which presents a more detailed discussion of HELP. To obtain information about any of these keywords simply type the word HELP followed by the keyword.

CHAPTER III
USEFUL FEATURES OF IFPS

3.1 Using IFPS to Ask Questions About the Model

3.1.1 WHAT IF
3.1.2 SENSITIVITY
3.1.3 GOAL SEEKING
3.1.4 ANALYZE
3.1.5 IMPACT ON
3.1.6 Finding Out Where You Are (CASELIST)

3.2 Built-In Functions (Financial, Forecasting, Mathematical)

3.2.1 Financial Functions
3.2.2 The PERIODS Statement
3.2.3 Statistical and Forecasting Functions
3.2.4 Mathematical Functions

3.3 Built-In Subroutines(Depreciation,Amortization)

CHAPTER III
USEFUL FEATURES OF IFPS

In Chapter II, we described the basic elements of IFPS. We showed you how to obtain IFPS at the terminal and how to construct simple models. At several points in Chapter II we used some of the built-in functions available in IFPS. In this chapter we explore these and various other useful features that are built into the modeling language. These features include the ability to ask questions and make decisions; the built-in functions for finance, forecasting, and mathematical applications; and built-in subroutines for depreciation and amortization.

3.1 USING IFPS TO ASK QUESTIONS ABOUT THE MODEL

In analyzing the results of your models, you will often be interested in finding out what would happen if conditions turn out to be different from what you assumed. You might ask such questions as:

> "What if sales are higher than the marketing department forecast?"
>
> "Will small changes in market size affect our profit?"
>
> "How many units will we have to sell to meet our net income goal?"
>
> "How much impact does a 1% change in sales have on profit?"

IFPS contains a number of commands that allow you to explore these questions in detail. We will discuss four of these commands in this section:

- WHAT IF
- SENSITIVITY
- GOAL SEEKING
- IMPACT ON

These commands all help you understand the effects of changes in assumptions on the measures of effectiveness in your model. In addition, we discuss the

- ANALYZE

command, a useful tool that helps you understand the interrelations that exist within your model.

3.1.1 WHAT IF

The WHAT IF command allows you to change the definition of one or more variables temporarily to see what such a change implies. Being an executive command like MODEL and SOLVE, WHAT IF does not require a line number. Suppose, for example, you are working with the Simple IFPS Model of Section 2.2 (Figure 2-3). You have used the LIST command to display it in front of you at your terminal and you want to find out what happens if sales start at 100 but grow at a rate of 15% rather than 25% per period. To investigate this possibility, you type the command:

```
WHAT IF
```

In response, the computer asks you to:

```
ENTER STATEMENTS
```

This is a request to tell the computer which variable definitions (that is, which lines) you want to change.

As you can see from Figure 3-1, you type in a complete IFPS statement, *without line numbers*, to define the temporary change that you want. What IFPS does in response to this WHAT IF is to replace the old definition of SALES with your new definition.

```
? what if
MODEL GRAY  VERSION OF  08/30/82  16:39 -- 6 COLUMNS 5 VARIABLES
WHAT IF CASE 1
ENTER STATEMENTS
? sales = 100,previous sales*1.15
? solve
ENTER SOLVE OPTIONS
? all


***** WHAT IF CASE 1 *****
1 WHAT IF STATEMENT PROCESSED

                              1        2        3        4        5        6

SALES                       100      115    132.3    152.1    174.9    201.1
EXPENSES                     75      100      125      150      175      175
NET INCOME                   25       15    7.250    2.088   -.0994    26.14

                                        RATIO ANALYSIS
PERCENT OF SALES
EXPENSE RATIO             .7500    .8696    .9452    .9863    1.001    .8701
NET INCOME RATIO          .2500    .1304    .0548    .0137   -.0006    .1299
```

FIGURE 3-1. WHAT IF

After you have specified all the WHAT IF changes you want, you type SOLVE as usual. IFPS asks you to enter SOLVE options. You can ask for ALL, in which case you obtain a complete printout as before. However, you may not need or want to print out an entire model for each WHAT IF case. You have the option of specifying which variables you want printed. For example, in Figure 3-2, we have asked only for SALES and NET INCOME. The idea is to list the names of the variables you want, in sequence, with commas between them.

```
? what if
WHAT IF CASE 2
ENTER STATEMENTS
? sales = 100,previous sales*1.15
? solve
ENTER SOLVE OPTIONS
? sales,net income


***** WHAT IF CASE 2 *****
2 WHAT IF STATEMENTS PROCESSED

                              1        2        3        4        5        6

SALES                       100      115    132.3    152.1    174.9    201.1
NET INCOME                   25       15    7.250    2.088   -.0994    26.14
```

FIGURE 3-2. SELECTING OUTPUT IN WHAT IF

You should know the following important things about the WHAT IF option:

1. Do not use line numbers. If you type a line number, IFPS assumes you are making a permanent rather than a temporary change in your model. This is not a fatal mistake, since your IFPS model now contains your WHAT IF condition. However, the line number has taken you out of the WHAT IF mode and has modified the original model. If you want your original model back, you have to retype the original line with its line number.

2. You can change several statements, not just one, in a particular WHAT IF case. For example, you might want to determine the effect of simultaneous changes into both sales and expenses. In this case you would type:

```
? WHAT IF
? SALES = 100, PREVIOUS * 1.15
? EXPENSES = 70, PREVIOUS + 20
? SOLVE
? ALL
```

3. Each WHAT IF case is evaluated with respect to the original model, referred to as the "base model". That is, if you run several WHAT IF cases in a row, the original model is restored each time.

4. If you want to see what happens if every value is changed by a constant

amount, you can write, for example,

```
SALES = SALES * 1.1
```

The result of this statement is to raise every SALES value in the base case by 10%. This form of "circular" definition (where the equal sign stands for "replace") is allowed in WHAT IF statements but is not allowed in the base model.

5. If you want to accumulate changes from one case to the next, you can do so by typing:

```
WHAT IF CONTINUE
```

Figure 3-3 adds a change in EXPENSES to the change in SALES of Figure 3-1 by use of WHAT IF CONTINUE.

```
? what if continue
WHAT IF CASE 3
ENTER STATEMENTS
? expenses = 70,previous + 20
? solve
ENTER SOLVE OPTIONS
? all

***** WHAT IF CASE 3 *****
3 WHAT IF STATEMENTS PROCESSED

                        1       2       3       4       5       6

SALES                 100     115   132.3   152.1   174.9   201.1
EXPENSES               70      90     110     130     150     170
NET INCOME             30      25   22.25   22.09   24.90   31.14

                              RATIO ANALYSIS
PERCENT OF SALES
EXPENSE RATIO       .7000   .7826   .8318   .8548   .8576   .8452
NET INCOME RATIO    .3000   .2174   .1682   .1452   .1424   .1548
```

FIGURE 3-3. WHAT IF CONTINUE

6. If you make WHAT IF changes and then run sensitivity analyses (see Section 3.1.2), the sensitivity analysis will be with respect to the WHAT IF conditions, not the base model. That is, you can combine WHAT IF and sensitivity analysis. Similarly, the GOAL SEEKING (Section 3.1.3) and the ANALYZE (Sec. 3.1.4) commands are combined with the previous WHAT IF command.

7. If you want to return to the original version of your model, just type BASE MODEL in response to a ?.

Figure 3-4 shows you how IFPS organizes storage and manages files. For now, we will concentrate only on the edit area and the WHAT IF area. We will discuss other portions of Figure 3-4 later. For the present what you need to understand is that your base model is located in the edit area. When you specify WHAT IF, in effect, a copy is made of your model, and placed in the WHAT IF area. The WHAT IF changes you specify are made on this copy on a line-for-line replacement basis. When you ask for SOLVE, the SOLVE command checks to see if you are in WHAT IF mode and runs the WHAT IF case rather than the base model. If you ask for another WHAT IF case, IFPS first makes a new copy of the base case (which is still in your edit area) and puts it in the WHAT IF area. It then makes the changes you specify in your new WHAT IF case. However, if you ask for WHAT IF CONTINUE, the previous WHAT IF case is left intact in the WHAT IF area and is modified. Thus, with WHAT IF CONTINUE you can either make aditional changes or you can modify some of your previous changes.

The WHAT IF area is also referred to in SENSITIVITY, GOAL SEEKING, and ANALYZE. In effect, these commands operate in a WHAT IF CONTINUE mode; that is, if you invoke them right after a WHAT IF case, they work on the WHAT IF case rather than on the base model.

3.1.2 SENSITIVITY

Sensitivity analysis is a special form of WHAT IF analysis. It is typically used when you are uncertain about the assumptions you made about a particular variable. What you want to find out is whether changes from the assumed values have major or minor impact on the results, and hence on your decision. In IFPS, sensitivity analysis allows you to step a variable through a number of values and print out the effects of these changes. Figure 3-5 shows you an example of a typical sensitivity analysis. When you type :

```
SENSITIVITY ANALYSIS
```

IFPS first asks you the name of the variable to be stepped and then asks you to enter the START, STOP, STEP PERCENTAGES. Note that IFPS does sensitivity analysis only in percentage terms. The START and STOP percentages refer to the range of sensitivity to be explored. Typically you would pick a negative value such as –10 or –20 as the start value and a positive value such 10 or 20 as the stop value. The step refers to the increment to be used in exploring between the start and stop values. In Figure 3-5, the start value is –10 per cent, the stop value is 10 percent, and the incremental step is 10 percent.

As you can see from the Figure, IFPS gives you a lot of output in sensitivity analysis. You receive three sets of data:

1. The new values of the variables,
2. The absolute change from the base value, and
3. The percentage change from the base value.

Because of the large amount of information given to you, it is wise to ask only for the values of the variables you need in decision making when IFPS asks you which variables are to be printed. Otherwise, you will drown in output and will find it difficult to interpret the results. You will also notice that the 0% change case is not given. IFPS assumes you know the values of the base case from solving the problem.

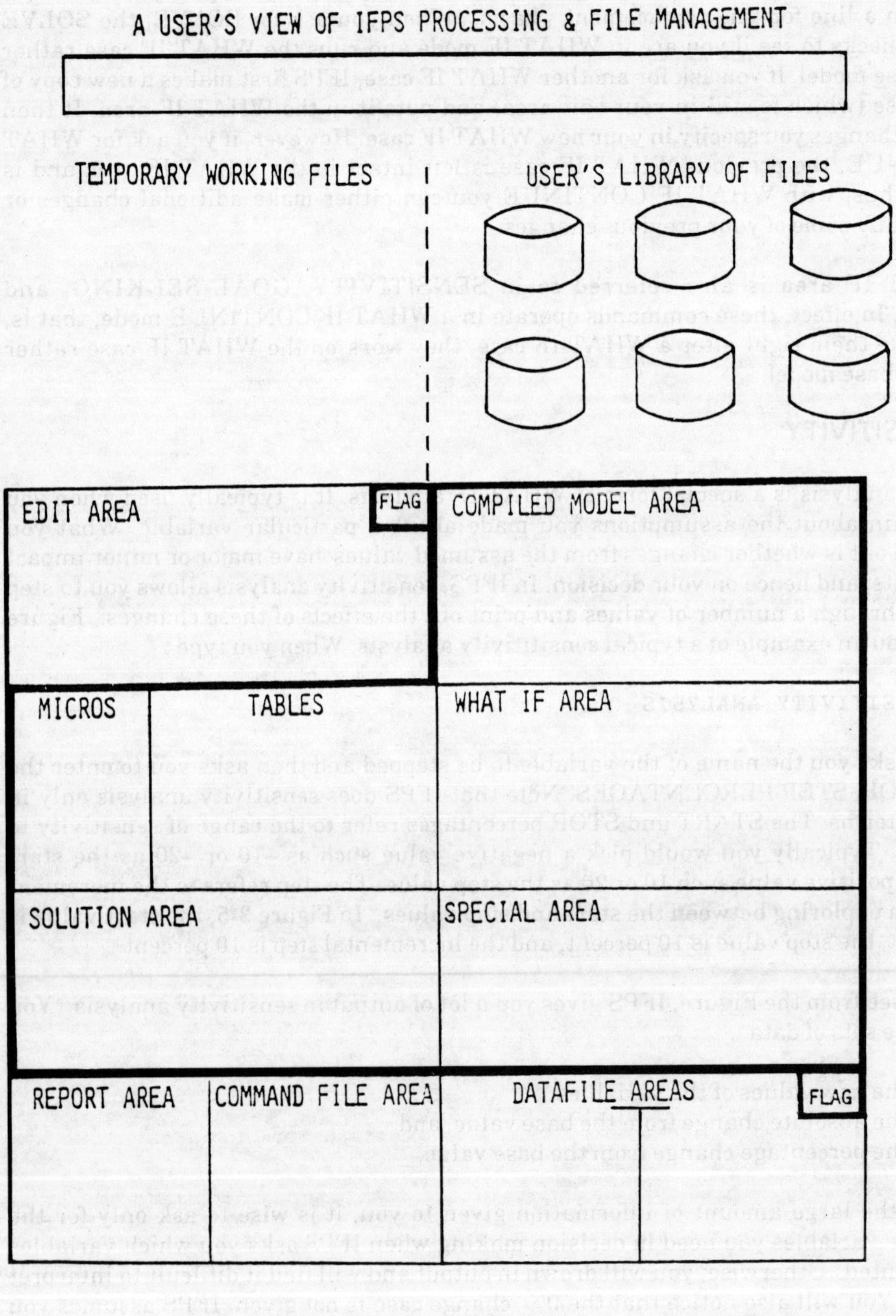

FIGURE 3-4. A USER'S VIEW OF IFPS PROCESSING AND FILE MANAGEMENT

```
? sensitivity analysis
ENTER VARIABLE TO BE STEPPED
? sales
ENTER START,STOP,STEP PERCENTAGES
?-10,10,10
ENTER VARIABLES TO BE PRINTED
? sales,net income,expenses

***** WHAT IF CASE 3 *****
2 WHAT IF STATEMENTS PROCESSED

SENSITIVITY ANALYSIS FOR   -10 PER CENT CHANGE IN SALES
    NEW VALUES

                        1        2        3        4        5        6

SALES                  90    103.5    119.0    136.9    157.4    181.0
NET INCOME             20    13.50    9.025    6.879    7.411    11.02
EXPENSES               70       90      110      130      150      170

    CHANGE FROM BASE

                        1        2        3        4        5        6

SALES                 -10   -11.50   -13.23   -15.21   -17.49   -20.11
NET INCOME            -10   -11.50   -13.23   -15.21   -17.49   -20.11
EXPENSES                0        0        0        0        0        0

    PERCENT CHANGE FROM BASE

                        1        2        3        4        5        6

SALES                 -10      -10      -10      -10      -10      -10
NET INCOME         -33.33      -46   -59.44   -68.86   -70.24   -64.60
EXPENSES                0        0        0        0        0        0
```

FIGURE 3-5. SENSITIVITY ANALYSIS
(This Figure Continued on the Next Page)

```
SENSITIVITY ANALYSIS FOR     10 PER CENT CHANGE IN SALES

     NEW VALUES

                              1       2       3       4       5       6

SALES                       110   126.5   145.5   167.3   192.4   221.2
NET INCOME                   40   36.50   35.48   37.30   42.39   51.25
EXPENSES                     70      90     110     130     150     170

     CHANGE FROM BASE

                              1       2       3       4       5       6

SALES                        10   11.50   13.23   15.21   17.49   20.11
NET INCOME                   10   11.50   13.23   15.21   17.49   20.11
EXPENSES                      0       0       0       0       0       0

     PERCENT CHANGE FROM BASE

                              1       2       3       4       5       6

SALES                        10      10      10      10      10      10
NET INCOME                33.33      46   59.44   68.86   70.24   64.60
EXPENSES                      0       0       0       0       0       0
```

FIGURE 3-5. SENSITIVITY ANALYSIS
(Continued)

3.1.3 GOAL SEEKING

Through GOAL SEEKING, you can find out the value a particular variable has to have in order to achieve a desired level of performance. You can specify your goal either as:

- Performance at a single point in time.
- Performance over the entire time horizon.

Thus, you might want a net income of $150 in Period 6 or you might require that the initial income is $25 and doubles every period. IFPS asks you which variable you want to adjust to reach your goal. If you have a point goal, then you have to specify a point adjustment (e.g., sales in Period 6); if you have a goal over the time horizon, you specify the variable to be adjusted in each period.

> *NOTE*: IFPS asks you first for the variable to be adjusted and second for the relation defining the goal.

Figure 3-6 illustrates the two GOAL SEEKING cases. Since you specify the goal, IFPS only prints out the values of the variable to be adjusted to reach the goal. If you want more detail than the values of the variable to be adjusted, you can follow your GOAL SEEKING command immediately with a SOLVE command.

```
? goal seeking
GOAL SEEKING CASE 1
ENTER NAME OF VARIABLE TO BE ADJUSTED TO ACHIEVE PERFORMANCE
? sales
ENTER COMPUTATIONAL STATEMENT FOR PERFORMANCE
? net income = 25, previous net income*2


***** GOAL SEEKING CASE 1 *****

                         1        2        3        4        5        6

SALES                  100      150      225      350      575      975

ENTER SOLVE OPTIONS
? goal seeking
GOAL SEEKING CASE 2
ENTER NAME OF VARIABLE TO BE ADJUSTED TO ACHIEVE PERFORMANCE
? sales(6)
ENTER COMPUTATIONAL STATEMENT FOR PERFORMANCE
? net income(6) = 150


***** GOAL SEEKING CASE 2 *****

                         1        2        3        4        5        6

SALES                  100      125    156.3    195.3    244.1      325

ENTER SOLVE OPTIONS
? all
                         1        2        3        4        5        6

SALES                  100      125    156.3    195.3    244.1      325
EXPENSES                75      100      125      150      175      175
NET INCOME              25       25    31.25    45.31    69.14      150

                               RATIO ANALYSIS
PERCENT OF SALES
EXPENSE RATIO        .7500    .8000    .8000    .7680    .7168    .5385
NET INCOME RATIO     .2500    .2000    .2000    .2320    .2832    .4615
```

FIGURE 3-6. GOAL SEEKING

You will find that IFPS has adjusted the values of all variables so that they are consistent with the goal you specified. The way that IFPS does goal seeking is by solving the problem "backwards". That is, it fixes your goal and then uses the relations in the model between your goal and the variable to be adjusted to give that variable the correct value. It also changes the values of all variables that depend on your goal. It does not, however, worry about consistency with respect to the variable being adjusted. You can see this by performing the following exercise.

EXERCISE: Consider the simple model:

```
5  COLUMNS 1
10 NET REVENUE = SALES -EXPENSES
20 SALES = 4.8* ADVERTISING
30 EXPENSES = 200 + ADVERTISING
40 ADVERTISING = 100
50 INVESTMENT = 170
60 INTERNAL RATE OF RETURN =IRR(NET REVENUE,INVESTMENT)
```

SOLVE this model. Then use GOAL SEEKING to determine the value of SALES if your goal is net revenue of 250. If you respond to ENTER SOLVE OPTIONS with ALL you will see that advertising expenditures have not changed even though sales have!

Also observe that the value of internal rate of return has changed to be consistent with the new net revenue.

> *MORAL:* Be careful in interpreting the results of a GOAL SEEKING run! The answers you receive may not be possible in the real world!

Operationally, GOAL SEEKING is treated by IFPS as an addition to any WHAT IF (and WHAT IF CONTINUE) statements. It is carried out in the area of storage labeled "special" in Figure 3-4.

3.1.4 ANALYZE

When developing a new model or trying to understand the relations that led to a complex or strange result, the ANALYZE command is a useful tool. As shown in Figure 3-7, when you ask IFPS to analyze a variable, you obtain a printout of:

- The line of the model defining the variable.
- The values of the variable for each period.
- The values of every variable whose name appears on the right hand side of the definition.

It is the last output that is the power of the ANALYZE command to help you in debugging. You can check each of the components that make up your definition of the variable to make sure that they make sense, and you can begin the process of tracing to find the source of errors.

ANALYZE also helps you see which terms in your definition contribute most the to value of a variable. For example, if you analyze SUBSCRIPTION SALES and find that MAIL SALES = 100000 while NEWSSTAND SALES = 5000 you might want to take action.

```
?analyze net income ratio

90 NET INCOME RATIO = NET INCOME/SALES


***** GOAL SEEKING CASE 2 *****


                              1        2        3        4        5        6

NET INCOME RATIO          .2500    .2000    .2000    .2320    .2832    .4615
NET INCOME                   25       25    31.25    45.31    69.14      150
SALES                       100      125    156.3    195.3    244.1      325
```

FIGURE 3-7. ANALYZE

Although you can usually find the same information by poring over the detailed printout from the model, the ANALYZE command highlights information and therefore can lead you quickly to defining issues for decision making.

3.1.5 IMPACT ON

The economist has long been interested in the effect that small changes in one or more variables have on an important decision variable. This is usually referred to as "marginal analysis". It is important because if a small change in one variable causes large and important changes in another, then you must obtain data with great accuracy; whereas, if the effects are unimportant, more approximate data can be used. In IFPS, the IMPACT ON command is used for marginal analysis.

Figure 3-8 illustrates the IMPACT ON command. In using the IMPACT ON command, you have to specify both the name of the variable to be impacted and the variable causing the impact. The variable being impacted is specified first. If you look at the data you will see that IFPS assumed a 1% increase in the variable to be changed, in our case SALES. The default value is 1%. If you want to examine a different percent change you specify the amount by putting a comma after the variable to be impacted and adding BY and the number of percent (but no percent sign!). For example, if you wanted to see the effect of a 15% change of sales on net income ratio, you would have typed:

```
?NET INCOME RATIO, BY 15
```

You are not limited to changing one variable. You can change several. However, each variable to be changed must be changed by the same amount.

```
? SOLVE
MODEL GRAY  VERSION OF  02/06/82  16:01 -- 6 COLUMNS 5 VARIABLES
ENTER SOLVE OPTIONS
? IMPACT ON
ENTER IMPACT VARIABLE
? NET INCOME RATIO
ENTER VARIABLES TO BE CHANGED
? SALES

     NEW VALUES
                          1      2      3      4      5      6

SALES                    101  126.3  157.8  197.3  246.6  308.2

NET INCOME RATIO       .2574  .2079  .2079  .2396  .2903  .4322
     CHANGE FROM BASE
NET INCOME RATIO       .0074  .0079  .0079  .0076  .0071  .0057
     PERCENT CHANGE FROM BASE
NET INCOME RATIO       2.970  3.960  3.960  3.278  2.506  1.331

ENTER MORE VARIABLES TO BE CHANGED OR NONE
```

FIGURE 3-8. IMPACT ON

EXERCISE: Enter the New Product Model shown in Figure 2-9 on your computer. Then perform the following steps:

1. Solve the model.
2. Use WHAT IF to determine the effect of using a 20% discount rate.
3. Use WHAT IF to determine the net present value if, in addition to requiring a 20% discount rate, you expect your share to be only 13% increasing by 0.3% per quarter. Would you still undertake the project under these conditions?
4. Make a SENSITIVITY run on market share, in which the market share ranges from −20% to +20% of the base model value in steps of 20%. Print out the effect on net revenue, internal rate of return, net present value, and market share.
5. Supposing your supervisor sets a goal of $600 net revenue in the first quarter, increasing by $100 per quarter thereafter. Determine the market share required to achieve this goal. In addition, use SOLVE to determine the rate of return and net present value implied by this goal.
6. Repeat the previous goal seeking exercise for a net revenue of $1000 increasing by $500 per quarter.
7. ANALYZE the operating expense and the net revenue in the base model.
8. Determine the IMPACT of a 5% decrease in market and in price on net present value.

3.1.6 Finding Out Where You Are (CASELIST)

Every so often, when you have been working with a large number of WHAT IF, WHAT IF CONTINUE, and GOAL SEEKING statements, you may find yourself in the position of not knowing exactly which conditions are currently in force. To find out where you are, you ask for SOLVE and then, in response to ENTER SOLVE OPTION, you type:

```
CASELIST
```

CASELIST tells you in detail what the WHAT IF and GOAL SEEKING conditions are. For example, you might see the following as output:

```
ENTER SOLVE OPTIONS
? CASELIST

WHAT IF CASE 2
WHAT IF STATEMENTS
   EXPENSES = 70,PREVIOUS +20
GOAL SEEKING CASE 3
GOAL SEEKING VARIABLE BEING ADJUSTED SALES
GOAL SEEKING PERFORMANCE STATEMENT
   NET INCOME = 130,PREVIOUS +30
```

3.2 BUILT-IN FUNCTIONS (FINANCIAL, FORECASTING, MATHEMATICAL)

IFPS contains three types of built-in functions that make life easier for you:

1. Financial functions,
2. Statistical functions including forecasting functions,
3. Mathematical functions.

We will describe each of these in turn.

To use a particular function, you must refer to it by its name and then specify the values to be used in computing its value. For example, to compute the net present value for each period, you have to specify the anticipated returns (that is, cash inflows), the discount rate, and the investment (that is, cash outflows) in the form:

```
NPVC(RETURN, DISCOUNT RATE,INVESTMENT).
```

NOTE: For all functions you have to provide the values in the exact sequence shown. You cannot be creative about it. If you put the value of the discount rate first in the NPVC function, for example, you will get the wrong answer. Although functions do a lot of computing work for you, you have to know the rules and follow them if they are to do you any good.

3.2.1 Financial Functions

The choice of appropriate financial effectiveness measures is, as you know, often a matter of corporate policy. Different measures can lead you to different conclusions about whether to accept or reject a particular investment. IFPS allows you to compute the measures of your choice including net present value, net terminal value, internal rate of return, benefit/cost ratio, and growth rate. Figure 3-9 shows the result of using these functions for a project requiring an initial investment of $1000 at the beginning of Year 1 and having returns of $400, $500, $500, and $600 at the end of Years 1, 2, 3, and 4. A discount rate of 15% is assumed.

```
MODEL FUNCT  VERSION OF  09/02/85  21:07
10 COLUMNS 1-4
20 INVESTMENT=1000,0
30 RETURNS =400,500,500,600
40 DISCOUNT RATE=.15
50 NET PRESENT VALUE =NPVC(RETURNS,DISCOUNT RATE,INVESTMENT)
60 NET TERMINAL VALUE = NTV(RETURNS,DISCOUNT RATE,INVESTMENT)
70 INTERNAL RATE OF RETURN =IRR(RETURNS,INVESTMENT)
80 BENEFIT COST RATIO=BCRATIO(RETURNS,DISCOUNT RATE,INVESTMENT)
90 GROWTH OF RETURNS = GROWTHRATE(RETURNS)
100 RECENT GROWTH = GROWTHRATE(RETURNS,2)
END OF MODEL
?solve
MODEL FUNCT  VERSION OF  09/02/85  15:12 -- 4 COLUMNS 9 VARIABLES
ENTER SOLVE OPTIONS
?all

                               1        2        3        4

INVESTMENT                  1000        0        0        0
RETURNS                      400      500      500      600
DISCOUNT RATE              .1500    .1500    .1500    .1500
NET PRESENT VALUE         -652.2   -274.1    54.66    397.7
NET TERMINAL VALUE          -750   -362.5    83.13    695.6
INTERNAL RATE OF RET                         .1814    .3229
BENEFIT COST RATIO         .3478    .7259    1.055    1.398
GROWTH OF RETURNS                   .2500    .1180    .1447
RECENT GROWTH                                    0    .0954
```

FIGURE 3-9. FINANCIAL FUNCTIONS (NPVC,NTV,IRR,BCRATIO,GROWTH RATE)

In Figure 3-9, the following considerations apply to the measures of effectiveness:

<u>Consideration 1.</u> The functions are defined in the following format:

NET PRESENT VALUE: NPVC(RETURN,DISCOUNT RATE, INVESTMENT)

NET TERMINAL VALUE: NTV(RETURN,DISCOUNT RATE, INVESTMENT)

INTERNAL RATE OF RETURN: IRR(RETURN,INVESTMENT)

BENEFIT/COST RATIO: BCRATIO(RETURN,DISCOUNT RATE, INVESTMENT)

GROWTHRATE: GROWTHRATE (VARIABLE) OR GROWTHRATE (VARIABLE, COLUMN)

Consideration 2. The return, discount rate, and investment can be defined elsewhere in the model (e.g., in Lines 20, 30, and 40 in Figure 3-9) or numerically in the function itself. For example, we could have written:

```
50 NET PRESENT VALUE = NPVC(RETURNS,.15,INVESTMENT)
```

On most computers (but not on some Control Data Computers operating under NOS or KRONOS), discount rate can be expressed as either a decimal (e.g., .15) or as a percentage (e.g., 15%). Control Data accepts only the decimal form.

Consideration 3. You do not have to use the word RETURNS or the word INVESTMENT in Lines 50 through 90. You can refer to any variable in your model (that is, the left-hand side of an equal sign) or use any arithmetic expression. For example, if you have several sources of income (e.g., DIRECT SALES, SALES THROUGH JOBBERS, MAIL SALES, EXPORT SALES), you can accumulate these sources into a single variable (e.g., NET SALES=DIRECT SALES + SALES THROUGH JOBBERS + MAIL SALES + EXPORT SALES) and call for NPVC(NET SALES,DISCOUNT RATE,INVESTMENT) or you could put all the information into the function by writing NPVC(DIRECT SALES+SALES THROUGH JOBBERS+MAIL SALES + EXPORT SALES, DISCOUNT RATE,INVESTMENT). Similarly, if you had several investments, you could accumulate them into a single variable.

Consideration 4. Investments (cash outflows) are assumed to take place at the beginning of a period and returns (cash inflows) are assumed to take place at the end of the period. These conventions are discussed further in Section 6.16.

Each of the financial functions is described briefly below. Additional descriptions with examples are given in Chapter VI.

NET PRESENT VALUE. The NPVC function determines the value of *all* investments and *all* income over the time of the calculations. The function is quite general. It allows investments to be made at the beginning of any period (not just the first period) and returns (not necessarily equal to one another) to occur at the end of any period. For each period, the function computes the present value of all cash flows up to that time. For example, in Figure 3-9, the present value of –274.1 in Period 2 is the result of the investment of $1000 and the returns of $400 and $500. In Period 3, the discounted return from the $500 received in that period is added to raise the net present value to 54.66.

The NPVC function is discussed in more detail in Section 6.2.1 in the Chapter on Financial Applications. In that section, we also discuss a more specialized function, NPV. The NPV function is used to find the present worth of an annuity which requires an initial investment at the beginning of Year 1 and has fixed annual payments thereafter for a specified lifetime.

NET TERMINAL VALUE. The NTV function computes the compounded cash value up to the end of the current period of all investments and returns. It is computed in the same way as the NPVC function, but both investments and returns are compounded rather than discounted back to the present. The NTV function is described further in Section 6.2.3.

INTERNAL RATE OF RETURN. THE IRR function prints out only *positive* values of the internal rate of return except in the last column. When multiple rates of return can be ascribed to a particular set of cash flows, IFPS prints out the smallest positive value. See Section 6.4.3 for a further discussion of IRR.

BENEFIT / COST RATIO. The BCRATIO function is based on the ratio of the net present value of the cash inflows divided by the net present value of the investments. It is really an alternative way of expressing the NPVC function. BCRATIO has a value smaller than 1.0 when the NPVC function is negative and a value greater than 1.0 when the NPVC function is positive. BCRATIO is discussed further in Section 6.4.4.

GROWTHRATE. GROWTHRATE measures the annual percentage growth in a variable with respect to some starting point. The growth rate is a measure of compound growth. As shown in Figure 3-9, it has 2 forms. In the first form, GROWTHRATE(RETURNS), the function computes the compound growth in the annual returns relative to column 1. Because column 1 is the standard, no data are shown. You will see a 25% growth in returns (from 400 to 500) shown in column 2. However, because the variable measures compound growth rate, when the returns remain flat at 500 in column 3, the average annual growth rate for the first two years is only 11.8%.

In the second form, GROWTHRATE(RETURNS,2), the function computes the growth rate relative to a specified column, in our case column 2. The idea here is that you may want to measure growth from some point other than the beginning year. For example, if a new sales manager were appointed at the end of Year 2, you might want to see what growth the new person produced.

GROWTHRATE assumes the columns represent years. If they represent some other time interval, you must include a PERIODS statement .

3.2.2 The PERIODS Statement

Unless told otherwise, the built-in financial functions assume that the discount rates and cash flows are annual values. If the cash flows are more frequent than annual (for example, monthly or quarterly) you have to tell IFPS about it by using the PERIODS statement. We saw an example of the PERIODS statement in the new product model shown in Figure 2-9, where the quarterly nature of the cash flows was indicated in line 200 by:

```
200 PERIODS 4
```

In general, the PERIODS statement requires a line number, the word PERIODS followed by a space, and the number of periods per year. The statement can be put any place in your model; the end of the model is a good place.

The periods statement converts the annual rate into a period rate by the formula:

$$\text{PERIOD RATE} = (1 + \text{ANNUAL RATE})^{1/\text{PERIODS}} - 1 \qquad (3\text{-}1)$$

The statement also results in giving the correct annualized rate for internal rate of return.

The PERIODS statement is needed only if you use the built-in financial functions (Section 3.2.1) or the built-in financial subroutines (Section 3.3) in your model. Its only role is to convert interest rates from and to annualized values.

3.2.3 Statistical And Forecasting Functions

IFPS provides both elementary statistical and elementary forecasting functions. The statistical functions, illustrated in Figure 3-10, are:

- MEAN
- MEDIAN
- STDDEV (for standard deviation)

The forecasting functions, which will be illustrated in Figures 3-10, 3-11, and 3-12, respectively, are:

- MOVAVG (for moving average)
- TREND (for trend extrapolation)
- POLYFIT(for fitting linear and quadratic functions to data)

```
MODEL STATFNCT  VERSION OF  08/30/82  16:38
10 COLUMNS 1-6
20  X=25,27,33,26,44,30
30 MEAN VALUE= MEAN(MATRIX(X,1),MATRIX(X,6))
40 MEDIAN VALUE= MEDIAN(MATRIX(X,1),MATRIX(X,6))
50 STANDARD DEVIATION = STDDEV(MATRIX(X,1),MATRIX(X,6))
END OF MODEL
?solve
MODEL STATFNCT  VERSION OF  08/30/82  16:38 -- 6 COLUMNS 4 VARIABLES
ENTER SOLVE OPTIONS
? all

                             1        2        3        4        5        6

X                           25       27       33       26       44       30
MEAN VALUE               30.83    30.83    30.83    30.83    30.83    30.83
MEDIAN VALUE                30       30       30       30       30       30
STANDARD DEVIATION       7.083    7.083    7.083    7.083    7.083    7.083
```

FIGURE 3-10. STATISTICAL FUNCTIONS (MEAN,MEDIAN,STDDEV)

MEAN. The MEAN function (Figure 3-10) allows you to find the average of the values of a particular variable across a set of columns. A typical reference to the MEAN function is:

AVERAGE COST = MEAN(MATRIX(COST,1),MATRIX(COST,6)) (3-2)

As described in Sections 2.8.8 and 4.4.2, MATRIX is used to refer to a location in the model. MATRIX(COST,1) in Equation (3-2) refers to the row labeled COST and to column 1, while MATRIX(COST,6) refers to the row labeled COST and to column 6. In using the MEAN function, then, you have to specify both a particular row and the number (or names) of the starting column and the ending column. One way of doing this is to use

MATRIX twice with the same row reference. Thus, if Equation (3-2) appears in an IFPS model (as it does in Line 30), it results in finding the average of the 6 values in columns 1 through 6.

MEDIAN. The MEDIAN function works in exactly the same way as the mean function, requiring matrix references to the starting and ending columns of a particular row. Instead of finding the average value of these numbers, IFPS selects the value such that half the numbers are smaller than the median and half the numbers are larger than the median. For example, if there are seven numbers, it chooses the fourth largest number, since there are three numbers which are smaller and three numbers which are larger. If there are six numbers, however, IFPS also chooses the fourth largest (as shown in Figure 3-10). (The usual approach in statistics texts is to take the average of the third and fourth values if there are six values; be sure to remember that IFPS does not do it this way!).

STDDEV. The STDDEV function finds the standard deviation of the sample defined by the MATRIX references. A typical STDDEV function is:

STD DEVIATION = STDDEV(MATRIX(COST,1),MATRIX(COST,6)) (3-3)

The STDDEV function is discussed in more detail in Section 7.1.5 where the relations among the standard deviation of the sample, the variance of the sample, the standard deviation of the population, and the variance of the population are shown.

MOVAVG. One simple forecast of what will happen is to assume that future values will be equal to the average of past values. A slightly more sophisticated forecast is to use only recent values. This can be done through the use of the MOVAVG function illustrated in Figure 3-11.

```
MODEL MOVAVG   VERSION OF   08/30/82   16:38
10 COLUMNS 1-6
20 X=25,27,33,26,44,30
30 Y=MOVAVG(X,.5,.5)
40 Z=MOVAVG(FUTURE X,.33,.33,.33)
50 W=MOVAVG(X,.5,.3,.2)
END OF MODEL
? solve
MODEL MOVAVG   VERSION OF   08/30/82   16:38 -- 6 COLUMNS 4 VARIABLES
ENTER SOLVE OPTIONS
?all
                         1        2        3        4        5        6

X                       25       27       33       26       44       30
Y                       25       26       30    29.50       35       37
Z                       26    28.33    28.67    34.33    33.33       37
W                       25    25.80    27.20    28.60    33.10    32.20
```

FIGURE 3-11. MOVING AVERAGE

To use the MOVAVG function, you specify the variable to be averaged and the relative weight to be given to each period, starting with the variable and working backwards in that row. In general form:

MOVAVG(variable, weight1,weight2,....weightn).

The last weight (weightn) refers to the current period and each preceding weight to a preceding period. For example:

MOVAVG(variable, weight1,weight2)

assigns weight2 to the current period and weight1 to the previous period. The weights allow you to give different importance to different past periods. The weights should add up to 1; however, if they do not, IFPS scales them for you automatically during the calculation so that they do add to 1.

Note that in Line 40 of Figure 3-11, the starting point for the variable is FUTURE X. FUTURE refers to one period from now (i.e. from the current column) just as PREVIOUS refers to one period ago. In Period 3, for example,

$$Z = \text{MOVAVG(FUTURE X,.333,.333,.333)} \tag{3-4}$$

finds the average of the value of X in periods 4, 3, and 2.

You must be careful in interpreting the the values computed for MOVAVG for the starting and ending columns in a particular row. If MOVAVG refers to a value that is undefined because it is outside the model, two things happen:

1. The values outside the model are discarded.
2. The weights are rescaled based on the remaining points.

For example, the value given in column 1 for Z is 26, which is the average of the X values in columns 1 and 2 since MOVAVG(FUTURE X,.33,.33,.33) in column 1 calls for the values in columns 2, 1, and 0.

Line 50 in Figure 3-11 shows an example of unequal weights. Here we take MOVAVG(X,.5,.3,.2), which implies the current value contributes less to the forecast than the previous value and the previous value contributing less than the value two periods ago. The value of 27.2 in Column 3 for W is obtained by taking 20% of 33, 30% of 27 and 50% of 25. (Check this!)

TREND. The TREND function performs simple linear regression. In Figure 3-12, sales are forecast from the trend line fitted to the relation between advertising and sales. To use TREND, you provide the model with historical values for two or more periods so that a regression line can be determined. In Figure 3-12, five periods of sales and advertising history are given and the sales anticipated in Period 6 for the proposed advertising budget of $35,000 is forecast.

```
MODEL TREND  VERSION OF   08/30/82  16:38
10 COLUMNS 1-6
20 ADVERTISING EXPENDITURE =50000,30000,45000,40000,30000,35000
30 SALES=1500000,1400000,1420000,1550000,1600000,'
31 TREND(ADVERTISING EXPENDITURE)
END OF MODEL
?solve
MODEL TREND  VERSION OF   08/30/82  16:38 -- 6 COLUMNS 2 VARIABLES
ENTER SOLVE OPTIONS
?all

                             1       2       3       4       5       6

ADVERTISING EXPENDIT     50000   30000   45000   40000   30000   35000
SALES                  1500000 1400000 1420000 1550000 1600000 1499375
```

FIGURE 3-12. TREND

In computing the TREND function, IFPS generates a linear regression function of the form:

$$a + bX$$

where a and b are the coefficients of the regression line. Normally, these coefficients are not displayed. However, if, at any time before you SOLVE for the trend line you enter OPTION H2 on a separate line, these coefficients are printed out for you from then until you QUIT.

Linear regression models (including the TREND function) are discussed further in Section 7.5.

POLYFIT. Whereas the TREND function deals with the effects of one variable (e.g., advertising) in your model on another (e.g., sales), POLYFIT extrapolates a single variable forward in time. As shown in Figure 3-13, the extrapolation can have three forms, denoted by POLYFIT(0), POLYFIT(1), or POLYFIT(2).

If POLYFIT(0) is used, all future values are assumed to be the same and equal to the average of the past values. For POLYFIT(1), a regression line is fitted to the data and is used to extrapolate to the next period. In POLYFIT(2), the extrapolation is based on fitting a quadratic equation to the data and then extrapolating.

In Figure 3-13, the same four data points are used as inputs. The values in columns 5 and 6 are extrapolation values that result from the three forms of the POLYFIT function.

```
MODEL POLY  VERSION OF  08/30/82  16:37
10 COLUMNS 1-6
20 SALES0=125,138,142,159,POLYFIT(0)
30 SALES1=125,138,142,159,POLYFIT(1)
40 SALES2=125,138,142,159,POLYFIT(2)
END OF MODEL
? solve
MODEL POLY  VERSION OF  08/30/82  16:37 -- 6 COLUMNS 3 VARIABLES
ENTER SOLVE OPTIONS
? all

                               1       2       3       4       5       6

SALES0                       125     138     142     159     141     141
SALES1                       125     138     142     159   167.5   178.1
SALES2                       125     138     142     159   172.5   189.1
```

FIGURE 3-13. POLYFIT

3.2.4 Mathematical Functions

Like BASIC and other computer programming languages, IFPS contains a number of built-in mathematical functions. These functions fall into three groups:

1. Functions of a single variable (natural logarithm, logarithm to the base 10, exponential, truncate, roundup, round, and absolute value).

2. Functions of two or more variables (raising to a power, maximum, and minimum).

3. Table look-up functions (step function, interpolation).

These functions are illustrated in Figure 3-14.

<u>*FUNCTIONS OF A SINGLE VARIABLE*</u>. The NATLOG, LOG10, and NATEXP functions compute logarithms and e to the power x. Two kinds of logarithms are provided. NATLOG refers to Naperian or "natural" logarithms that are defined to the base e, whereas LOG10 refers to ordinary logarithms defined to the base 10. The latter are what you learned first in high school. The NATLOG and NATEXP functions occasionally show up in financial models. The exponential function is also useful for obtaining exponentially distributed random variables in simulations (see Sec. 5.14). You may note one peculiarity: IFPS ignores signs on natural logarithms and logarithms to the base 10. That is, the rules of mathematics define logarithms only for positive numbers but IFPS ignores this restriction so that you don't stop the calculation with an error message. However, you have to be careful and recognize that logarithms of negative numbers are meaningless.

```
MODEL MATH  VERSION OF  09/02/85  23:18
10 COLUMNS 1-6
20 X=1,5,10,12.3,12.7,-5
30 NATURAL LOG=NATLOG(X)
40 LOG TO THE BASE 10 = LOG10(X)
50 E TO THE POWER X=NATEXP(X)
60 TRUNCATE =TRUNCATE(X)
70 ROUNDUP=ROUNDUP(X)
80 ROUND =ROUND(X)
90 ABSOLUTE VALUE=ABS(X)
100 *
110 *FUNCTIONS OF TWO AND MORE VARIABLES
120 *
130 Y= .5,2,3,3.5,4,5
140 X TO THE POWER Y =XPOWERY(X,Y)
150 Z=10
160 MAXIMUM OF X Y AND Z=MAXIMUM(X,Y,Z)
170 MINIMUM OF X Y AND Z=MINIMUM(X,Y,Z)
END OF MODEL
? solve
MODEL MATH  VERSION OF  09/02/85  23;18 -- 6 COLUMNS 13 VARIABLES
ENTER SOLVE OPTIONS
? all
                          1       2       3       4       5       6

X                         1       5      10   12.30   12.70      -5
NATURAL LOG               0   1.609   2.303   2.510   2.542   1.609
LOG TO THE BASE 10        0   .6990       1   1.090   1.104   .6990
E TO THE POWER X      2.718   148.4   22026  219696  327748   .0067
TRUNCATE                  1       5      10      12      12      -5
ROUNDUP                   1       5      10      13      13      -5
ROUND                     1       5      10      12      13      -5
ABSOLUTE VALUE            1       5      10   12.30   12.70       5

FUNCTIONS OF TWO AND MORE VARIABLES

Y                     .5000       2       3   3.500       4       5
X TO THE POWER Y          1      25    1000    6526   26014   -3125
Z                        10      10      10      10      10      10
MAXIMUM OF X Y AND Z     10      10      10   12.30   12.70      10
MINIMUM OF X Y AND Z  .5000       2       3   3.500       4      -5
```

FIGURE 3-14. MATHEMATICAL FUNCTIONS

The TRUNCATE, ROUNDUP, ROUND, and ABS functions are used to present numbers in uniform format. Suppose X = 12.30. TRUNCATE removes all fractional parts; therefore, TRUNCATE(X) = 12. ROUNDUP increases numbers with fractional parts to the next highest integer; therefore ROUNDUP(X) = 13. ROUND, on the other hand, finds the closest integer; therefore, ROUND(X) = 12.

IMPORTANT NOTE: TRUNCATE, ROUNDUP, and ROUND work on the absolute values of numbers. Thus, if X = –4.3, TRUNCATE (X) = –4, ROUNDUP(X) = –5, and ROUND(X) = –4.

ABS finds the absolute value of numbers; that is, it removes the minus sign from negative numbers but leaves positive numbers as they are.

FUNCTIONS OF TWO OR MORE VARIABLES. Of all the mathematical functions, the one you are most likely to use frequently is XPOWERY. This function allows you to raise any positive number X to any power Y and to raise any negative number to an integer power. It is also the function you use to obtain square roots, since IFPS does not have a built-in square root function. For example, to find the square root of 9, you would write:

```
XPOWERY(9,0.5)
```
(3-5)

where, of course, the 0.5 represents the one-half power for the square root. You can also do arithmetic inside a mathematical function. For example, you could have written XPOWERY(9,1/2) in Equation (3-5) to obtain the square root.

In the case of maximum and minimum functions, you have to specify the list whose maximum or minimum you want. In Lines 150 and 160 of Figure 3-14, three variables are used; you could just as easily have found the maximum or minimum of two or four or as many as nine variables.

INTERPOLATION ON. If you need a function that is not built-in to IFPS, you can represent it in your model by using INTERPOLATION ON. For example, suppose your market forecasts indicate the following relation between PRICE and SALES VOLUME:

PRICE	SALES VOLUME
1.50	10000
1.70	9000
1.85	8000
2.00	6500
2.10	5000

In graphical form:

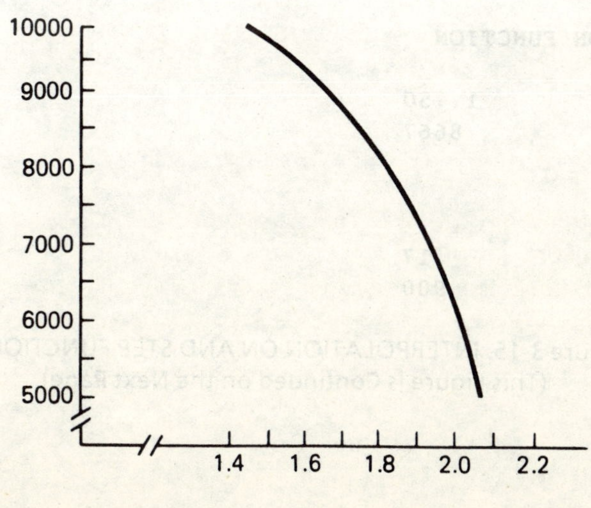

If you ask IFPS to find the SALES VOLUME at a price of 1.75, you are, in effect, asking it to read the graph for you. This is done with the INTERPOLATION ON function. For the forecast data, you would write:

```
10 PRICE = 1.75
20 SALES VOLUME=INTERPOLATION ON(PRICE,1.50,10000,1.70,9000',
       1.85, 8000, 2.00,6500,2.10,5000)
```

The INTERPOLATION ON function specifies the variable to be interpolated on (in our case, price) followed successively by the coordinates of points on the graph (in our case, prices and sales volumes). For example, the first pair of values corresponds to a price of 1.50 and a sales volume of 10000. When you specify a price for which the value is not given (e.g., 1.75), IFPS searches until it finds a value of price just greater than the one you asked for. It then assumes that the graph consists of a set of straight lines and computes an approximate value for your price by using "linear interpolation". Although the result is only approximate, it is perfectly adequate for most calculations. Figure 3-15 illustrates the INTERPOLATION ON function.

```
MODEL LISTFNCT  VERSION OF  11/22/82  15:18
10 COLUMNS  1
20 *
30 * INTERPOLATION ON FUNCTION
40 *
50 PRICE = 1.75
60 SALES VOLUME=INTERPOLATION ON(PRICE,1.50,10000,1.70,9000,1.85,'
70 8000,2.00,6500,2.10,5000)
80 *
90 * STEP FUNCTION
100 *
110 NO OF UNITS = 17
120 SALES PRICE=STEP(NO OF UNITS,1,1200,6,1000,11,900,21,800,51,700)
END OF MODEL
? solve
MODEL LISTFNCT  VERSION OF  11/22/82  15:18 -- 1 COLUMNS 4 VARIABLES
ENTER SOLVE OPTIONS
? all
                                         1


 INTERPOLATION ON FUNCTION

PRICE                               1.750
SALES VOLUME                         8667

 STEP FUNCTION

NO OF UNITS                            17
SALES PRICE                           900
```

Figure 3-15. INTERPOLATION ON AND STEP FUNCTION

(This Figure is Continued on the Next Page)

```
ENTER SOLVE OPTIONS
? what if
WHAT IF CASE 1
ENTER STATEMENTS
? price=1.35
?solve
ENTER SOLVE OPTIONS
? sales volume

***** WHAT IF CASE 1 *****
1 WHAT IF STATEMENT PROCESSED
INTERPOLATION VALUE OUT OF RANGE=          1.350
IN COMPUTATION OF VARIABLE SALES VOLUME

                              1


SALES VOLUME                  0
```

FIGURE 3-15 . INTERPOLATION ON AND STEP FUNCTION
(Continued)

NOTE: In technical terms, given two pairs of values, X1,Y1 and X2,Y2, to find the value of Y corresponding to an X value between X1 and X2, apply the formula:

$$Y = Y1 + (Y2\text{-}Y1)^* (X\text{-}X1)/(X2\text{-}X1) \quad (3\text{-}6)$$

For example, given the X,Y pairs (10,25) and (20,48), then if X = 13, application of Equation 3-6 results in:

$$Y = 25 + (48\text{-}25)^* (13\text{-}10)/(20\text{-}10) = 31.9$$

The rules for the INTERPOLATION ON function include:

1. Pairs of values must be presented in increasing order of the first variable. In our example, the prices increased from 1.50 to 2.10. If you specify, for example, 1.85,8000, 1.50,10000, 2.00,6500 you will get incorrect answers.

2. There is a trade-off between accuracy and speed of computation. The more pairs of values you provide, the more accurate the result. However the more values you provide, the slower the search process required to find the answer. The minimum number of data pairs is two, and the maximum is 49.

3. If you ask for a value that is outside the range included in your data, you will receive an error message. For example, in our example above, when you ask for PRICE of 1.35, IFPS tells you:

```
INTERPOLATION VALUE OUT OF RANGE    1.350
IN COMPUTATION OF VARIABLE SALES VOLUME
```

There is one exception, which occurs if you only specify two data pairs (that is, two points on the graph). Since two points define a straight line, IFPS is smart enough to extrapolate your straight line graph in both directions.

STEP FUNCTION. The STEP function can be used to represent data that are discontinuous such as prices with volume discounts. For example, if a manufacturer prices computer terminals as follows:

No. of Units	Price
1 - 5	1200
6 - 10	1000
11 - 20	900
21 - 50	800
>50	700

the graph would look as follows:

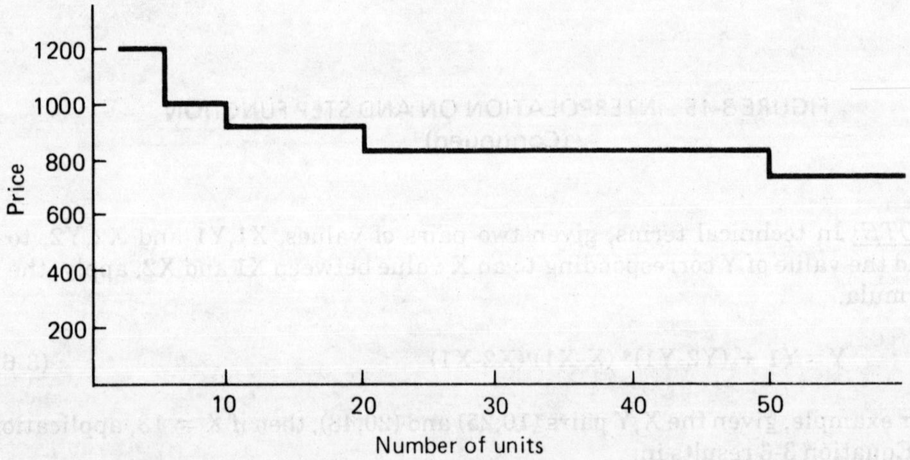

and the corresponding STEP function in IFPS would be:

```
PRICE= STEP(NO OF UNITS, 1,1200,6,1000,11,900,21,800,51,700)
```

As in the case of INTERPOLATION ON, you specify pairs of numbers, the first representing the minimum number of units to achieve that price and the second the corresponding price.

The STEP function can be extended to cover the case when each step has a functional form. To do so, you write expressions rather than constants for the second value of the pair. The STEP function is illustrated in Lines 90 through 120 of Figure 3-15.

EXERCISE: Consider the IFPS equation:

```
PRICE = STEP(NO OF UNITS, 1,1200,6,1000-5*NO OF UNITS,11,900-'
      4*NO OF UNITS,21,800-3*NO OF UNITS,51,750 - NO OF UNITS)
```

Plot the resulting price structure. (If you want the computer to do this exercise for you, have IFPS PLOT this function. PLOT is described in Section 4.3.)

3.3 BUILT-IN SUBROUTINES (DEPRECIATION, AMORTIZATION)

Depreciation and amortization calculations are performed using subroutines. Subroutines are similar to functions, but differ in two respects:

1. They do not have a left-hand side and equal sign. They occupy one line in a model.

2. They can produce three or more lines of output, rather than a single line which is the case for an ordinary variable.

The straight-line depreciation subroutine shown in Figure 3-16 is typical. The subroutine is called STLINE DEPR and the parentheses are followed by the names of three inputs and three outputs. The inputs represent the investment, the salvage value as a percent of investment, and the lifetime (in years). The outputs are the depreciation during the period, the current book value, and the cumulative depreciation to date.

If you do not want all the output printed, just leave a blank when you specify the subroutine; for example, STLINE DEPR(COST,0.10,10,,BOOK) will print only the book value of the investment depreciated over 10 years to 10% of its initial value. The "blank" is created when you put two commas next to each other with no information between them.

```
MODEL SURTN  VERSION OF  11/22/82  15:19
10 COLUMNS 1-6
20STLINE DEPR(INVESTMENT,SALVAGE,LIFE,PERIODDEPRECIATION,BOOKVALUE,'
30      CUMULATIVE DEPRECIATION)
40 INVESTMENT=150000,0
50 SALVAGE=0.05
60 LIFE=6
END OF MODEL
? solve
MODEL SURTN  VERSION OF  11/22/82  15:19 -- 6 COLUMNS 6 VARIABLES
ENTER SOLVE OPTIONS
? all

                             1       2       3       4       5       6

PERIODDEPRECIATION       23750   23750   23750   23750   23750   23750
BOOKVALUE               126250  102500   78750   55000   31250    7500
CUMULATIVE DEPRECIAT     23750   47500   71250   95000  118750  142500
INVESTMENT              150000       0       0       0       0       0
SALVAGE                  .0500   .0500   .0500   .0500   .0500   .0500
LIFE                         6       6       6       6       6       6
```

FIGURE 3-16. STRAIGHT-LINE DEPRECIATION SUBROUTINE

If you use the same name for an output variable in different depreciation calculations, the individual values will be added up and only the total will be printed out. For example,

```
STLINE DEPR(WIDGETS,0.10,5,DEPRECIATION)
DECBAL DEPR(TRUCKS,0.05,7,DEPRECIATION)
```

will add up the contributions of WIDGETS and TRUCKS to the DEPRECIATION account.

Depreciation subroutines other than straight line depreciation are set up as follows:

SUM OF THE YEAR DIGITS:

SUM DEPR(INVESTMENT, SALVAGE VALUE FRACTION, ASSET LIFE, PERIOD DEPRECIATION,BOOK VALUE,CUMULATIVE DEPRECIATION)

DECLINING BALANCE DEPRECIATION:

DECBAL DEPR(INVESTMENT,SALVAGE VALUE FRACTION,ASSET LIFE, ACCELERATION CONSTANT,SWITCHOVER, PERIOD DEPRECIATION, BOOK VALUE, CUMULATIVE DEPRECIATION)

In declining balance depreciation, the acceleration constant determines the percentage of book value used to calculate the depreciation expense. A 200% constant is represented by a 2.0, a 150% constant by 1.5. The subroutine also allows for a SWITCHOVER of depreciation methods as soon as the alternative method allows for greater depreciation expense. SWITCHOVER can have three values:

0 no switchover

1 switchover to straight line

2 switchover to sum-of-the-years digits.

GENERAL DECLINING BALANCE DEPRECIATION:

GENDECBAL DEPR(INVESTMENT, SALVAGE VALUE FRACTION, ASSET LIFE, ACCELERATION CONSTANT, SWITCHOVER, ALLOCATION, PERIOD DEPRECIATION, BOOK VALUE, CUMULATIVE DEPRECIATION)

This form of declining balance permits allocating a portion of the first year's accelerated depreciation in the first year of service. This is done by specifying the ALLOCATION fraction:

0 makes the routine defer the depreciation for a full year;

0.5 is the half-year convention, and

2 is the same as double declining balance.

ACRS DEPRECIATION: Under the Economic Recovery Act of 1981, an Accelerated Cost Recovery System (ACRS) was authorized. Under the ACRS method, asset cost is recovered in a shorter time than previously allowed for acquisitions in 1981 or later. The ACRS subroutine,

ACRS DEPR(CATEGORY, PURCHASE YEAR, COST,ANNUAL DEPRECIATION, BOOK VALUE, CUMULATIVE DEPRECIATION)

implements this method. Eligible property is divided in class-life categories of 3, 5, 10, and 15 years. Real estate must be classified as either regular or low-income. The value of CATEGORY must be one of the following numbers, corresponding to the desired category of property:

Category	Category of Property
3	3-year property class
5	5-year property class
10	10-year property class
15	15-year property class
1	Regular real estate
2	Low-income real estate

Figure 3-17 illustrates the ACRS depreciation subroutine.

```
MODEL ACRS  VERSION OF  11/22/82  15:30
10 COLUMNS 1-6
20 ACRS DEPR(CATEGORY,PURCHASE YEAR,INVESTMENT,PERIODDEPRECIATION,'
30 BOOKVALUE,CUMULATIVE DEPRECIATION)
40 *
50 CATEGORY = 5
60 *
70 INVESTMENT = 150000,0
80 PURCHASE YEAR = 1983, PREVIOUS + 1
END OF MODEL
? solve
MODEL ACRS  VERSION OF  11/22/82  15:30 -- 6 COLUMNS 6 VARIABLES
ENTER SOLVE OPTIONS
? all

                           1       2       3       4       5       6

PERIODDEPRECIATION     22500   33000   31500   31500   31500       0
BOOKVALUE             127500   94500   63000   31500       0       0
CUMULATIVE DEPRECIAT   22500   55500   87000  118500  150000  150000

CATEGORY                   5       5       5       5       5       5

INVESTMENT            150000       0       0       0       0       0
PURCHASE YEAR           1983    1984    1985    1986    1987    1988
```

FIGURE 3-17. ACRS DEPRECIATION

AMORTIZATION SUBROUTINE: The amortization subroutine is defined by:

AMORT(AMORTIZED LOAN, UNAMORTIZED LOAN, ANNUAL INTEREST RATE, ASSET LIFE, START COLUMN, PAYMENTS PER COLUMN, PAYMENT AMOUNT, PAYMENT TO INTEREST,PAYMENT TO PRINCIPAL, OUTSTANDING PRINCIPAL)

The first six quantities in the amortization subroutine are inputs. The amortized loan is reduced to zero over the life of the loan. The unamortized portion represents the balloon payment at the end (which may be zero). The nominal annual interest rate, the life of the loan in years, the time the loan is made (START COLUMN) and the number of payments per column are the other inputs. If the format is annual, the payments are the number of payments per year; if the PERIODS statement is used, the payments per column is the number of payments per period. As shown in Figure 3-18, the amortization subroutine provides output information on the payment, the interest, total payment made to principal, and the current outstanding balance.

```
MODEL AMORT  VERSION OF  08/30/82  16:35
10 COLUMNS 1-6
20 AMORT(100000,0,INTEREST RATE,6,1,1,PAYMENT,INTEREST,PRINCIPAL,'
21 BALANCE)
30 INTEREST RATE=.14
END OF MODEL
? solve
MODEL AMORT  VERSION OF  08/30/82  16:35 -- 6 COLUMNS 5 VARIABLES
ENTER SOLVE OPTIONS
? all

                          1      2      3      4      5      6

PAYMENT               25716  25716  25716  25716  25716  25716
INTEREST              14000  12360  10490   8358   5928   3158
PRINCIPAL             11716  13356  15226  17357  19787  22558
BALANCE               88284  74928  59703  42345  22558      0
INTEREST RATE         .1400  .1400  .1400  .1400  .1400  .1400
```

FIGURE 3-18. AMORTIZATION SUBROUTINE

CHAPTER IV
ADVANCED CAPABILITIES OF IFPS

4.6 Data Files

4.7 Generating Formatted Reports(GENREPORT)

4.8 Consolidation

4.9 An Example Involving Data Files, Reports, and Consolidation

4.10 Additional Editing Commands

4.11 Interacting with Your Mainframe's Command System (DIRECTORY, SYSTEM, EDIT)

CHAPTER IV
ADVANCED CAPABILITIES OF IFPS

The first three chapters are a primer on creating IFPS models. If you know and understand the concepts and ideas in these chapters, you can use IFPS as a personal tool to assist you in solving a wide variety of problems and to support you in many decision situations. You have learned how to set up a model, how to perform sensitivity analysis, how to use built-in functions, and how to approach problems involving uncertainty.

IFPS, of course, is more than a personal tool for solving small to medium scale problems. It also provides the capability for dealing with large scale problems and for communicating results within the organization. In this chapter we present additional capabilities of IFPS that are useful particularly for:

- plotting results
- creating reports in a format that improves communication between the creator and the users of models
- handling large volumes of data
- consolidating multiple models into a single report.

Finally, there are a number of convenience features in IFPS that allow you to deal with specific situations or to simplify the mechanics of IFPS. These features are discussed in Sections 4.4 and 4.5.

In the first reading of this Chapter, particularly if you are new to IFPS, you may want to skip Sections 4.6 (Data Files), 4.7 (Generating Formatted Reports) and 4.8 (Consolidation). As you gain skill and tackle larger problems, you will find these sections important for your work.

4.1 SOLVE OPTIONS

When IFPS asks you to ENTER SOLVE OPTIONS it is offering you choices on what information you want displayed on your video screen or hard copy terminal and on how you want the output to appear. That is, solve options are really display control options. No matter which solve options you specify, IFPS will perform the same calculations. The following sections outline some of the options available to you. Figure 4-1 shows examples of some of the solve options for the simple IFPS model shown in Figure 2-3 of Section 2.2.

4.1.1 Choosing Variables To Be Displayed

In most of the examples thus far, we asked IFPS to display the values of all the variables for each time period. Specifically, we replied ALL when IFPS asked us to enter solve options.

```
? solve
MODEL GRAY  VERSION OF  01/07/83  11:46 --  6 COLUMNS 5 VARIABLES
ENTER SOLVE OPTIONS
? columns 1,4,6
? sales thru net income

                                 1        4         6

SALES                          100    195.3     305.2
EXPENSES                        75      150       175
NET INCOME                      25    45.31     130.2

ENTER SOLVE OPTIONS
? invert
? sales thru net income

                             SALES  EXPENSES NET INCO
         1                     100        75       25
         4                   195.3       150    45.31
         6                   305.2       175    130.2

ENTER SOLVE OPTIONS
? columns 6,3,2,1
? normal
? sales,net income

                                 6        3         2         1

SALES                        305.2    156.3       125       100
NET INCOME                   130.2    31.25        25        25
```

FIGURE 4-1. EXAMPLE OF SOLVE OPTIONS

In some examples, such as those dealing with WHAT IF and SENSITIVITY in Chapter III, you may have noticed that we specified the names of only some variables and, when we did, obtained output only of the variables named. This capability for being selective in which rows are displayed is a general capability. The following are typical examples of this solve option.

ENTRY	RESULT
ALL	All variables shown
NET INCOME	Only the line containing NET INCOME diplayed
SALES THRU NET INCOME	All lines starting from SALES and including NET INCOME
SALES,NET INCOME	Only two lines are shown.

IMPORTANT POINTS YOU SHOULD KNOW:

- Even though you ask for only a partial display of results, IFPS solves the entire model internally. The results are the same no matter which variables you specify in the solve options.

- IFPS accepts only one line of variable names in response to ENTER SOLVE OPTIONS. If you have a long list of names, just keep typing the list without hitting the carriage return key. The terminal will automatically return for you. If you hit a carriage return, IFPS assumes you are through with your list and the remaining variable names you type are ignored. Thus, the variable list is always assumed to be the last line of the solve options and all other solve options must appear ahead of this line.

- THRU is a reserved word. You must use THRU rather than the more normal English spelling of "through." In a list of variables, you can mix single variables and groups of variables. For example, SALES THRU NET INCOME, NET INCOME RATIO is an acceptable specification of the solve option.

4.1.2 Choosing Columns to Be Displayed

In addition to being able to select which rows (i.e., variables) you want displayed, you can also select which columns should appear. This capability is useful, for example, if you have more than six columns and you do not need details for each period. To select columns, you specify the word COLUMNS followed by their values or names. For example,

```
COLUMNS 1-3,6,10
```

will print columns 1 through 3, column 6, and column 10. If you ask for COLUMNS 1986-1988, 1990, 1995 you will get those years.

IMPORTANT POINTS YOU SHOULD KNOW:

- Columns MUST be specified before variables in the solve option. (The reason is that IFPS begins generating output immediately after you specify one line of variable names.)

- Once you specify a columns option for a model, it remains in force for all subsequent SOLVE commands for that model unless you change it by specifying a different COLUMNS option. If you move from one model to another, the columns option is deleted.

- If you do not specify a columns option initially, you get all columns. If you have been using a COLUMNS option to restrict output and want to see all the columns, you must repeat the information in the COLUMNS line in your MODEL.

- Columns are always displayed in the order you specify. For example, COLUMNS 10, 1-3 will display column 10 before columns 1 through 3. That is, you can display columns in any order you want.

- A hyphen between two numbers (e.g., 1-3) implies all columns inclusively.

- If you have used names for column headings (e.g., QRT1, QRT2,....) you can specify either the name of the column or its numeric position. You can also use a hyphen to specify a set of columns. For example, if your headings are QRT1 through QRT9, it is perfectly legitimate for you to use COLUMNS 1-3, QRT7-QRT9 to display the first three and last three columns.

4.1.3. Inverting Rows and Columns

In working with some models you may be interested in the values in a large number of columns but only for a few variables. In this case you will find it handy to be able to interchange rows and columns by using the INVERT solve option. As shown in Figure 4-1, you can combine the INVERT option with the COLUMNS option and the selection of variables. Like the COLUMNS option, the INVERT option remains in force until changed. If you want to go back to the normal format, type NORMAL as a solve option.

4.1.4 Sorting the Order in Which Output Appears

IFPS allows you to present output in sorted order. Two kinds of sorts are possible:

- sort on name
- sort on value

In sorting on name, IFPS sequences variables in alphabetic order whereas in sort on value, IFPS examines one or more columns and sequences according to the values of the variables.

SORT ON NAME. A series of examples will demonstrate the SORT ON NAME options available.

```
ENTER SOLVE OPTIONS
?SORT ON NAME (ALL)
```

results in sequencing all variables in alphabetic order. Comments are removed when variables are sorted. The results obtained from sorting on name for MODEL GRAY are shown in Figure 4-2.

Sorting can also be done on specific lines and in ascending (A) or descending (D) order. For example,

```
SORT D ON NAME (SALES THRU NET INCOME)
```

will sort in descending alphabetical order (Z to A) the lines in the model between sales and net income.

```
? LIST
 MODEL GRAY  VERSION OF  10/03/85  23:12
 10 COLUMNS 1-6
 20 SALES = 100,PREVIOUS SALES *1.25
 30 EXPENSES = 75,100,125,150,175
 40 NET INCOME = SALES -EXPENSES
 50 *
 60 *                              RATIO ANALYSIS
 70 *PERCENT OF SALES
 80 EXPENSE RATIO = EXPENSES/SALES
 90 NET INCOME RATIO = NET INCOME/SALES
 END OF MODEL

 ? SOLVE
 MODEL GRAY  VERSION OF  10/03/85  23:12 -- 6 COLUMNS 5 VARIABLES
 ENTER SOLVE OPTIONS
 ? WIDTH 62 20 7
 ? SORT ON NAME(ALL)
                              1      2      3      4      5      6

 EXPENSE RATIO            .7500  .8000  .8000  .7680  .7168  .5734
 EXPENSES                    75    100    125    150    175    175
 NET INCOME                  25     25  31.25  45.31  69.14  130.2
 NET INCOME RATIO         .2500  .2000  .2000  .2320  .2832  .4266
 SALES                      100    125  156.3  195.3  244.1  305.2


 ENTER SOLVE OPTIONS
 ? SORT D ON NAME (SALES THRU NET INCOME)

                              1      2      3      4      5      6

 SALES                      100    125  156.3  195.3  244.1  305.2
 NET INCOME                  25     25  31.25  45.31  69.14  130.2
 EXPENSES                    75    100    125    150    175    175

 ENTER SOLVE OPTIONS
 ? SORT A ON 3 (L20 THRU L40)

                              1      2      3      4      5      6

 NET INCOME                  25     25  31.25  45.31  69.14  130.2
 EXPENSES                    75    100    125    150    175    175
 SALES                      100    125  156.3  195.3  244.1  305.2
```

FIGURE 4-2. SORT ON NAME AND SORT ON VALUE

SORT ON VALUE. In SORT ON VALUE, the rows of the model are ordered according to the values in a specific column of the model. For example,

```
ENTER SOLVE OPTIONS
?SORT A ON 3 (L20 thru L40)
```

the lines are presented in ascending (i.e., increasing) order according to their value in column 3. You can specify multiple columns. For example, SORT A ON COL3, COL2, COL6 (ALL) results in IFPS first sorting according to the values in column 3 (the first one you specify) and then using, successively, the values in column 2 and then column 6 to break ties if values are the same in column 3.

EXERCISE: Sort MODEL PRODUCT first by name and then in descending order by value in columns 2,5,7 for Lines 50 through 140.

4.1.5 Additional Solve Options

Other solve options available in IFPS are listed in Table 4-1. Options that are described as being able to restore features are the default options; that is, they are used automatically by IFPS if you do not specify another solve option first. For more detail on how they work, try them out on a simple model of your own.

TABLE 4-1

ADDITIONAL SOLVE OPTIONS

NOCOMMENTS	Does not display comment lines (i.e.lines beginning with a *). You can improve efficiency by using NOCOMMENTS.
COMMENTS	Restores comments for display.
NOINDENT	Eliminates all indentation of variable names. NOINDENT can improve efficiency.
INDENT	Restores indentation.
NAMEINDENT n	Allows you to indent variable names n spaces.
DOUBLE	Causes output to be printed out double spaced.
SINGLE	Restores single spacing.
SPACE n	When included in the variable list, leaves n blank lines in the output, where n is a number such as 1, 2, or 3.

ZEROSUP	Suppresses printing a variable (that is, an entire row) if all the values of the variable are zero in the columns selected for printout by the columns option.
ZEROPRINT	Restores printing of zero variables.
POSOPT+	Prefaces all positive numbers with a + sign.
POSOPTCR	Adds CR to all positive numbers.
POSOPT	Restores printing of positive numbers without + or CR.
NEGOPT	NEGOPT provides optional ways of printing negative numbers. Forms available include NEGOPT PAREN which puts negative numbers in parenthesis, NEGOPT -A which puts the minus sign after the number, NEGOPTDB which adds DB to the number, and NEGOPTCR which add CR to the number. The default option is NEGOPT, which prefaces numbers with a minus sign.

The solve options listed in Table 4-1, as well as options involving COLUMNS, remain in effect as long as you do not change them, but only as long as you work with the current model. If you issue a MODEL command you must ask for these solve options again if you want them to apply.

4.2 WIDTH AND OPT

WIDTH and OPT are really two special solve options and they must be preceded by a SOLVE command. They are sufficiently important that they warrant separate discussion.

WIDTH allows you to specify:

- the overall width of the display (that is, the number of characters on a line)
- the maximum number of characters to be shown for variable names
- the number of characters in each column
- the number of decimal places for each value.

Thus, WIDTH is a simple, yet powerful way of controlling how much information you display in a row and how you space information within a row.

The following is a typical example of the WIDTH command:

```
WIDTH  120  30  10  3
```

The word WIDTH is followed, in order, by the number of characters on the line (in our example, 120) the number of characters for variable names (30), the number of spaces in each column (10), and the number of decimal places in each value (3). If you do not specify WIDTH, IFPS uses the default values listed in Table 4-2. The allowed limits on the value of each parameter are also shown in the table.

TABLE 4-2

DEFAULT VALUES AND PARAMETERS OF THE WIDTH COMMAND

Parameter	Default Value	Allowable Range
Total numberof characters	78	20-132
Variable name length	24	1-100
Column width	9	1-32
Number of decimal places	–1	(–1)-9

If you use –1 for the number of decimal places, the location of the decimal point and the number of decimal places will vary. IFPS makes the choice based on the value to be displayed and the number of spaces available in a column. Another restriction on the number of decimal places is that it must be two less than the column width. Thus, for example, you cannot specify 78 20 3 2 but you can specify 78 20 4 2.

If you look at the default values, you see that there are 78 spaces available (typical of the number of columns on a CRT or a portable terminal), 24 of which are reserved for variable names. Hence 54 spaces are available for data. Since the column width is 9, the 54 spaces provide 6 columns. If you have 8 columns (as in the New Product Model of Section 2.7), you can put them all on one line by reducing the column width to 6 or by reducing the variable name space to 22 and the column width to 7. In the case of this book, we have 68 spaces on a line. Therefore, in Figure 4-3, we show you how to put 8 columns on a line by using 68 20 6. Here we use 20 spaces for the variable name and use 6 spaces for each column to present 8 columns of information on a line.

You can, if you so choose, specify only the first, first two, or first three parameters of the WIDTH command, For example,

```
WIDTH 132 30
```

request 132 characters and 30 spaces for names but leaves column width and decimal places at their default value.

Like other SOLVE options, once you specify a WIDTH command, it remains in force until you give another WIDTH command. However, the first parameter of the WIDTH command (total number of characters per line) is more powerful than a SOLVE option; it remains in force throughout an entire terminal session, even when you move from one MODEL to another. (You will find that all other specifications in SOLVE will return to their default values when you move from one MODEL to another.)

The OPT command is a subset of the WIDTH command. It allows you to specify the last three parameters of the WIDTH command and this command applies only while working

```
MODEL PRODUCT  VERSION OF  08/30/82  18:21 -- 8 COLUMNS 13 VARIABLES
ENTER SOLVE OPTIONS
? width 68 20 6
? all
                          1      2      3      4      5      6      7      8


             NEW PRODUCT MODEL

SALES VOLUME           1200   1277   1358   1442   1531   1623   1719   1820
MARKET                 8000   8240   8487   8742   9004   9274   9552   9839
MARKET SHARE          .1500  .1550  .1600  .1650  .1700  .1750  .1800  .1850
GROSS SALES            3000   3193   3395   3606   4209   4463   4728   5006
UNIT PRICE            2.500  2.500  2.500  2.500  2.750  2.750  2.750  2.750
OPERATING COST         2700   2874   3055   3245   3720   3944   4178   4423
PRODUCTION COST       1.250  1.250  1.250  1.250  1.350  1.350  1.350  1.350
OVERHEAD                  1      1      1      1  1.080  1.080  1.080  1.080
NET INCOME              300  319.3  339.5  360.6  489.8  519.4  550.2  582.5
INVESTMENT             2500      0      0      0      0      0      0      0

NET PRESENT VALUE     -2208  -1907  -1595  -1273-847.8-409.6  41.64  506.0
INTERNAL RATE OF RET                                             .1372  .3056

DISCOUNT RATE         .1200  .1200  .1200  .1200  .1200  .1200  .1200  .1200
```

FIGURE 4-3. USING WIDTH TO SHOW EIGHT COLUMNS

on your current model. For example,

```
OPT 14, 8, 2
```

indicates that you want 14 spaces for the variable name, eight spaces for each column and two decimal places. The OPT command allows you to change the appearance of your printout without having to repeat how many characters wide you want the printout.

4.3 PLOTTING RESULTS GRAPHICALLY

If you have results that you want to present in graphic form, you can ask IFPS to draw you a graph. Like WIDTH, PLOT is a SOLVE option that is so important it deserves a separate section of its own. In Section 4.3.1 we discuss the basic elements of obtaining a plot. If you are only interested in obtaining a quick plot of results for your own use, read Section 4.3.1 and skip Section 4.3.2. If, however, you want to label the graphs and/or use other specialized features, you should read Section 4.3.2, which discusses these features.

4.3.1 Basics of Plotting

To obtain graphic output, you type PLOT. IFPS solves your model and then enters a plotting subsystem. IFPS responds by asking you to ENTER PLOT OPTIONS. You need to:

1. Tell IFPS how you want to graph the data.

2. Tell IFPS what quantities you want plotted.

You do this by first asking for:

```
GRID 36,64,8
```

This is the largest graph you can obtain. It has 36 vertical lines, 64 horizontal spaces, and sets up both a horizontal and a vertical scale for you. The value 8 is a grid option that is explained in Sec. 4.3.2. IFPS uses periods for the horizontal axis. If you forget to specify the GRID, IFPS will use the 36,64,8 format by default.

You than tell IFPS which variables to PLOT, using the format PLOT variable1, variable2,... Note that the word PLOT followed by the names of variables, separated from one another by commas is required. In Figure 4-4 you see plots of three variables: sales, expenses, and net profit. IFPS uses numbers corresponding to the sequence in which you asked for the variables to draw the plots. For example, in Figure 4-4. sales are plotted using the symbol 1. IFPS automatically provides you with a legend indicating the meaning of each symbol.

If you want to draw several graphs, you can issue a series of PLOT commands without repeating the GRID command. If, however, you want to change the GRID specifications, you can do so by issuing another GRID command. A word of advice: Although IFPS lets you plot up to 9 variables on a single graph, don't ask for more than three for four variables on a single plot. Graphs become difficult to interpret if you try to present too much information.

If you are satisfied with the default (or with the current) GRID, you can use a single instruction to obtain your plot. For example, if you simply write:

```
PLOT SALES,EXPENSES,NET INCOME
```

and nothing else, you will get the same result as Figure 4-4. Try it!

4.3.2 Drawing More Sophisticated Graphs

We will now briefly discuss the various PLOT options available to you. These options must be specified before you give the list of variables to be plotted. Once specified, they remain in force until countermanded by you. This section has been written as a catalog explaining the various options, so you can come back to it when you need specific features. The best way to see the results of using these options is to sit down at a terminal and do each of the exercises.

GRID. If you want fewer than 36 vertical lines or fewer than 64 columns, you simply specify the appropriate number in the GRID command. For example, GRID 12,24,8 gives you 12 vertical lines and 24 rows.

You have probably wondered by now why you need the 8 in the GRID specification. Actually, you can use any value from 1 to 9 for this "grid option" position, but the appearance of the graph will change. Table 4-3 list the effects of the grid options.

```
? SOLVE
MODEL GRAY  VERSION OF  10/03/85  23:12 -- 6 COLUMNS 5 VARIABLES
? PLOT
ENTER PLOT OPTIONS
? GRID 36,64,8
? PLOT SALES, EXPENSES,NET INCOME

350



                                                                1
300




250
                                                    1



200                                     1

                                                    2           2

                            1
150                                     2

                1           2                                   3


100 1           2

    2
                                                    3

 50                                     3

    3           3           3


  0 +-----------+-----------+-----------+-----------+-----------+

    1           2           3           4           5           6


    1 - SALES
    2 - EXPENSES
    3 - NET INCOME
```

FIGURE 4-4. IFPS PLOT EXAMPLE

TABLE 4-3

GRID OPTIONS

Grid Option	Result
1	Horzontal and vertical grid lines
2	Horizontal grid lines, vertical axis
3	Vertical grid lines, horizontal axis
4	Horizontal and vertical axes, + sign at grid
5	Horizontal grid lines only
6	Vertical grid lines only
7	No axes or grid lines
8	Horizontal and vertical axes only
9	Closest grid line to zero used for horizontal and vertical axes.

EXERCISE: Plot the data shown in Figure 4-3 for each of the grid options listed in Table 4-4. Use only 20 vertical lines and 40 horizontal spaces.

TITLE. You can put titles on your graphs by specifying both the position of the title and its text. For example, if you specify:

```
TITLE 1 TOP CENTER/RESULTS OF SIMPLE IFPS MODEL
TITLE 2 LEFT CENTER/DOLLARS
```

the result is that shown in Figure 4-5. In general, you specify:

TITLE number location position/text

That is, begin with the word TITLE followed with a sequence number between 1 and 10. The sequence number determines the order of printing and allows you to select which lines you want to change as you move from one plot to the next. The location can contain any of the reserved words:

TOP above the plot
LEFT to the left of the vertical axis
BOTTOM below the plot

Position can refer either to:

CENTER which centers the text on the top, left, or bottom
MARGIN which left-justifies the text

Having positioned a line of the title, IFPS prints exactly what you put down after the /.

If you want to remove the entire title, you write:

```
TITLE CLEAR.
```

```
? plot
ENTER PLOT OPTIONS
? grid 36,64,8
? title 1 top center/results of simple ifps model
? title 2 left center/dollars
? plot sales,expenses,net income

                          RESULTS OF SIMPLE IFPS MODEL

   350



                                                                   1
   300




   250
                                                       1



D
O  200                                     1
L
L                                                      2           2
A
R                              1
S  150                                     2

                   1           2                                   3

   100 1           2
       2


                                                       3

    50                                     3
       3           3           3


     0 +-----------+-----------+-----------+-----------+-----------+

       1           2           3           4           5           6

         1 - SALES
         2 - EXPENSES
         3 - NET INCOME
```

FIGURE 4-5. CREATING TITLES AND LABELS ON A PLOT

EXERCISE: Expand the title of Figure 4-5 so that it lists the variables plotted and labels the time axis.

PLOTTING VARIABLES OTHER THAN COLUMN. If you want the horizontal axis to be a variable rather than a column heading, you use the VS option. For example,

```
VS COST
PLOT SALES, PROFIT
```

results in a plot of sales and profit against cost rather than time.

CHOOSING THE RANGE OF VALUES TO BE PLOTTED. You can select the minimum and maximum values of the vertical and horizontal axes by using the RANGE command. For example,

```
RANGE 0,250
```

plots only vertical axis values between 0 and 250. Similarly, RANGE 0,250,2,5 plots only values between 0 and 250 for periods 2 through 5. You must specify the vertical minimum and maximum. If you do not specify the horizontal maximum and minimum, the entire axis is plotted.

EXERCISE: Modify Figure 4-5 so that it shows only values between 0 and 200 and periods 2 through 4.

SCALE. The SCALE option allows you to divide all values by a constant factor before plotting the results. The general form is:

SCALE vertical constant, horizontal constant

For example,

```
SCALE 1000
TITLE 2 LEFT CENTER/THOUSANDS OF DOLLARS
```

results in plotting values in thousands of dollars and labeling the vertical axis accordingly. Scaling of the horizontal axis can be used only in conjunction with the VS option.

USING CHARACTERS OTHER THAN NUMBERS. If you don't like to see numbers on your plot, you can use any typewriter symbol by following the plot specification with a symbol specification. For example:

```
PLOT SALES/$/,EXPENSES/-/,PROFIT/#/
```

results in $ signs appearing for sales, – appearing for expenses, and # appearing for profit. The characters you can use depend on what is available on your terminal.

EXERCISE: Modify Figure 4-5 so that it shows sales in units of 100's of dollars and uses the symbols $, –, and #. Title the axes appropriately.

PUTTING TIME ON THE VERTICAL AXIS. If you want to turn your graph around so that the time period appears on the vertical rather than the horizontal axis, you can do so by specifying INVERT as a plot option. INVERT will remain in force until you specify

NORMAL to return time to the horizontal axis.

EXERCISE: Invert Figure 4-4.

WHAT YOU CAN DO WHEN VALUES OVERLAP. Every so often you will find that two or more variables take on the same value. The result is that you observe an * on the printout. The * calls attention to the fact that two or more variables are trying to occupy the same space and that, in fact, two or more curves cross at that point. If you want a character other than an *, you can use the SOVER option. For example SOVER $ puts a $ sign at these values. If you want to use the last character plotted, use SOVER LAST.

4.4 USEFUL CALCULATIONAL FEATURES (L, MATRIX, VMATRIX, SUM, IF, COLUMN)

4.4.1 Using Line Numbers Rather than Variable Names

If you choose, you can substitute the line number on which a variable is defined for the name of the variable. For example,

```
10 SALES = L20*L30
20 MARKET = 8000, PREVIOUS MARKET *1.05
30 MARKET SHARE = 0.15, PREVIOUS MARKET SHARE + 0.005
```

is just as valid as writing for Line 10

```
10 SALES = MARKET * MARKET SHARE
```

As shown above, line number references involve the letter L followed by a number. As you become more experienced with IFPS you will find the use of line number references particularly handy. You do have to be careful, however. If you ask IFPS to change line numbers with a RESEQUENCE command (see Section 4.5.3), line number references are corrected for you automatically. However, if for some reason you move the line on which a particular variable is defined, you have to change the references to that variable which are by line number and change them manually. If you are faced with this problem, the CROSSREF command explained in Section 4.5.7 will be of help in finding all references to the variable.

One of the risks of using line number references is that if you do it too often, the model loses its readability and hence loses one of the important advantages of IFPS as a communications tool. Fortunately, you can use the computer to interpret the line number references for you. As described in Section 4.5.8, IFPS has an EXPAND option on the LIST command that results in substituting names for line numbers.

4.4.2 Referring to a Single Number (MATRIX, VMATRIX)

If you want to refer to a single number in the model (e.g., the revenue for the year), you use MATRIX. The term comes from the idea that the output of an IFPS model is a two-dimensional matrix whose rows are the variables and whose columns are defined by the COLUMNS statement. For example, if the revenue for the year is given in column 4 of CUMULATIVE REVENUE, you can refer to it by:

```
MATRIX(CUMULATIVE REVENUE,4)
```

In general, the first term in parenthesis refers to the row (i.e., the variable) and the second term to the column. Figure 4-6 illustrates the use of MATRIX.

```
MODEL SIMPLE1   VERSION OF   08/30/82   18:04
10 COLUMNS 1-4
20 SALES = 100,PREVIOUS SALES *1.25
30 EXPENSES =75,100,125,150
40 NET REVENUE = SALES -EXPENSES
50 CUMULATIVE REVENUE = PREVIOUS + NET REVENUE
60*
70*NET REVENUE THIS QUARTER AS PERCENTAGE OF ANNUAL REVENUE
80*
90 PERCENT OF TOTAL REVENUE=NET REVENUE/MATRIX(CUMULATIVE REVENUE,4)
END OF MODEL
? solve
MODEL SIMPLE1   VERSION OF   08/30/82   18:04 -- 4 COLUMNS 5 VARIABLES
ENTER SOLVE OPTIONS
? all

                              1        2        3        4

SALES                       100      125    156.3    195.3
EXPENSES                     75      100      125      150
NET REVENUE                  25       25    31.25    45.31
CUMULATIVE REVENUE           25       50    81.25    126.6

NET REVENUE THIS QUARTER AS PERCENTAGE OF ANNUAL REVENUE

PERCENT OF TOTAL REV      .1975    .1975    .2469    .3580
```

FIGURE 4-6. USE OF MATRIX TO REFER TO A SINGLE VALUE

VMATRIX is an extension of the MATRIX idea. Whereas MATRIX requires you to specify a specific column either by column name or by column number, VMATRIX allows you to select the column to be used based on a computation. The general form is:

VMATRIX(VARIABLE NAME, COMPUTED COLUMN)

where VARIABLE NAME refers to a row and the column is determined from some computation.

EXERCISE: You anticipate production capacity to be 1000 units in Week 1 and to grow by 10 per week for each of the next 12 weeks if there is no strike. Call this base production. Unfortunately, you anticipate a strike starting several weeks from now. The strike will be of unknown duration. Once the strike is over, you anticipate you can work overtime for a number of weeks equal to the strike duration. During that time, your capacity will increase by 25% over that in the last week before the strike. After that, the growth will be 10 units per week starting from the prestrike production. Write a short model based on this situation using VMATRIX to define the actual production once the strike is over.

Assume that the strike will start in Week 3. Make a series of WHAT IF runs for strike durations of 2, 3, and 4 weeks.

HINT: Create a variable OFFSET to determine the week in the base production cycle that actual production will follow once the plant returns to normal after the strike.

4.4.3 IF Statements in IFPS

Just as in BASIC or FORTRAN, you can make your results depend on which conditions are true. For example, as shown in Figure 4-7, your tax rate may depend on the size of the year's profit.

The format for an IF statement, which always appears on the right of an = sign, is:

> IF the test is true, THEN assign the value shown, ELSE assign an alternative value.

The alternative value can be a number or an expression.The test conditions are always expressed with a period before them and after them. They are:

.LT. less than	.LE. less than or equal to
.GT. greater than	.GE. greater than or equal to
.EQ. equal to	.NE. not equal to

```
MODEL IF  VERSION OF  08/30/82  18:03
10 COLUMNS 1-6
20 PROFIT BEFORE TAX=25000,PREVIOUS PROFIT BEFORE TAX*1.2
30 TAX RATE=IF PROFIT BEFORE TAX.LE.30000 THEN .35 ELSE .48
40 TAX=TAX RATE*PROFIT BEFORE TAX
50 NET PROFIT = PROFIT BEFORE TAX - TAX
END OF MODEL
? solve
MODEL IF  VERSION OF  08/30/82  18:03 -- 6 COLUMNS 4 VARIABLES
ENTER SOLVE OPTIONS
? all
                          1       2       3       4       5       6

PROFIT BEFORE TAX     25000   30000   36000   43200   51840   62208
TAX RATE              .3500   .3500   .4800   .4800   .4800   .4800
TAX                    8750   10500   17280   20736   24883   29860
NET PROFIT            16250   19500   18720   22464   26957   32348
```

FIGURE 4-7. IF STATEMENT

Compound conditions can also be expressed. These compound conditions can involve

1. Requiring two conditions to be true (.AND.) or
2. Being satisfied if either one of two conditions is true (.OR.).

Thus, for example, you might specify a state income tax condition as:

```
TAX RATE=IF PROFIT BEFORE TAX .LE. 30000 THEN .05 ELSE'
          IF PROFIT BEFORE TAX .GE. 50000 .AND.'
          CARRYFORWARD .LT. 15000 THEN .10 ELSE .08
```

Note that this example also illustrates the possibility of using an IF statement within an ELSE statement.

As a second example, consider a policy in MODEL PRODUCTwhich set the price depending on MARKET or MARKET SHARE:

```
PRICE = IF MARKET .GT. 9000 .OR. MARKET SHARE .GT. .16 THEN'
        2.50 ELSE 2.75
```

4.4.4 SUM Function

In many models you will calculate the components of a quantity individually (e.g., the components of operating cost) and then add them up. That is, you will want to take totals or subtotals within a column. Rather than having to write out the names of all the variables or put down all the line numbers, you can simply use the SUM function.

The SUM function adds up all the variables specified and records the total. You can either list two variables (e.g., SUM(L20,L35) adds up the values of Lines 20 and 35) or you can use THRU to obtain all variables from the beginning to the end of a sequence (e.g., SUM(DOMESTIC SALES THRU INVESTMENT INCOME)). Unfortunately, putting more than two variable names in the list won't work. For example, trying to add Lines 20, 35, and 50 together by writing SUM(L20,L35,L50) won't work. You have to write L20 + L35 + L50.

An example of the usefulness of the SUM function can be seen in Figure 2-10 in Section 2.9. There, we wrote

```
370 TOTAL OPERATING EXPENSE = SUM(L290 THRU L350)
```

rather than the more cumbersome:

```
370 TOTAL OPERATING EXPENSE = ADVERTISING + COMMISSIONS + '
    SALARIES +PAYROLL TAXES + LEASES + NOTE INTEREST + '
    DEPRECIATION
```

You will generally find it advisable to use the SUM function in a line close to the variables being summed. The reason is that you can easily find the quantities being added and can check the model for correctness. When using THRU references in SUM commands you have to be careful not to include extraneous quantities. Although typically not a problem when setting up your model originally, extraneous quantities can appear if you insert a line that is in the middle of a THRU.

4.4.5 Working Across Rather than Down (COLUMN)

Almost all computational work in IFPS is done row by row, where each row represents a different variable. However, there are occasions when you want to put results in a column rather than a row. For example, you may want to have columns representing quarterly and annual results, where the column headings would be:

```
QUARTER1      QUARTER2      QUARTER3      QUARTER4      ANNUAL
```

where the first four columns represent the quarters and the last column represents the yearly total. One way of achieving this result, based on what we have discussed thus far, is to compute the annual value as:

```
PREVIOUS + PREVIOUS 2 + PREVIOUS 3 + PREVIOUS 4
```

This form is cumbersome to implement, and becomes much worse if you are, for example, trying to add monthly results into annual values. One alternative is to follow the approach used in the consolidation example, MODEL COMPANY, in Section 4.8.4. There we created separate lines for each cumulative total. A second alternative, one we believe you will find easier and more natural to implement, is to use the COLUMN computational statement.

> *NOTE:* The COLUMN computational statement is different from the definitions of COLUMNS at the beginning of a model.

The objective in using COLUMN is to define directly the values of an entire column of a model or of specific lines within a column. The following are typical examples of the COLUMN statement.

```
COLUMN 5 = 100*COLUMN 3/COLUMN 4
COLUMN 8 FOR SALES = COLUMN 7/.8
COLUMN 6 FOR L10 THRU L50 = C 4/C 3
COLUMN ANNUAL = SUM(C QUARTER 1 THRU C QUARTER 4)
```

The first example states that each element in column 5 is obtained by taking the ratio of column 3 to column 4 and multiplying by a hundred. That is, column 5 gives the percentage that column 3 is of column 4.

The second example defines only the value of sales in column 8. That is, FOR defines the row for which the expression on the right hand side is true. You can have a single variable (e.g. SALES), a list of variables (e.g., SALES,COST,PROFIT), or a THRU statement to define a set of variables. The latter is the case in the third example.

In the third example, we define column 6 for all lines from 10 through 50 in terms of the ratio of columns 4 and 3. Note that we use the abbreviation C for column.

> *NOTE*: You must write out the word COLUMN on the left hand side. However, it is not necessary to write out COLUMN on the right hand side. C can be used as an abbreviation. You can use either C3 or C 3 to refer to column 3.

The last example returns to the problem we posed at the beginning of this section, namely adding columns to obtain totals. This example could also have been written:

```
COLUMN 5 = SUM(C1 THRU C4)
```

That is, you can refer to columns either by their name or by their position.

4.4.6 Rules for COLUMN Computational Statements

COLUMN computational statements have several rules and limitations associated with them. You should go over the following list before you start using COLUMN statements.

LOCATION IN MODEL. Like variables, COLUMN statements can be in any order and are written as separate lines in the model.

> EXCEPTION: If you use FOR in a COLUMN statement, all the variables referenced after the FOR must have been defined previously, that is, they must have lower line numbers.

ORDER OF COMPUTATION. If any COLUMN statements are used in the model, IFPS partitions the model into two sections, the regular column section and the special column section. The location of the partition, let's call it *k*, is the first (lowest number) column referred to on the left-hand side of a COLUMN statement. For all columns before *k*, the usual row logic of IFPS applies; for column *k* and beyond you must use COLUMN computational statements to obtain answers.

> NOTE: The partition between row and column logic acts like a wall. You *cannot* use results from a COLUMN calculation in a row calculation. For example, the following sequence will not work:

```
10 COLUMN 4 = SUM (C1 THRU C3)
20 X = 10,20,30
30 Y = X + MATRIX(X,4)
```

> Try it and see what happens!

FORMAT. In general, the left-hand side has the word COLUMN and the name or number of the column to be computed. This column definition can be for the entire column or for part of a column, the latter if FOR is used. The right hand side can be any valid IFPS right hand side, including references to columns, with some specific exceptions.

> EXCEPTIONS for RIGHT HAND SIDE:
>
> 1. You cannot reference the functions NPVC, MOVAVG, TREND, OR POLYFIT.
>
> 2. You cannot reference subroutines such as those for amortization and depreciation.

ORDER OF SOLVING. IFPS performs COLUMN computations in column order, no matter what order the columns are referred to. For example,

```
70 COLUMN 4 FOR A,B = C 1 + C 3
80 COLUMN 5 FOR A,B, X THRU Z = C 1 + C 2
90 COLUMN 4 FOR X THRU Z = C 1/TOTAL SALES
```

results in IFPS evaluating all of the column 4 references before column 5.

RESOLUTION OF AMBIGUITY. If you accidentally define column entries twice, IFPS uses the first definition you give. For example,

```
10 COLUMN 4 FOR SALES = C 3
20 COLUMN 4 = SUM(C 1 THRU C3)
```

results in adding the values of columns 1 through 3 for all values in column 4 except the value of sales.

NOT DEFINING A VALUE. If you fail to define a value in a special COLUMN it will remain blank.

4.5 USEFUL COMMAND FEATURES (', !, RESEQUENCE, COPY, COMPILESAVE, CROSSREF, EXPAND)

4.5.1 What to Do If Your Expression Does Not Fit on One Line (')

If there is not enough space on one line for what you want to say, you have two options. If you restrain yourself and do not hit the RETURN or ENTER key when you reach the end of the line, IFPS will automatically continue the line for you. This feature is referred to as wrapping. However, there is a limit of how many characters you can put on a line whether or not it is wrapped. The limit depends on the computer you are using.

An alternative is for you to use the apostrophe (') as a special character. For example,

```
60 TOTAL EXPENSES=MATERIALS + LABOR +'
61 PREVIOUS ADVERTISING +  OVERHEAD
```

When you use the apostrophe at the end of a line, IFPS assumes that the next line in sequence will be a continuation of the current line. It does not expect an equal sign. If you are in AUTO mode, IFPS will automatically assign the continuation a line number for you.

IMPORTANT RULES:

1. You cannot split a variable name with an apostrophe. For example, you cannot split ANNUAL SALES between lines.

2. You cannot split a FOR, PREVIOUS, or FUTURE with an apostrophe.

4.5.2 What to Do if You Want to Use a Special Character in its Ordinary Meaning (!)

IFPS has a number of characters with special meaning. For example, in editing text you might write 10C/A/B/ to tell IFPS that you want to change A to B in Line 10. The / also has the ordinary meaning of division. What do you do if you want to change A/B to C/D? Writing C/A/B/C/D/ won't work. (Try it and see what happens.) The answer is to put an exclamation point in front of the division signs. That is, write:

```
C/A!/B/C!/D/
```

In general, if you want to use a form that is not normally allowed or understood by IFPS, you use an exclamation point to tell IFPS to follow you literally. Another example is:

```
X!-Y = X - Y
```

Here you want to tell IFPS that the variable name is X-Y; if you do not use the exclamation point, IFPS gives you an error message since arithmetic is not allowed in variable names. Try it and see.

The use of exclamation points does not work in certain instances. Specifically, you cannot use the exclamation point in model, report, or file names and you cannot use it in front of an apostrophe if the apostrophe is the last character in the line. The exclamation point will be shown when you list a model or a report but will not be shown when you SOLVE or create a report with GENREPORT.

4.5.3 Cleaning Up Line Numbers (RESEQUENCE)

If you have made many insertions in creating a model, report, or data file, you may feel that the line number system has become cumbersome. You can ask IFPS to renumber lines for you by using RESEQUENCE. Typical examples are:

```
RESEQUENCE MODEL PROFORMA 10 10
RESEQUENCE REPORT OUTPUT 1 3
```

In both cases you first tell IFPS to resequence, then you tell it whether it is a model or a report and give the corresponding name. The two numbers refer to, respectively, the number to be assigned to the first line and the increment to be used for successive lines. Thus, 10 10 tells IFPS to use 10,20,30,....for line numbers whereas 1 3 tells IFPS to use 1,4,7,.... In performing the resequencing, IFPS will automatically change line number references within a model (or a report) so that they are consistent.

If you ask for resequencing of a model, IFPS will ask you whether you have any reports or data files that relate to this model. The reason is that you may have line number references in the report that refer to the model. If you do not have a report or a data file, type NONE in response to the inquiry. Also type NONE as the last entry in the list of reports and the list of data files.

For example, if your model PROFORMA has REPORT STATMNT and DATAFILE RESULTS associated with it, the sequence might look as follows:

```
RESEQUENCE MODEL PROFORMA
ENTER NAME OF RELATED REPORT OR NONE
STATMNT
NONE

ENTER NAME OF RELATED DATAFILE OR NONE
RESULTS
NONE
```

You can ask to RESEQUENCE either the model you are working on or any other model. To keep things straight for itself, IFPS removes the model you are working on from the workspace and does not replace it when you are done. (The reason is that if you ask to resequence a different model than the one in your workspace, IFPS does not know whether you will want the one you had or the one you resequenced.) That is, IFPS performs the resequencing and then expects you to tell it what you want to do. Typically, you will want to ask for the MODEL you just resequenced; however, you can ask for anything else if you so choose. You cannot just go on as before with, say, LIST and expect to obtain a listing of the resequenced model. If you forget, IFPS gives you an error message asking you for new instructions.

4.5.4 Making a Duplicate Copy of a Model or Report (COPY)

A typical situation when working with IFPS is that you want to use variations of a particular model or create a new model that uses all or parts of an existing model within it. Rather than typing in a new model you can make a copy of the existing model and give it a new name. Examples of the COPY command are:

```
COPY MODEL ALPHA TO BETA
COPY REPORT  A TO B
COPY FILE DATA TO NEWDATA
```

The first command tells IFPS to make a copy of ALPHA and call it BETA. ALPHA and BETA are identical; they only differ in name. The sequence is the word COPY followed by the appropriate definition of model, report, or data file. TO is optional. Finally, you give the name to be assigned to the copy. This name should be different from an existing name in your file, otherwise you will erase the current version. Like RESEQUENCE, you lose what is in your workspace and have to tell IFPS what you want to do next.

4.5.5 Combining Several Models into a Single Model (COMBINE, COMBINESAVE)

If you are creating a large model, you may want to divide the work among several people each of whom is expert in a particular area. Participants create a model for their own area and tests it.

```
MODEL GRAY1  VERSION OF  09/03/85  20:39
10 COLUMNS 1-4
20 SALES=100,PREVIOUS SALES *1.25
30 EXPENSES = 75, PREVIOUS EXPENSES +25
40 NET INCOME = SALES - EXPENSES
END OF MODEL

MODEL GRAY2  VERSION OF  09/03/85  20:54
10 COLUMNS 1-4,TOTAL
100 AFTER TAX INCOME = 0.6 * NET INCOME
110 COLUMN TOTAL FOR SALES = SUM (C1 THRU C4)
120 COLUMN TOTAL FOR EXPENSES = SUM(C1 THRU C4)
130 COLUMN TOTAL FOR NET INCOME = SUM(C1 THRU C4)
140 COLUMN TOTAL FOR AFTER TAX INCOME = SUM(C1 THRU C4)
END OF MODEL
```

FIGURE 4-8. TWO SIMPLE MODELS TO BE COMBINED

The COMBINE command is an executive level command that allows you to paste the individual models together into one large, merged model. For example, you may want to combine a market forecast with a sales estimate, a production cost model, and a financial model to create a corporate model for a particular project. Figure 4-8 shows a simple example of two models. Note that the first model will SOLVE but the second model (MODEL GRAY2) will not SOLVE on its own. (Can you explain why? If you don't believe it, try it out on your computer!)

To create a single model from these two, you respond to a ? with:

```
?COMBINE SAVE GRAY1 GRAY2 AS GRAYTOT
```

The computer responds with:

```
COMBINED MODEL READY FOR EDIT OR SOLVE
```

If you LIST and SOLVE, you see Figure 4-9.

```
? COMBINE SAVE GRAY1 GRAY2 AS GRAYTOT
COMBINED MODEL READY FOR EDIT OR SOLVE
? LIST

 MODEL GRAYTOT  VERSION OF  05/05/86  11:28
 10 COLUMNS 1-4,TOTAL
 20 SALES=100,PREVIOUS SALES *1.25
 30 EXPENSES = 75, PREVIOUS EXPENSES +25
 40 NET INCOME = SALES - EXPENSES
 100 AFTER TAX INCOME = 0.6 * NET INCOME
 110 COLUMN TOTAL FOR SALES = SUM (C1 THRU C4)
 120 COLUMN TOTAL FOR EXPENSES = SUM(C1 THRU C4)
 130 COLUMN TOTAL FOR NET INCOME = SUM(C1 THRU C4)
 140 COLUMN TOTAL FOR AFTER TAX INCOME = SUM(C1 THRU C4)
 END OF MODEL
 ? SOLVE
 MODEL GRAYTOT  VERSION OF  05/05/86  11:28 -- 5 COLUMNS 4 VARIABLES
 ENTER SOLVE OPTIONS
 ? ALL

                               1      2      3      4  TOTAL

 SALES                       100    125  156.3  195.3  576.6
 EXPENSES                     75    100    125    150    450
 NET INCOME                   25     25  31.25  45.31  126.6
 AFTER TAX INCOME             15     15  18.75  27.19  75.94
```

FIGURE 4-9. RESULTS OF THE COMBINE COMMAND

In using the COMBINE command, the following points are important:

1. The form shown assumes you want to save the result in your file. In this form, you tell IFPS to COMBINE SAVE and give it a list of the models you want to combine. The SAVE is necessary if you want the combined model saved in your file.

If you are only interested in a temporary combination, you could have written:

```
?COMBINE GRAY1 GRAY2
```

The computer responds with:

```
ENTER MORE MODEL NAMES OR NONE
?
```

If you say NONE, the computer carries out the combination. However, this model will disappear if you go to another model or quit.

2. Use the same line number for defining the number and titles of columns in each model being merged. In this way you avoid having two different lines in the model which define the column headings, a fatal error.

3. The combined model has the number of columns of the last model COMBINEd. Thus, in our example, columns 1-4 and a total column appear in both MODEL GRAY2 and MODEL GRAYTOT.

4. COMBINE causes IFPS to merge the models according to line number. Good practice, therefore, is to use non-overlappling line numbers for each model being combined. The RESEQUENCE command discussed in Section 4.5.3 can be used to change line numbers to make sure there is no overlap.

4.5.6 Saving Time in Executing The Model (COMPILESAVE,COMPILEFILE)

Once you have completed a model which you plan to use many times, you may find it advantageous to save it in your files in the computer's own language (called "compiled" mode) rather than in the English-like wording that is IFPS. Typical situations include:

- A dummy model that will be used with many data files. (See Section 4.6 for a discussion of data files.)
- Debugging a REPORT format (Section 4.7) where you use GENREPORT over and over with a particular mode until you are satisfied with the format.
- Extensive sensitivy analysis.
- In Universal Consolidation (Sec. 10.1) where IFPS would recompile the same model several times as it combines models that represent the performance of hierarchical organizations.

Using the compiled form of the model saves you computer time (and computer costs) in these situations compared to using the MODEL .... SOLVE combination you would use ordinarily.

You can create a compiled form of the model in two ways:

COMPILESAVE
COMPILEFILE

In the first case, you save an existing model in compiled form. As shown below, with COMPILESAVE, every time you access the compiled model, you have to use the command COMPILEGET to retrieve it. COMPILEFILE is a statement placed within a model that eliminates the need for COMPILEGET. However, as indicated below, this advantage comes at a price of increased directory entries.

Three steps are involved in the COMPILESAVE process:

1. Ask IFPS for the model to be compiled by using the MODEL command.

2. Tell IFPS to create a compiled file and give the file a name. To do so, you issue a COMPILESAVE command where the word COMPILESAVE is followed by a name under which the file is to be saved.

3. When you are ready to retrieve the compiled file, you issue a COMPILEGET command, where the word COMPILEGET is followed by the name of the file that was previously compiled.

Figure 4-10 shows the sequence of steps followed. When you issue the COMPILEGET command, IFPS responds by asking you what SOLVE option you want. You can use any valid IFPS solve option or language command.

```
? model product
READY FOR EDIT, LAST LINE IS 200
? compilesave invest
MODEL PRODUCT  VERSION OF  08/30/82  18:21 -- 8 COLUMNS 13 VARIABLES
COMPILED MODEL PRODUCT VERSION OF 08/30/82 18:21 SAVED ON FILE
INVEST
? compileget invest
MODEL PRODUCT  VERSION OF  08/30/82  18:21 -- 8 COLUMNS 13 VARIABLES
ENTER SOLVE OPTIONS
```

FIGURE 4-10. COMPILESAVE AND COMPILEGET

The idea in COMPILEFILE is to to put a statement at the very beginning of a model (before the COLUMNS statement!) that will create a separate file for the compiled version. The model itself remains in the IFPS file where it was created. (See Sec. 2.1.3 and 2.1.4 for a discussion of IFPS files.)

Figure 4-11 illustrates COMPILEFILE. In this figure, Line 5 is the COMPILEFILE instruction. It consists of the word COMPILEFILE followed by the name of the file to be used. The file name must be a legitimate file name for your computer and should differ from an existing file name since you can erase the existing file.

```
? model simplec
READY FOR EDIT, LAST LINE IS 40
? LIST
MODEL SIMPLEC  VERSION OF  09/05/85  23:25
 1* Short Version of Model SIMPLE Set Up for Compilation
 5 COMPILEFILE SIMPCOMP
 10 COLUMNS 1-6
 20 REVENUE = 100,PREVIOUS REVENUE *1.25
 30 EXPENSES =75,100,125,150,175
 40 NET INCOME = REVENUE -EXPENSES
 END OF MODEL
 ?COMPILESAVE SIMPCOMP
 MODEL SIMPLEC  VERSION OF  09/05/85  23:25 -- 6 COLUMNS 3 VARIABLES
 COMPILED MODEL SIMPLEC VERSION OF 09/05/85 23:25 SAVED ON FILE
 SIMPCOMP
 ?SOLVE
 ENTER SOLVE OPTIONS
 ? WIDTH 62 20 7
 ? ALL

                                 1      2      3      4      5      6

  Short Version of Model SIMPLE Set Up for Compilation
 REVENUE                       100    125  156.3  195.3  244.1  305.2
 EXPENSES                       75    100    125    150    175    175
 NET INCOME                     25     25  31.25  45.31  69.14  130.2
```

FIGURE 4-11. COMPILEFILE

You must use the COMPILESAVE command followed by the name of the file as given in the model to create the compiled version. When the model is solved, the COMPILEFILE line does not print because it occurs ahead of the columns definition.

You should understand how COMPILEFILE works. You are allowed to SOLVE a model containing COMPILEFILE once to check it for correctness before you COMPILESAVE it. If you try to solve it more than once before COMPILESAVE you will get an error message. You can, however, edit it and then SOLVE it once again without an error message. Once you have compiled the model, you refer to it by its model name not its COMPILEFILE name. Thus, for example, if you want to retrieve the file in Figure 4-11 at some later time, you type MODEL SIMPLEC. Solving SIMPLEC automatically uses the compiled file SIMPCOMP without you having to COMPILEGET it.

COMPILEFILE can be a little tricky when the original model contains micros (see Sec. 9.6 for a discussion of micro).

4.5.7 Finding All References to a Variable (CROSSREF)

In a complicated model, making changes in one place can affect you in many other places. For example, if you decide you want to remove widgets from your product line, you will want to remove all references to widgets in your IFPS model. The CROSSREF command helps you keep track of what goes on in your model by showing you an alphabetized list of all variables in your model. In addition, for each variable it tells you the line on which it is defined and the lines on which it is referred to on the right hand side. Figure 4-12 illustrates the use of CROSSREF for the Simple IFPS Model of Section 2.2. Note that you have to tell IFPS to CROSSREF a particular model name; CROSSREF by itself is not enough. The rest follows automatically.

```
? crossref
INVALID MODEL NAME AFTER CROSSREF COMMAND
READY FOR EXECUTIVE COMMAND
? crossref simple
VARIABLE NAME                     DEFN    REFERENCES
EXPENSES                            30    40    80
EXPENSE RATIO                       80
NET INCOME                          40        90
NET INCOME RATIO                    90
REVENUE                             20        20    40    80    90
```

FIGURE 4-12. CROSSREF

In using CROSSREF you leave the IFPS model but not the file. You have to re-enter the MODEL command (including the name of the model) to continue.

4.5.8 Printing out Variable Names Rather than Line Numbers (EXPAND)

In Section 4.4.1 you saw how you could refer to variables by using the line number where they were defined (i.e., where they are on the left of the equal sign) rather than by their name. Thus, we wrote:

```
10 SALES = L20*L30
20 MARKET = 8000,PREVIOUS MARKET *1.05
30 MARKET SHARE = 0.15,PREVIOUS MARKET SHARE+0.005
```

If you want to see a listing that substitutes the names for the line numbers, all you have to do is type:

```
LIST EXPAND
```

The result for Line 10 will be:

```
10 SALES = MARKET * MARKET SHARE
```

The EXPAND feature is temporary. If you ask for list again, the original (unexpanded) version will be displayed. Similarly, if you ask for a printout of one or more lines, you will get the unexpanded version.

4.6 DATA FILES

If you want to solve the same model for a variety of conditions (e.g., different departments or divisions) or if you have a large amount of data (e.g., 30 historical periods), you may find it easier to place your input data into a data file rather than keeping it in the model. In this section we describe the basic features of data files. An advanced feature of data files, "tagged data files" is described in Section 9.7.

4.6.1 The Dummy Model

If you are going to use data files, there is no need for you to include the data in the model. Therefore, what you do is define the variable on the left-hand side of the equal sign and set it equal to 0. That is, you create a dummy model. The dummy model for the Simple IFPS Model of Section 2.7 is shown in Figure 4-13.

```
MODEL DUMMY  VERSION OF  11/22/82  15:38
10 COLUMNS 1-6
20 SALES=0
30 EXPENSES=0
40 NET INCOME=SALES-EXPENSES
50 EXPENSE RATIO=EXPENSES/SALES
60 NET INCOME RATIO=NET INCOME/SALES
END OF MODEL
```

FIGURE 4-13. DUMMY MODEL

4.6.2 The Data File

The data file contains the information to be substituted in the dummy model. Since you will provide data only for some lines of the model, not the entire model, you have to tell IFPS where you want the information to go. Therefore, you have to store both the identity of the line and the data in the data file. Information can be stored either by referring to the variable name or the line number. The data file associated with the dummy model of Figure 4-13 is shown in Figure 4-14. In this figure, SALES is referred to by line number (20) and EXPENSES is used directly. Note that you can put the number of the line on the left hand side and follow it with an equal sign. You can also refer to Line 20 by using L20 (see Section 4.4.1).

```
? list
1 20=100,125,160,195,245,330
2 EXPENSES=75,100,125,150,175,175
```

FIGURE 4-14. DATA FILE FOR DUMMY MODEL

4.6.3 Obtaining Answers with a Data File (MODEL ... USING)

The dummy model and the data file have to be brought together before you can solve the model. To do so, you change the way you retrieve the model from the file. Specifically, you ask for:

MODEL modelname USING datafile

where you substitute the appropriate model and data file names. For example, if your model is DUMMY and your data file is GDATA, you type:

```
MODEL DUMMY USING GDATA
```

You then tell IFPS to SOLVE in the usual way. The MODEL ...USING combination does not change the model; rather, it allows the model to use the data file values as it needs them.

A few words of caution. Because of the substitution process involved, if your data file does not contain information about a variable, IFPS simply uses the values in the model. This can result in 0's being used if you forget a line of data. On the other hand, if you have defined a variable in both the model and the data file, the data file normally takes precedence. (Refer to the *IFPS USER'S MANUAL* for information on PROTECT DATA.)

In our example, the growth in sales is replaced by the data file values. If the data file does not provide enough values for all columns, IFPS simply assumes the last value you gave it. On the other hand, if a line of your data file contains more values than there are columns in your model, you will receive an error message. You should make the necessary corrections before proceeding. The important point is that it is up to you to make sure you have the data values you need available to you in your data file.

4.6.4 Creating and Saving a New Data File (DATAFILE)

Creating a new data file involves the same sequence of steps as creating a new model. In response to a ? you type DATAFILE and IFPS asks you for a name. You are then told to BEGIN ENTERING NEW DATAFILE. Figure 4-15 shows you how the data file GDATA was created.

```
? datafile gdata
BEGIN ENTERING NEW DATA FILE
? 20=100,125,160,195,245,330
? expenses=75,100,125,150,175,175
? save
DATAFILE SAVED
```

FIGURE 4-15. CREATING AND SAVING A DATA FILE

Once a file is created, you must SAVE it. This is done by typing SAVE.

IFPS will help you remember by asking you whether you want to save the updated file or not. Type YES if you do.

<u>WARNING:</u> If you fail to SAVE a data file you lose it!!

<u>USING EXPRESSIONS IN DATAFILES.</u> The example shown in Figure 4-15 contains numbers for each data item. You are not limited in this way. You can use expressions involving:

FOR
PREVIOUS or FUTURE

within a data line. For example, you might write:

```
20 EXPENSES = 75 FOR 3, PREVIOUS +25
```

and IFPS knows that the values are 75,75,75,100,125,150 .

4.6.5 Finding Out What Is in a Data File

If you have a data file, you can find out what is in it by using either LIST or SOLVE. In response to a question mark you first tell IFPS you want the data file in your personal workspace. For example, you might ask for:

```
? DATAFILE BUDGET
```

You can then LIST it and obtain output such as was shown in Figure 4-14. If you want more easily readable ouput in column format, you can ask for SOLVE. This is done in Figure 4-16.

```
? solve
ENTER SOLVE OPTIONS
? all

                        1        2        3        4        5        6

L20                   100      125      160      195      245      330
EXPENSES               75      100      125      150      175      175
```

FIGURE 4-16. USING SOLVE TO EXAMINE THE CONTENTS OF A DATA FILE

EXERCISE: Create the dummy model and data file shown in this section and then SOLVE. Convince yourself that you obtain the same results as in Figure 2-5 in Section 2.2.

4.6.6 Changing a Data File

A data file is edited in exactly the same way as a model. You use the editing commands given in Sections 2.5 and Section 4.10 that explain how to correct mistakes. Be sure to SAVE the changed data file. IFPS will prompt you and ask you whether you want to SAVE. If you don't SAVE the changes, the old, unedited data file will remain in your permanent storage.

4.6.7 Storing the Output of a Model for Future Use as Data (STORENT)

If you want to use the results of one model as the inputs to a subsequent model, you can do so with the STORENT command (i.e., Store,No Tag) . This command has the form

STORENT datafile

STORENT derives its name from the fact that the data are "untagged"; that is, they are not identified as coming from a particular place (e.g., a model, a data file, or a particular what if case of a model). As discussed in Section 9.7, it is possible to "tag" datafiles so their origin is known and to use that information in models. The significance of tagging is that it creates a third dimension to the usually two-dimensional data that IFPS creates. See Section 9.7 for details on tagged data files.

When you give the STORENT command, IFPS immediately solves your model and then asks you which variables you want stored in the data file whose name you have given. If you respond ALL, it will put all output values in the file; if you give it a list of variable names, it will store only those variables. If you used a data file in the model, IFPS will also store all variables that appear in the model.

Figure 4-17 shows you the result of solving MODEL DUMMY (Section 4.6.1) using the GDATA data file in combination with the STORENT command. We chose to call the new data file GDATA, thereby replacing the original with the newly created data file. In this example we are replacing an existing data file. Therefore, since Line 20 was referred to by line number in the original version, it is also referred to as Line 20 in the new version.

```
? solve
MODEL DUMMY  VERSION OF  11/22/82  15:38 -- 6 COLUMNS 5 VARIABLES
ENTER SOLVE OPTIONS
? all

                            1       2       3       4       5       6

SALES                     100     125     160     195     245     330
EXPENSES                   75     100     125     150     175     175
NET INCOME                 25      25      35      45      70     155
EXPENSE RATIO           .7500   .8000   .7813   .7692   .7143   .5303
NET INCOME RATIO        .2500   .2000   .2188   .2308   .2857   .4697

ENTER SOLVE OPTIONS
? storent gdata
ENTER STORE OPTIONS
? all

STORE UPDATE COMPLETE

ENTER SOLVE OPTIONS
? datafile gdata
READY FOR EDIT, LAST LINE IS 5
? list
1 20=100,125,160,195,245,330
2 EXPENSES =75,100,125,150,175 FOR 2
3 NET INCOME=25 FOR 2,35,45,70,155
4 EXPENSE RATIO=.75,.8,.78125,.769231,.714286,.530303
5 NET INCOME RATIO=.25,.2,.21875,.230769,.285714,.469697
```

FIGURE 4-17. STORING MODEL OUTPUT AS A DATA FILE AND LISTING OF THE RESULTING DATA FILE

4.6.8 Combining Data from Several Files into a New File (DATASELECT)

A situation often encountered in practice is that data for a particular model or for a summary report are scattered among several data files. For example, you may have budget data in one file, actual data in another, and variance data in a third. Furthermore, each data set has quarterly and annual data and you need to create a single annual variance report that combines data from all three files. A simple approach to solving this problem is to use the DATASELECT command. With this command, you can select columns of data from one or more existing data files and combine them into a new data file that can then be used with any model.

Specifically, the DATASELECT command allows you to:

- Select data from an existing data file and put it in a new data file.
- Combine data from two or more data files into a new data file.
- Add (that is, consolidate) or subtract data from two or more files or multiply data by a factor when creating the new data file.

The DATASELECT command works on columns in the existing data files and creates columns in the new data file.

Combining these capabilities provides you with powerful data manipulation capability. For example, you can select columns from an existing data file and rearrange them. You can take a column and compute its ratio or percentage with respect to another column (e.g., percent profit or benefit/cost ratio). You can pick summary columns from several files and combine them into a master summary report for top management.

The DATASELECT command is particularly user friendly in that it prompts you through the sequence of steps required to create the new file. For convenience, we will refer to the new file as the "output" file and the files from which we obtain information as the "input" files.
Figure 4-18 leads you through a typical sequence. We will use this sequence again in our example in Section 4.9. What we are trying to do here is combine the annual data for budget, actual, and variance available in column 4 in each of three data files into a single data file. We also want to compute the percent variance of the actual from the budget.

The sequence of steps is as follows:

1. Type in the DATASELECT command. At this point IFPS drops its previous work and is ready to create a new data file.

2. IFPS asks you to tell it the number of columns in the output file you are creating (in our case four). The number of columns in the output file need have no relation to the number of columns in any of the input files.

3. IFPS keeps asking you for the name of the file from which to copy data and what you want to do with the data until you type in the word NONE to signify that you have finished creating the new file. ENTER DATAFILE NAME OR NONE in our case requires telling IFPS about the input files CBUDGET, CACTUAL, and CVAR.

```
?dataselect
ENTER NUMBER OF COLUMNS IN OUTPUT MATRIX
? 4
ENTER DATAFILE NAME OR NONE
? cactual
ENTER DIRECTIVE OR END
? 4 into 1
ENTER DIRECTIVE OR END
? end
ENTER DATAFILE NAME OR NONE
? cbudget
ENTER DIRECTIVE OR END
? 4 into 2
ENTER DIRECTIVE OR END
? end
ENTER DATAFILE NAME OR NONE
? cvar
ENTER DIRECTIVE OR END
? 4 into 4
ENTER DIRECTIVE OR END
? end
ENTER DATAFILE NAME OR NONE
?cavr
ENTER DIRECTIVE OR END
?4 into 4
ENTER DIRECTIVE OR END
?end
ENTER DATAFILE NAME OR NONE
? cbudget
ENTER DIRECTIVE OR END
? divide
ENTER DIRECTIVE OR END
? 4(.01) into 4
ENTER DIRECTIVE OR END
? end
ENTER DATAFILE NAME OR NONE
? none
ENTER OUTPUT FILENAME (STOREOPT OR NAOUTPUT)
? varann
DATA FILES SELECTED AND SAVED ON FILE VARANN
READY FOR EXECUTIVE COMMAND
? datafile varann
READY FOR EDIT, LAST LINE IS 4
? list
1 TOTAL UNITS=460 FOR 2,0 FOR 2
2 TOTAL REVENUE=1212.5,1181.25,-31.25,-2.57732
3 TOTAL COSTS=660,652,-8,-1.21212
4 NET PROFIT=552.5,529.25,-23.25,-4.20814
```

FIGURE 4-18. DATASELECT

4. For each input file you are asked to give a DIRECTIVE (or END if you are finished with that file). A DIRECTIVE can copy from any column in the input file to any column in the output file. You can also multiply the input column by any factor by putting the multiplier in parentheses. The format is:

Input column number(factor) INTO ouput column number

The factor is assumed to be equal to 1 unless you specify otherwise. INTO is a keyword to separate input from output column numbers.

You can list several DIRECTIVEs on one line by separating them with commas and you can do multiple column transfers using a format that is similar to the FOR-NEXT format used in BASIC for performing looping. For example,

```
?ENTER DIRECTIVE OR END
1-7 STEP 2 INTO 1-4, 9-11 INTO 5-9 STEP 2
```

copies columns 1, 3, 5, and 7 from the input file into the first four columns of the output file and then copies copies columns 9, 10, and 11 from the input file into columns 5, 7, and 9 of the output file.

5. We use the command DIVIDE to create percentage values in column 4 of the output file. We first copied column 4 of the file CVAR into both columns 3 and 4 of the output file. We then told IFPS to consider file CBUDGET again and gave the directive DIVIDE. When prompted again we said to divide column 4 of the input file CBUDGET (multiplied by the factor .01 to create percentages) into column 4 of the output file. Note that the input file is BUDGET and that we had previous copied data from the CVAR file into column 4 of the output file. For example, if the input file value is 70 and the output file value is 35 then this set of instructions results in 35/(70*.01) = 50.

In addition to the DIVIDE directive, the DATASELECT command provides a MULTIPLY directive. A typical sequence is:

```
MULTIPLY
1 INTO 3
```

In this sequence, column 1 of the data file multiplies column 3 of the output matrix and puts the result in column 3 of the output matrix.

6. Once you have created the new file, you respond to ENTER DATAFILE NAME OR NONE by typing NONE. IFPS asks you for a name for the output file. This name should be unique. You must be careful not to choose an existing file name, because if you do you will erase that file. In Figure 4-18 we use the name VARANN for annual variance.

7. Figure 4-18 also shows a listing of the data file VARANN to check the success of the DATASELECT process.,

4.6.9 Merging Multiple Data Files (MERGE)

The DATASELECT command discussed in the previous section allows sophisticated combinations of data. In some cases, all you want to do is combine several existing data files into one. This is done with the MERGE command. For example, the dialog:

```
?MERGE DAT1,DAT2,DAT3
ENTER MORE DATAFILE NAMES OR NONE
?NONE
ENTER OUTPUT FILE NAME
?DATA4
DATAFILES MERGED AND SAVED ON FILE DATA4
```

results in combining the three files DAT1, DAT2, DAT3 into a single data file DATA4. IFPS simply copies the file one after the other as illustrated below:

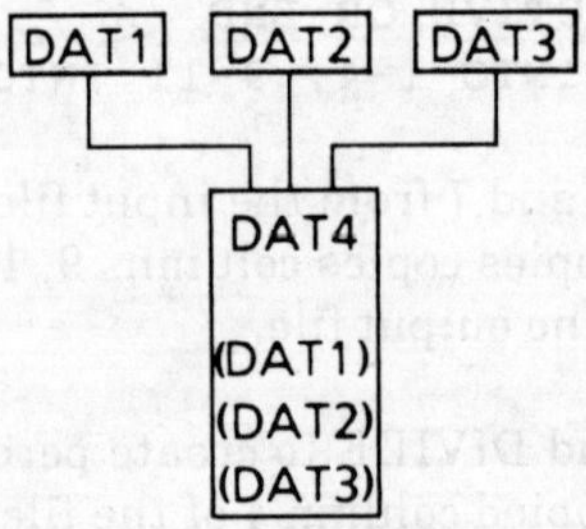

WARNING: IFPS does not check the data you MERGE.

For example, if you use the same variable name in two files or have a typing error, say, in one of the files, the MERGE operation will give you no warning that errors exist.

EXERCISE: Suppose DAT1, DAT2, DAT3 are three one-line data files having data as shown:

DAT1:	`20 = 200,300, 400 FOR 4`
DAT2:	`10 = 300,500, 650, (PREVIOUS +100) FOR 3`
DAT3:	`DEBT SERVICE = 150 FOR 6`

Create these data files and then MERGE them into a new file called DAT4. Print out all four files. Use the DIRECTORY (or CATALOG) command on your computer to see if the MERGE operation erased DAT1.

4.6.10 What To Do If You Don't Have a Piece of Data (NA, NAOUTPUT)

Even the best accounting systems sometimes do not provide a specific piece of data called for in your model. If you are working with data gathered in the field, you may find a large number of data points missing. The NA feature allows you to specify that a particular value of a variable is "Not Available." What you do is:

1. Tell IFPS how you will type in the not available values, followed by IS NA. The following are two examples of the way you do this:

```
NA IS NA
```

or

```
N/A IS NA
```

2. Type in the not available definition whenever you don't have the value. For example, if you used N/A, you might type:

L20 = 100,N/A,160, N/A FOR 2, 330

to indicate that data in columns 2,4,and 5 are not available for Line 20.

You can use any definition up to 10 characters (e.g., MISSING IS NA) but you must then use only that definition in the data file.

If you like, you can specify NA IS NULL. In this special case, IFPS expects only a comma. Thus,

```
NA IS NULL
L20 = 100,,160,,,330
```

is the same as our previous example.(Do you see why? Note the need for 2 commas because of the FOR 2)

> *IMPORTANT:* If you define data as "not available," IFPS does not use the NA elements in calculations. Any other row or column that depends on a "not available" piece of data is also considered "not available" and prints out the same way.

You can select how "not available" items will appear in your output when you SOLVE a model. Immediately after IFPS asks you to specify SOLVE options, you type NAOUTPUT followed by what you want to appear. For example,

```
ENTER SOLVE OPTIONS
?NAOUTPUT = ***
?ALL
```

would result in *** appearing for all undefined values.

4.7 GENERATING FORMATTED REPORTS (GENREPORT)

In presenting results to management, you will usually want to show your output in a neat format, one that is standard for your company. To obtain formatted reports in IFPS, you ask for GENREPORT rather than SOLVE. The format is:

GENREPORT reportname

where reportname refers to a separately defined (and saved) report format. The steps you follow are:

1. Create a MODEL.

2. Either create a REPORT format or use an existing one.

3. Call for GENREPORT rather than SOLVE.

Because GENREPORT creates a report according to the format that you have specified, you cannot choose options (such as printing out different variables each time you run the model) as you can when using SOLVE. However, you can include any SOLVE option within the report format.

Not being able to change the SOLVE options from run to run is not necessarily a disadvantage. In fact, if you are developing a particular model or running a long series of WHAT IF cases in which you use the same SOLVE options over and over, you will find it easier to create a REPORT that contains this repetitive information than to type the same information repeatedly.

Remember that the MODEL and the REPORT are separate. Therefore you can:

- Create different reports for the same model.
- Use a report with a number of models.

Furthermore, not every quantity computed in a model needs to be printed in a report.

4.7.1 Creating a New Report

When you are creating a new report format, you simply tell IFPS:

REPORT reportname

and IFPS will respond with BEGIN ENTERING NEW REPORT. If the report name has been used previously, IFPS will respond with READY FOR EDIT, LAST LINE IS __. As in the case of MODEL and DATAFILE, you can LIST a report, SAVE it, or use the standard editing commands listed in Section 2.5 and Section 4.10 to modify it.

We will now describe some of the formatting features available. There are many more than we have room for here; the *IFPS USER'S MANUAL* contains a complete description of the many options available. Rather than overloading you with detail, we will concentrate on:

- How to create a heading, blank lines, and underscores
- How to specify column headings
- How to specify variables to be displayed
- How to specify format within a line.

4.7.2 First Report Example

Figure 4-19 is a sample report for the Simple IFPS Model of Section 2.2. We will go over this sample report line by line. The results of generating output by using this report format are also shown in Figure 4-19.

Line 10 This line tells IFPS that only columns 1,4, and 6 are to be displayed. This is done in the same way as the SOLVE option. If you want all columns, Line 10 is unnecessary.

Lines 20 through 40 These lines define the report title. Headings can be entered in two ways:

```
*text
CENTER text
```

The * acts like a comment and results in displaying whatever is specified in exactly the spacing shown. If you type only a * on a line, the line is left blank. This is a convenient way of spacing. CENTER takes the text and puts it in the center of the line.

Line 50 COLUMN TITLES, results in headings of the colums being displayed. If this line is left out, headings are omitted. We will discuss column titles shortly.

Line 60 The names of the variables to be displayed must be given explicitly. Only the variables whose names are given appear. You will note, for example, that the expense ratio computed in the original program in Section 2.2 is not called for and hence does not appear. Several variables can be specified on one line, if they

```
REPORT PRODUCT  VERSION OF  08/30/82  18:20
10 COLUMNS 1,4,6
20 *
30 CENTER NEW PRODUCT FORECAST
40*
50 COLUMN TITLES
60 SALES,EXPENSES
70 UNDERLINE -
80 /PROFIT/NET INCOME
90*
100 NET INCOME RATIO
110 UNDERLINE=
END OF REPORT
? model gray
READY FOR EDIT, LAST LINE IS 90
? genreport product
MODEL GRAY  VERSION OF  01/07/83  11:46 -- 6 COLUMNS 5 VARIABLES

                              NEW PRODUCT FORECAST

                                      1         4         6
SALES                               100     195.3     305.2
EXPENSES                             75       150       175
                                -------   -------   -------
PROFIT                               25     45.31     130.2

NET INCOME RATIO                  .2500     .2320     .4266
                                =======   =======   =======
```

FIGURE 4-19. FIRST REPORT EXAMPLE

are separated by commas. If you want all lines in a model, specify ALL. If you want all lines between two points in the model use L20 THRU L95 or SALES THRU PROFITS. (See Section 4.4.1 for further discussion of the use of L to refer to line numbers.)

Line 70 UNDERLINE- creates a single underscore. See the description of Line 110 below.

Line 80 /PROFIT/NET INCOME. The / format causes a variable name to be replaced by the name you want to use in the output. Here NET INCOME in the model is to be replaced by PROFIT. The general format is to put / / around the name to be printed and follow it by the original name used in the model. Note that while this approach seems similar to that used for editing mistakes, it handles things in reverse order. In the case of reports you define the new name first and then give the original name found in the model.

Line 110 UNDERLINE= causes a double line to be displayed. If you do not specify either -- or = after UNDERLINE, you will get a single underscore.

4.7.3 The WIDTH Command

As explained in Section 4.2, the WIDTH command allows you to specify:

- the total length of the line in number of spaces
- the number of spaces to be used for the variable name
- the number of spaces to be used for each column
- the number of decimal places for each number.

In Figure 4-20, you will see the use of WIDTH 68,20,8,2 to indicate that you want 68 columns with 20 spaces for the variable name, 8 spaces for each column, and two decimal spaces for each number. Table 4-2 showed the default values and ranges allowed for each option.

The WIDTH command is the simplest formatting device. It provides the same format for all lines following the command. You can use multiple WIDTH commands within a report format; every time a new WIDTH is encountered, it governs everything that follows until the next WIDTH.

If you do not want to change the total length of the line, but do want to change other parameters, you can use the OPT statement instead of WIDTH. OPT was described in Section 4.2.

4.7.4 The COLUMN TITLES Command

You can have IFPS print the column titles you want by specifying the exact heading right after COLUMN TITLES. In the example in Figure 4-20, Lines 50 and 60 result in specifying the columns in terms of quarters rather than 1 through 6 as in the model. Multiple COLUMN TITLES lines can be used to produce more than one heading per column.

If you just specify COLUMN TITLES you obtain the headings given in the columns specification at the beginning of the model.

```
REPORT FORECAST0  VERSION OF  01/07/83  12:08
10 WIDTH 68,20,8,2
20 *
30 CENTER NEW PRODUCT FORECAST
40 *
50 COLUMN TITLES 1ST,2ND,3RD,4TH,5TH,6TH
60 COLUMN TITLES QTR,QTR,QTR,QTR,QTR,QTR
70 *
80 ALL
END OF REPORT
? model gray
READY FOR EDIT, LAST LINE IS 90
? genreport forecast0
MODEL GRAY  VERSION OF  01/07/83  11:46 -- 6 COLUMNS 5 VARIABLES


                          NEW PRODUCT FORECAST

                          1ST      2ND      3RD      4TH      5TH      6TH
                          QTR      QTR      QTR      QTR      QTR      QTR

SALES                   100.00   125.00   156.25   195.31   244.14   305.18
EXPENSES                 75.00   100.00   125.00   150.00   175.00   175.00
NET INCOME               25.00    25.00    31.25    45.31    69.14   130.18

                                   RATIO ANALYSIS
PERCENT OF SALES
EXPENSE RATIO              .75      .80      .80      .77      .72      .57
NET INCOME RATIO           .25      .20      .20      .23      .28      .43
```

FIGURE 4-20. WIDTH AND COLUMN TITLES

4.7.5 The FORMAT Command

If you want more control over format than is given by the WIDTH command, you can create a format for a line by using the FORMAT command. You may *not*, however, use WIDTH and FORMAT for the same line.

What you type in the FORMAT command is interpreted literally by IFPS, space by space.

The following are special editing symbols:

- A blank space will be displayed as a blank space.
- A 9 indicates any number.
- A single . indicates a decimal point.
- A , indicates a comma.

Examples of the FORMAT command are shown in Figure 4-21. Examine Line 10 of this figure and the resulting display. You will see that a string of periods indicates where text is to be shown. If ...... immediately follows the word FORMAT, the amount of space allocated to the variable name is the number of periods plus 6. If, as in line 10, the ...... appear in the middle of the line, the number of spaces is equal to the number of periods.

Using FORMAT requires meticulous attention to detail in planning. You literally have to count spaces to know where things will appear. Planning is particularly important if you use several format statements in a single report. It is easy to create columns that do not line up and it is easy to specify the wrong number of spaces. If you allocate too much space to a variable name, blank spaces will remain at the right end. If you allocate too little space, the name will be truncated.

```
REPORT FORECAST  VERSION OF  08/30/82  18:08
10 FORMAT 9999.99 9999.99 9999.99  ................. 9999.99 '
11 9999.99 99999.99
20*
30 CENTER NEW PRODUCT FORECAST
35 UNDERLINE=
40*
50 COLUMN TITLES 1ST,2ND,3RD,4TH,5TH,6TH
60 COLUMN TITLES QTR,QTR,QTR,QTR,QTR,QTR
70 *
80 SALES,EXPENSES,NET INCOME
85 UNDERLINE-
90*
100 EXPENSE RATIO,NET INCOME RATIO
END OF REPORT
? model gray
READY FOR EDIT, LAST LINE IS 90
? genreport forecast
MODEL GRAY  VERSION OF  08/30/82  18:20 -- 6 COLUMNS 5 VARIABLES

                              NEW PRODUCT FORECAST
                              ====================

  1ST      2ND      3RD                        4TH      5TH      6TH
  QTR      QTR      QTR                        QTR      QTR      QTR

 100.00   125.00   156.25   SALES             195.31   244.14   305.18
  75.00   100.00   125.00   EXPENSES          150.00   175.00   175.00
  25.00    25.00    31.25   NET INCOME         45.31    69.14   130.18
 ------  -------  -------                    -------  -------  -------

    .75      .80      .80  EXPENSE RATIO        .77      .72      .57
    .25      .20      .20  NET INCOME RATIO     .23      .28      .43
```

FIGURE 4-21. PUTTING NAMES IN THE MIDDLE

The FORMAT command is quite rich. Figure 4-22 illustrates other features of the command. In Figure 4-22, two format statements are used, one to obtain numbers with two decimal places and one to obtain numbers with four decimal places. You will also observe in Figure 4-22, that:

- If you want to use a format several times, you can use the square bracket option; for example, 3[9999.99]. In this case, the first symbol after the [should be a blank so that numbers do not run into one another.

- B and D will also print numbers. However, B will leave any entries that are zero blank, while D replaces a zero value with a single –. If you use () around a number, the result is to show negative numbers with a () around them rather than with a minus sign. (NOTE: each bracket of the parenthesis uses one space in the format.)

- Like WIDTH, a FORMAT is followed until a new format is encountered.

```
REPORT NEWPROD  VERSION OF  08/30/82  18:07
10 FORMAT .................. 3[ 9999.99] BBBB.BB (DDDD.DD) 9999.99
20*
30 CENTER NEW PRODUCT FORECAST
40 UNDERLINE=
50 SPACE 2
60 COLUMN TITLES 1981,1982,1983,1984,1985,1986
70 SALES,EXPENSES,NET INCOME
80 SPACE 3
90 FORMAT .................. 6[ 999.999]
100 EXPENSE RATIO,NET INCOME RATIO
END OF REPORT
? model gray
READY FOR EDIT, LAST LINE IS 90
? genreport newprod
```

```
                           NEW PRODUCT FORECAST
                           ====================


                        1981     1982     1983     1984     1985     1986
SALES                 100.00   125.00   156.25   195.31   244.14   305.18
EXPENSES               75.00   100.00   125.00   150.00   175.00   175.00
NET INCOME             25.00    25.00    31.25    45.31    69.14   130.18



EXPENSE RATIO           .750     .800     .800     .768     .717     .573
NET INCOME RATIO        .250     .200     .200     .232     .283     .427
```

FIGURE 4-22. LINE FORMATS

4.7.6The SPACE Command

If you want to leave several lines blank it is easier to use the SPACE command followed by a blank and the number of lines to be left blank than to use the * method described in Section 4.7.2. Lines 50 and 80 in Figure 4-18 show the use of SPACE 2 and SPACE 3.

4.7.7 Seeing What You have Created (TESTREPORT)

Writing report specifications can be a tedious task and one that is error prone. If you are writing complex report specifications, particularly for large models with many columns, you may want to preview what you have done. The TESTREPORT command lets you do this. As shown in Figure 4-23, if you type TESTREPORT in response to a ? while you are working on a report, you see a skeleton of what the report looks like. This example uses REPORT NEWPROD of Figure 4-22. The printout shows the text, spacing, and number format you have specified as they will actually look. By convention, TESTREPORT shows only one column of data.

```
? REPORT NEWPROD
READY FOR EDIT, LAST LINE IS 100
? TESTREPORT




                           NEW PRODUCT FORECAST
                           ====================



                     1981
SALES            00000.00
EXPENSES         00000.00
NET INCOME       00000.00




EXPENSE RATIO     000.000
NET INCOME RATIO  000.000
```

FIGURE 4-23. TESTREPORT APPLIED TO REPORT NEWPROD

4.7.8 A Report Format for the Pro Forma Profit and Loss Statement

In Section 2.9, we presented a pro forma profit and loss statement associated with a particular inventory policy. Figure 4-24a and 4-24b show a formatted version of the pro forma statement shown unformatted in Figure 2-10. For simplicity we have modified the model so that it shows only four months not 12 months. This report contains applications of many of the report features we have discussed here. Study Figure 4-24 and make sure you understand the relation between what is in the REPORT format and the result of using the GENREPORT command. You will see, for example, that the section providing input data and the quantities derived from input data are not included in the report. As implied earlier, not every line in the model has to be printed in the report.

```
REPORT PANDL  VERSION OF  01/07/83  13:15
10 WIDTH 68,30,8,0
20 CENTER 1983 BUDGET
30 CENTER FOR
40 CENTER ABC COMPANY
50 UNDERLINE-
60*
70 COLUMN TITLES JAN,FEB,MARCH,APR
80 UNDERLINE-
90 SPACE 1
100 GROSS SALES
110*COST OF GOODS SOLD
120/ BEGINNING FG INVENTORY/BEGINNING INVENTORY
130* COST OF GOODS MANUFACTURING
140/   DIRECT MATERIAL/MATERIAL COST
150/   DIRECT LABOR/DIRECT LABOR
160 UNDERLINE-
170/ TOTAL/COST OF MANUFACTURING
180*
190/ TOTAL CGM AND FG INV/TOTAL INVENTORY VALUE
200/ ENDING FG INVENTORY/ENDING INVENTORY VALUE
210 UNDERLINE-
220 COST OF GOODS SOLD
230*
240 GROSS PROFIT ON SALES
250*
260*OPERATING EXPENSES
270/ ADVERTISING/ADVERTISING
280/ COMMISSIONS/COMMISSIONS
290/ LEASES/LEASES
300/ NOTE INTEREST/NOTE INTEREST
310/ DEPRECIATION/DEPRECIATION
320UNDERLINE-
330/ TOTAL EXPENSES/TOTAL OPERATING EXPENSE
340*
350NET PROFIT BEFORE TAX
360*
370NET PROFIT$
380UNDERLINE=
END OF REPORT
```

a. Model

FIGURE 4-24. FORMATTED VERSION OF THE PRO FORMA BALANCE SHEET
(This Figure Continued on the Next Page)

```
? model profitloss
READY FOR EDIT, LAST LINE IS 610
?solve
ENTER SOLVE OPTIONS
? columns 1-4
? genreport pandl
MODEL PROFITLOSS   VERSION OF   08/30/82   18:07 -- 12 COLUMNS 29
VARIABLES



                                     1983 BUDGET
                                         FOR
                                     ABC COMPANY
                                     -----------

                                   JAN      FEB    MARCH      APR
                                ------   ------   ------   ------

GROSS SALES                    1075000  1525000  1825000  2125000
COST OF GOODS SOLD
 BEGINNING FG INVENTORY        1334000  2160500  2726000  3117500
 COST OF GOODS MANUFACTURING
   DIRECT MATERIAL             1075000  1075000  1075000  1075000
   DIRECT LABOR                 375000   375000   375000   375000
                                ------   ------   ------   ------
 TOTAL                         1450000  1450000  1450000  1450000

 TOTAL CGM AND FG INV          2784000  3610500  4176000  4567500
 ENDING FG INVENTORY           2160500  2726000  3117500  3335000
                                ------   ------   ------   ------
COST OF GOODS SOLD              623500   884500  1058500  1232500

GROSS PROFIT ON SALES           451500   640500   766500   892500

OPERATING EXPENSES
 ADVERTISING                     26875    26875    38125    45625
 COMMISSIONS                     53750    76250    91250   106250
 LEASES                          65000    65000    65000    65000
 NOTE INTEREST                    2500     2500     2500     2500
 DEPRECIATION                    50000    49000    48020    47060
                                ------   ------   ------   ------
 TOTAL EXPENSES                 274775   296275   321545   343085

NET PROFIT BEFORE TAX           176725   344225   444955   549415

NET PROFIT                      $95432  $185882  $240276  $296684
                                ======   ======   ======   ======
```

b. Output of GENREPORT

FIGURE 4-24. FORMATTED VERSION OF THE PRO FORMA BALANCE SHEET
(Continued)

The following comments about specific lines will help you follow the REPORT.

Line 10 uses WIDTH to define a 68-character line with 30 spaces used for the name of the variable and 8 spaces for each of the 4 columns. Numbers are to be printed as dollars since we provide 0 decimal places.

Lines 20 through 40 create a centered heading for the budget.

Line 50 provides the single underscore and Line 60 leaves a line blank.

Line 70 substitutes abbreviations for the names of the month for the column headings 1 through 6 in the original.

Line 90 is an alternate way of leaving a line blank.

Line 100 tells IFPS to print the gross sales line as is.

Line 110 uses the comment format to print a heading.

Line 120 uses the substitution feature. Note that the new name, given within the / / is substituted for exactly; therefore, when we leave the first space after the / blank we obtain a name that is indented.

Line 130 by leaving a space after the * indents the heading by one space.

Lines 140 through 200 substitute names to obtain output in the format desired. Note that in line 150 we have to use the substitution format, even though the variable names are the same, in order to achieve the desired indenting.

Lines 220 through 330 use the same ideas as previous lines. It is a general characteristic of reports that you use the same formats repeatedly to achieve a uniform look.

Line 370 NET PROFIT$ indicates that a $ sign should be put in front of every number.

Line 380 creates a final double underline.

Figure 4-24b shows the resulting output. Check the commands in Figure 4-24a against the output in Figure 4-24b and make sure you understand how each line of the output was specified.

4.8 CONSOLIDATION

In many modeling situations you reach a point where you want to combine the solutions of previous models. For example, you may have a model of your own firm and a potential acquisition and want to find out what the combined balance sheet would look like. You may have a forecast done at the beginning of the month and actual figures from the end of the month and want to find out about the variances in performance. You may have monthly results that you want to combine into quarterly results or quarterly results you want to combine into an annual report. CONSOLIDATE is a powerful command that allows you to produce composite reports from two or more models.

4.8.1 Simple, Additive Consolidation

It is important to recognize that CONSOLIDATE is a command in IFPS, just as MODEL or SOLVE are commands. CONSOLIDATE is closer in form to MODEL than to SOLVE which asks you to enter solve options. Just as in MODEL where you have to specify the name of the model, in CONSOLIDATE you have to specify the names of all the models to be consolidated. For example, if you want to consolidate the income statements from two divisions, you would type:

```
CONSOLIDATE DIVISION1 DIVISION2
```

where DIVISION1 and DIVISION2 are existing models. Note that you do *NOT* use a comma between the model names. The CONSOLIDATE command for two models is the simplest form of this command. The sequence of steps that occurs when you give this command is:

- The DIVISION1 model is solved.
- The DIVISION2 model is solved.
- The output from the two models is combined into a final solution matrix.

In the combination, if a variable has the same name in both models, its values are added up, period by period. If a variable appears in only one of the models, the values from that model will be included in the combination.

Once the combination is complete, you can ask IFPS to print out the results by either using SOLVE or, if you want to format your output, by GENREPORT.

> NOTE. You will not get any printout from CONSOLIDATE unless you ask for SOLVE or GENREPORT

The CONSOLIDATE command is not limited to two models. You can specify a long list of models if you so choose. The following is a typical sequence of steps you might see when you ask for CONSOLIDATE.

```
?CONSOLIDATE MODEL1 MODEL2 MODEL3
ENTER MORE MODEL OR DATA FILE NAMES OR NONE
?MODEL4 MODEL5
ENTER MORE MODEL OR DATA FILE NAMES OR NONE
?NONE
```

The above prompting sequence results in consolidating five models. When the consolidation is complete, IFPS tells you:

```
CONSOLIDATION COMPLETE, 5 MODELS
```

and you are ready to use SOLVE or GENREPORT to obtain output.

```
MODEL SIMPLE VERSION OF 08/30/82 18:06
10 COLUMNS 1-6
20 SALES = 100,PREVIOUS SALES*1.25
30 EXPENSES =75,100,125,150,175
40 NET INCOME = SALES -EXPENSES
50*
60 *                              RATIO ANALYSIS
70 *PERCENT OF REVENUE
80 EXPENSE RATIO = EXPENSES/SALES
90 NET INCOME RATIO = NET INCOME/SALES
END OF MODEL
? model simple2
READY FOR EDIT, LAST LINE IS 90
? list
MODEL SIMPLE2 VERSION OF 08/30/82 18:06
10 COLUMNS 1-6
20 SALES = 150,PREVIOUS SALES * 1.15
30 EXPENSES = 90,120,150,180
40 NET INCOME = SALES -EXPENSES
50 *
60 *                              RATIO ANALYSIS
70 *PERCENT OF SALES
80 EXPENSE RATIO = EXPENSES/SALES
90 NET INCOME RATIO = NET INCOME/SALES
END OF MODEL
? consolidate simple simple2
ENTER MORE MODEL NAMES OR NONE
? none
CONSOLIDATION COMPLETED 2 MODELS
? solve
ENTER SOLVE OPTIONS
? WIDTH 62 20 7
? ALL

                          1       2       3       4       5       6

SALES                   250   297.5   354.6   423.4   506.5   606.9
EXPENSES                165     220     275     330     355     355
NET INCOME               85   77.50   79.63   93.44   151.5   251.9

                                  RATIO ANALYSIS
PERCENT OF SALES
EXPENSE RATIO         1.350   1.496   1.556   1.557   1.403   1.170
NET INCOME RATIO      .6500   .5043   .4439   .4430   .5971    8299
```

FIGURE 4-25. CONSOLIDATION OF TWO MODELS

Figure 4-25 on the previous page illustrates this simple form of consolidation. In this figure we consider our Simple IFPS model from Chapter II and a similar model based on another product. The consolidation shows the results of consolidating these two models to assess their combined impact. (Can you explain why the ratios are WRONG?).

> <u>*SPECIAL WARNING ABOUT RATIOS:*</u> If you look at the Figure 4-25 output, you will see that the consolidation did exactly what it promised to do, namely added the values obtained from solving models SIMPLE and SIMPLE2. The results for **EXPENSE RATIO** and **NET INCOME RATIO**, however, are not what you would intuitively expect from consolidation. For example, in Period 1, the expense ratio for model SIMPLE is 75/100 =.75 and for model SIMPLE2 is 90/150=.60. If you add .75 and .60 you get 1.350, the value that is shown in Figure 4-25. However, if you consider the consolidated expenses (165) and consolidated sales (250) for Period 1 as shown in Figure 4-20, you compute an expense ratio of 165/250=.66. In practical terms, it is this latter value of .66 that you are interested in for the company as a whole. In general, straight consolidation only adds. Therefore many quantitites which are not additive (such as ratios!) are computed incorrectly. The way around this problem involves two steps:
>
> 1. Do not include non-additive variables in your model. You may have to modify an existing model to remove such variables.
>
> 2. Create a separate postprocessing model which computes these quantitites. The use of postprocessing models is described in Section 4.8.4.

EXERCISE: This exercise is a follow-up on Figure 4-25. It leads you through a series of steps that create correct expense and net income ratios.

1. Create Model DUMMY1 in your Models and Reports File. This model should consists of Lines 10 through 40 shown in Figure 4-13.

2. Create two data files, DIV1 and DIV2 that contain the data for Sales and Expenses in models SIMPLE and SIMPLE2, respectively. Remember that a line in a data file can be computational statements such as are used for sales.

3. Create Model COMPANY which has six columns and which defines expense ratio and net income ratio.

4. Consolidate DUMMY1 using DIV1 and DIV2 with COMPANY.

4.8.2 Weighted Consolidation

If you own only part of an organization (e.g., a 60% owned joint venture) you can weight the effect of the partial ownership by putting the weighting in parentheses after the model name. For example,

```
CONSOLIDATE CORPORATE SUBA(.60)
```

results in multiplying every value in the output of SUBA by .6 before it is consolidated with CORPORATE.

4.8.3 Variance Analysis

Variance analysis is made simple by using weighted consolidation. You take the budget and multiply it by −1. Thus,

```
CONSOLIDATE ACTUAL BUDGET(-1)
```

results in a variance report. That is, multiplying the budget by −1 and consolidating results in obtaining the difference between actual and budget. Figure 4-26 illustrates this use of consolidation for variance analysis.

```
MODEL ACTUAL   VERSION OF   08/30/82   18:06
1 COLUMNS 1-4
10 UNITS =97,112,126,125
20 PRICE =2.5 FOR 3,2.75
30 REVENUE = UNITS*PRICE
40 COSTS = 142,155,172,183
END OF MODEL
?solve
MODEL ACTUAL   VERSION OF   08/30/82   18:06 -- 4 COLUMNS 4 VARIABLES
ENTER SOLVE OPTIONS
? all
                          1        2        3        4

UNITS                    97      112      126      125
PRICE                 2.500    2.500    2.500    2.750
REVENUE               242.5      280      315    343.8
COSTS                   142      155      172      183
```

a. Model Actual

```
MODEL BUDGET   VERSION OF   08/30/82   18:05
1 COLUMNS 1-4
10 UNITS =100,110,120,130
20 PRICE =2.5,2.5,2.75
30 REVENUE =UNITS*PRICE
40 COSTS = 150,170
END OF MODEL
? solve
MODEL BUDGET   VERSION OF   08/30/82   18:05 -- 4 COLUMNS 4 VARIABLES
ENTER SOLVE OPTIONS
? all
                          1        2        3        4

UNITS                   100      110      120      130
PRICE                 2.500    2.500    2.750    2.750
REVENUE                 250      275      330    357.5
COSTS                   150      170      170      170
```

b. Model Budget

FIGURE 4-26. USING CONSOLIDATION FOR VARIANCE ANALYSIS
(This Figure Continued on the Next Page)

```
ENTER SOLVE OPTIONS
? consolidate actual budget(-1)
ENTER MORE MODEL NAMES OR NONE
? none
CONSOLIDATION COMPLETED 2 MODELS
? solve
ENTER SOLVE OPTIONS
? width 68 20 8
? all
                          1       2       3       4

UNITS                    -3       2       6      -5
PRICE                     0       0   -.2500      0
REVENUE              -7.500       5     -15  -13.75
COSTS                    -8     -15       2      13
```

c. Consolidation

FIGURE 4-26. USING CONSOLIDATION FOR VARIANCE ANALYSIS (Continued)

In this figure, a company has budgeted and actual data for the number of units to be sold, the price charged, and the costs incurred during each quarter during the past year. The consolidated report shows the variances between the actual and budgeted values.

4.8.4 Using the Consolidated Model in Computations (Postprocessing Models)

Consolidating several models into a single model can, as indicated above, give you a broader picture of the organization as a whole than observing models individually. The next step is to perform calculations based on the consolidated data. For example, you might want to sum several categories of expenses or you might want to add the anticipated corporate overhead and determine the rate that will have to be charged back to the divisions. IFPS allows you to create such a postprocessing model and apply it as part of the consolidation process. To tell IFPS you are adding a postprocessing model you use the reserved word WITH in the format

```
CONSOLIDATE DIVISION1 DIVISION2 WITH CORPORATE
```

where CORPORATE contains the postprocessing model. In response to this form of the CONSOLIDATE command, IFPS first solves DIVISION1 and DIVISION2 and consolidates the result and then solves the postprocessing model. After IFPS tells you CONSOLIDATION COMPLETED 2 MODELS, you give the command SOLVE (or GENREPORT if you want a REPORT). The model solved consists of both the consolidation and the postprocessing model CONSOLIDATE. The line numbers associated with the variables in the last model consolidated are still available to be referenced by the postprocessing model.

Several restrictions and rules apply when using postprocessing. They are:

- The postprocessing model should have different line numbers from those of the last model consolidated. In this way, you avoid overwriting lines from the consolidation with the postprocessing model.

- The variable names in the postprocessing model should be different from those in the last model consolidated. If the names are the same, the rule is that the values of the most recent occurrence of the name are to be used when variable names are referenced in a report or as a solve option.
- The postprocessing model must have at least as many columns defined as the consolidated model. If more columns are specified, the additional columns are computed by statements in the postprocessing model.

Figure 4-27 shows how postprocessing can be done on consolidated models. In this Figure, BUDGET and ACTUAL are the same as in Figure 4-26. Model COMPANY uses the results of each model to compute the quarterly profits and then to accumulate the values for the year. Thus, the values of total units through net profit represent the values for the entire year.

```
MODEL COMPANY  VERSION OF   08/30/82  18:05
1 COLUMNS 1-4
50 PROFIT = REVENUE - COSTS
60*
70 TOTAL UNITS = PREVIOUS + UNITS
80 TOTAL REVENUE =PREVIOUS + REVENUE
90 TOTAL COSTS=PREVIOUS +COSTS
100 NET PROFIT = PREVIOUS + PROFIT
END OF MODEL
? consolidate actual budget(-1) with company
CONSOLIDATION COMPLETED 2 MODELS
? solve
ENTER SOLVE OPTIONS
? all
                           1        2        3        4

UNITS                     -3        2        6       -5
PRICE                      0        0   -.2500        0
REVENUE               -7.500        5      -15   -13.75
COSTS                     -8      -15        2       13
PROFIT                 .5000       20      -17   -26.75

TOTAL UNITS               -3       -1        5        0
TOTAL REVENUE         -7.500   -2.500   -17.50   -31.25
TOTAL COSTS               -8      -23      -21       -8
NET PROFIT             .5000    20.50    3.500   -23.25
```

FIGURE 4-27. USING THE CONSOLIDATED MODEL IN COMPUTATIONS

4.8.5 Using Multiple Data Files with a Model

If you have a large model that requires several data files, you can combine CONSOLIDATE and USING to obtain both data files for solving the model. For example, you might ask for:

```
CONSOLIDATE PRODUCT USING DATA1 DATA2
```

where PRODUCT is a model name and DATA1 and DATA2 are data files. This approach leaves the individual data files intact for future use.

4.8.6 Creating Consolidated Data Files (CONSOLDF)

If you want to combine two or more data files into a single data file that you can store for use in future computations, you invoke the CONSOLDF command. The form of the CONSOLDF command is indicated by the example:

```
CONSOLDF DATA1 DATA2 NONE
```

The NONE is needed to tell IFPS that you have given it the names of all the files to be consolidated. IFPS responds with:

```
ENTER OUTPUT FILE NAME
```

and you type in a name for the consolidated data file. This name should differ from the names of existing data files; if it does not, you erase the existing data file.

Just as the CONSOLIDATE command allows you to add the values in two or more models, CONSOLDF allows you to add the values in two or more data files. Note that CONSOLDF command differs from the MERGE command in that CONSOLDF adds the values of variables in a data file, whereas MERGE simply copies two files into a single file.

VARIANCE ANALYSIS. Just as in CONSOLIDATE, you may put a factor after the name of any file. For example,

```
CONSOLDF  ACTUAL BUDGET(-1) NONE
```

creates a variance analysis data file. Note that the factor has to be put in parenthesis and that it multiplies every number in the data file.

CURRENCY CONVERSION. You can also use the CONSOLDF command to multiply a single data file by a constant. This is particularly useful for currency conversion. For example, if the French franc is selling at 20 cents, you could convert a data file of sales in France to dollars by:

```
CONSOLDF FRSALES  (0.20) NONE
```

Note that the file in francs still exists and can also be used. The general rule is that if you do not specify a data file before a conversion factor, the conversion factor affects all files.

CAUTION: CONSOLDF must be used with care because all numbers are added. This can lead to nonsense results as shown in Figure 4-28 in which each data file contains PRICE. CONSOLDF adds the prices, resulting in the sale of 175 items at $5.50! Furthermore, if the results of CONSOLDF are close to the original values you can easily overlook the error that you created.

```
? list datafile dat1
 FILE DAT1 05/05/86 11:15
 PRICE = 2.50
 SALES = 100
 END OF DATAFILE
 READY FOR EXECUTIVE COMMAND
 ? list datafile dat2
 FILE DAT2 05/05/86 11:15
 PRICE = 3.00
 SALES =75
 END OF DATAFILE
 READY FOR EXECUTIVE COMMAND
 ? consoldf dat1 dat2 none
 ENTER OUTPUT FILE NAME (STOREOPT OR NAOUTPUT)
 ? dat3
 DATA FILES CONSOLIDATED AND SAVED ON FILE DAT3
 READY FOR EXECUTIVE COMMAND
 ? list datafile dat3
 FILE DAT3 05/05/86 11:16
 COLUMNS 1
 PRICE=5.5
 SALES=175
 END OF DATAFILE
 READY FOR EXECUTIVE COMMAND
```

FIGURE 4-28. EXAMPLE OF PROBLEM THAT CAN RESULT WHEN USING CONSOLDF

4.8.7 Modeling Hierarchical Situations

In discussing consolidation we have thus far only considered situations in which the organizations involved (e.g., divisions) are all on the same level. However, many situations exist in which there are hierarchical structures; for example, DIVISION1 may have three groups each of which is a cost center of its own. These three groups have to be consolidated into DIVISION1 and then the divisions must be consolidated into a corporate report. IFPS has the capability for dealing with such hierarchies. The details are a bit more involved than what we have discussed here because you have to define the hierarchical structure first before you can undertake hierarchical consolidation. The details of how this is done are presented in detail in Section 10.1.

4.9 AN EXAMPLE INVOLVING DATA FILES, REPORTS, AND CONSOLIDATION

In this example we consider the company whose budget and actual quarter-by-quarter results were illustrated in Figures 4-26 and 4-27. What we want to do is create a simple, easy-to-read report for management that shows:

- The budget
- The actual
- The variance
- The percent variance

at the end of the year.

Given the data in quarterly form as in models ACTUAL and BUDGET shown in Figure 4-26, the following steps show one way of achieving this goal. This sequence of steps is illustrated in Figures 4-29 through 4-33.

1. Use model COMPANY and CONSOLIDATE to perform postprocessing and obtain annual data on the actual, budget, and variance. (Figure 4-29.)

2. Create data files by using the STORENT command on each of these three cases.

3. Use the DATASELECT feature of data files to create a new file that consists of the year-end figures and the percent variance, where the percent variance is computed by using divide and factor features available in DATASELECT. (Figure 4-30.)

4. Having put the required data into a data file, create a dummy model that can use the data file. (Figure 4-31.)

5. Write a REPORT that generates the desired format. (Figure 4-32.)

6. Use GENREPORT to obtain the output in the form needed by management. (Figure 4-33.)

Immediately after each CONSOLIDATE ... WITH is solved in Step 1, a data file (CACTUAL, CBUDGET, and CVAR) is created with STORENT in Step 2. Note that since we will need only the accumulated data for the year, we only save the total units, total revenue, total costs, and the net profit in these new files.

In Figure 4-30, the DATASELECT feature picks annual data (located in column 4) out of the CACTUAL, CBUDGET, and CVAR data files and puts them into a new file which we have called VARYEAR. This is Step 3. We then compute the percent variance by using the simple computational features available with DATASELECT. (Be sure to go over this figure line by line so that you understand what is being done. Go back to Section 4.6.8 which describes DATASELECT if you don't.) Figure 4-30 also shows you the contents of the newly created file VARYEAR.

```
? consolidate budget with company
CONSOLIDATION COMPLETED 1 MODELS
? solve
ENTER SOLVE OPTIONS
? all

                              1        2        3        4

UNITS                       100      110      120      130
PRICE                     2.500    2.500    2.750    2.750
REVENUE                     250      275      330    357.5
COSTS                       150      170      170      170
PROFIT                      100      105      160    187.5

TOTAL UNITS                 100      210      330      460
TOTAL REVENUE               250      525      855     1213
TOTAL COSTS                 150      320      490      660
NET PROFIT                  100      205      365    552.5

ENTER SOLVE OPTIONS
? storent cbudget

ENTER STORE OPTIONS
? total units thru net profit

ENTER MORE VARIABLES FOR STORE PROCESSING (OR NONE)
? none
STORE UPDATE COMPLETE
ENTER SOLVE OPTIONS
? consolidate actual with company
CONSOLIDATION COMPLETED 1 MODELS
? solve
ENTER SOLVE OPTIONS
? total units thru net profit

                              1        2        3        4

TOTAL UNITS                  97      209      335      460
TOTAL REVENUE             242.5    522.5    837.5     1181
TOTAL COSTS                 142      297      469      652
NET PROFIT                100.5    225.5    368.5    529.3
```

FIGURE 4-29. CONSOLIDATE...WITH AND STORENT TO OBTAIN DATA FILES

(This Figure Continued on the Next Page)

```
ENTER SOLVE OPTIONS
? storent cactual
ENTER STORE OPTIONS
total units thru net profit
ENTER MORE VARIABLES FOR STORE PROCESSING (OR NONE)
? none
STORE UPDATE COMPLETE
ENTER SOLVE OPTIONS
? consolidate actual with company
CONSOLIDATION COMPLETED 1 MODELS
? solve
ENTER SOLVE OPTIONS
? total units thru net profit
                          1        2        3        4

TOTAL UNITS              97      209      335      460
TOTAL REVENUE         242.5    522.5    837.5     1181
TOTAL COSTS             142      297      469      652
NET PROFIT            100.5    225.5    368.5    529.3

ENTER SOLVE OPTIONS
? storent cactual
ENTER STORE OPTIONS
? total units thru net profit
ENTER MORE VARIABLES FOR STORE PROCESSING (OR NONE)
? none
STORE UPDATE COMPLETE
ENTER SOLVE OPTIONS
? consolidate actual budget(-1) with company
CONSOLIDATION COMPLETED 2 MODELS
? solve
ENTER SOLVE OPTIONS
? total units thru net profit
                          1        2        3        4

TOTAL UNITS              -3       -1        5        0
TOTAL REVENUE        -7.500   -2.500   -17.50   -31.25
TOTAL COSTS              -8      -23      -21       -8
NET PROFIT            .5000    20.50    3.500   -23.25

ENTER SOLVE OPTIONS
? storent cvar
NEW DATA FILE WILL BE CREATED
ENTER STORE OPTIONS
? total units thru net profit
ENTER MORE VARIABLES FOR STORE PROCESSING (OR NONE)
? none
STORE UPDATE COMPLETE
```

FIGURE 4-29. CONSOLIDATE...WITH AND STORENT TO OBTAIN DATA FILES (CONTINUED)

```
?DATASELECT
ENTER NUMBER OF COLUMNS  IN OUTPUT MATRIX
? 4
ENTER DATAFILE NAME OR NONE
? cbudget
ENTER DIRECTIVE OR END
? 4 into 1
ENTER DIRECTIVE OR END
? end
ENTER DATAFILE NAME OR NONE
? cactual
ENTER DIRECTIVE OR END
? 4 into 2
ENTER DIRECTIVE OR END
? end
ENTER DATAFILE NAME OR NONE
? cvar
ENTER DIRECTIVE OR END
? 4 into 3, 4 into 4
ENTER DIRECTIVE OR END
? end
ENTER DATAFILE NAME OR NONE
? cbudget
ENTER DIRECTIVE OR END
? divide
ENTER DIRECTIVE OR END
? 4(.01) into 4
ENTER DIRECTIVE OR END
? end
ENTER DATAFILE NAME OR NONE
? none
ENTER OUTPUT FILENAME (STOREOPT OR NAOUTPUT)
? varyear
DATA FILES SELECTED AND SAVED ON FILE VARYEAR
READY FOR EXECUTIVE COMMAND
? datafile varyear
READY FOR EDIT, LAST LINE IS 4
? solve
ENTER SOLVE OPTIONS
? all

                              1       2        3        4

TOTAL UNITS                 460     460        0        0
TOTAL REVENUE              1213    1181   -31.25   -2.577
TOTAL COSTS                 660     652       -8   -1.212
NET PROFIT                552.5   529.3   -23.25   -4.208
```

FIGURE 4-30. USING DATASELECT TO CREATE THE ANNUAL VARIANCE FILE

```
MODEL X  VERSION OF  08/30/82  18:05
1 COLUMNS BUDGET,ACTUAL,VARIANCE,PERCENT
2 TOTAL UNITS =0
3 TOTAL REVENUE =0
4 TOTAL COSTS =0
5 NET PROFIT =0
END OF MODEL
? model x using varyear
? solve
MODEL X  VERSION OF  08/30/82  18:05 -- 4 COLUMNS 4 VARIABLES
ENTER SOLVE OPTIONS

? all

                          BUDGET  ACTUALVARIANCE PERCENT

TOTAL UNITS                  460     460       0       0
TOTAL REVENUE               1213    1181  -31.25  -2.577
TOTAL COSTS                  660     652      -8  -1.212
NET PROFIT                 552.5   529.3  -23.25  -4.208
```

FIGURE 4-31. DUMMY MODEL AND ITS SOLUTION

```
? report variance
READY FOR EDIT, LAST LINE IS 11
? list

REPORT VARIANCE  VERSION OF  08/30/82  18:04
1 FORMAT..........4[     99999.9  ]
2 CENTER COMPANY VARIANCE REPORT
3 CENTER (ANNUAL)
4 SPACE 2
5 COLUMNS 2,1,3,4
6 INVERT NOVAR
7 COLUMN TITLES SALES   ,REVENUE ,,NET    ,
8 COLUMN TITLES  UNITS  ,$     ,COSTS   ,PROFITS,
9 UNDERLINE-
10 DOUBLE
11 TOTAL UNITS THRU NET PROFIT
END OF REPORT
```

FIGURE 4-32. REPORT USED TO GENERATE FIGURE 4-33

```
? genreport variance
```

COMPANY VARIANCE REPORT
(ANNUAL)

	SALES UNITS	REVENUE $	COSTS	NET PROFITS
	-------	-------	-------	-------
ACTUAL	460.0	1181.3	652.0	529.3
BUDGET	460.0	1212.5	660.0	552.5
VARIANCE	.0	-31.3	-8.0	-23.3
PERCENT	.0	-2.6	-1.2	-4.2

FIGURE 4-33. VARIANCE REPORT FOR MANAGEMENT

Having VARYEAR as a data file, we next create the needed dummy model, which we call MODEL X, and which is shown in Figure 4-31 together with its output when using VARYEAR. This is Step 4.

The transformation of this output into the form desired by management (Steps 5 and 6) is shown in Figures 4-32 and 4-33. In Figure 4-33, we simply call for GENREPORT VARIANCE to obtain the desired answer. Of course, to do so, we previously had to create the report named VARIANCE (Fig. 4-32). Study Figure 4-32 and note the following points:

- Line 5 reorders the columns from the way that they are stored in the data file.
- Line 6 interchanges the rows and columns in the data file so that management can see actual, budget, and variance as rows rather than as columns.
- The column titles differ from the names under which the data are stored. This is perfectly all right.

EXERCISE: Figure 4-34 shows an alternate form of the variance report for management. Write a REPORT which will generate Figure 4-34.

COMPANY VARIANCE REPORT (ANNUAL)				
	BUDGET	ACTUAL	VARIANCE	PERCENT VARIANCE
	-------	-------	-------	-------
SALES UNITS	460.0	460.0	.0	.0
REVENUE $	1212.5	1181.3	-31.3	-2.6
COSTS	660.0	652.0	-8.0	-1.2
	-------	-------	-------	-------
NET PROFIT	552.5	529.3	-23.3	-4.2

FIGURE 4-34. ALTERNATE FORM OF THE VARIANCE REPORT

In this section we have taken you, step by step, through the use of CONSOLIDATE, DATAFILE, DATASELECT, and REPORT to create neatly formatted output. If you were using the information for your own purposes you might well have stopped after CONSOLIDATE...WITH since the answers you need can be obtained by looking at that output. However, the extra steps are often worthwhile if you need to present information to managers who are used to basing their decisions on information presented in a particular way.

4.10 ADDITIONAL EDITING COMMANDS

In Section 2.5 we presented a series of useful editing commands including:

- C for changing a portion of a line
- D for delete
- Listing a single line by typing its line number.
- Listing a group of lines by typing the first and last line numbers, separated by a comma.
- Replacing a line by retyping it with its line number.

You will find that these edit commands will be sufficient for most editing tasks. In this section we present some additional editing commands that will be helpful in specific situations.

4.10.1 Using " Rather Than / for Editing

IFPS will accept either a quotation mark (") or a slash mark (/) in editing commands. Thus, it is equally valid to write:

```
20C"ORF"ROF"
```

as it is to write:

```
20C/ORF/ROF/
```

4.10.2 Finding All Occurrences of a Specific Phrase

If you want to find all references to a particular variable or phrase or combination of letters, you can use the quote form of the editing command. For example,

```
"SALES"
```

The quote command searches the text of your model until it finds the first time that the combination of letters SALES is used and prints out the entire line. To find the second and later occurrences, you keep repeating the quote editing command.

Figure 4-35 shows you a search for all occurrences of the word SALES in the Simple IFPS Model.

```
? model simple
READY FOR EDIT, LAST LINE IS 90
? "sales"
20 SALES = 100,PREVIOUS SALES *1.25
? "sales"
40 NET INCOME = SALES -EXPENSES
? "sales"
70 *PERCENT OF SALES
? "sales"
80 EXPENSE RATIO = EXPENSES/SALES
? "sales"
90 NET INCOME RATIO = NET INCOME/SALES
? "sales"
20 SALES = 100,PREVIOUS SALES *1.25
```

FIGURE 4-35. FINDING ALL OCCURRENCES OF "SALES" IN THE SIMPLE IFPS MODEL

If you only want to find all references to a particular variable, then the CROSSREF command descibed in Section 4.5.6 is an easier method.

4.10.3 Changing All Occurrences of a Specific Phrase

The C edit command allows you to change a single occurrence of a specific phrase. For example, if you want to change SLAES to SALES in Line 20, you type

```
20C/SLAES/SALES/
```

If, however, you want to make the same change for every time a particular combination of letters or a particular phrase occurs, you can save yourself the tedium of finding and changing each occurrence by using the global change command. For example, if you want to change SALES to REVENUE throughout the Simple IFPS Model, you would type:

```
10,90G"SALES"REVENUE"
```

where the sequence is as follows:

- starting line number followed by a comma (10,)
- ending line number followed by no blank spaces (90)
- G
- quotation mark (or /)
- old text to be replaced (SALES)
- quotation mark (or /)
- new text to be inserted (REVENUE)
- quotation mark (or /).

If you forget the last quotation mark (or last /) IFPS assumes that the new text ends with the last letter that is not a blank space.

Figure 4-36 shows several examples of the global replace command.

```
10,90g"sales"revenue"
20 REVENUE = 100,PREVIOUS REVENUE *1.25
40 NET INCOME = REVENUE -EXPENSES
70 *PERCENT OF REVENUE
80 EXPENSE RATIO = EXPENSES/REVENUE
90 NET INCOME RATIO = NET INCOME/REVENUE
```

a. Use of "SALES"REVENUE"

```
? 10,90g/sales/revenue/
20 REVENUE = 100,PREVIOUS REVENUE *1.25
40 NET INCOME = REVENUE -EXPENSES
70 *PERCENT OF REVENUE
80 EXPENSE RATIO = EXPENSES/REVENUE
90 NET INCOME RATIO = NET INCOME/REVENUE
```

b. Use of /SALES/REVENUE/

FIGURE 4-36. ALTERNATE FORMS OF GLOBAL SEARCH
(This Figure Continued on the Next Page)

```
? 10,90g"sales"revenue
20 REVENUE = 100,PREVIOUS REVENUE *1.25
40 NET INCOME = REVENUE -EXPENSES
70 *PERCENT OF REVENUE
80 EXPENSE RATIO = EXPENSES/REVENUE
90 NET INCOME RATIO = NET INCOME/REVENUE
```

c. Use of "SALES" REVENUE

FIGURE 4-36. ALTERNATE FORMS OF GLOBAL SEARCH
(Continued)

4.10.4 Avoiding Retyping by Moving, Copying, and Adding to Lines (MOVE, COPY, APPEND)

Retyping existing material is always a pain. It is also risky because you may introduce new errors. Three commands allow you to avoid retyping:

MOVE which allows you to move one or more lines from one location to another.

COPY which allows you to copy one or more lines from one location to another.

APPEND which allows you to add material at the end of an existing line.

The MOVE and COPY command differ in that MOVE erases lines in one place and re-creates them in another whereas COPY makes a copy of the lines in a new place but also leaves them where they are.

MOVE and COPY. The following are examples of the MOVE and COPY commands:

```
5MOVE15
6,8MOVE20
10COPY23
15,20COPY38 0.5
```

The first of these commands, moves Line 5 to Line 15. The second moves Lines 6 through 8 to a position starting at Line 20. The first COPY command creates a copy of Line 10 at Line 23 whereas the second copies Line 15 through 20 to a position starting at Line 38 and incrementing line numbers by 0.5 (i.e., it creates lines 38, 38.5,39,...)

The following are general principles:

1. Begin with the source line or lines, then the word MOVE or COPY, and finally the first line where the moved or copied lines are to appear.

2. Don't put a space before or after the words MOVE or COPY.

3. If you want to MOVE or COPY a range of lines, specify the first and last line number separate by a comma.

4. The new line numbers will be separated by 1 unless you specify the interval that you want. Separate the interval by a space from the starting line number.

<u>**WARNING:**</u> **There are serious dangers associated with COPY and MOVE.**

Thse dangers include:

1. If you MOVE or COPY lines so they overlap existing line numbers, you will get an error message. For example, if you move Lines 6 through 8 to Lines starting at 20, as in the example, above, and you already have a Line 21, you will get an error message.

2. MOVE and COPY do *not* change cross-references to line numbers. You have to change these cross-references yourself. The reference can be either within the lines copied or moved or by some other line to the copies or moved lines.

3. If you COPY lines in a model, you will be repeating variable names. This can create errors if you are not careful.

APPEND. Here is an example of typical APPEND command interaction:

```
?30A
30 SALES = 25
ENTER TEXT TO BE APPENDED (OR END)
? ,PREVIOUS * 1.1
30 SALES = 25,PREVIOUS * 1.1
```

You type the line number followed by the letter A. IFPS displays the text of the initial line and you type in the information to be added. IFPS, in turn, shows you want the edited line looks like. This handshaking back and forth is designed to make sure you know what changes you have made.

If you are an experienced user, you may want to reduce the amount of printout needed for the APPEND transaction. You can eliminate the listing of the original line by putting a / after the A, typing the change, and putting another / at the end of the change. For example:

```
?30A/, PREVIOUS * 1.1/
30 SALES = 25, PREVIOUS * 1.1
```

4.10.5 Additional Editing Commands for Data Files and Data in Models

IFPS provides four additional editing commands that can be used with data. The data can be either in a data file or within a model. These commands are:

REMOVE column
INSERT column
CHANGE column
CHANGE variable

If you want only specific elements of a column or a variable, you add the word FOR. For example, to remove the values of sales and expenses in column 4, you would write

```
REMOVE 4 FOR SALES,EXPENSES
```

If you want to insert or change, you have to specify not only the column but also the new values. The following are typical examples:

```
INSERT 4 FOR X = 7
CHANGE 3RD QTR FOR SALES,EXPENSES=250,212
CHANGE SALES FOR 1983 THRU 1986 = 420,435,460,490
```

The first of these adds the value 7 to column 4 of the variable X. The second changes the current values of sales and expenses in the column labeled 3RD QTR to the values 250 and 212 respectively. The last example changes the variable sales in the columns named 1983, 1984, 1985, and 1986 to the new values indicated.

Figure 4-37shows examples of three of these editing commands. The following paragraphs describe these commands in more detail.

```
? model product
READY FOR EDIT, LAST LINE IS 200
? insert 5 for unit price = 2.65
NUMBER OF CHANGES PERFORMED WAS 1
? change 1 for market = 7000
NUMBER OF CHANGES PERFORMED WAS 1
? change 1140=3000,0
NUMBER OF CHANGES PERFORMED WAS 2
? 50,140p
50 SALES VOLUME =MARKET*MARKET SHARE
60 MARKET=7000,PREVIOUS MARKET*1.03
70 MARKET SHARE =0.15,PREVIOUS MARKET SHARE +0.005
80 GROSS SALES = SALES VOLUME * UNIT PRICE
90 UNIT PRICE=2.5 FOR 4,2.65,2.75
100 OPERATING COST=(PRODUCTION COST +OVERHEAD)*SALES VOLUME
110 PRODUCTION COST= 1.25 FOR 4,1.35
120 OVERHEAD=PRODUCTION COST*0.80
130 NET INCOME=GROSS SALES -OPERATING COST
140 INVESTMENT =3000,0
```

FIGURE 4-37. INSERT AND CHANGE EDITING COMMANDS

REMOVE. The REMOVE command deletes the data values indicated. It is the simplest of the data file editing commands.

INSERT. The INSERT command adds information which did not exist before. The insert command can always be used to insert data in the first column. However, it can be used for any subsequent column only if the previous column exists in the definition of the model and constant data are given for that column. Thus, if:

```
30 Z = 1,2,3
```

you cannot ask for

```
INSERT 5 FOR Z = 5
```

Similarly, if:

```
30 Z = 1, PREVIOUS +1
```

you cannot ask for:

```
INSERT 3 FOR Z = 4
```

CHANGE. You can change a data value only if that value already exists in the model. Variable names can be referenced by name or line number and columns can be referenced by name or number.

4.10.6 Full Screen Editing (EDIT)

> *NOTE.* The EDIT command is not available on all machines. It is implemented on CMS, CSS, Data General, DTSS, TOPS 20, TSO, UNIX, and VAX 11/ systems.

The editing system discussed thus far is a simple, straightforward line editor built into IFPS. That is, it works either on a single line at a time (such as C) or on a group of lines (e.g., D, MOVE, APPEND) that you specify. If you have written a large model in which you want to make a number of changes, you may find this line-by-line approach tedious. The purpose of the EDIT command is to allow you access to the full screen editor built into your mainframe.

The people who wrote IFPS chose this approach to full screen editing because it requires you to learn the details of only one editing system--the one on your own mainframe, which you probably know already--rather than having to learn their editing system as well.

You can call your system's full screen editor three ways:

EDIT
EDIT editorname
EDIT editorname filename

In the first case, you are sent to a standard editor and can proceed to change the model, report, or data set you are working on. If you have more than one editor on your system, you can specify which one you want. On a VAX for example, you might specify EDIT EDT if you have the EDT editor.

In working with a full screen editor controlled by your computer rather than by IFPS, you have to be careful about line numbers. Your computer's full screen editor does not renumber lines automatically. Thus, you have to type them in. In the full screen editor you should also be careful about cross-references to line numbers.

When you are finished using the full screen editor, leave it as you normally do at the end of an editing session. You are then automatically transferred back into IFPS at the point you were when you went to the editor. It will pay you at that point to use the RESEQUENCE command (Sec. 4.5.3) to clean up the line numbering.

4.11 INTERACTING WITH YOUR MAINFRAME'S COMMAND SYSTEM (DIRECTORY, SYSTEM, EDIT)

> NOTE. These commands are not available on all machines. They are implemented on CMS, CSS, DTSS, TOPS 20, TSO, UNIX, and VAX 11/ systems.

When you are working in IFPS, you are working inside a self-contained system. There are times, however, when you would like to get out of IFPS, do something, and get back into IFPS without having to QUIT. Three commands are available to you to go back and forth to the mainframe's own command system: DIRECTORY, SYSTEM, and EDIT.

DIRECTORY is the simplest of these commands. When you type DIRECTORY you are shown a list of all the files that you currently have in the computer. This command is particularly useful if you want to move between one IFPS file and another using the FILE command (Sec. 2.3). SYSTEM allows you to perform any command available to you in your computer's operating system. For example, you may want to PRINT some other file while you are working in IFPS or you may want to respond to an electronic mail message. Whenever you ask for DIRECTORY or SYSTEM, IFPS will give you instructions on how to reenter the system.

The EDIT command leads you to the text editing system built into your computer. If you have several different editors available, you specify which one you want. The general form is

```
EDIT editorname
```

where, for example, you might specify EDT on a VAX 11/ system. The EDIT command was discussed more fully in Section 4.10.6.

CHAPTER V
MONTE CARLO SIMULATION (RISK ANALYSIS)

CHAPTER V
MONTE CARLO SIMULATION (RISK ANALYSIS)

5.1 THE RATIONALE AND USE OF SIMULATION

In the models discussed in the first four chapters of this book, all input data and all relationships were assumed to be known precisely. Such models are called deterministic. Although this is often (but not always) the case when dealing with historical information (as in bookkeeping), it is rarely the case when making estimates about the future. The future is uncertain and hence, from a business point of view, risky. In making business decisions, these risks must be evaluated.

Consider the New Product Model of Section 2.7. In creating this model, we assumed that we knew precisely what costs and revenues would be each quarter over the next two years. That is, we used single point estimates for all quantities. Although we would know about some changes (e.g., increases in wages resulting from existing labor contracts) and could build them into the model (e.g., production cost increases from $1.25 to $1.35), other changes from the situation modeled would be much less certain. For example, we assumed that market share would start at 15 percent and grow by one-half percent per quarter. Such single point estimates typically reflect the average of the values anticipated. The real situation might be market shares of:

.15, .149,.155,.163,.173,.179,.185,.182.

over the eight-quarter time horizon. If this sequence occurs, is the venture still profitable? Supposing there is a different pattern of growth. What then?

One way of exploring the implications of uncertainty is to use the WHAT IF, SENSITIVITY, and GOAL SEEKING features of IFPS. These features allow you to explore alternative situations by modifying the model and determining the effects of changes. Although excellent for exploring the effects of changes in one or two variables or answering specific concerns about the assumptions by senior management, these features are not the most effective way of analyzing risk. A second approach is to make best case and worst case estimates. In this approach, estimates are made of the most favorable and most unfavorable value that each input variable could have. To obtain the best case, the most favorable values are assumed and to obtain the worst case, the most unfavorable values are used. Unfortunately, in the real world all variables do not take on their best values simultaneously nor do they all take on their worst values. Although very useful for examing the most extreme situations, the best case/worst case approach does not give insight into the range of situations which can realistically be expected. The alternative approach is to use simulation, the subject of this chapter.

Simulation is based on the concepts of probability and statistics. We will assume that you have an elementary knowledge of both. If you know nothing about these subjects, then you should first read and understand Sections 7.1 through 7.4. Better still, if you are a student, skip this chapter until you are well into a beginning course in statistics. If you are a professional, work with someone in your organization who is knowledgeable and can help you.

5.1.1 The Difference Between Modeling and Simulation

Until now, we have been concerned with building models. Modeling and simulation differ in that:

- **MODELING involves building a representation of a situation.**
- **SIMULATION involves performing sampling experiments on the model of the situation**

We have emphasized this distinction so that you will engrave it in your memory.

The key words in this definition of simulation are "sampling experiments."

In a sampling experiment, a large number of trials are made. Because of the presence of uncertainty, the outcome of each trial may be different from that of other trials. However, the commonly used concepts of statistics, such as mean and standard deviation, allow inferences to be made about the anticipated outcomes of the situation. In simulation, the sampling experiments are performed on the computer model, thereby allowing many trials to be made at little expense.

5.1.2 Modeling Uncertainty

If you are uncertain about a variable such as market share, you have two choices:

1. Ignore uncertainty by assuming that average or most likely values will occur.
2. Attempt to model the uncertainty.

In most modeling situations you have some idea as to the nature and extent of the uncertainties being faced. In the new product example, market share could theoretically range from 0 to 100 percent; however, based on market survey, historical experience, and analysis of the competition, you can estimate that market share will remain relatively stable from quarter to quarter and have long term growth. You might, in fact, be willing to state that market share would never increase by more than, say, two percent in a quarter nor that it would shrink by more than, say, one percent in a quarter. Furthermore, you may be willing to estimate that one-half percent linear growth is most likely. Such beliefs can be converted into the form of probability distributions and these probability distributions can be included explicitly in the IFPS model. We will discuss methods for modeling probability distributions in Sections 5.2 and 5.3. In technical terms, we have introduced a random variable (in our example, growth in market share) with a given probability distribution.

5.1.3 Using Random Variables

Although we cannot predict which value a random variable will take, we know that it will take on some value; the chances of a particular value are defined by the probability distribution. For example, if we roll a pair of dice, we cannot tell what the result will be until the roll ends. However, before the roll we know that there is a 1/36 chance of a 2 and a 1/6 chance of a 7.

In solving a model containing one or more random variables, we have to have a rule for deciding what value that random variable takes on. One way of making this decision is simply to assign a value from the probability distribution and proceed as if this is the value that had occurred. Doing this once leads to a particular outcome, a "scenario." Since in simulation we perform a sampling experiment, we repeat this process many times. Each time we come to a random variable, we choose a value from the probability distribution and use that value in determining the outcome. That is, we choose the value of the random variable so that the frequency of occurrence of particular values is related to the probability distribution. For example, in simulating dice, your experiment might involve generating 36,000 different rolls of the dice on the computer. However, you must arrange things in such a way that approximately 1000 times (that is, 1/36th of the time) the outcome is a two and approximately 6000 times the outcome is a seven. (Because of the nature of randomness you should not expect to observe exactly 1000 2's or exactly 6000 7's.)

5.1.4 The Simulation Procedure

In summary, the steps in running a simulation are:

1. Build a model that defines uncertainties and risks in terms of probability.

2. Perform a sampling experiment on the computer in which you run the model a large number of times. Each outcome gives you one possible scenario.

3. Perform statistical analyses on the outcome of the experiment.

4. Use the statistical results obtained for decision making.

You, as modeler, must introduce the uncertainty into your IFPS model. Having done so, you can instruct IFPS how many times you want the model to be run. IFPS makes these runs and presents you with a statistical analysis of the results. After examining the results, you can then ask for additional runs to gain better precision or you can make a decision based on the results presented.

5.1.5 Example: A Simple Simulation Experiment

Before proceeding with the details of how simulation is performed in IFPS, we present two simple examples of simulation which you can perform by hand. If you are an old hand in simulation, you can skip directly to Section 5.2. If you are new to it, read and understand these examples before proceeding.

Your friend Terri offers you \$7 to play the following game with her. A coin will be flipped as many times as needed until four tails have appeared. For each flip of the coin, you pay Terri \$1. For example, if the first four flips are tails, you receive \$7, pay \$4 and make a net profit of \$3. The chances of this happening are only 1 in 16. However, if it takes 12 flips until the 4th tail occurs, you lose \$5. Should you play? If not, can you make Terri a fair counterproposal as to how much she should pay you to play?

Although you can compute your expected winnings (or losses) by probability theory, the calculations are a bit messy. An alternative is to ask for a few minutes to think the proposition over and head for a nearby computer terminal. You remember how to generate random numbers and obtain the following sequence:

1,0,4,8,0,1,5,0,1,1,5,3,6,0,2,0,1,1,8,1,6,4,7,9,1,3,4,6,6,
9,1,4,1,9,4,6,2,5,9,0,3,6,2,0,7,2,0,9,6,9,9,9,5,7,0,9,9,0,
7,0,0,2,3,6,4,1,7,3,3

If you interpret 0 through 4 as tails and 5 through 9 as heads, you see that the first "play" of the game requires 5 flips (a profit of $2). That is, 1,0,4,8,0 corresponds to the sequence T,T,T,H,T (T=tail, H=head). Using this rule, succeeding plays of the game require 5,6,6,9,6,7,14,5, and 6 flips respectively. If you base your decision on the average number of flips observed in these 10 "plays" of the game you would decide to play since the average cost is $6.90 and you will receive $7.00 for playing. However, should you?

EXERCISE: Suppose you interpret 0 through 4 as heads and 5 through 9 as tails. Show that the average cost under this rule for the data given is $9.14 based on a sample of 7 plays requiring 64 flips.

This simple example points out an important characteristic and a problem of simulations. First, the computer can be used to generate random numbers that can be interpreted as the outcome of random events. Second, data interpretation from simulations requires care. If you terminated after the first simulated play of the game, you would expect a profit of $2. If you had used a sample of eight plays, your average cost would have been $7.13 and you would not play. The point is that the "results" of the simulation depend on the size of the sample used in the experiment. Sample size must be chosen with care based on statistical considerations. Although the mean is $6.90, the standard deviation of the sample is $2.76. It also turns out that the true average cost is $8 and that there is approximately a 36% chance of losing $2 or more. Is this risk acceptable to you?

5.1.6 Example: A Second Simple Simulation

The TAG Donut Shoppe buys fresh doughnuts each morning to serve to that day's customers. Doughnuts not sold that day are thrown away. Unfortunately, demand fluctuates. Based on past experience, demand has ranged from 24 to 28 dozen with the probabilities shown in Table 5-1.

TABLE 5-1

DEMAND FOR TAG DOUGHNUTS

Demand (Dozen)	Probability of Demand	Probability of This Demand or Less
23	0.0	0.0
24	0.2	0.2
25	0.1	0.3
26	0.3	0.6
27	0.3	0.9
28	0.1	1.0

TAG pays $2.00 per dozen and sells at $3.00 per dozen. How many dozen should TAG order each day?

It is not difficult to show that the optimal policy, if demand one day does not depend on any other day, is to buy 26 dozen. This policy results in an average daily profit of $24.50. The actual profit (P) on a given day is given by:

$$P = 3.00*D - 2.00*S \quad \text{if } D < S, \text{ and}$$
$$P = 1.00*S \quad \text{if } D >= S \quad (5\text{-}1)$$

In the second case, demand (D) equals or exceeds supply (S) and all doughnuts are sold at a profit of a dollar a dozen.

To simulate this situation, the procedure is similar to that used in the coin flipping example.

1. Decide on a daily supply, S
2. Determine demand
3. Compute profit from Equation 5-1
4. Repeat steps 2 and 3 a sufficient number of times to estimate the mean and variance of the profit associated with a supply policy, S.

Since the objective is to find that supply policy which yields a maximum profit, the procedure has to be repeated systematically for different levels of supply (i.e., for 24,25,26,...dozen) until a maximum is found. Note that in specifying the simulation procedure we tacitly assumed that the same size order should be placed each day. (Do you see why it should be the same?)

Three problems manifest themselves here.

1. How is demand to be determined?
2. How is supply to be selected?
3. How often do you repeat to be able to make a decision?

To determine demand, we use the column in Table 5-1 labeled "Probability of This Demand or Less." These values are the cumulative probability. First choose a random number between 0 and 1. Suppose it is .532. Then determine the interval in Table 5-1 in which this random number falls (.532 is between 0.3 and 0.6). Select as the demand the value corresponding to the upper end of the interval (26 dozen corresponds to 0.6). Thus, for the data in Table 5-1, if a random number is between 0 and .2, we assume 24 dozen; from .2 to .3 we assume 25 dozen, etc.

The use of random numbers between 0 and 1 to represent cumulative probabilities is one of the fundamental ideas in simulation. That is, you use the fact that the cumulative probability distribution for any random variable is uniformly distributed between 0 and 1. When you pick a random number between 0 and 1, therefore, you are picking a point on the cumulative probability distribution. By finding the corresponding value of the random variable, you have made the decision as to which value it takes on.

The second problem involves the choice of supply, S. Whereas in the coin flipping example, the profit depended only on the number of flips, here the profit depends on two variables, supply and demand. Supply is the decision variable, the one over which you have control, whereas demand is a random variable determined by "nature" or chance. One simple approach, then, is to try different values of S (by WHAT IF) until the one yielding the highest profit is found.

The third problem is a statistical one. Suppose you obtain the following data after 10 replications at each supply:

Supply,S	Average Profit	Std. Deviation of Average Profit
25	24.45	0.20
26	24.47	0.25
27	23.97	0.30

At first glance, the average profits indicate that you could narrow your choice of maximum down to S=25 or S=26 dozen and that the answer most likely is S=26. But can you? If you draw a 90% confidence interval around the average profits, you obtain the region inside which there is a 90% chance that the true mean lies. For our results, you obtain:

Supply,S	Lower Limit on Profit	Upper Limit on Profit
25	24.35	24.55
26	24.34	24.60
27	23.83	24.13

90% confidence intervals are computed from the fomulas:

$$\text{UPPER LIMIT} = \text{AVERAGE} + 1.65^{*}\ \text{STANDARD DEVIATION} / \sqrt{n}$$

$$\text{LOWER LIMIT} = \text{AVERAGE} - 1.65^{*}\text{STANDARD DEVIATION} / \sqrt{n}$$

where n is the number of replications.

The sketch below plots the confidence intervals for the three daily supplies:

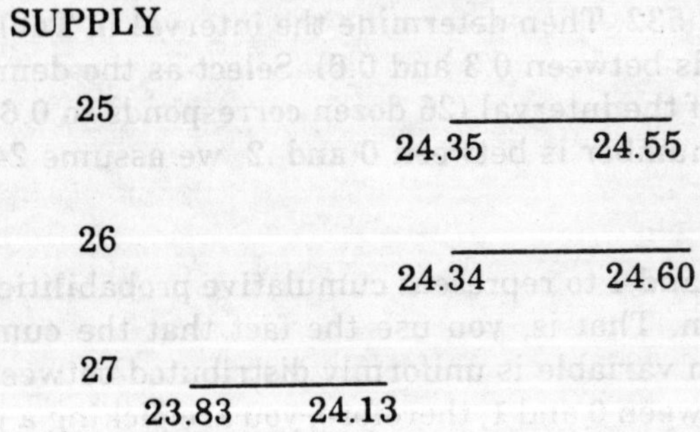

Because the confidence interval for S=27 is entirely below that of the other two choices, S =27 can be eliminated from further consideration. Since the limits for 25 and 26 overlap, you cannot make a choice between them. You can, however, reduce the size of the confidence interval (i.e., the difference between upper and lower limit) by increasing the number of replications. As the number of replications increases, the size of the confidence interval decreases; however, this decrease is slow. For example, quadrupling the replications halves the size of the confidence interval. Because of the importance of confidence intervals in making decisions, IFPS calculates confidence intervals for you. You will also see that IFPS allows you to increase the sample size through the use of the POOL command discussed in Section 5.11.

5.2 IFPS APPROACH TO SIMULATION

IFPS provides you with the capability for performing Monte Carlo Simulations. The term Monte Carlo was coined duringWorld War II when the major development of simulation took place. Analysts using the method on a classified project wanted a code word to describe it. Since chance events were being modeled it appeared appropriate to give the method a code name based on the biggest gambling casino which was then located in Monte Carlo.

The procedure you follow is to describe each quantity about which you are uncertain in terms of a probability distribution. The values of these distributions are random variables. When you ask for MONTE CARLO, IFPS solves the model a number of times with different combinations of values picked each time from the distributions you specified. The results of these replications are analyzed statistically by IFPS and you are given the statistical results. These statistical results can be interpreted in terms of the risks involved in the decision. For example, you may find out there is a 10% chance the internal rate of return will exceed 25% and a 90% chance that it will exceed 14%.

If you have a deterministic model, you will find that it is not necessary to change the basic structure of the model to incorporate risk into the analysis. All you have to do is express quantities in terms of probabilities rather than in terms of single point estimates. IFPS contains four built-in distributions (discussed in Section 5.3) and you also have the ability to model any arbitrary cumulative probability distribution of your choice (Section 5.4). Furthermore, as we discuss in Section 5.7, IFPS provides you with the ability to generate scenarios based on assigning high, low, mean, and median values to individual random variables.

5.3 BUILT-IN PROBABILITY DISTRIBUTIONS

Four built-in probability distributions are provided by IFPS:

UNIRAND	uniform distribution
TRIRAND	triangular distribution
T1090RAND	an alternate form of the triangular distribution
NORRAND	normal distribution

In addition, IFPS allows you to model any distribution of your choice through GENRAND and CUMRAND. We will discuss GENRAND and CUMRAND in Section 5.4.

For each of these probability distributions, you must specify the name of the distribution and two or more of its parameters. A typical specification is UNIRAND(10,30) which defines a probability distribution that is uniformly distributed between limits of 10 and 30. We now proceed to discuss each of the built-in distributions.

5.3.1 Uniform Probability Distribution (UNIRAND)

If all values in an interval are equally likely, then we have a uniform probability distribution. For example, in the following uniform distribution

all values between 10 and 30 are equally likely. To generate random values from this distribution, you would write, for example,

```
COST = UNIRAND(10,30)
```
(5-2)

In a simulation with many replications, each time IFPS reaches a statement containing UNIRAND(10,30), it selects a value at random between 10 and 30.

In general, UNIRAND(LOWER,UPPER) specifies a uniform distribution between the upper and lower limit. The LOWER limit must be less than the UPPER limit.

5.3.2 Triangular Probability Distribution (TRIRAND and T1090RAND)

The triangular distribution has been found to be particularly useful in modeling risk situations. Three arguments have to be supplied by you:

- the lower limit
- the most probable (maximum) value
- the upper limit

For example,

```
TRIRAND(0.96, 1.05,1.07)
```

tells IFPS to generate values from a triangular distribution of the form

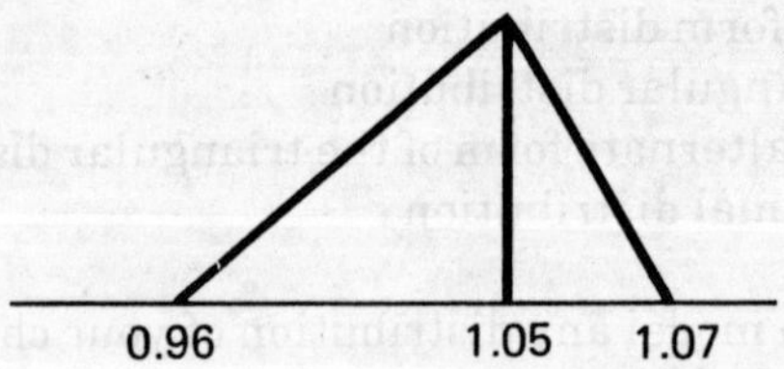

The triangular distribution is a convenient approximation when the range of possible values (i.e., upper and lower limits) is known and the distribution has a single peak. It also provides the capability for expressing the idea that risk is not symmetrically distributed around the most likely value.

The following statement is a typical IFPS application of TRIRAND:

```
MARKET = PREVIOUS MARKET*TRIRAND(0.96,1.05,1.07)
```

It models the idea that the market growth is uncertain, ranging from a 4% decrease (.96*PREVIOUS) to a 7% increase with the most likely value being a 5% increase (1.05*PREVIOUS).

If the most probable value is equal to the upper (or lower) limit, a right-angled triangular distribution is generated. For example, TRIRAND (10,10,30) generates the following distribution:

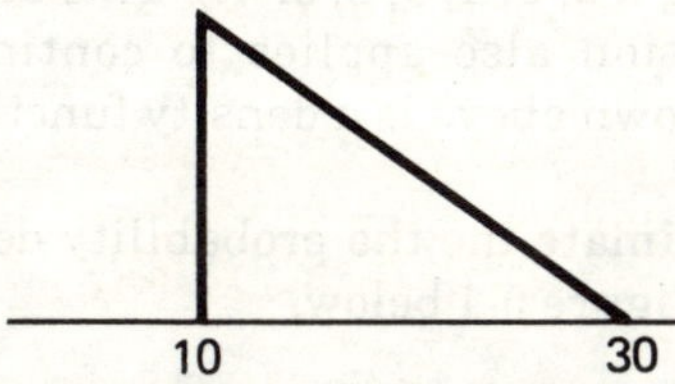

An alternative way of specifying a triangular distribution is to use the T1090RAND function. If you do not know precisely the smallest and largest value that a particular variable can take on, you may be able to estimate the 10th and 90th percentage points on the distribution. In this case, you would write

```
T1090RAND(0.97,1.05,1.065)
```

where .97 and 1.065 represent the 10th and 90th percentiles and 1.05 is the most likely value.

The most likely value of a triangular distribution is the mode, not the average. If the triangular distribution is symmetric (e.g., TRIRAND(10,20,30)) then the average value and the mode are the same. However, if the triangular distribution is skewed left as it is in TRIRAND(0.93,1.00,1.05) then the mean is less than the mode. If it is skewed right, the mean is larger than the mode. Incidentally, the mean of TRIRAND(a,b,c) is equal to (a+b+c)/3.

5.3.3 Normal Probability Distribution (NORRAND)

To generate a normally distributed random variable, you have to specify the mean and the standard deviation. For example,

```
NORRAND(100,10)
```

creates a normal distribution with a mean of 100 and a standard deviation of 10. This distribution is shown below.

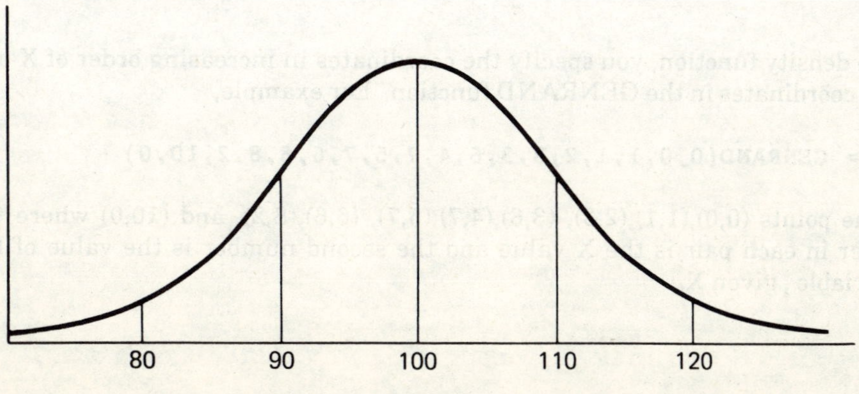

5.4 DEFINING YOUR OWN PROBABILITY DISTRIBUTIONS

Although many business situations can be described in terms of the built-in distributions, occasions where you need some other distribution do arise. In these cases, you can define either a generalized density function (GENRAND) or a generalized cumulative distribution (CUMRAND) to meet your requirements. As you recall, the density function represents the probability of a particular outcome (e.g., throwing a 2 with a pair of dice) whereas the cumulative distribution represents the probability of obtaining all values less than or equal to a given value (e.g., the cumulative distribution for 7 in throwing dice adds up the probabilities of throwing a 2, 3, 4, 5, 6, or 7.) This distinction between density function and cumulative distribution also applies to continuous distributions. For example, the normal distribution shown above is a density function.

In the GENRAND form you approximate the the probability density function with a series of straight lines as shown in Figure 5-1 below.

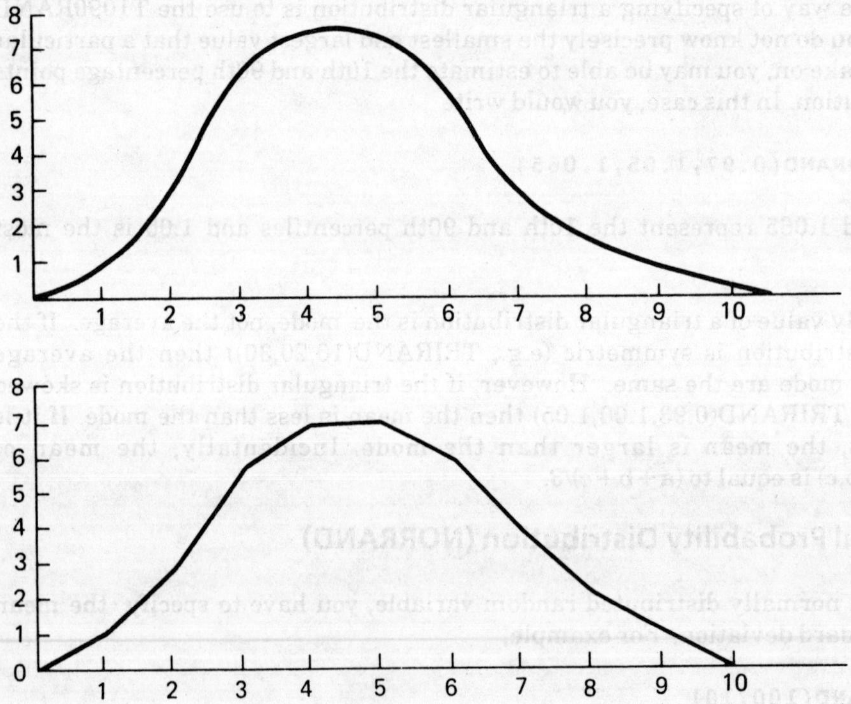

FIGURE 5-1. APPROXIMATING A PROBABILITY DENSITY FUNCTION WITH STRAIGHT LINES

To use the density function, you specify the coordinates in increasing order of X and include the coordinates in the GENRAND function. For example,

```
X = GENRAND(0,0,1,1,2,3,3,6,4,7,5,7,6,6,8,2,10,0)
```

specifies the points (0,0),(1,1),(2,3), (3,6),(4,7),(5,7), (6,6),(8,2), and (10,0) where the first number in each pair is the X value and the second number is the value of the random variable , given X.

EXERCISE: Use GENRAND to specify a triangular distribution with endpoints 0 and 5 and mode 4. Note that you will have to determine the height of the distribution at the mode.

If you know the cumulative probability distribution rather than the probability density function, you should use CUMRAND rather than GENRAND. In CUMRAND you specify the X value in equal increments of 10% of the cumulative distribution. For example, the figure shows

```
X = CUMRAND(0,3,5,6,7,7.5,8,8.5,9,10,12)
```

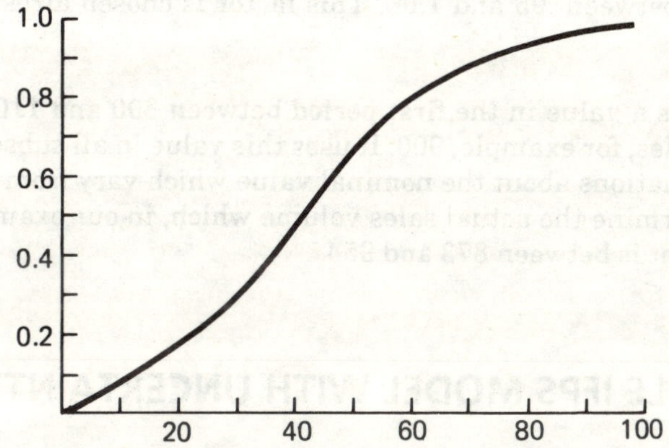

Here, 1/10 of the probability value is between 0 and 3, 1/10th between 3 and 5, etc. There is a 30 percent probability that the value will be less than or equal to 6.

Since IFPS fixes the Y values at 0, 10%, 20%,..., you need to specify only the 11 corresponding X values. A total of 11 values, MUST be included between the parentheses in CUMRAND.

5.5 CHOOSING THE SAME RANDOM NUMBER FOR ALL PERIODS OR A NEW VALUE FOR EACH PERIOD

A particular quantity (such as rental cost) may be uncertain initially but once determined stays fixed, whereas another quantity (such as sales volume) may fluctuate from period to period. IFPS allows you to model both kinds of situations. If you use:

UNIRAND,TRIRAND,T1090RAND,NORRAND,GENRAND,or CUMRAND

you will make the choice of value once and keep that same value in all following periods. However, if you add an R to any of these definitions of probability distributions, that is, if you use:

UNIRANDR,TRIRANDR,T1090RANDR,NORRANDR,GENRANDR,or CUMRANDR

you will obtain a different value each period.

You can combine the two forms. For example:

```
UNIT COST=TRIRAND(10,12,13),PREVIOUS UNIT COST*1.08*
                UNIRANDR( 0.95,1.06)
```

or:

```
SALES VOLUME=TRIRAND(800,1000,1100)*TRIRANDR(0.97,1.0,1.06)
```

In the first example, IFPS picks a unit cost in the first period. In subsequent periods the cost grows by 8% times a factor between .95 and 1.06. This factor is chosen afresh each period.

In the second example, IFPS picks a value in the first period between 800 and 1100 that represents the nominal level of sales; for example, 900. It uses this value in all subsequent periods. However, there are fluctuations about the nominal value which vary from period to period. These fluctuations determine the actual sales volume which, in our example, is between 97% and 106% of 900, that is between 873 and 954.

5.6 EXAMPLE: THE SIMPLE IFPS MODEL WITH UNCERTAINTY

Consider again the simple IFPS model introduced in Section 2.2. In that example, a product is to be marketed with sales most likely to be 100 during the first year and growing at 25% per year. Expenses are most likely to start at 75 and grow by 25 a year. Although these are the most likely estimates, the outcomes are by no means certain.

Initial sales may be as low as 90 and as high as 120, and sales growth each year may be smaller or larger than 25%. In fact, year-to-year sales growth may vary from being flat to being as high as 50% per year. Similarly, although initial expenses are known to be 75, expense growth is uncertain. Expense growth has a fixed component that will be known by the first year and a variable component that fluctuates from year to year. Figure 5-2 shows the resulting IFPS model.

```
MODEL MONTE  VERSION OF  12/29/80  14:55
10 COLUMNS 1-6
20 SALES=INITIAL SALES,PREVIOUS SALES* SALES GROWTH RATE
30 EXPENSES=75,PREVIOUS EXPENSES + 25 +FIXED EXPENSE GROWTH'
31 +VARIABLE EXPENSE GROWTH
40 NET INCOME=SALES-EXPENSES
50 *
60 *
70 *
80 INITIAL SALES=TRIRAND(90,100,120),0
90 SALES GROWTH RATE=1.25*UNIRANDR(0.8,1.2)
100 FIXED EXPENSE GROWTH =UNIRAND(-2,4)
110 VARIABLE EXPENSE GROWTH=UNIRANDR(-3,1)
```

FIGURE 5-2. SIMPLE IFPS MODEL WITH UNCERTAINTY

You can solve this model in two ways:

- By creating scenarios.
- By asking IFPS for a MONTE CARLO simulation.

We discuss these two methods in turn.

5.7 GENERATING SCENARIOS (HIGH,LOW, MEAN, MOSTP)

Before undertaking MONTE CARLO simulation runs, it is usually wise to examine the range of answers that can be anticipated. You may want to know what a typical (average or most probable) outcome is and what the best and worst situations would be. This combination of best, worst, and most likely scenarios is an excellent way of beginning to understand a situation and is often a convenient, short-hand way of communicating with management.

To allow the generation of scenarios, IFPS provides you four solve options:

- HIGH •LOW •MEAN •MOSTP

These options set the value of a probability distribution to its maximum, minimum, average, and most likely values. (In the case of NORRAND, the HIGH value is +2.5 standard deviations and the LOW value is −2.5 standard deviations.) The options can be chosen individually for each distribution. Thus, by mixing values, favorable and unfavorable scenarios can be created.

In the Simple IFPS Model with Uncertainty discussed in Section 5.6, the most favorable case occurs if:

- initial sales and sales growth rate are HIGH
- expense growth is LOW,

while the most unfavorable case occurs if:

- initial sales and sales growth rate are LOW
- expense growth rate is HIGH.

In general, the best case is obtained when all probability distributions are in your favor and the worst case is obtained when all distributions are against you. Figure 5-3 shows the results of running the best and worst cases for the Simple IFPS Model with Uncertainty. Figure 5-3 shows that you use one of the solve option words, such as HIGH, followed by a list of variables separated by commas to tell IFPS what you want. In general, you must first specify the levels you want the variables to have using HIGH, LOW, MEAN, and/or MOSTP, and then you must tell IFPS which variables you want printed (for example, ALL in Figure 5-3). Once you specify the variables to be printed, IFPS begins computing.

```
? solve
MODEL MONTE  VERSION OF  12/29/80  14:55 -- 6 COLUMNS 7 VARIABLES
ENTER SOLVE OPTIONS
? high initial sales ,sales growth rate
? low fixed expense growth,variable expense growth
? all

                             1       2       3       4       5       6

SALES                      120     180     270     405   607.5   911.3
EXPENSES                    75      95     115     135     155     175
NET INCOME                  45      85     155     270   452.5   736.3


INITIAL SALES              120       0       0       0       0       0
SALES GROWTH RATE        1.500   1.500   1.500   1.500   1.500   1.500
FIXED EXPENSE GROWTH        -2      -2      -2      -2      -2      -2
VARIABLE EXPENSE GROWTH     -3      -3      -3      -3      -3      -3

ENTER SOLVE OPTIONS
? low initial sales,sales growth rate,
? high fixed expense growth,variable expense growth
? all
                             1       2       3       4       5       6

SALES                       90      90      90      90      90      90
EXPENSES                    75     105     135     165     195     225
NET INCOME                  15     -15     -45     -75    -105    -135


INITIAL SALES               90       0       0       0       0       0
SALES GROWTH RATE            1       1       1       1       1       1
FIXED EXPENSE GROWTH         4       4       4       4       4       4
VARIABLE EXPENSE GROWTH      1       1       1       1       1       1
```

FIGURE 5-3. BEST CASE AND WORST CASE SOLUTIONS OF SIMPLE IFPS MODEL WITH UNCERTAINTY

You can use the modifier ALL with HIGH, LOW, etc. Thus, for example, the combination

```
?HIGH ALL
?ALL
```

sets all probabilistic variables to their high values and then prints out all lines of the solution.

Before proceeding to the most likely case, a word of caution is in order. The absolute best and absolute worst cases are easy to compute but can be dangerous to use for decision making, particularly for models of complex situations. It is rare indeed when all variables take on their absolutely most favorable or most unfavorable values. Therefore absolute best and absolute worst cases are not representative and give a distorted view of the upside and downside risk. A more reasonable approach is to set some variables to HIGH and LOW and leave others at their mean or most probable levels.

The MOSTP and MEAN values are the same for symmetric distributions (such as the uniform and the normal) but differ for non-symmetric triangular distributions. For example, for TRIRAND(90,100,120) the most probable value is 100 but the mean is 103.3. You can set variables to their most probable or their mean values. The results of these two cases will be slightly different. This can be seen from Figure 5-4 which shows what happens when you set all random variables first to their most probable value and then to their mean value.

```
? mostp all
? all
                              1       2       3       4       5       6

SALES                       100     125   156.3   195.3   244.1   305.2
EXPENSES                     75     100     125     150     175     200
NET INCOME                   25      25   31.25   45.31   69.14   105.2


INITIAL SALES               100       0       0       0       0       0
SALES GROWTH RATE         1.250   1.250   1.250   1.250   1.250   1.250
FIXED EXPENSE GROWTH          1       1       1       1       1       1
VARIABLE EXPENSE GROWTH      -1      -1      -1      -1      -1      -1
ENTER SOLVE OPTIONS
? mean all
? all
                              1       2       3       4       5       6

SALES                     103.3   129.2   161.5   201.8   252.3   315.3
EXPENSES                     75     100     125     150     175     200
NET INCOME                28.33   29.17   36.46   51.82   77.28   115.3


INITIAL SALES             103.3       0       0       0       0       0
SALES GROWTH RATE         1.250   1.250   1.250   1.250   1.250   1.250
FIXED EXPENSE GROWTH          1       1       1       1       1       1
VARIABLE EXPENSE GROWTH      -1      -1      -1      -1      -1      -1
```

FIGURE 5-4. MOST PROBABLE AND MEAN CASE SOLUTIONS FOR SIMPLE IFPS MODEL WITH UNCERTAINTY

WARNING: If you set each variable to its most likely value or if you set each variable to its mean value, the result is not necessarily the outcome with the highest probability of occurring or the average of all outcomes.

NOTE:

1. If you use SOLVE, your solution is COMPLETELY deterministic.

2. If you do not specify an option, IFPS will assign the MEAN value.

5.8 RUNNING A MONTE CARLO SIMULATION

In Monte Carlo simulation, the IFPS model is run many times, with each replication using a different combination of randomly drawn values from probability distributions. The objective is to obtain information not only on the average (i.e., expected) outcomes, but also on the distribution of the possible results (i.e., the risk) to be anticipated.

To start the process, you use the MONTE CARLO command in place of the SOLVE command. This command has the form:

MONTE CARLO number

where number refers to the number of iterations to be performed. If you leave out the number, IFPS will perform 100 iterations.

NOTE: The MONTE CARLO command is an expensive feature. The more iterations you ask for, the longer the computing time. If you double the number of iterations, you nearly double the cost and the waiting time at the terminal. For most problems, 100 iterations is perfectly adequate. However, see the discussion on interpreting MONTE CARLO results in Section 5.10 before deciding on sample size.

Once you have entered, for example, MONTE CARLO 100, IFPS responds with:

```
ENTER MONTE CARLO OPTIONS
```

At this point you have to tell IFPS:

- which variables you want analyzed
- the format to be used for output (e.g., histogram, frequency distribution), and
- the columns (i.e., the time periods) for which you want results printed out.

Two important default values for you to know about are:

- If you do not specify the colums for which you want data, you will automatically receive printout only for the last column of the model. The assumption is that the values at the end of the time period being investigated are the ones being used for decision making.

- For each variable for which you ask IFPS for a histogram, you will also receive a frequency distribution.

You may choose from the options listed in Table 5-2.

TABLE 5-2

MONTE CARLO OPTIONS

Option	Result
ALL	ALL columns for a variable will be analyzed.
COLUMNS	Only those columns specified will be analyzed. For example, COLUMNS 1,5,8,10 would give you those four columns, COLUMNS 4-6 would give you columns 4 through 6 inclusive.
FREQ	Generates a frequency distribution table for the variable. This is a cumulative observed probability distribution.
HIST	Generates a histogram and frequency distribution for the variable.
NORM	Generates a table of normal probability distribution percentile values based on the mean and standard deviation of the variable.
COMB	Generates both FREQ and NORM for the variable.

Once you have listed all the options you want, you MUST use:

NONE	Terminates option entry and starts the MONTE CARLO calculations.

<u>*NOTE:*</u> NONE *must* always be the last entry in the options list

For example, the sequence:

```
? MONTE CARLO 100
ENTER MONTE CARLO OPTIONS
? COLUMNS 1,4-6
ENTER MONTE CARLO OPTIONS
? HIST SALES, FREQ EXPENSES
ENTER MONTE CARLO OPTIONS
? COMB NET INCOME
ENTER MONTE CARLO OPTIONS
? NONE
```

tells IFPS that you want 100 replications in the MONTE CARLO process. Furthermore, you want printout for columns 1, 4, 5, and 6. (Do you see how column 5 is included?) This printout is to consist of a histogram and frequency distribution of sales, a frequency distribution for expenses, and both a frequency distribution and a normal distribution for net income. IFPS keeps prompting you, asking you to enter additional MONTE CARLO options. The only way to stop these requests is by using NONE to tell IFPS you are done.

Figure 5-5 shows the result of using the above sequence on the Simple IFPS Model With Uncertainty of Section 5.6, Figure 5-2. We will discuss the interpretation of this output in Section 5.10.

```
ENTER SOLVE OPTIONS
? monte carlo 100
ENTER MONTE CARLO OPTIONS
? columns 1,4,6
ENTER MONTE CARLO OPTIONS
? hist sales,freq expenses,comb net income,none
```

NORMAL APPROXIMATION TABLE

PROBABILITY OF VALUE BEING GREATER THAN INDICATED

	90	80	70	60	50	40	30	20	10
NET INCOME									
1	21.32	23.96	25.87	27.50	29.02	30.54	32.16	34.07	36.71
4	-5.6	14.9	29.7	42.4	54.2	66.0	78.7	93.5	114.0
6	-3.5	39.6	70.7	97.3	122.2	147.0	173.6	204.7	247.9

FREQUENCY TABLE

PROBABILITY OF VALUE BEING GREATER THAN INDICATED

	90	80	70	60	50	40	30	20	10
SALES									
1	96.0	99.1	100.5	101.9	103.7	105.5	106.8	109.4	113.2
4	154.4	166.8	172.2	184.1	199.2	208.6	225.9	238.8	269.0
6	215	242	259	276	304	334	363	400	464
EXPENSES									
1	75.0	75.0	75.0	75.0	75.0	75.0	75.0	75.0	75.0
4	144.0	145.4	146.9	149.2	150.5	151.6	153.4	155.1	156.4
6	189.3	192.5	195.1	198.0	200.4	203.2	206.2	208.1	210.9
NET INCOME									
1	21.00	24.07	25.55	26.93	28.65	30.49	31.78	34.41	38.17
4	6.8	14.2	23.6	33.2	49.6	60.7	72.8	88.6	117.7
6	12.5	40.5	56.6	81.0	103.8	132.1	156.1	206.7	258.4

FIGURE 5-5. MONTE CARLO SOLUTION OF THE SIMPLE IFPS MODEL WITH UNCERTAINTY
(This Figure Continued on the Next Page)

SAMPLE STATISTICS

	MEAN	STD DEV	SKEWNESS	KURTOSIS	10PC	CONF MEAN	90PC
SALES							
1	104.0	6.003	.1	2.4	103.2		104.8
4	204.4	46.01	.8	3.6	198.5		210.3
6	322.4	96.63	.7	2.9	310.1		334.8
EXPENSES							
1	75	0	.0	.0	75		75
4	150.2	4.962	-.2	2.4	149.6		150.9
6	200.3	8.249	-.2	2.1	199.2		201.3
NET INCOME							
1	29.02	6.003	.1	2.4	28.25		29.78
4	54.19	46.67	.7	3.5	48.22		60.17
6	122.2	98.09	.7	2.9	109.6		134.7

```
    HISTOGRAM FOR COLUMN        1 OF SALES
17- 18       * * *
15- 16       * * *
13- 14       * * *
11- 12       * * * *
 9- 10     * * * * *
 7-  8   * * * * * *   *
 5-  6   * * * * * * * *
 3-  4   * * * * * * * *
 1-  2 * * * * * * * * * *
       -------------------
             1     1     1
       9     0     0     1
       1     0     8     7
       .     .     .     .
       5     2     9     6
START      90.0  STOP     119.0 SIZE OF INTERVAL      2.90
```

FIGURE 5-5. MONTE CARLO SOLUTION OF THE SIMPLE IFPS MODEL WITH UNCERTAINTY
(This Figure Continued on the Next Page)

```
   HISTOGRAM FOR COLUMN        4 OF SALES
 27- 28     *
 25- 26     *
 23- 24     *
 21- 22     * *
 19- 20     * *
 17- 18     * * *
 15- 16     * * *
 13- 14     * * *
 11- 12   * * * *
  9- 10   * * * *   *
  7-  8   * * * * * * *  5-  6   * * * * * *
  3-  4   * * * * * * *
  1-  2 * * * * * * * *   *
        -------------------
        1     1     2     3
        2     9     7     4
        3     8     3     8
START   110.0  STOP    360.0 SIZE OF INTERVAL      25.00


   HISTOGRAM FOR COLUMN        6 OF SALES
 19- 20     * *
 17- 18     * *
 15- 16   * * *
 13- 14   * * * *
 11- 12   * * * *
  9- 10   * * * * *
  7-  8 * * * * * * *
  5-  6 * * * * * * * * *
  3-  4 * * * * * * * * *
  1-  2 * * * * * * * * * *
        -------------------
        1     3     4     5
        8     1     4     7
        2     4     6     8
START   160.0  STOP    600.0 SIZE OF INTERVAL      44.00
ENTER POOL OR MODELING LANGUAGE COMMAND
```

FIGURE 5-5. MONTE CARLO SOLUTION OF THE SIMPLE IFPS MODEL WITH UNCERTAINTY (Continued)

You can combine several options on one line as well as listing several variables. For example:

```
?MONTE CARLO 300
ENTER MONTE CARLO OPTIONS
?ALL FREQ HIST EXPENSES,NET INCOME
ENTER MONTE CARLO OPTIONS
?NONE
```

asks IFPS to make 300 iterations and print out both frequency distributions and histograms for all columns for the variable EXPENSES and the frequency distribution for NET INCOME. (IFPS prints out only frequency information unless you specify HIST in front of each variable or you use DEFAULT, which is discussed below.) This simple specification results in a large amount of data if you have, say, eight columns in your model!

If you want the same analysis for all variables, you can use the DEFAULT option. Here you first specify what you want, for example:

```
DEFAULT COLUMNS 1,4-6,COMB, HIST
```

and then specify the list of variables for which DEFAULT applies. For example:

```
?MONTE CARLO 200
ENTER MONTE CARLO OPTIONS
?DEFAULT COLUMNS 1,4-6, COMB, HIST
ENTER MONTE CARLO OPTIONS
?SALES,EXPENSES, NET INCOME,NONE
```

asks for 200 iterations and print outs on the variables SALES, EXPENSES, and NET INCOME. For all three variables information is to be printed out for columns 1, 4, 5 and 6 and a frequency distribution, a normal distribution, and a histogram are to be printed.

A few words about the use of commas in these MONTE CARLO options. If you have a list of variables, such as SALES, EXPENSES, NET INCOME you must separate them with commas. If you ask for different analyses on the same line, such as HIST SALES, FREQUENCY EXPENSES, you must separate the analyses by a comma. The default list must be separated by commas. However, if you want several analyses of the same variable, such as ALL FREQ HIST SALES, you do *not* put commas between the analyses to be performed. ALL FREQ HIST results in creating frequency distributions and histograms for all columns of the variable SALES.

5.9 THE STOP COMMAND (What To Do If You Make An Options Mistake)

When typing in the MONTE CARLO options it is quite easy to make a mistake or to change your mind as to what you want done. You can abort the Monte Carlo run by typing STOP in response to ENTER MONTE CARLO OPTIONS. However, you must type STOP before your type NONE.

If you use STOP, you cannot restart where you left off. You must start over with MONTE CARLO.

5.10 INTERPRETING MONTE CARLO RESULTS

Monte Carlo results are printed in a format that differs from the usual IFPS output. A SOLVE command results in a spread sheet that provides a single value for every row and column specified in the solve options. The MONTE CARLO options result in one or more probability distributions being displayed for each variable and column specified. Monte Carlo ouput is organized in the sequence:

- Normal Approximation Table
- Frequency Table
- Sample Statistics
- Histogram

Within each of these categories, IFPS presents results in the order in which the variables are specified and for each variable in the order in which the columns are specified. The data are given in a fixed format for each category. Before examining each of these outputs, you should be aware of the meaning of the percentile points shown for the Frequency Table and the Normal Approximation Table.

These tables provide the "probability of the value being greater than indicated." For example, a 90 indicates that 90% of the observations will be larger than the number shown; a 50 indicates 50% and a 10 indicates 10%. Thus, in Figure 5-5, 90 of the 100 replications resulted in SALES in time period 1 being above 96.0 and hence, by implication, 10 of the replications resulted in SALES less than or equal to 96.0. Similarly, in only 10 of the 100 replications were the SALES in time period 1 above 113.2 and hence by implication in 90 of the 100 replications they were at or below 113.2.

5.10.1 Frequency Table

The Frequency Table shows each time period as a row rather than a column. Thus,in Figure 5-5, columns 1, 4, 5, and 6 are shown as rows. For each variable and column, the 90th through 10th percentile points of the observed data are shown in equal increments. The frequency table therefore summarizes the actual experimental data points.

5.10.2 Normal Approximation Table

The Normal Approximation Table is based on the assumption that the variable being displayed comes from a normal probability distribution with mean and variance equal to the mean and variance computed from the data. Except for their mean and variance, the observed data are not used in creating this table! IFPS simply computes the percentile points on a standard normal distribution with that mean and variance. The result is that the 50th percentile point is always equal to the mean and that the distribution shown is symmetric. The 90th and 10th percentile points correspond to -1.28 and $+1.28$ standard deviations from the mean. For example, in Figure 5-5 for NET INCOME in column 1, the mean is 29.02 and the standard deviavion is 6.003 according to the Sample Statistics shown further down in in the printout. Hence the 90th percentile point is $6.003*1.28 =$ 7.68 units below the mean and the 10th percentile point is 7.68 units above the mean. These normal approximation points are different from the observed points, as you can see by looking at the Frequency Table results for NET INCOME in column 1.

When can you use the normal approximation? A simple way of checking is to look at the skewness and kurtosis values in the sample statistics. For a true normal distribution, the skewness is 0 and the kurtosis is 3.0. If the observed values are within 0.3 units of these theoretical values then the hypothesis of normality cannot be rejected. In this case, the normal approximation table can be used to make statements about risk (see Figure 5-6 in Section 5.12). However, if the data are not normally distributed, this table should not be used for risk statements.

5.10.3 Sample Statistics

A fixed set of statistics is provided about each distribution given in the Frequency Table. Table 5-3 lists and explains the information provided.

TABLE 5-3

DEFINITION OF SAMPLE STATISTICS PROVIDED IN MONTE CARLO

MEAN	Average value of the observations.
STD DEV	Standard deviation of the observed sample.
SKEWNESS	Measures the asymmetry of the distribution with respect to the observed mean. A skewness of 0 implies perfect symmetry.
KURTOSIS	Not a dread disease. Kurtosis measures the "peakedness" of the data compared to the peak of a normal distribution. The larger the kurtosis, the more peaked the data. Technically, kurtosis refers to the fourth moment of the observed data. Although a rather obscure measure for most purposes, it proves useful in IFPS because it allows testing if the normal approximation table can be used.
10PC	The 10PC value refers to the 10 percent level of the confidence interval around the mean. As we shall see below, the 10th and 90th percent level create an 80 percent confidence interval that can be used to assess whether additional replications are needed for making decisions.
90PC	The 90 percent level of the confidence interval around the mean.

5.10.4 Histogram

The histogram option, which is shown on a number of figures, is a plot of the observed distribution in simple graphic form. Visually, the histogram shows you the shape of the distribution. Reading the graph numerically, however, may appear tricky until you get the hang of it. The reason is that IFPS always scales the information so that it fits into a fixed format. The height of each column of asterisks tells you the number of data values observed in that interval (read from the vertical scale on the left). The numbers on the X axis (i.e., the horizontal axis) are printed vertically and should be read from top to bottom. These X axis values have to be used in conjunction with the information printed on the bottom of the plot; that is, the start and stop values and the size of the interval. The size of the interval tells you how big each division on the X axis is and saves you the trouble of trying to figure out the distance between successive X values. The start and stop values give you the left and right end points on the X axis. The actual numbers printed are located at the midpoints of their particular intervals and are shown only every third column. Because intervals on histograms are determined automatically by the computer in a uniform way and depend so strongly on the data, you should be very careful that you know what the numbers mean before trying to interpret them.

5.11 THE POOL COMMAND

After the results of a Monte Carlo analysis have been printed out, IFPS will give you the message:

```
ENTER POOL OR MODELING LANGUAGE COMMAND
```

MODELING LANGUAGE COMMAND refers to any command other than POOL. That is, you go on to whatever you need to do next during your session at the terminal. POOL is a specialized command that allows you to continue the present Monte Carlo run for additional iterations. If you believe you need additional iterations (samples, in statistical terms) to draw conclusions from the output, you type, say:

```
POOL 100
```

IFPS will run 100 additional iterations and then print out the Monte Carlo output for the combined data from all the iterations performed.

The POOL command should be used if the data indicate large standard deviations or the confidence interval around the mean is large. For example, in Figure 5-5, the observed mean of the NET INCOME in period 6 is 122.2, based on a sample of 100. The 80% confidence interval around this mean is 109.6 to 134.7. The width of this interval is 134.7 - 109.6 = 25.1. That is, there is an 80% probability that the true mean is between 109.6 and 134.7 and there is a 10% probability that it is below 109.6 or above 134.7. If this level of uncertainty is satisfactory, you can go on and continue your work. However, if it is not, you have the option of asking IFPS to run additional samples and give you a new estimate of the mean and a new confidence interval. Since the width of the confidence interval depends on $1/\sqrt{n}$ (see any statistics text for a discussion and the formula), increasing the sample size reduces the uncertainty; However, because of the square root factor, the rate of decrease is quite slow.

EXERCISE: (a) Enter the IFPS model of Figure 5-2 into your computer and run the model for the conditions shown in Figure 5-5. Use MONTE CARLO 100. You may get different output because of a different choice of random numbers by the computer.
(b) Use the POOL command to obtain a total sample of 200. Examine the output for the net income in Period 6. You should observe a different value of the mean and a smaller confidence interval around the mean.

5.12 EXAMPLE: THE NEW PRODUCT MODEL WITH UNCERTAINTY

The New Product Model was introduced in Section 2.7 and was illustrated in Figure 2-9. It is a market planning model that assumes that everything about the market, including its growth and the company's market share, is known. Furthermore, the model assumes that overhead costs would be fixed. These and other assumptions of the New Product Model can be modified to take uncertainty into account. An example of such an analysis is shown in Figure 5-6. In this figure, we use WHAT IF statements to introduce the uncertainty. Specifically, we ask what if:

1. Market growth is triangularly distributed with parameters (0.9, 1.02, 1.08)

2. Market share growth is uniformly distributed between (–0.002, 0.008)

3. Overhead cost relative to production cost is normally distributed with mean 80% and standard deviation of .5%.

The results indicate that under these conditions the expected internal rate of return is reduced from the 30% value in Figure 2-9 to 14.6% (see Column 8 of Figure 5-6) if all variables take on their expected values. When we make a Monte Carlo run with 200 replications, the mean rate of return observed is 14.43%. Furthermore, for the discount rate criterion that we want a 15% rate of return, we see that the investment meets this rate of return criterion slightly more than 50% of the time. On the other hand, the investment will return 11% or more 70 percent of the time. The risks associated with the investment in the new product are now much better defined. The decision can be based on a clearer understanding of the anticipated range of outcomes.

EXERCISE: Solve the New Product Model using the WHAT IF case shown in Figure 5-6 for each of the following conditions:

1. HIGH MARKET, HIGH MARKET SHARE, LOW OVERHEAD.

2. LOW MARKET, LOW MARKET SHARE, LOW OVERHEAD.

3. MOSTP for all variables.

Use IFPS to PLOT the results (see Section 4.3) for net income and net present value.

EXERCISE: Use MONTE CARLO 200 on the New Product Model with the WHAT IF conditions shown in Figure 5-6 and with the following additional changes:

1. Initial investment is uncertain. Assume a normal distribution with mean 2500 and standard deviation 500.

2. The initial market share is uncertain. Although its most likely value is 15%, there is a 10% chance it may be as low as 13% and you can be 90% sure that it will not exceed 21%. (HINT: Use T1090RAND).

(This EXERCISE continued following Figure 5-6.)

```
MODEL DECIDE  VERSION OF  06/06/82  13:32
10 COLUMNS 1-8
20 *
30 *
40 *NEW PRODUCT MODEL
50 *
60 SALES VOLUME=MARKET*MARKET SHARE
70 MARKET=8000,PREVIOUS MARKET*1.03
80 MARKET SHARE=0.15,PREVIOUS MARKET SHARE +0.005
90 GROSS SALES =SALES VOLUME *UNIT PRICE
100 UNIT PRICE =2.5 FOR 4,2.75 FOR 4
110 OPERATING COST =SALES VOLUME *(PRODUCTION COST + OVERHEAD)
120 PRODUCTION COST =1.25 FOR 4,1.35
130 OVERHEAD = PRODUCTION COST *0.80
135 NET INCOME =GROSS SALES -OPERATING COST
140 INVESTMENT =2500,0
150 RATE OF RETURN = IRR(NET INCOME,INVESTMENT)
160 NET PRESENT VALUE=NPVC(NET INCOME,DISCOUNT RATE,INVESTMENT)
170 DISCOUNT RATE =.15
180 PERIODS 4
END OF MODEL
? what if

WHAT IF CASE 1
ENTER STATEMENTS
? market =8000,previous*trirandr(0.90,1.02,1.08)
? market share = .15,previous + unirandr(-.002,.008)
? overhead = production cost * norrandr(0.80,.005)
? solve
ENTER SOLVE OPTIONS
? all
***** WHAT IF CASE 1 *****
3 WHAT IF STATEMENTS PROCESSED

                          1     2     3     4     5     6     7     8

NEW PRODUCT MODEL

SALES VOLUME           1200  1224  1248  1272  1296  1320  1344  1368
MARKET                 8000  8000  8000  8000  8000  8000  8000  8000
MARKET SHARE          .1500 .1530 .1560 .1590 .1620 .1650 .1680 .1710
GROSS SALES            3000  3060  3120  3180  3564  3630  3696  3762
UNIT PRICE            2.500 2.500 2.500 2.500 2.750 2.750 2.750 2.750
OPERATING COST         2700  2754  2808  2862  3149  3208  3266  3324
PRODUCTION COST       1.250 1.250 1.250 1.250 1.350 1.350 1.350 1.350
OVERHEAD                  1     1     1     1 1.080 1.080 1.080 1.080
NET INCOME              300   306   312   318 414.7 422.4 430.1 437.8
INVESTMENT             2500     0     0     0     0     0     0     0
RATE OF RETURN                                              .0012 .1465
NET PRESENT VALUE -2210 -1925 -1644 -1367 -1019-676.7-340.0-8.950
DISCOUNT RATE         .1500 .1500 .1500 .1500 .1500 .1500 .1500 .1500
```

FIGURE 5-6. NEW PRODUCT MODEL WITH UNCERTAINTY
(This Figure Continued on the Next Page)

```
ENTER SOLVE OPTIONS
? monte carlo 200
ENTER MONTE CARLO OPTIONS
? freq rate of return,,net present value,none

***** WHAT IF CASE 1 *****


                    FREQUENCY TABLE

    PROBABILITY OF VALUE BEING GREATER THAN INDICATED

          90      80      70      60      50      40      30      20      10

   RATE OF RETURN
   8    .069    .094    .112    .131    .152    .165    .176    .197    .220

   NET PRESENT VALUE
   8 -201.9  -142.4   -95.7   -49.0     4.3    37.1    66.5   118.2   179.8


                    SAMPLE STATISTICS

               MEAN    STD DEV SKEWNESS KURTOSIS  10PC CONF MEAN   90PC

   RATE OF RETURN
     8        .1443     .0591     -.2      2.7       .1389      .1496

   NET PRESENT VALUE
     8       -12.75     149.2     -.2      2.7      -26.26      .7557
ENTER POOL OR MODELING LANGUAGE COMMAND
```

FIGURE 5-6. NEW PRODUCT MODEL WITH UNCERTAINTY
(Continued)

3. The extent of the price increase after Period 4 is uncertain. You have the following three possibilities for prices (HINT: Use GENRAND.)

2.50	20% chance of happening
2.65	30% chance of happening
2.90	50% chance of happening

Obtain histograms of net income and net present value and obtain frequency and normal approximation tables for rate of return.

Based on the data from this Monte Carlo simulation, should the company invest or not? Explain.

```
ENTER SOLVE OPTIONS
? monte carlo 200
ENTER MONTE CARLO OPTIONS
? freq rate of return,,net present value,none

***** WHAT IF CASE 1 *****

                         FREQUENCY TABLE

        PROBABILITY OF VALUE BEING GREATER THAN INDICATED

           90      80      70      60      50      40      30      20      10

       RATE OF RETURN
       8  .069    .094    .112    .131    .152    .165    .176    .197    .220

       NET PRESENT VALUE
       8 -201.9 -142.4   -95.7   -49.0     4.3    37.1    66.5   118.2   179.8


                         SAMPLE STATISTICS

              MEAN    STD DEV SKEWNESS KURTOSIS  10PC CONF MEAN  90PC

       RATE OF RETURN
         8   .1443     .0591     -.2       2.7     .1389       .1496

       NET PRESENT VALUE
         8  -12.75     149.2     -.2       2.7    -26.26       .7557
ENTER POOL OR MODELING LANGUAGE COMMAND
```

FIGURE 5-6. NEW PRODUCT MODEL WITH UNCERTAINTY (Continued)

3. The extent of the price increase after Period 4 is uncertain. You have the following three possibilities for prices (HINT: Use GENRAND.)

2.50	20% chance of happening
2.65	30% chance of happening
2.90	50% chance of happening

Obtain histograms of net income and net present value and obtain frequency and normal approximation tables for rate of return.

Based on the data from this Monte Carlo simulation, should the company invest or not? Explain.

5.13 EXAMPLE: A RISK ANALYSIS MODEL

This model is based on the classic paper by David Bendel Hertz, "Risk Analysis in Capital Investment" *Harvard Business Review*, January-February 1964. Assume that a medium-sized chemical firm is considering a $10 million improvement program for its main plant. The improvement is expected to have a lifetime of 10 years. Management has determined that the key input factors in analyzing the profitability of this proposed capital investment are:

- Market size
- Selling price
- The company's market share
- Total investment
- Salvage value of the investment
- Operating costs
- Fixed costs

Unfortunately, all of these quantities have uncertainties associated with them. Table 5-4 lists these uncertainties.

TABLE 5-4

UNCERTAINTIES IN CAPITAL BUDGET

Quantity	Distribution	Values
Initial Market	Triangular	100000,250000,34000
Market Growth	Triangular	1, 1.03,1.06
Selling Price	Triangular	385,510,575
Market Share	Uniform	12% to 17%
Investment ($ Million)	Triangular	7,9.5,10.5
Operating Cost per unit	Triangular	370,435,545
Fixed Cost ($Thousands)	Triangular	250,300,375
Salvage Value	Triangular	3.5,4.5,5

The data in Table 5-4 indicate the great range of uncertainty that can be encountered. In building its forecast, the company knows that it has the option of closing the plant down if the selling price goes below the operating cost. In such a case, it would still have to pay the fixed costs.

Figure 5-7 shows the IFPS model for this situation. The various probability distributions shown in Table 5-4 have been incorporated into the model as well as the condition for shutting down. The shutdown condition is expressed by using the built-in maximum function to determine the revenue. If the selling price is below the operating cost, the revenue is 0; if it is above, there is a contribution from sales.

```
MODEL RISK   VERSION OF   06/06/82   13:41
10 *
20 *
30 *
40 *              RISK MODEL FOR CHEMICAL COMPANY
50 *
60 COLUMNS 1-10
70 MARKET=TRIRAND(100000,250000,340000),PREVIOUS*'
71 TRIRAND(1,1.03,1.06)
80 SELLING PRICE = TRIRAND(385,510,575)
90 MARKET SHARE = UNIRAND(.12,.17)
100 SALES VOLUME = MARKET * MARKET SHARE
110 INVESTMENT =TRIRAND(7,9.5,10.5)*1000000,0
120 LIFE = 10
130 OPERATING COST = TRIRAND(370,435,545)
140 FIXED COST = TRIRAND(250,300,375)*1000
150  REVENUE  =  MAXIMUM(0,(SELLING  PRICE  -  OPERATING  COST)*SALES
VOLUME)
160 NET INCOME = REVENUE - FIXED COST
170 SALVAGE VALUE =0 FOR 9,TRIRAND(3.5,4.5,5)*1000000
180 *
190 RATE OF RETURN =IRR(NET INCOME + SALVAGE VALUE,INVESTMENT)
200 *
END OF MODEL
```

FIGURE 5-7. RISK MODEL

Figure 5-8 shows the result of solving this model with all variables set to their expected values (the default option if no other specification is given). The results indicate a 9.92% internal rate of return.

A much richer set of information is obtained when we ask for MONTE CARLO 200 (Figure 5-9). We see that even by Year 10, the net income can fluctuate wildly (between a loss of over \$300,000 and a profit of over \$4 million). Furthermore, the rate of return on this investment ranges from –12.1% to 42.0% with only more than a 40% chance that it will exceed 15%.

The histograms indicate that there is a significant risk of losing money, resulting from shutdowns when the operating cost exceeds the selling price. If you are a manager facing this situation, you have to come to grips with the problems that would arise if the venture fails. If there is a significant chance of failure, you may well not want to take the risk even though the project's expected payout is above 10%.

```
? solve
MODEL RISK  VERSION OF  06/06/82  13:41 -- 10 COLUMNS 12 VARIABLES
ENTER SOLVE OPTIONS
? columns 1-3,8-10
? all
```

	1	2	3	8	9	10
RISK MODEL FOR CHEMICAL COMPANY						
MARKET	230000	236900	244007	282871	291357	300098
SELLING PRICE	490	490	490	490	490	490
MARKET SHARE	.1450	.1450	.1450	.1450	.1450	.1450
SALES VOLUME	33350	34351	35381	41016	42247	43514
INVESTMENT	9000000	0	0	0	0	0
LIFE	10	10	10	10	10	10
OPERATING COST	450	450	450	450	450	450
FIXED COST	308333	308333	308333	308333	308333	308333
REVENUE	1334000	1374020	1415241	1640652	1689871	1740567
NET INCOME	1025667	1065687	1106907	1332318	1381538	1432234
SALVAGE VALUE	0	0	0	0	0	4333333
RATE OF RETURN				.0093	.0357	.0992

FIGURE 5-8. EXPECTED VALUE SOLUTION OF THE RISK MODEL

EXERCISE: Suppose the firm can tell at the beginning of each year whether it has to shut the plant down because of low operating cost. It has an arrangement with the bank to carry a loan for $100,000 if they are shut down. That is, the company can shut down with only this fixed cost if revenue is less than operating cost. Modify Figure 5-7 to reflect these conditions and repeat the runs shown in Figures 5-8 and 5-9. Are there improvements in net income and internal rate of return? Are these improvements sufficient?

EXERCISE: Suppose the firm's policy is to shut down whenever revenue is less than fixed cost (i.e., the net income is negative). Are there improvements in net income and internal rate of return? How much are they? Are these improvements sufficient?

EXERCISE: Use IFPS to determine the minimum net income required to obtain an expected internal rate of return of 18%. Find this income based on most probable values. Repeat using MONTE CARLO. Use a criterion of exceeding 18% internal rate of return at least 50% of the time.

```
ENTER SOLVE OPTIONS
? monte carlo 200
ENTER MONTE CARLO OPTIONS
? hist net income
ENTER MONTE CARLO OPTIONS
? hist rate of return
ENTER MONTE CARLO OPTIONS
? none


                          FREQUENCY TABLE

            PROBABILITY OF VALUE BEING GREATER THAN INDICATED

           90     80     70     60     50     40     30     20     10

 NET INCOME
  10     -314   -282    189    794   1449   2222   3056   3659   4624
 *1000

 RATE OF RETURN
  10    -.121  -.109  -.050   .030   .107   .174   .252   .329   .420


                         SAMPLE STATISTICS

                 MEAN   STD DEV SKEWNESS KURTOSIS   10PC CONF MEAN   90PC

    NET INCOME
     10       1884388   2056701       .8      2.9     1698237      2070539

    RATE OF RETURN
     10         .1291     .2194       .6      2.6       .1093        .1490
```

FIGURE 5-9. MONTE CARLO SIMULATION OF RISK MODEL
(This Figure Is Continued on the Next Page)

```
    HISTOGRAM FOR COLUMN      10 OF NET INCOME
  57- 60  *
  53- 56  *
  49- 52  *
  45- 48  *
  41- 44  *
  37- 40  *
  33- 36  *
  29- 32  *
  25- 28  *
  21- 24  *
  17- 20  * * * *     *
  13- 16  * * * *   * *
   9- 12  * * * * * * * * *
   5-  8  * * * * * * * * * * *
   1-  4  * * * * * * * * * * * * *   *
          -----------------------------
                1     3     5     6
          -     6     3     0     7
          8     3     5     7     9
          1     7     7     6     6
          4     9     3     7     1
          3     6     6     6     6
          3     7     7     7     7
START -368000.0  STOP   8229000 SIZE OF INTERVAL  573133.3

    HISTOGRAM FOR COLUMN      10 OF RATE OF RETURN
  49- 52  *
  45- 48  *
  41- 44  *
  37- 40  *
  33- 36  *
  29- 32  *
  25- 28  *
  21- 24  *
  17- 20  * * * * * * *
  13- 16  * * * * * * * *
   9- 12  * * * * * * * * *   *
   5-  8  * * * * * * * * *   *
   1-  4  * * * * * * * * * * * *     *
          -----------------------------
          -
          .     .     .     .     .
          1     0     2     4     6
          2     8     8     8     9
          1     2     5     8     2
START       -.2  STOP        .9 SIZE OF INTERVAL       .07
ENTER POOL OR MODELING LANGUAGE COMMAND
```

FIGURE 5-9. MONTE CARLO SIMULATION OF RISK MODEL
(Continued)

5.14 EXAMPLE: TESTING THE IFPS RANDOM NUMBER GENERATOR

> *NOTE:* The problem discussed in this section is primarily of interest to the professional in simulation. We present it here to illustrate the use of the IFPS MONTE CARLO commands. You can skip this section without losing continuity or missing any new points.

A critical consideration in simulation is the effectiveness of generating random numbers. In this example, we show you how to generate:

- random numbers between 0 and 1
- random integers between 0 and 9
- normally distributed random numbers with mean 0 and standard deviation 1 (or arbitrary mean and standard deviation)
- exponentially distributed random numbers.

We also show you how to test the random numbers generated to determine if they are indeed randomly selected from the desired probability distribution.

Figure 5-10 shows the IFPS model for generating these four kinds of numbers. As shown in Figure 5-10 (and discussed in Section 5.3), UNIRAND (0,1) and UNIRANDR(0,1) generate random numbers uniformly distributed between 0 and 1. These numbers are decimals. Because they are uniformly distributed, we should expect that the first digit of these numbers should also be uniformly distributed. That is, we should expect as many numbers to start with .0 as with .3 as with .6 or with .9. Therefore, a simple way to generate uniformly distributed random integers between 0 and 9 is to use the first digit of the random numbers created by UNIRAND. To do so, we multiply the random number by 10 and then delete the decimal part by using the TRUNCATE function described in Section 3.2.4. For example, if the random number is:

.35721,

multipyling it by 10 results in:

3.5721.

Truncating the decimal part (in this case, truncating .5721) leaves 3.

```
MODEL RANDNOS   VERSION OF   02/06/81   21:13
1 COLUMNS 1-12
2 RANDOM NUMBER=UNIRANDR(0,1)
3 RANDOM INTEGER = TRUNCATE(10*RANDOM NUMBER)
4 SUM=RANDOM NUMBER,PREVIOUS SUM+RANDOM NUMBER
5 Z=SUM-6
6 EXPRANDOM=-NATLOG(RANDOM NUMBER)
END OF MODEL
```

FIGURE 5-10. MODEL FOR TESTING RANDOM NUMBER GENERATION IN IFPS

One approximate way of obtaining normally distributed random numbers is to use the Law of Large Numbers of probability theory. This law states that if you add up a large number of values each of which was drawn independently from any particular probability distribution, the result will be a number drawn from a normal distribution. Specifically, if you use a sample of size n, the normal distribution will have a mean equal to n times the mean of the original distribution and a variance equal to n times the variance of the original distribution. It turns out that in theory a "large number" is really infinite but in practice, it is relatively small. For the uniform distribution a sample of size 12 is more than adequate.

We therefore use the fact that the mean of the uniform distribution is one-half and its variance is 1/12. If we add 12 uniform random numbers, the resulting sum should be a sample drawn from a normal distribution that has a mean of 12*0.5 = 6 and a variance of 12*(1/12) = 1. To obtain a normal distribution with a mean of 0, we simply subtract 6 from every sum. In IFPS terms, we create 12 columns and:

```
SUM = RANDOM NUMBER, PREVIOUS SUM + RANDOM NUMBER
```

gives us a normally distributed number in Column 12. If we then subtract 6, that is,

```
Z = SUM - 6
```

the result should be a normal random number with mean equal to 0 and variance equal to 1. If you look at tables of the normal distribution in any text, you will find it is the normal with mean 0 and variance 1 (hence standard deviation equal to 1) that is tabulated.

In practical terms, you can obtain random numbers with any mean, M, and any standard deviation, S, by using the standard formula from statistics that:

```
X = Z*S + M
```

The exponential distribution, which shows up in simulating waiting lines and other phenomena where events occur at random, is defined by:

```
EXPRANDOM = - NATLOG(RANDOM NUMBER)
```

In this form, you generate an exponential distribution with mean 1. If you want a mean M, you take:

```
EXPRANDOM = - M*NATLOG(RANDOM NUMBER)
```

To illustrate what happens when you ask IFPS to generate random numbers from these four distributions, Figure 5-11 shows the results for samples of 1000 random numbers. (To keep memory space requirements and costs reasonable, IFPS has a built-in limit of 1000 replications.) This sample size is usually considered small for testing random numbers; however, the observed means and standard deviations are quite close to the theoretical means and standard deviations, and the histograms show that the observed distributions have the shapes anticipated for these distributions. There is, of course, some fluctuation but that is to be anticipated by the nature of randomness. Do you agree?

```
? monte carlo 200
MODEL RANDNOS  VERSION OF  02/06/81  21:13 -- 12 COLUMNS 5 VARIABLES
ENTER MONTE CARLO OPTIONS
? hist random number,none

                          FREQUENCY TABLE

            PROBABILITY OF VALUE BEING GREATER THAN INDICATED

          90      80      70      60      50      40      30      20      10

RANDOM NUMBER
  12     .124    .245    .340    .444    .505    .579    .674    780    .910
                          SAMPLE STATISTICS

                MEAN    STD DEV SKEWNESS KURTOSIS  10PC CONF MEAN   90PC

    RANDOM NUMBER
      12      .5114     .2748       .0      2.0       .4865       .5363


   HISTOGRAM FOR COLUMN        12 OF RANDOM NUMBER
 21- 22                 *
 19- 20               * *
 17- 18               * *           *
 15- 16         *   * * *     *     *
 13- 14 *       *   * * *     *   * *
 11- 12 * * *   * * * * * * * *   * *
  9- 10 * * *   * * * * * * * *   * *
  7-  8 * * * * * * * * * * * *   * *
  5-  6 * * * * * * * * * * * *   * *
  3-  4 * * * * * * * * * * * * * * *
  1-  2 * * * * * * * * * * * * * * *
        -----------------------------

        .     .     .     .     .
        0     2     4     6     8
        4     4     3     3     3
        4     0     7     4     0

START          .0  STOP        1.0 SIZE OF INTERVAL          .07
ENTER POOL OR MODELING LANGUAGE COMMAND
```

a. Uniform Random Numbers

FIGURE 5-11. RESULTS OF TESTING RANDOM NUMBER GENERATION IN IFPS

(This Figure Continued on the Next Page)

```
? monte carlo 200
ENTER MONTE CARLO OPTIONS
? hist random integer,none

                   FREQUENCY TABLE

     PROBABILITY OF VALUE BEING GREATER THAN INDICATED

          90     80     70     60     50     40     30     20     10

 RANDOM INTEGER
   12   1.00   2.00   3.00   4.00   5.00   5.00   6.00   7.00   8.00   8.50


                   SAMPLE STATISTICS

              MEAN    STD DEV SKEWNESS KURTOSIS  10PC CONF MEAN  90PC

    RANDOM INTEGER
      12     4.500     2.778      .0      1.9      4.249      4.751


    HISTOGRAM FOR COLUMN        12 OF RANDOM INTEGER
27- 28                  *
25- 26              *   *
23- 24        *     *   *
21- 22        *     *   * *
19- 20  *     *     *   * *         *
17- 18  * *   *     *   * *   *     *
15- 16  * *   *     *   * *   *   * *
13- 14  * *   * *   *   * *   *   * *
11- 12  * *   * *   *   * *   *   * *
 9- 10  * *   * *   *   * *   *   * *
 7-  8  * *   * *   *   * *   *   * *
 5-  6  * *   * *   *   * *   *   * *
 3-  4  * *   * *   *   * *   *   * *
 1-  2  * *   * *   *   * *   *   * *
        ------------------------------
              2     3     5      7
        .     .     .     .      .
        3     1     9     7      5
        0     2     4     6      8
START       .0  STOP        9.1 SIZE OF INTERVAL       .61
ENTER POOL OR MODELING LANGUAGE COMMAND
```

b. Uniform Random Integers

FIGURE 5-11. RESULTS OF TESTING RANDOM NUMBER GENERATION IN IFPS
(This Figure Continued on the Next Page)

```
? monte carlo 200
ENTER MONTE CARLO OPTIONS
? comb hist z,none


                   NORMAL APPROXIMATION TABLE

        PROBABILITY OF VALUE BEING GREATER THAN INDICATED

          90      80      70      60      50      40      30      20      10
 Z
   12 -1.267   -.843   -.537   -.276   -.032    .213    .474    .780   1.204

                   FREQUENCY TABLE

        PROBABILITY OF VALUE BEING GREATER THAN INDICATED

          90      80      70      60      50      40      30      20      10

 Z
   12 -1.365   -.835   -.515   -.206   -.026    .199    .407    .797   1.153

                   SAMPLE STATISTICS

             MEAN   STD DEV SKEWNESS KURTOSIS  10PC CONF MEAN   90PC

 Z
      12    -.0316     .9639       .0     2.7     -.1189        .0556

     HISTOGRAM FOR COLUMN       12 OF Z
  34- 36                   *
  31- 33                   *
  28- 30                   *
  25- 27                   * *
  22- 24                 * * *
  19- 21               * * * *   *
  16- 18               * * * * * *
  13- 15           * * * * * * * *
  10- 12           * * * * * * * *
   7-  9       * * * * * * * * * * *
   4-  6     * * * * * * * * * * * *   *
   1-  3   * * * * * * * * * * * * *   *
           -----------------------------
           -     -
           2     1     -           1
           .     .     .     .     .
           3     3     3     6     6
           3     3     3     7     7
START       -2.5  STOP        2.5 SIZE OF INTERVAL       .33
```

c. Normally Distributed Random Numbers

FIGURE 5-11. RESULTS OF TESTING RANDOM NUMBER GENERATION IN IFPS
(This Figure Continued on the Next Page)

```
? monte carlo 200
ENTER MONTE CARLO OPTIONS
? hist exprandom,none

                    FREQUENCY TABLE

     PROBABILITY OF VALUE BEING GREATER THAN INDICATED

          90     80     70     60     50     40     30     20     10
EXPRANDOM
   12   .120   .193   .318   .468   .629   .895  1.176  1.549  2.143

                    SAMPLE STATISTICS

          MEAN   STD DEV SKEWNESS KURTOSIS  10PC CONF MEAN   90PC

EXPRANDOM
     12    .9254    .8638      1.4      4.9       .8472       1.004


     HISTOGRAM FOR COLUMN        12 OF EXPRANDOM
  53- 56  *
  49- 52  *
  45- 48  *
  41- 44  * *
  37- 40  * *
  33- 36  * *
  29- 32  * *
  25- 28  * *
  21- 24  * * * *
  17- 20  * * * *
  13- 16  * * * * *
   9- 12  * * * * * *   *
   5-  8  * * * * * * * *
   1-  4  * * * * * * * * * * * * *   *
          -----------------------------
                1     1     2     3
          .     .     .     .     .
          1     0     9     8     7
          5     5     5     5     5
START         .0  STOP        4.5 SIZE OF INTERVAL       .30
ENTER POOL OR MODELING LANGUAGE COMMAND
```

FIGURE 5-11. RESULTS OF TESTING RANDOM NUMBER GENERATION IN IFPS
(Continued)

EXERCISE: Write an IFPS model that creates

1. Uniformly distributed numbers between 0 and 10
2. Uniformly distributed integers between 0 and 99
3. Normally distributed numbers with mean 20 and standard deviation 5
4. Exponentially distributed numbers with mean 6

Obtain a frequency distribution and histogram for each distribution based on a sample of 1000.

EXERCISE: Our argument that IFPS generates adequate random numbers was based on the "reasonable" agreement of the means, variances, frequency distributions, and histograms produced. Such an argument is not mathematically adequate. What you have to do is test the observed distribution against the theoretical distribution. The simplest such test, given cumulative probability distributions as is the case here, is the Kolmogorov-Smirnov (usually abbreviated K-S) test. If you know something about statistics, go back to one of the standard statistics textbooks and perform a K-S test on the data shown in Figure 5-11.

CHAPTER VI
APPLICATIONS IN FINANCE

6.9 Analyzing Project Proposals--Break-Even and Sensitivity Analysis

6.10 Using Scenarios to Evaluate Project Proposals

6.11 Using Simulation to Evaluate Project Proposals

6.12 The Black-Scholes Formula for Call Options

6.13 Financial Ratio Analysis

6.14 Cash Management Model

6.15 Pro Forma Financial Forecast Models

6.16 Addendum: Year 0 vs. Year 1

CHAPTER VI
APPLICATIONS IN FINANCE

6.1 INTRODUCTION

This chapter shows you how to use IFPS in problems of corporate finance. Financial problems, particularly financial forecasts, were the inspiration for IFPS. Thus, as you saw in Section 3.2, IFPS has many built-in features that make financial calculations simple, including built-in capabilities for net present value, internal rate of return, and depreciation calculations.

In writing this chapter, we have followed the sequence of presentation and used many of the examples in the book *PRINCIPLES OF CORPORATE FINANCE* by Richard Brealey and Stewart Myers (McGraw-Hill, 1981). If you need more information about a particular method or topic, you can refer to the Brealey and Myers book or to any similar introductory finance text. We have tried to present the following material in such a way that if you have a working understanding of finance concepts you can use this chapter to solve finance problems without having to refer to outside sources.

6.2 NET PRESENT VALUE

The concept of present value is fundamental to finance. It is assumed that an individual or a firm values a dollar today more than a dollar tomorrow. Furthermore, the amount of the decrease in value between today and tomorrow is expressed in terms of a "discount factor." The discount factor is given as:

$$\text{DISCOUNT FACTOR} = 1/(1+r)$$

where r is the rate of return; that is, the reward that investors demand for accepting delayed payment.

In general, in financial calculations we are interested in a series of investments by us and returns to us over time. Typically, these occur at one year intervals, with the assumption made that investments occur at the beginning of the year and returns occur at the end of the year. The general formula for finding NET PRESENT VALUE is:

$$\text{NPV} = \Sigma\, C(t) / (1+r)^t \qquad (6\text{-}1)$$

where: NPV is net present value,
C(t) is the cash flow at time t,
r is the rate or return or "discount rate" at time t.

Note that in this formula, a plus sign is assumed for returns and a minus sign for investments requiring cash outlays.

As shown in Section 3.2, IFPS contains built-in net present value functions. The three functions available are:

```
NPVC(RETURN,DISCOUNT RATE,INVESTMENT)

NPV(YEARLY RETURN,DISCOUNT RATE,LIFE,INVESTMENT)

NTV(RETURN,DISCOUNT RATE,INVESTMENT)
```

6.2.1 NPVC

The NPVC function computes the net present value each year for all investments and returns made up to that point. Figure 6-1 shows the net present value for an investment of $150,000 at the beginning of Year 1 followed by an investment of $100,000 at the beginning of Year 2 and leading to a return of $300,000 at the end of Year 2. Such a stream of cash flows might occur, for example, in a commercial construction venture.

```
MODEL NPV  VERSION OF  08/24/81   20:53
10 COLUMNS 1-2
20 * THIS MODEL ILLUSTRATES THE NPVC FUNCTION
30 *
40 NET PRESENT VALUE=NPVC(RETURN,DISCOUNT RATE,INVESTMENT)
50 INVESTMENT=150000,100000
60 RETURN=0,300000
70 DISCOUNT RATE=0.07
END OF MODEL
? solve
MODEL NPV  VERSION OF  08/24/81   20:53 -- 2 COLUMNS 4 VARIABLES
ENTER SOLVE OPTIONS
?all

                                    1          2

 THIS MODEL ILLUSTRATES THE NPVC FUNCTION

NET PRESENT VALUE             -150000      18574
INVESTMENT                     150000     100000
RETURN                              0     300000
DISCOUNT RATE                   .0700      .0700
```

FIGURE 6-1. NPVC FUNCTION

Note the following points about this IFPS model:

1. Investment and returns are shown year-by-year on separate lines. RETURN in the NPVC function can refer to any variable in the problem or to a combination of variables in an expression. If you have several sources of income (e.g., DIRECT SALES, SALES THROUGH JOBBERS, EXPORT SALES) you can accumulate these sources into a single variable (e.g., NET

SALES = DIRECT SALES + SALES THROUGH JOBBERS + EXPORT SALES). Alternatively, you could write NPVC(DIRECT SALES + SALES THROUGH JOBBERS + EXPORT SALES, DISCOUNT RATE, INVESTMENT). The same considerations apply to investments.

If in doubt as to what the conventions are, do a little testing. Take an example worked out in detail in your reference text and write an IFPS model that replicates it. Make sure you get the two to match and that you understand why they match.

If this particular convention troubles you, turn to Section 6.16 at the end of this chapter and you will find an additional discussion of the great Year 0 vs. Year 1 controversy.

2. Whereas the formula treats investments as negative numbers, IFPS shows investments as positive numbers. IFPS can do this because it asks you to specify investments and returns separately in the built-in financial functions.

3. The discount rate used is a constant. However, we could just as easily have specified a variable or any IFPS expression and thereby used a different discount rate for each period.

WARNING. Some texts, including Brealey and Myers, define the initial investment as occurring at the end of Year 0 rather than at the start of Year 1. This difference does not change the numerical answers; however, it does cause the data presentation formats to differ from those of IFPS. Be sure to understand the conventions followed in any reference text that you may use. Watch out for the difference!

EXERCISE: Write an IFPS program using data from Figure 6-1 that computes net present value directly from the formula.

6.2.2 NPV

The NPV function is used for the special case of an annuity, that is, a single initial investment made now that pays a fixed return for a fixed number of years (called the life of the annuity). Figure 6-2 shows an example of the NPV function. In this example, the present value of an annuity paying $5000 per year for 20 years is computed on the assumption of no investment (e.g., an inheritance) and a 10% discount rate.

EXERCISE: Use the model given in Figure 6-2 to determine the present value of an annuity that requires a $20000 investment and which pays $4000 a year for 15 years. Assume a 20% discount rate.

6.2.3 NTV

The NTV function determines the net terminal value. It is computed the same way as the NPVC function except that values are compounded rather than discounted. Equation (6-1) is modified such that

$$NTV = \Sigma C(t) * (1 + r) \qquad (6\text{-}2)$$

```
MODEL NPV2   VERSION OF  12/28/82  11:45
10 *THIS MODEL ILLUSTRATES THE NPV FUNCTION
20 COLUMNS 1
30 YEARLY RETURN=50000
40 DISCOUNT RATE=.10
50 LIFE =20
60 INVESTMENT=0
70 *
80 PRESENT VALUE = NPV(YEARLY RETURN,DISCOUNT RATE,LIFE,INVESTMENT)
END OF MODEL
? solve
MODEL NPV2   VERSION OF  12/28/82  11:45 -- 1 COLUMNS 5 VARIABLES
ENTER SOLVE OPTIONS
? aLL
                                    1

THIS MODEL ILLUSTRATES THE NPV FUNCTION
YEARLY RETURN                   50000
DISCOUNT RATE                   .1000
LIFE                               20
INVESTMENT                          0

PRESENT VALUE                  425678
```

FIGURE 6-2. NPV FUNCTION FOR FINDING NET PRESENT VALUE OF AN ANNUITY

Thus, NTV can be used to find the balance in a savings account if money is deposited today and left there for a period of time. Figure 6-3 illustrates NTV for the same stream of investments as Figure 6-1.

```
MODEL NTV   VERSION OF  08/24/81  20:57
10 COLUMNS 1-2
20 *THIS MODEL ILLUSTRATES THE NTV FUNCTION
30 *
40 NET TERMINAL VALUE = NTV(RETURN,DISCOUNT RATE,INVESTMENT)
50 INVESTMENT=150000,100000
60 RETURN = 0,300000
70 DISCOUNT RATE=.07
END OF MODEL
? solve
MODEL NTV   VERSION OF  08/24/81  20:57 -- 2 COLUMNS 4 VARIABLES
ENTER SOLVE OPTIONS
? all
                                    1         2

THIS MODEL ILLUSTRATES THE NTV FUNCTION

NET TERMINAL VALUE            -160500     21265
INVESTMENT                     150000    100000
RETURN                              0    300000
DISCOUNT RATE                   .0700     .0700
```

FIGURE 6-3. NTV FUNCTION FOR FINDING NET TERMINAL VALUE

6.2.4 Non-Annual Payments

Thus far in this section we have assumed that all transactions are yearly. If they are periodic (e.g., monthly, quarterly), then the PERIODS statement described in Section 3.2 must be used. PERIODS can be put anywhere in the model, although putting it right after the COLUMNS statement or as the last statement in the model is good practice. When PERIODS is specified, IFPS assumes all rates are given as annual rates and automatically converts them to periodic rates. Compounding is performed correctly in all built-in financial functions. With the PERIODS statement, IFPS regards each column as being one period rather than one year.

6.3 PRESENT VALUE OF BONDS AND STOCKS

6.3.1 A Bond's Yield to Maturity

When you buy a bond and hold it to maturity, you receive periodic interest payments and you receive the face value of the bond at maturity. If the interest offered is less than the current market interest rate, the bond is sold for less than its face value. That is, it is discounted. The investor wants to determine the present value of the bond since that is the amount the investor should pay for it.

For example if a bond yields:

1983	1984	1985	1986	1987	1988
87.50	87.50	87.50	87.50	87.50	1087.50

and the market interest rate is 10.2%, then the model shown in Figure 6-4 can be used to determine its value. This is a simple present value calculation with 0 investment. The present value of the bond is shown in the 1988 column of Figure 6-4 to be $937.20.

EXERCISE: Assume that you buy a bond for $937.22 with the cash flows shown above. Determine the internal rate of return.

EXERCISE: Suppose the bond pays $43.75 every six months. Modify Figure 6-4 to determine the present value of the bond with semi-annual payments. *Hint:* Double the number of columns, change the payments, and use the PERIODS statement.

6.3.2 Value of a Common Stock

Finding the value of a common stock is slightly more complicated than finding the value of a bond because a stock has two forms of return, dividends and price appreciation. Furthermore, both the dividends and the appreciation can vary over time, and the stock has an infinite life. Consider the simple case in which both the current dividend and the current stock price are expected to have the same growth rate. Then, we can make the following statments:

1. We make an initial investment at the beginning of Year 1.

2. At the end of Year 1 we receive a dividend and the (future) price of the stock increases by the growth rate.

```
MODEL BONDYIEL  VERSION OF  04/12/86  21:32
10 * BOND VALUE EXAMPLE
20 *
30 COLUMNS 1983-1988
40 CASH FLOWS = 87.5 FOR 5,1087.5
50 PAYMENTS=0
60 MARKET INTEREST RATE=.102
70 PRESENT VALUE= NPVC(CASH FLOWS,MARKET INTEREST RATE,PAYMENTS)
END OF MODEL
? SOLVE
ENTER SOLVE OPTIONS
? ALL
```

	1983	1984	1985	1986	1987	1988
BOND VALUE EXAMPLE						
CASH FLOWS	87.50	87.50	87.50	87.50	87.50	1088
PAYMENTS	0	0	0	0	0	0
MARKET INTEREST RATE	.1020	.1020	.1020	.1020	.1020	.1020
PRESENT VALUE	79.40	151.5	216.8	276.2	330.0	937.2

FIGURE 6-4. FINDING THE PRESENT VALUE OF A BOND GIVEN THE MARKET INTEREST RATE

3. At the end of each subsequent year, the dividend and the future price of the stock increases by the growth rate.

4. The net present value of the stream of annual dividends can be obtained by using the NPVC function.

5. The present value of the future price of the stock requires more care in computation. Unlike dividends, which we receive annually, we can sell the stock only once. Therefore, we must compute the present value of a single payment received in the future. The NPVC function cannot be used for this purpose because if would compute the present value of all the possible sales combined. Rather, we must use some other approach. In Figure 6-5 we have chosen to compute the net present value of the payment directly. It is obtained from the formula:

$$\text{NPV OF FUTURE PRICE} = \text{FUT PRICE} / (1 + \text{DISCOUNT RATE})^{n} \quad (6\text{-}3)$$

where FUT PRICE refers to the future price.

An alternative approach is to use two statements and compute the difference between the current period's and the previous period's NPVC values. In Figure 6-5, we would replace lines 50 and 60with:

```
60 CUMULATIVE NPV = NPVC(FUT PRICE,DISCOUNT RATE,0)
64 PREVIOUS NPV = PREVIOUS CUMULATIVE NPV
62 NPV OF FUTURE PRICE = CUMULATIVE NPV - PREVIOUS NPV
```

6. The total present value is obtained by adding the results of steps 4 and 5.

Figure 6-5 illustrates the computation of common stock value under the assumption that a growth stock selling for $100 will have a 10% annual increase in dividends and, as a result, a 10% annual increase in price. The discount rate (=capitalization rate) is assumed to be 15%.

```
MODEL STOCKVALUE  VERSION OF  12/28/82  11:53
10 COLUMNS 1-20
20 DIVIDEND =INITIAL DIVIDEND,PREVIOUS DIVIDEND * GROWTH RATE
30 FUT PRICE=INVESTMENT *GROWTH RATE,PREVIOUS*GROWTH RATE
40 NPV OF DIVIDENDS = NPVC(DIVIDEND,DISCOUNT RATE,PAYMENT)
50 NPV OF FUT PRICE =INVESTMENT*GROWTH RATE/(1+DISCOUNT RATE),'
60 PREVIOUS*GROWTH RATE/(1+DISCOUNT RATE)
70 TOTAL PRESENT VALUE=NPV OF DIVIDENDS + NPV OF FUT PRICE
80 *
90 *
100 INVESTMENT=100,0
110 INITIAL DIVIDEND=5,0
120 PAYMENT=0
130 DISCOUNT RATE=.15
140 GROWTH RATE =1.1
END OF MODEL
? solve
MODEL  STOCKVALUE   VERSION OF   12/28/82  11:53 -- 20 COLUMNS  10
VARIABLES
ENTER SOLVE OPTIONS
? columns 1,2,5,10,15,20
? all
```

	1	2	5	10	15	20
DIVIDEND	5	5.500	7.321	11.79	18.99	30.58
FUT PRICE	110	121	161.1	259.4	417.7	672.7
NPV OF DIVIDENDS	4.348	8.507	19.93	35.89	48.66	58.89
NPV OF FUT PRICE	95.65	91.49	80.07	64.11	51.34	41.11
TOTAL PRESENT VALUE	100	100	100	100	100	100
INVESTMENT	100	0	0	0	0	0
INITIAL DIVIDEND	5	0	0	0	0	0
PAYMENT	0	0	0	0	0	0
DISCOUNT RATE	.1500	.1500	.1500	.1500	.1500	.1500
GROWTH RATE	1.100	1.100	1.100	1.100	1.100	1.100

FIGURE 6-5. VALUE OF A COMMON STOCK
(This Figure Continued on the Next Page)

```
ENTER SOLVE OPTIONS
? what if
WHAT IF CASE 1
ENTER STATEMENTS
? npv of fut price = fut price/xpowery(1+discount rate,n)
WARNING - NEW VARIABLE WAS CREATED
? n = previous + 1
? solve
ENTER SOLVE OPTIONS
? npv of fut price


***** WHAT IF CASE 1 *****
2 WHAT IF STATEMENTS PROCESSED

                          1       2       5      10      15      20

NPV OF FUT PRICE      95.65   91.49   80.07   64.11   51.34   41.11
```

FIGURE 6-5. VALUE OF A COMMON STOCK
(Continued)

In Figure 6-5 the net present value of the future price is computed in two ways. In the model, the investment increases by the growth rate and is reduced by the discount rate each year, with the values each year being computed from the values in the previous year. In the alternative form, shown in the WHAT IF case, the net present value is computed directly by applying Equation (6-3). The results are identical; however, the direct computation from Equation (6-3) is less efficient computationally. Note that in the direct computation, done in the WHAT IF case, we have to use a separate line to establish the year number, N.

If we assume a constant growth rate, g, for dividends from now into perpetuity, then we can estimate the discount rate (or capitalization rate for a stock), r, from the formula:

$$r = (\text{DIVIDEND/PRESENT VALUE OF STOCK}) + g \qquad (6\text{-}4)$$

That is, the capitalization rate of a stock is the sum of the dividend yield and the dividend growth rate,g. The dividend and the current stock price are known. If growth is financed internally, the growth rate is estimated by multiplying the "plowback ratio" by the "return on equity." The plowback ratio refers to the fraction of the year's earnings reinvested in the firm and can be found by taking (1 – DIVIDEND/EARNINGS PER SHARE). The return on equity is the ratio EARNINGS PER SHARE/BOOK EQUITY PER SHARE. Earnings per share and book equity per share are known quantities that can be obtained from published data.

Figure 6-6 shows the IFPS model for determining capitalization rate. Like many IFPS models you will see in this book, it is quite straightforward once you have gone through the series of steps needed to understand the process being modeled. The input values of dividend rate, selling price, earnings per share, and book value per share shown are based on American Telephone and Telegraph performance in 1982/1983. AT&T has a history of declaring dividends that are approximately 60% of earnings per share.

```
MODEL CAPRATE  VERSION OF  04/12/86  21:41
10 * CAPITALIZATION  RATE  -- CURRENT DATA ONLY
20 *
30 COLUMNS 1
40 DIVIDEND YIELD=DIVIDEND RATE/SELLING PRICE
50 PLOWBACK RATIO =1-DIVIDEND RATE/EARNINGS PER SHARE
60 RETURN ON EQUITY = EARNINGS PER SHARE/BOOK EQUITY PER SHARE
70 DIVIDEND GROWTH RATE=PLOWBACK RATIO*RETURN ON EQUITY
80 CAPITALIZATION RATE= DIVIDEND YIELD +DIVIDEND GROWTH RATE
90 *
100 *     INPUT DATA
110 DIVIDEND RATE =5.40
120 SELLING PRICE = 60.00
130 EARNINGS PER SHARE = DIVIDEND RATE/0.60
140 BOOK EQUITY PER SHARE =69.23
END OF MODEL
?solve
MODEL CAPRATE  VERSION OF  04/12/86  21:41 -- 1 COLUMNS 9 VARIABLES
ENTER SOLVE OPTIONS
? ALL

                                          1

 CAPITALIZATION  RATE  -- CURRENT DATA ONLY

DIVIDEND YIELD                         .0900
PLOWBACK RATIO                         .4000
RETURN ON EQUITY                       .1300
DIVIDEND GROWTH RATE                   .0520
CAPITALIZATION RATE                    .1420

     INPUT DATA
DIVIDEND RATE                          5.400
SELLING PRICE                             60
EARNINGS PER SHARE                         9
BOOK EQUITY PER SHARE                  69.23
```

FIGURE 6-6. ESTIMATING CAPITALIZATION RATE BASED ON CURRENT DATA ONLY

6.3.3 Capitalization Rate Taking Future Estimated Changes into Account

The previous model of capitalization rate assumed that growth could be maintained at current levels forever. This is an optimistic assumption, particularly for high growth firms that exceed the growth in Gross National Product by considerable amounts. An alternative model assumes that the current growth will continue for a fixed time and growth will then drop to a lower rate.

In the previous model, we could solve Equation (6-4) for the present value of the stock:

$$\text{PRESENT VALUE OF STOCK} = \text{DIVIDEND} / (r\text{-}g) \qquad (6\text{-}5)$$

In this case, it turns out that the appropriate model is to take the present value of the stream of earnings for the number of years that the current growth rate is expected to continue, and then to apply Equation (6-5). In formula terms,

$$PRESENT\ VALUE\ OF\ STOCK = \sum_{I=1}^{K-1} \frac{DIV(I)}{(1+r)^I} + \frac{P(K)}{r-g} \qquad (6\text{-}6)$$

where: DIV(I) is the dividend in Year I.
P(K) us the stock price in Year K when the growth rate changes
g is the growth rate
r is the discount rate.

Figure 6-7 implements this model. In the example shown, the current dividend of 50 cents on a $50 stock price grows by 20% annually for three years and then grows by only 8% per year. It can then be shown that the capitalization rate must be greater than 8% (the eventual growth rate) but less than the capitalization rate obtained from Equation (6-4) for the initial growth rate.

```
MODEL CAPRTE2  VERSION OF  04/12/86  21:54
10 *CAPITALIZATION RATE--TAKING FUTURE ESTIMATED CHANGES INTO ACCOUNT
20 *
30 COLUMNS 1-4
40 BOOK EQUITY =10,PREVIOUS+PREVIOUS EARNINGS PER SHARE -'
41     PREVIOUS DIVIDEND
50 EARNINGS PER SHARE = RETURN ON EQUITY * BOOK EQUITY
52 RETURN ON EQUITY =  .25 FOR 2,.16
54 PAYOUT RATIO =.2 FOR 2,.5
60 DIVIDEND = EARNINGS PER SHARE * PAYOUT RATIO
70 DENOMINATOR=1+CAPITALIZATION RATE,PREVIOUS*'
71 (1+CAPITALIZATION RATE) FOR 2,'
72 PREVIOUS *(CAPITALIZATION RATE -G)
80 PRESENT VALUE OF STOCK =DIVIDEND/DENOMINATOR,'
81 PREVIOUS+DIVIDEND/DENOMINATOR
90 *
100*INPUT DATA
110 *
120 INITIAL DIVIDEND =.50,0
130 INITIAL STOCK PRICE = 50,0
140 DIVIDEND GROWTH RATE=1.2 FOR 3,1.08
150 G=0 FOR 3,.08
160 RETURN ON EQUITY =.25 FOR 2, .16
170 CAPITALIZATION RATE = .21
END OF MODEL
```

a. Model

FIGURE 6-7. ESTIMATING THE CAPITALIZATION RATE TAKING FUTURE ESTIMATED CHANGES INTO ACCOUNT
(This Figure Continued on Next Page)

EXERCISE. Show that if the current dividend is 50 cents, the current stock price is $50 and the current growth rate is 20%, then the maximum capitalization rate is 21%.

```
? solve
MODEL CAPRTE2  VERSION OF   12/28/82  12:07 -- 4 COLUMNS 7 VARIABLES
ENTER SOLVE OPTIONS
? all
                                      1        2        3        4

CAPITALIZATION RATE--TAKING FUTURE ESTIMATED CHANGES INTO ACCOUNT

BOOK EQUITY                          10       12    14.40    15.55
EARNINGS PER SHARE                2.500        3    2.304    2.488
RETURN ON EQUITY                  .2500    .2500    .1600    .1600
PAYOUT RATIO                      .2000    .2000    .5000    .5000
DIVIDEND                          .5000    .6000    1.152    1.244
DENOMINATOR                       1.210    1.464    1.772    .2303
PRESENT VALUE OF STOCK            .4132    .8230    1.473    6.876

INPUT DATA

INITIAL DIVIDEND                  .5000        0        0        0
INITIAL STOCK PRICE                  50        0        0        0
DIVIDEND GROWTH RATE              1.200    1.200    1.200    1.080
G                                     0        0        0    .0800
RETURN ON EQUITY                  .2500    .2500    .1600    .1600
CAPITALIZATION RATE               .2100    .2100    .2100    .2100
```

b. Results Based on 21% Capitalization Rate

FIGURE 6-7. ESTIMATING THE CAPITALIZATION RATE TAKING FUTURE ESTIMATED CHANGES INTO ACCOUNT
(This Figure Continued on Next Page)

The problem the analyst faces is how to determine r. It cannot be done directly; it has to be done by successive approximation. In Figure 6-7b we show one such approximation scheme, called "interval halving." We know, initially, that the value of the capitalization rate has to be between 8% and 21%; in fact it cannot be equal to 8% since Equation (6-6) would then require division by 0. For simplicity, assume that the capitalization rate is between 8.1% and 21%. You will note in Figure 6-7 that we set the capitalization rate at 21% initially in the model and use a WHAT IF case t(Figure 6-7c) o compute the present value of the stock for 8.1%. The results indicate that 21% implies a present value of the stock of $6.88 (too low) and 8.1% implies a present value of $986.80 (too high). We can conclude from these two answers that the capitalization rate that yields the current $50 value of the stock has to be between 8% and 21%. We can depict the situation as follows:

PV $698.90 ———————————————— $6.88

Yield (%) 8.1 ———————————————— 21

It is clear that we should pick a value in the interval from 8.1% to 21%. The easiest thing to do is to divide the interval in half and pick, say 14% for the next try. (We could have picked the exact half-way point, 14.55%, but precision is not needed in this process until we are close to the answer.) Since 14% yields a value of $15.67, we can conclude that the

```
WHAT IF CASE 1
ENTER STATEMENTS
? CAPITALIZATION RATE =.081
? SOLVE
ENTER SOLVE OPTIONS
? PRESENT VALUE OF STOCK,CAPITALIZATION RATE
***** WHAT IF CASE 1 *****
1 WHAT IF STATEMENT PROCESSED

                                 1        2        3        4

PRESENT VALUE OF STOCK       .4625    .9760    1.888    986.8
CAPITALIZATION RATE          .0810    .0810    .0810    .0810

ENTER SOLVE OPTIONS
? WHAT IF
WHAT IF CASE 2
ENTER STATEMENTS
? CAPITALIZATION RATE =.14
? SOLVE
ENTER SOLVE OPTIONS
? PRESENT VALUE OF STOCK,CAPITALIZATION RATE
***** WHAT IF CASE 2 *****
1 WHAT IF STATEMENT PROCESSED

                                 1        2        3        4

PRESENT VALUE OF STOCK       .4386    .9003    1.678    15.67
CAPITALIZATION RATE          .1400    .1400    .1400    .1400

ENTER SOLVE OPTIONS
? WHAT IF
WHAT IF CASE 3
ENTER STATEMENTS
? CAPITALIZATION RATE =.11
? SOLVE
ENTER SOLVE OPTIONS
? PRESENT VALUE OF STOCK, CAPITALIZATION RATE
***** WHAT IF CASE 3 *****
1 WHAT IF STATEMENT PROCESSED

                                 1        2        3        4

PRESENT VALUE OF STOCK       .4505    .9374    1.780    32.10
CAPITALIZATION RATE          .1100    .1100    .1100    .1100
```

c. Results Based on 8.1%, 14%, and 11%

FIGURE 6-7. ESTIMATING THE CAPITALIZATION RATE TAKING FUTURE ESTIMATED CHANGES INTO ACCOUNT

(This Figure Continued on the Next Page)

```
WHAT IF CASE 4
ENTER STATEMENTS
? CAPITALIZATION RATE =.10
? SOLVE
ENTER SOLVE OPTIONS
? PRESENT VALUE OF STOCK,CAPITALIZATION RATE
***** WHAT IF CASE 4 *****
1 WHAT IF STATEMENT PROCESSED

                                  1         2         3         4

PRESENT VALUE OF STOCK        .4545     .9504     1.816     48.55
CAPITALIZATION RATE           .1000     .1000     .1000     .1000
WHAT IF CASE 5
ENTER STATEMENTS
? CAPITALIZATION RATE =.099
? SOLVE
ENTER SOLVE OPTIONS
? PRESENT VALUE OF STOCK,CAPITALIZATION RATE
***** WHAT IF CASE 5 *****
1 WHAT IF STATEMENT PROCESSED

                                  1         2         3         4

PRESENT VALUE OF STOCK        .4550     .9517     1.820     51.15
CAPITALIZATION RATE           .0990     .0990     .0990     .0990
```

d. Results Based on 10% and 9.9%

FIGURE 6-7. ESTIMATING THE CAPITALIZATION RATE TAKING FUTURE ESTIMATED CHANGES INTO ACCOUNT
(Continued)

correct value is between 8.1% and 14% since all values above 14% would lead to even smaller present values. (Do you see why? If not, try it on the computer for a few values between 14% and 21% and convince yourself.) Dividing the interval in half again and again, each time choosing the capitalization rate integer, we find that the closest answer to the nearest 0.1% is 9.9%. (Only the results for 10% and 9.9% are shown in Figure 6.7d) The diagram below shows the sequence of steps followed.

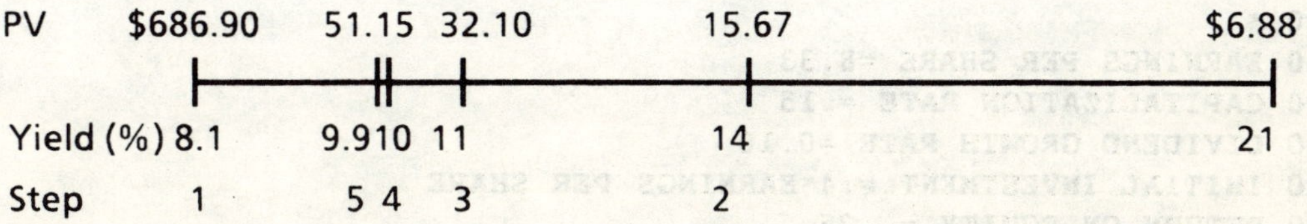

6.3.4 Present Value of Growth Opportunities

For a growth stock, it is appropriate to consider its value as consisting of two components:

1. the present value of a level stream of earnings, and

2. the present value resulting from growth opportunities.

The present value of the level stream of earnings is simply the earnings per share divided by the capitalization rate (i.e., EPS/R). The present value of growth opportunities (PVGO) is given by:

$$PVGO = NPV(1)/(r\text{-}g) \tag{6-7}$$

where NPV(1) is determined by considering the investment (a negative number!) in growth at the beginning in Year 1 (the amount plowed back from earnings) plus the return from this investment assumed to continue into perpetuity. This return is obtained by taking the investment times the return on equity and dividing by the capitalization rate.

Figure 6-8 illustrates the calculation of the present value of growth opportunities for Fledgling Electronics, a firm whose earnings per share are $8.33, dividend growth rate is 10%, and capitalization rate is 15%. Fledgling plows back 40% of its dividend into growth. It is assumed that this growth equity is able to earn 25%. The results show the portion of the stock price due to level earnings and due to growth opportunities.

```
MODEL GROOPP  VERSION OF  12/28/82  12:29
10 *PRESENT VALUE OF GROWTH OPPORTUNITIES
20 *
30 * FLEDGLING ELECTRONICS EXAMPLE
40 *
50 COLUMNS 1
60 PV OF LEVEL EARNINGS =EARNINGS PER SHARE/CAPITALIZATION RATE
70 PV OF GROWTH OPPORTUNITIES =NPV1/(CAPITALIZATION RATE -'
71 DIVIDEND GROWTH RATE)
80 NPV1=-INITIAL INVESTMENT+INITIAL INVESTMENT*RETURN ON EQUITY/'
81 CAPITALIZATION RATE
90 *
100 SHARE PRICE = PV OF LEVEL EARNINGS +PV OF GROWTH OPPORTUNITIES
110 *
120 *INPUT DATA
130 *
140 EARNINGS PER SHARE =8.33
150 CAPITALIZATION RATE =.15
160 DIVIDEND GROWTH RATE =0.10
170 INITIAL INVESTMENT =.4*EARNINGS PER SHARE
180 RETURN ON EQUITY = .25
END OF MODEL
```

FIGURE 6-8. PRESENT VALUE OF GROWTH OPPORTUNITIES FOR A STOCK
(This Figure Continued on the Next Page)

```
? solve
MODEL GROOPP  VERSION OF  04/12/86  22:31 -- 1 COLUMNS 9 VARIABLES
ENTER SOLVE OPTIONS
? ALL

                                         1

PRESENT VALUE OF GROWTH OPPORTUNITIES

 FLEDGLING ELECTRONICS EXAMPLE

PV OF LEVEL EARNINGS           55.55
PV OF GROWTH OPPORTUNITI       44.44
NPV1                           2.222

SHARE PRICE                   100.00

INPUT DATA

EARNINGS PER SHARE             8.333
CAPITALIZATION RATE            .1500
DIVIDEND GROWTH RATE           .1000
INITIAL INVESTMENT             3.333
RETURN ON EQUITY               .2500
```

FIGURE 6-8. PRESENT VALUE OF GROWTH OPPORTUNITIES FOR A STOCK (Continued)

6.4 ALTERNATIVE CRITERIA FOR INVESTMENT DECISIONS

In this section we consider various alternative criteria for evaluating investment decisions. Each of these criteria can be implemented in a relatively straightforward way in IFPS. We will present these criteria without comment as to their relative virtues and faults; we leave these arguments to the various finance texts. All of these criteria are being used in practice. In many cases the choice of criterion within a particular firm is based on historical rather than technical reasons; that is, it has always been done that way.

The five criteria are:

1. Net Present Value
2. Payback Period
3. Average Return on Book Value
4. Internal Rate of Return
5. Profitability Index.

Net present value was discussed extensively in Sections 6.2 and 6.3. Therefore, in Figure 6-9 which illustrates all five criteria, we simply show the net present value calculation for comparison.

The stream of incomes that we consider is as follows:

- A $2000 investment at the beginning of Year 1.
- A $1000 return at the end of Years 1 and 2, followed by $5000 at the end of Year 3.
- A discount rate of 10%.

```
MODEL CRITERIA  VERSION OF  12/28/82  12:36
10 *THIS MODEL ALLOWS EVALUATING INVESTMENTS BY FIVE DIFFERENT'
11 * CRITERIA:
20 *
30 *1)PRESENT VALUE 2)PAYBACK 3) AVERAGE RETURN ON BOOK 4)IRR'
31 * 5)PROFITABILITY INDEX
40 *
50 COLUMNS 1-3
60 INVESTMENT =2000,0
70 RETURN =1000,1000,5000
80 DISCOUNT RATE =.10
90 NET PRESENT VALUE = NPVC(RETURN,DISCOUNT RATE,INVESTMENT)
100 *
110 PAYBACK AMOUNT =-INVESTMENT + RETURN,PREVIOUS + RETURN
120 DISCOUNTED PAYBACK=IF NPVC(RETURN,DISCOUNT RATE,INVESTMENT).LT.'
121 0 THEN 0 ELSE 1
130 *
140 GROSS BOOK VALUE =2000
150 AVERAGE INVESTMENT=(GROSS BOOK VALUE-SALVAGE VALUE)/2
160 NET INCOME=1000,1000,5000
170 CUMULATIVE INCOME=NET INCOME,PREVIOUS +NET INCOME
180 AVG NET INCOME = CUMULATIVE INCOME/NYEARS
190 SALVAGE VALUE=0
200 NYEARS=1,PREVIOUS +1
210 AVG BOOK RATE OF RETURN = AVG NET INCOME/AVERAGE INVESTMENT
220 *
230 INTERNAL RATE OF RETURN =IRR(RETURN,INVESTMENT)
240 *
250 PRESENT VALUE =NPVC(RETURN,DISCOUNT RATE,0)
260 INITIAL INVESTMENT=INVESTMENT,PREVIOUS
270 PROFITABILITY INDEX = PRESENT VALUE/INITIAL INVESTMENT
280 BENEFIT COST RATIO=BCRATIO(RETURN,DISCOUNT RATE,INVESTMENT)
END OF MODEL
```

a. Model

FIGURE 6-9. ALTERNATIVE INVESTMENT CRITERIA
(This Figure Continued on the Next Page)

```
? solve
MODEL CRITERIA  VERSION OF   12/28/82   12:36 -- 3 COLUMNS 19
VARIABLES
ENTER SOLVE OPTIONS
? all
                                      1         2          3

THIS MODEL ALLOWS EVALUATING INVESTMENTS BY FIVE DIFFERENT CRITERIA:

1)PRESENT  VALUE  2)PAYBACK  3)  AVERAGE  RETURN  ON  BOOK  4)IRR
5)PROFITABILITY INDEX

INVESTMENT                         2000         0          0
RETURN                             1000      1000       5000
DISCOUNT RATE                     .1000     .1000      .1000
NET PRESENT VALUE                 -1091    -264.5       3492

PAYBACK AMOUNT                    -1000         0       5000
DISCOUNTED PAYBACK                    0         0          1

GROSS BOOK VALUE                   2000      2000       2000
AVERAGE INVESTMENT                 1000      1000       1000
NET INCOME                         1000      1000       5000
CUMULATIVE INCOME                  1000      2000       7000
AVG NET INCOME                     1000      1000       2333
SALVAGE VALUE                         0         0          0
NYEARS                                1         2          3
AVG BOOK RATE OF RETURN               1         1      2.333

INTERNAL RATE OF RETURN                         0      .6815

PRESENT VALUE                     909.1      1736       5492
INITIAL INVESTMENT                 2000      2000       2000
PROFITABILITY INDEX               .4545     .8678      2.746
BENEFIT COST RATIO                .4545     .8678      2.746
```

FIGURE 6-9. ALTERNATIVE INVESTMENT CRITERIA
(Continued)

6.4.1 Payback Period

The payback period is determined by finding the time, in years, at which the forecasted cash flow (without discounting!) equals the initial investment. Typically, companies specify a number of years and accept projects for which the payback amount, given by equation (6-8), is positive within that time.

$$\text{PAYBACK AMOUNT} = -\text{INVESTMENT} + \text{SUM OF RETURNS} \tag{6-8}$$

Contributions to return that occur beyond the cutoff time are ignored. In Figure 6-9, the payback period is two years, for at that time the payback exactly equals the investment.

A modified form of the payback period considers discounted cash flows. The discounted payback period is the time at which the net present value becomes positive. A quick way of highlighting this time on your output is to use the IF...THEN...ELSE construction in IFPS. Specifically, if the net present value of the cash flow (i.e., NPVC) is negative, show a 0 in your output, whereas if the NPVC value is 0 or positive show a 1. This is what is done in Line 120 of the model and results in showing that the discounted payback becomes positive in the third year under the assumed 10% discount rate.

6.4.2 Average Return on Book Value

This criterion is given by equation (6-9):

AVG. RETURN ON BOOK VALUE = AVG. RETURN/AVERAGE INVESTMENT (6-9)

A project is accepted if this ratio is better than some pre-specified value, such as the average for the company or the industry.

To compute the average return, you divide the cumulative return (undiscounted) by the time since the start of the project. The average investment is, similarly, the initial investment divided by time if straight line depreciation is used.

EXERCISE: Revise the calculation for average book value in Figure 6-9 under the assumption of 3-year life and the declining balance depreciation. *Hint:* Use the built-in depreciation functions available in IFPS (Section 3.3).

6.4.3 Internal Rate of Return

The internal rate of return is defined as that interest rate for which the net present value equals 0 at the end of the time horizon. That is, if we had chosen the internal rate of return as the discount rate, we would have a project which just broke even in net present value terms. Computing the internal rate of return directly is difficult task, requiring a successive approximation technique such as interval halving which we used in Section 6.3.3 for determining capitalization rate. Fortunately, IFPS contains a built-in internal rate of return function, IRR. As explained in Section 3.2, this function prints blanks for negative rates of returns (except in the last column). Typically, an investment is accepted if its internal rate of return is greater than the opportunity cost of obtaining capital on the open market.

The internal rate of return sometimes leads to difficulties. Specifically, if the total cumulative cash flow changes sign more than once, you may find that there are multiple rates of return. If there is only one change of sign from negative to positive, then the internal rate of return is defined uniquely. This is true, for example, in the simple case of of a single investment at the start of Year 1. If there are both negative and positive values of internal rate of return, IFPS will choose the smallest positive one; of there are several values that are all positive, IFPS will choose the smallest positive value. If you suspect multiple rates, you can use the modified internal rate of return function provided in IFPS. This function is defined by:

MIRR(RETURN,DISCOUNT RATE,INVESTMENT) (6-10)

What MIRR does is first compute the difference between the return in one year and the investment at the beginning of the next year. (Remember that the convention in IFPS is that investments are made at the beginning of a year.) If this difference is negative, it treats the amount as an investment and "returns" this investment to the start of the first year, using the discount rate. MIRR then computes an internal rate of return based on an effective initial investment and only positive cash flows thereafter. MIRR, like IRR, is an annual rate.

6.4.4 Profitability Index (or Benefit/Cost Ratio)

The profitability index is the ratio of the present value of returns to the initial investment. The profitability index can be computed directly from this definition by determining the value of the NPVC function with no investment and dividing by the investment. Alternatively, the built-in BCRATIO function can be used since, if you examine the definition of profitability index, you see that it is the ratio of benefits (i.e., returns on investment) divided by costs (investment). The BCRATIO function is given by:

BCRATIO (RETURN,DISCOUNT RATE,INVESTMENT) (6-11)

6.5 OPTIMAL TIMING FOR SELLING AN ASSET OR MAKING AN INVESTMENT

Suppose you have an asset whose current value you know, and you can forecast, to some extent, what its value will be in the future. For example, you own a valuable painting. Similarly, suppose you have a choice as to whether to make an investment now or later where the value of the investment may be larger if made later. You face the same problem in either case; namely, what is the best time to act.

Figure 6-10 shows the calculations involved in making such a decision. The example assumes that the current value is $50,000 and that you have determined, by some means, the value of the asset or the investment at the end of each of the next five years. The model computes the present value of the asset at each point in time.

Note that you do not obtain the right answer if you simply compute the NPVC function for this purpose. (Try it and see!) The NPVC function assumes that you receive a payment every period. However, if you own a single asset (or make a single investment) which you hold for a period of time and then sell, you receive only one payment and it occurs when you sell. (For example, you receive no income from owning a painting.) Therefore, you must compute the present value of each of the sales prices. One way of doing so is to take the difference between NPVC and the previous NPVC. If you think about it, you recognize that the NPVC function computes the present worth of all payments from Period 1 to the current period (e.g., from Period 1 through Period 5) whereas the previous NPVC value computes the present worth of all payments up to one period ago (e.g., in Period 5, PREVIOUS NPVC covers Periods 1 through 4). The difference therefore is just the present value of the current payment (e.g., Period 5).

WARNING: In some implementations of IFPS, you will obtain the wrong answer if PREVIOUS refers to an NPVC statement on the same line. For example:

PRESENT VALUE = NPVC(INCOME,INTEREST,0) − PREVIOUS PRESENT VALUE

```
MODEL OPTIME  VERSION OF  01/20/82  15:42
10 COLUMNS 1-5
20*
30*OPTIMAL TIMING OF AN INVESTMENT
40*
50 CURRENT VALUE=50,0
60 NET FUT VALUE =64.4,77.5,89.4,100,109.4
70 PCT CHANGE IN VALUE = 100*(NET FUT VALUE -CURRENT VALUE)/'
71 CURRENT VALUE, 100*(NET FUT VALUE-PREVIOUS NET FUT VALUE)'
72 /PREVIOUS NET FUT VALUE
80 CUMULATIVE NPV =NPVC(NET FUT VALUE,DISCOUNT RATE,CURRENT VALUE)
90 NET PRESENT VALUE = CUMULATIVE NPV - PREVIOUS CUMULATIVE NPV
100*
110 DISCOUNT RATE =.1
120*
130* NOTE1: CURRENT VALUE IS AT BEGINNING OF YEAR 1
140* NOTE2: NET FUT VALUE IS NET FUTURE VALUE AT END OF YEAR
END OF MODEL
? solve
MODEL OPTIME  VERSION OF  01/20/82  15:42 -- 5 COLUMNS 6 VARIABLES
ENTER SOLVE OPTIONS
? all
```

OPTIMAL TIMING OF AN INVESTMENT	1	2	3	4	5
CURRENT VALUE	50	0	0	0	0
NET FUT VALUE	64.40	77.50	89.40	100	109.4
PCT CHANGE IN VALUE	28.80	20.34	15.35	11.86	9.400
CUMULATIVE NPV	8.545	72.60	139.8	208.1	276.0
NET PRESENT VALUE	8.545	64.05	67.17	68.30	67.93
DISCOUNT RATE	.1000	.1000	.1000	.1000	.1000

```
 NOTE1: CURRENT VALUE IS AT BEGINNING OF YEAR 1
 NOTE2: NET FUT VALUE IS NET FUTURE VALUE AT END OF YEAR
```

FIGURE 6-10. OPTIMAL TIMING OF AN INVESTMENT

Lines 80 and 90 in Figure 6-10 show the computation of the present value of the single payment. You will note that Line 80 shows the cumulative present value, whereas Line 90 pinpoints the present value from a single sale by taking the difference between the current and previous cumulative values.

EXERCISE: An alternate way of computing the value of a single payment at the end of Year N is the relation:

```
NET PRESENT VALUE = PAYMENT*DISCOUNT FACTOR
```

where in Figure 6-10 the payment is the NET FUT VALUE of the asset. The discount factor is 1/(1+DISCOUNT RATE) raised to the Nth power (see Section 6.2). Modify Figure 6-10 so that it uses this form.

To determine the optimal timing, examine the net present values computed. The best time to act will be when the present value is largest. In Figure 6-10, this time is at the end of Year 4.

This model, like all the models you see in this chapter, implicitly assumes that the discount rate describes the rate of return you could obtain if you made an alternative investment. In the case of selling an asset, as long as the rate of return from the asset is greater than the discount rate, you hold it. In the case of making an investment, you do not make it until the rate of return from future earnings exceeds the discount rate.

EXERCISE: Run the model of Figure 6-10 for discount rates of 8, 10, and 20% and determine the optimum time for selling the asset.

6.6 A LARGER EXAMPLE -- THE GUANO PROJECT

Until now in this chapter we have considered very specific calculations involving determination of value. At this point we will undertake a more ambitious example in which we put together projections for both profitability and cash flows. It is these larger, integrated models that are the rationale for using financial planning languages. You now know enough, if you have followed the text, to be able to undertake such a larger calculation.

Consider the following situtation. You have the opportunity to invest $10,000 in plant and machinery at the start of a project for processing guano. (Guano is obtained from the droppings of the guano bird and is used as fertilizer.) The project will last six years and, during the seventh year, you expect to be able to sell the machinery for scrap and receive $1000. The IRS will let you depreciate your investment over the six-year life to a $500 book value. Your firm uses straight line depreciation. Your operating groups have made estimates of working capital, sales, operating and other costs. Your tax rate is estimated to be 46%. Finally, if you decide to undertake the project you estimate that you will incur operating costs of $4,000 to start up the project. Being operating costs, these pre-investment costs are tax deductible (we assume you are making a profit and have income to offset these costs) and hence their net cost to you is

$4000*(1-TAX RATE) = $4000*(1-0.46) = $2,160.

Figure 6-11 shows the model for this scenario. You will note that there are really three models shown: (1) projections of after tax-profits without taking inflation into account, (2) projections of after-tax profits with inflation, and (3) a cash flow analysis. The reason for including all three in one IFPS Model is that the data are interconnected and some data are repeated. The initial projections do not take inflation into account. However, some input variables (specifically, working capital, sales, operating costs, other costs) are subject to inflation, which is assumed to be 10% annually. Other variables (e.g., depreciation) are not. The second set of projections, therefore, modifies the first by multiplying the input data by an inflation factor. The inflation factor is simply the value of $1 compounded at a 10% annual rate. The cash flow analysis uses the projections with inflation to derive the net present value of the investment, under the assumption that you have a 20% discount rate.

```
MODEL GUANO  VERSION OF  05/07/86   22:26
10 COLUMNS 1-7
20 *
30 * A GUANO PROJECT -- PROJECTIONS WITHOUT INFLATION
40 *
50 CAPITAL INVESTMENT=10000,0
60 SALVAGE VALUE =0 FOR 5, 1000
70 STLINE DEPR(CAPITAL INVESTMENT,.05,6,DEPRCIATION,'
80 YR END BOOK VALUE,ACCUM DEPRECIATION)
90 WORKING CAPITAL = 500,1065,2450,3340,2225,1130,0
100 TOTAL BOOK VALUE = YR END BOOK VALUE + WORKING CAPITAL FOR 6,0
110 *
120 PREINVESTMENT COSTS =4000*(1-.46),0
130 *
140 ANNUAL SALES =475,10650,24500,33400,22250,11130,0
150 OPERATING COSTS= 761,6388,14690,20043,13345,6678,0
160 OTHER COSTS=2000,0
170 PRETAX PROFIT = ANNUAL SALES - OPERATING COSTS -OTHER COSTS'
180 -DEPRCIATION FOR 6, SALVAGE VALUE -PREVIOUS YR END BOOK VALUE
190 TAX AT 46 PERCENT=PRETAX PROFIT*.46
200 PROFIT AFTER TAX=PRETAX PROFIT-TAX AT 46 PERCENT
210 *
220 *A GUANO MODEL PROJECTIONS WITH INFLATION
230 *
240 CAPITAL INVESTMENT = L50
250 SALVAGE VALUE = L60*INFLATION FACTOR
260 STLINE DEPR(CAPITAL INVESTMENT,.05,6,DEPRECIATION,'
270 YEAR END BOOK VALUE,ACCUMULATED DEPRECIATION)
280 WORKING CAPITAL =L90*INFLATION FACTOR
290 TOTAL BOOK VALUE = YEAR END BOOK VALUE + WORKING CAPITAL
300 *
310 PREINVESTMENT COSTS = L120
320 *
330 SALES=L140*INFLATION FACTOR
340 OPERATING COSTS =L150 *INFLATION FACTOR
350 OTHER COSTS=L160* INFLATION FACTOR
360 PRETAX PROFIT = L330-L340-L350-DEPRECIATION FOR 6,SALVAGE VALUE'
370 -PREVIOUS YEAR END BOOK VALUE
380 TAX AT 46 PERCENT=PRETAX PROFIT*.46
390 PROFIT AFTER TAX = PRETAX PROFIT -TAX AT 46 PERCENT
400 INFLATION FACTOR = 1.1,PREVIOUS * 1.1
410 *
420 *
```

FIGURE 6-11. THE GUANO PROJECT

(This Figure Continued on the Next Page)

```
430 * CASH FLOW ANALYSIS
440 *
450 INCOME FROM SALES=SALES
460 COSTS FROM OPERATIONS = OPERATING COSTS
470 OTHER COST=OTHER COSTS
480 TAX ON OPERATIONS =TAX AT 46 PERCENT FOR 6,0
490 *
500 CASH FLOW FROM OPERATIONS = L450 -L460-L470-L480
510 *
520 CHANGE IN WORKING CAPITAL=PREVIOUS WORKING CAPITAL'
521 -WORKING CAPITAL
530 CAPITAL INVESTMENT AND DISPOSAL = CAPITAL INVESTMENT FOR 6, '
540 SALVAGE VALUE - TAX AT 46 PERCENT
550*
560 TOTAL INFLOWS = CASH FLOW FROM OPERATIONS +'
570 CHANGE IN WORKING CAPITAL FOR 6,SALVAGE VALUE'
580 -TAX AT 46 PERCENT + CHANGE IN WORKING CAPITAL
590 TOTAL OUTFLOWS =CAPITAL INVESTMENT +PREINVESTMENT COSTS,0
600 NET CASH FLOW =TOTAL INFLOWS-TOTAL OUTFLOWS
610 NET PRESENT VALUE =NPVC(TOTAL INFLOWS,DISCOUNT RATE,'
620 TOTAL OUTFLOWS)
630 *
640 DISCOUNT RATE =.20
END OF MODEL
? SOLVE

MODEL GUANO  VERSION OF  05/07/86  22:26 -- 7 COLUMNS 41 VARIABLES
ENTER SOLVE OPTIONS
? ALL
```

A GUANO PROJECT -- PROJECTIONS WITHOUT INFLATION	1	2	3	4	5	6	7
CAPITAL INVESTMENT	10000	0	0	0	0	0	0
SALVAGE VALUE	0	0	0	0	0	1000	1000
DEPRCIATION	1583	1583	1583	1583	1583	1583	0
YR END BOOK VALUE	8417	6833	5250	3667	2083	500	500
ACCUM DEPRECIATION	1583	3167	4750	6333	7917	9500	9500
WORKING CAPITAL	500	1065	2450	3340	2225	1130	0
TOTAL BOOK VALUE	8917	7898	7700	7007	4308	1630	0
PREINVESTMENT COSTS	2160	0	0	0	0	0	0
ANNUAL SALES	475	10650	24500	33400	22250	11130	0
OPERATING COSTS	761	6388	14690	20043	13345	6678	0
OTHER COSTS	2000	0	0	0	0	0	0
PRETAX PROFIT	-3869	2679	8227	11774	7322	2869	500
TAX AT 46 PERCENT	-1780	1232	3784	5416	3368	1320	230
PROFIT AFTER TAX	-2089	1446	4442	6358	3954	1549	270

FIGURE 6-11. THE GUANO PROJECT

(This Figure Continued on the Next Page)

A GUANO MODEL PROJECTIONS WITH INFLATION

CAPITAL INVESTMENT	10000	0	0	0	0	0	0
SALVAGE VALUE	0	0	0	0	0	1772	1949
DEPRECIATION	1583	1583	1583	1583	1583	1583	0
YEAR END BOOK VALUE	8417	6833	5250	3667	2083	500	500
ACCUMULATED DEPRECIA	1583	3167	4750	6333	7917	9500	9500
WORKING CAPITAL	550	1289	3261	4890	3583	2002	0
TOTAL BOOK VALUE	8967	8122	8511	8557	5667	2502	500
PREINVESTMENT COSTS	2160	0	0	0	0	0	0
SALES	522.5	12887	32610	48901	35834	19717	0
OPERATING COSTS	837.1	7729	19552	29345	21492	11830	0
OTHER COSTS	2200	0	0	0	0	0	0
PRETAX PROFIT	-4098	3574	11474	17973	12758	6304	1449
TAX AT 46 PERCENT	-1885	1644	5278	8267	5869	2900	666.4
PROFIT AFTER TAX	-2213	1930	6196	9705	6889	3404	782.3
INFLATION FACTOR	1.100	1.210	1.331	1.464	1.611	1.772	1.949

CASH FLOW ANALYSIS

INCOME FROM SALES	522.5	12887	32610	48901	35834	19717	0
COSTS FROM OPERATION	837.1	7729	19552	29345	21492	11830	0
OTHER COST	2200	0	0	0	0	0	0
TAX ON OPERATIONS	-1885	1644	5278	8267	5869	2900	0
CASH FLOW FROM OPERA	-629.6	3513	7779	11289	8473	4987	0
CHANGE IN WORKING CA	-550	-738.7	-1972	-1629	1307	1582	2002
CAPITAL INVESTMENT A	10000	0	0	0	0	0	1282
TOTAL INFLOWS	-1180	2774	5807	9659	9780	6569	3284
TOTAL OUTFLOWS	12160	0	0	0	0	0	0
NET CASH FLOW	-13340	2774	5807	9659	9780	6569	3284
NET PRESENT VALUE	-13143	-11216	-7856	-3197	732.7	2933	3849
DISCOUNT RATE	.2000	.2000	.2000	.2000	.2000	.2000	.2000

FIGURE 6-11. THE GUANO PROJECT
(Continued)

As you go over this model and read the results you should note the following:

- The capital investment occurs at the start of Year 1. The salvage value refers to the anticipated sale for scrap. The difference between book value and what you realize from the sale for scrap is taxable income in Year 7.

- In using the straight line depreciation function, the salvage fraction is 5%, since you will write the investment down from $10,000 to $500. That is, at the end of its life, the investment is worth 5% of what it was at the beginning.

- The depreciation function computes and prints out the annual depreciation, year-end book value, and accumulated depreciation in that order.

- Working capital is an input. Total book value is obtained by adding working capital to year-end book value.

- Pre-investment costs are shown at the beginning of Year 1. These costs are called out separately since, although they form part of the investment costs for determining present value in cash flow analysis, they are not capitalized and hence not depreciated.

- The salvage value in Year 7 results in a profit after taxes which, in turn, contributes to the present value in the cash flow analysis.

- In the cash flow analysis, the cash flow from operations is the difference between sales income and outflows for costs and taxes. To find the total inflows, add in the change in working capital.

- The contribution to cash flow from salvage is obtained by subtracting the taxes paid ($666) from the proceeds realized ($1948).

Figure 6-11 also illustrates several points about IFPS.

- The same variable name is used several times; for example, SALES, WORKING CAPITAL, OTHER COSTS. IFPS can give strange results if you are not careful about such multiple use. The rule followed is that the value used is the most recent previous one for which data is given. When in doubt, use line number references since line numbers are absolute values and do not need to be interpreted. You will see some examples where variables are repeated to improve readability, and the reference on the righthand side is to the previous mention of the same variable.

- In the case of the STLINE DEPR function, different names are used for the output variables (depreciation, year-dend book value, and accumulated depreication) in Lines 70 and 80 and 260 and 270 .This use of multiple names for output variables is mandatory because IFPS adds up all depreciation values with the same name. In our case, all we want to do is repeat the information.

- Because of the need for repetition and the linkages that exist, we wrote a single model containing all three cases. However, we used the ability in the SOLVE option to print only a portion of the model to create separate printouts of the three cases.

EXERCISE: Rewrite Figure 6-11 with a minimum number of lines; that is, without duplicating any information. Then use the SOLVE option to select lines of printout so as to duplicate the output obtained in Figure 6-11.

6.7 MEAN AND VARIANCE OF THE RETURN FROM A PORTFOLIO OF TWO STOCKS

The simplest portfolio is one consisting of two assets, such as stocks. Figure 6-12 illustrates the computation of the mean and variance of such a portfolio.

In this calculation it is assumed that a different amount is invested in each stock and that each has a different rate of return and different standard deviation of the rate of return associated with it. Furthermore, the formulas allow for the returns from the two investments to be correlated (e.g., if the stocks are in the same industry, their prices may move up and down together). The formulas themselves, written in IFPS style, are the standard formulas for expected value (mean) and variance (see Section 7.1). Specifically:

$$\text{MEAN} = \text{INVESTMENT1*RETURN1} + \text{INVESTMENT2*RETURN2} \tag{6-12}$$

$$\begin{aligned}\text{VARIANCE} = {} & \text{INVESTMENT1*INVESTMENT1*VARIANCE1} \\ & + \text{INVESTMENT2*INVESTMENT2*VARIANCE2} \\ & + \text{2*INVESTMENT1*INVESTMENT2} \\ & \quad \text{*CORRELATION COEFFICIENT12*STD.DEVIATION1} \\ & \quad \text{*STANDARD DEVIATION2}\end{aligned} \tag{6-13}$$

In both equations the investment and the return are expressed as percentages. This can also be seen in Figure 6-12 where 33% of the investment is in Stock 1. Note that you need information on both the investments and on the correlation between them to use these formulas.

```
MODEL MEANVAR  VERSION OF  05/07/86  22:31
10 COLUMNS 1
20 *
30 *MEAN AND VARIANCE OF A PORTFOLIO OF TWO STOCKS
40 *
50 INVEST1=.33
60 INVEST2=1-INVEST1
70 RETURN1= .21
80 RETURN2 =.15
90 STD DEVIATION1=.40
100STD DEVIATION2=.20
110 CORRELATION=.2
115*
120 VARIANCE1=STD DEVIATION1*STD DEVIATION1
130 VARIANCE2=STD DEVIATION2*STD DEVIATION2
140*
150 MEAN = INVEST1*RETURN1 + INVEST2*RETURN2
160 VARIANCE=INVEST1*INVEST1*VARIANCE1+INVEST2*INVEST2*VARIANCE2 +'
161 2*INVEST1*INVEST2*CORRELATION*STD DEVIATION1*STD DEVIATION2
170 STANDARD DEVIATION = XPOWERY(VARIANCE,0.5)
END OF MODEL
```

FIGURE 6-12. MEAN AND VARIANCE OF THE RETURN FROM A PORTFOLIO OF TWO STOCKS

(This Figure Continued on the Next Page)

```
? SOLVE
MODEL MEANVAR  VERSION OF  05/07/86  22:31 -- 1 COLUMNS 12 VARIABLES
ENTER SOLVE OPTIONS
? ALL

                                    1

MEAN AND VARIANCE OF A PORTFOLIO OF TWO STOCKS

INVEST1                          .3300
INVEST2                          .6700
RETURN1                          .2100
RETURN2                          .1500
STD DEVIATION1                   .4000
STD DEVIATION2                   .2000
CORRELATION                      .2000

VARIANCE1                        .1600
VARIANCE2                        .0400

MEAN                             .1698
VARIANCE                         .0425
STANDARD DEVIATION               .2060
```

FIGURE 6-12. MEAN AND VARIANCE OF THE RETURN FROM A PORTFOLIO OF TWO STOCKS
(Continued)

EXERCISE: Extend the formula for the average return from a given portfolio (i.e., Equation (6-12)) to a portfolio containing n stocks, where n could be 3, 4, 5, etc. Implement your formula in an IFPS program in which you evaluate the average return of a portfolio consisting of 20% returning 8%, 30% returning 12%, 42% returning 15%, and 8% losing 3%.

EXERCISE: (more difficult) Look up the general formula for finding the variance of a portfolio containing many stocks. Implement this formula in IFPS for the following data:

INVESTMENT No.	Amt.	RETURN	STD.DEV.	CORRELATION COEFFICIENTS i-1	i-2	i-3	i-4
1:	20%	8%	4%	-	.34	.78	.95
2:	30%	12%	7%	.34	-	.43	.05
3:	42%	15%	9%	.78	.43	-	.50
4:	8%	–3%	5%	.95	.05	.50	-

The correlation coefficients in column i-1 ,for example, refer to the correlations between 1-1, 2-1, 3-1, and 4-1.

6.8 CAPITAL ASSET PRICING MODEL

The Capital Asset Pricing Model is a simple model that relates the risk and return associated with investments. The key quantity in this model is beta, a measure of how sensitive the return on an investment is to movements in the market. Beta is really the ratio of the standard deviation of a well-diversified portfolio of assets compared to the standard deviation of a market portfolio. The beta of the market is 1.0. The beta of risk-free treasury bonds is 0.0. A beta of, say, 2.0 implies an investment that outperforms the market when the market is going up but goes down much faster than the market when the market return is less than the risk-free rate. A beta of, 0.3 implies the investment is relatively insensitive to market fluctuations.

The concept of beta is related to the concept of risk premium, that is the additional return that must be offered investors to induce them to accept the risk associated with a given investment. Risks are expressed in terms of annual rates of return and three quantities are of interests

1. The risk-free rate, rf, (e.g. Treasury bills)

2. The market risk, rm, (based on a portfolio consisting of all assets; historically, the market risk has averaged about 8.8% above the risk-free rate).

3. The expected rate of return of the investment, r.

These quantities are related to one another and beta by:

$$r = beta*rm + (1\text{-}beta)*rf \tag{6-14}$$

The expected risk premium is (r – rf) and the expected market risk premium is (rm–rf). Figures 6-13 and 6-14 show small IFPS models for finding r and for finding beta given the other quantities.

```
MODEL BETA  VERSION OF  09/12/81   13:04
10 COLUMNS 1
20*
30*  CAPITAL ASSET PRICING MODEL
40*
50 RISK= BETA *RETURN OF MARKET + (1-BETA)*RISK FREE RATE
60*
70 RISK PREMIUM = RISK - RISK FREE RATE
80 MARKET RISK PREMIUM = RETURN OF MARKET - RISK FREE RATE
90*
100*DATA
110*
120 RISK FREE RATE=.08
130 RETURN OF MARKET =.168
140 BETA =.8
END OF MODEL
```

FIGURE 6-13. SOLVING THE CAPITAL ASSET PRICING MODEL TO DETERMINE RISK
(This Figure Continued on the Next Page)

```
? solve
MODEL BETA  VERSION OF  09/12/81  13:04 -- 1 COLUMNS 6 VARIABLES
ENTER SOLVE OPTIONS
? all
                                    1

 CAPITAL ASSET PRICING MODEL

RISK                             .1504

RISK PREMIUM                     .0704
MARKET RISK PREMIUM              .0880

DATA

RISK FREE RATE                   .0800
RETURN OF MARKET                 .1680
BETA                             .8000
```

FIGURE 6-13. SOLVING THE CAPITAL ASSET PRICING MODEL TO DETERMINE RISK (Continued)

The concept of beta can be extended to leveraged investments; that is, investments in which part of the capital is obtained by borrowing. If you view the interest paid on the borrowing as rf and let rE be the return on equity, then:

$$r^*(DEBT + EQUITY) = rf^*DEBT + rE^*EQUITY \qquad (6\text{-}15)$$

Solving for the rate of return:

$$r = rf^*DEBT/(DEBT+EQUITY)+rE^*EQUITY/(DEBT+EQUITY) \qquad (6\text{-}16)$$

that is, the expected return on the total investment is a weighted average of the return on the debt, rf, and on the equity investment, rE.

The same approach applies to a firm and its leveraging of capital investment. The beta for an asset which is partly financed by borrowing is similar to Equation (6-16):

$$\begin{aligned} beta(ASSET) = {} & beta(DEBT)^*DEBT/(DEBT + EQUITY) \\ & + beta(EQUITY)^*EQUITY/(DEBT+EQUITY) \end{aligned} \qquad (6\text{-}17)$$

If you assume that the debt is risk free, then beta(DEBT) = 0. You can then solve Equation (6-17) for beta(EQUITY):

$$beta(EQUITY) = beta(ASSET)^*(1 + DEBT/EQUITY) \qquad (6\text{-}18)$$

Equation (6-18)shows that the risk (i.e., beta) increases with debt. For example, if you borrow an amount equal to your investment, DEBT/EQUITY=1 and your risk has doubled since then beta(EQUITY)= 2*beta(ASSET).

```
MODEL BETA2  VERSION OF  05/25/82  15:12
10 COLUMNS 1
20 *
30* FINDING BETA
40 BETA=(REQUIRED RATE OF RETURN-RISK FREE RATE)/(RETURN OF MARKET'
41 -RISK FREE RATE)
50*
60*DATA
70*
80 REQUIRED RATE OF RETURN = .12
90 RETURN OF MARKET = .168
100 RISK FREE RATE = .08
END OF MODEL
? solve
MODEL BETA2  VERSION OF  05/25/82  15:12 -- 1 COLUMNS 4 VARIABLES
ENTER SOLVE OPTIONS
? all

                                        1

 FINDING BETA

BETA                              .4545

DATA

REQUIRED RATE OF RETURN           .1200
RETURN OF MARKET                  .1680
RISK FREE RATE                    .0800
```

FIGURE 6-14. SOLVING THE CAPITAL ASSET PRICING MODEL TO FIND BETA

Figure 6-15 illustrates the effect of leverage on return. A total investment of $20,000 based on $10,000 cash and $10,000 debt at 5% interest is assumed. Figure 6-15 shows the percentage return on the cash investment for different percentage returns on the asset. The results are also plotted in Figure 6-15 using the IFPS PLOT routine. (See Sec. 4.3 for the options available to you in PLOT.)

It will help you to interpret the plot by connecting the points with the same numbers to obtain curves for the results. The curve for interest (shown by numeral 2) is horizontal, reflecting the risk-free investment. The curve for percentage return on asset (shown as 1) goes through the origin with a slope of 1. (Do you see why?) The percentage return on investment (shown as 3) has a slope of 2 which reflects the fact that beta (EQUITY) = 2*BETA(ASSET) for this case where equity equals debt.

The PLOT routine, although giving very simple plots, is helpful in visualizing the answers. However, you have to be careful in how you set your plots up. You will notice that in Figure 6-15 we carefully labeled COLUMNS so that (1) the headings would be the same as percent return on asset and (2) so that they would be equally spaced. The reason for this choice was twofold:

- The plot routine uses column headings for labeling the X axis.
- Equal spacing of values assures that the linear relation of Equation (6-18) would be reflected in linearity in the output. Non-equal spacing would have resulted in distortion (i.e., non-linearity).

6.9 ANALYZING PROJECT PROPOSALS--Break-Even and Sensitivity Analysis

Managers, when presented with a project proposal, usually try to ascertain the range of conditions they may face because of the risks involved. A variety of analyses help in understanding these risks. The approaches used include:

- break-even analysis
- sensitivity analysis
- scenarios
- simulation

In this and the following two sections we will explore these approaches in terms of a particular example, the Electric Car Project. The situation is relatively straightforward. A manufacturer is considering whether or not to enter the market for electrically powered vehicles. He has the following estimates from his marketing group: For an investment of $150 million, revenues of $375 million will be generated for each of the next 10 years. The annual variable cost is estimated to be $300 million, the annual fixed cost $30 million, and annual straight line depreciation $15 million. The company has a 50% marginal tax rate and a 10% opportunity cost of capital. The resultant IFPS model, shown in Figure 6-16, indicates a net present value of $34.4 million.

```
MODEL LEVERAGE  VERSION OF  09/07/81  15:23
10 COLUMNS -10,0,10,20,30,40
20 *
30 * EXAMPLE OF POSSIBLE OUTCOMES OF LEVERAGED INVESTMENT
40 * $10000 INVESTED AND $10000 BORROWED
45 * VARIOUS RETURNS ON ASSET
50*
60 PCT RETURN ON ASSET = -10,PREVIOUS +10
70 DOLLAR RETURN = TOTAL INVESTMENT * PCT RETURN ON ASSET/100
80 INTEREST = AMT BORROWED * INTEREST RATE
85 PCT INTEREST ON DEBT =100*INTEREST RATE
90 NET DOLLAR RETURN = DOLLAR RETURN - INTEREST
100 PCT RETURN ON INVESTMENT = 100*NET DOLLAR RETURN/INVESTMENT
110*
120* DATA
130*
140 INVESTMENT=10000
150 AMT BORROWED =10000
160 TOTAL INVESTMENT =INVESTMENT + AMT BORROWED
170 INTEREST RATE = .05
END OF MODEL
? solve
MODEL LEVERAGE  VERSION OF  09/07/81  15:23 -- 6 COLUMNS 10
VARIABLES
ENTER SOLVE OPTIONS
? all
                          -10        0       10       20       30       40


 EXAMPLE OF POSSIBLE OUTCOMES OF LEVERAGED INVESTMENT
 $10000 INVESTED AND $10000 BORROWED
 VARIOUS RETURNS ON ASSET

PCT RETURN ON ASSET       -10        0       10       20       30       40
DOLLAR RETURN           -2000        0     2000     4000     6000     8000
INTEREST                  500      500      500      500      500      500
NET DOLLAR RETURN       -2500     -500     1500     3500     5500     7500
PCT INTEREST ON DEBT        5        5        5        5        5        5
PCT RETURN ON INVEST      -25       -5       15       35       55       75

 DATA

INVESTMENT              10000    10000    10000    10000    10000    10000
AMT BORROWED            10000    10000    10000    10000    10000    10000
TOTAL INVESTMENT        20000    20000    20000    20000    20000    20000
INTEREST RATE           .0500    .0500    .0500    .0500    .0500    .0500
```

FIGURE 6-15. FINDING THE POSSIBLE OUTCOMES OF A LEVERAGED INVESTMENT USING THE CAPITAL ASSET PRICING MODEL
(This Figure Continued on the Next Page)

```
ENTER SOLVE OPTIONS
? plot
pct return on asset, pct interest on debt,pct return on investment



    80
                                                                   3



    60
                                                       3



    40                                                             1
                                           3
                                                       1


    20                                     1
                               3
                               1

       2           2           2           2           2           2
     0 +-----------1-----------+-----------+-----------+-----------+
                   3

       1

   -20
       3



      -10         0          10          20          30          40

       1 - PCT RETURN ON ASSET
       2 - PCT INTEREST ON DEBT
       3 - PCT RETURN ON INVESTMENT
```

FIGURE 6-15. FINDING THE POSSIBLE OUTCOMES OF A LEVERAGED INVESTMENT USING THE CAPITAL ASSET PRICING MODEL
(Continued)

```
MODEL CAR  VERSION OF  09/07/81  20:20
1 COLUMNS 1-10
10 * ELECTRIC CAR PROJECT FORECASTS
20 *
30 INVESTMENT=150,0
40 REVENUE =375
50 VARIABLE COST=300
60 FIXED COST =30
70 DEPRECIATION =15
80 PRETAX PROFIT =REVENUE-VARIABLE COST-FIXED COST -DEPRECIATION
90 TAX = .5 *PRETAX PROFIT
100 *
110 NET PROFIT = PRETAX PROFIT -TAX
120*
130 OPERATING CASH FLOW =NET PROFIT + DEPRECIATION
140 DISCOUNT RATE =.1
150*
160 NET PRESENT VALUE = NPVC(OPERATING CASH FLOW,'
161 DISCOUNT RATE,INVESTMENT)
END OF MODEL
? solve
MODEL CAR  VERSION OF  09/07/81  20:20 -- 10 COLUMNS 11 VARIABLES
ENTER SOLVE OPTIONS
? all
```

	1	2	5	10
ELECTRIC CAR PROJECT FORECASTS				
INVESTMENT	150	0	0	0
REVENUE	375	375	375	375
VARIABLE COST	300	300	300	300
FIXED COST	30	30	30	30
DEPRECIATION	15	15	15	15
PRETAX PROFIT	30	30	30	30
TAX	15	15	15	15
NET PROFIT	15	15	15	15
OPERATING CASH FLOW	30	30	30	30
DISCOUNT RATE	.1000	.1000	.1000	.1000
NET PRESENT VALUE	-122.7	-97.93	-36.28	34.34

FIGURE 6-16. ELECTRIC CAR MODEL: ASSUMPTIONS NOT SHOWN

So far, so good. However, the model presented as in Figure 6-16 hides the assumptions made. It is essential that the assumptions made be spelled out because you cannot understand the results otherwise. Figure 6-17 is a modification of Figure 6-16 which shows that the following assumptions were made by marketing:

1. The total market for cars will be 10 million units.

2. Your company's share of the market will be 1% of the total car market.

3. You will be able to price individual cars at $3750.

4. You will be able to produce cars at $3000 per unit variable cost.

5. Fixed costs will be $30 million.

The model in Figure 6-17 is more complex because you have to derive some of the quantities (e.g, unit sales) and because you have to be careful about scaling quantities so they are in compatible units. For example, revenue must be divided by 1 million to put it in the same units as the costs so that profit can be computed.

```
MODEL CAR2  VERSION OF  09/10/81  22:19
1 COLUMNS 1-10
10 * ELECTRIC CAR PROJECT FORECASTS INCLUDING ASSUMPTIONS
20*
30 INVESTMENT=150,0
40 REVENUE = UNIT SALES * PRICE PER UNIT/1000000
50 VARIABLE COST = VARIABLE COST PER UNIT * UNIT SALES/1000000
60 FIXED COST = L230
70 DEPRECIATION = 15
80 PRETAX PROFIT= REVENUE-VARIABLE COST-FIXED COST-DEPRECIATION
90 TAX = .5* PRETAX PROFIT
100*
110 NET PROFIT = PRETAX PROFIT - TAX
120 OPERATING CASH FLOW =NET PROFIT + DEPRECIATION
130*
140 NET PRESENT VALUE = NPVC(OPERATING CASH FLOW,'
141 DISCOUNT RATE,INVESTMENT)
150*
160*ASSUMPTIONS
170*
180 TOTAL MARKET =10000000
190 MARKET SHARE = .01
200 UNIT SALES =TOTAL MARKET * MARKET SHARE
210 PRICE PER UNIT = 3750
220 VARIABLE COST PER UNIT =3000
230 FIXED COST =30
240 DISCOUNT RATE =.1
END OF MODEL
```

FIGURE 6-17. ELECTRIC CAR MODEL: ASSUMPTIONS SHOWN

(This Figure Continued on the Next Page)

```
? solve
MODEL CAR2  VERSION OF  09/10/81  22:19 -- 10 COLUMNS 17 VARIABLES
ENTER SOLVE OPTIONS
? all
                              1        2        5       10

 ELECTRIC CAR PROJECT FORECASTS INCLUDING ASSUMPTIONS

INVESTMENT                  150        0        0        0
REVENUE                     375      375      375      375
VARIABLE COST               300      300      300      300
FIXED COST                   30       30       30       30
DEPRECIATION                 15       15       15       15
PRETAX PROFIT                30       30       30       30
TAX                          15       15       15       15

NET PROFIT                   15       15       15       15
OPERATING CASH FLOW          30       30       30       30

NET PRESENT VALUE        -122.7   -97.93   -36.28    34.34

ASSUMPTIONS

TOTAL MARKET                1E7      1E7      1E7      1E7
MARKET SHARE              .0100    .0100    .0100    .0100
UNIT SALES               100000   100000   100000   100000
PRICE PER UNIT             3750     3750     3750     3750
VARIABLE COST PER UN       3000     3000     3000     3000
FIXED COST                   30       30       30       30
DISCOUNT RATE             .1000    .1000    .1000    .1000
```

FIGURE 6-17. ELECTRIC CAR MODEL: ASSUMPTIONS SHOWN (Continued)

All four of the above assumptions are subject to challenge. The analysis methods are really designed to determine the risks involved if the assumptions turn out not to be true. The simplest form of analysis of the assumptions is break-even analysis. Break-even analysis is used to determine the conditions under which the net present value of an investment is 0; that is, the point at which you are indifferent between undertaking and not undertaking the investment. Typically, break-even analysis is done on one variable at a time. The variables used most often are sales and cost. Since we are trying to find the point at which net present value is 0, we can again use the interval halving technique first described in Section 6.3.3 and illustrated in Figure 6-7. This is done in Figure 6-18 for a break-even analysis on sales. The result is that the project will break even if unit sales are as low as 85,000, all other things remaining the same. From a finance point of view, it is important to recognize that the appropriate criterion for break-even is zero net present value, not an accounting break-even of cash in equals cash out. The latter is the kind of calculation done for payback period (See Section 6.4.1.)

```
? what if
WHAT IF CASE 1
ENTER STATEMENTS
? unit sales = 50000
? solve
ENTER SOLVE OPTIONS
? column 10
? net present value

***** WHAT IF CASE 1 *****
1 WHAT IF STATEMENT PROCESSED


                                  10

NET PRESENT VALUE          -80.87

ENTER SOLVE OPTIONS
? what if
WHAT IF CASE 2
ENTER STATEMENTS
? unit sales = 75000
? solve
ENTER SOLVE OPTIONS
? net present value


***** WHAT IF CASE 2 *****
1 WHAT IF STATEMENT PROCESSED
                                  10

NET PRESENT VALUE          -23.27

ENTER SOLVE OPTIONS
? what if
WHAT IF CASE 3
ENTER STATEMENTS
? unit sales = 87500
? solve
ENTER SOLVE OPTIONS
? net present value


***** WHAT IF CASE 3 *****
1 WHAT IF STATEMENT PROCESSED

                                  10

NET PRESENT VALUE           5.534
```

FIGURE 6-18. BREAK-EVEN ANALYSIS ON ELECTRIC CAR PROJECT

(This Figure Continued on the Next Page)

EXERCISE: Use the SENSITIVITY analysis feature of IFPS to find the break-even point for sales. Assume that you do not know the answer given above and find a rational way of applying sensitivity analysis to solve the problem.

The major problem with sensitivity analysis is that it assumes that changes are independent of one another and therefore that changes in one assumption will not affect other assumptions. This is usually not true. For example, if you come in with a high unit variable cost for your car you are likely to have to raise your price which, in turn, may reduce your market share. Scenarios and simulation, discussed in the next two sections, are a way of overcoming these shortcomings.

6.10 USING SCENARIOS TO EVALUATE PROJECT PROPOSALS

A scenario is a set of assumptions made about future outcomes. Typically, a manager will use a number of alternative scenarios as a way of understanding the risks in a project. A scenario usually revolves around one or two ideas or combinations of ideas which are carried through to their logical conclusion. A good scenario must meet three criteria:

1. The conditions assumed must be logically consistent.

2. The conditions must be possible, that is, they could happen.

3. The conditions must be plausible, that is, they must be believable to a decision maker.

The simplest use of scenarios involves assuming that there are three possible outcomes, a worst-worst case in which everything goes wrong (e.g., total market down, costs up), a nominal case in which everything occurs at the expected value (i.e. the initial calculation which serves as a base case), and a best-best case in which everything is favorable (e.g., total market up, costs down). The best-best and worst-worst scenarios rarely happen in the real world; thus, they are not plausible. However, they are often used to bracket the range of outcomes that have to be considered. The easiest way to create a scenario in IFPS is to run a WHAT IF case in which a number of variables are changed simultaneously. For example, to obtain worst-worst and best-best scenarios for the electric car example of Figure 6-17, you could use the set of pessimistic and optimistic values, respectively, given in the EXERCISE above in two WHAT IF cases. Figure 6-19 shows the worst-worst case results. Note that in this case, some values are higher (e.g., unit variable cost and fixed cost) while others are lower (e.g., market size and market share). More important, the worst-worst case is not plausible since a firm faced with a selling price below its variable cost would either go on a cost-reduction program or would withdraw from the market

EXERCISE: Use the set of optimistic values in the previous EXERCISE to obtain a best-best case. You should find a net present value of 240 million.

The net present value results of the worst-worst case (loss of 238 million), the nominal case of Figure 6-17 (gain of 34 million) and of the best-best case (gain of 240 million) are sufficiently broad that they really don't help in decision making. Under these conditions, you may want to examine specific consistent, possible, plausible scenarios. One such scenario would be the possibility of another sharp rise in world oil prices combined with a

```
? what if
WHAT IF CASE 1
ENTER STATEMENTS
? total market = 9000000
? market share =.004
? price per unit = 3500
? variable cost per unit = 3600
? fixed cost = 40
? solve
ENTER SOLVE OPTIONS
? L30 thru L140


***** WHAT IF CASE 1 *****
5 WHAT IF STATEMENTS PROCESSED
```

	1	2	5	10
INVESTMENT	150	0	0	0
REVENUE	126	126	126	126
VARIABLE COST	129.6	129.6	129.6	129.6
FIXED COST	40	40	40	40
DEPRECIATION	15	15	15	15
PRETAX PROFIT	-58.60	-58.60	-58.60	-58.60
TAX	-29.30	-29.30	-29.30	-29.30
NET PROFIT	-29.30	-29.30	-29.30	-29.30
OPERATING CASH FLOW	-14.30	-14.30	-14.30	-14.30
NET PRESENT VALUE	-163	-174.8	-204.2	-237.9

FIGURE 6-19. WORST-WORST CASE FOR ELECTRIC CAR PROJECT

recession and inflation. In such a case, the total market might go down precipitously, even below the pessimistic estimate (say, to 8 million units) but the market share for electric cars might go up (say, to 1.3%). Because unit variable cost and fixed costs would go up under inflation, price would also have to go up. The details of the assumptions and the results of this scenario are shown in Figure 6-20.

EXERCISE: Suppose you learn that a competitor is working on a steam-powered car that would compete with the electric car. If this development is successful, it would enter the market three years from now and would reduce your market share by 0.1% each year (i.e., to 0.9% in Year 4, 0.8% in Year 5, etc.). You also expect that you should be able to achieve production economies by the start of Year 5 that would reduce the unit variable cost to $2800 and would allow you to reduce price. You estimate that each $100 in price reduction allows you to gain 0.1% of the market. Set up and run this scenario. (Hint: You may have to experiment to determine what pricing policy is appropriate under these conditions.) What do you conclude from the results? What probability would you assign to the occurrence of this scenario? Justify your estimate. Based on your estimate of probability of occurrence, how seriously would the results affect your decision?

```
WHAT IF CASE 2
ENTER STATEMENTS
? total market = 8000000
? market share = .013
? price per unit = 4313
? variable cost per unit = 3450
? fixed cost =35
? solve
ENTER SOLVE OPTIONS
? L30 thru L140

***** WHAT IF CASE 2 *****
5 WHAT IF STATEMENTS PROCESSED
```

	1	2	5	10
INVESTMENT	150	0	0	0
REVENUE	448.6	448.6	448.6	448.6
VARIABLE COST	358.8	358.8	358.8	358.8
FIXED COST	35	35	35	35
DEPRECIATION	15	15	15	15
PRETAX PROFIT	39.75	39.75	39.75	39.75
TAX	19.88	19.88	19.88	19.88
NET PROFIT	19.88	19.88	19.88	19.88
OPERATING CASH FLOW	34.88	34.88	34.88	34.88
NET PRESENT VALUE	-118.3	-89.47	-17.79	64.30

FIGURE 6-20. HIGH OIL PRICE AND RECESSION SCENARIO FOR ELECTRIC CAR PROJECT

6.11 USING SIMULATION TO EVALUATE PROJECT PROPOSALS

In this section we discuss the use of simulation to evaluate risky investments. Before reading this section, go back to Chapter V, which describes the use of probability distributions and MONTE CARLO commands in IFPS as a way of running financial simulations. Once you have mastered that Chapter, return to this section.

As a first step consider the case in which the annual total market is expected to range from a pessimistic 9 million to an optimistic 11 million, with an average market of 10 million. If we believe that all values between 9 and 11 million are equally likely, we could represent the probability distribution of sales by a uniform distribution and use the UNIRAND function. If, however, we believe that the further away from 10 million the less likely the outcome, we may want to use a triangular distribution of the form TRIRAND(9000000,10000000,11000000). This is done in Figure 6-21. Here we introduce three WHAT IF cases for the Electric Car Model. The total market is represented by a triangular distribution as follows:

WHAT IF CASE	TOTAL MARKET
3	TRIRAND (9000000,10000000,11000000)
4	TRIRANDR(9000000,10000000,11000000)
5	10000000*TRIRAND(.9,1,1.1),PREVIOUS*TRIRAND(.9,1,1.1)

In the first case, in each Monte Carlo iteration, a market value is picked at the beginning of Year 1 and followed for all ten years. In the second, the total market varies from year to year, picking a different value between 9 and 11 million each year. The most interesting case is the last one, in which a value is picked from the distribution in the first year, and the value in each subsequent year depends on the value in the previous year. The results in Figure 6-21 show that, on the average, the first two cases are little different than the deterministic case; however, if the forecast fluctuations from year to year are tied together, the net present value increases from 34 to approximately 38. (Can you explain why these results should occur?)

```
WHAT IF CASE 3
ENTER STATEMENTS
? total market = trirand(9000000,10000000,11000000)
? monte carlo 200
ENTER MONTE CARLO OPTIONS
? net present value,none

***** WHAT IF CASE 3 *****

                    FREQUENCY TABLE

 PROBABILITY OF VALUE BEING GREATER THAN INDICATED

          90     80     70     60     50     40     30     20     10

 NET PRESENT VALUE
   10   20.1   24.2   26.9   30.0   33.8   36.0   39.5   41.8   46.3

                    SAMPLE STATISTICS

              MEAN   STD DEV SKEWNESS KURTOSIS  10PC CONF MEAN  90PC

   NET PRESENT VALUE
     10     33.21     9.826       .1       2.3       32.32      34.10
```

FIGURE 6-21. UNCERTAINTY IN MARKET FOR ELECTRIC CAR PROJECT:Simulation Results
(This Figure Cntinued on the Next Page)

```
? what if
WHAT IF CASE 4
ENTER STATEMENTS
? total market = trirandr(9000000,10000000,11000000)
? monte carlo 200
ENTER MONTE CARLO OPTIONS
? frequency net present value,none

***** WHAT IF CASE 4 *****

                    FREQUENCY TABLE

  PROBABILITY OF VALUE BEING GREATER THAN INDICATED
          90     80     70     60     50     40     30     20     10

 NET PRESENT VALUE
   10  30.08  31.88  32.72  33.41  34.24  35.05  36.28  37.36  38.14

                    SAMPLE STATISTICS

             MEAN   STD DEV SKEWNESS KURTOSIS  10PC CONF MEAN  90PC

   NET PRESENT VALUE
     10     34.38    3.106      .1       2.5       34.10      34.66

? what if
WHAT IF CASE 5
ENTER STATEMENTS
? total market=10000000*trirand(.9,1,1.1),previous*trirand(.9,1,1.1)
? monte carlo 200
ENTER MONTE CARLO OPTIONS
? frequency net present value,none

***** WHAT IF CASE 5 *****

                    FREQUENCY TABLE

  PROBABILITY OF VALUE BEING GREATER THAN INDICATED
          90     80     70     60     50     40     30     20     10

 NET PRESENT VALUE
   10   -9.4    3.8   15.1   22.8   32.4   40.9   51.9   68.9   94.2

                    SAMPLE STATISTICS

             MEAN   STD DEV SKEWNESS KURTOSIS  10PC CONF MEAN  90PC

   NET PRESENT VALUE
     10     37.01   37.08      .5       2.6       33.66      40.37
```

FIGURE 6-21. UNCERTAINTY IN MARKET FOR ELECTRIC CAR PROJECT: Simulation Results (Continued)

A more sophisticated simulation introduces probability distributions for all of the variables. This is done in Figure 6-22 where we show the result of using triangular distributions for each of the input values. The end points of these distributions are the pessimistic and optimistic values used in the exercises above. When all variables are allowed to vary simultaneously, the result is a decrease in the expected net present value! In fact, the net present value becomes negative because the average net profit is reduced to five and hence the operating cash flow is reduced from 30 to 20. Here, as a user of the model you must be very careful in interpreting results. Why did this happen? Introducing uncertainty into which variables or combination of variables caused the reduction of operating cash flow? Given that the frequency table indicates that the net present value is positive less than 40% of the time, do you still undertake the project? The independent setting of variable cost per unit and price per unit can lead you to combinations in which you sell the car for less than your variable cost. Should you change your model to make price per unit be, say, 1.25*variable cost or perhaps model a more sophisticated pricing scheme that takes both variable and fixed costs into account since realistic pricing would do so? The point of the matter is that you have to be very careful in using simulation to make sure that you represent possible cases accurately. In particular, as Figure 6-22 illustrates so vividly, you must look for interactions among variables and must modify your model so that you represent these interactions correctly. They can affect the validity of your results.

One final note. The model used for simulation can also be used to create scenarios. All you have to do is decide which probability distributions should take on their HIGH,MOSTP, MEAN, or LOW values (see Section 5.7 for a discussion of these options).

EXERCISE: Revise the model in Figure 6-22 to reflect the relation between price per unit and variable and fixed costs. State and justify the assumptions that you make about this relation. Run your revised model and analyze the results for reasonableness and accuracy.

EXERCISE: Use the HIGH and LOW options to create the best-best and worst-worst scenarios of Section 6-10.

6.12 THE BLACK-SCHOLES FORMULA FOR CALL OPTIONS

Options allow investors the right to buy or sell stocks at agreed-upon prices at some time in the future. The right to buy is a "call option" and the right to sell is a "put option." The problem faced by the investor is whether or not to buy the option at its market price.

The Black-Scholes formula for the appropriate price of a call option is based on the assumption that call options are priced in such a way that the average return on portfolios in which all risk is hedged away equals the risk-free rate of interest. (Recall the Capital Asset Pricing Model which was discussed in Section 6.8). The formula appears at first glance to be quite complex. It is given by:

PV OF CALL OPTION = P*N(d1)-EX*exp(-rf*t)*N(d2) (6-16)

where P is the current price of the stock
N(d) is the cumulative normal probability density function evaluated at d
EX is the exercise price of the option
rf is the risk free rate

```
? what if
WHAT IF CASE 6
ENTER STATEMENTS
? total market = trirandr(9000000,10000000,11000000)
? market share = trirand(.004,.01,.016)
? price per unit = trirand(3500,3750,3800)
? fixed cost = trirand(20,30,40)
? monte carlo 200
ENTER MONTE CARLO OPTIONS
? freq

***** WHAT IF CASE 6 *****

                         FREQUENCY TABLE

  PROBABILITY OF VALUE BEING GREATER THAN INDICATED

           90       80       70       60       50       40       30       20       10

 OPERATING CASH FLOW
   10   13.97    17.01    20.67    22.74    24.77    26.92    28.60    33.02    37.85

 NET PROFIT
   10   -1.03     2.01     5.67     7.74     9.77    11.92    13.60    18.02    22.85

 NET PRESENT VALUE
   10   -67.3    -45.2    -23.6     -9.9      2.6     12.9     28.7     53.9     83.6

                        SAMPLE STATISTICS

                 MEAN     STD DEV SKEWNESS KURTOSIS   10PC CONF MEAN  90PC

   OPERATING CASH FLOW
     10         25.26      9.204       .4        2.8        24.43      26.09

   NET PROFIT
     10         10.26      9.204       .4        2.8        9.426      11.09

   NET PRESENT VALUE
     10         5.695      57.40       .4        2.8        .4997      10.89
```

FIGURE 6-22. ELECTRIC AR SIMULATION WITH INPUTS TRIANGULARLY DISTRIBUTED

t is the time to exercise date (in years)
and d1 and d2 are given respectively by:

$$d1 = (\log(P/EX) + rf{*}t + VARIANCE{*}t/2)/(STD\ DEVIATION{*}\sqrt{t})$$

$$d2 = (\log(P/EX) + rf{*}t - VARIANCE{*}t/2)/(STD\ DEVIATION{*}\sqrt{t})$$

These formulas are quite formidable when evaluated by hand, with the aid of a hand-calculator, or even through the use of tables. However, IFPS has the needed built-in functions to make this evaluation quite simple. Figure 6-23 shows the implementation of the formula in IFPS, including a sample set of data. The natural log function (NATLOG), the exponential function (NATEXP), and the XPOWERY function (see Section 3.2.4) are used to obtain the needed log, e to the x, and square root. Perhaps most unfamiliar is the use of INTERPOLATION ON to represent the normal distribution.

```
MODEL BLKSCHO  VERSION OF  09/15/81  21:17
10 COLUMNS 1
20* BLACK-SCHOLES FORMULA
30*
40 PRESENT VALUE OF CALL=PRICE*CUMPROB1-EXERCISE PRICE*'
41  CUMPROB2/NATEXP(RFT)
45 PRESENT VALUE OF PUT=PRESENT VALUE OF CALL - PRICE + '
46  EXERCISE PRICE/XPOWERY((1+RISK FREE RATE),TIME TO EXERCISE)
50*
60*
70 D1 =(NATLOG(PRICE/EXERCISE PRICE)+ RFT+PERIOD VARIANCE OF ROR *'
71 TIME TO EXERCISE/2)/DENOMINATOR
80 D2=(NATLOG(PRICE/EXERCISE PRICE)+RFT - PERIOD VARIANCE OF ROR *'
81 TIME TO EXERCISE/2)/DENOMINATOR
90*
100 CUMPROB1=INTERPOLATION ON(D1,-5,0,-2,.023,-1.5,.067,-1.2,.115,'
101 -1,.159 ,-.8,.21,-.6,.274,0,.5,.6,.726,.8,.788,1,.841,1.2,'
102 .884,1.5,.93,2,.997,5,1)
110 CUMPROB2=INTERPOLATION ON(D2,-5,0,-2,.023,-1.5,.067,-1.2,.115,'
111 -1,.159,-.8,.21,-.6,.274,0,.5,.6,.726,.8,.788,1,.84,1.2,.884,'
112 1.5,.93,2,.977,5,1)
120*
130*INPUT DATA
140*
200 PRICE=140
210 EXERCISE PRICE =160
220 RISK FREE RATE =.12
230 TIME TO EXERCISE =4
240 RFT = RISK FREE RATE *TIME TO EXERCISE
250 STD DEVIATION OF ROR =.40
260 PERIOD VARIANCE OF ROR=STD DEVIATION OF ROR*STD DEVIATION OF ROR
270 DENOMINATOR= STD DEVIATION OF ROR * XPOWERY(TIME TO EXERCISE,.5)
END OF MODEL
```

FIGURE 6-23. BLACK-SCHOLES MODEL
(This Figure Continued on the Next Page)

```
? solve
MODEL BLKSCHO  VERSION OF  09/15/81  21:17 -- 1 COLUMNS 13 VARIABLES
ENTER SOLVE OPTIONS
? all
                                             1

 BLACK-SCHOLES FORMULA

PRESENT VALUE OF CALL          60.81
PRESENT VALUE OF PUT           22.49

D1                             .8331
D2                             .0331

CUMPROB1                       .7968
CUMPROB2                       .5125

INPUT DATA

PRICE                            140
EXERCISE PRICE                   160
RISK FREE RATE                 .1200
TIME TO EXERCISE                   4
RFT                            .4800
STD DEVIATION OF ROR           .4000
PERIOD VARIANCE OF ROR         .1600
DENOMINATOR                    .8000
```

FIGURE 6-23. BLACK-SCHOLES MODEL
(Continued)

The normal distribution cannot be evaluated directly; however, you can use IFPS to look up the value in a table just as you would do if you were solving the problem by hand. IFPS allows you to specify tables through the INTERPOLATION ON function (see Section 3.2.4). You first give the name of the variable (in our case either d1 or d2) and then the table in which the value of the variable is to be looked up. The table is specified as successive pairs of values. For example, in Figure 6-23, we specify -5 standard deviations as 0, -2 standard deviations as .023, -1.5 standard deviations as .067, etc. What IFPS does is find the interval in which the value of the variable occurs and then performs linear interpolation within the interval to find the answer. Thus, for example, if d1 happened to be 0.4, IFPS would first determine that 0.4 falls between the table values of 0 and 0.6. Next, it would find that since 0.4 is two-thirds of the way between 0 and 0.6, the value of d1 should be 2/3 of the way between 0.5 and 0.72, that is that d1 = 0.6507.

In constructing the INTERPOLATION ON function, you are constrained in three ways:

- A maximum of 49 pairs of numbers can be used to define the function. The pairs must be in increasing order of the first variable.

- If you call for a value outside the region of definition during computation, you will receive an error message.

- Your table cannot exceed the maximum line length of IFPS (155 characters). If you have more data than the maximum line length, use the ' the apostrophe) to indicate that the statement is continued on the next line. The next line must have a line number.

6.13 FINANCIAL RATIO ANALYSIS

Although modern textbooks on finance warn their readers that the use of ratios based on current balance sheets and income statements is simplistic, such ratios are still very popular and useful ways of evaluating company performance. We will not get into the middle of this controversy here; our attitude is that if you want to use these ratios it is your choice, and you do so knowing the risks. Figure 6-24 is an IFPS model that includes most of the commonly used ratios. The model shows three types of indicators:

- Indicators of leverage.
- Indicators of liquidity.
- Indicators of efficiency.

The ratios are quite simple to compute once you have the needed balance sheets and income statements. The data in Figure 6-24 are based on balance sheets for two years and a current income statement. Although the indicators of leverage and liquidity depend only on the current year, most of the efficiency indicators are based on the changes in the balance sheet with respect to the previous year. You should be able to determine the specific indicators both from the names of the variables in the output and from their definition in Lines 510 through 840 of the model.

The balance sheet and income statement are input data and are printed out separately from the financial ratios. All three, however, are included in the same IFPS model. We have used the COLUMNS option in SOLVE to print out information in neat, simple form suitable for management use. In the present case with some data involving two years and some one year, the IFPS model creates two full columns; however only some portions of the second column (i.e., in the balance sheet) are needed.

You may also note a seeming contradiction in the program. The columns in the balance sheet are presented in the order 1982 and 1981, that is, most recent year first as is the custom in accounting presentations. As a result, the references to the 1981 column have to be "FUTURE" even though 1981 is a previous year. IFPS requires you to refer to columns to the right of the current column as "FUTURE". If you do not feel comfortable with this form of reference, you can use the MATRIX reference. We have used MATRIX(ACCOUNTS RECEIVABLE,2) in Line 761 in place of FUTURE ACCOUNTS RECEIVABLE. The same numeric result is obtained either way.

Finally, a note on format. You will notice that SALES TO NET WORKING CAPITAL RATIO requires over 30 letters. If we had ignored this length, IFPS would have arbitrarily chopped the name to fit the 24 column format available for variable names. To get around this limitation, we used the WIDTH command, described in Section 4.2. The WIDTH statement is shown in Figure 6-24. It is used as a SOLVE option and is included before the specification of COLUMNS. Rather than using the default options on WIDTH (that is, a 78 column wide output, with the first 24 used for the variable name, and 6 columns each 9 spaces wide), we used **WIDTH 68 40 9** to indicate that:

1. The results should be displayed over 68 columns .
2. Variable names should occupy 40 spaces.
3. Each column should contain 9 digits.

The WIDTH option is a simple way to achieve some of the features that are available through creating a REPORT (Section 4.7)

```
MODEL RATIOS  VERSION OF  04/17/86  00:51
10 COLUMNS 1982,1981
20 *
30 * THIS MODEL SHOWS A BALANCE SHEET AND INCOME STATEMENT
40 * IT USES THIS INFORMATION TO COMPUTE STANDARD FINANCIAL RATIOS
50 *
60 * BALANCE SHEET
70 *
80 *ASSETS
90 CASH&MRKTBLE SECURITIES=83,72
100 ACCOUNTS RECEIVABLE =1312,1204
110 INVENTORIES =1270,1514
115 OTHER CURRENT ASSETS = 85,67
120 *
130 TOTAL CURRENT ASSETS = L90+L100+L110+L115
140 PLANT AND EQUIPMENT = 2230,2264
150 OTHER LONG TERM ASSETS = 213,233
160 *
170 TOTAL ASSETS = TOTAL CURRENT ASSETS+L140+L150
180 *
200 *
210 *LIABILITIES
240 *
250 CURRENT LIABILITIES = 1174,1330
260 LONG TERM DEBT AND CAPITAL LEASES = 1037,1158
270 OTHER LONG TERM LIABILITIES =525,491
280 SHAREHOLDERS EQUITY = 2457,2375
290 *
310 TOTAL LIABILITIES = L250+L260+L270+L280
320 *
330 *
340 * INCOME STATEMENT
350 *
360 NET SALES =8689,0
370 COST OF GOODS SOLD = 6756,0
380 SELLING ADM &GEN EXPENSE=1300,0
390 OTHER INCOME = 19,0
400 *
410 EARNINGS BEFORE INT&TAX=L360-L370-L380+L390
420 INTEREST=191,0
430 *
```

FIGURE 6-24. FINANCIAL RATIOS

(This Figure Continued on the Next Page)

```
440 EARNINGS BEFORE TAX=L410-L420
450 TAX = 213,0
460 *
470 NET INCOME =EARNINGS BEFORE TAX-TAX
472*
473* OTHER FINANCIAL INFORMATION
474* ---------------------------
476 DEPRECIATION =239,0
478 CURRENT COST OF INVENTORIES =1752,0
480 MARKET VALUE OF EQUITY = 2588,0
481 MARKET VALUE OF ASSETS = MARKET VALUE OF EQUITY '
482 + TOTAL LIABILITIES -SHAREHOLDERS EQUITY
484 CURRENT COST OF PLANT AND EQUIPMENT =3794,0
486 MILLIONS OF SHARES = 73.933,0
488 EARNINGS PER SHARE =3.35,0
490 DIVIDEND PER SHARE =1.40,0
492 SHARE PRICE = 35,0
494 CURRENT COST OF ALL ASSETS =7239,0
500 *
510 *INDICATORS OF LEVERAGE
520 *---------- -- --------
525 DEBT RATIO = LONG TERM DEBT AND CAPITAL LEASES/'
526 (LONG TERM DEBT AND CAPITAL LEASES + SHAREHOLDERS EQUITY),0
528 DEBT EQUITY RATIO = LONG TERM DEBT AND CAPITAL LEASES'
529 /SHAREHOLDERS EQUITY,0
540 TIMES INTEREST EARNED = EARNINGS BEFORE INT&TAX/INTEREST,0
550 *
560 *INDICATORS OF LIQUIDITY
570 *---------- -- ---------
580 NET WORKING CAPITAL TO NET ASSETS = (TOTAL CURRENT ASSETS -'
590 CURRENT LIABILITIES)/TOTAL ASSETS,0
600 CURRENT RATIO = TOTAL CURRENT ASSETS/CURRENT LIABILITIES,0
610 QUICK RATIO= (TOTAL CURRENT ASSETS -INVENTORIES)/'
611 CURRENT LIABILITIES,0
620 CASH RATIO = CASH&MRKTBLE SECURITIES/CURRENT LIABILITIES,0
622 INTERVAL MEASURE = (TOTAL CURRENT ASSETS-INVENTORIES)*365/'
624 (COST OF GOODS SOLD + SELLING ADM &GEN EXPENSE),0
630 *
640 *INDICATORS OF EFFICIENCY
650 *---------- -- ----------
660 SALES TO TOTAL ASSETS = NET SALES/((TOTAL ASSETS +'
661 FUTURE TOTAL ASSETS)/2),0
670 SALES TO NET WORKING CAPITAL=NET SALES/(( TOTAL CURRENT ASSETS+'
680 FUTURE TOTAL CURRENT ASSETS-CURRENT LIABILITIES -'
681 FUTURE CURRENT LIABILITIES)/2),0
690 RETURN ON TOTAL ASSETS IN PCT = 100*(EARNINGS BEFORE INT&TAX -
700 TAX)/((TOTAL ASSETS + FUTURE TOTAL ASSETS)/2),0
710 RETURN ON EQUITY IN PCT =100*NET INCOME/'
720 ((SHAREHOLDERS EQUITY+FUTURE SHAREHOLDERS EQUITY)/2),0
```

FIGURE 6-24. FINANCIAL RATIOS
(This Figure Continued on the Next Page)

```
730 NET PROFIT MARGIN IN PCT=100*(EARNINGS BEFORE INT&TAX-'
740 TAX)/NET SALES,0
750 INVENTORY TURNOVER =COST OF GOODS SOLD/'
751 ((INVENTORIES+FUTURE INVENTORIES)/2),0
760 AVERAGE COLLECTION PERIOD IN DAYS=((ACCOUNTS RECEIVABLE +'
761 MATRIX(ACCOUNTS RECEIVABLE,2))/2)/(NET SALES/365),0
770 PAYOUT RATIO = DIVIDEND PER SHARE/EARNINGS PER SHARE,0
780 PLOWBACK RATIO =1-PAYOUT RATIO,0
790 GROWTH IN EQUITY FROM PLOWBACK = PLOWBACK RATIO*'
791 RETURN ON EQUITY IN PCT/100
795*
800*MARKET VALUE RATIOS
805*------------------
810 PRICE EARNINGS RATIO = SHARE PRICE/EARNINGS PER SHARE,0
820 DIVIDEND YIELD = DIVIDEND PER SHARE/SHARE PRICE,0
830 MARKET TO BOOK RATIO = SHARE PRICE/(SHAREHOLDERS EQUITY/'
831 MILLIONS OF SHARES),0
840 TOBINS Q = MARKET VALUE OF ASSETS/CURRENT COST OF ALL ASSETS,0
END OF MODEL
? solve
ENTER SOLVE OPTIONS
? L50 thru L310
```

	1982	1981
BALANCE SHEET		
ASSETS		
CASH&MRKTBLE SECURITIES	83	72
ACCOUNTS RECEIVABLE	1312	1204
INVENTORIES	1270	1514
OTHER CURRENT ASSETS	85	67
TOTAL CURRENT ASSETS	2750	2857
PLANT AND EQUIPMENT	2230	2264
OTHER LONG TERM ASSETS	213	233
TOTAL ASSETS	5193	5354
LIABILITIES		
CURRENT LIABILITIES	1174	1330
LONG TERM DEBT AND CAPIT	1037	1158
OTHER LONG TERM LIABILIT	525	491
SHAREHOLDERS EQUITY	2457	2375
TOTAL LIABILITIES	5193	5354

FIGURE 6-24. FINANCIAL RATIOS
(This Figure Continued on the Next Page)

```
ENTER SOLVE OPTIONS
? width 68 40 9
? column 1
? L340 thru L840
                                                    1982

 INCOME STATEMENT

NET SALES                                           8689
COST OF GOODS SOLD                                  6756
SELLING ADM &GEN EXPENSE                            1300
OTHER INCOME                                          19

EARNINGS BEFORE INT&TAX                              652
INTEREST                                             191

EARNINGS BEFORE TAX                                  461
TAX                                                  213

NET INCOME                                           248

 OTHER FINANCIAL INFORMATION
 ---------------------------

DEPRECIATION                                         239
CURRENT COST OF INVENTORIES                         1752
MARKET VALUE OF EQUITY                              2588
MARKET VALUE OF ASSETS                              5324
CURRENT COST OF PLANT AND EQUIPMENT                 3794
MILLIONS OF SHARES                                 73.93
EARNINGS PER SHARE                                 3.350
DIVIDEND PER SHARE                                 1.400
SHARE PRICE                                           35
CURRENT COST OF ALL ASSETS                          7239

INDICATORS OF LEVERAGE
---------- --------

DEBT RATIO                                         .2968
DEBT EQUITY RATIO                                  .4221
TIMES INTEREST EARNED                              3.414

INDICATORS OF LIQUIDITY
---------- -- ---------

NET WORKING CAPITAL TO NET ASSETS                  .3035
CURRENT RATIO                                      2.342
QUICK RATIO                                        1.261
CASH RATIO                                         .0707
INTERVAL MEASURE                                   67.06
```

FIGURE 6-24. FINANCIAL RATIOS

(This Figure Continued on the Next Page)

```
INDICATORS OF EFFICIENCY
---------- -- ----------
SALES TO TOTAL ASSETS                          1.648
SALES TO NET WORKING CAPITAL                   5.600
RETURN ON TOTAL ASSETS IN PCT                  8.325
RETURN ON EQUITY IN PCT                        10.26
NET PROFIT MARGIN IN PCT                       5.052
INVENTORY TURNOVER                             4.853
AVERAGE COLLECTION PERIOD IN DAYS              52.84
PAYOUT RATIO                                   .4179
PLOWBACK RATIO                                 .5821
GROWTH IN EQUITY FROM PLOWBACK                 .0598

MARKET VALUE RATIOS
------------------

PRICE EARNINGS RATIO                           10.45
DIVIDEND YIELD                                 .0400
MARKET TO BOOK RATIO                           1.053
TOBINS Q                                      .7355
```

FIGURE 6-24. FINANCIAL RATIOS
(Continued)

In going through Figure 6-24, note one fine point on the use of parentheses. In Lines 660 through 830 some of the ratios involve averages such as average assets. The result is a quantity of the form A/B/C. IFPS can give you wrong answers unless you use parentheses to avoid ambiguity. For example, 3/(4/5) = 3.75 whereas (3/4)/5 = 0.15. In general, extra parentheses don't hurt you but too few parentheses can cause you trouble. Statements starting on Lines 660, 670, and 710 are typical examples where the extra parentheses are needed. If you don't believe the need for them, try the model with the parentheses deleted.

6.14 CASH MANAGEMENT MODEL

The management of the cash balance of a firm can be modeled in terms of inventory theory. Although we will discuss inventory ideas in much more detail in Chapter VIII, we can see these ideas intuitively and use them to understand the Miller-Orr model for cash management.

A firm generally has a policy to keep a minimum amount of cash on hand to run its day-to-day affairs. The amount is sometimes determined by requirements imposed by the firm's banks. There is also a maximum desirable amount. This maximum reflects a trade-off between the transaction cost of investing in a liquid investment such as Treasury bills and the cost of lost interest because cash is not invested. Cash can be considered to be like any other good that the company keeps in its inventory. The Miller-Orr model assumes that you know the minimum cash balance required, the variance of daily cash flows, the daily interest rate, and the transaction cost for each sale or purchase of securities.

The Miller-Orr model applies the principles of inventory theory to the foregoing information to compute the spread between the maximum and minimum cash limits. The relation used is:

$$\text{SPREAD} = 3*(.75*\text{TRANSACTION COST}*\text{VARIANCE OF CASH FLOWS/INTEREST RATE})^{.333} \quad (6\text{-}20)$$

Knowing the minimum cash balance and the spread, you can compute the maximum cash balance and the return point:

$$\text{MAXIMUM CASH BALANCE} = \text{MINIMUM CASH BALANCE} + \text{SPREAD} \quad (6\text{-}21)$$

$$\text{RETURN POINT} = \text{MINIMUM CASH BALANCE} + \text{SPREAD}/3 \quad (6\text{-}22)$$

These formulas tell us that whenever the cash balance reaches the maximum, we should invest the difference between the maximum cash balance and the return point; similarly, whenever the minimum cash balance is reached, we should sell sufficient securities to reach the return point. Note that the return point is not midway between maximum and minimum cash balance, but one-third of the distance between them and on the low side.

Figure 6-25 shows the Miller-Orr model in IFPS and applies it to a particular example. As usual, the XPOWERY function is used; in this case to compute the cube root needed in determining the spread according to Equation (6-20).

6.15 PRO FORMA FINANCIAL FORECAST MODELS

We conclude this chapter by presenting a generalized financial forecast model that allows you to create:

- Income statements
- Sources and uses of funds
- Balance sheets

for as many years as you please. The choice of number of years is incorporated in the COLUMNS statement. In a typical financial planning model you make estimates of the revenues anticipated in future years, external variables over which your firm has little or no control (e.g., interest rates), and policy variables such as dividend payout.

Figure 6-26 shows a generalized five-year pro forma forecast, with 1983 assumed as the current year. As you read through this model you will see that it is really an accounting model that is based on the following assumptions:

- The anticipated growth of the business, i.e., revenues and stock issues.
- Relations between revenues and other quantities. Specifically, the cost of goods sold, the value of fixed assets, and the net working capital are assumed proportional to revenues. These are expressed as ratios in the list of assumptions.
- Dividend payout is proportional to net income.

```
MODEL MILLEROR  VERSION OF  05/07/86  22:43
10 COLUMNS 1
20*
30* MILLER-ORR CASH MANAGEMENT MODEL
40*
50 SPREAD = 3*XPOWERY(0.75*TRANSACTION COST *'
51 VARIANCE OF CASH FLOWS/INTEREST RATE IN PERCENT *.01,.33333)
60*
70 UPPER LIMIT = MINIMUM CASH BALANCE + SPREAD
80 RETURN POINT = MINIMUM CASH BALANCE + SPREAD/3
90*
100*DECISION RULES
110*
120 INVESTMENT AT UPPER LIMIT = UPPER LIMIT - RETURN POINT
130 SECURITY SALES AT MINIMUM CASH BALANCE = RETURN POINT'
131 - MINIMUM CASH BALANCE
140*
150* DATA
160*
170 MINIMUM CASH BALANCE =10000
180 STD DEVIATION OF CASH FLOWS = 2500
190 VARIANCE OF CASH FLOWS = XPOWERY(STD DEVIATION OF CASH FLOWS,2)
200 INTEREST RATE IN PERCENT =.025
210 TRANSACTION COST = 20
END OF MODEL

? SOLVE
ENTER SOLVE OPTIONS
? ALL

                                                   1

 MILLER-ORR CASH MANAGEMENT MODEL

SPREAD                                          1004

UPPER LIMIT                                    11004
RETURN POINT                                   10335

DECISION RULES

INVESTMENT AT UPPER LIMIT                      669.4
SECURITY SALES AT MINIMUM CASH                 334.7

 DATA

MINIMUM CASH BALANCE                           10000
STD DEVIATION OF CASH FLOWS                     2500
VARIANCE OF CASH FLOWS                       6250000
INTEREST RATE IN PERCENT                       .0250
TRANSACTION COST                                  20
```

FIGURE 6-25. MILLER-ORR CASH MANAGEMENT MODEL

- Current (i.e., 1983) data on revenues, debt, and equity as well as current and anticipated tax and interest rates.
- Changes in working capital and investment in 1983 are arbitrarily set to 0 since data were not given; however, in a real company you would have this information.

In using this model, you should view it as a basis for creating financial forecasts that are tailored to the situation of your own company and its accounting conventions. You will want to add and delete lines. You will also want to modify the assumptions to fit your expectations. In the simple model shown here, for example, growth is at a constant rate, tax and interest rates are fixed, and dividends are proportional to net income rather than being constant. You may believe that more complex situations will prevail and can easily include them in your model. We will ask you to do this in the exercises that follow.

EXERCISE: Modify Figure 6-26 to reflect the following conditions: Interest rates are expected to be stable for two years and then to increase 1% per year for the next three years. The corporate tax rate will go down to 35% in 1986. You anticipate a stock issue of $300,000 in 1987 and of $200,000 in 1988. Revenues will grow 30% for two years but will then grow at only 10%. The company's president has announced that the 1984 dividend will be $60 and that the dividend will stay at that level through the 1980's. To improve productivity, the company plans to become more capital intensive. As a result, fixed assets will grow from 37% in 1984 to 40% in 1987 (1% increase annually) but will be fixed thereafter. Run the model with these changes included.

```
MODEL FORECAST  VERSION OF  04/17/86  01:00
10 COLUMNS 1983-1988
20 *
30 *A GENERALIZED FIVE YEAR PRO FORMA FORECAST
40 *
50 *INCOME STATEMENT
60 *------ ---------
70 *
80 REVENUES = L620
90 COST OF GOODS SOLD = COST OF GOODS SOLD RATIO*REVENUES
100 *
110 EARNINGS BEFORE INTEREST&TAX=REVENUES-COST OF GOODS SOLD
120 INTEREST = INTEREST RATE * DEBT
130 *
140 EARNINGS BEFORE TAX = EARNINGS BEFORE INTEREST&TAX-INTEREST
150 TAX = TAX RATE * EARNINGS BEFORE TAX
160 *
170 NET INCOME =EARNINGS BEFORE TAX - TAX
180 *
190 *SOURCES AND USES OF FUNDS
200 *------- --- ---- -- -----
210 *
220 *SOURCES
230    NET INCOME = L170
240    DEPRECIATION = DEPRECIATION PERCENTAGE*FIXED ASSETS
250 *
```

FIGURE 6-26. A GENERALIZED FIVE-YEAR PRO FORMA FORECAST
(This Figure Continued on the Next Page)

```
260   OPERATING CASH FLOW =NET INCOME +DEPRECIATION
270     BORROWING =0,CHANGE IN NET WRKNG CAPITAL + INVESTMENT +'
280     DIVIDENDS - NET INCOME -DEPRECIATION-STOCK ISSUES
290     STOCK ISSUES = L630
300 *
310     TOTAL SOURCES =OPERATING CASH FLOW+BORROWING+STOCK ISSUES
320 *
330 *
340 *USES
350     CHANGE IN NET WRKNG CAPITAL = 40, NET WORKING CAPITAL'
360     -PREVIOUS NET WORKING CAPITAL
370     INVESTMENT=140,DEPRECIATION+FIXED ASSETS-PREVIOUS FIXED ASSETS
380     DIVIDENDS = DIVIDEND PAYOUT RATIO * NET INCOME
390     *
400 TOTAL USES=CHANGE IN NET WRKNG CAPITAL+INVESTMENT+DIVIDENDS
410 *
420 *
430 *BALANCE SHEETS
440 *--------------
450 *
460 *ASSETS
470     NET WORKING CAPITAL =NET WORKING CAPITAL RATIO * REVENUES
480     FIXED ASSETS =FIXED ASSETS RATIO *REVENUES
490 *
500     TOTAL ASSETS = NET WORKING CAPITAL + FIXED ASSETS
510 *
520 *LIABILITIES
530     DEBT=INITIAL DEBT,BORROWING + PREVIOUS DEBT
540     BOOK EQUITY=INITIAL EQUITY,PREVIOUS BOOK EQUITY+NET INCOME-'
550     DIVIDENDS + STOCK ISSUES
560 *
570     TOTAL LIABILITIES = DEBT + BOOK EQUITY
580 *
590 *ASSUMPTIONS
600 *-----------
610 *
620 REVENUES =2160,PREVIOUS * 1.3
630 STOCK ISSUES =64,0
640 COST OF GOODS SOLD RATIO = .9
650 INTEREST RATE = .09
660 TAX RATE = .50
670 DEPRECIATION PERCENTAGE = .10
680 DIVIDEND PAYOUT RATIO =.60
690 NET WORKING CAPITAL RATIO =.093
700 FIXED ASSETS RATIO = .37
710 INITIAL DEBT = 400,0
720 INITIAL EQUITY =600,0
END OF MODEL
```

FIGURE 6-26. A GENERALIZED FIVE-YEAR PRO FORMA FORECAST

(This Figure Continued on the Next Page)

```
? SOLVE
SIMULTANEOUS EQUATIONS DETECTED - DO YOU WANT TO PRINT THE VARIABLES
INVOLVED
? NO
MODEL  FORECAST   VERSION  OF   04/17/86   01:00  --  6  COLUMNS  34
VARIABLES

ENTER SOLVE OPTIONS
? WIDTH 62 20 7
? L50 THRU L400
```

	1983	1984	1985	1986	1987	1988
INCOME STATEMENT						
------ ---------						
REVENUES	2160	2808	3650	4746	6169	8020
COST OF GOODS SOLD	1944	2527	3285	4271	5552	7218
EARNINGS BEFORE INTE	216	280.8	365.0	474.6	616.9	802.0
INTEREST	36	59.01	89.15	128.6	180.0	247.1
EARNINGS BEFORE TAX	180	221.8	275.9	346.0	436.9	554.8
TAX	90	110.9	137.9	173.0	218.5	277.4
NET INCOME	90	110.9	137.9	173.0	218.5	277.4
SOURCES AND USES OF FUNDS						
------- --- ---- -- -----						
SOURCES						
NET INCOME	90	110.9	137.9	173.0	218.5	277.4
DEPRECIATION	79.92	103.9	135.1	175.6	228.3	296.7
OPERATING CASH FL	169.9	214.8	273.0	348.6	446.7	574.2
BORROWING	0	255.7	334.9	437.8	571.8	745.9
STOCK ISSUES	64	0	0	0	0	0
TOTAL SOURCES	233.9	470.5	607.9	786.4	1018	1320
USES						
CHANGE IN NET WRK	40	60.26	78.34	101.8	132.4	172.1
INVESTMENT	140	343.7	446.8	580.8	755.0	981.5
DIVIDENDS	54	66.54	82.77	103.8	131.1	166.5
TOTAL USES	234	470.5	607.9	786.4	1018	1320

FIGURE 6-26. A GENERALIZED FIVE-YEAR PRO FORMA FORECAST

(This Figure Continued on the Next Page)

```
ENTER SOLVE OPTIONS
? L430 THRU L720

                            1983    1984    1985    1986    1987    1988

BALANCE SHEETS
------- ------

ASSETS
  NET WORKING CAPIT    200.9   261.1   339.5   441.3   573.7   745.9
   FIXED ASSETS            799.2    1039    1351    1756    2283    2967
TOTAL ASSETS          1000    1300    1690    2197    2856    3713

LIABILITIES
  DEBT                     400   655.7   990.5    1428    2000    2746
  BOOK EQUITY              600   644.4   699.5   768.7   856.1   967.1

  TOTAL LIABILITIES       1000    1300    1690    2197    2856    3713

ASSUMPTIONS
-----------

REVENUES                  2160    2808    3650    4746    6169    8020
STOCK ISSUES                64       0       0       0       0       0
COST OF GOODS SOLD R     .9000   .9000   .9000   .9000   .9000   .9000
INTEREST RATE            .0900   .0900   .0900   .0900   .0900   .0900
TAX RATE                 .5000   .5000   .5000   .5000   .5000   .5000
DEPRECIATION PERCENT     .1000   .1000   .1000   .1000   .1000   .1000
DIVIDEND PAYOUT RATI     .6000   .6000   .6000   .6000   .6000   .6000
NET WORKING CAPITAL      .0930   .0930   .0930   .0930   .0930   .0930
FIXED ASSETS RATIO       .3700   .3700   .3700   .3700   .3700   .3700
INITIAL DEBT               400       0       0       0       0       0
INITIAL EQUITY             600       0       0       0       0       0
```

FIGURE 6-26. A GENERALIZED FIVE-YEAR PRO FORMA FORECAST
(Continued)

EXERCISE: Suppose you anticipate inflation in the next five years to be 2% below the interest rate. Assume that the data generated in the previous exercise are in absolute, not current, dollars. Modify the model in the previous exercise to create results in current dollars. Discuss how the future looks in current dollar terms.

If you try to solve this model on your computer, you will find that the response to SOLVE will be:

```
SIMULTANEOUS EQUATIONS DETECTED-DO YOU WANT TO PRINT VARIABLES
INVOLVED
```

If you respond YES, IFPS will display a list of variables which form a set of simultaneous equations. In the case of Figure 6-26, these variables are:

```
120 INTEREST
140 EARNINGS BEFORE TAX
150 TAX
170 NET INCOME
380 DIVIDENDS
270 BORROWING
530 DEBT
```

After providing the list, IFPS will ask you:

```
DO YOU WANT TO PROCEED WITH COMPILATION
```

If you respond YES, IFPS will proceed and attempt to solve the simultaneous equations. It uses the "Gauss-Seidel" method (an interative technique) to solve the simultaneous equations in each column independently. Because of this method of solution, you cannot have any FUTURE references in any column for the definitions of the variables involved in the simultaneous equations. Furthermore, under some conditions you may require many iterations. If too many iterations are required, IFPS may tell you:

```
NO CONVERGENCE FOR SIMULTANEOUS EQUATIONS IN COLUMN ...
```

If you know that you have simultaneous equations and want to avoid having to answer questions, you can put the statement SIMULTANEOUS AUTO anywhere in your model and IFPS will find all sets of simultaneous equations and will try to perform the necessary calculations.

CAUTION: Simultaneous equations and their solution can be a tricky business. Success is not guaranteed and seemingly simple situations can lead to trouble. Trouble can include the NO CONVERGENCE statement or, worse, incorrect answers without any message telling you that the answers are wrong. Try the exercises below to see what can happen to you.

In general it is good practice, if simultaneous equations exist, for you to:

- Check that the equations correspond to the situation being modeled.
- Check as many of the numbers produced as possible to make sure that they are correct and consistent with the assumptions of the model.

EXERCISE: Solve the following model:

```
10 COLUMNS 1-3
20 X = 2*Y +1
30 Y = 3*X +2
```

EXERCISE: Solve the following model:

```
10 COLUMNS 1
20 INCOME =1000
30 EXPENSES = 2200
40 BORROW = 1000 + DEFICIT
50 DEFICIT = EXPENSES   - INCOME - BORROW
```

If you did the foregoing exercises correctly, you found that you had simultaneous equations. IFPS could not solve them. Can you explain why IFPS could not get the solutions to converge?

6.16 ADDENDUM: YEAR 0 VS. YEAR 1

As we pointed out in Section 6.1, IFPS uses the convention that all investments occur at the beginning of a year and all returns occur at the end of a year. This differs from the convention followed in some finance texts that places the initial investment at the end of Year 0 and all subsequent investments at the end of subsequent years. The difference in approach reflects different viewpoints on what "present" means in "net present value." It is usually assumed that "present" refers to the time at which the first investment is made. Up to the point of initial commitment of funds, the project could be scrapped at no additional cost (a simplification in that we treat as sunk cost the cost of analyst and managerial time in reaching a decision). Furthermore, if the project is undertaken, returns occur only some time after the initial investment. To make this distinction between initial investment and later returns, many finance texts choose different year numbers for the initial investment and the initial returns.

In a modeling language such as IFPS, investments and returns are both calculated. Each variable must either be specified or computed for every column. It is more convenient to start both sets of calculations in the first column. The alternative would be to create a column to represent Year 0 and to set the value of every return to 0 in this column. In the author's personal view, this creates an artificiality that can easily lead to clerical errors in setting up the model.

You can see the difference between the two approaches in Figure 6-27. This figure shows the same problem modeled with a Year 1 and a Year 0 approach. Note that in the YEAR 0 approach the number of columns is increased by one and that all returns start with 0. You also have to define the NPVC and IRR functions differently. That is, you compute the difference between return and investment (i.e., the net return) and delete explicit reference to investment in these functions. Finally, the present values computed by IFPS are with respect to the BEGINNING of YEAR 0. You are interested in the returns at the end of YEAR 0 (which is equal to the beginning of YEAR 1). To make the results conform to your idea of what "present" represents, you have to multiply by (1 + DISCOUNT RATE). (Can you explain why?)

If you feel more comfortable starting with Year 0, by all means do so. However, be careful that your IFPS model correctly reflects your choice.

```
MODEL FIRST  VERSION OF  02/03/82  13:57
10 COLUMNS 1-5
20 INVESTMENT = LAND + BUILDING
30 RETURN = SALES -COSTS
40 PRESENT VALUE = NPVC(RETURN,DISCOUNT RATE,INVESTMENT)
50 IRR = IRR(RETURN,INVESTMENT)
60 *
70 * INPUT DATA
80 *
90 LAND = 200,0
100 BUILDING = 100,150,0
110*
120 SALES =500,600,700
130 COSTS = SUM (MATERIALS THRU LABOR)
140 MATERIALS = 10 + 0.20*SALES
150 OVERHEAD =50,60,70
160 LABOR = 20 + 0.40*SALES
170*
180 DISCOUNT RATE = 0.20
END OF MODEL
? solve
MODEL FIRST  VERSION OF  02/03/82  13:57 -- 5 COLUMNS 12 VARIABLES
ENTER SOLVE OPTIONS
? all

                            1        2        3        4        5

INVESTMENT                300      150        0        0        0
RETURN                    120      150      180      180      180
PRESENT VALUE            -200   -220.8   -116.7   -29.86    42.48
IRR                                           0    .1604    .2462

 INPUT DATA

LAND                      200        0        0        0        0
BUILDING                  100      150        0        0        0

SALES                     500      600      700      700      700
COSTS                     380      450      520      520      520
MATERIALS                 110      130      150      150      150
OVERHEAD                   50       60       70       70       70
LABOR                     220      260      300      300      300

DISCOUNT RATE           .2000    .2000    .2000    .2000    .2000
```

a. Investments Assumed to Occur at Start of Year 1

FIGURE 6-27. COMPARISON OF YEAR 1 AND YEAR 0 CONVENTIONS FOR INITIAL INVESTMENT

(This Figure Continued on Next Page)

```
MODEL SECOND  VERSION OF  02/03/82  14:00
10 COLUMNS 0-5
20 INVESTMENT = LAND + BUILDING
30 RETURN = SALES -COSTS
40 PRESENT VALUE=NPVC(RETURN-INVESTMENT,DISCOUNT RATE,0)'
41 *(1+DISCOUNT RATE)
50 IRR = IRR(RETURN-INVESTMENT,0)
60 *
70 * INPUT DATA
80 *
90 LAND = 200,0
100 BUILDING = 100,150,0
110*
120 SALES =0,500,600,700
130 COSTS = SUM (MATERIALS THRU LABOR)
140 MATERIALS = 0,10 + 0.20*SALES
150 OVERHEAD =0,50,60,70
160 LABOR = 0,20 + 0.40*SALES
170*
180 DISCOUNT RATE = 0.20
END OF MODEL
? solve
MODEL SECOND  VERSION OF  02/03/82  14:00 -- 6 COLUMNS 12 VARIABLES
ENTER SOLVE OPTIONS
? all
```

	0	1	2	3	4	5
INVESTMENT	300	150	0	0	0	0
RETURN	0	120	150	180	180	180
PRESENT VALUE	-300	-325	-220.8	-116.7	-29.86	42.48
IRR				0	.1604	.2462
INPUT DATA						
LAND	200	0	0	0	0	0
BUILDING	100	150	0	0	0	0
SALES	0	500	600	700	700	700
COSTS	0	380	450	520	520	520
MATERIALS	0	110	130	150	150	150
OVERHEAD	0	50	60	70	70	70
LABOR	0	220	260	300	300	300
DISCOUNT RATE	.2000	.2000	.2000	.2000	.2000	.2000

b. Investments Assumed to Occur at the End of Year 0

FIGURE 6-27. COMPARISON OF YEAR 1 AND YEAR 0 CONVENTIONS FOR INITIAL INVESTMENT
(Continued)

CHAPTER VII
APPLICATIONS IN STATISTICS

CHAPTER VII
APPLICATIONS IN STATISTICS

This chapter shows you how to use IFPS in problems involving statistics. Statistical techniques are needed in solving many problems in finance, marketing, accounting, economics, and other disciplines. As you will see from the examples shown in this chapter, IFPS, because of its ability to lay out information in matrix form and its WHAT IF capabilities, is often an easy way to understand what is going on in a statistical procedure. In other words, it is a way of de-mystifying statistics as well as a way of communicating results to management in a meaningful way.

As in Chapter VI, we have used many of the examples in an existing text. In this case, we used *STATISTICS FOR BUSINESS AND ECONOMICS* by Marion G. Sobol and Martin K. Starr (McGraw-Hill, 1982). If you need more information about a particular method or topic you can refer to the book by Sobol and Starr or to any similar introductory statistics text for business applications. We have tried, however, to present the following material in such a way that if you have a working understanding of statistical concepts, you can use this chapter to solve statistical problems without having to refer to outside sources.

This chapter contains a representative sample of IFPS applications in statistics. It is intended to show you what can be done and to encourage you to build your own IFPS models to solve statistical problems you encounter in your work.

7.1 SUMMARY MEASURES -- MEAN, VARIANCE, STANDARD DEVIATION

7.1.1 Mean and Moving Average

If you gather a large amount of data about a particular subject, you usually will find it easier to communicate your results to management by summarizing the information into a few commonly understood numbers. The simplest of these are the mean, the variance, and the standard deviation.

The mean is simply the average value of the numbers. It is obtained by adding all the data values, X, and dividing by n, the number of data points. In formula terms:

$$\text{MEAN} = (X1 + X2 + X3 + \ldots Xn) / n \qquad (7\text{-}1)$$

where X1,X2,...are the observations and n is the number of observations.

IFPS has a built-in function for finding the mean. As shown in Figure 7-1, you follow these steps:

1. Specify the number of columns to be equal to the number of observations.

2. Type in your X values.

3. Ask for the average by using the MEAN function.

The MEAN function requires two inputs, the location of the first observation and the last observation (Your X1 and Xn). Since you are referring to two columns in a particular row, you must use MATRIX. For example, to find the mean of 10 numbers, you ask for:

AVERAGE = MEAN(MATRIX(X,1),MATRIX(X,10))

As described in Section 4.4.2, MATRIX refers to a particular column of a variable. In Figure 7-1 we use MATRIX to define the values of a variable X whose values are given in columns 1 and 10.

```
MODEL STAT1  VERSION OF  08/27/82  22:18
5 COLUMNS 1-10
10 X=15,18,25,30,14,42,63,220,49,42
20*
30*          AVERAGE AND MOVING AVERAGE
40*
50 AVERAGE=MEAN(MATRIX(X,1),MATRIX(X,10))
60 MOVINGAVERAGE1=MOVAVG(X,.5,.5)
70 MOVINGAVERAGE2=MOVAVG(FUTURE X,.33,.33,.33)
END OF MODEL
?solve
ENTER SOLVE OPTIONS
? all

                          1     2     3     4     5     6     7     8     9    10

X                        15    18    25    30    14    42    63   220    49    42

     AVERAGE AND MOVING AVERAGE

AVERAGE                51.8  51.8  51.8  51.8  51.8  51.8  51.8  51.8  51.8  51.8
MOVINGAVERAGE1           15  16.5  21.5  27.5    22    28  52.5   142   135  45.5
MOVINGAVERAGE2         16.5  19.3  24.3    23  28.7  39.7   108   111   104  45.5
```

FIGURE 7-1. AVERAGE AND MOVING AVERAGE

When dealing with data that occur over time (for example, weekly sales or quarterly profits), the average of all the data we have may tell us very little because things change over time. However, we may want to smooth out random fluctuations to be able to observe the changes over time. A simple way to do this is to take a "moving average". Here we average data obtained over a specific time period. As shown in Figure 7-1, IFPS has a built-in moving average function, MOVAVG. To use this moving average function, you specify the variable to be averaged and the relative weight to be given to each period starting from (n-1) columns before the current one and working up to the current column. In general form:

MOVAVG(variable,weight1,weight2,...weightn) (7-2)

The weights do not have to be equal. However, they should add up to 1. If they do not, IFPS adjusts them in proportion so that they do. Note that in the second example of MOVAVG in Figure 7-1 (Line 70) the averaging begins with the next period (i.e., FUTURE). This form is useful in forecasting (see Section 7.7).

If the MOVAVG function specifies a column before the first or after the last, IFPS recognizes that the data points in these columns do not exist and uses only the data available. Thus, for example, MOVINGAVERAGE1 has a value of 15 in column 1 because the average is based on just that data point. Similarly, the value of MOVINGAVERAGE in column 10 is 45.5 because it is the average of just the last two points.

EXERCISE: In each implementation of IFPS there is a limit on the number of columns you can have (e.g., 250 on the CDC-6600 computer). This limits the number of data points that can be averaged using the model of Figure 7-1. Modify Figure 7-1 so that it can average, say 600 data points. Note that with large amounts of information, you will want to use the data features of IFPS described in Section 4.6.

EXERCISE: Write an IFPS model that finds the moving average using the mean function. Assume that the data points are to be equally weighted and are to include the current point and the three previous points. Your model need not match the results obtained by the MOVINGAVERAGE function for columns 1, 2, and 3.

7.1.2 Mean of Grouped Data

When data have been grouped into categories, that is, into a "frequency distribution", computing the mean becomes slightly more complicated. What is conventionally done is to assume that all the observations in the interval lie at the midpoint of the interval. For example, suppose data on weekly earnings of sales people are given by the following table:

SALARIES	65 75	75 85	85 95	95 105	105 115	115 125	125 135
PEOPLE	5	10	20	36	22	12	5

You treat these data as if there were five people earning $70, 10 people earning $80, etc. In terms of a simple formula:

$$\text{Average} = \Sigma f^*m/n \qquad (7\text{-}3)$$

where f is number in each interval, m is the midpoint of the interval and n is the total number of individuals. Figure 7-2 shows how to implement this procedure in IFPS. The data shown for total earnings, total sales people, and average earnings are cumulative; that is, each column is obtained from all the data from column 1 to the current column.

EXERCISE: Write an alternative version of Figure 7-2 using the MEAN function to find average earnings. What do you sacrifice by using the MEAN function?

```
MODEL STAT2  VERSION OF   08/23/82   00:08
1 COLUMNS 1-7
10*
20*        MEAN FOR GROUPED DATA
30*
40 BOTTOM OF RANGE = 65,PREVIOUS+10
50 TOP OF RANGE =BOTTOM OF RANGE+10
60 MIDPOINT OF RANGE=BOTTOM OF RANGE+(TOP OF RANGE'
61 - BOTTOM OF RANGE)/2
70 NUMBER OF EMPLOYEES =5,10,20,36,22,12,5
80 TOTAL EARNINGS =PREVIOUS +NUMBER OF EMPLOYEES*MIDPOINT OF RANGE
90 TOTAL EMPLOYEES=PREVIOUS+NUMBER OF EMPLOYEES
100 AVERAGE EARNINGS=TOTAL EARNINGS/TOTAL EMPLOYEES
END OF MODEL
? solve
MODEL STAT2  VERSION OF   08/23/82   00:08 -- 7 COLUMNS 7 VARIABLES
ENTER SOLVE OPTIONS
? all
                           1      2      3      4      5      6      7

         MEAN FOR GROUPED DATA

BOTTOM OF RANGE           65     75     85     95    105    115    125
TOP OF RANGE              75     85     95    105    115    125    135
MIDPOINT OF RANGE         70     80     90    100    110    120    130
NUMBER OF EMPLOYEES        5     10     20     36     22     12      5
TOTAL EARNINGS           350   1150   2950   6550   8970  10410  11060
TOTAL EMPLOYEES            5     15     35     71     93    105    110
AVERAGE EARNINGS          70  76.67  84.29  92.25  96.45  99.14  100.5
```

FIGURE 7-2. MEAN FOR GROUPED DATA

7.1.3 Average of Weighted Data

Suppose you want to find the average GPA of students at six universities that play in the same football conference. The data are as follows:

SCHOOL	AU	BU	CU	DU	EU	GU
STUDENTS(1000's)	28.4	17.6	14.4	8.9	11.7	14.3
GPA	2.43	2.37	2.39	2.79	2.56	2.22

Simply averaging the six GPA's given to obtain 2.46 (check this!) does not take into account the different sizes of the schools. The correct way to deal with the problem is to apply the formula:

$$\text{Weighted Average} = \Sigma w^*X / \Sigma w \qquad (7\text{-}4)$$

where w is the weight (in our case the number of students) and X is the observed value (i.e., the grade point average). Equation (7-4) tells you to multiply each observation by the number of students who generated it and to divide by the total number of students in the six schools. This approach is implemented in IFPS in Figure 7-3.

```
MODEL STAT3  VERSION OF  08/27/82  22:49
10 COLUMNS 1-6
20 *
30 *        MEAN FOR WEIGHTED DATA
40 *
50 THOUSANDS OF STUDENTS = 28.4,17.6,14.4,8.9,11.7,14.3
60 GPA = 2.43,2.37,2.39,2.79,2.56,2.29
70 TOTAL GRADEPOINTS=GPA*THOUSANDS OF STUDENTS
80 *
90 CUMULATIVE GRADEPOINTS = PREVIOUS + TOTAL GRADEPOINTS
100CUMULATIVE NO OF STUDENTS=PREVIOUS+THOUSANDS OF STUDENTS
110WEIGHTED AVG GPA=CUMULATIVE GRADEPOINTS/CUMULATIVE NO OF STUDENTS
120*
END OF MODEL
? solve
MODEL STAT3  VERSION OF  08/27/82  22:49 -- 6 COLUMNS 6 VARIABLES
ENTER SOLVE OPTIONS
? all

                                 1       2       3       4       5       6

     MEAN FOR WEIGHTED DATA

THOUSANDS OF STUDENTS        28.40   17.60   14.40   8.900   11.70   14.30
GPA                          2.430   2.370   2.390   2.790   2.560   2.290
TOTAL GRADE POINTS           69.01   41.71   34.42   24.83   29.95   32.75

CUMULATIVE GRADEPOINTS       69.01   110.7   145.1   170.0   199.9   232.7
CUMULATIVE NO OF STUDENTS    28.40      46   60.40   69.30      81   95.30
WEIGHTED AVG GPA             2.430   2.407   2.403   2.453   2.468   2.441
```

FIGURE 7-3. MEAN FOR WEIGHTED DATA

7.1.4 Median

The mean is a good way of describing data when observations are relatively close together or the frequency distribution is nearly symmetric. For the data used in Figure 7-1 this was not the case; the mean was larger than 8 of the 10 numbers because of the very large value of 220. When there are a few observations that are very different from the rest, the median is a better way of describing the data in terms of a single, most typical value. In simple terms, the median is the middle value of a set of observations. An equal number of observed values are above the median and below the median. For example, for observations of 1, 3, 5, 7, and 29, the mean is 15 and the median is 5.

The median is obtained by ordering the values of the observations in increasing (or decreasing) order and taking the middle observed value. This is easy to do if there are an odd number of observations (e.g., take the 3rd value of 5) but slightly more difficult if there is an even number of observations. The convention that is followed in statistics for an even number of observations is to take the average of the two middle values. For example, if we observe 1, 3, 5, 7, 9, and 29 we take the average of 5 and 7; that is, the median is 6.

Figure 7-4 uses the same data as Figure 7-1 and shows that all you need to do is replace the reserved word MEAN by the reserved word MEDIAN to use the MEDIAN function.

```
MODEL STAT4  VERSION OF  09/01/82  20:54
10 COLUMNS 1-10
20 DATA = 15,18,25,30,14,42,63,220,49,42
30 AVERAGE=MEAN(MATRIX(DATA,1),MATRIX(DATA,10))
40 MEDIAN=MEDIAN(MATRIX(DATA,1),MATRIX(DATA,10))
50 MOVING MEDIAN=MEDIAN(PREVIOUS 2 DATA,FUTURE DATA)
END OF MODEL
? solve
MODEL STAT4  VERSION OF  09/01/82  20:54 -- 10 COLUMNS 4 VARIABLES
ENTER SOLVE OPTIONS
? all

                    1    2    3    4    5    6    7    8    9   10

DATA               15   18   25   30   14   42   63  220   49   42
AVERAGE          51.8 51.8 51.8 51.8 51.8 51.8 51.8 51.8 51.8 51.8
MEDIAN             36   36   36   36   36   36   36   36   36   36
MOVING MEDIAN    16.5   18 21.5 21.5 27.5   36 52.5   56   56   49
```

FIGURE 7-4. MEDIAN

EXERCISE: Finding the median of a frequency distribution is slightly more complicated. The problem is that you first have to find the group in which the middle observation occurs and then have to estimate the value of that middle observation. Use the data in Section 7.1.2 on the earnings of sales people and write an IFPS model to determine the median. Note that the sample contains 110 observations. Because a frequency distribution for the purpose of finding the median is considered continuous, you have to find the 110/2 or 55th value. To do so, you will first have to find that the 55th observation lies in the fourth interval and then you will have to assume that the observations are uniformly distributed within the fourth interval. You will find the following formula helpful:

$$\text{MEDIAN} = L + ((n/2 - \Sigma f(L-1)) / f(L)) * X(L) \tag{7-5}$$

where L is the bottom of the range containing the median,
n is the total sample size,
f(L-1) is the total sample up to the median class,
f(L) is the number in the median class, and
X(L) is the size of the interval containing the median.

In our case, L=95, n=110, f(L-1)=35, f(L)=36, and X(L)=10.

This is not a simple exercise. Don't try to sit at a terminal and write the solution. Think about how to do it first and write it out on scratch paper. You will find it useful to use IF...THEN...ELSE. (see Section 4.4.3).

7.1.5 Measures of Dispersion

In the preceding sections we have discussed various ways of obtaining a single number, either the mean or the median, for summarizing data. Although such a single number is useful, it does not tell the whole story. You can obtain the same median, for example, from 1, 2, 3, 4, 5 and from –10, –5, 3, 11, 27; however, these two sets of data are quite different. The usual approach therefore is to characterize data in terms of two or more numbers, one of which indicates a central location while the others measure the dispersion around this center. This subsection deals with measures of dispersion. It includes discussions of:

- standard deviation and variance of a sample and a population
- skewness
- kurtosis
- average deviation and range
- confidence interval
- coefficient of variation

You have encountered almost all these measures previously when you examined the output from Monte Carlo calculations in Chapter V. Figure 7-5 shows how to compute each of these measures in IFPS. The data in Figures 7-1 and 7-4 are used. Figure 7-5 repeats the observed data and the mean and median from the previous figures.

STANDARD DEVIATION OF THE SAMPLE. IFPS has a built-in function for computing the standard deviation of a sample, STDDEV. As in the case of the MEAN and MATRIX function you specify the locations of the first and last points by using the MATRIX form. That is, you write

STDDEV(MATRIX(OBSERVED DATA,1),MATRIX(OBSERVED DATA,n)) (7-6)

where OBSERVED DATA contains the values observed and n refers to the number of columns of data.(In Figure 7-5, n=10). What STDDEV computes is:

$$\text{STDDEV} = \sqrt{\Sigma(\text{X - MEAN})^2/(\text{N-1})} \qquad (7\text{-}7)$$

This is known as the standard deviation of the sample since it takes into account that we only estimate the mean from the data, we do not know its underlying (i.e., true) value. In Equation (7-7), X represents observed values and MEAN the average of the observed values computed by using the MEAN function.

VARIANCE OF THE SAMPLE. The variance of the sample is obtained by squaring the standard deviation.

```
MODEL STAT5  VERSION OF  09/01/82  22:37
10 COLUMNS 1-10
20 OBSERVED DATA = 15,18,25,30,14,42,63,220,49,42
25*
30 MEAN=MEAN(MATRIX(OBSERVED DATA,1),MATRIX(OBSERVED DATA,10))
40 MEDIAN=MEDIAN(MATRIX(OBSERVED DATA,1),MATRIX(OBSERVED DATA,10))
45*
50 STD DEV OF SAMPLE=STDDEV(MATRIX(OBSERVED DATA,1),'
51 MATRIX(OBSERVED DATA,10))
60 SAMPLE VARIANCE=XPOWERY(STD DEV OF SAMPLE,2)
70*
80*DIRECT CALCULATION OF VARIANCE OF POPULATION
90*
100 VARIANCE=0 FOR 9,SUM OF SQUARES/NCOL-MEAN*MEAN
110 STD DEVIATION=XPOWERY(VARIANCE,0.5)
120*
130*OTHER MEASURES OF DISPERSION
140*
150 SKEWNESS=3*(MEAN-MEDIAN)/STD DEV OF SAMPLE
160*
170 KURTOSIS = 0 FOR 9,(SUM OF 4TH POWERS/NCOL)/'
180 XPOWERY(SAMPLE VARIANCE,2)
190*
200 AVERAGE DEVIATION=PREVIOUS +ABS(OBSERVED DATA-MEAN)/NCOL
210*
220 RANGE = LARGEST VALUE - SMALLEST VALUE
225*
230 LOWER CONFIDENCE LIMIT = MEAN - 1.65*STD DEV OF SAMPLE
240 UPPER CONFIDENCE LIMIT= MEAN +1.65*STD DEV OF SAMPLE
250*
260 COEFFICIENT OF VARIATION = STD DEV OF SAMPLE*100/MEAN
270*
280*     INTERMEDIATE CALCULATIONS AND VALUES
290*
300 SUM OF SQUARES =PREVIOUS +OBSERVED DATA*OBSERVED DATA
310 NCOL=10
320 SUM OF 4TH POWERS =PREVIOUS +XPOWERY((OBSERVED DATA-MEAN),4)
330 LARGEST VALUE =OBSERVED DATA,MAXIMUM(PREVIOUS,OBSERVED DATA)
340 SMALLEST VALUE =OBSERVED DATA,MINIMUM(OBSERVED DATA,PREVIOUS)
END OF MODEL
```

FIGURE 7-5. MEASURES OF DISPERSION
(This Figure Continued on the Next Page)

```
? solve
MODEL STAT5 VERSION OF  09/01/82  22:37 -- 10 COLUMNS 19 VARIABLES
ENTER SOLVE OPTIONS
? all

                        1    2    3    4    5    6    7    8    9   10

OBSERVED DATA          15   18   25   30   14   42   63  220   49   42

MEAN                 51.8 51.8 51.8 51.8 51.8 51.8 51.8 51.8 51.8 51.8
MEDIAN                 42   42   42   42   42   42   42   42   42   42

STD DEV OF SAMPLE    61.2 61.2 61.2 61.2 61.2 61.2 61.2 61.2 61.2 61.2
SAMPLE VARIANCE      3748 3748 3748 3748 3748 3748 3748 3748 3748 3748

DIRECT CALCULATION OF VARIANCE OF POPULATION

VARIANCE                0    0    0    0    0    0    0    0    0 3374
STD DEVIATION           0    0    0    0    0    0    0    0    0 58.1

OTHER MEASURES OF DISPERSION

SKEWNESS             .480 .480 .480 .480 .480 .480 .480 .480 .480 .480

KURTOSIS                0    0    0    0    0    0    0    0    0 5.74

AVERAGE DEVIATION    3.68 7.06 9.74 11.9 15.7 16.7 17.8 34.6 34.9 35.9

RANGE                   0    3   10   15   16   28   49  206  206  206

LOWER CONFIDENCE L-49.2-49.2-49.2-49.2-49.2-49.2-49.2-49.2-49.2-49.2
UPPER CONFIDENCE L    153  153  153  153  153  153  153  153  153  153

COEFFICIENT OF VAR    118  118  118  118  118  118  118  118  118  118

     INTERMEDIATE CALCULATIONS AND VALUES

SUM OF SQUARES        225  549 1174 2074 2270 4034 8003  6E4  6E4  6E4
NCOL                   10   10   10   10   10   10   10   10   10   10
SUM OF 4TH POWERS     2E6  3E6  4E6  4E6  6E6  6E6  6E6  8E8  8E8  8E8
LARGEST VALUE          15   18   25   30   30   42   63  220  220  220
SMALLEST VALUE         15   15   15   15   14   14   14   14   14   14
```

FIGURE 7-5. MEASURES OF DISPERSION
(Continued)

DIRECT CALCULATION OF VARIANCE AND STANDARD DEVIATION. In Figure 7-5 we also show an alternate way of computing the variance that does not use the STDDEV function (Line 100). It is based on the computational formula for the variance of the population:

$$\text{VARIANCE} = (\Sigma X^2 / N) - \text{MEAN}^2 \qquad (7\text{-}8)$$

Note that here we assume that the population mean is known and hence we can divide by N rather than N-1. As a result, the variance and standard deviation of the population are smaller than the variance and standard deviation of the sample. In Figure 7-5, the population standard deviation is 58.1 whereas the sample standard deviation is 61.2.

EXERCISE: Modify Line 100 in Figure 7-5 so that it computes the variance of the sample rather than the variance of the population.

The variance is also called the "second moment" around the mean. This terminology comes from physics where the same calculation is performed in mechanics. You can see the origin of the name if you rewrite Equation (7-8) in the form:

$$\text{VARIANCE} = \Sigma\ (\text{OBSERVED DATA} - \text{MEAN})^2 / N \qquad (7\text{-}9)$$

That is, you add up the second powers of the differences between the observed data and the average value. We will use the concept of moment again when we discuss kurtosis later in this subsection.

SKEWNESS. Skewness refers to the symmetry or lack of symmetry of a frequency distribution that has a single peak. Skewness is usually measured in terms of the Pearson Coefficient of Skewness which is given by:

$$\text{SKEWNESS} = 3 * (\text{MEAN} - \text{MEDIAN}) / \text{STANDARD DEVIATION} \qquad (7\text{-}10)$$

where STANDARD DEVIATION is the standard deviation of the sample as is Equation (7-7). If the mean is equal to the median, then the skewness is equal to 0 and the distribution is symmetric. However, the more the the mean and median differ in location, the more asymmetric the distribution and hence the larger the value of skewness. If the Pearson Coefficient of Skewness is positive, then the mean is bigger than the median and the distribution typically has a long tail to the right; whereas if it is negative there is a tail to the left. Values of skewness larger than +1 or smaller than -1 indicate significant skewness.

KURTOSIS. The next measure of dispersion, kurtosis (a word that comes from the Greek), measures how big the peak of a distribution is. As shown below, distributions having the same mean can be relatively peaked or flat:

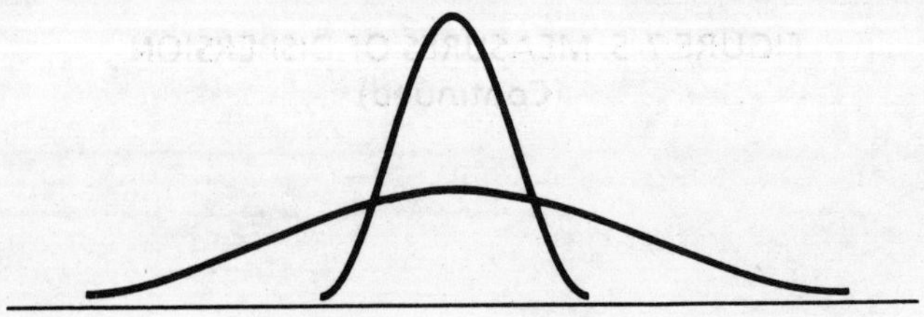

The more peaked the distribution, the greater the kurtosis. As a reference, you will find that the kurtosis of a normal distribution is equal to 3. Kurtosis is computed from the ratio:

$$\text{KURTOSIS} = \text{M4}/(\text{VARIANCE})^2 \tag{7-11}$$

where M4 represents what is called the fourth moment about the mean. M4 is computed from the relation:

$$\text{M4} = \Sigma\ (\text{OBSERVED DATA - MEAN})^4\ /\text{N} \tag{7-12}$$

As you can see, the fourth moment has the same form as the variance of the population except that it adds up the fourth power rather than the square of the deviation from the mean. In Figure 7-5 the cumulative sum of the fourth power of (OBSERVED DATA –MEAN) is computed in Line 320 and used in Line 170 to compute kurtosis. Since the values of the fourth power are over a million and we provide only six spaces for printing out the values, IFPS reports them in the exponential form (e.g.,2E6). However, the exact values are kept inside memory and the value of kurtosis shown is based on the exact value, not the approximation printed in exponential form.

The skewness and kurtosis values that you saw in Monte Carlosimulation (see Section 5.10) help you decide whether the normal distribution is a suitable approximation to a variable or not. If the skewness is close to 0 and the kurtosis is close to 3, then the normal approximation is valid and you can use the results of the NORM option in Monte Carlo.

AVERAGE DEVIATION. The average deviation measures how close individual values are to the mean. The average deviation is given by:

$$\text{AVERAGE DEVIATION} = \Sigma\ (\text{ABSOLUTE VALUE}\ (\text{X - MEAN})\ )/\ n \tag{7-13}$$

Unlike the standard deviation which adds up the square of the difference between observed and mean values, the average deviation is a linear measure and hence does not weight outlying points as heavily.

RANGE. The range is simply the difference between the largest and smallest values observed. It is a relatively poor measure of dispersion since a single outlying point can affect the result drastically. For example (1,2,3,4,5) has a range of (5-1) = 4 whereas (1,2,3,4,11) has a range of (11-1) = 10.

In computing the RANGE we used the IFPS MAXIMUM and MINIMUM functions to find the largest and smallest values of the data. Since these functions take the largest (or smallest) value of their arguments, we compare the previous maximum (or minimum) with the current data point. If the current data point is larger (smaller) than any before it, this point becomes the new maximum (minimum).

CONFIDENCE INTERVALS. The mean value computed from a set of data is, of course, only an estimate of the true mean of the total population if the sample represents only a fraction of the total population. The question to be resolved is "How good is the estimate of the mean?". The usual way to resolve this issue is to define a "confidence interval". This interval is constructed in such a way that a specified percentage of the time (e.g., 90% or

95%) the interval determined by the procedure contains the true mean.

In Monte Carlo simulation (Section 5.1.6), one of the standard statistics provided is the 90% confidence interval for the mean. It is obtained by computing:

$$\text{LOWER LIMIT (10\%)} = \text{MEAN} - 1.65^{*}\text{STD DEVIATION} / \sqrt{N} \quad (7\text{-}14)$$

$$\text{UPPER LIMIT (90\%)} = \text{MEAN} + 1.65^{*}\text{STD DEVIATION} / \sqrt{N} \quad (7\text{-}15)$$

These formulas are standard. If you want to obtain a 95% confidence interval, you replace 1.65 by 1.96. Between them the lower limit and the upper limit define the range of values inside which you expect the true mean to lie. In Figure 7-5, for example, the sample mean is 51.8 and the 90% confidence limits are –49.2 and 153. In this case the limits are quite broad because we have only a few data points and they scatter. As the sample size increases, the confidence limits typically get closer to the estimate of the mean. However, this convergence is slow, decreasing as the square root of the sample size, N. Thus, you typically need four times as many points as you have if you want to cut the width of the confidence interval in half.

COEFFICIENT OF VARIATION. The population coefficient of variation measures the ratio of the standard deviation of the sample to the mean. It is given by:

$$\text{COEFFICIENT OF VARIATION} = \text{STD DEVIATION}^{*}100/\text{MEAN} \quad (7\text{-}16)$$

This is a percentage measure and can therefore be used to compare the variability of different distributions. The coefficient of variation is particularly useful when you are comparing quantities that are expressed in different units (e.g., family income in dollars and family living space in square feet) or when comparing quantities in the same units but of different orders of magnitude (e.g., Gross National Product in millions and personal income in thousands) In Figure 7-5, the coefficient of variation is 118% since the mean is 51.8 and the standard deviation is 61.2.

7.2 PERMUTATIONS AND COMBINATIONS

In computing probabilities it is often necessary to determine how many different ways particular outcomes can occur. There are two cases to consider:

- The order in which events occur is important (i.e., permutation).
- The order in which events occur is immaterial (i.e., combination).

For example, HT (two coin flips resulting in "heads," H followed by "tails",T) is a different permutation than TH since H and T are in different order, whereas HT and TH are the same combination.

We are usually interested in determining the number of permutations or the number of combinations of n things taken k at a time. For example, how many ways can you pick 3 numbers out of 5? Symbolically, we write, ${}_5P_3$ or ${}_5C_3$ for permutations and combinations, respectively.

To compute permutations we recognize that if we have n objects (e.g., numbers) then we can select the first one n different ways. However, once the first one is selected, there are only (n-1) objects left, so there are only (n-1) ways to pick it. In general, if we want to pick x objects out of n,

$$ {}_nP_x = n*(n-1)*(n-2)*...*(n-x) \tag{7-17}$$

This can be done recursively. That is, the relation:

$$ {}_nP_x = {}_nP_{x-1} *(n-x+1), \qquad x=1,2,...,n \tag{7-18}$$

holds, where ${}_nP_0 = 1$.

Figure 7-6 shows this form of the computation in IFPS. In using this model you should be careful. Permutations become very large numbers very fast because you are multiplying integers.

```
MODEL PERMUTE  VERSION OF  08/31/82  22:56
10 COLUMNS 0-5
20 * MODEL FOR COMPUTING PERMUTATIONS
30 *
40PERMUTATIONS =1,PREVIOUS*(N-X+1)
50*
55 N=5
60 X=0,PREVIOUS+1
END OF MODEL
? solve
MODEL PERMUTE  VESION OF  08/31/82  22:56 -- 6 COLUMNS 3 VARIABLES
ENTER SOLVE OPTIONS
? all

                                0     1     2     3     4     5
 MODEL FOR COMPUTING PERMUTATIONS

PERMUTATIONS                    1     5    20    60   120   120

N                               5     5     5     5     5     5
X                               0     1     2     3     4     5
```

FIGURE 7-6. PERMUTATIONS

Combinations are much smaller numbers than permutations since each combination includes many permutations. The formula for combinations is:

$$ {}_nC_x = {}_nP_x / x! \tag{7-19}$$

Like permutations, combinations can be calculated recursively. Specifically,

$$ {}_nC_0 = 1, $$

and

$$ {}_nC_x = {}_nC_{x-1} * (n-x+1)/x \tag{7-20}$$

Equation (7-20) is implemented in IFPS in Figure 7-7 which shows how to compute combinations for n things taken 1, 2, and so on up to n at a time. Note that we provide 20 columns in our COLUMNS definition but use only six in our SOLVE option since we chose n=5. To use this model for other values of n, you need only change n with a WHAT IF statement. If you have values of n greater than 20 you also have to change the COLUMNS definition.

```
MODEL COMBINE  VERSION OF  08/31/82  23:00
10 COLUMNS 0-20
20*
30*MODEL FOR COMPUTING COMBINATORIALS
40*
50 COMBINATORIAL = 1,PREVIOUS*(N-X+1)/X
60 *
80 N=5
90 X= 0,PREVIOUS +1
100*
END OF MODEL
? solve
MODEL COMBINE  VERSION OF  08/31/82  23:00 -- 21 COLUMNS 3 VARIABLES
ENTER SOLVE OPTIONS
? columns 0-5
? all
                                  0      1      2      3      4      5

MODEL FOR COMPUTING COMBINATORIALS

COMBINATORIAL                     1      5     10     10      5      1

 DATA
N                                 5      5      5      5      5      5
X                                 0      1      2      3      4      5
```

FIGURE 7-7. COMBINATIONS

EXERCISE: Suppose you are trying to form a committee of six, with three representatives from Department A and three from Department B. Department A has seven people and Department B has nine people. How many different committees can you form? This is a standard probability problem. Set up the appropriate combinatorials and then use IFPS to obtain your numeric answer.

EXERCISE: Suppose the order in which people are appointed to your committee determines their seniority. How many "different" committees can you form in this case?

7.3 PROBABILITY DISTRIBUTIONS

To understand probability distributions we must begin with random variables. Random variables are numerical descriptions of the outcome of experiments. The specific outcome of a particular situation may be unknown beforehand, but we usually can say something about the possible outcomes and we can say it in numeric terms. For example, if you inspect a shipment of 100 television sets, you may observe anywhere between 0 and 100 defective sets. Furthermore, you may even have prior information as to the probability of 0 or 1 or 2 or more than 2 defective sets. The numeric values of these probabilities form a probability distribution. In this section, we describe how to determine the values of two standard probability distributions using IFPS:

- Binomial distribution.
- Poisson distribution.

If you want to find a single value from a particular binomial or Poisson distribution, you will do better by using your hand caclulator; however the power of using IFPS comes in creating a table of values each of which can then be used in larger calculations.

7.3.1 Binomial Distribution

The binomial probability distribution arises in situations in which there are two possible outcomes, such as heads and tails. If there is a probability, p, of one outcome (e.g., heads), then the probability of the other outcome must be (1–p). Usually, we set q = 1–p and talk about a probability p of a favorable outcome and q of an unfavorable outcome. The binomial probability distribution occurs if we perform an experiment (e.g., flipping a coin) a fixed number of times. Each experiment has the same two possible outcomes with probability p and q respectively. The question is what is the probability of 0,1, 2, ..., x, ...n successes (e.g., heads) in n trials. The probability of x successes in n trials with probability p of success on each trial is denoted by P(X). The formula for the binomial probability distribution involves computing:

$$P(X) = {}_{n}C_{x}\, p^{x} q^{n-x} \tag{7-21}$$

We showed how to compute the combinatorial x in the previous section. Here we have to multiply the combinatorial by powers of p and q. The IFPS program for accomplishing this is shown in Figure 7-8. You will see in the figure that the easy way to perform this calculation and to obtain the entire distribution for a given probability p and number of trials n is to use the fact that:

$$P(X) = P(X\text{-}1)^{*}\,(n-x+1)^{*}p\,/\,(q^{*}x) \tag{7-22}$$

where P(0) is given by q^n. The quantity P(0) represents the case of no successes (e.g., all tails). Equation (7-22) shows that, for given n and p, the probability for x successes is computed by multiplying the probability for (x-1) successes by a constant that depends on the probability of success p, the number of trials, n, and the number of successes x.

If you look at the IFPS program in Figure 7-8, you will see that we have specified columns 0 to 20 simply to allow you to compute binomial probabilities for up to 20 trials; if you have more than that, you will have to change the COLUMNS statement in Line 10. To obtain results for other than the sample values of n and p given (n=5 and p=0.3), use WHAT IF statements to put in your data. Finally, print out only the columns through n by specifying the number of columns you need as a SOLVE option. Note, however, that you must specify column numbers numerically. You can't say COLUMNS 0-N; you must say, for example, COLUMNS 0-5.

```
MODEL BINOMIAL  VERSION OF  08/31/82  23:05
10 COLUMNS 0-20
20*MODEL FOR COMPUTING BINOMIAL PROBABILITIES
25*X SUCCESSES IN N TRIALS WITH PROBABILITY OF SUCCESS P PER TRIAL
30 *
40 BINOMIAL XNP=XPOWERY(Q,N),PREVIOUS*(P*(N-X+1))/(Q*X)
50 CUMULATIVE BINOMIAL XNP=PREVIOUS + BINOMIAL XNP
55*
60*DATA
70 P=.3
80 Q=1-P
90 N=5
100 X=0,PREVIOUS+1
END OF MODEL
? solve
MODEL BINOMIAL  VERSION OF  08/31/82  23:05--21 COLUMNS 6 VARIABLES
ENTER SOLVE OPTIONS
? columns 0-5
? all
                             0       1       2       3       4       5

MODEL FOR COMPUTING BINOMIAL PROBABILITIES
X SUCCESSES IN N TRIALS WITH PROBABILITY OF SUCCESS P PER TRIAL

BINOMIAL XNP               .1681   .3602   .3087   .1323   .0284   .0024
CUMULATIVE BINOMIAL        .1681   .5282   .8369   .9692   .9976       1

DATA
P                          .3000   .3000   .3000   .3000   .3000   .3000
Q                          .7000   .7000   .7000   .7000   .7000   .7000
N                              5       5       5       5       5       5
X                              0       1       2       3       4       5
```

FIGURE 7-8. BINOMIAL DISTRIBUTION

In Figure 7-8 you will find not only the binomial probability distribution for the input data values of n and p, but also the cumulative distribution. The cumulative distribution is found by adding up all the values from x = 0 through the current value of x. Thus, in the example, if x = 0, both the binomial probability and the cumulative probability distribution have a value of 0.1681. For x = 1, the binomial probability is 0.3602 and the the cumulative distribution is equal to 0.1681 + 0.3602 or 0.5283 (Note: IFPS displays rounded answers; hence the cumulative shown on the output may differ slightly from the answer you obtain by adding up the output values of the individual probabilities.)

7.3.2 Poisson Distribution

The Poisson distribution describes the probability of 0, 1, 2, or more events occurring in a fixed time interval where we know that:

- Events occur "at random"
- The average number of occurrences in the time interval is m.

This distribution describes, for example, random arrivals at service facilities such as trucks at terminals, phone calls at a switchboard, or customers at a fast food restaurant. The form of the distribution is:

$$P(x) = m^x / (NATEXP(m)*x!) \qquad x=0,1,2,... \quad (7\text{-}23)$$

As in the case of the binomial distributions, it is easier to calculate this distribution recursively in IFPS. Equation (7-23) can be rewritten as:

$$P(x) = P(x\text{-}1)*\ m/x \qquad (7\text{-}24)$$

where P(0) = 1/NATEXP(m) as in Equation (7-23). This form of computing the Poisson distribution is illustrated in Figure 7-9. This figure shows both the probability of exactly x arrivals and the probability of up to x arrivals (that is, the cumulative probability distribution).

The Poisson distribution differs from the binomial in that it has, at least in theory, an infinite number of terms; practically, however, the individual probabilities become small as x becomes larger.

EXERCISE: Suppose customers arrive at random at a fast food restaurant at a rate of 20 per hour. Compute the probability of exactly 0, 1, 2, 3, ... arrivals during a 10-minute interval by modifying Figure 7-9. Write a model that combines Figure 7-9 with the models for mean and variance of Section 7.1 to compute the mean and variance of this Poisson distribution. You should find the mean is equal to the input value and, furthermore, that the mean and the variance of the Poisson distribution are equal.

EXERCISE: The Poisson distribution is considered a good approximation to the binomial distribution if the number of binomial trials is 20 or more and the probability of success, p, is 5% or less. Since the mean of the binomial is equal to n*p, you approximate the binomial with a Poisson whose mean is equal to n*p. Write a model that combines Figure 7-8 and Figure 7-9 and computes both the binomial and its Poisson approximation for n=20 and p=.05. Compare the binomial and the Poisson by using the plot feature of IFPS to plot the cumulative distributions.

EXERCISE: Repeat the previous exercise for the case n=5, p=.05 and for the case n=20, p=.60. Again, plot the results to compare the answers.

7.4 CHI-SQUARE TESTS OF GOODNESS OF FIT AND INDEPENDENCE

The chi-square distribution is a tabulated probability distribution that is used in testing two hypotheses:

1. The agreement between an observed distribution and an assumed distribution.

2. The independence of two variables.

```
MODEL POISSON  VERSION OF  09/22/81  19:04
10 COLUMNS 0-20
20*POISSON DISTRIBUTION FOR MEAN M
30*
40 X= 0,PREVIOUS+1
50 PROBABILITY OF X=1/NATEXP(MEAN),PREVIOUS*MEAN/X
60 CUMULATIVE PROBABILITY = PREVIOUS + PROBABILITY OF X
70*
80*DATA
90*----
100 MEAN = 5
? solve
MODEL POISSON  VERSION OF  09/22/81  19:04 -- 21 COLUMNS 4 VARIABLES
ENTER SOLVE OPTIONS
? columns 0-17
? all
                              0       1       2       3       4       5
POISSON DISTRIBUTION FOR MEAN M

X                             0       1       2       3       4       5
PROBABILITY OF X          .0067   .0337   .0842   .1404   .1755   .1755
CUMULATIVE PROBABILI      .0067   .0404   .1247   .2650   .4405   .6160

DATA
----
MEAN                          5       5       5       5       5       5

                              6       7       8       9      10      11
POISSON DISTRIBUTION FOR MEAN M

X                             6       7       8       9      10      11
PROBABILITY OF X          .1462   .1044   .0653   .0363   .0181   .0082
CUMULATIVE PROBABILI      .7622   .8666   .9319   .9682   .9863   .9945
DATA
----
MEAN                          5       5       5       5       5       5

                             12      13      14      15      16      17
POISSON DISTRIBUTION FOR MEAN M

X                            12      13      14      15      16      17
PROBABILITY OF X          .0034   .0013   .0005   .0002       0       0
CUMULATIVE PROBABILI      .9980   .9993   .9998   .9999       1       1

DATA
----
MEAN                          5       5       5       5       5       5
```

FIGURE 7-9. POISSON DISTRIBUTION

These are quite different problems. In the first case, we typically have a notion based on theory or analysis that a phenomenon should follow some specified distribution and we want to see if that notion is correct. That is, we want to see how well the hypothesized distribution fits the data. Such a test is called a "goodness of fit" test. For example, we believe that if we throw an honest pair of dice, a 2 should show up 1/36th of the time, a 7 should show up 6/36th of the time, etc. If we throw a pair of dice 3600 times and observe 105 2's and 585 7's, can we reject the hypothesis that this is a fair pair of dice?

Figure 7-10 shows how such a goodness of fit test is conducted in IFPS. The input data are the observed and expected number of times of each outcome from 2 through 12 in throwing a pair of dice 3600 times. These values are used to compute the value of chi-square from the formula:

$$\chi^2 = \Sigma((\text{OBSERVED} - \text{EXPECTED})^2 / (\text{EXPECTED}) \qquad (7\text{-}25)$$

where the observed and expected values are taken column by column. The program computes the individual terms of the sum and cumulates values as it goes along. The result is the chi-square value shown in the last column.

```
MODEL CHISQ1  VERSION OF  07/09/81  22:38
10 COLUMNS 2-12
20*
30*    DETERMINING GOODNESS OF FIT
40*
50 OBSERVED=95,190,315,380,470,640,510,420,280,210,90
60 EXPECTED=100,200,300,400,500,600,500,400,300,200,100
70 CHISQUARE TERMS=(OBSERVED-EXPECTED)*(OBSERVED-EXPECTED)/EXPECTED
80 CHISQUARE= PREVIOUS + CHISQUARE TERMS
? solve
MODEL CHISQ1  VERSION OF  07/09/81  22:38 -- 11 COLUMNS 4 VARIABLES
ENTER SOLVE OPTIONS
? all
                              2       3       4       5       6       7

    DETERMINING GOODNESS OF FIT

OBSERVED                     95     190     315     380     470     640
EXPECTED                    100     200     300     400     500     600
CHISQUARE TERMS           .2500   .5000   .7500       1   1.800   2.667
CHISQUARE                 .2500   .7500   1.500   2.500   4.300   6.967

                              8       9      10      11      12
     DETERMINING GOODNESS OF FIT

OBSERVED                    510     420     280     210      90
EXPECTED                    500     400     300     200     100
CHISQUARE TERMS           .2000       1   1.333   .5000       1
CHISQUARE                 7.167   8.167   9.500      10      11
```

FIGURE 7-10. USING CHI-SQUARE TO DETERMINE GOODNESS OF FIT

To use this result we need two additional pieces of data: the degrees of freedom and the desired probability level. For a simple distribution such as this one, the number of degrees of freedom is one less than the number of categories (in our case 11 categories implies 10 degrees of freedom). The usual probability level is 5%. Look up the test value for the degrees of freedom and probability level in a chi-square table in your favorite statistics book. If the chi-square value you observe is greater than the test value from the table, you reject the hypothesis that the observed distribution fits the assumed distribution. In Figure 7-10, the observed chi-square value was 11. The tabulated value for ten degrees of freedom and 5% is 18.307. Therefore, we cannot reject the hypothesis that the dice are fair.

In the second case, we are interested in whether two characteristics depend on one another or not. For example, supposing we are trying to determine whether support of a particular candidate is independent of the education level of voters. Then the hypothesis to be tested is that the chance of preferring a candidate is independent of educational level. The best evidence of this would be that the chance of supporting a candidate is the same whether the voter had some high school, was a high school graduate, had some college, or was a college graduate.

To determine whether this is so or not we set up a contingency table, such as the following, for three candidates whom we shall call Jones, Kenner, and Hartz:

	SOME HS	HS GRAD	SOME COL	COLLEGE	TOTAL
JONES	50	80	60	30	220
KENNER	20	60	80	20	180
HARTZ	30	60	60	50	200
TOTAL	100	200	200	100	600
EXPECTED VOTES					
JONES EXPECTED	36.67	73.33	73.33	36.67	220
KENNER EXPECTED	30.00	60.00	60.00	30.00	180
HARTZ EXPECTED	33.33	66.67	66.67	33.33	200

The first three lines above represent actual experience. The expected votes for each candidate are computed from the row and column totals. Since 100 out of 600 have some high school, we should expect one-sixth of each candidates' supporters to be in the some high school category; for example, we should expect 30 out of Kenner's 180 supporters to have some high school.

We are now at the point where we can apply Equation (7-25) and determine the value of chi-square. This is done in Figure 7-11. This figure looks like our table above. Adding up the data in each column is done in the usual way in Line 70. Finding the row totals on the right, however, is somewhat more difficult. We could have used the available COLUMNS command and written:

```
COLUMN 5 = SUM(COLUMN 1 THRU COLUMN 4)
```

However, IFPS is basically a row logic not a column logic language. Although you can compute the value in a given column, such as column 5, you cannot use the COLUMN command results for computation. For contingency tables we use the row totals in computing the expected values. To get around this difficulty, we show two alternate ways of performing the calculations. The first of these, shown in Figure 7-11a, keeps the same

```
MODEL CHISQ2  VERSION OF  08/22/82  21:08
10 COLUMNS SOME HS,HS,SOME COLLEGE,COLLEGE,TOTAL
20*CHI SQUARE TEST OF INDEPENDENCE
30*
40 JONES=50,80,60,30,PREVIOUS+PREVIOUS 2 + PREVIOUS 3 + PREVIOUS 4
50 KENNER=20,60,80,20,PREVIOUS+PREVIOUS 2 +PREVIOUS 3 + PREVIOUS 4
60 HARTZ = 30,60,60,50,PREVIOUS+PREVIOUS 2 + PREVIOUS 3 + PREVIOUS 4
70 TOTAL =JONES + KENNER + HARTZ
80*
90* EXPECTED VOTES
95*
100 JONES EXPECTED= MATRIX(JONES,5)*TOTAL/MATRIX(TOTAL,5)
110 KENNER EXPECTED=MATRIX(KENNER,5)*TOTAL/MATRIX(TOTAL,5)
120 HARTZ EXPECTED = MATRIX(HARTZ,5)*TOTAL/MATRIX(TOTAL,5)
130*
140 CHISQ ROW1 =XPOWERY((JONES-JONES EXPECTED),2)/JONES EXPECTED
150 CHISQ ROW2 =XPOWERY((KENNER-KENNER EXPECTED),2)/KENNER EXPECTED
160 CHISQ ROW3=XPOWERY((HARTZ-HARTZ EXPECTED),2)/HARTZ EXPECTED
170*
180 CHISQUARE = PREVIOUS + CHISQ ROW1 + CHISQ ROW2 +CHISQ ROW3
END OF MODEL
? solve
MODEL CHISQ2  VERSION OF  08/22/82  23:44 -- 5 COLUMNS 11 VARIABLES
ENTER SOLVE OPTIONS
? all
```

	SOME HS	HS	SOME COL	COLLEGE	TOTAL
CHI SQUARE TEST OF INDEPENDENCE					
JONES	50	80	60	30	220
KENNER	20	60	80	20	180
HARTZ	30	60	60	50	200
TOTAL	100	200	200	100	600
EXPECTED VOTES					
JONES EXPECTED	36.67	73.33	73.33	36.67	220
KENNER EXPECTED	30	60	60	30	180
HARTZ EXPECTED	33.33	66.67	66.67	33.33	200
CHISQ ROW1	4.848	.6061	2.424	1.212	0
CHISQ ROW2	3.333	0	6.667	3.333	0
CHISQ ROW3	.3333	.6667	.6667	8.333	0
CHISQUARE	8.515	9.788	19.55	32.42	32.42

a. Standard Form

FIGURE 7-11. CHI-SQUARE TEST OF INDEPENDENCE
(This Figure Continued on the Next Page)

```
MODEL CHISQ3  VERSION OF  09/07/82  22:02
10 COLUMNS JONES,KENNR,HARTZ,TOTAL,EXPJ,EXPK,EXPH,CHIJ,CHIK,CHIH,'
11 TOTCH
20 SOME HS=50,20,30
30 HS GRAD=80,60,60
40 SOME COL = 60,80,60
50 COLLEGE GRAD=30,20,50
60 TOTAL = SUM(SOME HS THRU COLLEGE GRAD)
65*
70 COLUMN TOTAL = C JONES + C KENNR + C HARTZ
80 COLUMN EXPJ =MATRIX(TOTAL,1)*C TOTAL/MATRIX(TOTAL ,4)
90 COLUMN EXPK= MATRIX(TOTAL,2)*C TOTAL/MATRIX(TOTAL,4)
100 COLUMN EXPH= MATRIX(TOTAL,3)*C TOTAL/MATRIX(TOTAL,4)
110 COLUMN CHIJ=XPOWERY(C JONES-C EXPJ,2)/C EXPJ
120 COLUMN CHIK=XPOWERY(C KENNR-C EXPK,2)/C EXPK
130 COLUMN CHIH=XPOWERY(C HARTZ-C EXPH,2)/C EXPH
140 COLUMN TOTCH FOR SOME HS THRU COLLEGE GRAD=C CHIJ'
141 +C CHIK +C CHIH
150 COLUMN TOTCHFOR TOTAL=SUM(SOME HS THRU COLLEGE GRAD)
END OF MODEL
? solve
MODEL CHISQ3  VERSION OF  09/07/82  22:02 -- 11 COLUMNS 5 VARIABLES
ENTER SOLVE OPTIONS
? width 68 13 5
? all
```

	JONES	KENNR	HARTZ	TOTAL	EXPJ	EXPK	EXPH	CHIJ	CHIK	CHIH	TOTCH
SOME HS	50	20	30	100	36.7	30	33.3	4.85	3.33	.333	8.52
HS GRAD	80	60	60	200	73.3	60	66.7	.606	0	.667	1.27
SOME COL	60	80	60	200	73.3	60	66.7	2.42	6.67	.667	9.76
COLLEGE GRAD	30	20	50	100	36.7	30	33.3	1.21	3.33	8.33	12.9
TOTAL	220	180	200	600	220	180	200	0	0	0	32.4

b. Alternate Form

FIGURE 7-11 CHI-SQUARE TEST OF INDEPENDENCE
(Continued)

output format as above but requires computing the row totals in a rather cumbersome way. The PREVIOUS command is used to refer to each of the earlier numbers in the row. We also had to be very careful and use MATRIX references to retrieve these row totals in computing expected values. This is not entirely satisfactory because it becomes awkward if there are many observations. The observed and expected values are then used to apply Equation 7-25 and find the contribution of each element of the table to chi-square. The final chi-square value appears in the lower right hand corner and is equal in our example to 32.42.

The alternate form, shown in Figure 7-11b, inverts the rows and the columns, showing the categories as rows and what was previously row information as columns. It is also an example of using the COLUMN commands (Section 4.4.5) in calculations. Go over both forms; you will find that one or the other methods is easier for you to use.

The number of degrees of freedom for a test of independence is determined differently than for a test of goodness of fit. Specifically, if r is the number of rows and c is the number of columns, then the number of degrees of freedom is equal to (r-1)*(c-1). In our case we have 3 rows and 4 columns; therefore we have (3-1)*(4-1) = 6 degrees of freedom. At the 5% level and six degrees of freedom, the chi-square table gives a test value of 12.592. Since the observed value is 32.42, we must reject the hypothesis that the chance of supporting a given candidate does not depend on educational level.

EXERCISE: Rewrite Figure 7-11a so that it has only four columns, SOME HS, HS, SOME COL and COLLEGE. That is, do not show the totals column explicitly. You will have to compute the values in the totals column as separate rows; however, you can suppress these intermediate calculations in your printout. The resulting format is different but the results should be the same. Which do you prefer?

7.5 LINEAR REGRESSION

In this section (and in the next section) we are concerned with using data for prediction. The simplest case is one in which there are two variables, for example, soda consumption and temperature, which we believe are related. If we can find the relation between the variables, then given the value of one (e.g., temperature),we can use the relationship to forecast the value of the other (e.g., soda consumption).

In general, if we do not know the relation between the variables we must infer the relationship from a sample of data. Usually, it is possible to plot sample data in the form of "scatter diagrams" such as this one:

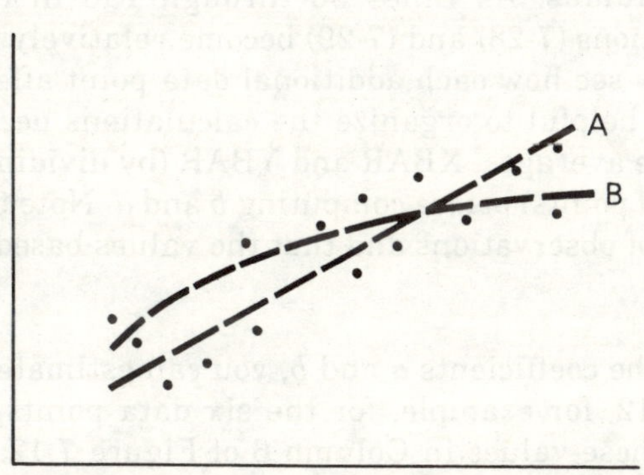

The relation may appear to be linear (Curve A) or curvilinear (Curve B) as shown by the dashed lines. The first decision you have to make is what form of the relational is appropriate. (You can, of course, try several forms and pick the one that fits best according to test; we will discuss these tests later.) To illustrate the procedure we will assume a linear relation, that is, a relation of the form:

$$Y = a + bX \tag{7-26}$$

Here Y refers to the value of Y that is computed given a value of X. The problem, thus, is to determine the values of the coefficients a and b in such a way as to specify the straight line that best fits the sample data that we have.

Although "best fits" is a simple-sounding criteria, we must have some way of operationalizing it. A number of criteria are possible; however, the standard way the problem of obtaining the best fit is solved is to find those values of *a* and *b* for which:

$$\Sigma (Y - Y_C)^2 \qquad (7\text{-}27)$$

is a minimum and for which $\Sigma(Y - Y_C) = 0$. The first criterion makes the total squared deviation of the observed values from the computed values as small as possible. Since this line may not be unique, we impose the additional constraint that the average deviation of the observations from the computed values must be 0; this means that the line goes through the average value of the observed X's and Y's. (Do you see why?)

7.5.1 Computing the Regression Coefficients

The coefficients *a* and *b* in Equation(7-26) are computed from the following relations:

$$b = \frac{SUM(X*Y) - n*XBAR*YBAR}{SUM(X*X) - n*XBAR*XBAR} \qquad (7\text{-}28)$$

$$a = YBAR - b*XBAR \qquad (7\text{-}29)$$

where SUM refers to adding up all values (e.g., SUM(X*Y) = XY in the conventional notation of mathematics), and XBAR and YBAR are the average values of X and Y, respectively, computed as in Section 7.1.1. These calculations are shown in Figure 7-12. For simplicity of presentation, we have used only six data points; however the relations are valid for any number of data points up to the IFPS limit for your computer on the maximum number of columns. As Lines 50 through 190 in Figure 7-12 show, the seemingly complex Equations (7-28) and (7-29) become relatively simple when expressed in IFPS. You can literally see how each additional data point affects the estimate of the coefficients *a* and *b*. It is helpful to organize the calculations neatly, first obtaining the needed sums and then the averages XBAR and YBAR (by dividing the sum of the X and Y values by the number of points) before computing *b* and *a*. Note that the values of *b* and *a* depend on the number of observations and that the values based on all the data appear in the last column.

Once you have obtained the coefficients *a* and *b*, you can estimate the value of Y for any value of X. In Figure 7-12, for example, for the six data points given, $a = -2.545$ and $b = 34.49$. You will find these values in Column 6 of Figure 7-12. The values of *a* and *b* given in Columns 2 through 5 represent the values of *a* using all the data up to that point; for example, the value in column 4 is based on the first four observed values. Based on the six data points available,

$$Y = -2.545 + 34.49X \qquad (7\text{-}30)$$

Hence, if you want to know the expected value of Y if X=1.8, simply substitute 1.8 for X in Equation (7-30) to obtain Y=59.534. This is also done in Figure 7-12.

Before proceeding further, a few words are in order about the relation between the REGRESS model shown in Figure 7-12 and the TREND and POLYFIT functions described in Section 3.2.3. As you recall, in the TREND function you supply X and Y

```
 MODEL REGRESS  VERSION OF  01/12/83  19:36
10 COLUMNS 1-6
30 * SUMS
50 SUMX=PREVIOUS +X
60 SUMY=PREVIOUS +Y
70 SUMXY=PREVIOUS +X*Y
80 SUMXSQUARE=PREVIOUS+X*X
90 SUMYSQUARE=PREVIOUS+Y*Y
100 *
110 * AVERAGES
120 *
130 XBAR=SUMX/N
140 YBAR=SUMY/N
150 *
160 *A AND B COEFFICIENTS OF REGRESSION LINE
170 *
180 B=0,(SUMXY -N*XBAR*YBAR)/(SUMXSQUARE-N*XBAR*XBAR)
190 A=0,YBAR-B*XBAR
200 *
210 * ESTIMATION
220 *
230 X TO BE ESTIMATED= 1.8
240 Y TO BE ESTIMATED= A+B*X TO BE ESTIMATED
250 *
260 *COEFFICIENT OF DETERMINATION,RSQUARE, AND CORRELATION'
261 COEFFICIENT,R
270 *
280 RSQUARE=0,0, (A*SUMY +B*SUMXY-N*YBAR*YBAR)/'
281 (SUMYSQUARE-N*YBAR*YBAR)
290 R=XPOWERY(RSQUARE,0.5)*MULTIPLIER
300 MULTIPLIER = IF B.GT.0 THEN 1 ELSE (-1)
310 *
320 *T STATISTIC--TEST FOR POPULATION CORRELATION COEFFICIENT RHO=0
330 *
340 T = 0,0,R/XPOWERY((1-RSQUARE)/(N-2),.5)
350 *
360 *CONFIDENCE INTERVAL FOR REGRESSION COEFFICIENT B
370 *
380 STD ERROR OF ESTIMATE=0,0,XPOWERY((SUMYSQUARE-A*SUMY-B*SUMXY)'
381 /(N-2),.5)
390 DENOMINATOR1 =0,0,SUMXSQUARE-N*XBAR*XBAR
400 STD ERROR OF REGRESSION COEFFICIENT = 0,0,'
410 STD ERROR OF ESTIMATE/XPOWERY(DENOMINATOR1,0.5)
420 UPPER CONFIDENCE LIMIT=B+TCRITICAL*'
421 STD ERROR OF REGRESSION COEFFICIENT
430 LOWER CONFIDENCE LIMIT=B-TCRITICAL*'
431 STD ERROR OF REGRESSION COEFFICIENT
440 *INPUT DATA
480 X=1.7,3,2,1.5,0.6,1.5
490 Y=50,100,75,45,20,50
500 TCRITICAL = 2.776
510 N=1,PREVIOUS +1
```

FIGURE 7-12. LINEAR REGRESSION

(This Figure is Continued on the Next Page)

```
? solve
MODEL REGRESS  VERSION OF  01/12/83  19:36 -- 6 COLUMNS 24 VARIABLES
ENTER SOLVE OPTIONS
? all
                                1       2       3       4       5       6
 SUMS

SUMX                        1.700   4.700   6.700   8.200   8.800   10.30
SUMY                           50     150     225     270     290     340
SUMXY                          85     385     535   602.5   614.5   689.5
SUMXSQUARE                  2.890   11.89   15.89   18.14   18.50   20.75
SUMYSQUARE                   2500   12500   18125   20150   20550   23050

 AVERAGES

XBAR                        1.700   2.350   2.233   2.050   1.760   1.717
YBAR                           50      75      75   67.50      58   56.67

A AND B COEFFICIENCTS OF REGRESSION LINE

B                               0   38.46   35.07   36.84   34.56   34.49
A                               0  -15.38  -3.327  -8.026  -2.829  -2.545

 ESTIMATION

X TO BE ESTIMATED           1.800   1.800   1.800   1.800   1.800   1.800
Y TO BE ESTIMATED               0   53.85   59.80   58.29   59.38   59.54

COEFFICIENT OF DETERMINATION,RSQUARE, AND CORRELATION COEFFICIENT,R

RSQUARE                         0       0   .9119   .9378   .9646   .9649
R                               0       0   .9549   .9684   .9821   .9823
MULTIPLIER                     -1       1       1       1       1       1
 T STATISTIC--TEST FOR POPULATION CORRELATION COEFFICIENT RHO=0

T                               0       0   3.217   5.491   9.039   10.48

CONFIDENCE INTERVAL FOR REGRESSION COEFFICIENT B

STD ERROR OF ESTIMATE           0       0   10.50   7.737   6.636   5.764
DENOMINATOR1                    0       0   .9267   1.330   3.012   3.068
STD ERROR OF REGRESSION CO      0       0   10.90   6.709   3.824   3.291
UPPER CONFIDENCE LIMIT          0   38.46   65.34   55.47   45.18   43.63
LOWER CONFIDENCE LIMIT          0   38.46   4.805   18.22   23.95   25.36

 INPUT DATA

X                           1.700       3       2   1.500   .6000   1.500
Y                              50     100      75      45      20      50
TCRITICAL                   2.776   2.776   2.776   2.776   2.776   2.776
N                               1       2       3       4       5       6
```

FIGURE 7-12. LINEAR REGRESSION
(Continued)

values for as many X,Y combinations as you have data. You then give IFPS the X value(s) you want and ask for TREND(X) values to be shown as Y. In this form you do not need the linear regression program since IFPS does linear regression for you; however you do need to run an extra column beyond the data for each X value for which you want an estimate. If, in response to SOLVE OPTIONS you specify

```
OPTION H2
```

IFPS will also print out for you the *a* and *b* coefficients of the linear regression equation as well as the coefficient of determination, called R^2 (which is discussed in Section 7.5.2). Figure 7-13 illustrates the TREND function and OPTION H2.

```
MODEL TREND  VERSION OF  09/01/82  19:45
10 COLUMNS 1-7
20*
30*USING TREND FUNCTION AND OPTION H2 FOR FORECASTING
40*
50 X=1.7,3.0,2.0,1.5,.6,1.5,1.8
60 Y=50,100,75,45,20,50,TREND(X)
END OF MODEL
? OPTION H2
READY FOR MODELING LANGUAGE COMMAND
? solve
MODEL TREND  VERSION OF  09/01/82  19:45 -- 7 COLUMNS 2 VARIABLES
ENTER SOLVE OPTIONS
? all
TREND FUNCTION COEFFICIENTS-LINE 60       34.49 * IND VAR +    -2.545
R SQUARED IS       .9649

                                1        2        3        4      5        6      7


USING TREND FUNCTION AND OPTION H2 FOR FORECASTING

X                           1.700        3        2    1.500  .6000    1.500  1.800
Y                              50      100       75       45     20       50  59.54
```

FIGURE 7-13. USING THE TREND FUNCTION AND OPTION H2 FOR REGRESSION ANALYSIS

Since both the linear regression equation and the forecast points are available much more simply with the use of TREND than by creating the REGRESS model, why write the REGRESS model? The answer is that TREND gives you only the *a* and *b* coefficients of Equation (7-26), not the additional richness of information about the extent of the association between the variables that can be obtained from the calculations done in the REGRESS model.

Linear regression is also performed by POLYFIT(1). Here, the X values are assumed to correspond to the integers 1, 2, 3,....corresponding to the column numbers. Suppose you have six values of Y and ask for POLYFIT(1) in column 7. IFPS will treat the first six values as a time series (see Section 7.7), fit a regression line through the points and use the regression line to forecast the value in the next time interval. Again, POLYFIT(1) is much more limited than the REGRESS model.

7.5.2 Correlation Analysis

In correlation analyis, the basic objective is to determine the degree of association between variables. The stronger the association, the better able we are to forecast the value of the dependent variable (Y) given the value of the independent variable (X).

In correlation analysis, the usual assumptions made are somewhat stronger than in regression analysis. Specifically, in correlation analysis it is assumed that:

- Both X and Y are random variables.
- Both X and Y are normally distributed; however the two distributions need not be independent.
- The standard deviations of Y are the same for all values of X and the standard deviations of X are the same for all values of Y.

These assumptions differ from the regression model, where only Y is assumed to be a random variable and the Y values are treated as a random sample taken from the conditional probability distribution of Y given X.

The degree of correlation between Y and X is usually expressed in terms of two quantitites: the coefficient of determination, R^2 , and the correlation coefficient, r. As implied by the notation, the coefficient of determination is just the square of the correlation coefficient. The coefficient of determination is a ratio that compares the variation of the Y values around the regression line to the variation of the Y values around the average value of Y. As usual, when we talk about variation in statistics we mean the sum of the squared deviations. In equation terms, the coefficient of determination is given by:

$$R^2 = 1 - \frac{\Sigma(Y - Y_C)^2}{\Sigma(Y - YBAR)^2} \qquad (7\text{-}31)$$

The value of the coefficient of determination is usually interpreted as the fraction of the variation in Y that is accounted for ("explained") by the regression equation that relates X and Y. Note that if Y_c is equal to YBAR for all values of Y, then no new information is obtained from the regression equation since no matter what X we specify, we always forecast the same Y. In this case, the coefficient of determination is equal to 0. At the other extreme, if theY value always falls directly on the regression line, then knowing X forecasts Y perfectly and the coefficient of determination turns out to be equal to 1. In practice, values of the coefficient of determination of 0 and 1 are almost never observed; rather the values are between 0 and 1.

In calculating the coefficient of determination in Figure 7-12, we have used a slightly different form of Equation (7-31) that is equivalent to it. In this form, we use the coefficients *a* and *b* and the other quantities we have already calculated. Specifically, we compute

$$R^2 = \frac{A*SUMY + B*SUMXY - N*YBAR*YBAR}{SUMYSQUARE - N*YBAR*YBAR} \tag{7-32}$$

EXERCISE: Equation (7-32) does not take sample size into account. If you wanted to be precise for small samples, you would modify Equation (7-32) by dividing the numerator by (N-2) and the denominator by (N-1). Change Lines 280 and 281 in Figure 7-12 to this "corrected" sample coefficient of determination.

In calculations, the correlation coefficient, r, is determined by taking the square root of R^2. In taking square roots, we have to make a choice between the positive and negative square root. If the Y value increases with increasing X, the regression line has positive slope and the regression coefficient, *b*, is positive whereas if the Y value decreases as X increases,the slope and *b* are both negative. To indicate the direction of the relation, the + square root is chosen if *b* is positive and the – square root is chosen if b is negative. These two cases are illustrated below for perfect correlation (r = –1 and r = 1):

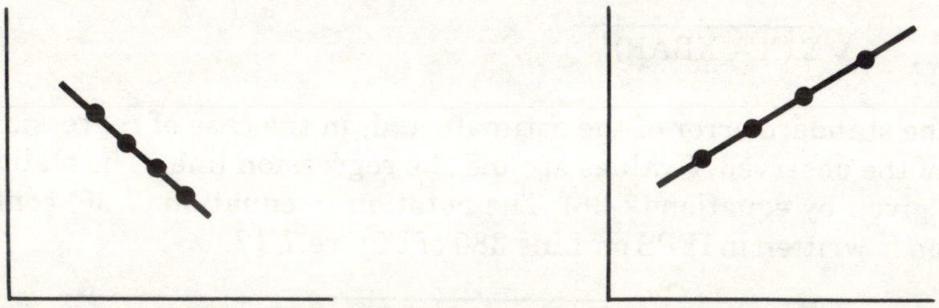

r = –1 r = +1

In IFPS we can pick the positive or negative sign by using the IF ... THEN ....ELSE construct. The XPOWERY function requires a positive input for numbers raised to a fractional power such as 0.5, and always gives a positive output. In Line 300 of Figure 7-12 we use IF...THEN...ELSE to compute a multiplier which has the value 1 if the slope, *b*, is positive and –1 if the slope, *b*, is negative. This multiplier is used in Line 290 to obtain the desired result.

7.5.3 Statistical Inferences in Regression

In most statistical analyses we want not only to estimate a particular value such as a mean or standard deviation or correlation coefficient, we also want to measure how good the estimate is. We have seen this once before, in Section 7.1.5, where we computed the confidence interval to measure the quality of the estimate of the mean. In this section we examine the quality of the regression and of the correlation coefficients.

The first case which we consider is the correlation coefficient r. If, based on a sample, we compute a value for r that is non-zero, we imply that Y and X are related. We want to protect against the possibility that there is, in fact, no correlation between X and Y even though we computed one on the basis of the sample that we observed. To do so, we must run a hypothesis test. Our null hypothesis is that the correlation of the underlying population is 0 and our alternative hypothesis is that the correlation is not zero. (We have not explained the formalism of hypothesis testing in this chapter; if you are not familiar with it, refer to any standard statistics text.) The usual approach to testing this hypothesis is to compute the statistic

$$t = r / \sqrt{(1-r*r)/(N-2)} \tag{7-33}$$

This statistic has a t distribution with (N-2) degrees of freedom, where N is the number of observations in the sample. Once you have computed t from Equation (7-33), you look up the 5% level of significance for this number of degrees of freedom. If the absolute value of t is greater than the tabulated value, you can reject the hypothesis of no association between X and Y in the population. In Figure 7-12, for example, the value of 10.48 is far larger than the table value of 2.776 for the 5% level of the t distribution with four degrees of freedom.

The second case we consider is the regression coefficient *b*. Being a slope of a straight line, *b* estimates the incremental change in Y for each unit increase in X based on the sample. Computing a confidence interval for *b* allows us to judge the quality of this estimate. The 95% confidence interval is given by:

$$b + t^* s_b \qquad (7\text{-}34)$$

where t is the 5% level of the t distribution for (N-2) degrees of freedom and s_b is the estimated standard deviation of the sampling distribution. The problem, therefore, is to determine this standard deviation. It is given by:

$$s_b = s_{Y,X} \; / \sqrt{\Sigma\,(X - XBAR)^2} \qquad (7\text{-}35)$$

where $s_{Y,X}$ is the standard error of the estimate and, in the case of regression, measures the dispersion of the observed Y values around the regression line. The standard error of the estimate is given by equation (7-36). The notation in equation (7-36) conforms to the way the equation is written in IFPS on Line 380 of Figure 7-12.

$$s_{Y,X} = \sqrt{(SUMYSQUARE - A^*SUMY - B^*SUMXY)\,/\,(N\text{-}2)} \qquad (7\text{-}36)$$

All the terms of Equation (7-36) were computed in finding the *a* and *b* coefficients of the regression equation. Thus, first finding the standard error of the estimate, then using the standard error of the estimate to estimate the standard deviation of the sampling distribution of the value of *b*, leads us to finding the upper and lower limits of the confidence interval on *b*. All of these steps are shown in Lines 380 to 431 of Figure 7-12.

7.6 MULTIPLE REGRESSION

<u>*NOTE:*</u> This section is based on the Stepwise Multiple Linear Regression (MLR) routine provided by IFPS in many (but not all implementations). To determine whether your computer facility has the MLR routine available, use the executive command EXECUTE MLR. If you receive an error message indicating that IFPS does not understand you, MLR is not implemented on your computer.

In the previous section we considered the problem of finding the straight line which best describes the relation between an independent variable X and a dependent variable Y. Many real situations are more complex, with two or more independent variables, X1, X2, ... affecting the values of the dependent variable Y. For example, the number of passengers boarding the flights of an airline in a given city (Y) may depend on the population of the metropolitan area (X1), the population of the cities that can be reached nonstop (X2), the number of flights per day (X3), and the number of competitor flights per day (X4).

The extension from one independent variable to several independent variables is straightforward, although messy to model because it is necessary to keep track of the subscripts. Therefore, many IFPS installations provide a multiple regression routine, called MLR. This section describes this routine.

The multiple linear regression equation for n independent variables is given by:

$$YC = A + B1*X1 + B2*X2 + \dots + Bn*Xn \tag{7-37}$$

where A, B1, ... Bn are regression coefficients that are selected in such a way as to minimize the difference between the predicted values of YC and the observed values Y.

<u>*COEFFICIENT OF MULTIPLE DETERMINATION (R2)*</u>. Just as the coefficient of determination, R2, indicated the quality of the fit of the regression equation to the data (i.e., the percentage of the variation explained by the equation), so the coefficient of multiple determination measures the goodness of fit for multiple regression. The value of R2 can range between 0 (no relation exists) and 1 (perfect fit).

<u>*CORRELATION COEFFICIENTS.*</u> In linear regression, the correlation coefficient, r, was just the square root of R2. In multiple linear regression it is possible to calculate correlation coefficients between each pair of variables; for example, between X1 and X3. A value of a correlation coefficient close to 1 for a pair of variables indicates that "autocolinearity" exists. This implies that X1 and X3 have a similar effect on the outcome and including both is redundant. In practice this means that when both variables are used in the calculations, the first one chosen captures most of the effect and the second one adds little. The appropriate response to autocolinearity is to delete one of the variables and, incidentally, simplify the calculation.

<u>*RESIDUALS.*</u> A residual is the difference between the actual value Y and the computed value YC. The MLR routine will print out both the values of the residuals and a quantity called "the standard error of the residuals." This quantity is a measure of the variance of the observed values of Y around the regression equation.

<u>*STEPWISE PROCEDURE*</u>. In multiple regression analysis, you may follow one of two alternative strategies. The simpler one is to select a set of variables and compute equation (7-37). The alternative is to begin with one variable to estimate the dependent variable and then add other variables one at a time. This stepwise approach is the one followed by the MLR routine.

As a user of the routine, you have the option of deciding the order in which variables are to be added or you can let IFPS do it for you. In the latter case, IFPS chooses variables in the order of their F-ratio values. The F-ratio measures the ratio of the explained variance to the unexplained variance. The larger the F-ratio value the more of the variance is explained and hence the more likely the variable is to improve the correlation. The limitation of this approach is that it considers variables one at a time and neglects the possibility that combinations of two or more variables may do better than a single variable.

<u>*PREPARING THE DATA FILE.*</u> The MLR package is separate from other parts of IFPS. This means that you have to use it with a data file. You can't use it directly in a model. The first step in running MLR, therefore, is to create the data file (Sec. 4.6) if you don't have it available. When working with a model, you can create a data file from the output of solving the model using the STORENT command of Section 4.6.7.

To understand how MLR works, we will use the data file shown in Figure 7-14. This data file represents information on sales in 12 cities where your firm has branches. For each city, the population, number of competitors with comparable product in each market, the sales, and the traffic count in 1000's entering your establishment in that city are shown. The objective in the example that follows is to find a regression equation that can be used to forecast sales based on one or more of these variables. (This example was developed by EXECUCOM Systems Corporation, and is used with their permission.)

```
? DATAFILE MULREG
READY FOR EDIT, LAST LINE IS 5
? LIST
1 POPULATION IN MILLIONS=1.7,3.0,2.0,1.5,.6,1.5,2.3,5.1,3.2,4.8,'
2 6.6,2.2
3 NO OF COMPETITORS = 6,7,5,2,3,4,5,3,1,2,4,3
4 SALES = 50,100,75,45,20,50,70,150,70,80,170,80
5 MEDIAN FAMILY INCOME = 15,20, 27,33,12,17,22,12,15,22,18,21
6 DAILY TRAFFIC IN THOUSANDS=19,16,16,18,15,8,19,25,12,19, 30,11
```

FIGURE 7-14. DATA FILE FOR MULTIPLE REGRESSION EXAMPLE

RUNNING MLR. To run MLR, you enter the IFPS command:

```
?EXECUTE MLR
```

You are then asked to ENTER DATA FILE NAME and the name of the dependent variable. In the example, shown in Figure 7-15, we want to use multiple regression to forecast SALES.

PRELIMINARY DATA EXPLORATION. Before proceeding with the regression analysis, you will proably want to make use of some of the preliminary capabilities that are provided. The first of these is a listing of the variables. As shown in Figure 7-15, once you have specified the dependent variable, IFPS prompts you and asks whether you want to see the variable names. If you answer YES (and I recommend that you answer yes), you see a list of the variables in the data file including the depended variable. IFPS will refer to variables in its MLR output by variable number *not* by variable name. Therefore, this list is important to you.

```
ENTER SOLVE OPTIONS
? EXECUTE MLR
SAVE UPDATED DATA FILE MULREG (YES OR NO)
? YES
ENTER DATA FILE NAME
? MULREG
5 VARIABLES PROCESSED, 12 COLUMNS
ENTER NAME OF DEPENDENT VARIABLE
? SALES
DO YOU WANT A LIST OF NUMBER VERSUS VARIABLE NAME (Y=YES)
? Y
```

FIGURE 7-15. PRELIMINARY ANALYSIS OF DATA USING MLR PACKAGE
(This Figure Is Continued on the Next Page)

```
1 POPULATION IN MILLIONS
2 NO OF COMPETITORS
3 MEDIAN FAMILY INCOME
4 DAILY TRAFFIC IN THOUSANDS
5 SALES
DO YOU WANT TO PRINT MEANS AND STD DEV (Y=YES)
? Y
  AVERAGES...
VAR(1)=     2.875
VAR(2)=     3.750
VAR(3)=     19.50
VAR(4)=     17.33
VAR(5)=        80
  STANDARD DEVIATIONS...
VAR(1)=     1.772
VAR(2)=     1.765
VAR(3)=     6.142
VAR(4)=     5.975
VAR(5)=     42.91
DO YOU WANT TO PRINT CORRELATION COEFF (Y=YES)
? Y
  SIMPLE CORRELATION COEFFICIENTS...
          1       2       3       4       5
  1  1.000
  2  -.139   1.000
  3  -.172   -.021   1.000
  4   .732    .103   -.054   1.000
  5   .911    .090   -.166    .723   1.000
```

FIGURE 7-15. PRELIMINARY ANALYSIS OF DATA USING MLR PACKAGE (Continued)

ANALYZING THE INPUT INFORMATION. In addition to giving you the multiple linear regression solution, the MLR package provides information about the input data itself. Specifically, you can ask for:

- Mean value of each variable
- Standard deviation of each variable
- Correlation coefficient matrix.

The mean and variance were discussed in Section 7.1. As described in Section 7.5.2, the correlation coefficients measure the extent to which each pair of variables is related. A correlation coefficient close to either 1 or -1 indicates that the value of one of the two variables nearly perfectly forecasts the value of the second variable and vice versa. A value of 0, indicates no relationship. In general, values of the correlation coefficient close to 1 (or -1) indicate that using both variables will explain little more about the dependent variable than using just one of the variables. In this example, several pairs of variables have high correlation coefficients. For example, there is a strong positive correlation between sales and both population in millions (.931) and daily traffic in thousands (.723) as well as between daily traffic count and population (.732). The implication is that it may pay to recast some of the variables. For example, you may want to consider the traffic count per thousand people.

REGRESSION ANALYSIS. Once the preliminaries are completed, you are ready to run the multiple linear regression. The idea in MLR is that you add (or delete) one variable at a time to try to improve the coefficient of determination, R2. You can either specify the variables that are to enter or you can have the computer make the selection for you.

LETTING THE COMPUTER SELECT THE VARIABLES TO ENTER. If you answer N to the prompt "DO YOU WANT TO SELECT THE VARIABLES TO ENTER", IFPS performs classical linear stepwise regression by choosing the variable with the hghest F ratio. You can see how this works by examining Figure 7-16.

```
DO YOU WANT TO SELECT VARIABLES TO ENTER (Y=YES)
?N
STEP NUMBER 1
MULTIPLE CORRELATION COEFFICIENT    .911
R SQUARED                           .829
STANDARD ERROR FOR RESIDUALS      18.608
F RATIO      F(1,10)=      48.4838
CONSTANT TERM =         16.62
 VAR COEFFICIENT     STD DEV        F-VALUE
  1       22.05      3.166         48.48
STEP NUMBER 2
MULTIPLE CORRELATION COEFFICIENT    .936
R SQUARED                           .877
STANDARD ERROR FOR RESIDUALS      16.650
F RATIO      F(2,9)=       32.0221
CONSTANT TERM =         -5.638
 VAR COEFFICIENT     STD DEV        F-VALUE
  1       22.79      2.861         63.45
  2       5.367      2.873         3.490
STEP NUMBER 3
MULTIPLE CORRELATION COEFFICIENT    .937
R SQUARED                           .877
STANDARD ERROR FOR RESIDUALS      17.638
F RATIO      F(3,8)=       19.0295
CONSTANT TERM =         -7.045
 VAR COEFFICIENT     STD DEV        F-VALUE
  1       22.29      4.647         23.01
  2       5.230      3.195         2.680
  4       .1929      1.372         .0197
 OBS      ACTUAL     ESTIMATES      RESIDUAL
  1        50.00       65.90         -15.90
  2       100.00       99.53          .4729
  3        75.00       66.77          8.225
  4        45.00       40.32          4.676
  5        20.00       24.91         -4.913
  6        50.00       48.86          1.144
  7        70.00       74.04         -4.041
  8       150.00      127.16          22.84
  9        70.00       71.83         -1.834
 10        80.00      114.08         -34.08
 11       170.00      166.79          3.212
 12        80.00       59.81          20.19
```

FIGURE 7-16. MULTIPLE LINEAR REGRESSION - VARIABLES SELECTED BY IFPS

SELECTING VARIABLES TO ENTER OR LEAVE. If you respond to the IFPS prompt

```
? DO YOU WANT TO SELECT VARIABLES TO ENTER (Y=YES)
```

with Y, you can make the variable selection. You can see the dialog in Figure 7-17. IFPS allows you to choose among four decisions:

1. Add a variable. To do so, simply type the variable number or name.

2. Remove a variable. Type REMOVE followed by the variable number or name.

3. Type out the residual errors based on the variables currently in the regression. Type RESID.

4. Terminate the MLR routine by typing END.

To help you select variables, IFPS prompts you with:

```
? CANDIDATES (Y=YES)
```

The list produced shows the F ratio, among other quantitites. The larger the F ratio, the more accuracy is increased if that variable is brought into the solution. Be aware that this is a one-at-a-time technique and that you may get better results if you select two or three variables at a time.

```
DO YOU WANT TO SELECT VARIABLES TO ENTER (Y=YES)
? Y
CANDIDATES (Y=YES)
? Y
CANDIDATE   CORRELATION   F RATIO   COEFFICIENTS

     1          .0000       48.48          22.05
     2          .0000         .08          2.190
     3          .0000         .28         -1.157
     4          .0000       10.98          5.195
     5          .0000       42.91
ENTER NUMBER OF FIRST VARIABLE
? 1
STEP NUMBER 1
MULTIPLE CORRELATION COEFFICIENT       .911
R SQUARED                              .829
STANDARD ERROR FOR RESIDUALS         18.608
F RATIO       F(1,10)=         48.4838
CONSTANT TERM =           16.62
 VAR COEFFICIENT      STD DEV       F-VALUE
  1      22.05        3.166          48.48
CANDIDATES (Y=YES)
? Y
```

FIGURE 7-17. USER CHOICE OF VARIABLES TO ENTER MULTIPLE LINEAR REGRESSION
(This Figure Is Continued on the Next Page)

```
CANDIDATE    CORRELATION   F RATIO    COEFFICIENTS

   2            .1388         3.49         5.367
   5            .9105        18.61
ENTER VAR NUMBER, REMOVE VAR NUMBER, RESID, OR END
? 2
STEP NUMBER 2
MULTIPLE CORRELATION COEFFICIENT    .936
R SQUARED                           .877
STANDARD ERROR FOR RESIDUALS      16.650
F RATIO     F(2,9)=        32.0221
CONSTANT TERM =          -5.638
 VAR COEFFICIENT      STD DEV      F-VALUE
  1        22.79       2.861        63.45
  2        5.367       2.873        3.490
CANDIDATES (Y=YES)
? Y
CANDIDATE    CORRELATION   F RATIO    COEFFICIENTS
    5           .9364        16.65
ENTER VAR NUMBER, REMOVE VAR NUMBER, RESID, OR END
? END
```

FIGURE 7-17.USER CHOICE OF VARIABLES TO ENTER MULTIPLE LINEAR REGRESSION (Continued)

TERMINATING THE MULTIPLE REGRESSION. You should terminate the multiple regression either when you have no more variables left to include or when you believe that adding or deleting another variable will not lead to a significant improvement. If the coefficient of determination, R^2, is approaching 1.0, you can, of course, terminate.

GETTING OUT OF THE MLR PACKAGE. When you are done using the MLR package, you can get out of it by giving any executive or modeling command. For example, you might ask for MODEL PRODUCT. If you are done with your session, you can QUIT.

USING THE REGRESSION COEFFICIENTS. The MLR package is relatively standalone. It does not automatically transfer its results to where you want to use them because IFPS does not know what your purpose was in running MLR. Therefore, you must copy the coefficients created by the package into your working model. Usually, this involves having a printout or copying values from the screen. For example, the results of Figure 7-17 indicate that the regression equation being computed is:

SALES = -5.638 + 22.79*POPULATION IN MILLIONS'
+ 5.367*NO OF COMPETITORS

since the values of the coefficients are 22.79 for Variable 1 and 5.367 for Variable 2. You can use this equation in models involving SALES with the variables shown. Remember however, that the coefficients of the regression equation depend on the data in the data file. If you get additional data or have different data, you have to run MLR again.

7.7 TIME SERIES AND FORECASTING

The term "time series" refers to a set of values about a specific quantity that was obtained at different points in time. For example, you may have sales data for your department obtained daily or you may be keeping monthly records on the U.S. balance of trade. You can use time series data to forecast future values if you believe that the trends and patterns observed in the past will continue without changes in the underlying causal relationships. If events occur that change these relations (e.g., a three month strike by your principal supplier or a sharp increase in oil prices) then, no matter how well you apply them, the methods of this section will be useless in obtaining reliable or accurate forecasts.

In this section we will consider both short-term and long-term forecasting based on historical data.

7.7.1 Short-Term Forecasting

By short-term forecasting, we mean forecasts that deal only with the next period. The following are five methods of making such forecasts:

1. Arithmetic mean.
2. Moving average
3. Trend extrapolation
4. Exponential smoothing
5. Double exponential smoothing.

Figure 7-18 illustrates the various short-range forecasting methods. We show 12 periods of historical data (sales in thousands of dollars in each of the previous 12 quarters, Line 60). The forecast value is shown in the last column. Note that the value of sales in the last column is the same as in Column 12. This corresponds to a forecast that says the next period will be identical to the present period. Is this a good method of forecasting?

The arithmetic mean and the moving average were discussed in Section 7.1. The arithmetic mean forecast simply assumes that the next period will be the average of all the values observed in the past. The mean of all the historical data is thus used as the forecast for the next period. All previous periods are weighted equally. A quick way of obtaining this forecast is to use POLYFIT(0). As described in Section 3.2.3, POLYFIT(0) computes the mean of all previous values of a variable

The moving average forecast assumes that the older the data, the less relevant they are to the future. Thus, in a moving average forecast, choices have to be made of how many previous historical periods to use and how the weights should be assigned to each period used. You might use a moving average forecast if you are forecasting a quantity repetitively, such as next month's sales and believe that only the last few months are relevant. The forecast value is equal to the moving average value. In Figure 7-18, the moving average forecast is based on three periods weighted equally. (i.e., .333 each) In the exercise below we ask you to compute moving averages for different periods and unequal weightings.

```
MODEL FORECAS2  VERSION OF  09/01/82  20:11
10 COLUMNS 1-12,FRCST
20 *
30 * INPUT DATA
40*  =========
50 *
60 ACTUAL SALES=13.1,12.0,15.8,11.4,14.0,15.3,17.6,13.0,15.2,'
61 16.4,19.2, 14.7,0
70*
80*MOVING AVERAGE
85*=============
90*
100 MOVING AVERAGE = 0,0,0,MOVAVG(SALES,.333,.333,.333,0)
110*
120 *FORECASTS USING THE POLYFIT FUNCTION
123*=================================
130*
140 MEAN = SALES FOR 12,POLYFIT(0)
150 LINEAR REGRESSION = SALES FOR 12,POLYFIT(1)
160 QUADRATIC REGRESSION = SALES FOR 12,POLYFIT(2)
170*
180*EXPONENTIAL SMOOTHING
183*=====================
190*
200 EXPFORECAST = SALES,PREVIOUS SALES,PREVIOUS EXPFORECAST +ALPHA*'
201 (PREVIOUS SALES-PREVIOUS EXPFORECAST)
210 ALPHA = .2
220*
230*DOUBLE EXPONENTIAL SMOOTHING
235*========================
240*
250DOUBLESMOOTH = SALES,PREVIOUS SALES,2*PREVIOUS EXPFORECAST-'
251 PREVIOUS 2 F2FUNCTION
260 F2FUNCTION=SALES,ALPHA*EXPFORECAST+(1-ALPHA)*PREVIOUS F2FUNCTION
END OF MODEL
ENTER SOLVE OPTIONS
? all

                                 1      2      3      4      5      6      7

 INPUT DATA
 =========

ACTUAL SALES                 13.10     12  15.80  11.40     14  15.30  17.60

MOVING AVERAGE
=============

MOVING AVERAGE                   0      0      0  13.63  13.07  13.73  13.57
```

FIGURE 7-18. VARIOUS FORECASTING METHODS
(This Figure Continued on the Next Page)

```
FORECASTS USING THE POLYFIT FUNCTION
====================================

MEAN                 13.10     12  15.80  11.40     14  15.30  17.60
LINEAR REGRESSION    13.10     12  15.80  11.40     14  15.30  17.60
QUADRATIC REGRESSIO  13.10     12  15.80  11.40     14  15.30  17.60
EXPONENTIAL SMOOTHING
=====================

EXPFORECAST          13.10  13.10  12.88  13.46  13.05  13.24  13.65
ALPHA                .2000  .2000  .2000  .2000  .2000  .2000  .2000

DOUBLE EXPONENTIAL SMOOTHING
============================

DOUBLESMOOTH         13.10  13.10  13.10  12.66  13.87  12.96  13.36
F2FUNCTION           13.10  13.10  13.06  13.14  13.12  13.14  13.25

                         8      9     10     11     12  FRCST

 INPUT DATA
 ==========

ACTUAL SALES            13  15.20  16.40  19.20  14.70      0

MOVING AVERAGE
==============

MOVING AVERAGE       15.63  15.30  15.27  14.87  16.93  16.77
 FORECASTS USING THE POLYFIT FUNCTION
====================================

MEAN                    13  15.20  16.40  19.20  14.70  14.81
LINEAR REGRESSION       13  15.20  16.40  19.20  14.70  17.19
QUADRATIC REGRESSION    13  15.20  16.40  19.20  14.70  16.85
EXPONENTIAL SMOOTHING
=====================
EXPFORECAST          14.44  14.15  14.36  14.77  15.66  15.47
ALPHA                .2000  .2000  .2000  .2000  .2000  .2000
DOUBLE EXPONENTIAL SMOOTHING
============================

DOUBLESMOOTH         14.16  15.64  14.82  15.11  15.77  17.34
F2FUNCTION           13.49  13.62  13.77  13.97  14.31  14.54
```

FIGURE 7-18. VARIOUS FORECASTING METHODS
(Continued)

If there are definite trends in the data (e.g. sales are growing), a simple form of short-term forecasting is to apply the methodology of linear regression (Section 7.5). You find the appropriate regression equation based on the past values and then evaluate the regression equation for the next period. The POLYFIT(1) function can be used for this purpose. Although it uses the identical calculation methods, this approach to forecasting is not simply an application of regression analysis since the assumptions of regression analysis are not satisfied. Rather this form finds the best-fitting line and uses the extrapolation of the line to the next period as the forecast. Figure 7-15 also shows the use of POLYFIT(2) which extrapolates on the basis of the best-fitting quadratic equation.

EXERCISE: Modify Figure 7-18 to compute the following quantities:

1. The moving average forecast, based on the last six periods weighted equally.

2. The error in the moving average forecast, based on the difference between the forecast and actual values.

3. The trend forecast for each period. To obtain this forecast you must use the TREND function described in Section 3.2. You may find this a little tricky to do; however, try to find a clever way of making this computation.

4. The error in the trend forecast, based on the difference between the forecast and actual values.

Exponential smoothing is a short-term forecasting method that gives weight to all the historical points, but weights recent points more heavily than old ones. Exponential smoothing is defined by a recursive relationship:

$$\text{EXPFORECAST} = \text{PREVIOUS EXPFORECAST} + \text{ALPHA} \\ (\text{PREVIOUS ACTUAL} - \text{PREVIOUS EXPFORECAST}) \quad (7\text{-}41)$$

That is, the forecast for this period is the same as the forecast for last period but modified by the difference between the observed value and the previous forecast value. ALPHA is a constant of proportionality (between 0 and 1) that determines the extent of the influence of the observed values. For example, if ALPHA is zero, then EXPFORECAST = PREVIOUS EXPFORECAST and actual values are ignored, whereas if ALPHA = 1, the forecast is simply the last observed value. Typically, values between 0.1 and 0.3 are used for ALPHA; a value of 0.2 is used in Figure 7-18 (Line 210). When starting this process, the first data point is used as the first forecast (since we have no history at that time, all we can assume is that the first period will be repeated). The formula is then applied iteratively on all the historical data. The last value computed is the forecast.

EXERCISE: Use WHAT IF statements on the model of Figure 7-18 to observe the effect of ALPHA on the forecasts. Specifically, use ALPHA values of .1, .3, .5, .7, and .9 and print out the exponential smoothing forecast values. For each case, PLOT the observed and forecast values. Which value of ALPHA gives the best forecast?

EXERCISE: It can be shown that exponential smoothing is equivalent to an N period moving average if N is chosen so that

$$N = (2/\text{ALPHA}) - 1 \quad (7\text{-}42)$$

Verify this by using Equation (7-42) to find N for ALPHA values of 0.1, 0.333, 0.4, and 0.5. Use WHAT IF statements to modify Figure 7-18 to find both the moving average and exponential smoothing forecasts for these combinations of ALPHA and N.

Double exponential smoothing, while slightly more difficult to compute (it requires one more line in your IFPS model and has a slightly more complex form than exponential smoothing), provides a way of improving exponential smoothing so that it usually tends to follow actual values more closely. It is widely used in marketing applications. The basic relation for double exponential smoothing is:

```
DOUBLESMOOTH = 2*PREVIOUS EXPFORECAST
                -PREVIOUS 2 F2FUNCTION          (7-43)
```

where DOUBLESMOOTH is the double exponential smoothing forecast and EXPFORECAST is the exponential smoothing forecast shown in Equation (7-41). F2FUNCTION is called the double smoothing function. It is computed from the relation:

```
F2FUNCTION = ALPHA * EXPFORECAST +
             (1 - ALPHA) *PREVIOUS F2FUNCTION   (7-44)
```

If you look closely at F2FUNCTION you will see that it requires two periods of historical data. The exponential smoothing forecast depends on the previous period's observed data and hence the PREVIOUS F2FUNCTION depends on data observed two periods ago. Going through the same analysis will show you that the DOUBLESMOOTH forecast uses a minimum of three periods of historical data and hence the first meaningful DOUBLESMOOTH forecast is for Period 4.

EXERCISE: Use WHAT IF statements with Figure 7-18 to determine the effect of ALPHA on the DOUBLESMOOTH forecast. Use ALPHA values of .1, .3, .5, .7, and .9. In each case, PLOT the actual and forecast values. Does DOUBLESMOOTH provide more accurate forecasts than exponential smoothing? What is the best value of ALPHA for the data shown?

7.7.2 Long-Term Forecasting

If you have a large amount of historical time series data available and you believe that the underlying phenomena will continue into the future, then the classical time series model can be used as a long-term forecasting method. When you plot historical time series, you will usually find that the data appear complex and are difficult to interpret. The reason is that many phenomena are occurring and they interact with one another. In the classical time series model, the changes over time are assumed to contain four components:

1. Trend, T.
2. Cyclical fluctuations, C.
3. Seasonal variations, S.
4. Irregular movements, I.

that interact with one another to produce the observed time series. The model attempts to separate these components, obtain forecasts for each of them, and then combine these individual forecasts into a composite forecast of future values.

Trend refers to long-term movements caused by underlying factors (e.g., demographic, technological, taste changes). *Cyclical fluctuations*, such as business cycles, are movements around the trend. Typically, they are several years in duration. *Seasonal variations* are much shorter cycles, completed within a year and repeating from year to year. For example, air conditioner and snow shovel sales exhibit strong seasonal variations. *Irregular movements* refers to the very short-term fluctuations in time series that follow no pattern. They are what is left over when the first three components have been accounted for.

One form of the classical time series model assumes that the values, Y, of a time series are the product of the four components, that is:

$$Y = T * C * S * I \tag{7-45}$$

To find the trend component, the method of least squares is used, that is, the arithmetic of regression analysis. We will consider the simple case of an arithmetic straight line trend. We assume that the trend is of the form:

$$Y_t = a + b * X \tag{7-46}$$

where Y_t is the computed trend value for period X. To simplify the calculations, the time periods are measured with respect to the arithmetic mean (i.e., middle) of the historical data. For example, if we have data on the period 1961-1981, we choose 1970 as X=0, 1971 as X=1, 1972 as X=2, 1969 as X= −1, 1968 as X = −2, etc. Since the average value of X is 0, the equations that define the coefficients *a* and *b* simplify to:

$$a = \text{YBAR} \tag{7-47}$$

$$b = \text{SUMXY/SUMXSQUARED} \tag{7-48}$$

Here YBAR is the average of the observed values, Y; SUMXY is the sum of the products of X and Y, and SUMXSQUARED is the sum of the squares of the X values. Figure 7-19 illustrates the computation of the trend line for a simple set of 24 data points. We have written the model in a general form. Specifically, we have chosen to input the variable NPERIODS to represent the number of periods of data, and we have computed the initial value of X by taking −(NPERIODS −1)/2. Note that if you want to use this model for a different number of periods, you have to be careful and change the reference to the number of data points everywhere it occurs; specifically in Line 10 (number of columns), and Line 170 (NPERIODS).

```
MODEL TLINEB  VERSION OF  08/22/82  23:09
10 COLUMNS 1-24
20 *
30* INPUT DATA
40*
50 X=-(NPERIODS -1)/2,PREVIOUS+1
60 Y= 13.1,12.0,15.8,11.4,14.0,15.3,17.6,14.0,15.2,16.4,19.2,14.7,'
61 15.6,15.5,17.2,16.7,16.8,16.5,17.4,14.4,17.0,19.4,19.2,16.7
70*
80 * COMPUTATION OF TREND LINE COEFFICIENTS
90*
```

FIGURE 7-19. COMPUATION OF THE TREND LINE FORECAST
(This Figure Continued on the Next Page)

```
100 SUMY=PREVIOUS + Y
110 SUMXSQUARED=PREVIOUS +X*X
120 SUMXY= PREVIOUS + X*Y
130*
140 A= SUMY/NPERIODS
150 B= SUMXY/SUMXSQUARED
160*
170 NPERIODS = 24
END OF MODEL
? solve
MODEL TLINEB  VERSION OF  08/22/82  23:09 -- 24 COLUMNS 8 VARIABLES
ENTER SOLVE OPTIONS
? all
              1    2    3    4    5    6    7    8    9   10   11   12

 INPUT DATA

X           -11.5-10.5-9.50-8.50-7.50-6.50-5.50-4.50-3.50-2.50-1.50-.500
Y            13.1   12 15.8 11.4   14 15.3 17.6   14 15.2 16.4 19.2 14.7

 COMPUTATION OF TREND LINE COEFFICIENTS

SUMY         13.1 25.1 40.9 52.3 66.3 81.6 99.2  113  128  145  164  179
SUMXSQUA      132  243  333  405  461  504  534  554  566  573  575  575
SUMXY        -151 -277 -427 -524 -629 -728 -825 -888 -941 -982-1011-1018

A            .546 1.05 1.70 2.18 2.76 3.40 4.13 4.72 5.35 6.03 6.83 7.45
B           -1.14-1.14-1.28-1.29-1.36-1.45-1.55-1.60-1.66-1.72-1.76-1.77

NPERIODS       24   24   24   24   24   24   24   24   24   24   24   24


             13   14   15   16   17   18   19   20   21   22   23   24

 INPUT DATA

X            .500 1.50 2.50 3.50 4.50 5.50 6.50 7.50 8.50 9.50 10.5 11.5
Y            15.6 15.5 17.2 16.7 16.8 16.5 17.4 14.4   17 19.4 19.2 16.7

 COMPUTATION OF TREND LINE COEFFICIENTS

SUMY          194  210  227  244  261  277  294  309  326  345  364  381
SUMXSQUAR     575  578  584  596  616  647  689  745  817  908 1018 1150
SUMXY       -1010 -987 -944 -886 -810 -719 -606 -498 -354 -170 32.1  224

A            8.10 8.74 9.46 10.2 10.9 11.5 12.3 12.9 13.6 14.4 15.2 15.9
B           -1.76-1.71-1.62-1.49-1.31-1.11-.880-.669-.433-.187 .032 .195

NPERIODS       24   24   24   24   24   24   24   24   24   24   24   24
```

FIGURE 7-19. COMPUTATION OF THE TREND LINE FORECAST
(Continued)

We next turn to seasonal variations. To make meaningful comparisons you would like to remove the effects of these variations, that is, to deseasonalize the data. To do so, the most widely used technique is the ratio-to-moving-average method. We will illustrate this method for the case of quarterly data and leave it as an exercise for you to deal with monthly data.

The basic idea in deseasonalizing data is to find a number which represents the ratio between the observed value in a given period and the value that would have been observed if seasonal effects had not been present (that is, the average value for the year). Once these ratios have been found for each quarter, every observed value is divided by the ratio for its quarter. For example, if sales in the fourth quarter are 30% above average sales for the year, then it would be appropriate to divide fourth quarter sales by 1.3. The ratios, called seasonal indices, are found by applying the ratio to moving average method shown in Figures 7-20 and 7-21. It is easier to use separate models to determine the seasonal indices than to attempt to compute them as an integral part of the forecasting model. (If you do not believe this assertion, write a single IFPS model that performs the entire seasonal index problem and judge the level of difficulty for yourself.)

In Figure 7-20, we convert the observed data for each quarter into a percentage number relative to a four-quarter (i.e., annual) average centered at the observed point. To do so, we perform the following steps:

1. Compute four-quarter moving totals. These totals are the sum of the current value of the data and the previous three values. If we divide this total by four, we have a four-quarter average. However, by their definition, these averages lie midway between the second and third quarter of the data. We would like to obtain averages that lie at the same level as the data, that is, a centered moving average.

2. Add the current and next four-quarter moving total.

3. Divide the number obtained in Step 2 by 8 to obtain a centered moving average.

4. Divide the original data by the centered moving average obtained in Step 3.

```
MODEL MOVAVGPCT   VERSION OF   01/12/83   20:06
10 COLUMNS 1-24
20 *
30 SALES = 13.1,12,15.8,11.4,14.0,15.3,17.6,13.0,15.2,16.4,19.2,'
40 14.7,15.6,15.5,17.2,16.7,16.8,16.5,17.4,14.4,17.0,19.4,19.2,16.7
50 MOV TOT=0,0,FUTURE SALES+SALES+PREVIOUS SALES+'
51 PREVIOUS 2 SALES FOR 21,0
60 MOV TOT8=0,0,MOV TOT +FUTURE MOV TOT FOR 20,0
70 MOVING AVG = MOV TOT8/8
80 SALES INDX=0,0, 100*SALES/MOVING AVG FOR 20,0,0
END OF MODEL
```

FIGURE 7-20. SALES INDEX BASED ON MOVING AVERAGES: 24 QUARTERS OF DATA

(This Figure is Continued on the Next Page)

```
? solve
MODEL MOVAVGPCT VERSION OF 01/12/83  20:06 -- 24 COLUMNS 5 VARIABLES
? invert
? all
```

	SALES	MOV TOT	MOV TOT8	MOVING AVG	SALES INDX
1	13.10	0	0	0	0
2	12	0	0	0	0
3	15.80	52.30	105.5	13.19	119.8
4	11.40	53.20	109.7	13.71	83.14
5	14	56.50	114.8	14.35	97.56
6	15.30	58.30	118.2	14.78	103.6
7	17.60	59.90	121	15.13	116.4
8	13	61.10	123.3	15.41	84.35
9	15.20	62.20	126	15.75	96.51
10	16.40	63.80	129.3	16.16	101.5
11	19.20	65.50	131.4	16.43	116.9
12	14.70	65.90	130.9	16.36	89.84
13	15.60	65	128	16	97.50
14	15.50	63	128	16	96.88
15	17.20	65	131.2	16.40	104.9
16	16.70	66.20	133.4	16.68	100.1
17	16.80	67.20	134.6	16.83	99.85
18	16.50	67.40	132.5	16.56	99.62
19	17.40	65.10	130.4	16.30	106.7
20	14.40	65.30	133.5	16.69	86.29
21	17	68.20	138.2	17.28	98.41
22	19.40	70	142.3	17.79	109.1
23	19.20	72.30	0	0	0
24	16.70	0	0	0	0

FIGURE 7-20. SALES INDEX BASED ON MOVING AVERAGES: 24 QUARTERS OF DATA (Continued)

```
MODEL SEASONAL  VERSION OF  01/12/83  19:54
10 COLUMNS 1-4
20 *
30 *QUARTERLY INPUT DATA
40 *
50 Q1=.976,.965,.975,.998
60 Q2= 1.035,1.015,.969,.996
70 Q3= 1.163,1.169,1.049,1.067
80 Q4= .844,.899,1.002,.863
90 *
100 *COMPUTATION OF MAXIMUM AND MINIMUM
110 *
120 MAXQ1=Q1,MAXIMUM(PREVIOUS,Q1)
130 MAXQ2=Q2,MAXIMUM(PREVIOUS,Q2)
140 MAXQ3=Q3,MAXIMUM(PREVIOUS,Q3)
150 MAXQ4=Q4,MAXIMUM(PREVIOUS,Q4)
160 MINQ1=Q1,MINIMUM(PREVIOUS,Q1)
170 MINQ2=Q2,MINIMUM(PREVIOUS,Q2)
180 MINQ3=Q3,MINIMUM(PREVIOUS,Q3)
190 MINQ4=Q4,MINIMUM(PREVIOUS,Q4)
200 *
210 *COMPUTATION OF SUM OF QUARTERLY DATA
220 *
230 SUMQ1=PREVIOUS+Q1
240 SUMQ2=PREVIOUS+Q2
250 SUMQ3=PREVIOUS+Q3
260 SUMQ4=PREVIOUS+Q4
270 *
280 *COMPUTATION OF REDUCED MEANS
290 *
300 MEANQ1=0,0,(SUMQ1-MAXQ1-MINQ1)/(N-2)
310 MEANQ2=0,0,(SUMQ2-MAXQ2-MINQ2)/(N-2)
320 MEANQ3=0,0,(SUMQ3-MAXQ3-MINQ3)/(N-2)
330 MEANQ4=0,0,(SUMQ4-MAXQ4-MINQ4)/(N-2)
340 TOTMEAN=SUM(L300 THRU L330)
350 *
360 *COMPUTATION OF SEASONAL INDEXES
370 *
380 ADJ FACTOR=0,0,400/TOTMEAN
390 INDEX1=ADJ FACTOR*MEANQ1
400 INDEX2=ADJ FACTOR*MEANQ2
410 INDEX3 =ADJ FACTOR*MEANQ3
420 INDEX4=ADJ FACTOR*MEANQ4
430 *
440 N=PREVIOUS+1
END OF MODEL
```

FIGURE 7-21. SEASONAL INDEXES
(This Figure is Continued on the Next Page)

```
? solve
MODEL SEASONAL VERSION OF  01/12/83  19:54 -- 4 COLUMNS 27 VARIABLES
ENTER SOLVE OPTIONS
? all

                          1        2        3        4

QUARTERLY INPUT DATA

Q1                    .9760    .9650    .9750    .9980
Q2                    1.035    1.015    .9690    .9960
Q3                    1.163    1.169    1.049    1.067
Q4                    .8440    .8990    1.002    .8630
COMPUTATION OF MAXIMUM AND MINIMUM

MAXQ1                 .9760    .9760    .9760    .9980
MAXQ2                 1.035    1.035    1.035    1.035
MAXQ3                 1.163    1.169    1.169    1.169
MAXQ4                 .8440    .8990    1.002    1.002
MINQ1                 .9760    .9650    .9650    .9650
MINQ2                 1.035    1.015    .9690    .9690
MINQ3                 1.163    1.163    1.049    1.049
MINQ4                 .8440    .8440    .8440    .8440

COMPUTATION OF SUM OF QUARTERLY DATA

SUMQ1                 .9760    1.941    2.916    3.914
SUMQ2                 1.035    2.050    3.019    4.015
SUMQ3                 1.163    2.332    3.381    4.448
SUMQ4                 .8440    1.743    2.745    3.608

COMPUTATION OF REDUCED MEANS

MEANQ1                    0        0    .9750    .9755
MEANQ2                    0        0    1.015    1.006
MEANQ3                    0        0    1.163    1.115
MEANQ4                    0        0    .8990    .8810
TOTMEAN                   0        0    4.052    3.977
COMPUTATION OF SEASONAL INDEXES

ADJ FACTOR                0        0    98.72    100.6
INDEX1                    0        0    96.25    98.11
INDEX2                    0        0    100.2    101.1
INDEX3                    0        0    114.8    112.1
INDEX4                    0        0    88.75    88.61

N                         1        2        3        4
```

FIGURE 7-21. SEASONAL INDEXES
(Continued)

The SALES INDX results shown in Figure 7-20 are divided by 100 and used as input data for Figure 7-21. We have used only the data in columns 5 through 20. These inputs are labeled Q1, Q2, Q3, and Q4. Note that rather than listing the data sequentially, we have separated it by quarters. The convention in doing these calculations is to remove the largest and the smallest value observed. Such a procedure eliminates outlying values that may be due to unusual conditions in the past (e.g., a heat wave, a strike). In IFPS this means we have to compute the maximum and minumum of the values for each quarter. This is done in Figure 7-21 by using the MAXIMUM and MINIMUM functions. Note that we chose the initial values as the starting values for these calculations and then successively chose either the previously observed maximum (or minimum) or the current value, depending on which is larger. The mean for each quarter is computed in Lines 300 through 330 by using the relation:

$$\text{MEAN} = ((\Sigma Q_i) - \text{MAX } Q_i - \text{MIN } Q_i) / (N-2) \qquad (7\text{-}49)$$

That is, we add up all the values for quarter i and then subtract the largest and smallest values observed in that quarter. We then divide by the number of observations considered, that is (N-2).

The foregoing mean values look like seasonal indices but they are not. The reason is that if you add them up they do not have the desired average value of 100. To obtain an average of 100, we perform the following steps:

1. Add up the means. In our case the total in Q4 is 3.977.

2. Divide 400 by the sum of the means. The result of this division is an adjustment factor.

3. Multiply each mean by the adjustment factor. The results are the seasonal indices, S.

Note that the indices just computed are one form of index number, the subject of Section 7.8 which follows.

EXERCISE: For clarity of presentation, Figure 7-21 separates input data, maximum, minimum, sum, and mean by quarters. Although visually helpful, this formulation results in a complex input requirements, a lengthy model and long printout. Write an IFPS program that allows you to write each of these quantities in a single line, with the data input in the sequence of occurrence (e.g., .976, 1.035, 1.163, .844, .965 ...). You will be find PREVIOUS 4 helpful in doing this.

EXERCISE: Modify the previous exercise so that the model is applicable to monthly input data.

Let us review where we now stand. We had defined a model:

$$Y = T * S * C * I. \qquad (7\text{-}45)$$

If we divide both sides by the seasonal index S that we have just computed, we obtain a forecast Y/S which has seasonal effects removed from it:

$$Y/S = T * C * I \tag{7-50}$$

We turn now to the cyclic values. If we divide the deseasonalized forecast by the trend line:

$$Y/ST = C*I \tag{7-51}$$

the cyclic component modified by the irregular component remains. If we assume that the irregular component is random, its average value will be 1, and we can approximate the cyclic components by dividing the observed values by the product of the seasonal and trend values. The cyclic component shown in Figure 7-22 is interpreted in the same way as the seasonal index in that values below one indicate a reduction from the trend values while values above one indicate values above the trend due to cyclic effects.

```
MODEL RECOMPOSE   VERSION OF   08/22/82   23:04
10 COLUMNS 1-6
20 TREND = A + B*NCOL
30 SEASONAL = .979,1.016,1.135,.870,PREVIOUS 4 SEASONAL
40 CYCLIC =1.02,1.04,1.06,1.05,1.03
50 *
60 FORECAST = TREND * SEASONAL *CYCLIC
70 *INPUT DATA
80 *
90 A= 12.42
100 B=.3668
110 NCOL=13,PREVIOUS + 1
END OF MODEL
MODEL RECOMPOSE VERSION OF   08/22/82   23:04 -- 6 COLUMNS 7 VARIABLES
ENTER SOLVE OPTIONS
? all
                          1        2        3        4        5        6

TREND                 17.19    17.56    17.92    18.29    18.66    19.02
SEASONAL             0.9790    1.016    1.135    .8700    .9790    1.016
CYCLIC                1.020    1.040    1.060    1.050    1.030    1.030

FORECAST              17.16    18.55    21.56    16.78    18.81    19.91

INPUT DATA

A                     12.42    12.42    12.42    12.42    12.42    12.42
B                     .3668    .3668    .3668    .3668    .3668    .3668
NCOL                     13       14       15       16       17       18
```

FIGURE 7-22. FORECASTS BASED ON TREND, SEASONAL AND CYCLIC FACTORS

Using the historical cyclic data to infer a general form for the cyclic pattern is a relatively complex art which is made more difficult by the fact that the data are based on the product C*I which contains the irregular component. We will not attempt to discuss the intricacies here. Rather we will assume that the cyclic component has been established based on the historical data. (If pressed to do it, you may simply have to draw a smooth curve through the historical cyclic data and then extrapolate it into the future by eye. An alternative is to attempt to fit a simple sine wave to the data based on the time from peak to peak and the swing in amplitude from peak to trough.

Thus far we have spent considerable time to decompose the observed data into trend, seasonal, and cyclic components. Once we know these components, we can recompose these results to obtain forecasts. This is done in Figure 7-22 where we show a forecast for six quarters based on the analysis of the time series data used in Figures 7-19 through 7-21. To compute the trend, we use the a and b coefficients of the trend line $a + b$*X. The initial value is for quarter 13 (shown as the initial value of NCOL). Since the trend line is linear with slope b, we increase by b from quarter to quarter. The seasonal index (Line 30) is given numerically for the first four quarters and then uses the value four quarters previously because the seasonal index repeats every four quarters. We have approximated the cyclic factor and simply provided input values; you might want to do a more substantial analysis for your own problems. Finally, we have multiplied the three factors together (assuming the irregular factor, which cannot be forecast anyway, to be equal to 1) to obtain the forecast values.

7.8 INDEX NUMBERS

Index numbers are pervasive in our society. The evening news tells us about the latest values of the consumer price index, the wholesale price index, the Dow Jones Average, and many others. These index numbers provide a handy shorthand for understanding the movement of economic trends over time. In this section, we will describe the underlying concept of index numbers and show how to compute them using IFPS.

An index number is a ratio that relates prices (or other quantities) at two different points in time. Typically, a particular year (or group of years) is chosen as the base year and current values are compared to the values in the base year. For example, the consumer price index for all urban consumers has used 1967 as the base year. This index stood at 242.5 in April 1980, indicating that prices were 2.425 times as great in April 1980 than in the base year of 1967. Note that the index multiplies the ratio by 100 (242.5 rather than 2.425).

Indexes typically measure the change in a group of items, often referred to as a market basket. For illustrative purposes, we will consider the simplified market basket shown in Table 7-1. This market basket might reflect a high school student's weekly snack diet.

Figure 7-23 shows the IFPS model using this price and purchase information to generate various index numbers. We begin by considering "aggregative index numbers," that is, index numbers that consider only the total price. If we add up the values in the price column in 1980 ($1.90) and the values in the price column in 1970 ($1.20) and take their ratio times 100 we obtain:

$$\text{Aggregative price index} = 100 * (1.90/1.20) = 158.33$$

This is an unweighted index since it does not take into account how much of each item was consumed.

TABLE 7-1

MARKET BASKET

COMMODITY	PRICE 1970	PRICE 1980	AMOUNT 1970	AMOUNT 1980
Coffee	.10	.25	20	15
Hamburgers	.50	.65	5	6
French Fries	.20	.40	5	4
Ice Cream Cone	.25	.40	3	3
Chocolate Bar	.15	.20	1	2

```
MODEL INDEX  VERSION OF  01/12/83  20:17
10 COLUMNS 1-5
20 *
30 * COMMODITY PRICES
40 *
50 PRICES 1970 = .1,.5,.2,.25,.15
60 PRICES 1980 = .25,.65,.4,.4,.2
70 *
80 TOTAL 1970 COST = PREVIOUS + PRICES 1970
90 TOTAL 1980 COST = PREVIOUS + PRICES 1980
100 *
110 UNWEIGHTED AGGREGATIVE INDEX=100*TOTAL 1980 COST/TOTAL 1970 COST
120 *
130 PRICE RATIO 1980 TO 1970 = PRICES 1980/PRICES 1970
140 CUMULATIVE 1980 TO 1970 PRICE RATIO=PREVIOUS+'
141 PRICE RATIO 1980 TO 1970
150 UNWEIGHTED INDEX OF PRICE RELATIVES = '
160 CUMULATIVE 1980 TO 1970 PRICE RATIO *100/NCOL
170 *
180 * PURCHASES
190 *
200 PURCHASES 1970 = 20,5,5,3,1
210 PURCHASES 1980 =15,6,4,3,2
220 *
230 *    LASPEYRES INDEX
250 COSTS 1980 = PRICES 1980* PURCHASES 1970
260 COSTS 1970 = PRICES 1970 * PURCHASES 1970
270 CUMULATIVE 1980 COSTS = PREVIOUS + COSTS 1980
280 CUMULATIVE 1970 COSTS = PREVIOUS + COSTS 1970
290 LASPEYRES INDEX=100*CUMULATIVE 1980 COSTS/CUMULATIVE 1970 COSTS
300 *
```

FIGURE 7-23. INDEX NUMBERS

(This Figure Continued on the Next Page)

```
310 *       PAASCHE INDEX
330 COST 1980 = PRICES 1980 * PURCHASES 1980
340 COST 1970 = PRICES 1970 * PURCHASES 1980
350 CUMULATIVE 1980 COST = PREVIOUS + COST 1980
360 CUMULATIVE 1970 COST = PREVIOUS + COST 1970
370 PAASCHE INDEX = 100*CUMULATIVE 1980 COST /CUMULATIVE 1970 COST
380 *
390 NCOL=PREVIOUS + 1
END OF MODEL
? solve
ENTER SOLVE OPTIONS
? all
                                        1       2       3       4       5

 COMMODITY PRICES

PRICES 1970                            .10     .50     .20     .25     .15
PRICES 1980                            .25     .65     .40     .40     .20

TOTAL 1970 COST                        .10     .60     .80    1.05    1.20
TOTAL 1980 COST                        .25     .90    1.30    1.70    1.90

UNWEIGHTED AGGREGATIVE INDEX        250.00  150.00  162.50  161.90  158.33

PRICE RATIO 1980 TO 1970              2.50    1.30    2.00    1.60    1.33
CUMULATIVE 1980 TO 1970 PRICE RAT     2.50    3.80    5.80    7.40    8.73
UNWEIGHTED INDEX OF PRICE RELATIV   250.00  190.00  193.33  185.00  174.67

 PURCHASES

PURCHASES 1970                       20.00    5.00    5.00    3.00    1.00
PURCHASES 1980                       15.00    6.00    4.00    3.00    2.00

     LASPEYRES INDEX
COSTS 1980                            5.00    3.25    2.00    1.20     .20
COSTS 1970                            2.00    2.50    1.00     .75     .15
CUMULATIVE 1980 COSTS                 5.00    8.25   10.25   11.45   11.65
CUMULATIVE 1970 COSTS                 2.00    4.50    5.50    6.25    6.40
LASPEYRES INDEX                     250.00  183.33  186.36  183.20  182.03

      PAASCHE INDEX
COST 1980                             3.75    3.90    1.60    1.20     .40
COST 1970                             1.50    3.00     .80     .75     .30
CUMULATIVE 1980 COST                  3.75    7.65    9.25   10.45   10.85
CUMULATIVE 1970 COST                  1.50    4.50    5.30    6.05    6.35
PAASCHE INDEX                       250.00  170.00  174.53  172.73  170.87

NCOL                                  1.00    2.00    3.00    4.00    5.00
```

FIGURE 7-23. INDEX NUMBERS
(Continued)

EXERCISE: Add gasoline to the market basket in Table 7-1. Its price was $0.42 per gallon in 1970 and $1.23 in 1980. Consumption went from six gallons to four gallons per week during that time. Determine the aggregative price index for this augmented market basket.

An alternate way of computing an unweighted index is to consider the relative prices of each item and average these relative prices. The relative price of an item is the ratio of its current price to its price in the base year. For example, for coffee in Table 7-1, the relative price of coffee in 1980 compared to 1970 is 250 (i.e., 100*(.25/.10)). This form of index is called the unweighted index of price relatives. Note that for our market basket it is 100*(8.73/5) or 174.60. Here, 8.73 is the sum of the price ratios and we divide by 5 to obtain the average of a market basket containing five items. In general, the two types of unweighted indexes give different answers.

Neither of these simple indexes is appropriate when the amount purchased differs for each item. What we would like to know is how much actual expenditures have risen. Therefore, we have to multiply the unit cost by the amount purchased. For example, in 1970 20*0.20 = $4.00 was spent on coffee. At this point we have to decide which consumption pattern we will compare: the 1970 market basket or the 1980 market basket. The first case, called the Laspeyres index, assumes that we want to know how much a 1970 market basket would cost us if we bought it today. It takes the ratio of the the total cost of the 1970 market basket in 1980 to its cost in 1970. (See Lines 230 through 290 of Figure 7-23). The second case, called the Paasche index, assumes that we don't care about consumption patterns in the past but are interested in how much more today's market basket costs us compared to a point in the past. It takes the ratio of the total cost of the 1980 market basket in 1980 to its cost in 1970. (See Lines 310 through 370 of Figure 7-23.) The results, for the Laspeyres index and the Paasche indices, respectively, as shown in Figure 7-23, are 182.03 and 170.87. The advantage of the Laspeyres index is that it always measures the same basket thereby providing continuity and requiring no data gathering on changing tastes. The Paasche index accounts for taste changes and includes substitutions made by consumers that reflect different rates of inflation on different items, but requires new data to be gathered each time on the market basket.

EXERCISE: Compute the Laspeyres index for a weighted index of price relatives for the market basket of Table 7-1. That is, multiply the price relative of each item in 1980 by the total cost in 1970 (unit cost times number of units) for each item to obtain the current cost. Show that the Laspeyres index is the same for both methods of computation.

EXERCISE: Compute the Paasche index for a weighted index of price relatives for the market basket of Table 7-1.

EXERCISE: Compute the Laspeyres and Paasche indices with gasoline added to the market basket as in the first exercise in this section.

CHAPTER VIII
APPLICATIONS IN PRODUCTION AND OPERATIONS MANAGEMENT

CHAPTER VIII
APPLICATIONS IN PRODUCTION AND OPERATIONS MANAGEMENT

This chapter shows you how to apply IFPS to problems in production and operations management (P/OM). The area of production and operations management has become increasingly important in recent years throughout the world as competition makes improvements in productivity necessary for survival. Many of the management techniques of P/OM involve financial analysis and can be well modeled in IFPS. In this chapter we present two such methods (break-even analysis and equipment replacement analysis). Some problems involve statistical techniques (particularly forecasting) and simulation which have been discussed earlier in this book. We present examples of these problems and of others which are unique to P/OM, such as inventory models and materials requirements planning (MRP).

As in Chapters VI and VII, we have taken many of the examples from an existing text. In this this chapter we use *OPERATIONS MANAGEMENT : Decision Making in the Operations Function (2nd Edition)* by Roger G. Schroeder (McGraw-Hill, 1985). If you need more information about a particular method or topic, you can refer to the Schroeder book or to any similar introductory text in P/OM. We have tried, however, to present the sampling of topics from P/OM in such a way that if you have a working understanding of the underlying concepts you can use this chapter to solve P/OM problems without having to refer to outside sources.

8.1 BREAK-EVEN ANALYSIS

In making decisions involving production and operations management, financial considerations are equally important to technical considerations. Break-even analysis, described in Section 6.9 in the chapter on Financial Applications, is so fundamental to financial decision making in P/OM that we present a second discussion here. Simply put, break-even occurs when present value of revenue equals present value of expenses, that is, profit equals zero.

Consider a simple situation in which a company is trying to decide whether to invest $10 million into automation equipment for a portion of its production line. The situation of the company is as follows:

Annual sales	$60.0 million
Current expenses	$37.8 million
Annual production volume	200,000 units

Of its current expenses, $10.2 million are fixed costs. Its current break-even quantity can be obtained from the formula:

$$BREAKEVEN\ VOLUME = \frac{FIXED\ COST}{UNIT\ PRICE - UNIT\ VARIABLE\ COST} \qquad (8-1)$$

This formula expresses the usual idea that the profit is zero when the markup (excess of price over variable cost) times the volume of sales is just sufficient to cover the fixed cost. As shown in Figure 8-1, before investment, the company actually breaks even at annual sales of 6296 units (that is, 62.96 *100 units since production is defined in units of hundreds.)

```
MODEL EVEN  VERSION OF  05/11/86  22:42
10 COLUMNS 1-5
20 *
25*   ALL DOLLAR VALUES IN (000'S)
27*
30 *    BEFORE INVESTMENT
40 *
50 SALES=60000
60 EXPENSES=37800
70 ANNUAL PRODUCTION  = 200
80 FIXED COST = 10200
90 *
100 VARIABLE COST = EXPENSES - FIXED COST
110 UNIT VARIABLE COST = VARIABLE COST/ANNUAL PRODUCTION
120 UNIT PRICE = SALES/ANNUAL PRODUCTION
130 PROFIT=SALES-EXPENSES
140 BREAKEVEN VOLUME = FIXED COST/(UNIT PRICE - UNIT VARIABLE COST)
150 *
160 *     AFTER INVESTMENT -- NO TAX CASE
170 *
180 DEPRECIATION=2000
190 VARIABLE COST SAVING = 7000
200 UNIT VARIABLE COST SAVING=VARIABLE COST SAVING/ANNUALPRODUCTION
210 BREAK EVEN = (FIXED COST +DEPRECIATION)/(UNIT PRICE - '
211 UNIT VARIABLE COST + UNIT VARIABLE COST SAVING)
220 *
230 *   FINANCIAL MEASURES
240 *
250 INVESTMENT=10000,0
260 TOTAL SAVINGS=VARIABLE COST SAVING + DEPRECIATION
270 DISCOUNT RATE = .25
280 PRESENT VALUE=NPVC(TOTAL SAVINGS,DISCOUNT RATE,INVESTMENT)
290 RATE OF RETURN=IRR(TOTAL SAVINGS,INVESTMENT)
300 *
310 *     AFTER INVESTMENT -- 46 PERCENT TAX RATE CASE
320 *
330 TAX RATE =.46
340 NET SAVINGS =DEPRECIATION*TAX RATE+VARIABLE COST SAVING*'
341      (1-TAX RATE)
350 NET PRESENT VALUE=NPVC(NET SAVINGS,DISCOUNT RATE,0)
360 NET RATE OF RETURN=IRR(NET SAVINGS,INVESTMENT)
END OF MODEL
```

FIGURE 8-1.BREAK-EVEN ANALYSIS
(This Figure Continued on the Next Page)

```
? solve
MODEL EVEN  VERSION OF  05/11/86  22:42 -- 5 COLUMNS 22 VARIABLES
ENTER SOLVE OPTIONS
? width 62 22 8
? all
```

	1	2	3	4	5
ALL DOLLAR VALUES IN (000'S)					
BEFORE INVESTMENT					
SALES	60000	60000	60000	60000	60000
EXPENSES	37800	37800	37800	37800	37800
ANNUAL PRODUCTION	200	200	200	200	200
FIXED COST	10200	10200	10200	10200	10200
VARIABLE COST	27600	27600	27600	27600	27600
UNIT VARIABLE COST	138	138	138	138	138
UNIT PRICE	300	300	300	300	300
PROFIT	22200	22200	22200	22200	22200
BREAKEVEN VOLUME	62.96	62.96	62.96	62.96	62.96
AFTER INVESTMENT -- NO TAX CASE					
DEPRECIATION	2000	2000	2000	2000	2000
VARIABLE COST SAVING	7000	7000	7000	7000	7000
UNIT VARIABLE COST SAV	35	35	35	35	35
BREAK EVEN	61.93	61.93	61.93	61.93	61.93
FINANCIAL MEASURES					
INVESTMENT	10000	0	0	0	0
TOTAL SAVINGS	9000	9000	9000	9000	9000
DISCOUNT RATE	.2500	.2500	.2500	.2500	.2500
PRESENT VALUE	-2800	2960	7568	11254	14204
RATE OF RETURN		.5000	.7245	.8175	.8595
AFTER INVESTMENT -- 46 PERCENT TAX RATE CASE					
TAX RATE	.4600	.4600	.4600	.4600	.4600
NET SAVINGS	4700	4700	4700	4700	4700
NET PRESENT VALUE	3760	6768	9174	11100	12640
NET RATE OF RETURN			.1936	.3108	.3740

FIGURE 8-1. BREAK-EVEN ANALYSIS
(Continued)

The $10 million investment (Line 250) would result in annual variable cost savings of $7 million at the current volume of 200,000 units. The company will depreciate the equipment on a straight line basis over five years (i.e., at $2 million/year). It insists on a 25% rate of return on its investments. Figure 8-1 also shows the analysis with the investment. First we compute the break-even volume with the investment, adding the depreciation to our fixed cost and reducing the variable cost by the variable cost saving. The results show that the break-even volume decreased slightly to 6193 units.

We next consider the time value of money for the investment of $10 million which is to be offset by the savings in variable cost and the depreciation. The measures of effectiveness are the net present value and the internal rate of return. The results show that financial break-even occurs during the second year (since present value becomes positive) and the rate of return on the investment is 85.95 % for the five-year time horizon.

These results are quite favorable for the investment; however, they do not present the whole picture. To be more realistic, we must consider tax effects. The company's marginal tax rate was 46%. The savings from depreciation must therefore be multiplied by the tax rate since only the taxes are saved, while the variable cost savings must be multiplied by (1 - tax rate) since only the after-tax savings accrue to the company. With taxes included the project still passes the company's rate of return criterion, but by much less since the rate of return is 37.4 percent. The present value of the investment is approximately $12.6 million.

Note that Figure 8-1 also allows you to determine the payback period with discounting taken into account. Specifically, the present value exceeds the 10 million dollar investment during Year 4.

The sequence of steps followed in Figure 8-1 is by no means the only way to analyze the problem. Figure 8-2 shows the same problem organized in the way accountants think about the problem. In this form of the analysis, we first compute the profit on sales (i.e., the current value of the operation shown in Line 90). We then compute the value with the investment (labeled INVESTMENT VALUE) and, after a series of steps (read these over and make sure you understand lines 160 through 190) arrive at the NET AFTER TAXES, which is used to compute the present value net after-tax of the stream of savings. This net present value after taxes is $12.64 million as in Figure 8-1.

EXERCISE: Consider the following revenue stream associated with a new product:

Year After Release	1	2	3	4	5	6	7
Revenue (million $)	0.2	0.5	1.2	1.8	2.0	1.0	0.6

If your company requires a 15% rate of return on its investments, what is the maximum you should be willing to spend for design, tooling, introductory advertising, and similar initial investment expenses? This is a straightforward application of the IFPS NPVC function. The answer is that the maximum investment you would be willing to make is $4.02 million.

EXERCISE: Use IFPS to determine for what lease period you should be indifferent between buying an automobile for personal use at $10,000 or leasing it at $550 per month. Assume you can invest in a money fund that guarantees you 1% per month after taxes. Assume further that all other expenses will be the same in either case.

EXERCISE: Reformulate the model of Figure 8-1 so that break-even volume is not computed directly. Rather, use GOAL SEEKING to find the break-even volume. Note that you will have to formulate the problem in such a way that profit depends on the annual production.

```
MODEL EVEN2  VERSION OF  08/31/82  08:29
10COLUMNS 1-5
20*
30*BREAKEVEN ANALYSIS DONE IN ACCOUNTING STYLE
40*
50 SALES = 60000
60 FIXED COST =10200
70 INITIAL DEPRECIATION =0
80 VARIABLE COST = 27600
90 CURRENT VALUE = SALES -FIXED COST - VARIABLE COST
100*
110* WITH INVESTMENT
120*
130 INVESTMENT DEPRECIATION =2000
140 INVESTMENT VARIABLE COST = 20600
150 INVESTMENT VALUE = SALES -FIXED COST -INVESTMENT VARIABLE COST
160 VALUE DIFFERENCE = INVESTMENT VALUE - CURRENT VALUE
170 DIFFERENCE WITH DEPRECIATION = VALUE DIFFERENCE'
171 -(INVESTMENT DEPRECIATION - INITIAL DEPRECIATION)
180 TAX INCREASE = DIFFERENCE WITH DEPRECIATION *0.46
190 NET AFTER TAXES = VALUE DIFFERENCE -TAX INCREASE
200 PRESENT VALUE NET AFTER TAXES = NPVC(NET AFTER TAXES,0.25,0)
END OF MODEL
? SOLVE
MODEL EV  VERSION OF  05/11/86  23:06 -- 5 COLUMNS 13 VARIABLES
ENTER SOLVE OPTIONS
? ALL
                                  1        2        3        4        5


BREAKEVEN ANALYSIS DONE IN ACCOUNTING STYLE

SALES                         60000    60000    60000    60000    60000
FIXED COST                    10200    10200    10200    10200    10200
INITIAL DEPRECIATION              0        0        0        0        0
VARIABLE COST                 27600    27600    27600    27600    27600
CURRENT VALUE                 22200    22200    22200    22200    22200

 WITH INVESTMENT

INVESTMENT DEPRECIATION        2000     2000     2000     2000     2000
INVESTMENT VARIABLE COST      20600    20600    20600    20600    20600
INVESTMENT VALUE              29200    29200    29200    29200    29200
VALUE DIFFERENCE               7000     7000     7000     7000     7000
DIFFERENCE WITH DEPRECIA       5000     5000     5000     5000     5000
TAX INCREASE                   2300     2300     2300     2300     2300
NET AFTER TAXES                4700     4700     4700     4700     4700
PRESENT VALUE NET AFTER        3760     6768     9174    11100    12640
```

FIGURE 8-2. BREAK-EVEN ANALYSIS IN ACCOUNTING FORMAT

8.2. AGGREGATE SCHEDULING

In a job shop, planning is done at three levels: aggregate scheduling, shop loading, and sequencing. Aggregate scheduling involves determining the total resources (labor, raw materials, supplies, facilities) that have to be available for a given period (e.g., a quarter). Shop loading involves the assignment of actual work on hand to individual facilities. Sequencing determines the order in which work is to be done at each facility. Both shop loading and sequencing must be done much more often than aggregate scheduling because they have to take into account day-to-day changes that occur. These three levels of planning are interrelated. In this section, we shall be concerned with the first level, aggregate scheduling.

8.2.1 Production Forecasting

Aggregate scheduling involves predicting the demand for resources. Therefore, the aggregate scheduling process begins with forecasts of these demands. Usually, some of the information is on hand from orders already in process or booked. However, we can anticipate that new orders will come into the job shop, some of which will have to be started during the planning period. The short-range forecasting methods described in Section 7.7 are usually employed to make the needed forecasts. The following four exercises describe a simple operations management situation. You are asked to use the methods of moving averages, weighted moving averages, exponential smoothing, and regression respectively to obtain forecasts for this situation. You should write IFPS models for each method. Refer to Chapter 7 for the details of the methods and for sample IFPS models.

EXERCISE: The maintenance department of a large real estate complex assigns crews to different tasks. These task are completed in batches before another task in undertaken. For example, parking lot care last year required the following number of crew hours:

Month	Crew Hours	Month	Crew Hours	Month	Crew Hours
Jan	250	May	200	Sept	250
Feb	200	June	80	Oct	200
March	200	July	100	Nov	220
Apr	200	Aug	120	Dec	280

Use a moving average based on six- month history to "predict" the crew requirements for July of last year through January of this year. Determine the magnitude of the error in the "forecast" by comparing your prediction for July though December with the actual crew hours.

What if you used a three-month moving average? Are the results more accurate?

EXERCISE: If you examine the maintenance department data given in the previous exercise you can see that recent months requirements are closer to next month's than those several months ago. A weighted moving average might be more appropriate. Use a weighted six-month moving average on the maintenance department data with weights of 0.1, 0.1, 0.1, 0.2, 0.2, and 0.3. Again determine the magnitude of the error and compare with the error obtained with unweighted moving averages for six months and for three months.

EXERCISE: Use exponential smoothing (Section 7.7.1) on the maintenance department data. Use WHAT IF statements to find the value of ALPHA that most closely predicts the values for July through December. Use this value of ALPHA as your forecast for January.

EXERCISE: Use POLYFIT(1) and POLYFIT(2) to forecast January. To check the validity of these methods, use POLYFIT(1) and POLYFIT(2) to forecast each month from August to December. Determine the error between the regression forecasts defined by the POLYFIT functions and the observed values. Are these errors acceptable? (Sections 3.2.3 and 7.7.1 discuss POLYFIT.)

8.2.2 Trading Off Overtime, Work Force, and Inventory

Demand is almost never constant over time. It fluctuates week to week or month to month. You have several policy options available to you, including:

1. level work force,
2. level work force plus overtime, or
3. "chase" strategy.

In a level work force policy, you determine the total need over the time horizon (e.g., a year) and produce to inventory to meet demand. If you anticipate periods of peak load, you may want to use a smaller work force and use overtime to meet the peak. In the "chase" strategy, you hire and lay off workers each period so that you create no inventory and meet demand exactly. These three are only some of the policies available to you. Each policy can be modeled in IFPS. In fact, you can create a basic model and then use WHAT IF to explore other options.

An example is shown in Figure 8-3 for the level work force case. The scenario modeled is that of a brewery where each worker produces 10,000 gallons of beer per month on regular time. The brewery has 40 workers. Company rules allow overtime use of 20% in only a three-month period. Sales are forecast at the levels shown in Line 80 of the model. All demand must be met and stockouts are not allowed.

The number of workers required is determined by adding the monthly sales forecasts (in 1000's of gallons) for the year, dividing by 12 to obtain the monthly average, and then dividing by the average worker's production of 10,000 gallons. Workers are assumed to be paid $1000/month on regular time and are paid overtime at 150% of regular time. It costs $1000 to hire and $2000 to lay off a worker. Inventory cost is 6 cents per gallon. Starting inventory is 50,000 gallons and an inventory of 50,000 gallons is desired at the end of the year.

As shown in Figure 8-3, the level work force policy requires 45 workers and costs $726,500. Five workers have to be hired. The first WHAT IF case explores the implications of allowing overtime. Note the definition of the overtime percentage as a fraction of all direct calculations. This policy requires only 43 workers but has a higher total cost since the overtime costs are not compensated for by reductions in regular wages, inventory, and hiring costs. The second WHAT IF case models the chase policy. Here the number of workers just equals the sales and inventory is kept fixed at 50,000. The result is a net cost savings of over $50,000 at the expense of a hire/layoff policy that shuttles work force between 30 and 65. Although a lower cost policy, is it implementable in real labor markets?

```
MODEL TRADE1  VERSION OF  05/12/86  12:17
10 COLUMNS 1-12,TOTAL
20 *
39*RESOURCES
40*
50 REGULAR WORKERS =45
60 OVERTIME PERCENT =0
70 UNITS PRODUCED =REGULAR WORKERS *10*(1+OVERTIME PERCENT)
80 SALES FORECAST=300,300,350,400,450,500,650,600,475,475,450,450
90 END OF MONTH INVENTORY = STARTING INVENTORY+UNITS PRODUCED -'
91 SALES FORECAST
100*
110*COSTS (000'S)
120 REGULAR TIME =REGULAR WORKERS
130 OVERTIME =OVERTIME PERCENT*REGULAR TIME *1.5
140 HIRE OR LAYOFF COST=IF INITIAL WORKFORCE.GT.REGULAR WORKERS'
141 THEN 2*(INITIAL WORKFORCE-REGULAR WORKERS) ELSE'
142 REGULAR WORKERS -INITIAL WORKFORCE
150 INVENTORY CARRY =STARTING INVENTORY *.06
160 TOTAL COST =SUM(REGULAR TIME THRU INVENTORY CARRY)
170*
180*INITIAL CONDITIONS
190*
200 INITIAL INVENTORY =50,0
210 INITIAL WORKFORCE=40,PREVIOUS REGULAR WORKERS
220 STARTING INVENTORY =50,PREVIOUS END OF MONTH INVENTORY
260 COLUMN TOTAL FOR UNITS PRODUCED,SALES FORECAST =SUM(C1 THRU C12)
270 COLUMN TOTAL FOR REGULAR TIME THRU TOTAL COST =SUM(C1 THRU C12)
END OF MODEL
? SOLVE
MODEL TRADE1  VERSION OF  05/12/86  12:17 -- 13 COLUMNS 13 VARIABLES
ENTER SOLVE OPTIONS
? ALL
```

	1	2	3	4	5	6	7
RESOURCES							
REGULAR WORKERS	45	45	45	45	45	45	45
OVERTIME PERCENT	0	0	0	0	0	0	0
UNITS PRODUCED	450	450	450	450	450	450	450
SALES FORECAST	300	300	350	400	450	500	650
END OF MONTH INVENTO	200	350	450	500	500	450	250
COSTS (000'S)							
REGULAR TIME	45	45	45	45	45	45	45
OVERTIME	0	0	0	0	0	0	0
HIRE OR LAYOFF COST	5	0	0	0	0	0	0
INVENTORY CARRY	3	12	21	27	30	30	27
TOTAL COST	53	57	66	72	75	75	72

FIGURE 8-3. TRADE-OFFS AMONG OVERTIME, WORK-FORCE AND INVENTORY IN AGGREGATE SCHEDULING

(This Figure is Continued On the Next Page)

```
INITIAL CONDITIONS

INITIAL INVENTORY        50     0     0     0     0     0     0
INITIAL WORKFORCE        40    45    45    45    45    45    45
STARTING INVENTORY       50   200   350   450   500   500   450

                          8     9    10    11    12 TOTAL
RESOURCES

REGULAR WORKERS          45    45    45    45    45
OVERTIME PERCENT          0     0     0     0     0
UNITS PRODUCED          450   450   450   450   450  5400
SALES FORECAST          600   475   475   450   450  5400
END OF MONTH INVENTO    100    75    50    50    50

COSTS (000'S)
REGULAR TIME             45    45    45    45    45   540
OVERTIME                  0     0     0     0     0     0
HIRE OR LAYOFF COST       0     0     0     0     0     5
INVENTORY CARRY          15     6 4.500     3     3 181.5
TOTAL COST               60    51 49.50    48    48 726.5

 INITIAL CONDITIONS

INITIAL INVENTORY         0     0     0     0     0
INITIAL WORKFORCE        45    45    45    45    45
STARTING INVENTORY      250   100    75    50    50

ENTER SOLVE OPTIONS
? WHAT IF
WHAT IF CASE 1
ENTER STATEMENTS
? REGULAR WORKERS =43
? OVERTIME PERCENT =0 FOR 5,.2 FOR 3,0
? SOLVE
ENTER SOLVE OPTIONS
?L50THRU L160

***** WHAT IF CASE 1 *****
2 WHAT IF STATEMENTS PROCESSED

                          1     2     3     4     5     6     7
RESOURCES

REGULAR WORKERS          43    43    43    43    43    43    43
OVERTIME PERCENT          0     0     0     0     0 .2000 .2000
UNITS PRODUCED          430   430   430   430   430   516   516
SALES FORECAST          300   300   350   400   450   500   650
END OF MONTH INVENTO    180   310   390   420   400   416   282
```

FIGURE 8-3. TRADE-OFFS AMONG OVERTIME, WORK-FORCE AND INVENTORY IN AGGREGATE SCHEDULING

(This Figure is Continued On the Next Page)

```
COSTS(000'S)
REGULAR TIME               43     43     43     43     43     43     43
OVERTIME                    0      0      0      0      0  12.90  12.90
HIRE OR LAYOFF COST         3      0      0      0      0      0      0
INVENTORY CARRY             3  10.80  18.60  23.40  25.20     24  24.96
TOTAL COST                 49  53.80  61.60  66.40  68.20  79.90  80.86

                            8      9     10     11     12  TOTAL

RESOURCES

REGULAR WORKERS            43     43     43     43     43
OVERTIME PERCENT        .2000      0      0      0      0
UNITS PRODUCED            516    430    430    430    430   5418
SALES FORECAST            600    475    475    450    450   5400
END OF MONTH INVENTO      198    153    108     88     68

COSTS(000'S)
REGULAR TIME               43     43     43     43     43    516
OVERTIME                12.90      0      0      0      0  38.70
HIRE OR LAYOFF COST         0      0      0      0      0      3
INVENTORY CARRY         16.92  11.88  9.180  6.480  5.280  179.7
TOTAL COST              72.82  54.88  52.18  49.48  48.28  737.4

WHAT IF CASE 2
ENTER STATEMENTS
? REGULAR WORKERS =ROUNDUP(SALES FORECAST/10)
? SOLVE
ENTER SOLVE OPTIONS
? L50 through L160

***** WHAT IF CASE 2 *****
1 WHAT IF STATEMENT PROCESSED

                            1      2      3      4      5      6      7

RESOURCES

REGULAR WORKERS            30     30     35     40     45     50     65
OVERTIME PERCENT            0      0      0      0      0      0      0
UNITS PRODUCED            300    300    350    400    450    500    650
SALES FORECAST            300    300    350    400    450    500    650
END OF MONTH INVENTO       50     50     50     50     50     50     50
```

FIGURE 8-3. TRADE-OFFS AMONG OVERTIME, WORK-FORCE AND INVENTORY IN AGGREGATE SCHEDULING
(This Figure is Continued On the Next Page)

COSTS (000'S)							
REGULAR TIME	30	30	35	40	45	50	65
OVERTIME	0	0	0	0	0	0	0
HIRE OR LAYOFF COST	20	0	5	5	5	5	15
INVENTORY CARRY	3	3	3	3	3	3	3
TOTAL COST	53	33	43	48	53	58	83

	8	9	10	11	12	TOTAL
RESOURCES						
REGULAR WORKERS	60	48	48	45	45	
OVERTIME PERCENT	0	0	0	0	0	
UNITS PRODUCED	600	480	480	450	450	5410
SALES FORECAST	600	475	475	450	450	5400
END OF MONTH INVENTO	50	55	60	60	60	
COSTS(000'S)						
REGULAR TIME	60	48	48	45	45	541
OVERTIME	0	0	0	0	0	0
HIRE OR LAYOFF COST	10	24	0	6	0	95
INVENTORY CARRY	3	3	3.300	3.600	3.600	37.50
TOTAL COST	73	75	51.30	54.60	48.60	673.5

FIGURE 8-3. TRADE-OFFS AMONG OVERTIME, WORK-FORCE AND INVENTORY IN AGGREGATE SCHEDULING (Continued)

One final IFPS note. In deciding on the number of workers in a given month, we took the work force and rounded it up to the next higher worker if a fraction of a worker is required, since we can't hire a part of a person.

EXERCISE: Suppose, because of a local Octoberfest, the forecast demand in Period 10 has been increased to 900,000 gallons. Rerun the three policies under this condition.

EXERCISE: Suppose in the previous exercise, the demand for months 11 and 12 drops to 300 following the Octoberfest. Can you meet the no stockout criterion in the level workforce or the level workforce with overtime cases? If not, can you devise a simple, inexpensive policy to avoid stockouts other than the "chase" policy?

Suppose your company policy does not allow more than 10 hires in a given month or more than 10 layoffs because of limits on training and fear of unionization. Develop a plan which takes these limits into account.

8.2.3 Linear Decision Rules -- The HMMS Model

Thus far, we have considered trading off work force size, overtime, and inventory in a simple manner. A more sophisticated model for this tradeoff was devised by Holt, Modigliani, Muth, and Simon and is known as the HMMS model. (Incidentally, both Professors Modigliani and Simon have since won the Nobel Prize in Economics.) The model assumes quadratic costs and as a result, provides decisions about work force and production rate that are linear.

The HMMS model involves adding up six components of cost. These components and their definitions are given in Table 8-1, where C1 through C9 represent various constants in the model.

TABLE 8-1

COST COMPONENTS OF THE HMMS MODEL

REGULAR PRODUCTION COST	C1 * WORK FORCE
HIRING COST	C2 * (CHANGE IN WORK FORCE)^2
OVERTIME1	C3 * (PRODUCTION -C4*WORK FORCE)^2
OVERTIME2	C5 * PRODUCTION
OVERTIME3	–C6*WORK FORCE
INVENTORY	C7*(TOTAL INVENTORY – C8 – C9*DEMAND)^2

As you examine Table 8-1, you will see that the model again depends on work force, production, and inventory. A representative set of assumptions is used in Figure 8-4, where the HMMS model is implemented in IFPS. The components of cost are shown in Lines 90 through 140. Values are assigned to the constants in Lines 170 through 250. These constants represent unit costs associated with payroll, hiring and firing, overtime, and inventory. Total costs for each period and cumultative costs are shown in Lines 270 and 280.

The demand and conditions in Figure 8-4 are identical to those in Figure 8-3, with cost coefficient values added.

EXERCISE: Use WHAT IF statements to modify Figure 8-4 for the following conditions:

1. A constant work force of 43 with 20% overtime allowed in Periods 6,7, and 8.
2. The "chase strategy" described in the previous section.
3. A policy of your own devising that has as small a total cost as you can find.

```
MODEL HMMS1  VERSION OF  05/14/86  20:20
10 COLUMNS 1-6
20 SALES FORECAST = 300,300,350,400,450,500
30 WORK FORCE = 43
40 UNITS PRODUCED = WORK FORCE*10
50 CHANGE IN WORK FORCE=WORK FORCE-INITIAL WORK FORCE,WORK FORCE -'
51 PREVIOUS WORK FORCE
60 CURRENT INVENTORY =UNITS PRODUCED -SALES FORECAST
70 TOTAL INVENTORY = CURRENT INVENTORY,PREVIOUS+CURRENT INVENTORY
80*
90 REGULAR PRODUCTION COST = C1*WORK FORCE
100 HIRING COST =C2*XPOWERY(CHANGE IN WORK FORCE,2)
110 OVERTIME1 = C3*XPOWERY(UNITS PRODUCED - C4*WORKFORCE,2)
120 OVERTIME2=C5*UNITS PRODUCED -C6*WORK FORCE
130 INVENTORY=C7*XPOWERY(TOTAL INVENTORY-C8-C9*SALES FORECAST,2)
140 INITIAL WORK FORCE = 40
170 C1=1
180 C2=1.5
190 C3=.2
200 C4= 10
210 C5 =2
220 C6=20
230 C7=.06
240 C8 = 50
250 C9=.2
260 *
270 COST =SUM (L90,L130)
280 TOTAL COST = PREVIOUS TOTAL COST+COST
END OF MODEL
? SOLVE
MODEL HMMS1  VERSION OF  05/14/86  20:20 -- 6 COLUMNS 23 VARIABLES
ENTER SOLVE OPTIONS
? WIDTH 62 20 6
? ALL
```

	1	2	3	4	5	6
SALES FORECAST	300	300	350	400	450	500
WORK FORCE	43	43	43	43	43	43
UNITS PRODUCED	430	430	430	430	430	430
CHANGE IN WORK FORCE	3	0	0	0	0	0
CURRENT INVENTORY	130	130	80	30	-20	-70
TOTAL INVENTORY	130	260	340	370	350	280
REGULAR PRODUCTION COST	43	43	43	43	43	43
HIRING COST	13.50	0	0	0	0	0
OVERTIME1	0	0	0	0	0	0
OVERTIME2	0	0	0	0	0	0
INVENTORY	24	1350	2904	3456	2646	1014
INITIAL WORK FORCE	40	40	40	40	40	40

FIGURE 8-4. LINEAR DECISION RULE MODEL
(This Figure is Continued on the Next Page)

C1	1	1	1	1	1	1
C2	1.500	1.500	1.500	1.500	1.500	1.500
C3	.2000	.2000	.2000	.2000	.2000	.2000
C4	10	10	10	10	10	10
C5	2	2	2	2	2	2
C6	20	20	20	20	20	20
C7	.0600	.0600	.0600	.0600	.0600	.0600
C8	50	50	50	50	50	50
C9	.2000	.2000	.2000	.2000	.2000	.2000
COST	80.50	1393	2947	3499	2689	1057
TOTAL COST	80.50	1474	4421	7920	10609	11666

FIGURE 8-4. LINEAR DECISION RULE MODEL
(Continued)

8.3 INVENTORY

Inventory refers to items kept in stock for use in the production process or for sale. A very simple case is shown in the following drawing:

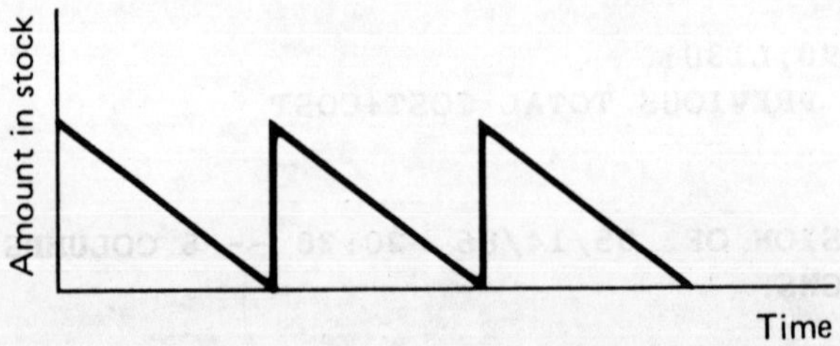

Here an order is placed at time 0, and received instantaneously. Demand results in withdrawal at a constant rate. At time T, the initial supply is exhausted and another order is placed. Restocking is again instantaneous. This process can be assumed to repeat itself. The decision problem you have is how many to order; that is, what is the optimum order quantity? Once you know the demand, you also know the order quantity and the time between reorders.

This seemingly simple problem is an economic one because there are costs associated with both the ordering and the holding of inventory. In fact, if we consider more general inventory situations, we have the following economic structure:

1. Carrying cost: Cost of storing, financing, guarding inventory (\$/item-year)

2. Reorder cost: Fixed cost of placing an order (\$/order)

3. Shortage cost: Cost of not meeting demand due to stockout (\$/unit-year)

4. Price break: Discounts due to quantity purchases.

More complex models allow for producing (or delivery of) goods at the same time that they are used up, salvage value for items not sold, lead time to account for the time between placing an order and receiving it, uncertain demand patterns, etc. Many problems that do not at first appear to be inventory models really are. One example is the amount of cash kept in the till by a supermarket or a bank. Here the carrying cost is lost interest, order cost is armored car delivery, and stockout costs are lost sales. Another example is flight attendants for airlines. Since these are hired in groups there will often be a surplus when a new class graduates. Thus, carrying costs are wages and fringes, order costs are training costs for a class, and shortage cost are the costs of cancelled flights if flight attendants are not available. In this section we will consider several simple inventory models to demonstrate how IFPS can be used to help in understanding the inventory process and in computing the optimal policy based on an inventory model. We will discuss the following situations:

- No shortages allowed, instant replenishment, constant withdrawal.
- No shortages allowed, constant delivery, constant withdrawal.
- The first case above with quantity discounts.

8.3.1 Simple EOQ Model

This case, described by the drawing above, assumes instant delivery, no shortages allowed, and a constant withdrawal rate. The total inventory cost is the sum of the carrying cost and the order cost. The components that go into the total cost are:

1. The average number of units carried in stock, which is equal to half the number of units purchased per order, that is, the lot size, Q.

2. The average dollar inventory, which is the unit cost, C, times the average number of units carried in stock, i.e., CQ/2.

3. The annual carrying cost per unit, which is expressed as the product of the interest rate, i, times the unit cost. Multiplying this quantity by the average inventory gives the carrying cost.

4. The number of orders placed per year, which is obtained by dividing the annual demand, D, by the order quantity (i.e., by the lot size).

5. The cost per order placed, (setup cost), S. Multiplying the cost per order placed by the number of orders yields the order cost.

The total inventory cost is given by:

$$TC = SD/Q + iCQ/2 \qquad (8\text{-}2)$$

All quantities on the right side of equation (8-2) are known except the order quantity, Q. It can be shown that the optimal size of the order quantity is given by:

$$Q = \sqrt{2*S*D/i*C} \tag{8-3}$$

It turns out that for this optimal value of Q, (called the Economic Order Quantity, or EOQ), the order cost and the carrying cost are equal. These results are implemented in the model shown in the top half of Figure 8-5 (lines 20 through 70.) The numerical results shown are based on the following input assumptions: an item (e.g., a bolt) costs six cents, has a 15% interest rate per unit, and an annual demand of 200,000 units.

EXERCISE: Check that the order quantity defined in Lines 40 and 41 in Figure 8-5 is optimal. To do so, expand the model shown in Lines 40 through 70 so that it uses 11 columns that specify order quantities spaced at intervals of 500 starting at 27,500. You should find that the total costs are larger, but only slightly, even for order quantities well away from the optimum.

8.3.2 Economic Lot Size Model - Uniform Lot Delivery

As a second case, consider a situation which is identical to the previous one except that you can produce the item in your own shop. Assume that you can produce at a constant rate, which is greater than the demand for the product. Thus, as shown below, an inventory builds up and you alternate between producing and not producing. The decision you now have to make is how big the production run should be.

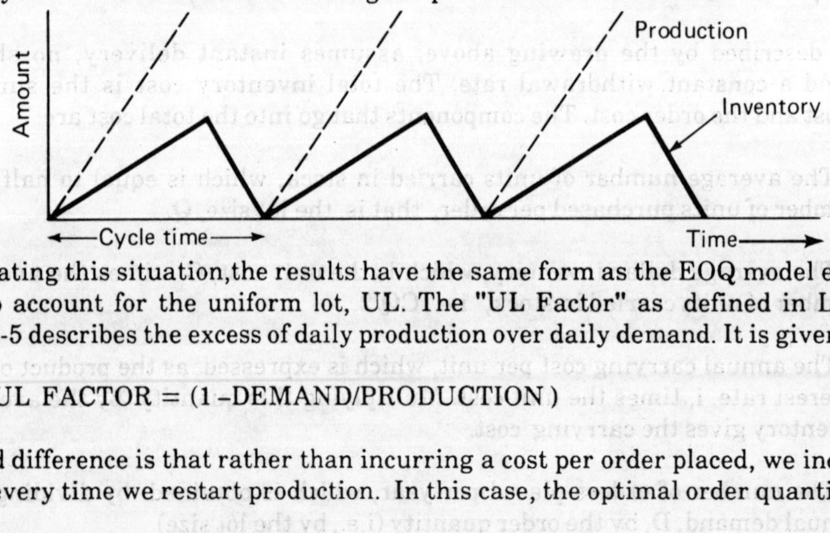

In evaluating this situation,the results have the same form as the EOQ model except for a factor to account for the uniform lot, UL. The "UL Factor" as defined in Line 110 of Figure 8-5 describes the excess of daily production over daily demand. It is given by:

$$\text{UL FACTOR} = (1-\text{DEMAND}/\text{PRODUCTION}) \tag{8-4}$$

A second difference is that rather than incurring a cost per order placed, we incur a setup cost, S, every time we restart production. In this case, the optimal order quantity is given by:

$$Q = \sqrt{(2*S*D)/(i*C*\text{UL FACTOR})} \tag{8-5}$$

As shown in Figure 8-5, as a result of production, the order quantity increases (from 141.4 to 200) and the inventory cost decreases (from 70.71 to 50) compared to the EOQ case. This results from the fact that you use up some of the items as they are produced. Hence, the average inventory and the maximum inventory are less than for EOQ. Figure 8-5 also shows the length of the production run in days, the time between production runs and the cycle time, which is the time from the start of one production cycle to the next. The data used to illustrate continuous delivery are based on the same situation as for the EOQ model. It is assumed that there is a cost of $10 per setup, that there is daily production of 8 units, and 250 working days per year.

```
MODEL INVENTOR  VERSION OF  05/14/86  20:46
10 COLUMNS 1
20 * SIMPLE EOQ MODEL
30*
40 ORDER QUANTITY = XPOWERY((2*ANNUAL DEMAND*COST PER ORDER)/'
41(COST*INTEREST RATE ),0.5)
50 CARRYING COST = 0.5*COST * ORDER QUANTITY*INTEREST RATE
60 ORDER COST =(ANNUAL DEMAND /ORDER QUANTITY)*COST PER ORDER
70 TOTAL COST = CARRYING COST + ORDER COST
80*
90*UNIFORM LOT DELIVERY (UL)
100 *
110 UL FACTOR = 1-DAILY DEMAND/DAILY PRODUCTION
120 UL ORDER QUANTITY = XPOWERY((2*ANNUAL DEMAND*COST PER SETUP)'
121/(COST*INTEREST RATE*UL FACTOR),0.5)
130 UL CARRYING COST = 0.5* COST*UL ORDER QUANTITY*UL FACTOR'
131*INTEREST RATE
140 UL ORDER COST =(ANNUAL DEMAND/UL ORDER QUANTITY)*COST PER SETUP
150 TOTAL UL COST = UL CARRYING COST + UL ORDER COST
160*
170 LENGTH OF PRODUCTION RUN IN DAYS = UL ORDER QUANTITY/'
171 DAILY PRODUCTION
180 TIME BETWEEN PRODUCTION RUNS = UL ORDER QUANTITY*UL FACTOR'
181 /DAILY DEMAND
185 TOTAL CYCLE TIME = L170 +L180
190 AVERAGE UL INVENTORY =0.5*UL ORDER QUANTITY *UL FACTOR
200 MAXIMUM UL INVENTORY = 2*AVERAGE UL INVENTORY
300 *
310 *INPUT DATA
320*
330 COST = 5
340 INTEREST RATE =.2
350 COST PER ORDER =10.00
360 ANNUAL DEMAND = 1000
370 DAILY PRODUCTION = 8
380 DAILY DEMAND = ANNUAL DEMAND/250
390 COST PER SETUP =10.00
END OF MODEL
```

FIGURE 8-5. SIMPLE EOQ AND CONTINUOUS DELIVERY INVENTORY MODELS
(This Figure is Continued on the Next Page)

```
? solve
ENTER SOLVE OPTIONS
? ALL

                                              1
 SIMPLE EOQ MODEL

ORDER QUANTITY                            141.4
CARRYING COST                             70.71
ORDER COST                                70.71
TOTAL COST                                141.4

UNIFORM LOT DELIVERY (UL)

UL FACTOR                                 .5000
UL ORDER QUANTITY                           200
UL CARRYING COST                             50
UL ORDER COST                                50
TOTAL UL COST                               100

LENGTH OF PRODUCTION RUN                     25
TIME BETWEEN PRODUCTION                      25
TOTAL CYCLE TIME                             50
AVERAGE UL INVENTORY                         50
MAXIMUM UL INVENTORY                        100

INPUT DATA

COST                                          5
INTEREST RATE                             .2000
COST PER ORDER                               10
ANNUAL DEMAND                              1000
DAILY PRODUCTION                              8
DAILY DEMAND                                  4
COST PER SETUP                               10
```

FIGURE 8-5. SIMPLE EOQ AND CONTINUOUS DELIVERY INVENTORY MODELS (Continued)

8.3.3 Quantity Discounts

The EOQ model is based on the assumption of a fixed price. If a supplier offers a discount when large quantities are ordered, then it is possible to trade off additional inventory cost (resulting from ordering a non-optimal quantity) for the cost saving. Thus, the decision to be made is whether to order the EOQ or the minimum quantity for which the price break is obtained. The steps followed are:

1. Compute the economic order quantity and total inventory cost for the undiscounted price as in Section 8.3.1 above.

2. Compute the economic order quantity with the discounted price. (Note that this quantity will typically be larger than without the discount. Can you see why from Equation 8-2?). If this quantity is less than the minimum quantity required for the discount, then recognize that you will have to order the minimum.

3. Compute the total inventory cost for the discounted quantity.

4. Compare the total costs for the two cases and pick the lower one. The total cost is defined by Equation (8-6).

$$\text{Total Cost} = \text{Inventory Cost} + \text{Cost of Goods} \tag{8-6}$$

This procedure is illustrated in Figure 8-6. You will see the model uses IF...THEN...ELSE to make choices as to which quantity is best with the discount and which quantity to select based on total cost.

```
MODEL DISCOUNT  VERSION OF  05/14/86  20:55
10 COLUMNS 1
20 * SIMPLE EOQ MODEL
30*
40 ORDER QUANTITY = XPOWERY((2*ANNUAL DEMAND*COST PER ORDER)/(COST'
41 *INTEREST RATE),0.5)
50 CARRYING COST = 0.5 * COST * ORDER QUANTITY*INTEREST RATE
60 ORDER COST =(ANNUAL DEMAND /ORDER QUANTITY)*COST PER ORDER
70 TOTAL INVENTORY COST = CARRYING COST + ORDER COST
80*
90 * EOQ WITH DISCOUNT
100*
110 DISCOUNT EOQ = XPOWERY((2*ANNUAL DEMAND*COST PER ORDER)/'
111 (DISCOUNT COST*INTEREST RATE),0.5)
120 DISCOUNT ORDER QUANTITY = IF DISCOUNT EOQ .GT.'
121 DISCOUNT MINIMUM QUANTITY THEN DISCOUNT EOQ'
122 ELSE DISCOUNT MINIMUM QUANTITY
130 DISCOUNT CARRYING COST=0.5*DISCOUNT COST*'
131 DISCOUNT ORDER QUANTITY*INTEREST RATE
140 DISCOUNT ORDER COST=(ANNUAL DEMAND/DISCOUNT ORDER QUANTITY)*'
141 COST PER ORDER
150 DISCOUNT TOTAL INVENTORY COST = DISCOUNT CARRYING COST+'
151 DISCOUNT ORDER COST
160*
170* OPTIMAL POLICY
175*
180 EOQ TOTAL COST =TOTAL INVENTORY COST + ANNUAL DEMAND*COST
185 DISCOUNT TOTAL COST=DISCOUNT TOTAL INVENTORY COST+'
186 ANNUAL DEMAND * DISCOUNT COST
```

FIGURE 8-6. OPTIMAL INVENTORY WITH QUANTITY DISCOUNTS
(This Figure Continued on the Next Page)

```
190 OPTIMAL ORDER QUANTITY = IF DISCOUNT TOTAL COST .LT.'
191 EOQ TOTAL COST THEN DISCOUNT ORDER QUANTITY ELSE ORDER QUANTITY
200 OPTIMAL TOTAL COST = IF DISCOUNT TOTAL COST .LT.'
201 EOQ TOTAL COST THEN DISCOUNT TOTAL COST ELSE EOQ TOTAL COST
300 *
310 *INPUT DATA
320*
330 COST = 5
340 INTEREST RATE =.20
350 COST PER ORDER = 10.00
360 ANNUAL DEMAND =1000
370 DISCOUNT COST =4.50
380 DISCOUNT  MINIMUM QUANTITY =200
END OF MODEL
? SOLVE
MODEL DISCOUNT  VERSION OF  05/14/86  20:55 -- 1 COLUMNS 19
VARIABLES
ENTER SOLVE OPTIONS
? ALL

                                        1
 SIMPLE EOQ MODEL

ORDER QUANTITY                      141.4
CARRYING COST                       70.71
ORDER COST                          70.71
TOTAL INVENTORY COST                141.4

 EOQ WITH DISCOUNT

DISCOUNT EOQ                        149.1
DISCOUNT ORDER QUANTITY               200
DISCOUNT CARRYING COST                 90
DISCOUNT ORDER COST                    50
DISCOUNT TOTAL INVENTORY              140

 OPTIMAL POLICY

EOQ TOTAL COST                       5141
DISCOUNT TOTAL COST                  4640
OPTIMAL ORDER QUANTITY                200
OPTIMAL TOTAL COST                   4640

 INPUT DATA

COST                                    5
INTEREST RATE                       .2000
COST PER ORDER                         10
ANNUAL DEMAND                        1000
DISCOUNT COST                       4.500
DISCOUNT MINIMUM QUANTITY             200
```

FIGURE 8-6. OPTIMAL INVENTORY WITH QUANTITY DISCOUNT
(Continued)

EXERCISE: In Figure 8-6, a discount is offered for quantities of 200 or more. Suppose the supplier offers to sell at 4.25 cents if you order at least 500. Modify the model in Figure 8-6 and determine the optimal inventory policy.

8.4 MATERIALS REQUIREMENTS PLANNING (MRP)

Materials Requirements Planning (MRP) is an information systems approach to keeping track of demands in complex, hierarchical production systems. It is particularly useful where demand is in batches rather than continuous and where there are complex relations among materials, semi-finished components, components, and end products.

MRP requires three sets of inputs:

1. A master production schedule.
2. A record of production structure.
3. Inventory on hand and on order, and an order policy.

These three inputs are organized by MRP to produce a schedule of orders and production. To achieve this organization, MRP uses the concepts of:

- Dependent demand
- Net requirement
- Lead time offsetting

which we will now describe. Dependent demand can be seen from an example. Suppose you offer a lettuce and tomato salad in your restaurant with each entree. The demand (and the portion) determine the number of heads of lettuce and the number of tomatoes you need. However, what do you do if your customers can order entrees with salad, chef's salads, and budget blue plates which contain a wedge of lettuce? The demand for lettuce is thus a function of all menu items that contain lettuce. In definitional terms:

Dependent Demand = total demand for an ingredient, material, or part.

Net requirement refers to the amount that has to be ordered. It is determined by the accounting relation:

Net Requirement = Total Required − On Hand − In Process − Receipts.

For example, consider truck engines. The net number required is equal to the total number required for final truck assembly less those in inventory, those on the assembly line being completed, and those scheduled to be received from subcontractors.

Lead time is the time between placing an order and receiving it. Offsetting by the lead time involves placing orders at (need time – lead time). Lead time may differ from item to item. For example, you may have to order labels one week, wrappings two weeks, and crates three weeks before you can ship an order.

As an example of MRP, consider a factory that produces tables. (This example is given on p. 428 of Schroeder.) As shown inFigure 8-7 , the table consists of a top and a leg assembly. The figure also shows the bill of materials in the form of a "goes into" diagram. The leg assembly consists of four legs that are tied together by two short rails and two long rails. The operations that are performed and the lead times involved are, as follows:

Assemble table	1
Finish leg assembly	1
Purchase legs	1
Purchase short rails	1
Purchase long rails	1
Purchase top	2

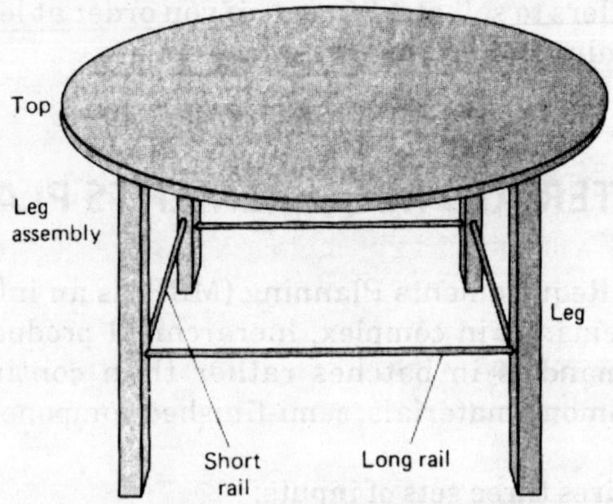

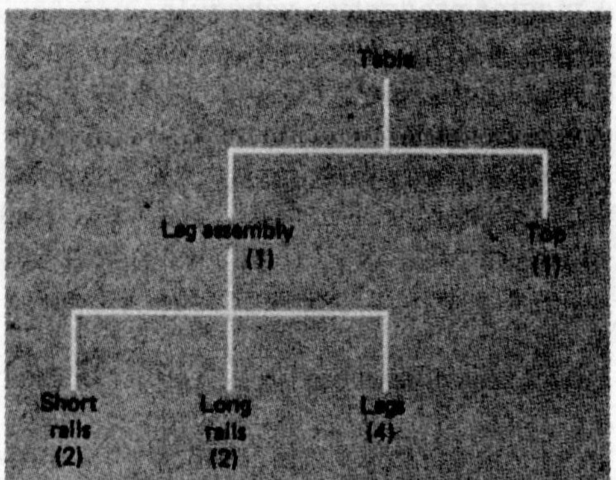

Suppose we want to plan to meet the following shipping schedule:

End of Week	4	5	6
Amt. to ship	200	150	100

At present, 50 tables are on hand. We want 0 inventory at the end of Week 6. In addition, 50 tops , 50 short rails, 100 leg assemblies, and 150 legs are on hand.

Figure 8-8 shows the IFPS model for materials requirements planning for this example. For each item the amount required is determined by the assembly in which it is used. The amount on order is determined by the initial data. The amount on hand is the initial inventory plus the amount ordered one lead time ago less the amount required (which is assumed to be used up). An order is placed whenever the amount on hand is less than the amount required, offset by the lead time.

EXERCISE: Suppose there are economic order quantities (EOQ) associated with each component. Modify Figure 8-8 so that the plan calls for ordering EOQ whenever the amount on hand is less the amount required offset by the lead time. Assume that the EOQ for legs is 200, for short rails and long rails is 150, and for tops is 125. Assume you are willing to have inventory at the end of Week 6.

Software packages specifically designed for MRP are available commercially. These packages provide capabilities for handling many hundreds of items using a firm's own numbering system for materials, parts, etc. The purpose of presenting the MRP model here is to illustrate the MRP concept and to show how IFPS can be used to keep track of small products.

```
MODEL MRP1  VERSION OF  05/14/86  22:33
10 COLUMNS 1-6
20*Tables (=TA)
30 TA GROSS REQT =0,0,0,200,150,100
40 TA ON HAND =50,0
45 TA INVENTORY=PREVIOUS+TA ON HAND+PREVIOUS TA NET REQT -'
46 PREVIOUS TA GROSS REQT
50 TA NET REQT= IF (TA GROSS REQT .GT.0) .AND. (TA GROSS REQT .GT.'
51 TA INVENTORY) THEN TA GROSS REQT -TA INVENTORY ELSE 0
60 TA PLANNED ORDER RELEASE = FUTURE TA NET REQT
90*Tops   (=TO)
100 TOP GROSS REQUIREMENT =TA PLANNED ORDER RELEASE
110 TOP ON HAND OR SCHEDULED = 50,50,0
120 TOP INVENTORY =PREVIOUS +TOP ON HAND OR SCHEDULED+'
121 PREVIOUS TOP NET REQUIREMENTS-PREVIOUS TOP GROSS REQUIREMENT
125 TOP NET REQUIREMENTS = IF (TOP GROSS REQUIREMENT .GT. 0) .AND.'
126 (TOP GROSS REQUIREMENT .GT. TOP INVENTORY) THEN L100-L120 ELSE 0
130 TOP PLANNED ORDER RELEASE = FUTURE 2 L125
190*Leg Assembly (=LA)
200 LA GROSS REQUIREMENTS = TA PLANNED ORDER RELEASE
210 LA ON HAND =100,0
215 LA INVENTORY=PREVIOUS+LA ON HAND+PREVIOUS LA NET REQUIREMENTS-'
216 PREVIOUS LA GROSS REQUIREMENTS
220 LA NET REQUIREMENTS = IF (LA GROSS REQUIREMENTS .GT. 0) .AND.'
221 (LA GROSS REQUIREMENTS-LA INVENTORY .GT.0) THEN L200-L215 ELSE 0
230 LA PLANNED ORDER RELEASE =FUTURE L220
290*Leg (=LG)
300 LG GROSS REQUIREMENTS=4*LA PLANNED ORDER RELEASE
310 LG ON HAND OR SCHEDULED =150,100,0
315 LG INVENTORY=PREVIOUS+LG ON HAND OR SCHEDULED+'
316 PREVIOUS LG NET REQUIREMENTS - PREVIOUS LG GROSS REQUIREMENTS
320 LG NET REQUIREMENTS = IF (LG GROSS REQUIREMENTS .GT. 0) .AND.'
321 (LG GROSS REQUIREMENTS .GT. LG INVENTORY) THEN L300-L315 ELSE 0
330 LG PLANNED ORDER RELEASE = FUTURE L320
END OF MODEL
```

FIGURE 8-8. MATERIALS REQUIREMENTS PLANNING

(This Figure is Continued on the Next page)

```
?SOLVE
ENTER SOLVE OPTIONS
? ALL

                          1     2     3     4     5     6

Tables (=TA)
TA GROSS REQT             0     0     0   200   150   100
TA ON HAND               50     0     0     0     0     0
TA INVENTORY             50    50    50    50     0     0
TA NET REQT               0     0     0   150   150   100
TA PLANNED ORDER REL      0     0   150   150   100     0
Tops   (=TO)
TOP GROSS REQUIREMEN      0     0   150   150   100     0
TOP ON HAND OR SCHED     50    50     0     0     0     0
TOP INVENTORY            50   100   100     0     0     0
TOP NET REQUIREMENTS      0     0    50   150   100     0
TOP PLANNED ORDER RE     50   150   100     0     0     0
Leg Assembly (=LA)
LA GROSS REQUIREMENT      0     0   150   150   100     0
LA ON HAND              100     0     0     0     0     0
LA INVENTORY            100   100   100     0     0     0
LA NET REQUIREMENTS       0     0    50   150   100     0
LA PLANNED ORDER REL      0    50   150   100     0     0
Leg (=LG)
LG GROSS REQUIREMENT      0   200   600   400     0     0
LG ON HAND OR SCHEDU    150   100     0     0     0     0
LG INVENTORY            150   250    50     0     0     0
LG NET REQUIREMENTS       0     0   550   400     0     0
LG PLANNED ORDER REL      0   550   400     0     0     0
```

FIGURE 8-8. MATERIALS REQUIREMENTS PLANNING (Continued)

8.5 DISTRIBUTION REQUIREMENTS PLANNING(DRP)

Distribution Requirements Planning is analogous to MRP but is concerned with distributing products rather than producing them. You start with the demand for the forthcoming time periods and the inventory on hand. You draw down the inventory until it reaches the safety stock level. Assuming you know the lead time, you can create a master schedule for shipments to make sure that the amount on hand is larger than the safety stock. The format and the ouput are very similar to that for MRP. An example, with the assumptions stated explicitly, is shown in Figure 8-9.

The data in Figure 8-9 indicate the real strength of the DRP model. Each of the three regional distribution centers (Los Angeles, Denver, and St. Louis) are supplied from a central supply. The model indicates the required stock at the central supply and makes sure that orders are placed to the factory or to the outside supplier. In the example, an EOQ of 2000 is assumed at the central supply.

```
MODEL DRP  VERSION OF  05/14/86  23:50
10 COLUMNS 1-8
20*LOS ANGELES
30 LA GROSS REQUIREMENT =120
40 LA PROJECTED ON HAND = 450,PREVIOUS-LA GROSS REQUIREMENT+'
41 LA PLANNED RECEIPT
50 LA PLANNED RECEIPT =0, IF (PREVIOUS LA PROJECTED ON HAND -'
51   LA GROSS REQUIREMENT).LT. LA SAFETY STOCK THEN'
52   LA ORDER QUANTITY ELSE 0
60 LA PLANNED SHIPMENT = FUTURE LA PLANNED RECEIPT
100*DENVER
110 DEN GROSS REQUIREMENT =50
120 DEN PROJECTED ON HAND=170,PREVIOUS-DEN GROSS REQUIREMENT +'
121 DEN PLANNED RECEIPT
130 DEN PLANNED RECEIPT =0, IF (PREVIOUS DEN PROJECTED ON HAND -'
131     DEN GROSS REQUIREMENT) .LT. DEN SAFETY STOCK'
132     THEN DEN ORDER QUANTITY ELSE 0
140 DEN PLANNED SHIPMENT = FUTURE DEN PLANNED RECEIPT
200*ST. LOUIS
210 STL GROSS REQUIREMENT =250
220 STL PROJECTED ON HAND =800,PREVIOUS -STL GROSS REQUIREMENT +'
221 STL PLANNED RECEIPT
230 STL PLANNED RECEIPT =0, IF (PREVIOUS STL PROJECTED ON HAND -'
231     STL GROSS REQUIREMENT) .LT. STL SAFETY STOCK THEN'
232     STL ORDER QUANTITY ELSE 0
240 STL PLANNED SHIPMENT = FUTURE STL PLANNED RECEIPT
300*CENTRAL SUPPLY
310 GROSS REQUIREMENT = LA PLANNED SHIPMENT  + DEN PLANNED SHIPMENT'
311     + STL PLANNED SHIPMENT
320 PROJECTED ON HAND =1200,PREVIOUS +MASTER SCHEDULE RECEIPT '
321     - GROSS REQUIREMENT
330 MASTER SCHEDULE RECEIPT =0,0, IF PREVIOUS PROJECTED ON HAND -'
331    GROSS REQUIREMENT .LT. CENTRAL SAFETY STOCK'
332    THEN CENTRAL ORDER QUANTITY ELSE 0
340 MASTER SCHEDULE SHIPMENT = FUTURE 2 MASTER SCHEDULE RECEIPT
400*ORDER QUANTITIES
410 LA ORDER QUANTITY =800
420 DEN ORDER QUANTITY = 600
430 STL ORDER QUANTITY = 1000
440 CENTRAL ORDER QUANTITY = 2000
500*SAFETY STOCK
510 LA SAFETY STOCK =80
520 DEN SAFETY STOCK =40
530 STL SAFETY STOCK =100
540 CENTRAL SAFETY STOCK = 260
END OF MODEL
```

FIGURE 8-9. DISTRIBUTION REQUIREMENTS PLANNING
(This Figure is Continued on the Next Page)

```
? SOLVE
ENTER SOLVE OPTIONS
? ALL
```

	1	2	3	4	5	6	7	8
LOS ANGELES								
LA GROSS REQUIREMENT	120	120	120	120	120	120	120	120
LA PROJECTED ON HAND	450	330	210	90	770	650	530	410
LA PLANNED RECEIPT	0	0	0	0	800	0	0	0
LA PLANNED SHIPMENT	0	0	0	800	0	0	0	0
DENVER								
DEN GROSS REQUIREMEN	50	50	50	50	50	50	50	50
DEN PROJECTED ON HAN	170	120	70	620	570	520	470	420
DEN PLANNED RECEIPT	0	0	0	600	0	0	0	0
DEN PLANNED SHIPMENT	0	0	600	0	0	0	0	0
ST. LOUIS								
STL GROSS REQUIREMEN	250	250	250	250	250	250	250	250
STL PROJECTED ON HAN	800	550	300	1050	800	550	300	1050
STL PLANNED RECEIPT	0	0	0	1000	0	0	0	1000
STL PLANNED SHIPMENT	0	0	1000	0	0	0	1000	0
CENTRAL SUPPLY								
GROSS REQUIREMENT	0	0	1600	800	0	0	1000	0
PROJECTED ON HAND	1200	1200	1600	800	800	800	1800	1800
MASTER SCHEDULE RECE	0	0	2000	0	0	0	2000	0
MASTER SCHEDULE SHIP	2000	0	0	0	2000	0	0	0
ORDER QUANTITIES								
LA ORDER QUANTITY	800	800	800	800	800	800	800	800
DEN ORDER QUANTITY	600	600	600	600	600	600	600	600
STL ORDER QUANTITY	1000	1000	1000	1000	1000	1000	1000	1000
CENTRAL ORDER QUANTI	2000	2000	2000	2000	2000	2000	2000	2000
SAFETY STOCK								
LA SAFETY STOCK	80	80	80	80	80	80	80	80
DEN SAFETY STOCK	40	40	40	40	40	40	40	40
STL SAFETY STOCK	100	100	100	100	100	100	100	100
CENTRAL SAFETY STOCK	260	260	260	260	260	260	260	260

FIGURE 8-9. DISTRIBUTION REQUIREMENTS PLANNING (Continued)

An alternative way of running a distribution network is to use the "push system." In this system, material is allocated by the factory or central supply forward to the distribution facilities rather than being pulled backward from one level to the next as it is in DRP. The push system assumes that lot size is irrelevant at the distribution center level, since moving stock from the central supply to the distribution center does not change the total inventory that the company as a whole is carrying.

A push system considers the requirements of each distribution center. When a distribution center requires inventory because it has reached its safety stock level, inventory is pushed out from the central supply facility if it is available. When shipments are made, each distribution center receives its "fair share." If more stock is available than is needed to bring all distribution centers to their order points, stock is allocated on an equal-weeks-supply basis. If not enough is available to fill the reorder point, a fair share covers lead time at all locations plus the same fraction of safety stock.

EXERCISE (Push System): Modify Figure 8-9 to model the push system. Assume gross requirements at the distribution centers are the forcast demands. Compute the projected inventory for each distribution center, assuming no new shipments from the central supply facility. Assume that inventory will be pushed as soon as one or more distribution centers reach their safety stock level. (Remember to take lead time into account!) The economic order quantity for the central supply is 2000 units. Central supply has 1200 on hand initially, of which it must keep a safety stock of 260.

CHAPTER IX
FOR THE PROFESSIONAL USER

9.1 Command Files

9.1.1 The Basic Elements of Command Files (Instructions and Directives)
9.1.2 Command File Operations
9.1.3 Simple Directives (Information Display and Input)
9.1.4 Flow Control Directive
9.1.5 Advanced Command File Directives (!ONERROR, !REPEAT, !REPEAT NEST, !CALL !IF)

9.2 Generating Many Model Statements with Only a Few Lines (GENERATE)

9.3 Creating and Using Sets (SETFILE and SETNAME)

9.3.1 Creating a SETFILE
9.3.2 Activating a SETFILE (SETNAME)
9.3.3 Using a SETFILE in a Model
9.3.4 Using SETFILE and Command Files Together

9.4 Creating Your Own IFPS Functions and Subroutines (FORMULA, SUBTASK)

9.4.1 FORMULAS
9.4.2 SUBTASKS

9.5 The DEFINITION Function

9.6 Creating Different Names Each Time a Model or Report is Solved (MICRO, MICROCOMPUTE)

9.6.1 MICRO Expressions
9.6.2 Built-In Micros in IFPS
9.6.3 Calculating Values for MICROs
9.6.4 Using MICRO Expressions in Reports

9.7 Tagged Data Files

9.7.1 Creating and Adding to Tagged Data Files (STORE)
9.7.2 Using Tagged Variables in Models (DFNAME)
9.7.3 Obtaining a View of the Data (SELECT)

CHAPTER IX
FOR THE PROFESSIONAL USER

9.1 COMMAND FILES

The professional (or power) user of IFPS is an individual who creates large models that use data files and report files extensively. Often, the professional user is called upon to create models that can be operated simply (and without knowing IFPS) by managers and others in the organization. To aid the professional users in managing complex tasks, IFPS contains Command Files which allow you to automate many of the command sequences that you usually perform manually in IFPS.

The simplest way of thinking about Command Files is that they contain a list of the commands that you would enter in an interactive session. For example:

```
FILE COMPROD
1 !COMMENT  This Command File retrieves the New Product
2 !COMMENT  Model set up for use with datafile DATA1, lists
3 !COMMENT the model and solves it
4 MODEL PRODUCT1 USING DATA1
5 LIST
6 SOLVE
7 ALL
END OF CMDFILE
```

When you type:

```
? COMMANDS COMPROD
```

This Command File takes MODEL PRODUCT1, lists it, and solves it using data file DATA1. (Don't worry about the ! in Lines 1,2, and 3. We will explain it shortly.)

Command Files differ from models in that they are procedural rather than non-procedural. That is, the order in which you say things does matter. In our example, you have to say SOLVE before you say ALL. Otherwise, IFPS would not understand you. Thus, Command Files are like conventional computer programs in which you give instructions to the machine in the sequence in which they are to be done.

As you will see in going through this section, Command Files are very powerful tools.

- They make production tasks easier. For example, they can use the same model and generate the same reports each time they are called. Thus, if you have new data each month, you can run a new report quickly.
- Theycreate complex applications that combine several models or several reports. A particularly important application is in hierarchical consolidation discussed in Section 10.1.

- They allow unsophisticated users to interact with IFPS models through menus, prompts for input data, etc.

9.1.1 The Basic Elements of Command Files (Instructions and Directives)

A Command File consists of:

- Instructions and
- Directives

listed in sequence.

An instruction is an ordinary command that you give IFPS such as SOLVE, LIST, WIDTH, or INVERT. In a Command File, you can, in fact, include any instruction that you give IFPS interactively from a terminal.

Directives, on the other hand, are specific to Command Files. You can recognize directives because they consist of an exclamation point followed by a keyword. Typical directives are:

!COMMENT	treats the rest of the line as a comment.
!MESSAGE	types out the line on the screen for the user.
!INPUT	requires an answer from the user.
!MENU	creates menus.
!PAUSE	causes the program to wait for a carriage return.

9.1.2 Command File Operations

CREATING A COMMAND FILE. Just as you use the keyword MODEL to obtain a model and REPORT to obtain a report, you use the keyword

```
CMDFILE
```

to obtain a Command File. Each Command File must have its own name. For example, if you want to create the file COMPROD you would type:

```
CMDFILE COMPROD
```

When you create a new Command File, IFPS prompts you with:

```
BEGIN ENTERING NEW COMMAND FILE
1 ?
```

Note that IFPS prompts you automatically with Line 1 and will continue to prompt you with line numbers increasing by one. Line numbers are essential in Command Files because you have to distinguish between a command you want to include in the Command File and a command to be executed right now.

The line numbering convention leads to a special case. If you want to include an instruction that depends on line numbers, (for example, 10,100P to list Lines 10 through 100) you have to first reenter the current line number. Thus,

```
12 ? 12 10,100P
```

is correct in defining a line in the Command File but

```
12 ? 10,100P
```

results in IFPS attempting to print lines 10 through 100 of the Command File.

If you want to leave the automatic numbering mode, you must enter END in response to a ?.

MODIFYING AN EXISTING COMMAND FILE. If you made a mistake in entering a line or want to change an existing line, you can use the standard IFPS editing commands (Sec. 2.5). If you want to return to prompted automatic numbering, you can use the AUTO command (Sec. 2.2.2).

SAVING AND RETRIEVING A COMMAND FILE When you are satisfied with your Command File, you can save it in your personal library. You use the SAVE command just as with Models or Reports. The result, however, is slightly different. Rather than adding the Command File to the current Models and Reports File, the SAVE command results in a separate file being created in your library. The advantage of this approach is that the Command File can be retrieved and used with any model, not just the models in a particular Models and Reports File for which it was created.

If you want to retrieve an existing Command File from your personal library, you type CMDFILE followed by the name of the file. This puts your Command File in your workspace and allows you to edit it.

RUNNING A COMMAND FILE To run a Command File, you type the word COMMANDS followed by the name of the Command File. For example, we ran COMPROD by typing COMMANDS COMPROD.

> *NOTE*: IFPS will forgive you if you type COMMAND rather than COMMANDS.

When you run (i.e., execute) a Command File, IFPS treats the Command File as if it were an ordinary computer program such as a BASIC program. It executes the file one line at a time in sequence. It stops executing when it reaches the end of the file or an !EXIT directive (see Table 9-1).

IFPS executes your Command File from its location in your private library. It does not bring the Command File into your workspace to execute it. In fact, if you have just created a Command File, IFPS will insist that you save the file before executing the COMMANDS instruction. As a result, the Command File will not be in your workspace after execution.

EXERCISE: Create FILE COMPROD shown at the beginning of this section on your computer.

- If you make a mistake in typing it in, use the edit commands to correct.
- Save the file.
- If you do not have a MODEL PRODUCT1 or a data file DATA1, create a simple model and a simple data file.

- Execute the Command File
- After execution, issue a LIST command. You should obtain a listing of MODEL PRODUCT1. Explain why IFPS produced a listing of PRODUCT1 rather than a listing of COMPROD.

9.1.3 Simple Directives (Information Display and Input)

Directives are written with an ! in front of them. If a directive, such as !COMMENT in our example, requires more than one line, each line must start with the name of the directive.

INFORMATION DISPLAY DIRECTIVES. IFPS provides three directives for showing (or not showing) information at the terminal. They are:

!COMMENT	allows you to put comments in the Command File. These comments are printed out only when you list the Command File.
!MESSAGE	prints out the line on the screen.
!SUPPRESS	stops printing out information at the terminal until SUPPRESS OFF is encountered.

INPUT DIRECTIVES. Input directives allow the user to enter information from the terminal.

!INPUT	allows input of one line of text.
!INPUTC	allows input of more than one line of text.
!EXIT	must be the last line typed by the user after an !INPUTC. The reason the user has to type a directive is that there is no other way that IFPS can tell that a multiple line input is complete.

EXAMPLE. Figure 9-1 shows a simple Command File (named COMPROD1) for running WHAT IF cases on MODEL PRODUCT for different discount rates.

```
cmdfile comprod1
READY FOR EDIT, LAST LINE IS 9
? list

1 !COMMENT Runs a WHAT IF Case on Discount Rate for MODEL
2 !COMMENT PRODUCT and prints NPV and IRR in period 8
3 MODEL PRODUCT
4 WHAT IF
5!MESSAGE type DISCOUNT RATE = followed by the value you want
6!INPUT for example: DISCOUNT RATE =.12
7 SOLVE
8 COLUMN 8
9 NET PRESENT VALUE,INTERNAL RATE OF RETURN
```

FIGURE 9-1. A SIMPLE COMMAND FILE

The following is a detailed explanation of Figure 9-1.

Lines 1 and 2 are comments.
Line 3 brings MODEL PRODUCT into the workspace
Line 4 tells IFPS that you want to do a WHAT IF case.
Line 5 prints a message to the user telling them what to do.
Line 6 requests one lineinput. Note that you can give explanations as part of the input request.
Line 7 tells IFPS to solve the WHAT IF Case
Lines 8 and 9 specify that only Net Present Value and Internal Rate of Return for Column 8 should be printed out.

The results of using this Command File are shown in Figure 9-2.

```
commands comprodl

? MODEL PRODUCT
READY FOR EDIT, LAST LINE IS 200
? WHAT IF
MODEL PRODUCT  VERSION OF  10/22/85  20:47 -- 8 COLUMNS 13 VARIABLES

WHAT IF CASE 1
ENTER STATEMENTS
type DISCOUNT RATE = followed by the value you want
INPUT for example: DISCOUNT RATE =.12
? DISCOUNT RATE =.10

? SOLVE
ENTER SOLVE OPTIONS
? COLUMN 8
? NET PRESENT VALUE,INTERNAL RATE OF RETURN

***** WHAT IF CASE 1 *****
1 WHAT IF STATEMENT PROCESSED

                                          8

NET PRESENT VALUE                     573.3
INTERNAL RATE OF RETURN               .3056

ENTER SOLVE OPTIONS
END OF COMMAND FILE(S)
```

FIGURE 9-2. RESULTS OF USING THE SIMPLE COMMAND FILE

Note the IFPS prompt for saving a Command File that is new or has been modfied and not yet saved. In going over Figure 9-2 you will see that IFPS executed the Command File in sequence and that the printout looks the same as if you had issued the same instructions.

9.1.4 Flow Control Directives

Just as procedural languages include instructions that allow you to move to different parts of a program (e.g., GO TO, SUBROUTINE), you can adjust the order in which a Command File is executed. Table 9-1 describes some of the flow control directives.

TABLE 9-1

FLOW CONTROL DIRECTIVES

!EXIT — Ends execution of the Command File.

!GOTO n — Makes line n the next line to be executed.
Example: **GOTO 35**. (GOTO must be one word)
This is a simple way of changing the "top-down" order in which Command Files are executed.

!MENU — !MENU implements the choices in a "menu" on the screen.
The menu itself is created with messages.
In effect, !MENU is equivalent to a multiple GO TO such as ON ...GOTO in BASIC. Typically, the user will be given messages on the screen that represent a set of numbered choices. Depending on which choice the user makes, !MENU transfers control to the line in the Command File that implements that choice.

Example:

```
1!MESSAGE TYPE 1 IF ALWAYS, 2 IF SOMETIMES
2!MESSAGE 3 IF NEVER
3!MENU 10,20,30
```

Explanation:
The !MESSAGE lines tell the user what to do.
The !MENU line results in a prompt appearingon the screen:

```
ENTER SELECTION NUMBER
```

If the user types a 1, Line 10 is executed next.
If the user types a 2, Line 20 is executed next.
If the user types a 3, Line 30 is executed next
If the user types anything else, a prompt appears.

!COND — !COND is put in front of a command which is executed only if the user responds to the question DO YOU WISH TO EXECUTE: with YES.

Example:
!COND LIST
This statement results in

```
DO YOU WISH TO EXECUTE: LIST
?
```

appearing on the screen. If you type YES, listing takes place. If you type NO, listing is skipped. The only other legal response is STOP, which ends execution of the Command File. Any other answer results in a prompt.

!CONDS !CONDS has the same effect as !COND. However, it is used with a preceding message and does not print out the "do you wish to execute." Example:

```
1!MESSAGE DO YOU WANT TO LIST THE MODEL?
2!MESSAGE TYPE YES OR NO
3!CONDS  LIST
```

!PAUSE !PAUSE stops execution until you type a carriage return. It is used when you want the user to look at the screen and absorb what is on it before proceeding or as a way to stop scrolling. Typically, !PAUSE follows:

```
!MESSAGE HIT CARRIAGE RETURN TO CONTINUE.
```

!SKIP n !SKIP is a specialized form of !GOTO. Rather than moving to a specified line number in your Command File, it simply skips over the number of lines you tell it to skip. For example, !SKIP 1 tells IFPS to ignore the next line and execute line after that.

EXAMPLE. Figure 9-3 shows a more sophisticated Command File for asking questions of MODEL PRODUCT. The user is given five choices through messages. Lines on which only !MESSAGE appears are used to create blanks that separate the choices and make them more easily readable on the screen.

```
? cmdfile comprod2
READY FOR EDIT, LAST LINE IS 71
? list
1 !COMMENT EXAMPLE OF USING FLOW CONTROL  IN A COMMAND FILE
2 MODEL PRODUCT
3!MESSAGE
4!MESSAGE ENTER 1,2,3,4 OR 5 DEPENDING ON WHAT YOU WANT TO DO
5!MESSAGE
6!MESSAGE    1 = WHAT IF
7!MESSAGE
8!MESSAGE    2 = WHAT IF CONTINUE
9!MESSAGE
10!MESSAGE   3 = GOAL SEEK
11!MESSAGE
12!MESSAGE   4 = BASE CASE
13!MESSAGE
14!MESSAGE   5 = END THE RUN
15!MESSAGE
16!MESSAGE
17!MENU 20,30,40,60,70
20!COMMENT WHAT IF
21WHAT IF
22!MESSAGE INPUT CHANGES YOU WANT. MAKE SURE YOUR LAST LINE IS: !END
23!INPUTC
24 SOLVE
25 COLUMN 8
26 NET PRESENT VALUE,INTERNAL RATE OF RETURN
27!GOTO 4
```

FIGURE 9-3. A COMMAND FILE FOR CREATING A MENU
(This Figure is Continued on the Next Page)

```
30!COMMENT WHAT IF CONTINUE
31 WHAT IF CONTINUE
32!MESSAGE ENTER THE WHAT IF CHANGES YOU WANT TO ADD
33!MESSAGE MAKE SURE YOUR YOUR LAST LINE IS !END
34!GOTO 23
40!COMMENT GOAL SEEK
41 GOAL SEEK
42!INPUT
43!INPUT
44!MESSAGE DO YOU WANT TO SEE DETAILED OUTPUT. TYPE: YES OR NO
45!CONDS !GOTO 50
46!GOTO 4
50 WIDTH 62 14 6
51 COLUMNS 1-8
52 ALL
53!GOTO 4
60!COMMENT RETURN TO BASE CASE
61 BASE
62!GOTO 4
70!COMMENT END THE RUN
71!EXIT
```

FIGURE 9-3. A COMMAND FILE FOR CREATING A MENU
(Continued)

The MENU command in Line 17 acts like a traffic cop, directing the user to Line 20 if they want WHAT IF, Line 30 if they want WHAT IF CONTINUE, Line 40 if they want to GOAL SEEK, Line 60 if they want to return to the BASE case, and Line 70 if they want to QUIT.

Lines 20 to 27 perform the WHAT IF. !INPUTC is used to allow several conditions to be entered for a WHAT IF case. When the WHAT IF actions are completed, the GOTO 4 in Line 27 causes the menu to reappear.

Lines 30 to 34 perform WHAT IF CONTINUE. Since much of the WHAT IF CONTINUE repeats the actions of WHAT IF, GOTO 23 in Line 34 allows reusing the same code. (Do you see how?)

Goal seeking is executed by Lines 40 through 53. As you recall from Section 3.1.3, GOAL SEEK requires two inputs. Hence, two !INPUT statements are provided in Lines 42 and 43. The WIDTH command is used in Line 50 to make sure that the printout fits within the space available in this book.

> *IMPORTANT NOTE:* In Command Files you have to know exactly what happens and provide for it.

Line 45 shows an example of !CONDS. Here, if the user types YES, control is transferred to Line 50 with a !GOTO and the complete results of GOAL SEEKING are presented. If the response is NO, the user sees the menu again. Using a command that begins with a ! is perfectly legal for !CONDS.

Lines 60 to 62 restore the BASE case and Lines 70 and 71 use the !EXIT directive to complete the Command File.

```
? command comprod2

? MODEL PRODUCT
READY FOR EDIT, LAST LINE IS 200

ENTER 1,2,3,4 OR 5 DEPENDING ON WHAT YOU WANT TO DO

1 = WHAT IF

2 = WHAT IF CONTINUE

3 = GOAL SEEK

4 = BASE CASE

5 = END THE RUN

ENTER SELECTION NUMBER
? 1

? WHAT IF
MODEL PRODUCT  VERSION OF  10/22/85  20:47 -- 8 COLUMNS 13 VARIABLES

WHAT IF CASE 1
ENTER STATEMENTS
INPUT CHANGES YOU WANT. MAKE SURE YOUR LAST LINE IS: !END
? INVESTMENT =3000,0
? DISCOUNT RATE =.12
? !END
? SOLVE
ENTER SOLVE OPTIONS
? COLUMN 8
? NET PRESENT VALUE,INTERNAL RATE OF RETURN

***** WHAT IF CASE 1 *****
2 WHAT IF STATEMENTS PROCESSED

                                    8

NET PRESENT VALUE              5.984
INTERNAL RATE OF RETURN        .1218

ENTER SOLVE OPTIONS
ENTER 1,2,3,4 OR 5 DEPENDING ON WHAT YOU WANT TO DO

1 = WHAT IF

2 = WHAT IF CONTINUE
```

FIGURE 9-4. USING !MENU,!GOTO, !CONDS,!EXIT, AND !SKIP IN COMMAND FILES
(This Figure is Continued on the Next Page)

```
3 = GOAL SEEK

4 = BASE CASE

5 = END THE RUN

ENTER SELECTION NUMBER
? 2

? WHAT IF CONTINUE
WHAT IF CASE 2
ENTER STATEMENTS
ENTER THE WHAT IF CHANGES YOU WANT TO ADD
MAKE SURE YOUR YOUR LAST LINE IS !END
? INVESTMENT =2000,0
? !END
? SOLVE
ENTER SOLVE OPTIONS
? COLUMN 8
? NET PRESENT VALUE,INTERNAL RATE OF RETURN

***** WHAT IF CASE 2 *****
3 WHAT IF STATEMENTS PROCESSED

                                  8

NET PRESENT VALUE              1006
INTERNAL RATE OF RETURN       .5865

ENTER SOLVE OPTIONS
ENTER 1,2,3,4 OR 5 DEPENDING ON WHAT YOU WANT TO DO

1 = WHAT IF

2 = WHAT IF CONTINUE

3 = GOAL SEEK

4 = BASE CASE

5 = END THE RUN

ENTER SELECTION NUMBER
? 4

? BASE
ENTER 1,2,3,4 OR 5 DEPENDING ON WHAT YOU WANT TO DO
```

FIGURE 9-4. USING !MENU,!GOTO, !CONDS,!EXIT, AND !SKIP IN COMMAND FILES

(This Figure is Continued on the Next Page)

```
1 = WHAT IF

2 = WHAT IF CONTINUE

3 = GOAL SEEK

4 = BASE CASE

5 = END THE RUN

ENTER SELECTION NUMBER
? 3
? GOAL SEEK
GOAL SEEKING CASE 1
ENTER NAME OF VARIABLE(S) TO BE ADJUSTED TO ACHIEVE PERFORMANCE
? MARKET SHARE
ENTER 1 COMPUTATIONAL STATEMENT(S) FOR PERFORMANCE
? NET REVENUE = 300,PREVIOUS+50


***** GOAL SEEKING CASE 1 *****

                                  8

MARKET SHARE                   .2064

ENTER SOLVE OPTIONS
DO YOU WANT TO SEE DETAILED OUTPUT. TYPE: YES OR NO
? YES

? WIDTH 62 14 6
? COLUMNS 1-8
? ALL

***** GOAL SEEKING CASE 1 *****

                    1     2     3     4     5     6     7     8


            NEW PRODUCT MODEL

SALES            1200  1400  1600  1800  1563  1719  1875  2031
MARKET           8000  8240  8487  8742  9004  9274  9552  9839
MARKET SHARE    .1500 .1699 .1885 .2059 .1735 .1853 .1963 .2064
GROSS REVENUE    3000  3500  4000  4500  4297  4727  5156  5586
PRICE           2.500 2.500 2.500 2.500 2.750 2.750 2.750 2.750
OPERATING EXPE   2700  3150  3600  4050  3797  4177  4556  4936
PRODUCTION COS  1.250 1.250 1.250 1.250 1.350 1.350 1.350 1.350
OVERHEAD            1     1     1     1 1.080 1.080 1.080 1.080
```

FIGURE 9-4. USING !MENU,!GOTO, !CONDS,!EXIT, AND !SKIP IN COMMAND FILES
(This Figure is Continued on the Next Page)

```
NET REVENUE        300    350    400    450    500    550    600    650
INVESTMENT        2500      0      0      0      0      0      0      0

NET PRESENT VA -2210  -1884  -1524  -1132-712.6-266.6 203.2 694.7
INTERNAL RATE                                    .0209 .2372 .4139

DISCOUNT RATE  .1500 .1500 .1500 .1500 .1500 .1500 .1500 .1500

ENTER SOLVE OPTIONS
ENTER 1,2,3,4 OR 5 DEPENDING ON WHAT YOU WANT TO DO

1 = WHAT IF

2 = WHAT IF CONTINUE

3 = GOAL SEEK

4 = BASE CASE

5 = END THE RUN


ENTER SELECTION NUMBER
? 5

EXIT FROM COMMAND FILE(S)
```

FIGURE 9-4. USING !MENU,!GOTO, !CONDS,!EXIT, AND !SKIP IN COMMAND FILES (Continued)

Figure 9-4 illustrates the sequence of events when Command File COMPROD2 is called. Two WHAT IF conditions are specified and then one of them is modified with a WHAT IF CONTINUE. Return to the BASE case precedes GOAL SEEK. A YES response to the !CONDS message (Line 45) during GOAL SEEK results in the complete printout. of the goal seeking case that starts at the bottom of the previous page. Finally, the run is terminated.

9.1.5 Advanced Command File Directives (!ONERROR, !REPEAT, !REPEAT NEST, !CALL, !IF)

The four preceding subsections showed you how to create and use Command Files and illustrated the simpler directives available. Command Files are extremely powerful and can relieve both the power user and the novice of many repetitive chores. For example:

!ONERROR

allows you to carry out a specific action (such as typing a message or exiting the Command File) if an execution error is encountered. An example is shown in Figure 9-5.

```
1!COMMENT   EXAMPLE OF !ONERROR, !SUPPRESS,SPOOLING
2!ONERROR !MESSAGE ERROR ENCOUNTERED
3!SUPPRESS
4 SPOOL OUTFILE
5 MODEL GRAY
6!SUPPRESS OFF
7 GENREPORT FORECAS0
8!SUPPRESS
9 SPOOL CLOSE
10!EXIT
? commands comprod3
? GENREPORT FORECAS0
MODEL GRAY  VERSION OF  10/03/85  23:12 -- 6 COLUMNS 5 VARIABLES
                              NEW PRODUCT FORECAST

                   1ST      2ND      3RD      4TH      5TH      6TH
                   QTR      QTR      QTR      QTR      QTR      QTR
SALES            100.00   125.00   156.25   195.31   244.14   305.18
EXPENSES          75.00   100.00   125.00   150.00   175.00   175.00
NET INOME         25.00    25.00    31.25    45.31    69.14   130.18

                                   RATIO ANALYSIS
PERCENT OF SALES
EXPENSE RATIO      .75      .80      .80      .77      .72      .57
NET INCOME RATIO   .25      .20      .20      .23      .28      .43
EXIT FROM COMMAND FILE(S)
```

FIGURE 9-5 !ONERROR, !SUPPRESS, !EXIT, SPOOLING

!REPEAT. You can perform looping (equivalent to FOR...NEXT in BASIC or DO in FORTRAN) by using the combination:

```
!REPEAT WHILE ...
...
!NEXT
```

Figure 9-6 illustrates the procedure. !REPEAT WHILE in Line 1 is followed by a list of parameters and the values they take on successively. In this example, there are three divisions, EAST0, MIDWEST and SOUTHWST and correspondingly three reports, ERPT, MRPT, and SWRPT. The statement:

```
1!REPEAT WHILE PARAM 1 IS EAST0, WEST, SOUTHWST;'
2 PARAM 2 IS ERPT, MRPT,SWRPT
```

tells IFPS to substitute first EAST0, then WEST, and then SOUTHWST for &1 and ERPT,MRPT,and SWRPT for &2 when it encounters these two symbols. (NOTE: Parameters are indicated by an ampersand (&) in front of the numerical value; for example &2 refers to parameter 2). As a result, IFPS creates three reports.

```
? cmdfile comprod7
READY FOR EDIT, LAST LINE IS 5
? list
1 !REPEAT WHILE PARAM 1 IS EASTO,MIDWEST,SOUTHWST;'
2 PARAM 2 IS ERPT,MRPT,SWRPT
3 MODEL SIMPLEO USING &1
4 GENREPORT &2
5 !NEXT

? commands comprod7
? MODEL SIMPLEO USING EASTO
READY FOR EDIT, LAST LINE IS 50
? GENREPORT ERPT

MODEL SIMPLEO  VERSION OF  03/02/86  23:40 -- 5 COLUMNS 3 VARIABLES


                       NEW PRODUCT RESULTS
                          EAST DIVISION

                      1        2        3        4      YEAR
REVENUES            150      200      130      225       705
EXPENSES            120      150      180      210       660
                 ------   ------   ------   ------    ------
PROFIT               30       50      -50       15        45
                 ======   ======   ======   ======    ======


? MODEL SIMPLEO USING MIDWEST
READY FOR EDIT, LAST LINE IS 50
? GENREPORT MRPT
MODEL SIMPLEO  VERSION OF  03/02/86  23:40 -- 5 COLUMNS 3 VARIABLES


                       NEW PRODUCT RESULTS
                        MIDWEST DIVISION

                      1        2        3        4      YEAR
REVENUES            100      125      150       80       455
EXPENSES             75      100      120      110       405
                 ------   ------   ------   ------    ------
PROFIT               25       25       30      -30        50
                 ======   ======   ======   ======    ======
```

FIGURE 9-6. !REPEAT WHILE...NEXT

(This Figure is Continued on the Next Page)

```
? MODEL SIMPLE0 USING SOUTHWST
READY FOR EDIT, LAST LINE IS 50
? GENREPORT SWRPT
MODEL SIMPLE0  VERSION OF  03/02/86  23:40 -- 5 COLUMNS 3 VARIABLES

                         NEW PRODUCT RESULTS
                         SOUTHWEST DIVISION

                             1      2      3      4    YEAR
REVENUES                    80     50     30    120     280
EXPENSES                    50     70     80     90     290
                        ------ ------ ------ ------  ------
PROFIT                      30    -20    -50     30     -10
                        ====== ====== ====== ======  ======

END OF COMMAND FILE(S)
```

a. Command File and Resulting Reports

```
MODEL SIMPLE0  VERSION OF  03/02/86  23:40
10 COLUMNS 1-4,YEAR
20 REVENUES=0
30 EXPENSES =0
40 PROFIT =REVENUES-EXPENSES
50 COLUMN YEAR =SUM(C 1 THRU C 4)
END OF MODEL
? datafile east0
READY FOR EDIT, LAST LINE IS 2
? list
1 REVENUES =150,200,130,225
2 EXPENSES = 120,150,180,210
? datafile midwest
READY FOR EDIT, LAST LINE IS 2
? list
1 REVENUES=100,125,150,80
2 EXPENSES =75,100,120,110
?datafile southwst
READY FOR EDIT LAST LINE IS 2
?list
1 REVENUES= 80, 50,30, 120
2 EXPENSES =50,70,80,90
REPORT ERPT  VERSION OF  03/02/86  23:40
10 COLUMNS 1-4,YEAR
15 WIDTH 62,20,8
20*
30 CENTER NEW PRODUCT RESULTS
40 CENTER EAST DIVISION
```

FIGURE 9-6. !REPEAT WHILE...NEXT

(This Figure is Continued on the Next Page)

```
50*
60 COLUMN TITLES
70 REVENUES, EXPENSES
80 UNDERLINE -
90 PROFIT
100 UNDERLINE =
END OF REPORT

REPORT MRPT  VERSION OF  03/02/86  23:42
10 COLUMNS 1-4,YEAR
20 WIDTH 62,20,8
20*
30 CENTER NEW PRODUCT RESULTS
40 CENTER MIDWEST DIVISION
50*
60 COLUMN TITLES
70 REVENUES, EXPENSES
80 UNDERLINE -
90 PROFIT
100 UNDERLINE =
END OF REPORT

REPORT SWRPT  VERSION OF  03/02/86  23:42
10 COLUMNS 1-4,YEAR
15 WIDTH 62,20,8
20*
30 CENTER NEW PRODUCT RESULTS
40 CENTER SOUTHWEST DIVISION
50*
60 COLUMN TITLES
70 REVENUES, EXPENSES
80 UNDERLINE -
90 PROFIT
100 UNDERLINE =
END OF REPORT
```

b. Model and Data Used

FIGURE 9-6. !REPEAT WHILE...NEXT
(Continued)

Note that the sequence in the REPEAT statement (Line 1 of COMPROD7, Figure 9-6) is:

- REPEAT WHILE
- PARAM
- parameter number
- IS
- parameter values
- ;

followed by the next parameter list for as many parameter lists as you want to use. However, you cannot continue a !REPEAT directive onto a second line. No punctuation is needed after the last list. (If you need longer lists than you can fit on one line, you can use SETFILE as described in Section 9.3.)

The !REPEAT directive is followed by a series of commands each of which are carried out in order until a !NEXT is encountered. The !NEXT tells IFPS it has come to the end of the loop and now needs to repeat.

The data used to generate the reports are shown in Figure 9-6b.

REPEAT NEST. It is also possible to nest parameter substitutions by calling for !REPEAT NEST rather than !REPEAT. The example shown in Figure 9-7 creates twelve reports, using the Data files:

AW AX AY AZ BW BX BY BZ CW CX CY CZ

in that order.

```
1!REPEAT NEST WHILE PARAM 1 IS A,B,C; PARAM2 IS W,X,Y,Z
2 MODEL PROFIT USING &1&2
3 GENREPORT BALANCE
4 !NEXT
5 !EXIT
```

FIGURE 9-7. !REPEAT NEST

The !REPEAT NEST is equivalent to:

```
FOR I = A,B,C
FOR J = W,X,Y,Z
...
NEXT J
NEXT I
```

in BASIC.

RECURSION THROUGH !CALL. You can have one Command File call another by using the !CALL directive. A simple example is shown in Figure 9-8. !CALL is part of an extensive nesting capability in Command Files which allows you to imbed one Command File in another. If you want to come back to the previous level, a !RETURN directive is available. The !CALL, !RETURN combination has to be used carefully because it is possible to get into an endless loop. Nesting of Command Files is discussed further in Section 9.3 where nesting is applied to SETFILES which allow you to deal with sets of data.

!IF. The !IF directive gives you the ability to make command execution dependent on values generated by the model. The general form is:

!IF (test is true) THEN .....

where the test can have either:

- numeric form (.LT., .LE., .EQ., .GE., .GT., .NE.), or
- text form (.HAS., .IS.)

```
? cmdfile comprod4
READY FOR EDIT, LAST LINE IS 5
? list
1!COMMENT EXAMPLE OF !CALL
3!MESSAGE DO YOU WANT TO ASK QUESTIONS OF THE MODEL (YES OR NO)
4!CONDS !CALL COMPROD2
5!EXIT
? commands comprod4

DO YOU WANT TO ASK QUESTIONS OF THE MODEL (YES OR NO)
? YES
? CALL COMPROD2
? MODEL PRODUCT

ENTER 1,2,3,4 OR 5 DEPENDING ON WHAT YOU WANT TO DO

1 = WHAT IF

2 = WHAT IF CONTINUE

3 = GOAL SEEK

4 = BASE CASE

5 = END THE RUN

ENTER SELECTION NUMBER
? 5
EXIT FROM COMMAND FILE(S)
```

FIGURE 9-8. !CALL

The !IF test differs from the IF...THEN...ELSE... test for model values discussed in Section 4.4.3 in that ELSE is not provided. Thus, when an !IF test fails (i.e., the logical result is FALSE), the Command File moves on to the next statement in sequence. For example,

```
200!IF NET PRESENT VALUE (6) .GT. 0 THEN GENEREPORT ACCEPT
```

would generate a report urging management to accept a proposal for which the net present value is positive in Period 6. If the net present value, however, is zero or negative, Line 200 is ignored.

The text mode lets Command Files depend on the ability to match text. Two types of matches can be tested:

> *a* .HAS. *b*
> *a* .IS. *b*

.HAS. asks whether text *a* contains text *b*, whereas .IS. asks whether text *a* is identical to text *b*. Thus, for example,

YEARLY .HAS. YEAR	is true
YEAR .HAS. YEARLY	is false
YEARLY .IS. YEAR	is false.

<u>*OTHER FEATURES*</u>. Among the Command File features not discussed here are the ability to use the same notation and ideas as in MICROS (Sec. 9.6) for substitution of values and for passing parameters. The *IFPS USER's MANUAL* describes these additional capabilities.

9.2 GENERATING MANY MODEL STATEMENTS WITH ONLY A FEW LINES (GENERATE)

When you get to large models that deal with complex corporate operations, you often wind up with many statements that are quite similar. For example, you may be dealing with sales, price, income, and costs from each of five sales offices on each of seven products. The names of the variables change only slightly, e.g., **SALES OF PRODUCTA BY NEW YORK, SALES OF PRODUCTC BY CHICAGO.** Typing the sames lines over and over is tedious, time consuming, and error prone. The GENERATE statement in IFPS allows you to create a "shell" which you write once and which provides a model statement for each case you specify. A simple example of a model containing a GENERATE statement is shown in Figure 9-9. The result of this GENERATE statement is shown in Figure 9-10.

```
? model simplgen
READY FOR EDIT, LAST LINE IS 30
? list
MODEL SIMPLGEN  VERSION OF  09/12/85  23:16
1 COLUMNS 1-4
5 GENERATE L10 THRU L30 AT L100 FOR GHQ, 1 THRU 2
10 REVENUE # = 0
20 EXPENSES # = 0
30 NET INCOME # = REVENUE # - EXPENSES #
END OF MODEL
```

FIGURE 9-9. SIMPLE EXAMPLE OF A GENERATE STATEMENT

```
? list generate
MODEL SIMPLGEN  VERSION OF  09/12/85  23:16
1 COLUMNS 1-4
100 REVENUE GHQ = 0
101 REVENUE 1 = 0
102 REVENUE 2 = 0
103 EXPENSES GHQ = 0
104 EXPENSES 1 = 0
105 EXPENSES 2 = 0
106 NET INCOME GHQ = REVENUE GHQ - EXPENSES GHQ
107 NET INCOME 1 = REVENUE 1 - EXPENSES 1
108 NET INCOME 2 = REVENUE 2 - EXPENSES 2
END OF MODEL
```

FIGURE 9-10. MODEL CREATED BY USING GENERATE STATEMENT IN FIGURE 9-9

If you examine Figure 9-9 you will see the pattern followed in using the GENERATE statement.

1. You specify a GENERATE statement that contains:
   - the names of the variables or lines to be replicated (L10 THRU L30 in Figure 9-9).
   - the reserved word AT signals IFPS that you are about to tell it where the lines being generated should be put.
   - the starting line number.
   - FOR.
   - the name to be substituted for each replication.

   That is, you tell IFPS that you will give it some dummy statements at a particular location and it is to copy them several times starting at a particular point. Each time it copies them, it creates a different case.

2. You use a # sign in each statement to be copied to indicate where the substitution is to be made.

3. If you want to have data on the right hand side, you have to provide it through a data file since it will be different in each replication. Therefore, as is customary in models using data files, the right-hand side is set equal to 0. (Figure 9-9, L10 and L20).

4. If the variable is defined the same way in each replication, then you can use # signs on both sides of the equal sign (L30 in Figure 9-9).

To see the result of your GENERATE statement, you can use LIST GENERATE.

As shown in Figure 9-10, LIST GENERATE gives you the full model you specified. (It is similar to LIST EXPAND discussed in Section 4.5.7 but LIST EXPAND does not give the same results as LIST GENERATE. Try it!).

Figure 9-11 illustrates what you can expect to see if you SOLVE a model containing a GENERATE statement. You obtain exactly what you see in the model shown with LIST GENERATE (Figure 9-9).

9.3 CREATING AND USING SETS (SETFILE AND SETNAME)

In IFPS it is possible to give a list of variables a name, that is to create a "set". For example, you might want to refer to the set of SALES DIVISIONS which consists of your EAST, MIDWEST, and SOUTHWEST offices. Sets are a powerful tool because they allow you to solve models and create reports for each member of the set. We present them at this point because, in order to use them, you have to apply the ideas of Command Files introduced in Section 9.1 and GENERATE from Section 9.2

To use sets, you need to do three things:

1. Create a SETFILE. A SETFILE contains the definitions of the sets you will use. It is analogous to a DATAFILE but you use names rather than numbers.

```
? solve
MODEL SIMPLGEN  VERSION OF  09/12/85  23:16 -- 4 COLUMNS 9 VARIABLES
ENTER SOLVE OPTIONS
? all

                          1        2        3        4
REVENUE GHQ               0        0        0        0
REVENUE 1                 0        0        0        0
REVENUE 2                 0        0        0        0
EXPENSES GHQ              0        0        0        0
EXPENSES 1                0        0        0        0
EXPENSES 2                0        0        0        0

NET INCOME GHQ            0        0        0        0
NET INCOME 1              0        0        0        0
NET INCOME 2              0        0        0        0
```

FIGURE 9-11. SOLVING THE SIMPLE EXAMPLE OF THE GENERATE STATEMENT

2. Activate the set by giving a SETNAME command at the Executive Level before you ask for a model from your file.
3. Create a small model that uses GENERATE NEST or create a Command File that uses the !REPEAT or !REPEAT NEST directive with the SETFILE to create the large amounts of output you need.

We will now describe how you accomplish each of these steps in turn.

9.3.1 Creating a SETFILE

A SETFILE is created in the same way as a data file. You begin by telling IFPS you want a SETFILE. For example,

```
?SETFILE DIVISIONS
```

You then build the SETFILE like a data file. However, you put names rather than numbers on the right hand side of the = signs. Figure 9-12 illustrates the creation of a simple SETFILE for two sets, one representing three divisions, and the other representing four departments.

```
?SETFILE DIVISIONS
BEGIN ENTERING NEW SETFILE
DIVISION = EAST,MIDWEST, SOUTHWEST
DEPT = ADMINISTRATION,MARKETING, ENGINEERING, PRODUCTION
```

FIGURE 9-12. CREATING A SETFILE FOR TWO SETS

The names on the right are called set variables. Set variables, unlike regular variables, are restricted to one word, no more than 12 letters long. Thus, DIVISIONS is a legal name but DIV NAMES is not. In addition, set variables must begin with a letter and may not be IFPS reserved words.

9.3.2 Activating a SETFILE (SETNAME)

If you want to use a SETFILE in your model, you must tell IFPS to activate the SETFILE before you ask for the model. That is, IFPS first brings the SETFILE to the working files area (Figure 3-4 in Chapter 3) so that it is available for reference in the model. The way you do this is to use SETNAME followed by the name of the SETFILE. For example,

```
?SETNAME DIVISIONS
```

IFPS responds by telling you how many sets are included in the SETFILE and that it is ready for a modeling command. A typical dialog would be:

```
2 SETS ACTIVE
?MODEL SETFILE USING EXPENSES
READY FOR EDIT LAST LINE IS 51
?LIST
```

You can activate several SETFILES with a single SETNAME. For example,

```
?SETNAME DIVISIONS, ACCOUNTS, PRODUCTS
```

would activate three separate SETFILES. Note that they are listed one after another, separated by commas.

SETNAME can be used inside a Command File, as described in Section 9.3.4 below. Because a Command File calls for many actions, you may find it useful to switch the SETFILE off by using the command:

```
SETNAME OFF
```

The result of SETNAME OFF is that all SETFILES are no longer active. You can then use the name of the SETFILE as a variable.

9.3.3 Using a SETFILE in a Model

The use of SETFILE in a Model is illustrated in Figure 9-13. You will note that we have used the nested form of the GENERATE statement to cycle through departments for each division using the sequence DIVISION; DEPT in Line 20. The semicolon is needed to separate the names of the sets. Furthermore, we have used the substitution symbols ##1 and ##2 to tell IFPS to replace the first and second symbols by the corresponding names of the division and department.

In general, in models you use the GENERATE NEST form as a quick way of cycling through a SETFILE.

```
?SETNAME DIVISIONS
2 SETS ACTIVE
?MODEL RESOURCE USING STAFFING

10 COLUMNS 1-4
20 GENERATE NEST L30 AT L40 FOR DIVISION; DEPT
30 ##1 ##2 = 0
END OF MODEL
?SOLVE
ENTER SOLVE OPTIONS
?ALL

                                  1      2      3      4
EAST ADMINISTRATION               0      0      0      0
EAST MARKETING                    0      0      0      0
EAST ENGINEERING                  0      0      0      0
EAST PRODUCTION                   0      0      0      0
MIDWEST ADMINISTRATION            0      0      0      0
MIDWEST MARKETING                 0      0      0      0
MIDWEST ENGINEERING               0      0      0      0
MIDWEST PRODUCTION                0      0      0      0
SOUTHWEST ADMINISTRATION          0      0      0      0
SOUTHWEST MARKETING               0      0      0      0
SOUTHWEST ENGINEERING             0      0      0      0
SOUTHWEST PRODUCTION              0      0      0      0
```

FIGURE 9-13. USING SETFILES IN A MODEL

9.3.4 Using SETFILE and Command Files Together

The real power of using SETFILE comes when the SETFILES are called through a Command File. The directives

```
!REPEAT
!REPEAT NEST
```

allow you to create a template Command File that you can customize to the appropriate sets at the time you SOLVE or generate reports. Figure 9-14 uses the SETFILE DIVISIONS in combination with the !REPEAT NEST directive.

```
?SETNAME DIVISIONS
1 !REPEAT NEST WHILE PARAM 1 IS DIVISION;PARAM 2 IS DEPT
2 MODEL COST USING &1&2
3 GENREPORT &1RPT
4 !NEXT
```

FIGURE 9-14. USING !REPEAT NEST WITH SETFILES

The four lines in Figure 9-14 generate 12 reports, one for each combination of division and department in SETFILE DIVISIONS.

9.4 CREATING YOUR OWN IFPS FUNCTIONS AND SUBROUTINES (FORMULA, SUBTASK)

In Chapter 3 you learned about built-in functions and subroutines in IFPS. They allow you to perform financial, statistical, and mathematical operations such as net present value, depreciation, median, and logarithm. As is the case with any computer language, the number of functions that can be provided is limited. It is also a corollary of Parkinson's law that no matter how many functions are available, you will need one that is not provided.

Almost all functions are based on combining simple operations. Thus, the major value of a built-in function is that it eliminates the need for your writing out the routine that creates it. If you have an unusual function, then you can, with a little research, find out how it is defined and calculate it. If it is to be used in only one model, then you should define it within that model. However, if the function is one that is common to your business or to a number of models that you are using, it will pay you to create and store a FORMULA or SUBTASK.

FORMULA and SUBTASK are comparable, respectively, to IFPS functions and subroutines. They even look the same as functions and subroutines when used in a model. Once you define and store them, you can use them in any model.

The main difference between a FORMULA and a SUBTASK is that:

- A FORMULA creates a single number.
- A SUBTASK can create one or more values that define different variables.

9.4.1 FORMULAS

You need to know two things about formulas:

1. How to create and store them for future use.
2. How to use them in a model.

CREATING A FORMULA. A FORMULA, just like a MODEL, has to be written and saved if it is to be used. Figure 9-15 is an example of creating a formula for computing financial leverage (see Section 6.13).

```
FORMULA LEVERAGE  VERSION OF  05/01/86  20:27
10 INPUTS DEBT,EQUITY
20 LEVERAGE = DEBT/(DEBT +EQUITY)
END OF FORMULA
? PRESERVE LEVRATIO
   FORMULA LEVERAGE  VERSION OF  05/01/86  20:27 -- 1 COLUMNS 3
VARIABLES
OPERATION PRESERVED ON FILE LEVRATIO
```

FIGURE 9-15. CREATING A FORMULA

The sequence of steps followed is:

1. Tell IFPS that you want a FORMULA and give it a name.
2. Specify the INPUTS to be used. The word INPUTS must precede the names of the variables. (Line 10)

3.Specify the formula. The name of the formula appears on the left of the equal sign and the definition of the formula in terms of the INPUT variables appears on the right. (Line 20)

Having defined the FORMULA, you next need to put it into your permanent files. This is a two-step procedure:

STEP 1. SAVE. This puts the formula into the Models and Reports File on which you are working.

STEP 2. PRESERVE. This step creates a separate permanent file which contains a compiled version of your FORMULA. You have to specify PRESERVE and follow it with a file name. It is this file name that creates a separate file. The file name must be a legal file name for your computer system and should be different from an existing file, otherwise you erase the existing file. In Figure 9-15, the formula LEVERAGE is preserved in file LEVRATIO.

TESTING A FORMULA. Once you've created your formula, you will want to test it to make sure it is correct. To do so, you SOLVE as shown in Figure 9-16. IFPS will prompt you for a value of each input variable and then show you both the inputs and the outputs. (*HINT:* In testing a formula, use simple values which you can use to hand-calculate the value of the function.)

```
? SOLVE
ENTER VALUE FOR INPUT VARIABLE: DEBT
? 1000
ENTER VALUE FOR INPUT VARIABLE: EQUITY
? 2000
ENTER SOLVE OPTIONS
? ALL


                                    1

DEBT                             1000
EQUITY                           2000
LEVERAGE                        .3333
```

FIGURE 9-16. TESTING A FORMULA

In addition to SOLVE, you can also use WHAT IF, SENSITIVITY, and ANALYZE with a formula.

USING A FORMULA IN A MODEL. Once you have created, saved, and preserved a formula, you can use it in a model. Figure 9-17 is an example of using the LEVERAGE formula.

```
MODEL RATIO1  VERSION OF  09/10/85  23:40
10 ACCESS FORMULA LEVERAGE,LEVRATIO
20 COLUMNS 1-2
30 FINANCIAL LEVERAGE = LEVERAGE(LONG TERM DEBT, STOCKHOLDERS
EQUITY)
40 LONG TERM DEBT = 1000,2000
50 STOCKHOLDERS EQUITY = 2000
60 LEV1=LEVERAGE(LONG TERM DEBT,STOCKHOLDERS EQUITY),PREVIOUS+1
END OF MODEL
? SOLVE
MODEL RATIO1  VERSION OF  09/10/85  23:40 -- 2 COLUMNS 4 VARIABLES
ENTER SOLVE OPTIONS
? ALL

                                  1        2

FINANCIAL LEVERAGE             .3333    .5000
LONG TERM DEBT                  1000     2000
STOCKHOLDERS EQUITY             2000     2000
LEV1                           .3333    1.333

ENTER SOLVE OPTIONS
```

FIGURE 9-17. USING A FORMULA IN A MODEL

You will note that a line appears ahead of the columns statement with the keywords ACCESS FORMULA followed by:

1. The name of the formula
2. The name of the file in which the formula is preserved.

Both the formula name and the file name are required. This can be a nuisance when you have created a lot of formulas. A simple way of keeping track of things is to include a remark statement in the formula definition which gives the name of the file. For example, you might add:

```
30*PRESERVED ON FILE LEVRATIO
```

ACCESS tells IFPS what formulas you will use in your model. You can then use the formula as often as you like in the model.

In the Figure, the LEVERAGE formula is used in Line 30. The names given in parenthesis in Line 30 are used as inputs and replace the variable names in Figure 9-15. You of course have to provide values for each variable (Lines 40 and 50).

THE ONE COLUMN LIMIT ON FORMULAS. You MUST keep your definition of formulas within the present column. As a result, you cannot have a formula depend on PREVIOUS, FUTURE, MATRIX, or SUM. Most financial, statistical, and random number generating functions cannot be used. You also cannot PLOT, STORE, COMBINE, CONSOLIDATE, or CROSSREF with formulas.

9.4.2 SUBTASKS

CREATING A SUBTASK. SUBTASK is identical to FORMULA except that you can create several output variables rather than a single variable. An example of creating and testing a SUBTASK is shown in Figure 9-18.

```
SUBTASK LIQUID  VERSION OF  09/10/85  23:47
1 INPUTS CURRENT ASSETS, CURRENT LIABILITIES, TOTAL
ASSETS,INVENTORIES
2 OUTPUTS NET WORKING CAPITAL TO NET ASSETS, CURRENT RATIO, QUICK
RATIO
3 NET WORKING CAPITAL TO NET ASSETS = (CURRENT ASSETS-'
4 CURRENT LIABILITIES)/TOTAL ASSETS
5 CURRENT RATIO = CURRENT ASSETS/CURRENT LIABILITIES
6 QUICK RATIO = (CURRENT ASSETS-INVENTORIES)/CURRENT LIABILITIES
END OF SUBTASK
? SAVE

MODELS AND REPORTS SAVED ON FILE CH9
? SOLVE
SUBTASK LIQUID  VERSION OF  09/10/85  23:47 -- 1 COLUMNS 7 VARIABLES

ENTER VALUE FOR INPUT VARIABLE: CURRENT ASSETS
? 100
ENTER VALUE FOR INPUT VARIABLE: CURRENT LIABILITIES
? 80
ENTER VALUE FOR INPUT VARIABLE: TOTAL ASSETS
? 135
ENTER VALUE FOR INPUT VARIABLE: INVENTORIES
? 30
ENTER SOLVE OPTIONS
? ALL

                                  1

CURRENT ASSETS                  100
CURRENT LIABILITIES              80
TOTAL ASSETS                    135
INVENTORIES                      30
NET WORKING CAPITAL TO N      .1481
CURRENT RATIO                 1.250
QUICK RATIO                   .8750

ENTER SOLVE OPTIONS
? PRESERVE LIQUIDITY
```

FIGURE 9-18. DEFINING AND TESTING A SUBTASK

The example creates three measures of liquidity (see Section 6.13): net working capital to net assets, current ratio, and quick ratio.

In defining a SUBTASK you have to specify both the INPUTS (Line 1) and the OUTPUTS (Line 2). You then write a relation for each output variable.

As shown in Figure 9-18, it is good practice to test the SUBTASK by solving it before using the PRESERVE command. Both SAVE and PRESERVE are required.

USING A SUBTASK IN A MODEL. Figure 9-19 illustrates the use of a subtask. Just as for a formula, the ACCESS statement has to be used for subtasks. The rules for subroutines discussed in Section 3.3 also apply to subtasks.

```
MODEL RATIO2  VERSION OF  09/10/85  23:58 -- 1 COLUMNS 7 VARIABLES
ENTER SOLVE OPTIONS
? ALL

                                    1

CURRENT ASSETS                   1000
CURRENT LIABILITIES               500
TOTAL ASSETS                     2000
INVENTORIES                       300
NET CAPITAL TO NET ASSET        .2500
CURRENT RATIO                       2
QUICK RATIO                     1.400

ENTER SOLVE OPTIONS
```

FIGURE 9-19. USING A SUBTASK IN A MODEL

WARNING: The one-column limitations for formulas also apply to subtasks.

9.5 THE DEFINITION FUNCTION

The DEFINITION function allows you to define the value of one cell in the IFPS spreadsheet in terms of the definition (not the value) in another cell in the spreadsheet. The main uses of the DEFINITION function are for:

- Recursion (that is, definitions that repeat).
- Eliminating the need to enter the same data twice.
- Reducing typing required for complicated definitions.

Figure 9-20 shows an example of using the DEFINITION for recursion. The model shows the sales for each quarter over a two-year period. The sales for the first year are cumulated by quarters and then the sales for the second year are cumulated by quarters. Columns 4 and 8 of CUMSALES show the annual totals. What DEFINITION (PREVIOUS 4) in Line 60 does is tell IFPS to define the variable CUMSALES in columns 5 through 8 in the same way it was defined in columns 1 through 4.

The important point here is that using the definition of a variable in a column is different than using its value in that column. The WHAT IF case in Figure 9-20 illustrates that when PREVIOUS 4 is used, the values in columns 1 through 4 are simply repeated.

In FIGURE 9-20 DEFINITION is used to refer to another column in the same variable.

```
MODEL SALEDATA  VERSION OF  09/05/85  22:56
10 COLUMNS 1-8
20*THE 8 COLUMNS ARE QUARTERS OVER A 2 YEAR PERIOD
30*THE FIRST FOUR COLUMNS OF CUMSALES REPRESENT YEAR 1
40*THE SECOND FOUR COLUMNS OF CUMSALES REPRESENT YEAR 2
50 SALES =200,260,320,220,240,310,350,270
60 CUMSALES =SALES,PREVIOUS+SALES FOR 3,DEFINITION(PREVIOUS 4)
END OF MODEL
?SOLVE

MODEL SALEDATA  VERSION OF  09/05/85  22:56 -- 8 COLUMNS 2 VARIABLES

ENTER SOLVE OPTIONS
? WIDTH 62,20,5
? ALL

                          1    2    3    4    5    6    7    8

THE 8 COLUMNS ARE QUARTERS OVER A 2 YEAR PERIOD
THE FIRST FOUR COLUMNS OF CUMSALES REPRESENT YEAR 1
THE SECOND FOUR COLUMNS OF CUMSALES REPRESENT YEAR 2
SALES                   200  260  320  220  240  310  350  270
CUMSALES                200  460  780 1000  240  550  900 1170

ENTER SOLVE OPTIONS
? WHAT IF

WHAT IF CASE 1
ENTER STATEMENTS
? CUMSALES=SALES,PREVIOUS+SALES FOOR  R 3, PREVIOUS 4
? SOLVE
ENTER SOLVE OPTIONS
? L50,L60

***** WHAT IF CASE 1 *****
1 WHAT IF STATEMENT PROCESSED
                          1    2    3    4    5    6    7    8

SALES                   200  260  320  220  240  310  350  270
CUMSALES                200  460  780 1000  200  460  780 1000
```

FIGURE 9-20. USE OF THE DEFINITION FUNCTION FOR RECURSION

Either PREVIOUS or FUTURE references can be used. A DEFINITION can also refer to a different variable. For example,

```
DEFINITION (SALES, 1)
```

refers to using the definition of the variable SALES in Column 1. In general, the two elements in parenthesis refer to row (i.e., variable name or line number) and column.

Columns can be put in either explicitly by number or they can be computed from some expression.

DEFINITION can also be used in COLUMN statements. For example,

```
COLUMN YEAR FOR CASH = DEFINITION(NET RECEIPTS ,4)
```

CAUTIONS:

1. Be careful of circular definitions. That is, a DEFINITION function cannot define a value that depends on itself for calculation. This can be a problem if you use PREVIOUS and FUTURE and wind up with one definition using another.

2. You cannot use DEFINITION in an arithmetic expression. You will get an error message if you write:

```
INCOME = DEFINITION(PREVIOUS SALES) * INFLATION FACTOR
```

9.6 CREATING DIFFERENT NAMES AND VALUES EACH TIME A MODEL OR REPORT IS SOLVED (MICRO, MICROCOMPUTE)

9.6.1 MICRO Expressions

MICRO expressions provide a way of writing general (i.e., generic) models and reports that can be custom tailored so that each time they are solved they apply to the specific situation being considered. As you will see, there is little reason to use a MICRO in a model that contains all its own data. However, it is extremely useful if the model is to be used with a large number of different data files (Sec. 4.6).

MICROs are written like ordinary expressions but are surrounded by ampersands (&). For example,

```
&PRODUCT&
```

defines a MICRO named "product." This MICRO acts as a "placeholder" for whatever product you want to consider. To use this MICRO you have to tell IFPS, at the time you SOLVE the model, what name to substitute for &PRODUCT&. This substitution is usually indicated in the data file. That is, you specify the substitutions to be made for MICROs at the beginning of the data file that you are using. A typical example of such a substitution is:

```
MICRO&PRODUCT&MODEM&
```

which tells IFPS to replace &PRODUCT& by MODEM wherever &PRODUCT& appears.

Figure 9-21 illustrates the use of MICROS. It shows MODEL SIMPLE from Chapter II (Figure 2-3) rewritten with MICROs and solved using data files. As you examine Figure 9-21, you will see that the substitutions to be used are listed first in data file MICRO2. For example, the MICRO &COST& is to be replaced by EXPENSES. The data refer to the actual name to be used (e.g., EXPENSES), not the name of the MICRO (e.g., &COST&). The MICROs used in the model are explained in the data file, even though data do not have to be provided for all of them.

The model in Figure 9-21 is written entirely in terms of MICROs. When you ask for it together with a data file (MODEL MICRO1 USING MICRO2) the result of SOLVE is to make the appropriate substitutions.

```
? DATAFILE MICRO2
READY FOR EDIT, LAST LINE IS 5
? LIST
1 MICRO &INCOME&SALES&
2 MICRO &COST&EXPENSES&
3 MICRO &NET&NET INCOME&
4 20 = 100,125,160,195,245,330
5 EXPENSES = 75,100,125,150,175
? MODEL MICRO1 USING S MICRO2
READY FOR EDIT, LAST LINE IS 40
? LIST
MODEL MICRO1  VERSION OF  09/12/85  22:44
10 COLUMNS 1-6
20 &INCOME&=0
30 &COST&=0
40 &NET& = &INCOME&-&COST&
END OF MODEL
? SOLVE

MODEL MICRO1  VERSION OF  09/12/85  22:44 -- 6 COLUMNS 3 VARIABLES
ENTER SOLVE OPTIONS
? WIDTH 62 24 5
? ALL


                          1    2    3    4    5    6

SALES                   100  125  160  195  245  330
EXPENSES                 75  100  125  150  175  175
NET INCOME               25   25   35   45   70  155
```

FIGURE 9-21. CREATING AND USING MICROS

NOTE: If you do not provide a MICRO statement, IFPS will prompt you for one when you SOLVE. For example, if you write:

```
90 PRICE = 2.50 FOR &MOS&, 2.75
```

in you model and do not define &MOS&, IFPS will prompt you:

```
ENTER DEFINITION FOR: MOS
?
```

and you would enter the number of months the price will stay at 2.50. If you enter, say, 4, then Line 90 would be interpreted as:

```
90 PRICE = 2.50 FOR 4, 2.75
```

Under most conditions, this on-line data entry mode is inefficient and you should avoid it.

9.6.2 Built-in MICROs in IFPS

IFPS provides you with several built-in MICROs that allow you to adjust your model so that it reflects the current date and time, the current model name, etc. When you use one of these MICROs, you do not have to define it. IFPS automatically substitutes the meaning of the MICRO into your model. The built-in MICROs include:

MICRO	Substitution
&DATE&	Defines current date in the form MM/DD/YY
&TIME&	The current time in HH:MM
&MONTH&	The current month as an integer (e.g., 9)
&MONTHA&	The current month as a three letter abbreviation (e.g., SEP)
&DAY&	The current day of the month
&YEAR&	The current year in four-digit form
&MNAME&	The name of the current model
&DFNAME&	The name of the last data file in the USING statement

Because the built-in MICROs are defined by IFPS itself, you can use them without a MICRO statement. For example,

```
10 COLUMNS 1980-&YEAR&
```

creates columns from 1980 through the present year.

9.6.3 Calculating Values for MICROs

Usually, a MICRO performs a text substitution. However, you can also use MICRO expressions to define numerical values. To do so, you use the MICROCOMPUTE statement. For example,

```
10 MICROCOMPUTE &PROJECT MONTH&  &MONTH& + 12 &
...
60 COLUMN PROJ YTD = SUM(C13 THRU C&PROJ MONTH&)
```

Line 10 defines the value of PROJECT MONTH as being the number of the current month (Remember: &MONTH& is a built-in MICRO in IFPS) + 12. In general, you first specify the name of the MICRO (in our case &PROJECT MONTH&) and then a computational statement for it. The computational statement can have a MICRO in it. In our case, we use the built-in MICRO and add 12 to it. The MICROCOMPUTE statement is terminated by an additional ampersand.

In Line 60, the year to date is computed by summing over the columns starting in column 13 and ending in in the current month. The current month number is computed from the MICROCOMPUTE statement.

9.6.4 Using MICRO Expressions in Reports

MICROs can be used in reports as well as in models. They work in exactly the same way. The built-in MICROs, for example, are a handy way of customizing the title block in reports to the current date and for having one report that handles multiple products. For example,

```
10 MICROCOMPUTE &START&  &DATE& - 9 &
20 CENTER &DEPARTMENT& REWORK REPORT
30 CENTER FOR WEEK BEGINNING &START&
```

might represent a rework report on the previous week that each department generates on Wednesday.

9.7 TAGGED DATA FILES

In Section 4.6 we discussed various aspects of data files. We showed how data files are created and used with models (Sec. 4.6.1 through 4.6.6). We also described how:

- model outputs could be retained as data (STORENT, Sec. 4.6.7)
- data from several files could be combined through DATASELECT and MERGE (Sec. 4.6.8 and 4.6.9).
- how the NA feature allows you to leave data cells blank (Sec. 4.10).

The data files described in Section 4.6 were created in "untagged" format. That is, they represented data in the usual two-dimensional spreadsheet format. For example, the following is a data file for a model with three columns:

```
FILE DATA0
1 SALES = 100,130,160
2 EXPENSES = 75,100,125
```

Each row represents the values associated with one variable. However, in a variety of situations you may want to define data in three dimensions and store them in the same data file. For example, you may want to keep data on two divisions together. The third dimension is added by "tagging" the data. This is done by putting the tag in square brackets after the variable name. Figure 9-22 is an example: that shows a tagged data file and a model that might use this information.

```
FILE DATATAG
1 SALES[DIV1]=100,130,160
2 EXPENSES[DIV1]=75,100,125
3 SALES[DIV2]=150,170,190
4 EXPENSES[DIV2]=80,110,140
```

a. Sample Tagged Data File

FIGURE 9-22. TAGGED DATA FILE
(This Figure is Continued on the Next Page)

```
MODEL TAG1
10 COLUMNS 1-3
20 TOTAL SALES=SALES[DIV1]+SALES[DIV2]
30 TOTAL EXPENSES=EXPENSES[DIV1]+EXPENSES[DIV2]
40 GROSS PROFIT =TOTAL SALES-TOTAL EXPENSES
END OF MODEL
?solve model tag1 using dfname
ENTER DATAFILE NAME FOR TAGGED VARIABLES (OR NONE)
? datatag,none
MODEL TAG1  VERSION OF  05/02/86  21:14 -- 3 COLUMNS 7 VARIABLES
ENTER SOLVE OPTIONS
? all

                                     1         2         3


TOTAL SALES                        250       300       350
TOTAL EXPENSES                     155       210       265
GROSS PROFIT                        95        90        85
```

FIGURE 9-22. TAGGED DATA FILE
(Continued)

In model TAG1, TOTAL SALES are computed in Line 20 by looking up the values of the sales in division1 and division 2 in the tagged data file DATATAG. Note that tagged data files create an exception from the normal rule in IFPS that if a value is used on the right of an equal sign it must be defined to the left of an equal sign. When IFPS encounters [] after a variable name it recognizes that the values will come from a data file not from another row in the model.

The basic idea of tagged data files is shown in Fig. 9-23.

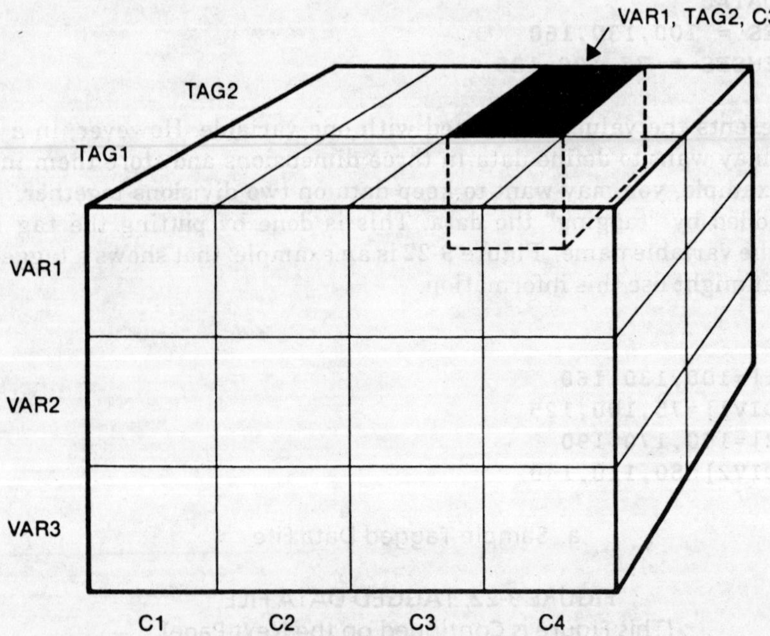

FIGURE 9-23. BASIC CONCEPT OF TAGGED DATA FILES

Each tag, in effect, creates a separate spreadsheet. Three parameters describe a particular value: its variable name, its column name, and its tag name. As described in Section 9.7.2, you can retrieve the data by selecting any one of these three parameters.

9.7.1 Creating and Adding to Tagged Data Files (STORE)

A tagged data file can be created (or added to) in two ways:

1. Copying an existing data file into a tagged data file.

2. Solve a model and store the results with a tag.

For example, to create a tagged data file from data file DATA0 shown above, you would go through the following sequence:

```
?datafile DATA0
?STORE DATATAG
NEW DATA FILE WILL BE CREATED
ENTER STORE OPTIONS
?TAG DIV1
?ALL

STORE UPDATE COMPLETE
```

As a result, you would have two files, DATA0 and DATATAG. If you list DATATAG at this point, the result is:

```
1 SALES[DIV1] = 100,130,160
2 EXPENSES[DIV1] = 75,100,115
```

The printout STORE UPDATE COMPLETE indicates that the storing of tagged data files is an update operation. That is, STORE changes an existing data file to reflect new values. If these values did not exist previously, they are simply added at the end of the file. To illustrate how data are added and to show how STORE can be used to save model solutions, consider MODEL TAG0 shown in Figure 9-24.

```
MODEL TAG0
10 COLUMNS 1-3
20 SALES = 150,170,190
30 EXPENSES = 80,110,140
40 GROSS PROFIT = SALES-EXPENSES
END OF MODEL
```

FIGURE 9-24. STORING TAGGED DATA FILES
(This Figure is Continued on the Next Page)

```
?SOLVE
ENTER SOLVE OPTIONS
STORE DATATAG
MODEL TAG0 VERSION OF ../../..  3 COLUMNS 3 VARIABLES
ENTER STORE OPTIONS
?TAG DIV2
?SALES,EXPENSES
ENTER MORE VARIABLES FOR STORE PROCESSING (OR NONE)
?NONE
STORE UPDATE COMPLETE
```

FIGURE 9-24. STORING TAGGED DATA FILES
(Continued)

In the dialog shown after MODEL TAG0 in Figure 9-24, IFPS is asked to solve the model and store the results in a tagged data file. The tag DIV2 was specified as were the variables SALES and EXPENSES. The prompt to enter more variables or to type NONE is required to tell IFPS that you have completed entering the list of variables to be stored. The result of this sequence is Lines 3 and 4 of FILE DATATAG that was shown in Figure 9-22.

In general, the STORE command is followed by a request for STORE options. TAG is just one of these options. Other options include:

COLUMNS	Specifies which columns should be stored. The default is ALL.
INVERT	Inverts columns and variables before storing them.
NAPRINT NO	Prevents storing NA data
SCALE	Scales values by the factor specified.
ZEROSUP	Suppresses storing variables whose value is 0 in all columns.

WARNING: If you do not specify a TAG option, IFPS automatically assigns the model name as the tag.

9.7.2 Using Tagged Variables in Models (DFNAME)

When you use a tagged variable in a model, you have to specify the tagged data file in which the values of the variable are stored. This can be done in several ways.

1. Specify the name of the tagged data file in response to a ?
2. Specify the data files with a USING command when calling the model.
3. Have IFPS prompt you for the data file.

We will discuss each of these methods in turn.

SPECIFYING THE DATA FILE WITH DFNAME. You can tell IFPS the name of a file containing tagged data by giving the DFNAME command in response to a ?. For example:

```
?DFNAME  DATATAG
```

When you SOLVE the model, IFPS looks in the data file specified with a DFNAME to find each of the tagged variables in the model. It uses the ones it finds and then prompts you (see below) for any others it may need.

DFNAME acts like an on-off switch. When you specify a particular data file with DFNAME, IFPS looks for tagged data in that file until you either specify a different DFNAME or you instruct IFPS to turn DFNAME off by typing

```
?DFNAME NONE
```

<u>*SPECIFYING TAGGED DATA FILES WITH USING.*</u> You can obtain tagged data in the same way you obtain untagged data by specifying the data file you are USING. For example,

```
?MODEL TAG1 USING DATATAG
```

results in IFPS associating DATATAG with model TAG0 when you SOLVE or use GENREPORT.

In general, you do not see the individual values of tagged variables referred to on the right- hand side. However, if you enter ALL as a SOLVE option, IFPS appends the data to the end of the output.

EXERCISE: Enter MODEL TAG1 and data file DATATAG into your computer. Call for MODEL TAG1 USING DATATAG. Solve the model, requesting ALL variables. Observe the output.

If you ask IFPS to SOLVE a model or give a GENREPORT command without having specified the tagged data files with either DFNAME or USING, IFPS will prompt you with:

```
ENTER DATAFILE NAME FOR TAGGED VARIABLES (OR NONE)
```

IFPS repeats this prompt until you have entered the names of enough data files to define value for all the tagged variables.

9.7.3 Obtaining a View of the Data (SELECT)

As shown in Figure 9-23, tagged data files provide information in three dimensions: (1) variable name, (2) column name, and (3) tag name. If you want to see all the information associated with a particular name, you can do so with the SELECT command. This command has three forms:

- SELECT TAG
- SELECT VARIABLE
- SELECT COLUMN

For example, if you want to see data associated with the tag DIV1, you would specify:

```
?SELECT TAG DIV1
```

Figure 9-25 illustrates all three forms of the SELECT command for datafile DATATAG.

```
?datafile datatag
READY FOR EDIT. LAST LINE IS 4
?LIST
1 SALES[DIV1]=100,130,160
2 EXPENSES[DIV1]=75,100,125
3 SALES[DIV2]=150,170,190
4 EXPENSES[DIV2]=80,110,140

?SELECT TAG DIV1
MATRIX HAS 2 ROWS 4 COLUMNS
?SOLVE
ALL

               1          2          3
SALES          100        130        160
EXPENSES       75         100        125

ENTER SOLVE OPTIONS
?SELECT VARIABLE SALES
MATRIX HAS 2 ROWS 3 COLUMNS
?SOLVE
ENTER SOLVE OPTIONS
?ALL
                   1          2          3
DIV1               100        130        160
DIV2               150        170        190
ENTER SOLVE OPTIONS
SELECT COLUMN 2
MATRIX HAS 2 ROWS AND 2 COLUMNS
?SOLVE
ENTER SOLVE OPTIONS
?ALL

                   DIV1       DIV2
SALES              130        170
EXPENSES           100        110
```

FIGURE 9-25 THE SELECT COMMAND

When you issue a SELECT command, IFPS first tells you how many rows and columns are in the matrix. You must then SOLVE and specify the SOLVE options you want.

In general,

SELECT TAG	displays variable names vs. columns
SELECT VARIABLE	displays tag names vs. columns
SELECT COLUMN	displays variable names vs. tag names

The SELECT command can be used only to display tagged data. For large data sets, it is often useful to INVERT before using the SELECT command so that the data can be read more easily.

EXERCISE: Ask for INVERT and then repeat Figure 9-25.

CHAPTER X
UNIVERSAL CONSOLIDATION AND RELATIONAL DATA BASE

10.1 Universal Consolidation

10.2 DIMENSION - The IFPS Data Base

CHAPTER X
UNIVERSAL CONSOLIDATION AND RELATIONAL DATA BASE

This chapter presents two capabilities of IFPS that allow the user to deal with problems of the size usually encountered in large firms. These capabilities are:

- universal consolidation
- data base management

Consolidation was introduced in Section 4.8. There you were introduced to the ideas needed to add the solutions of one or more models or data files through the use of the CONSOLIDATE and CONSOLDF commands. These models and files were assumed to be at the same level in the organization and were combined to obtain grand totals (e.g., from three divisions) or variances between planned and actual performance. In many organizations, the financial structures are more complex, representing hierarchies and networks. Universal Consolidation, discussed in Section 10.1, lets you work with these organiza-tional forms.

Data files were introduced in Section 4.6 as a way of using a variety of data sets with the same model. For example, you can analyze sales each month by recording the current month's results into a data file and solving the sales model using the latest data file. Many organizations today prefer to keep data such as sales figures in a corporate data base. IFPS/DIMENSION* has been created to provide a relational data base for use with IFPS models. The data base is of the "relational" type. Section 10.2. describes the features of IFPS/DIMENSION.

10.1 UNIVERSAL CONSOLIDATION

Universal consolidation allows you to analyze parts of your business, either singly or in any combination you want. It takes into account that businesses have complex organizational structures and that each unit and group in the organization maintains separate profit and loss records that need to be combined to achieve managerial control.

10.1.1 Organizational Structures

Organizational structures can be described either as hierarchicies or as networks. Hierarchical structure refers to the situation shown in Figure 10-1 in which each unit in the organization reports to the next higher unit. Eventually, a top level (which we shall

*IFPS/DIMENSION is available for many models of International Business Machines Corporation and Digital Equipment Corporation mainframes and minis. Check with your computer center to determine whether it is available to you.

refer to here as CORPORATE) is reached.

a. Hierarchical Structure

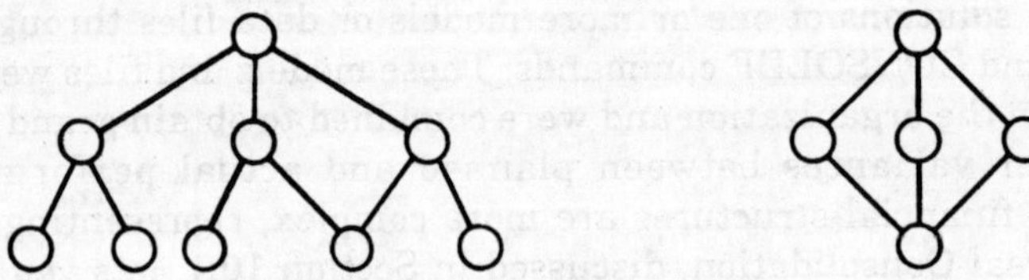

b. Network Structure

FIGURE 10-1. HIERARCHICAL AND NETWORK STRUCTURES

Network structure differs from hierarchical structure in that particular units may report upward to two or more units. A representative network structure is shown in Figure 10-1b. For example, a firm may organize by product groups (chemicals, electronics, steel) and by regions (East, West, International). An office selling chemicals in the East would report to both the Chemicals Group and to the Eastern Region. As shown in the example of Figure 10-2, not all products need be sold in each region.

In complex organizations, you may observe several hierarchies and networks all intermixed.

During Universal Consolidation, data are gathered at the lowest levels of the organization and serve as input to the model. When combined with output from any postprocessing models (Sec. 4.8.4), the solutions serve as input to the next level of the hierarchy. In effect, each data file "goes into" the next level up.

An important consideration in many organizations is allocated cost, particularly overhead, that is determined at the top of the hierarchy and assigned to lower levels on some basis. Universal Consolidation iterates back and forth among the different levels until these allocations converge.

Because managers at all levels want to be able to see how they and the organizations that report to them are performing, Universal Consolidation permits generating reports at each level; that is, you can create reports about intermediate results as well as about the total consolidation.

10.1.2 Defining a STRUCTURE

For Universal Consolidation to work, you have to define a STRUCTURE. A STRUCTURE is a road map for IFPS, telling it how you want the consolidation to work. It contains:

1. The names of the data files involved in the consolidation.
2. The hierachical and/or network relations among files.
3. What reports are to be created.
4. Which output data are to be stored as data bases for further processing.
5. The name of the file where the compiled version of the structure and the current status of the consolidation are stored.

Figure 10.2 shows the STRUCTURE for the network hierarchy given in Figure 10-1. The hierarchy defined here is used to determine the corporate income statement by consolidating the income statements from its divisions.

```
structure companyl
READY FOR EDIT, LAST LINE IS 19
? list
STRUCTURE COMPANY1  VERSION OF   02/25/86   22:52
1 DEFINE CORPORAT AS INCOME USING CHEMICAL ELECTRO STEEL
2 DEFINE CHEMICAL AS INCOME USING CHEMEAST CHEMINTL
3 DEFINE ELECTRO  AS INCOME USING ELECEAST ELECWEST ELECINTL
4 DEFINE STEEL    AS INCOME USING STEELEAS STEELWES
5 *
6 DEFINE EAST AS INCOME USING CHEMEAST ELECEAST STEELEAS
7 DEFINE WEST AS INCOME USING ELECWEST STEELWES
8 DEFINE INTL AS INCOME USING CHEMINTL ELECINTL
9 *
10 GENREPORT COMPANY FROM DATAFILE CORPORAT
11 GENREPORT DIVISION FROM DATAFILE CHEMICAL
12 GENREPORT DIVISION FROM DATAFILE ELECTRO
13 GENREPORT DIVISION FROM DATAFILE STEEL
14 GENREPORT REGION FROM DATAFILE EAST
15 GENREPORT REGION FROM DATAFILE WEST
16 GENREPORT REGION FROM DATAFILE INTL
17 DEFINESTATUS CORP1
18 STORE RESULTS FROM INCOME
19 SALES,GROSS INCOME,NET INCOME
END OF STRUCTURE
```

FIGURE 10-2. DEFINITION OF A STRUCTURE

To create or edit a STRUCTURE, you type the command STRUCTURE followed by its name. (If you forget to give a name, IFPS prompts you.) The STRUCTURE command activates a subsystem which has its own vocabulary; in this case, directives and commands. You can enter directives into a STRUCTURE in any order since STRUCTUREs are nonprocedural.

As you examine Figure 10-2 you will see that a STRUCTURE is a separate element of IFPS, like a MODEL or a REPORT. It is stored in a Models and Reports File. The STRUCTURE defines a set of data files which are created through consolidations. Since there is one data file per node in the STRUCTURE, these data files are referred to as node files. A STRUCTURE consists of a set of "directives", that is, instructions to IFPS to define relations among elements. The following is a line-by-line description of the STRUCTURE presented in Figure 10-2. In this structure, income statements, labeled INCOME, are prepared.

Line 1 shows that Corporate results are the sum (i.e., consolidation) of the results of three product lines: chemical, electronics, and steel. Note that this consolidation, like the ones that follow, creates a new data file. In this case, it is CORPORAT.

Lines 2 through 4 define the components of each product line in terms of its constituent divisions. In the figure, these divisions are named in terms of the product they produce and their location.

Lines 6 through 8 show how the regional data (east,west, and international) are to be consolidated.

Line 10 produces a report for the company as a whole from the data file CORPORAT.

Lines 11 through 16 create reports for each division and each region from their respective consolidated files. Note that three separate reports (shown in Figure 10-3) were created to customize the outputs. The report formats differ only in their headings. Note, too, the use of &DFNAME& which is a built-in IFPS micro that allows you to substitute the name of the data file. (See Sec. 9.6).

Line 17 uses the directive DEFINESTATUS to ask that the status list begin with the company as a whole and include all portions of the structure beyond that. DEFINESTATUS is described in Section 10.1.3.

Lines 18 and 19 use the directive STORE (Line 18) to create a data file RESULTS from model INCOME. This data file is really a three dimensional data base (Line 19) that includes the variables sales, gross income, and net income from each of the node files that was created.

10.1.3 Directives Available for Use in a STRUCTURE

Table 10-1 describes the directives available for creating a STRUCTURE. You will see that some of the directives are IFPS commands (e.g., GENREPORT, STORENT, STORE) with which you are familiar, while others (e.g., DEFINE, DEFINESTATUS, ALLOCATE) are not. The following paragraphs describe the terms that are new.

DEFINE DIRECTIVE. The DEFINE directive specifies a node and the associated data file (called node file) in a hierarchy or a network. One DEFINE directive is required for each node. Figure 10-4 shows how the node file is built up. The figure should be read from the bottom up to see the progression from individual data files to the node file.

```
REPORT COMPANY  VERSION OF  02/25/86  22:26
10 FORMAT ...............4[ 9999.99]
20*
30 CENTER CONSOLIDATED COMPANY INCOME
40 UNDERLINE=
50 SPACE 1
60 COLUMN TITLES 1ST,2ND,3RD,4TH
70 COLUMN TITLES QTR,QTR,QTR,QTR
80 SPACE 2
90 SALES,EXPENSES,GROSS INCOME,OVERHEAD,NET INCOME
END OF REPORT

? report division
READY FOR EDIT, LAST LINE IS 90
? list
REPORT DIVISION  VERSION OF  02/25/86  23:04
10 FORMAT ...............4[ 9999.99]
20*
25*      CONSOLIDATED REPORT FOR
30*      &DFNAME& DIVISION
50 SPACE 1
60 COLUMN TITLES 1ST,2ND,3RD,4TH
70 COLUMN TITLES QTR,QTR,QTR,QTR
80 SPACE 2
90 SALES,EXPENSES,GROSS INCOME,OVERHEAD,NET INCOME
END OF REPORT

? report region
READY FOR EDIT, LAST LINE IS 90
? list
REPORT REGION  VERSION OF  02/25/86  23:05
10 FORMAT ...............4[ 9999.99]
20*
25*      CONSOLIDATED REPORT FOR
30*      &DFNAME& REGION
50 SPACE 1
60 COLUMN TITLES 1ST,2ND,3RD,4TH
70 COLUMN TITLES QTR,QTR,QTR,QTR
80 SPACE 2
90 SALES,EXPENSES,GROSS INCOME,OVERHEAD,NET INCOME
END OF REPORT
```

FIGURE 10-3. CUSTOMIZED REPORTS CALLED FOR BY STRUCTURE OF FIGURE 10-2.

TABLE 10-1

SUMMARY OF DIRECTIVES

DEFINE	Gives a name to a node file and specifies the data files and models to be used to create the node file. A structure MUST contain one or more directives.
GENREPORT	Creates a formatted report.
STORENT	Specifies which variables are to be included (untagged) in the node file. The default value is all variables.
STORE	Similar to STORENT but tags the file with the name of the node file or data file (see Sec. 9.7 on tagged data f iles). STORE makes it easier to collect intermediate results.
COMMENT	Creates a line of text that can be used for documentation for the STRUCTURE. (An * or C followed by a space may be used in place of COMMENT.)
DEFINESTATUS	Gives the name of the file that will store the compiled STRUCTURE. A STRUCTURE *MUST* contain ONE (and no more than one) DEFINESTATUS.
SCALE	Used to scale all variables in a model solution. SCALE is useful for currency conversion and variance analysis. You can specify variables to be excluded from scaling.
ALLOCATE	Creates a tagged data file and defines the variables involved in allocation. Only one ALLOCATE directive may be issued in a STRUCTURE. See the discussion of allocation for a more thorough discussion of the allocation process used by IFPS.

A DEFINE statement must specify:

- A unique *node name* (which becomes the name of the data file it creates)
- Which *data files* are to be consolidated into the new data file
- Which *model* is to be used for the consolidation.

In addition, a DEFINE statement indicates which postprocessing model (PPMODEL in Figure 10-4), if any, is to be used and which reports are to be created. The general form of the DEFINE statement is:

```
DEFINE node file name'

    AS modelname USING datafile 1,datafile 2,...'
    WITH postprocessing modelname USING datafile..'
    ONLY ONTO reportfile
```

Here the ' are the usual continuations of a single statement.

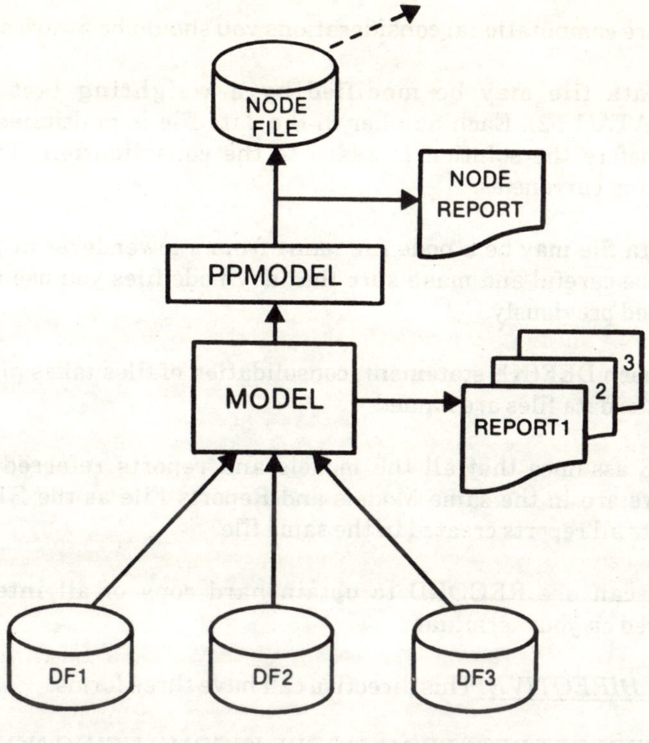

FIGURE 10-4. BUILDING A NODE FILE

Note that there are four keywords involved in the DEFINE: AS, USING, WITH, and ONLY ONTO.

- AS introduces the model to be used.
- USING defines the data files to be consolidated.
- WITH specifies the postprocessing model.
- ONLY ONTO specifies which report file is to contain the results.

If you say ONTO you get a copy of the report in both the file and at the terminal; whereas, if you say ONLY ONTO, you store the file but do not see output at your terminal. Skipping ONTO results in the report appearing at your terminal but not being saved in storage.

EXERCISE: Describe the results of each of the following DEFINE statements:

```
DEFINE SOUTHREG AS AREAMOD USING TEXDATA,ALADATA,GADATA ONTO SOTHREG
DEFINE NORTHREG AS AREAMOD USING MICHDATA,OHIODATA,ILLDATA'
   WITH POSTMOD USING POSTDAT ONLY ONTO NORTHREP
```

The following are computational considerations you should be aware of:

1. A data file may be modified by a weighting factor; for example, BRITDATA(1.52). Each number in the data file is multiplied by the weighting factor before the solution is added to the consolidation. This is one way of converting currencies.

2. A data file may be a node file name from a lower level in the structure. You should be careful and make sure that any node files you use as a data file were computed previously.

4. For each DEFINE statement, consolidation of files takes place in the order in which the data files are named.

5. IFPS assumes that all the models and reports referred to in a DEFINE directive are in the same Models and Reports File as the STRUCTURE. IFPS also puts all reports created in the same file.

6. You can use RECORD to obtain hard copy of all intermediate results displayed on your terminal.

GENREPORT DIRECTIVE. This directive can have three forms:

1. GENREPORT RPT1 FROM MODEL INCOME USING NORTHDAT, EASTDAT

2. GENREPORT RPT1 FROM MODEL INCOME

3. GENREPORT RPT1 FROM DATAFILE CORPORAT

The first case specifies the report(s) to be created; the model to be reported, and the data files to be used. A report is created whenever the model is solved with the data files named. The second case differs from the first in that the USING option is omitted. In case 2, a report is generated whenever the model is solved, irrespective of which data file is used. In the third case, the FROM DATAFILE form, the report is generated from the solution of the data file. This form is typically used to print out a node file.

EXERCISE: Describe the results of each of the following GENREPORT directives:

```
GENREPORT BALSHEET,INCOME FROM BUDGET
GENREPORT BALSHEET,INCOME FROM DATAFILE CORPORAT
GENREPORT BALSHEET,INCOME FROM MODEL DIVISION USING NORDATA,EASTDAT
GENREPORT VARIANCE FROM MODEL CORP USING VARDATA
```

STORE and STORENT DIRECTIVE. By default, all results of consolidation are stored in nontagged form. If you want to limit the information sent to the next higher level of the hierarchy you can do so by using a STORENT directive. The advantage is that you save storage space since only the data specified in the STORENT are kept. For example,

```
STORENT FROM CHEMEAST
SALES THROUGH NET INCOME
```

results in only the variables starting at SALES and ending at NET INCOME being stored for further use. Note that you put the STORENT directive on one line and specify the variables to be stored on the next.

The STORE directive allows you to keep results from several different node files in a single data file. This approach helps you create reports that involve data from several nodes. You can store values of variables both before consolidation and from a node file after consolidation. An example of the STORE directive is shown in Figure 10-2 (Lines 18 and 19):

```
STORE RESULTS FROM INCOME
SALES,GROSS INCOME,NET INCOME
```

This directive tells IFPS to store the variables from SALES through NET INCOME obtained from Model INCOME in the data file named RESULTS.

In general, you write either

STORE datafilename
or STORE datafilename FROM modelname

followed by a list of variables.

NOTE: If you need information only from some columns (e.g., the annual totals or the last four quarters) you can use:

STORENT COLUMNS a-b FROM modelname
or STORE datafilename COLUMNS a-b
or STORE datafilename COLUMNS a-b FROM modelname.

For example, you might write:

```
STORE RESULTS COLUMNS 5-8 FROM INCOME
```

NOTE: Although the STORENT and STORE commands limit what is saved in storage, they do not affect what is reported. You can use GENREPORT to give you any solution output you want from a given node.

DEFINESTATUS DIRECTIVE. This directive has the form:

DEFINESTATUS filename

For example,

```
DEFINESTATUS CORP1
```

It tells IFPS the name of the file in which the compiled version of the STRUCTURE is to be stored; in our example, the file CORP1. You MUST include one (and no more than one) DEFINESTATUS directive in each structure.

SCALE DIRECTIVE. The SCALE directive provides a way of converting currencies and other quantities so that the consolidated results have common measures such as dollars or meters.

The most general form of the SCALE directive is:

SCALE MULTIPLY BY variablename, EXCLUDE variable list
or SCALE BY variablename,EXCLUDE variable list

The "variablename" refers to the variable that contains the scale factor to be used. SCALE MULTIPLY BY results in each output being multiplied by the scale factor, whereas SCALE BY results in each output being divided by the scale factor.

The keyword EXCLUDE and the variable list that follows are optional. If you do not want to scale a variable, you can put it on the EXCLUDE list. For example, if your model (to be used with data files) were:

```
10 NUMBER OF UNITS SOLD = 0
20 UNIT PRICE = 0
30 RECEIPTS = NUMBER OF UNITS SOLD * UNIT PRICE
40 FRANC =155
50 END
```

Your SCALE directive would be:

```
SCALE  MULTIPLY  BY  FRANC,  EXCLUDE  NUMBER  OF  UNITS  SOLD,'
RECEIPTS,FRANC
```

Here NUMBER OF UNITS SOLD and FRANC are absolute values, and RECEIPTS contains UNIT PRICE values that have already been scaled.

EXERCISE: Write an alternate form of this SCALE command that puts UNIT PRICE on the EXCLUDE list.

ALLOCATE DIRECTIVE. The ALLOCATE directive tells IFPS how to divide costs incurred at a given node in a hierarchy among nodes lower down in the hierarchy. For example, you may have pension and administrative expense incurred by the company as a whole and want to allocate these costs among the various plants according to the number of their employees.

The allocation process follows a set pattern of calculation. The ALLOCATE directive creates a special tagged data file (Sec. 9.7) that automatically collects data values during consolidation for the variables designated in the ALLOCATE directive.

IMPORTANT: You may give only *one* ALLOCATE directive in a STRUCTURE.

The ALLOCATE directive has the following form:

ALLOCATE datafile FROM nodefile1, nodefile 2,...nodefilen
list of distinct variable names

It is written over two lines. For example,

```
50 ALLOCATE DFALLOCATE FROM COMPANY
51 PENSION FUND, ADMINISTRATIVE EXPENSES
```

The data file refers to the tagged data file (e.g., DFALLOCATE in our example) which will collect values during consolidation. The list of nodes is optional; however, the program will run more efficiently if you specify which nodes are involved. The usual case is to specify the top node in the hierarchy (e.g., COMPANY) where the allocation is from corporate to the all lower levels. The variable names must be listed explicitly; the THRU form is not accepted in this case. The variables should be untagged and must be defined on the left side of an equal sign in one or more models of the STRUCTURE.

The allocate process works in the following way. After consolidation is completed and the node files have been created, the list of variables in the ALLOCATE directive is checked. If this list contains any variables that are also included in models that have been consolidated, then the values of these variables are stored in the ALLOCATE file and are available for use. IFPS then iterates back through the models and uses the values in the allocation formulas. For example, suppose you have a statement for a division.

```
PENSION ALLOCATION=CORPORATE PENSION*DIVISION EMPLOYEES/TOTAL
EMPLOYEES
```

In the initial pass, since the consolidation starts at the bottom of the hierarchy, neither the amount in the corporate pension fund nor the total employees in the company are known. The result is that the Pension Allocation is 0. However, at the end of the initial pass, the corporate pension fund and the total employees are available from consolidation, and are put into the data file created by the ALLOCATE Directive. In the second pass, these values are used to compute the allocation.

The allocation process is described in detail in the IFPS User's Manual. Allocation requires attention to detail to set it up correctly.

10.1.4 Commands Used in Preparing and Editing a Structure

When preparing or editing a STRUCTURE, you have available to you many of the commands you usually use in creating or editing models. Specifically, you can use:

AUTO COMPILEFILE END LIST SAVE HELP

Of these, COMPILEFILE is particularly useful in Universal Consolidation. If you put:

COMPILEFILE filename

into a model before any other statement (with the exception of comments), the model will compile as soon as it is error free. More important, the compiled version will be used rather than the IFPS model with the result that calculations are speeded up.

10.1.5 Executing Universal Consolidation

After you have defined your STRUCTURE, created your models, and prepared your reports and data files, you are ready to carry out Universal Consolidation.

Your first step is to ask IFPS for the STRUCTURE you will use. Note that the STRUCTURE must be in the same Models and Reports File as the models and reports you define in the STRUCTURE. In our example case you would type:

```
?STRUCTURE COMPANY
```

It is a good idea to LIST the structure to make sure it is correct before you proceed. This simple check can save you both time and cost. In our example, the result of listing is the structure that was shown in Figure 10-2.

STATUSLIST. As a second check on the correctness of the STRUCTURE, you can ask for STATUSLIST. As shown in Figure 10-5, STATUSLIST gives you the following information:

- The number of signficant digits and decimal places in the output.
- Each file and subfile in the hierarchy. (STATUSLIST will also show you information about the changes you have made from the base case.)

RECOMPILE. As a third check on the correctness of the structure, you can ask for RECOMPILE. If the compilation is successful, the compiles structure will be saved on the file which you named in the DEFINESTATUS line. If the compilation is unsuccessful, you will see an error message on the screen. The RECOMPILE command is shown at the bottom of Figure 10-5.

CONSOLIDATE. Having convinced yourself that the structure is right, you next ask IFPS to perform universal consolidation. The simplest form is simply to type:

```
?CONSOLIDATE
```

The results are shown in Figure 10-6. You will note that the results are not shown in the order in which the directives are given in the STRUCTURE. Rather, IFPS goes down the STRUCTURE and tries to execute each line. If it can't, it goes on to the next. In our case, the data file CORPORAT depends on the consolidation of three divisions (CHEMICAL, ELECTRO, STEEL), which are themselves the results of consolidations. Thus, IFPS first consolidates CHEMICAL and prints out the result, followed by ELECTRO and STEEL. It can then consolidate CORPORAT. Finally, IFPS provides the consolidation by region.

When it is done, IFPS tells you that consolidation is completed and how many nodes were consolidated.

ALTERNATE FORMS OF THE CONSOLIDATE COMMAND. In addition to CONSOLIDATE, four other commands can be used:

CONSOLIDATE RECALCULATE
RECALCULATE
CONSOLIDATE THRU nodefile
CONSOLIDATE THRU nodefile RECALCULATE

These commands are useful because IFPS tries to consolidate with minimum calculation. If you have modified or altered only one or two nodes, IFPS will only recompute that portion of the STRUCTURE which has changed. CONSOLIDATE RECALCULATE (and RECALCULATE, which is equivalent) will recompute the entire STRUCTURE whether or not there have been changes.

You also have the ability to consolidate only a portion of the STRUCTURE. To do so, you issue the command CONSOLIDATE THRU. IFPS begins at that node and recomputes back up to the top node. If you add RECALCULATE, calculations are made at all nodes on the way up. Otherwise, calculations are made only where there have been changes.

```
? structure companyl
READY FOR EDIT, LAST LINE IS 19
? statuslist

CURRENT STORE OPTIONS ARE:
          6 SIGNIFICANT DIGITS
          2 DECIMAL PLACES
----------------------------------------------------------------------

NODE FILE CORPORAT

   NODE FILE CHEMICAL

      NODE FILE CHEMEAST
      NODE FILE CHEMINTL

   NODE FILE ELECTRO

      NODE FILE ELECEAST
      NODE FILE ELECWEST
      NODE FILE ELECINTL

   NODE FILE STEEL

      NODE FILE STEELEAS
      NODE FILE STEELWES
----------------------------------------------------------------------

NODE FILE EAST

   NODE FILE CHEMEAST
   NODE FILE ELECEAST
   NODE FILE STEELEAS
----------------------------------------------------------------------

NODE FILE WEST

   NODE FILE ELECWEST
   NODE FILE STEELWES
----------------------------------------------------------------------

NODE FILE INTL

   NODE FILE CHEMINTL
   NODE FILE ELECINTL
----------------------------------------------------------------------

? recompile
```

FIGURE 10-5. STATUSLIST AND RECOMPILE

```
? consolidate

     CONSOLIDATED REPORT FOR
     CHEMICAL DIVISION

                        1ST      2ND      3RD      4TH
                        QTR      QTR      QTR      QTR

SALES                850.00   950.00  1100.00  1150.00
EXPENSES             300.00   375.00   460.00   490.00
GROSS INCOME         550.00   575.00   640.00   660.00
OVERHEAD             390.00   430.00   510.00   540.00
NET INCOME           160.00   145.00   130.00   120.00

     CONSOLIDATED REPORT FOR
     ELECTRO DIVISION

                        1ST      2ND      3RD      4TH
                        QTR      QTR      QTR      QTR

SALES                350.00   440.00   525.00   580.00
EXPENSES             120.00   145.00   170.00   195.00
GROSS INCOME         230.00   295.00   355.00   385.00
OVERHEAD             180.00   226.50   270.00   300.00
NET INCOME            50.00    68.50    85.00    85.00

     CONSOLIDATED REPORT FOR
     STEEL DIVISION

                        1ST      2ND      3RD      4TH
                        QTR      QTR      QTR      QTR

SALES                 22.00    33.00    38.50    50.00
EXPENSES              11.00    16.50    26.50    28.00
GROSS INCOME          11.00    16.50    12.00    22.00
OVERHEAD               6.60     9.90    11.55    15.00
NET INCOME             4.40     6.60      .45     7.00

              CONSOLIDATED COMPANY INCOME
              ===========================

                        1ST      2ND      3RD      4TH
                        QTR      QTR      QTR      QTR

SALES               1222.00  1423.00  1663.50  1780.00
EXPENSES             431.00   536.50   656.50   713.00
GROSS INCOME         791.00   886.50  1007.00  1067.00
OVERHEAD             576.60   666.40   791.55   855.00
NET INCOME           214.40   220.10   215.45   212.00
```

FIGURE 10-6. RESULT OF UNIVERSAL CONSOLIDATION
(This Figure is Continued on the Next Page)

```
        CONSOLIDATED REPORT FOR
        EAST REGION

                         1ST      2ND      3RD      4TH
                         QTR      QTR      QTR      QTR

SALES                 470.00   605.00   585.00   555.00
EXPENSES              150.00   215.00   245.00   235.00
GROSS INCOME          320.00   390.00   340.00   320.00
OVERHEAD              196.00   251.50   245.50   233.50
NET INCOME            124.00   138.50    94.50    86.50

        CONSOLIDATED REPORT FOR
        WEST REGION

                         1ST      2ND      3RD      4TH
                         QTR      QTR      QTR      QTR


SALES                 202.00   253.00   303.50   325.00
EXPENSES               61.00    71.50    81.50    93.00
GROSS INCOME          141.00   181.50   222.00   232.00
OVERHEAD              100.60   125.90   151.05   161.50
NET INCOME             40.40    55.60    70.95    70.50

        CONSOLIDATED REPORT FOR
        INTL REGION

                         1ST      2ND      3RD      4TH
                         QTR      QTR      QTR      QTR

SALES                 550.00   565.00   775.00   900.00
EXPENSES              220.00   250.00   330.00   385.00
GROSS INCOME          330.00   315.00   445.00   515.00
OVERHEAD              280.00   289.00   395.00   460.00
NET INCOME             50.00    26.00    50.00    55.00

CONSOLIDATION COMPLETED - 7 NODES COMPUTED
```

FIGURE 10-6. RESULT OF UNIVERSAL CONSOLIDATION
(Continued)

If your STRUCTURE includes an ALLOCATE directive, it is good practice always to use RECALCULATE. In this way, you make sure that all needed reallocations are made.

10.1.6 Exploring Changes in the Consolidations (ALTER, MODIFIED)

In Universal Consolidation, WHAT IF cases can be explored in two ways:

1. Use the ALTER command.
2. Use the MODIFIED command.

The ALTER command allows temporary WHAT IF changes to variables that feed into one or more nodefiles. A typical form of this command (shown in Figure 10-7) is:

```
?ALTER ELECTRO FROM ELECINTL
```

This form of the ALTER command tells IFPS that you want to make a change at node ELECTRO by making a change in ELECINTL. IFPS responds by asking:

```
ENTER STATEMENTS
?
```

and you respond with the temporary changes you want. For example,

```
?OVERHEAD = .4*SALES
```

You must use variable names followed by equal signs for changes. IFPS assumes that the ALTER command is completed if you type any command. In the example above, only a single change statement is given (reducing the overhead rate); however, you can enter as many as you want. Furthermore, you can give several ALTER statements, one after the other. You might want to do that if you want to make changes that affect different node files. ALTER statements remain in effect until you give a BASE command (See Sec. 10.1.7).

The general form of the ALTER command is:

ALTER nodefile1 FROM dfname1, nodefile2 FROM dfname2,...

The data file name is optional; if you do not include it IFPS assumes you want to make a change in the node file rather than in one of its data files. If you use ALL instead of a node file name, you are changing all nodes. For example:

```
ALTER ALL FROM STEELWEST
```

Typically, you will follow an ALTER statement with a CONSOLIDATE statement. As shown in Figure 10-7, if you specify only a node file, IFPS only prints out the changes at that node. However, if you specify multiple nodes that are affected by the change, you get output for each node.

You use the MODIFIED command to tell IFPS that one or more data files (or node files) have been changed. For example:

```
MODIFIED ELECWEST
```

The only node that cannot be modified is the highest level one in the STRUCTURE (e.g., CORPORAT in our example).

In a typical application, where you run the same consolidation from time to time (e.g., monthly or quarterly) you want to tell IFPS it should not assume that the data are the same and hence give no output. In the example shown, in Figure 10-7, the data for ELECWEST have been changed to reflect a restatement of overhead and its modification is noted. As shown in Figure 10-7, MODIFIED and ALTER can be used together.

10.1.7 Getting Back to the Original Case (BASE)

ALTER is like WHAT IF CONTINUE. That is, it is cumulative. If you have been making a series of changes and need to get back to the original STRUCTURE, type either:

```
      BASE
   or BASE MODEL.
```

The BASE command removes all ALTER statements currently in effect.

10.1.8 Knowing Where your Are (More on STATUSLIST, ALTERLIST)

If you have been making a series of changes with MODIFIED and ALTER, you may want to know where you are currently. You can do so in two ways: by invoking STATUSLIST (Sec. 10.1.5) or by giving an ALTERLIST command.

In the case of STATUSLIST, the output shown in Figure 10-6 is augmented. Specifically, notations are added to let you know that a particular node is "NOT A BASE CASE SOLUTION" or "INPUT DATA FILE(S) CREATED OR MODIFIED."

The ALTERLIST gives you more detail about the changes that were made. For each ALTER command, you are shown which node was affected, the data files involved, and the specific WHAT IF changes that you made.

Figure 10-8 shows the STATUSLIST and the ALTERLIST for the MODIFIED and ALTER changes made in Figure 10-7.

```
?datafile electwest
READY FOR EDIT, LAST LINE IS 3
? list
1 SALES = 200,250,300,320
2 EXPENSES=60,70,80,90
3 OVERHEAD = .5*SALES
? 3 OVERHEAD =.7 6*SALES
SAVE
```

a. Modifying Datafile ELECWEST

```
? STRUCTURE COMPANY1
READY FOR EDIT, LAST LINE IS 19
? ALTER ELECTRO FROM ELECINTL
ENTER STATEMENTS
? OVERHEAD=.4*SALE
```

b. Altering Datafile ELECINTL

FIGURE 10-7. ALTER AND MODIFIED
(This Figure is Continued on the Next Page)

```
? MODIFIED ELECWEST
? CONSOLIDATE

     CONSOLIDATED REPORT FOR
     ELECTRO DIVISION

                    1ST      2ND      3RD      4TH
                    QTR      QTR      QTR      QTR

SALES            350.00   440.00   525.00   580.00
EXPENSES         120.00   145.00   170.00   195.00
GROSS INCOME     230.00   295.00   355.00   385.00
OVERHEAD         190.00   238.50   285.00   312.00
NET INCOME        40.00    56.50    70.00    73.00


           CONSOLIDATED COMPANY INCOME
           ===========================

                    1ST      2ND      3RD      4TH
                    QTR      QTR      QTR      QTR

SALES           1222.00  1423.00  1663.50  1780.00
EXPENSES         431.00   536.50   656.50   713.00
GROSS INCOME     791.00   886.50  1007.00  1067.00
OVERHEAD         586.60   678.40   806.55   867.00
NET INCOME       204.40   208.10   200.45   200.00

     CONSOLIDATED REPORT FOR
     WEST REGION

                    1ST      2ND      3RD      4TH
                    QTR      QTR      QTR      QTR

SALES            202.00   253.00   303.50   325.00
EXPENSES          61.00    71.50    81.50    93.00
GROSS INCOME     141.00   181.50   222.00   232.00
OVERHEAD         120.60   150.90   181.05   193.50
NET INCOME        20.40    30.60    40.95    38.50

CONSOLIDATION COMPLETED - 3 NODES COMPUTED
```

c. Consolidtation Using Modified ELECTINTL and Altered ELECWEST

FIGURE 10-7. ALTER AND MODIFIED
(Continued)

```
 ? alterlist
ALTER
       NODE FILE ELECTRO FROM NODE FILE ELECINTL
               OVERHEAD = .4*SALES
? statuslist

CURRENT STORE OPTIONS ARE:
        6 SIGNIFICANT DIGITS
        2 DECIMAL PLACES
-------------------------------------------------------------
NODE FILE CORPORAT -   INPUT NODE(S) CREATED OR MODIFIED
                   -  NOT BASE CASE SOLUTION

  NODE FILE CHEMICAL

     NODE FILE CHEMEAST
     NODE FILE CHEMINTL

  NODE FILE ELECTRO -  INPUT NODE(S) REATED OR MODIFIED
                    -  NOT BASE CASE SOLUTION

     NODE FILE ELECEAST
     NODE FILE ELECWEST
     NODE FILE ELECINTL

  NODE FILE STEEL

     NODE FILE STEELEAS
     NODE FILE STEELWES

-------------------------------------------------------------
NODE FILE EAST

   NODE FILE CHEMEAST
   NODE FILE ELECEAST
   NODE FILE STEELEAS
-------------------------------------------------------------
NODE FILE WEST  -INPUT NODE(S) CREATED OR MODIFIED

   NODE FILE ELECWEST
   NODE FILE STEELWES
-------------------------------------------------------------
NODE FILE INTL

   NODE FILE CHEMINTL
   NODE FILE ELECINTL
-------------------------------------------------------------
```

FIGURE 10-8. STATUSLIST AND ALTERLIST FOR FIGURE 10-7

10.2 DIMENSION - THE IFPS DATA BASE

10.2.1 Perspective on Data Bases in IFPS

When IFPS was created as one of the original fourth generation languages, it was conceived of as a modeling language for senior staff and managers. As the size of models became larger, it became clear that IFPS would have to interact with corporate data bases. As a result, a product called IFPS/DATASPAN was introduced which allowed data to be extracted from other systems to create IFPS data files. The next logical step was to create a data base management system,IFPS/DIMENSION, as an integral part of IFPS.

10.2.2 Overview of DIMENSION

In Sections 4.6 (Data Files) and 9.7 (Tagged Data Files) we showed how IFPS data files support two- and three-dimensional data structures. Text fields are limited to variable names and tags. IFPS/DIMENSION extends the capabilities of data files. IFPS/ DIMENSION is a

- multidimensional
- relational

data base management system. It allows, in effect, an unlimited number of fields of texts and data. As in any relational data base, flexible keys provide access to data.

Relational data bases consist of a collection of two-dimensional tables known as "relations." These tables appear to be quite similar to IFPS data files but differ from them in that, rather than allowing only one number per column, each entry is a "field" that can be either numeric or alphabetic. As shown in Figure 10-9, a relation consists of a table with rows (known as *records*) and columns (*fields*).

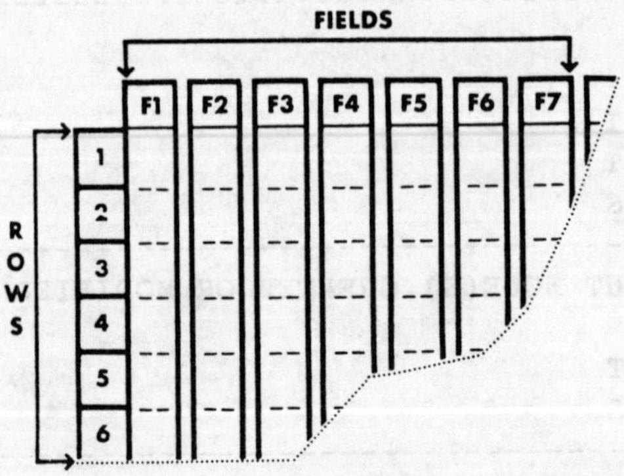

FIGURE 10-9. STRUCTURE OF A RELATIONAL DATABASE SHOWING FIELDS

Unlike a data file, which is tied to a specific model, a relation is independent of a specific model. That is, you can:

- use the same relation with many models.
- use a number of relations in the same model.

A relational data base can be created separately from any IFPS model. However, you can also store the results of solving an IFPS model or the values in a data file in a relational data base.

FIELDS. Fields are items of information that are recorded in columns. A given field may contain text or numbers. You usually specify the format of each field. Formats include

- real numbers (i.e., numbers with decimal points)
- integer numbers (i.e., numbers without decimal points)
- text

Examples of fields are variable name, value in the first quarter, address, and zip code.

RELATIONS. A relation may contain only one type of record. That is, each record in a particular relation contains the same fields in the same sequence. The records may be in any order or may be sequenced in a particular way (e.g., increasing in part number) You may, however, have several relations within a file.

A particular data field may be referred to in several relations. This is the advantage of the relational data base: a given item of data may be used in a number of relations but needs to be stored only once.

Figure 10-10 is an example of a relation. It consists of five fields (Account, QTR1 through QTR4) and has three rows.(PRICE, UNITS, AND COST RATE)

ACCOUNT	QTR1	QTR2	QTR3	QTR4
PRICE	.5000	.5000	.5000	.5000
UNITS	1000	1200	1200	1350
COST RATE	.2500	.3000	.3000	.3000

FIGURE 10-10. EXAMPLE OF A RELATION

RELATIONAL DATA BASE FUNCTIONS. With the IFPS relational data base you can perform the following functions:

1. Define relations.
2. Modify existing relations,
3. Solve models using relations defined in the database,
4. Store the solutions of models and data files into either existing or new relations,
5. Create new relations by combining existing relations,
6. Retrieve specific data from the relations for use in analysis and reporting through inquiries, and
7. Retrieve specific data from relations for use inUniversal Consolidation.

DIMENSION SUBSYSTEMS. As shown in Figure 10-11, IFPS/DIMENSION contains three subsystems:

- the database subsystem
- the relation subsystem
- the query subsystem.

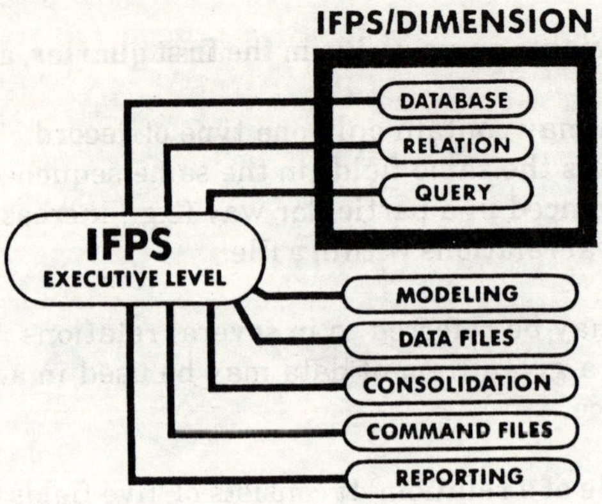

FIGURE 10-11. IFPS/DIMENSION SUBSYSTEMS

- The *Database* subsystem lets you define the fields and relations in a new data base and keep track of the structure of the data base.
- You enter and edit data through the *Relation* subsystem.
- The *Query* subsystem allows you to ask questions of the database. It lets you analyze relations, format data, and report data to the user.

The other subsystems in IFPS (e.g., modeling, consolidation, and command files) are integrated with DIMENSION. For example, you can access data in relations from models and you can transfer model outputs to Dimension relations.

10.2.3 Accessing Data Bases (DATABASE)

To use DIMENSION, you have to tell IFPS that you want to work with data bases. The command:

```
?DATABASE
```

is required. If, for some reason, you forget and issue a command that is valid within DIMENSION, IFPS will prompt you. The following is an example of the interaction in such a prompt:

```
?storedb company
THIS IS A SUBSYSTEM COMMAND
PLEASE ENTER THE APPROPRIATE SUBSYSTEM BEFORE ISSUING THIS
COMMAND
?database
ENTER DATABASE NAME AND PASSWORD
```

```
?company
DATABASE COMPANY DOES NOT EXIST
IF YOU WISH TO CREATE THIS DATABASE, ENTER A FIELD COMMAND
```

In this particular example, the data base COMPANY did not exist previously and will have to be created.

The DATABASE command tells IFPS that you will be using a specific data base. It is required because data bases are stored separately from models and reports and hence you have to attach them to your current work.

In the jargon of IFPS, when you use the data base command, you "open" the data base. A data base has to be opened whenever you:

- create,
- change,
- query, or
- use

a data base.

In what follows, we will use the same data as in Section 10.1 (Universal Consolidation). So that you don't have to flip back to Section 10.1, we will repeat the information here. As shown in Figure 10-12, this data base represents a multi-divisional company. CORPORATE has three divisions, CHEMICAL, ELECTRO and STEEL which operate in three regions (EAST, WEST, INTL). For each division, data are available on sales, expenses, and overhead for each of the last four quarters. It is this data that is to be put into the data base called COMPANY. We will create data base COMPANY in three ways:

1. Directly (Sec.10.2.4), including entering the data (Sec. 10.2.5)
2. From the output of models (Sec. 10.2.5)
3. From data in existing data files (Sec. 10.2.6)

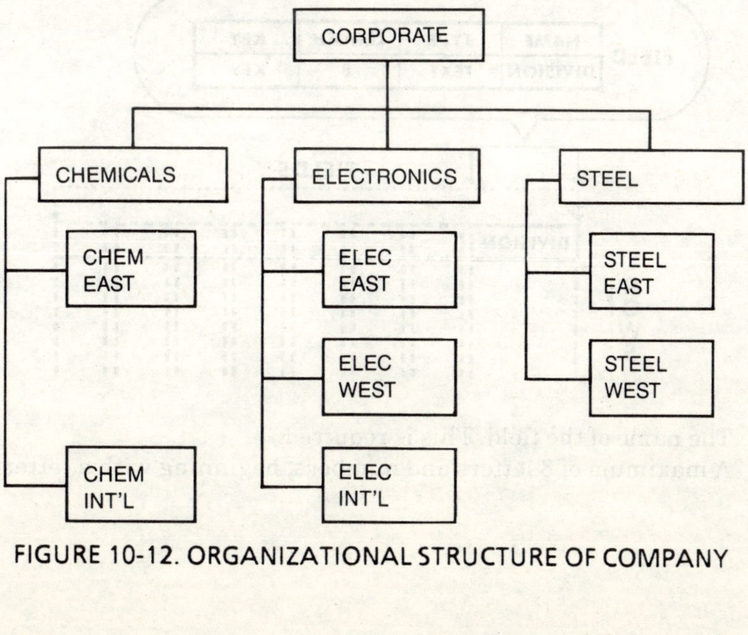

FIGURE 10-12. ORGANIZATIONAL STRUCTURE OF COMPANY

10.2.4 Creating Data Bases Directly (DATABASE, FIELD, RELATION...WITH, LISTFLDS, LISTREL)

To define a data base, you have to specify its fields (i.e., its columns)and its relations (i.e., how the fields are to be put together). The data itself forms the rows.

As implied by the dialog above, the sequence is:

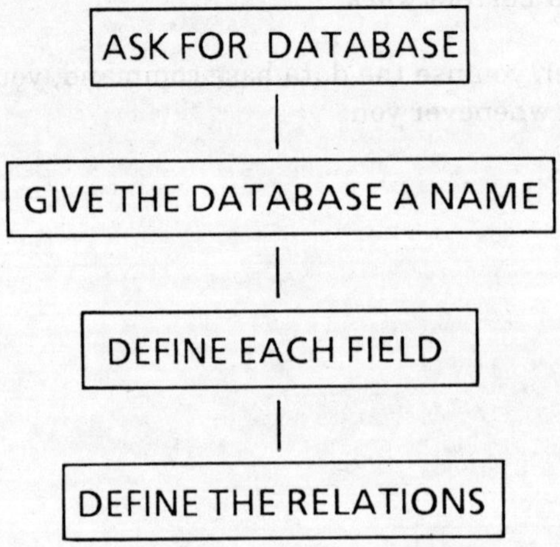

Figure 10-13 shows the sequence of commands used to define data base COMPANY. In response to calling the DATABASE sUbsystem and giving the data base a name (note that you can do this in one statement!), you are told that the data base does not exist. However, it will be created if you give it a field command. You then proceed to list each of the fields you want in the data base followed by the relations in order.

DEFINING FIELDS. A field definition consists of the word FIELD followed by definition of the four components as shown in the sketch below

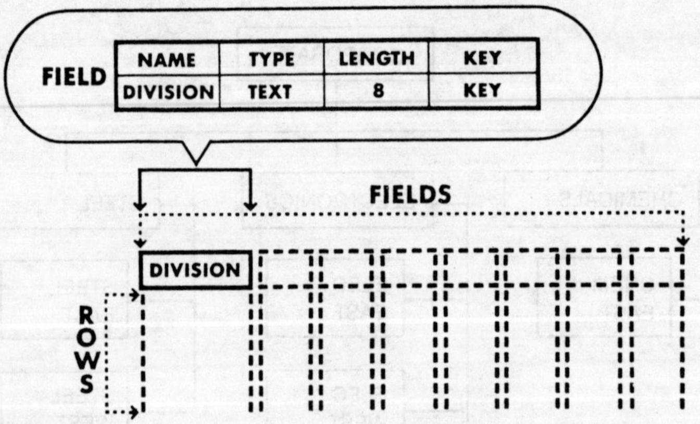

1. Name: The name of the field. This is required.
A maximum of 8 letters and numbers, beginning with a letter.

```
? database company
DATABASE COMPANY DOES NOT EXIST
IF YOU WISH TO CREATE THIS DATABASE, ENTER A FIELD COMMAND
? field division text 8 key
? field region text 4 key
? field account text 12
? field qtr1 real
? field qtr2 real
? field qtr3
? field qtr4
? relation product with division,region,account,qtr1,qtr2,qtr3,qtr4
? relation region with region,division,account,qtr1,qtr2,qtr3,qtr4
? listflds

DATABASE COMPANY

FIELD     TYPE    LENGTH  KEY  RELATION
-----     ----    ------  ---  --------
DIVISION  TEXT        8   YES
REGION    TEXT        4   YES
ACCOUNT   TEXT       12
QTR1      REAL        1
QTR2      REAL        1
QTR3      REAL        1
QTR4      REAL        1
DIVISION  TEXT        8   YES  PRODUCT
REGION    TEXT        4   YES  PRODUCT
ACCOUNT   TEXT       12        PRODUCT
QTR1      REAL        1        PRODUCT
QTR2      REAL        1        PRODUCT
QTR3      REAL        1        PRODUCT
QTR4      REAL        1        PRODUCT
REGION    TEXT        4   YES  REGION
DIVISION  TEXT        8   YES  REGION
ACCOUNT   TEXT       12        REGION
QTR1      REAL        1        REGION
QTR2      REAL        1        REGION
QTR3      REAL        1        REGION
QTR4      REAL        1        REGION
```

FIGURE 10-13. DEFINING FIELDS AND RELATIONS IN DATABASE COMPANY

2. Type: Three options are available:REAL, INT, TEXT

•REAL refers to numbers with decimal points.
•INT refers to numbers without decimal points.
The default type (if you don't specify) is REAL.

3. Length The number of characters in the field. If you want a variable number, specify VAR.
The default lengths are 1 for REAL and INT and 8 characters for TEXT.
The maximum length is 150 characters.

4. Key This component is entirely optional. If you specify KEY for a particular field, IFPS creates an index file for that field. This index file (which is separate from the data) orders the values within the field in either numeric or alphabetic order.Keys speed up computation if you use the variable for search or retrieval. However, there is a considerable setup cost. Therefore, use keys with discretion.

If you examine the definition of fields in Figure 10-13, you will see that division, region, and account have been set up as text fields with division and region (the two ways we intend to search and analyze data) defined as key. The numeric data for each quarter have been defined as real. Note that we have chosen to use the default definition of REAL for QTR3 and QTR4. This is perfectly all right.

DEFINING RELATIONS. The following is a typical RELATION...WITH command:

```
RELATION PRODUCT WITH DIVISION,REGION,ACCOUNT,INCOME
```

You specify the identifier RELATION followed by the name of the relation (PRODUCT in this example), the word WITH, and then a list of the names of the fields in the relation. The list of fields is equivalent to defining column names in a model.

LISTING THE DATABASE FIELDS AND RELATIONS. Figure 10-13 also shows the fields and the relations in which they appear. To obtain this list, you use the command:

```
LISTFLDS
```

The result of LISTFLDS is a listing of the fields in the order you defined them followed by a listing of the fields in each relation you defined in the order you defined them. Thus, in the figure, all the fields of relation PRODUCT and of relation REGION follow the definition of the fields themselves.

You can obtain a listing of the status of a relation by using the command:

```
LISTREL
```

As shown in Figure 10-14, you are shown the fields in the relation and the current number of rows defined in the relation.

```
? listrel product
                RELATION: PRODUCT

LAST MOD: 05/01/86              READ PASSWORD:    NONE
DATABASE: COMPANY               MODIFY PASSWORD:  NONE

NAME         TYPE    LENGTH    KEY
----         ----    ------    ---
DIVISION     TEXT         8    YES
REGION       TEXT         4    YES
ACCOUNT      TEXT        12
QTR1         REAL         1
QTR2         REAL         1
QTR3         REAL         1
QTR4         REAL         1

CURRENT NUMBER OF ROWS= 0
```

FIGURE 10-14. USING LISTREL

SPACE CONSIDERATIONS. When you create a data base, IFPS automatically sets up three files of equal size in your directory of equal length. A minimum block size is allocated to each file whether you use it or not. If you have limited file space assigned to you (e.g., student accounts) or if your budget is charged for storage space at a high rate, you should be careful in the number of data bases you set up. At the other end, the initial allocation is not a limit. The amount of space allocated will increase if you use up more than the default amount provided initially. If you have questions, consult your computer center operations group.

10.2.5 Entering Data Directly into a Relation (AUTO, LIST, SIZE)

ENTERING DATA. Having defined the data base, you are ready to enter data into it. This is done in the RELATION subsystem. You can enter this subsystem only if you have opened the data file with a DATAFILE command. The process is shown in Figure 10-15.

Your first step is to ask for the relation by name; e.g.,

```
RELATION PRODUCT
```

You are told the number of rows currently in the relation. You then have to specify the names of the fields in which you want to enter data. For example

```
FIELDS DIVISION, REGION, ACCOUNT, QTR4
```

If you want to enter data in all fields in a relation, use FIELDS ALL. It will then help you to give the command AUTO. AUTO prompts you for fields in the order in which they occur, one field at a time. As you use the AUTO feature, you may rapidly become tired of the prompts. In that case, you can enter several items of data in sequence or enter the entire row. You must, however, obtain a new prompt for each new row. This idea is illustrated in Figure 10-15. We entered the data for rows 1 and 2 one field at a time. For row 3, however, we entered the data for all four quarters on the same line. Then, for the remaining rows, we entered the entire row in response to the DIVISION prompt.

```
? relation product
RELATION HAS 0 ROWS
READY FOR RELATION COMMAND
? fields are all
? auto
1 DIVISION ? chemical
1 REGION ? east
1 ACCOUNT ? sales
1 QTR1 ? 350
1 QTR2 ? 450
1 QTR3 ? 400
1 QTR4 ? 350
2 DIVISION ? chemical
2 REGION ? east
2 ACCOUNT ? expenses
2 QTR1 ? 100
2 QTR2 ? 150
2 QTR3 ? 150
2 QTR4 ? 140
3 DIVISION ? chemical
3 REGION ? east
3 ACCOUNT ? overhead
3 QTR1 ? 140,180,160,140
4 DIVISION ? chemical,intl,sales,500,500,700,800
5 DIVISION ? chemical intl,expenses,200,225,300,350
6 DIVISION ? chemical,intl,overhead,250,250,350,400
7 DIVISION ? end
END OF AUTO INPUT
READY FOR RELATION COMMAND
```

FIGURE 10-15. ENTERING DATA INTO A RELATION

When you have completed entering data, you must tell IFPS you are done so that you can go on to something else. You type

END

in response to a prompt.

> *NOTE:* If you have the same data repeated a number of times, you can use FOR. For example,
>
> **100 FOR 4**
>
> If you already have some data in the relation, IFPS will prompt you with the next available line number. For example, if you have entered 6 rows of a relation, you will be prompted for row 7.

Text fields store upper and lower case data in the same way that you enter them. (see Figure 10-16.)

LISTING DATA. To check the data you have in a relation, you can use the LIST command. This is done in Figure 10-16. Figure 10-16 also shows the use of the SIZE option. This option specifies the number of characters and format in which a field is to be displayed. For TEXT and INT fields, only the number of characters is needed. For REAL fields, the number of decimals places can be specified. For example:

```
SIZE ACCOUNT 10
SIZE QTR1 9 2
```

```
READY FOR RELATION COMMAND
? size division 9
? size region 5
? size account 9
? size all real 6 2
? fields are all
? list

ROW  DIVISION   REGIO  ACCOUNT      QTR1    QTR2    QTR3    QTR4
---  ---------  -----  ---------  ------  ------  ------  ------
  1  chemical   east   sales      350.00  450.00  400.00  350.00
  2  chemical   east   expenses   100.00  150.00  150.00  140.00
  3  chemical   east   overhead   140.00  180.00  160.00  140.00
  4  chemical   intl   sales      500.00  500.00  700.00  800.00
  5  chemical   expe   200        225.00  300.00  350.00  400.00
  6  chemical   intl   overhead   250.00  250.00  350.00  400.00
```

FIGURE 10-16. LISTING A RELATION WITH THE LIST COMMAND

In the case of REAL, the first digit represents the total spaces (remember to leave one space for the decimal point!) and the second the number of decimal places. If you do not specify decimal places, IFPS gives you a floating decimal point based on the size of the number.

You can specify that all numbers of a given type have the same field size by saying SIZE ALL. For example:

```
SIZE ALL REAL 9 2
```

DELETING ALL DATA FROM A RELATION. Every so often you may want to update all the data in a relation. To do so, you use the

```
DELETE DATA
```

command. In the example shown in Figure 10-17, RELATION PRODUCT contained 6 rows. Following DELETE DATA, a listing of the relation shows it contained 0 rows.

DELETE DATA is one of several commands available for changing and editing relations. Additional commands are described in Section 10.2.10.

```
? relation product
RELATION HAS 6 ROWS
READY FOR RELATION COMMAND
? delete data
ALL ROWS DELETED FROM RELATION PRODUCT
? list
? relation product
RELATION HAS 0 ROWS
READY FOR RELATION COMMAND
```

FIGURE 10-17. DELETING ALL DATA FROM A RELATION

10.2.6 Using Model Output to Enter Data in a Relation (STOREDB)

The STOREDB command is used to enter data into a relation directly from the solution of a model. The advantages of this procedure are:

1. You do not have to enter data by hand.
2. The results of solving a model can be retrieved for later use.

The procedure is straightforward.

1. Open the data base with a DATABASE command (if you have not already done so).
2. Ask for a model.
3. Give the STOREDB command followed by the name of the relation.

There are two cases: you have not defined the relation previously or you call for an existing relation.

CREATING A NEW RELATION FROM A MODEL. If a relation does not exist, IFPS will go through the following typical sequence:

```
?storedb country
MODEL INCOME1 VERSION OF 03/16/86 23:54--4 COLS 5 VARS
RELATION DOES NOT EXIST
DO YOU WANT TO CREATE A NEW RELATION (YES OR NO)
?yes
ENTER STORE OPTIONS
```

At this point you must specify the relation in terms of the variables and columns of the model and the other conditions in the relation. For example, you might ask for:

```
?VARIABLE IS ACCOUNT 8
?COUNTRY IS "NORWAY" 8
?COLUMNS 1-4 ARE QTR1 THROUGH QTR4 REAL 6
?SALES,EXPENSES, OVERHEAD, NONE
```

The result of this series of instructions is a relation whose fields are ACCOUNT, COUNTRY, QTR1, QTR2, QTR3, QTR4 and whose rows are the sales, expenses, and overhead of goods sold in Norway.

Three conventions are used here:

1. VARIABLE IS — tells IFPS that the name of the variable in the model is to be put into the field named. In our example, the variables are to be in the account field.
2. COLUMNS ...ARE — specifies the fields into which each column is to be put.
3. variables,..NONE — The last line of the definition always contains the names of the variables to be added as rows of data in the relation. The last item in the list must be NONE. This variable list corresponds to the variable list in a solve option and may include some or all variables.

Figure 10-18 illustrates how you can create a relation from a model output. The figure shows a listing of the model, the dialog used to create the relation, and a listing of the resulting data in the relation. The listing of the relation shows that only the lines requested in the variable list (under STORE OPTIONS) are stored in the relation.

IF a model has not been solved, STOREDB first solves the model and then updates the relation. If the model has been solved, STOREDB takes data from the model according to instructions. It is therefore possible to give several STOREDB commands following a SOLVE command if you want to put data into two or more relations.

```
? database company
DATABASE COMPANY OPENED
? model income1
READY FOR EDIT, LAST LINE IS 60
? list
MODEL INCOME1  VERSION OF  03/16/86  23:54
10 COLUMNS QTR1,QTR2,QTR3,QTR4
20 SALES=350,450,400,350
30 EXPENSES = 100,150,160,140
40 GROSS INCOME = SALES -EXPENSES
50 OVERHEAD = .4*SALES
60 NET INCOME = GROSS INCOME -OVERHEAD
END OF MODEL
? storedb country
MODEL INCOME1  VERSION OF  03/16/86  23:54 -- 4 COLUMNS 5 VARIABLES
RELATION DOES NOT EXIST
DO YOU WANT TO CREATE A NEW RELATION (YES OR NO)
? yes
ENTER STORE OPTIONS
? variable is account 8
? country is "NORWAY" 8
? columns 1-4 are QTR1,QTR2,QTR3,QTR4
? SALES,EXPENSES,OVERHEAD
ENTER MORE VARIABLES FOR STORE PROCESSING (OR NONE)
? NONE
STOREDB UPDATE COMPLETE
```

FIGURE 10-18. CREATING A RELATION FROM A MODEL

(This Figure is Continued on the Next Page)

```
? RELATION COUNTRY
RELATION HAS 3 ROWS
READY FOR RELATION COMMAND
? LIST

ROW ACCOUNT        COUNTRY      QTR1      QTR2      QTR3      QTR4
--- ------------   ----------   --------  --------  --------  --------
  1 SALES          NORWAY       350       450       400       350
  2 EXPENSES       NORWAY       100       150       160       140
  3 OVERHEAD       NORWAY       140       180       160       140
```

FIGURE 10-18. CREATING A RELATION FROM A MODEL
(Continued)

USING MODEL OUTPUT TO UPDATE AN EXISTING RELATION. If a relation has already been defined, you can add data to the relation from a model output. As shown in Figure 10-19, the only difference between adding to an existing relation and defining a new relation is that you need to specify only the field names since field attributes such as length and type are already defined.

```
? MODEL INCOME1
READY FOR EDIT, LAST LINE IS 60
? STOREDB REGION
MODEL INCOME1  VERSION OF  03/16/86  23:54 -- 4 COLUMNS 5 VARIABLES
RELATION REGION HAS 3 TEXT FIELD(S) AND 4 DATA FIELDS
ENTER STORE OPTIONS
? VARIABLE IS ACCOUNT
? COLUMNS 1-4 ARE QTR1 THRU QTR4
? DIVISION IS "CHEMICAL"
? REGION IS "EAST"
? SALES,EXPENSES,OVERHEAD,NONE
STOREDB UPDATE COMPLETE
? RELATION REGION
RELATION HAS 3 ROWS
READY FOR RELATION COMMAND
? LIST

ROW REGI DIVISION ACCOUNT              QTR1      QTR2      QTR3      QTR4
--- ---- -------- ------------     --------  --------  --------  --------
  1 EAST CHEMICAL SALES                 350       450       400       350
  2 EAST CHEMICAL EXPENSES              100       150       160       140
  3 EAST CHEMICAL OVERHEAD              140       180       160       140
```

FIGURE 10-19. CREATING DATA IN AN EXISTING RELATION FROM A MODEL

USING DATAFILES WITH A MODEL TO UPDATE A RELATION . Data files can be used either with models or directly to create or update a relation. In Figure 10-20, a data file (CHEMINTL) is used together with a model (INCOME) to add to a relation (REGION). The only differences from the previous case are that the original data were stored in a data file and that the MODEL ... USING form (Sec. 4.6.3) combines the model and the data file.

```
? MODEL INCOME USING CHEMINTL
READY FOR EDIT, LAST LINE IS 60
? STOREDB REGION
MODEL INCOME  VERSION OF  03/16/86  23:55 -- 4 COLUMNS 5 VARIABLES
RELATION REGION HAS 3 TEXT FIELD(S) AND 4 DATA FIELDS
ENTER STORE OPTIONS
? VARIABLE IS ACCOUNT
? COLUMNS 1-4 ARE QTR1 THRU QTR4
? REGION IS "INT"
? DIVISION IS "CHEMICAL"
? SALES,EXPENSES,OVERHEAD
ENTER MORE VARIABLES FOR STORE PROCESSING (OR NONE)
? NONE
STOREDB UPDATE COMPLETE
? RELATION REGION
RELATION HAS 6 ROWS
READY FOR RELATION COMMAND
? LIST

ROW  REGI  DIVISION  ACCOUNT           QTR1        QTR2        QTR3        QTR4
---  ----  --------  ------------ ------  ----------  ----------  ----------
  1  EAST  CHEMICAL  SALES              350         450         400         350
  2  EAST  CHEMICAL  EXPENSES           100         150         160         140
  3  EAST  CHEMICAL  OVERHEAD           140         180         160         140
  4  INT   CHEMICAL  SALES              500         500         700         800
  5  INT   CHEMICAL  EXPENSES           200         225         300         350
  6  INT   CHEMICAL  OVERHEAD           250         250         350         400
```

FIGURE 10-20. UPDATING DATA IN AN EXISTING RELATION FROM A MODEL USING DATA FILES

UPDATING A RELATION FROM A DATAFILE. If data to be included in a relation are in a data file, they can be transferred by using the following sequence:

1. Call the data file.

2. Solve the data file

3. STOREDB

In Figure 10-21we start with an empty relation. The data file is called and listed. After solving the data file, we ask use STOREDB to move data to the relation. We then list the relation to show that the data have been moved.

```
? RELATION REGION
RELATION HAS 6 ROWS
READY FOR RELATION COMMAND
? DATAFILE CHEMEAST
READY FOR EDIT, LAST LINE IS 3
? LIST
1 SALES=350,450,400,350
2 EXPENSES = 100,150,160,140
3 OVERHEAD =140,180,160,140? SOLVE

ENTER SOLVE OPTIONS
? STOREDB REGION
RELATION REGION HAS 3 TEXT FIELD(S) AND 4 DATA FIELDS
ENTER STORE OPTIONS
? VARIABLE IS ACCOUNT
? COLUMNS 1-4 ARE QTR1 THRU QTR4
? REGION IS "EAST"
? DIVISION IS "CHEMICAL"
? ALL

STOREDB UPDATE COMPLETE
? RELATION REGION
RELATION HAS 6 ROWS
READY FOR RELATION COMMAND
? LIST

ROW  REGI  DIVISION  ACCOUNT          QTR1      QTR2      QTR3      QTR4
---  ----  --------  ------------  --------  --------  --------  --------
  1  EAST  CHEMICAL  SALES              350       450       400       350
  2  EAST  CHEMICAL  EXPENSES           100       150       160       140
  3  EAST  CHEMICAL  OVERHEAD           140       180       160       140
  4  INT   CHEMICAL  SALES              500       500       700       800
  5  INT   CHEMICAL  EXPENSES           200       225       300       350
  6  INT   CHEMICAL  OVERHEAD           250       250       350       400
```

FIGURE 10-21. SOLVING A DATA FILE TO UPDATE A RELATION

10.2.7 Solving a Model Using the Data Base (DBDEFINE, DBDATA, GETDB, CONSOLDB)

In the previous three subsections we have shown three different ways of getting data into a data base:

- Creating the data base directly (Sec. 10.2.4).
- Entering data into an existing relation (10.2.5).
- Using model and data file output (Sec. 10.2.6).

In this and the following sections we will be concerned with using the data that already exist in a data file. This can be done in two ways: (1) Solving a model using data in a data base, or (2) using the QUERY subsystem. Item (1) is discussed in this subsection and item (2) in the following three subsections.

DEFINING THE DATA TO BE USED . Data bases, like data files, can be used to put data into models. As was shown in Section 4.6, a model could be used with a data file through:

MODEL name USING datafilename

That is, you selected the data file by referring to it at the time you solved the model. In the case of data bases, you have to do two things:

1. Open the data base or data bases
2. Define the relations within the model by using DBDEFINE.

The DBDEFINE statement has the form:

DBDEFINE name FROM relation

Each DBDEFINE is given a name (for example SUBSET), followed by the word FROM and the name of the relation being used. By setting up the DBDEFINE statement in this way, IFPS not only allows you to select the relation but lets you create subsets of the relation which apply only to the current model. You do this by using three types of modifying statements following DBDEFINE:

VARIABLE IS	selects the text field in the relation to be used as the IFPS variable (i.e. the right hands side of the equal sign).
COLUMNS ARE	selects the fields to be used for the columns in the IFPS model. These must be numeric (not text) fields.
WHERE	restricts the rows to be referenced further. Restrictions are written in the form of logical relations using the logical variables (EQ, NE, GT, GE, LT, AND, and OR). Up to five AND and/or OR conditions can be used in a WHERE statement.

Thus, the combination of DBDEFINE, VARIABLE IS, COLUMNS ARE, and WHERE specify the portions of the data base to be used. You still need to specify where the data go. This is done with the DBDATA statement. The following, taken from Figure 10-22 is an example:

```
100 SALES = DBDATA FROM SUBSET
```

Here DBDATA is a keyword followed by FROM and the name of a DBDEFINE. Line 100 tells IFPS that the right hand side is to be obtained according to the specification given by the DBDEFINE named SUBSET.

Figure 10-22 is an example of a model that uses DBDEFINE to extract data from data base COMPANY. The model uses data on the CHEMEAST division stored in the data base to obtain annual totals and to compute a profit ratio. The information to be used from the data base is defined by Lines 50 through 80:

Lines 50	DBDEFINE is named SUBSET and uses the relation PRODUCT (see Fig. 10-6)
Line 60	The ACCOUNT field will serve as the variable name.
Line 70	The fields labeled QTR1,QTR2,QTR3,and QTR4 will be columns 1 through 4.
Line 80	Only rows for which the field DIVISION is CHEMICAL and the field REGION is EAST are to be used. Note use of " " marks in this line. IFPS matches the name in the field with the " " specification.

```
? DATABASE COMPANY
DATABASE COMPANY OPENED
?MODEL CHEMEAST   VERSION OF   05/04/86  12:45
10 COLUMNS QTR1,QTR2,QTR3,QTR4,YEAR
20*
30*ANNUAL PROFITABILITY REPORT FOR CHEMEAST OBTAINED BY USING DBDEFINE
40*
50 DBDEFINE SUBSET FROM PRODUCT
60 VARIABLE IS ACCOUNT
70 COLUMNS ARE QTR1 THRU QTR4
80 WHERE DIVISION EQ "CHEMICAL" AND REGION EQ "EAST"
90*
100 SALES = DBDATA FROM SUBSET
120 EXPENSES = DBDATA FROM SUBSET
130 OVERHEAD = DBDATA FROM SUBSET
140 PROFIT = SALES - EXPENSES - OVERHEAD
150*
160 PROFIT RATIO = PROFIT/SALES
180COLUMN YEAR FOR SALES THRU PROFIT =SUM(C1 THRU C4)
190COLUMN YEAR FOR PROFIT RATIO =PROFIT/SALES
END OF MODEL
? SOLVE
MODEL CHEMEAST   VERSION OF   05/04/86   12:45 -- 5 COLUMNS 5 VARIABLES
ENTER SOLVE OPTIONS
? WIDTH 62 20 7
? ALL
                              QTR1    QTR2    QTR3    QTR4    YEAR

ANNUAL PROFITABILITY REPORT FOR CHEMEAST OBTAINED BY USING DBDEFINE

SALES                          350     450     400     350    1550
EXPENSES                       100     150     160     140     550
OVERHEAD                       140     180     160     140     620
PROFIT                         110     120      90      70     390

PROFIT RATIO                 .3143   .2667   .2000   .2000   .2452
```

FIGURE 10-22. USING DBDEFINE TO OBTAIN DATA FOR SOLVING A MODEL

The sales, expenses, and overhead data are picked out of the data base by putting DBDATA FROM SUBSET on the right hand sides of Lines 100 through 130.

The model computes the profit and the profit ratio from the data. The COLUMNS statements (Lines 180 and 190) create the annualized values.

EXERCISE: Figure 10-22 is written specifically for data on CHEMEAST. You can generalize the model by writing &PRODUCT& in place of "CHEMICAL" and &REGION& in place of "EAST". Make this change and rerun Figure 10-22 for the International division of electronics and the West division of steel.

DEALING WITH LARGE AMOUNTS OF DATA . The approach used in Figure 10-22 is excellent when you are dealing with small amounts of data. However, if you are uncertain about the amount of data you have and want a row of output for each data item, you add GETDB statement(s) to the DBDEFINE specification. GETDB generates a separate variable for each row that matches its specifications. These specifications include:

- the line number in the model that contains the "template" which defines how much data are to be used. This line number must be the next line in the model following the GETDB statement. (GETDB L100),
- AT
- the line number that IFPS will assign to the first statement that is generated by the GETDB (AT 120)
- FROM follwed by the name of the DBDEFINE,
- BY and an increment to indicate the increment in line number between successive statements (BY 10),
- LIMIT and a number to indicate the maximum number of lines to be generated (LIMIT 5).

Both BY and LIMIT are optional. The default values are BY 1 and LIMIT 100.

Figure 10-23 shows how the CHEMEAST report of Figure 10-22 would be written in the GETDB form. Note that DEFINEDB, COLUMNS, and WHERE are still used but VARIABLE (which was Line 60 in Figure 10-22 and defined ACCOUNT as the variable name) is no longer needed.

Line 90 — The GETDB statement tells IFPS to look at Line 100 (the next line in the model!) and put statements into the model starting at Line 110 in increments of 10 according to the DBDEFINE named subset.

Line 100 — This is the "template" line. It tells IFPS to use each ACCOUNT field that satisfies the DBDEFINE. Remember that the FOR 4 is required. You *must* give IFPS reference to as many columns as you obtain data from the data base.

Line 150 — This line was Line 140 in Figure 10-22. It had to be moved because the template created Lines 110 through 140. (How could we have gotten around this problem?)

In general, the template (Line 100 in our case) has the definition of the field (or fields) to be used on the left-hand side and DBDATA on the right-hand side.

```
?DATABASE COMPANY
DATABASE COMPANY OPENED
MODEL CHEMEAS1  VERSION OF  05/04/86  12:57
10 COLUMNS QTR1,QTR2,QTR3,QTR4,YEAR
20*
30*ANNUAL PROFITABILITY REPORT FOR CHEMEAST OBTAINED BY USING DBDEFINI
40*
50 DBDEFINE SUBSET FROM PRODUCT
70 COLUMNS ARE QTR1 THRU QTR4
80 WHERE DIVISION EQ "CHEMICAL" AND REGION EQ "EAST"
90 GETDB L100 AT L110 BY 10 FROM SUBSET
100 ACCOUNT = DBDATA FOR 4
150 PROFIT=SALES-EXPENSES-OVERHEAD
160 PROFIT RATIO = PROFIT/SALES
170*
180COLUMN YEAR FOR SALES THRU PROFIT =SUM(C1 THRU C4)
190COLUMN YEAR FOR PROFIT RATIO =PROFIT/SALES
END OF MODEL
? SOLVE

MODEL CHEMEAS1  VERSION OF  05/04/86  12:57 -- 5 COLUMNS 5 VARIABLES
ENTER SOLVE OPTIONS
? WIDTH 62 20 7
? ALL

                         QTR1   QTR2   QTR3   QTR4   YEAR


ANNUAL PROFITABILITY REPORT FOR CHEMEAST OBTAINED BY USING DBDEFINE

SALES                     350    450    400    350   1550
EXPENSES                  100    150    160    140    550
OVERHEAD                  140    180    160    140    620
PROFIT                    110    120     80     70    380
PROFIT RATIO            .3143  .2667  .2000  .2000  .2452
```

FIGURE 10-23. USING GETDB WITH DBDEFINE TO OBTAIN DATA FOR SOLVING A MODEL

EXERCISE: The WHERE line is not needed if you specify the fields completely. Thus, Line 100 could be written

```
100 ACCOUNT "CHEMICAL" "EAST" = DBDATA FOR 4
```

The result will be output variables of the form

```
OVERHEAD CHEMICAL EAST
```

Make this change in Figure 10-23 and solve. You will get an error message involving undefined variables. The reason is that the variables profit and profit ratio refer to variables named sales, expenses, and overhead. Change the names of these variables in Lines 150 and 160 appropriately and solve again.

CONSOLIDATING DIRECTLY FROM A DATA BASE. The GETDB concept can be extended directly for use in consolidation by using CONSOLDB in place of GETDB. The main difference is that in CONSOLDB you set up broader categories to make sure you get all the pieces and that consolidation really takes place. For example, if we want to consolidate all the data in data base COMPANY, we would write Lines 50 through 100 in Figure 10-23 as:

```
50 DBDEFINE SUBSET FROM PRODUCT
70 COLUMNS ARE QTR1 THROUGH QTR4
90 CONSOLDB L100 AT L101 BY 1 FROM SUBSET
100 ACCOUNT = DBDATA FOR 4
```

EXERCISE: Change Figure 10-23 as indicated and SOLVE.

10.2.8 Asking Simple Questions of the Data Base (QUERY, LIST, WHERE, FIELDS ARE, BREAK ON, REVIEW)

In our discussion thus far of IFPS/DIMENSION we have concentrated on creating the data base, putting data into it, and using information in a data base when solving a model. In this section and the next one we discuss how you can get information out of the data base to be able to use it. As Figure 10-11 showed, IFPS/DIMENSION contains a QUERY subsystem which allows you to analyze data in a data base and create reports directly from it. Among other things in the QUERY subsystem, you can look at data in a single relation or in two relations simultaneously; you can perform simple computations (such as addition in a column or a row); and you can store the results of your query as a new relation. In this section, we will concentrate on asking simple questions of the data base. The fancier, more complex inquiries and capabilities are discussed in Sections 10.2.9 and 10.2.10.

ENTERING THE QUERY SUBSYSTEM (QUERY). To enter the QUERY subsystem, you have to do two things:

1. Open the data base by typing DATABASE followed by name of the data base.

2. Use the key word QUERY followed by the name of the relation.

Step 1 is needed only if the data base you are using is not open.

LISTING THE ENTIRE DATA BASE (LIST). The simplest QUERY operation is to list the entire data base. This is done with the LIST command. The sequence of QUERY and LIST is illustrated in Figure 10-24. The figure shows all the data in relation PRODUCT, which was defined in Figure 10-14. In the rest of this section, we will use the data in relation PRODUCT to illustrate the various QUERY options.

LIST is more general than just listing the entire data base. In general, whenever you ask for LIST, you obtain the set of fields and rows you have defined in the QUERY subsystem.

SELECTING DATA FROM THE RELATION (WHERE, FIELDS ARE, BREAK ON). For a large data base (and even for a small one), you generally want to see only part of the information stored. You can select:

- Rows by using WHERE
- Columns by using FIELDS ARE

```
?QUERY PRODUCT
READY FOR QUERY COMMAND
? LIST

DIVISION  REGI  ACCOUNT          QTR1      QTR2      QTR3      QTR4
--------  ----  ------------   --------  --------  --------  --------

CHEMICAL  EAST  SALES             350       450       400       350
CHEMICAL  EAST  EXPENSES          100       150       160       140
CHEMICAL  EAST  OVERHEAD          140       180       160       140
CHEMICAL  INTL  SALES             500       500       700       800
CHEMICAL  INTL  EXPENSES          200       225       300       350
CHEMICAL  INTL  OVERHEAD          250       250       350       400
ELECTRO   EAST  SALES             100       125       150       160
ELECTRO   EAST  EXPENSES           40        50        60        70
ELECTRO   EAST  OVERHEAD           50     62.50        75        80
ELECTRO   WEST  SALES             200       250       300       320
ELECTRO   WEST  EXPENSES           60        70        80        90
ELECTRO   WEST  OVERHEAD          100       125       150       160
ELECTRO   INTL  SALES              50        65        75       100
ELECTRO   INTL  EXPENSES           20        25        30        35
ELECTRO   INTL  OVERHEAD           30        39        45        60
STEEL     EAST  SALES              20        30        35        45
STEEL     EAST  EXPENSES           10        15        25        25
STEEL     EAST  OVERHEAD            6         9     10.50     13.50
STEEL     WEST  SALES               2         3     3.500         5
STEEL     WEST  EXPENSES            1     1.500     1.500         3
STEEL     WEST  OVERHEAD        .6000     .9000     1.050     1.500
```

FIGURE 10-24. QUERY AND LIST COMMANDS

If you want the data organized by some characteristic, you can sort and sequence them by using:

```
BREAK ON
```

For example, in dealing with relation PRODUCT, we may want to see only the international data. To do so, you type in

```
? WHERE REGION EQ "INTL"
```

Note the sequence that you follow. You type WHERE, the name of the field(s) on which the selection is to be based, and the condition to be imposed. In this case, the field is "region" and the condition is "equal international." In general, you can use any logical operator:

Operator	Meaning	Operator	Meaning
EQ	Equal	NE	Not Equal
GT	Greater than	GE	Greater or equal
LT	Less than	LE	Less or equal
AND	Both true	OR	Either true

For example, you might specify

```
WHERE ACCOUNT EQ "SALES" AND (QTR1 GT 175 OR QTR4 LE 50)
```

to select units with first quarter sales above 175 or fourth quarter sales of 50 or below.

If you simply ask for WHERE you will see a listing of all the data in each row in the order in which they are stored. To make some sense out of the data, you can add two other conditions:

1. FIELDS ARE selects the columns you want shown. FIELDS ARE is followed by a list of the columns you want in the order you want them.

2. BREAK ON sorts the rows of the data by category. You specify the fields on which you want the sorting to be performed; e.g., ACCOUNT, DIVISION.

Figure 10-25 shows the result of listing data selected by WHERE, FIELDS ARE and BREAK ON. The fields shown are those specified by BREAK ON and FIELDS ARE. Note that the data are given in order of account and within account by division even though the data are stored differently in the data base. Thus, BREAK ON and FIELDS ARE are simple ways of specifying output format.

```
? QUERY  PRODUCT
READY FOR QUERY COMMAND
? WHERE REGION EQ "INTL"
? FIELDS ARE QTR1 THRU QTR4
? BREAK ON ACCOUNT, DIVISION
? LIST
```

ACCOUNT	DIVISION	QTR1	QTR2	QTR3	QTR4
EXPENSES	CHEMICAL	200	225	300	350
	ELECTRO	20	25	30	35
OVERHEAD	CHEMICAL	250	250	350	400
	ELECTRO	30	39	45	60
SALES	CHEMICAL	500	500	700	800
	ELECTRO	50	65	75	100

FIGURE 10-25. SELECTING DATA BY WHERE, FIELDS ARE, BREAK ON

SIMPLE EDITING COMMANDS (CENTER, LINEWIDTH, SIZE). Format commands similar to those available for reports are available for queries. Figure 10-26 shows three of these commands.

- CENTER allows you to type a title, centered.

- LINEWIDTH specifies the number of characters on a line. The word LINEWIDTH should be followed by a number. If it is not, 78 characters per line is the default value.

- SIZE specifies the number of characters in a field. The first number you specify is the number of characters, the second the number of decimal places. For example, SIZE 10 3 specifies 10 characters and three decimal places. (Remember that the decimal point takes up one character.) The default SIZE is 8 characters.

```
? QUERY PRODUCT
READY FOR QUERY COMMAND
? WHERE REGION  EQ "INTL"
? FIELDS ARE QTR1 THRU QTR4
? BREAK ON ACCOUNT,DIVISION
? CENTER INTERNATIONAL RESULTS BY ACCOUNT
? LINEWIDTH 50
? SIZE ACCOUNT 8
? SIZE QTR1 THRU QTR4 6
? LIST

               INTERNATIONAL RESULTS BY ACCOUNT

ACCOUNT   DIVISION     QTR1      QTR2     QTR3     QTR4
--------  --------   ------    ------   ------   ------
EXPENSES  CHEMICAL      200       225      300      350
          ELECTRO        20        25       30       35
OVERHEAD  CHEMICAL      250       250      350      400
          ELECTRO        30        39       45       60
SALES     CHEMICAL      500       500      700      800
          ELECTRO        50        65       75      100


? REVIEW
FIELDS ARE QTR1 THRU QTR4
WHERE REGION EQ "INTL"
BREAK ON ACCOUNT,DIVISION
SIZE ACCOUNT 8
SIZE QTR1 THRU QTR4 6
CENTER INTERNATIONAL RESULTS BY ACCOUNT
LINEWIDTH 50
```

FIGURE 10-26.USING EDITING COMMANDS (CENTER,LINEWIDTH,SIZE) AND REVIEW

FINDING OUT WHERE YOU ARE (REVIEW). Because QUERY commands remain in force until you change them, you may, from time to time, want to check the current set of instructions. The REVIEW command, which is similar to CASELIST for WHAT IF (See Sec. 3.1.6), lets you do so. An example is shown in Figure 10-26.

10.2.9 Asking Questions of the Data Base that Create New Data (COMPUTE, SUM, SUBTOTAL, TOTAL, ACROSS, SAVE AS)

Elementary computational and merging capabilities are provided in IFPS/DIMENSION which, in effect, create new information. You can store these results in new relations within the data base.

COMPUTING NEW VARIABLES (COMPUTE). From a management point of view, you are often more interested in values computed from the data than the raw information stored in the data base. For example, you may have quarterly results in the data base but you are interested in the total for the year. To obtain annual data, you use the COMPUTE statement; for example:

```
?COMPUTE YEAR = SUM(QTR1 THRU QTR4)
```

The COMPUTE statement creates a new field, YEAR, by adding up the results for the fields starting in QTR1 and ending in QTR4. In effect, you have added a field to the relation. THRU allows specifying a set of fields stored next to one another in a relation. You can also pick specific columns. If you were comparing, say, the first quarter of last year with the first quarter of this year, you might have said: COMPUTE FIRST = QTR1 + QTR5. In general, you can use

1. Any arithmetic operator (+,-,*,/)
2. IF/THEN/ELSE
3. SUM

to define a computational expression involving fields. For example, if sales tax is 6.5%. you might ask for NET SALES = GROSS SALES/1.065.

You can print out the results for a computed variable such as YEAR as a separate column if you put your FIELDS ARE statement *after* your COMPUTE statement. This is one of the few places in IFPS where you have to be procedural; that is, you have to define the variable before you can use it. The reason is that the FIELDS ARE statement checks the the relation and gives you an error message if a field is not yet defined.

Figure 10-27 illustrates the COMPUTE COMMAND. In Figure 10-27, data are obtained for the costs for domestic divisions (note the use of NE with REGION and ACCOUNT).

ADDING TOTAL AND SUBTOTAL ROWS (TOTAL, SUBTOTAL). You can obtain a grand total for selected columns by using the TOTAL option and you can obtain intermediate subtotals with the SUBTOTAL option. As shown in Figure 10-27, the SUBTOTAL option requires you to specify which fields you want subtotaled and the major category by which you want the subtotal. The general form is:

SUBTOTAL names of fields FOR break on fields

That is, you specify the columns you want, separated by commas; use the word FOR; and then list the fields from your BREAK ON categories. In Figure 10-27, for example, the BREAK ON category is ACCOUNT, and hence subtotals are provided for EXPENSES and OVERHEAD. IFPS puts an * in front of the computed subtotal names.

A grand total is added to the output if you specify TOTAL.

ORGANIZING ROWS AND COLUMNS (ACROSS, DESC). Analogous to the INVERT command available in SOLVE options, ACROSS interchanges the rows and columns of a relation when they are displayed. Figure 10-28 illustrates the use of ACROSS. In this example, the results for the fourth quarter are presented for the international region. The quarter and region are specified by use of FIELDS ARE and WHERE. The BREAK ON command organizes the output by divisions. The ACROSS command makes rows in the relation (such as sales) become columns.

```
? QUERY PRODUCT
READY FOR QUERY COMMAND
? WHERE REGION NE "INTL" AND ACCOUNT NE "SALES"
? COMPUTE YEAR =SUM(QTR1 THRU QTR4)
? FIELDS ARE ACCOUNT,REGION,DIVISION,QTR1 THRU QTR4,YEAR
? BREAK ON "ACCOUNT"
? SUBTOTAL QTR1 THRU QTR4,YEAR FOR ACCOUNT
? TOTAL QTR1 THRU QTR4,YEAR
? CENTER COSTS FOR DOMESTIC DIVISIONS
? LIST
                      COSTS FOR DOMESTIC DIVISIONS

ACCOUN   REGI  DIVISION QTR1       QTR2       QTR3       QTR4       YEAR
------   ----  -------- ----      -----      -----      -----      -----
EXPENSES EAST  CHEMICAL  100        150        160        140        550
         EAST  ELECTRO    40         50         60         70        220
         WEST  ELECTRO    60         70         80         90        300
         EAST  STEEL      10         15         25         25         75
         WEST  STEEL       1      1.500      1.500          3          7
                        ----      -----      -----      -----      -----
*EXPENSES                211      286.5      326.5        328       1152

OVERHEAD EAST  CHEMICAL  140        180        160        140        620
         EAST  ELECTRO    50      62.50         75         80      267.5
         WEST  ELECTRO   100        125        150        160        535
         EAST  STEEL       6          9      10.50      13.50         39
         WEST  STEEL   .6000      .9000      1.050      1.500       4.05
                        ----      -----      -----      -----      -----
*OVERHEAD              296.6      377.4      396.6        395       1466
                        ----      -----      -----      -----      -----
*GRAND TOTAL           507.6      663.9      723.1        723       2618
```

FIGURE 10-27. COMPUTING ROW AND COLUMN TOTALS AND SUBTOTALS (COMPUTE, SUBTOTAL, TOTAL)

```
? QUERY PRODUCT
READY FOR QUERY COMMAND
? FIELDS ARE QTR4
? WHERE REGION EQ "INTL"
? BREAK ON DIVISION
? ACROSS ACCOUNT DESC
? SIZE ALL REAL 12 2
? CENTER  FOURTH QUARTER RESULTS FOR INTERNATIONAL REGION
? LIST
           FOURTH QUARTER RESULTS FOR INTERNATIONAL REGION

                   SALES        OVERHEAD        EXPENSES
DIVISION            QTR4            QTR4            QTR4
--------    ------------    ------------    ------------
CHEMICAL          800.00          400.00          350.00
ELECTRO           100.00           60.00           35.00
```

FIGURE 10-28. ORGANIZING DATA USING THE ACROSS COMMAND

In Figure 10-28, DESC is used to put the column headings in descending alphabetical order (i.e. SALES, OVERHEAD,EXPENSES) rather than the usual increasing alphabetical order. Alphabetic order is the default value. (DESC can, in fact, be used anywhere IFPS orders in increasing sequence of number or letter; for example you might write BREAK ON DIVISION DESC.)

Finally, note the expression SIZE ALL REAL 12 2 in Figure 10-28. SIZE ALL makes each number have the same format. In our example, we therefore specify that all numbers should have two decimal places.

COMBINING TWO RELATIONS INTO A NEW RELATION (SAVE AS). The QUERY subsystem allows you to combine data from two relations and, if you like, save the combined data as a new relation. Figure 10-29 illustrates the process. In this figure, data from relation PRODUCT, which we have used throughout our discussion of QUERY, is combined with a relation called STAFF. For our purposes, it is sufficient to know that STAFF contains within it the number of people in each office. The example computes the total sales and the average commission per sales person. The sales are in millions and the commissions are 2% on each million of sales.

To ask a question of two relations, you have to give both their names, separated by a comma, in the query statement. For example,

```
?QUERY PRODUCT,STAFF
```

The implication is that both relations are stored in the data base. The next step is to define those fields that are *common* to both relations, followed by the fields which are unique. Here the relations share a common field, the name of the relation has to be given before the name of the field and separated by a period. In the example, DIVISION and REGION are common to the two relations. This is expressed as:

PRODUCT.DIVISION EQ STAFF.DIVISION
PRODUCT.REGION EQ STAFF.REGION

That is, the information is given in the order:

- Name of the first relation in the QUERY statement
- A period
- Name of the field in the first relation
- EQ
- Name of the second relation in the QUERY statement
- A period
- Name of the field in the second relation.

In Figure 10-29, the field ACCOUNT is unique to the PRODUCT relation.

Two computations are performed. One computes TOTALSALES by adding up fields QTR1 through QTR4. The next computes the average commission by dividing the TOTALSALES obtained from PRODUCT by the size of the STAFF obtained from STAFF. The multipliers in this compute statement reflect the commission and the conversion to actual dollars.

The average commission data is made usable for management by giving sales in millions and commissions in actual dollars and cents. Furthermore, salary and staff are totaled but average commission is not since adding the averages would be meaningless.

Having created the average commission table, you can save it as a new relation. This is done in Figure 10-29 by using the SAVE AS command. All that is required is the words SAVE AS followed by a legal (no more than 8 letters) name for a relation. The resulting relation is listed in Figure 10-30. Note that once a relation has been defined, IFPS asks for a relation command. LIST, in Figure 10-30, is in response to this request.

```
? QUERY PRODUCT,STAFF
READY FOR QUERY COMMAND
? WHERE PRODUCT.DIVISION EQ STAFF.DIVISION AND PRODUCT.REGION EQ'
? STAFF.REGION AND ACCOUNT EQ "SALES"
? COMPUTE TOTALSALES =SUM(QTR1 THRU QTR4)
? COMPUTE AVGCOMMISSION = SUM(QTR1 THRU QTR4)*.20/STAFF
? FIELDS ARE DIVISION,REGION,TOTALSALES,STAFF,AVGCOMMISSION
? BREAK ON DIVISION
? SIZE ALL REAL 10 2
? LINEWIDTH 60
? TOTAL TOTALSALES,STAFF
? CENTER AVERAGE COMMISSION($10,000'S)
? LIST


                 AVERAGE COMMISSION($10,000'S)

DIVISION  REGI    TOTALSAL      STAFF    AVGCOMMI
________  ____  __________  __________  __________

CHEMICAL  EAST     1550.00          45        6.89
          INTL     2500.00          60        8.33
ELECTRO   EAST      535.00          20        5.35
          WEST     1070.00          30        7.13
          INTL      290.00          15        3.87
STEEL     EAST      130.00          12        2.17
          WEST       13.50           6         .45
                __________  __________
*GRAND TOTAL       6088.50         188


READY FOR QUERY COMMAND
? SAVE AS AVGCOMM
SAVE AS OPERATION COMPLETE
? RELATION AVGCOMM
RELATION HAS 7 ROWS
READY FOR RELATION COMMAND
```

FIGURE 10-29. COMBINING DATA FROM TWO RELATIONS AND SAVING THE RESULT AS A NEW RELATION (SAVE AS)

```
? LIST

ROW  DIVISION  REGI  TOTALSAL     STAFF  AVGCOMMI
---  --------  ----  --------  --------  --------
  1  CHEMICAL  EAST      1550        45     6.889
  2  CHEMICAL  INTL      2500        60     8.333
  3  ELECTRO   EAST       535        20     5.350
  4  ELECTRO   WEST      1070        30     7.133
  5  ELECTRO   INTL       290        15     3.867
  6  STEEL     EAST       130        12     2.167
  7  STEEL     WEST     13.50         6     .4500
```

FIGURE 10-30. LISTING OF THE RELATION CREATED IN FIGURE 10-29

10.2.10 Editing the Data Base

A number of editing commands are available to you to make it easier for you to deal with data entry and data update. The following is a list of some of these commands, with an example for each.

The editing commands fall into two categories: those that deal with the individual rows and those that deal with the data base or relation as a whole.

EDITING COMMAND FOR ROWS.

CHANGE The CHANGE command helps you correct data that are wrong. For example, suppose you typed "chemical" instead of "CHEMICAL". To correct this spelling, you would type:

```
CHANGE 1 THRU 3 FOR DIVISION = CHEMICAL FOR 3
```

That is, you specify CHANGE followed by the rows to be changed, the fields to be changed, the equal sign, and the correct values. You must specify as many values as are to be changed. In our example, we wanted to change three rows, therefore we had to specify that CHEMICAL was to be substituted three times. If you don't give IFPS enough data it will prompt you for the missing information.

The following are other examples of CHANGE:

```
CHANGE 2 FOR REGION = "WEST"
CHANGE 1,6 FOR QTR1,QTR3 = 100,300
```

DELETE You can delete rows by simply giving the row number followed by D. If you want to delete a group of rows, you give the first and last row numbers.

```
23D
15,26D
```

PRINT You can obtain a listing of the whole data base with LIST. If you want to see only specific rows, you use the PRINT form which consists of the row number followed by a "P".

```
10P
10,35P
```

EDITING COMMANDS FOR DATA BASE AND RELATIONS

BUILD KEY Allows you to add a KEY field to a relation. It is usually wise to wait until the data base is in use to select the key fields since storing keys uses up memory.

```
BUILD KEY FOR ACCOUNT IN PRODUCT
```

The words BUILD KEY FOR is followed by the name of the field, IN, and the name of the relation.

DELETE KEY Similar to BUILD KEY, but removes key field designation.

```
DELETE KEY FOR ACCOUNT IN PRODUCT
```

ADD FIELD Used to add a field to a relation. The simplest example is:

```
?ADD FIELD CUSTOMER TO PRODUCT
SUCCESSFUL OPERATION WITH 8 ROWS
```

A new field, CUSTOMER, has been added as the last item in the definition of the relation PRODUCT. IFPS replies by telling you that your instruction has been accomplished and the change made in all 8 rows of the relation.

If the field does not exist in the data base, you must first specify it by a FIELD command.

RENAME Lets you change the name of a field or a relation. You must specify the old name and the new name. If you want to make a change in only one relation, you may do so. The default is field name. If you want to change a relation name you have to specify it.

```
RENAME REGION TO AREA
RENAME REGION TO AREA IN PRODUCT
RENAME RELATION PRODUCT TO SERVICE
```

DELETE You can delete a relation, an entire data base, or all the data in a relation.

```
DELETE RELATION REGION
DELETE DATABASE COMPANY
DELETE DATA
```

```
DELETE DATA FROM RELATION REGION
```

<u>WARNING:</u> Delete is a powerful command. There is no "undo" in IFPS.

<u>WARNING:</u> DELETE only marks items for deletion. It does not physically delete them. This is done only with the COMPRESS command.

COMPRESS Any row you marked for deletion remains physically in the data base as a blank line until you type COMPRESS. Compress removes the rows makes storage space available.

<u>WARNING:</u> COMPRESS uses a large amount of CPU time and is expensive to run!

LIMIT LIST, PRINT, DELETE, and CHANGE commands process line numbers between 1 and 1000. To increase the number of lines in the data base, you have to declare a new limit.

LIMIT 2000.

If you want the data base to expand and contract as you add to it or delete, you would ask for LIMIT $.

EXERCISE: Create the six lines of relation PRODUCT shown in Figure 10-30. Edit this relation as follows:

1. Change INTL to WEST for CHEMICAL
2. Print out rows 4, 5, and 6
3. Add ACCOUNT as a key field. Show your action with LISTREL.
4. Delete ACCOUNT as a key field. Show your action with LISTREL
5. Add a field CUSTOMER to the relation.
6. Add customers named VERMONT and NORWAY by using the CHANGE command.
7. Change the name of the REGION field to LOCATION.
8. Add data for a new region, MIDW. Use any values that you please which are three digits.
9. Delete the data for the East region
10. Compress this shorter data base.
11. Delete all data from relation PRODUCT.

APPENDICES

APPENDIX I
HELP COMMANDS

This Appendix describes the HELP commands available in IFPS. It is an expansion of Section 2.10. You should read and be familiar with section 2.10 before strating to use this Appendix as a reference.

A1.1 HELP and HELP HELP

If you type HELP or if you type HELP HELP you will receive the following index

```
?help

HELP Command
Form(s)
 (1)   HELP
 (2)   HELP HELP
 (3)   HELP WHERE
 (4)   HELP CONTENTS
 (5)   HELP *
 (6)   HELP keyword
Usage
       "HELP" and "HELP HELP" provide this message telling how to
       use the HELP command.
       "HELP WHERE" identifies which subsystem the user is currently
       in, along with the currently active file, and specific
       model, report, or structure, as appropriate.
       "HELP CONTENTS" produces a table of contents outlining major
       categories within IFPS.  Instructions are also given for a
       subsequent HELP command for each category, to list all
       corresponding keywords for which help is available.
       "HELP *" prints a list of all keywords available with the
       HELP command.
       "HELP keyword" prints the HELP message for the specified
       keyword.  Valid from any level of IFPS.  Control will remain
       at the level where HELP was entered.

READY FOR EXECUTIVE COMMAND
```

A1.2 HELP WHERE

HELP WHERE tells you here you are in IFPS. For example, if you are in a file named SAMPLE and are working on a model named GRAY, you would see the following three lines in rdesponse to HELP WHERE:

```
? help where

SUBSYSTEM: MODELING
MODEL NAME: GRAY
MODELS AND REPORTS FILE : SAMPLE
READY FOR MODELING LANGUAGE COMMAND
```

A1.3 HELP CONTENTS

HELP CONTENTS divides IFPS into thirteen categories and allows you to obtain a list of keywords that apply to each category. HELP CONTENTS results in the following printout:

```
? help contents

CONTENTS of HELP File
The IFPS  HELP  file  is  organized  into  the  categories shown
below.  For a listing of the commands/options in any category,
enter:HELP category  where  "category" is the keyword identifier
shown to the left of  the  desired category (for instance, HELP
RLS10).


         RLS10    Release 10.0 Commands/Options
         UC       Universal Consolidation
         SROPTS   SOLVE/Report Options
         EXECS    Executive Level Commands
         MODS     Modeling Language Commands
         CMDS     Command File Commands
         DATA     Datafile Subsystem Commands; STORE/STORENT Options
         FUNCS    IFPS Functions & Subroutines
         STMTS    Special Modeling Statements
         SYS      System-dependent Characteristics & Special Helps
         DB       Database Subsystem
         REL      Relation Subsystem
         QRY      Query Subsystem
```

HELP CONTENTS is a subject index. If you want to see the keywords in each category you type HELP followed by the category's name. For example, HELP FUNCS gives you a list of all the built-in functions and subroutines in IFPS. The following example is a list of the keywords in the MODS category.

```
? help mods

MODS - MODELING LANGUAGE COMMANDS
* List of Modeling language commands:
ANALYZE      DEFINITION   HELP       OPTION     RECOMPILE   STORE
AUTO         DFNAME       IMPACT     OPTIONA    RECORD      STOREDB
BASE MODEL   END          LINK       thru       SAVE        STORENT
COMMANDS     GENERATE     LIST       OPTIONP    SENSITIVITY USING
COMPILEGET   GENREPORT    MONTE      PLOT       SOLVE       WHAT IF
COMPILESAVE  GOAL         NORECORD   PRESERVE   SPOOL
```

A1.4 HELP *

HELP * provides you with a list of all the keywords available within the HELP command. This table of contents for help is shown on the next page.

A1.5 HELP KEYWORD

You can obtain an explanation for each keyowrd contained in HELP * by typing the word HELP followed by the keyword. We show you two typical examples below: HELP ABS and HELP SOLVE . The first is a mathematical function that gives the absolute value of a number or expression. The second describes the SOLVE command. Here you will notice that all uses of SOLVE are discussed, such as SUBTASK, with which you may not be familiar or you may not be interested in. This is typical of what you will find in HELP. You will have to decide what is relevant and what is not relevant. *Hint:* Don't spend a lot of time trying to trace down portions of a HELP explanation that seems obscure to you. It usually (but unfortuntately, not always) refeers to a part of IFPS that is not of concern to you at the moment.

```
? help abs

ABS Function
Form
        ABS(expression)
where  "expression" is a variable name or an indicated calculation
involving some variable(s).
Usage
        Computes the algebraic absolute value of the designated
expression. Valid in a computational statement.

? help solve

SOLVE Command
Form(s)
        SOLVE
Usage
        Directs IFPS to solve (execute) the currently active
model or to display a data file with its values in columns.
Numerous SOLVE options are then available to select/format printed
output of the solution.
        Valid in the Modeling subsystem, with a Formula or Subtask,
or in the Datafile subsystem.
```

```
? help*

                   IFPS/Plus 2.0 TOPICS
ABS            COPYL          GROWTHRATE     NAMEINDENT     !PARAMCOMPUTE  SPOOL
ACCESS         CPROMPT        HELP           NAOUTPUT       PASSWORDS      SROPTS
ACROSS         CROSSREF       HIGH           NAPRINT        !PAUSE         STATUSLIST
ACRS           !CSETPARAM     !IF            NATEST         PERIODS        STDDEV
ADDFIELDS      CUMRAND        !IFRC          NATEXP         PLOT           STEP
ALLOCATE       CURRENCY       IMPACT         NATLOG         POLYFIT        STLINE
ALTER          D              INDENT         NEGOPT         POSOPT         STMTS
ALTERLIST      DATA           !INPUT         NEWPAGE        PRESERVE       STORE
AMORT          DATABASE       !INPUTC        NOAUTOST       PRINT          STOREDB
ANALYZE        DATAFILE       INPUTS         NOCOMMAS       PROMPT         STOREDBUC
APPEND         DATASELECT     INSERT         NOCOMMENTS     PROTECT        STOREDF
AUTO           DATE           INTERPOLATIO   NODEFORM       QRY            STORENT
BASE           DB             INVERT         NOINDENT       QUERY          STOREOPT
BCRATIO        DBDATA         IRR            NOLEGEND       QUIT           STRUCTURE
BREAKHEADER    DBDEFINE       KEY            NOMATCH        RANGE          SUBROUTINE
BREAKON        DECBAL         LASTLINE       NOPAGE         RECALCULATE    SUBTASK
BUILDKEY       DEFAULTMOD     LEFTMARGIN     NORECORD       RECOMPILE      SUBTOTAL
!CALL          DEFAULTREL     LEGEND         NORMAL         RECORD         SUBTOTALS
CASELIST       DEFINE         LIMIT          NORRAND        REL            SUM
CATALOG        DEFINESTATUS   LINENUM        NOSCALE        RELATION       SUMDEPR
CENTER         DEFINITION     LINEWIDTH      NPV            REMOVE         !SUPPRESS
CENTRE         DELETE         LINK           NPVC           RENAME         SYS
CHANGE         DFNAME         LIST           NTV            !REPEAT        SYSTEM
CIRR           DIRECTORY      LISTFLDS       !ONERROR       REPORT         TAB
!CLEARRC       DOUBLE         LISTREL        OPT            RESEQUENCE     TAG
CMDFILE        EDIT           LOAD           OPTION         !RETURN        TESTREPORT
CMDS           END            LOG10          OPTIONA        REVIEW         TIME
COLTITLES      EXECS          LOW            OPTIONB        RLS10          TITLE
COLUMN         EXECUTE        MATRIX         OPTIONC        ROUND          TOPICS
COLUMNS        !EXIT          MAXIMUM        OPTIOND        SAVE           TOTAL
COMBINE        EXPAND         MDIRR          OPTIONE        SAVEAS         TOTALS
COMDEC         FIELD          MEAN           OPTIONF        SCALE          TRACE
COMMANDS       FIELDSARE      MEDIAN         OPTIONG        SCALEUC        TREND
COMMAS         FILE           !MENU          OPTIONH        SCREENSIZE     TRIRAND
COMMENT        FILENAME       MERGE          OPTIONI        SELECT         TRUNCATE
COMMENTS       FILENAMES      !MESSAGE       OPTIONJ        SENSITIVITY    TYPE
COMPILEFILE    FORMAT         MICRO          OPTIONK        SETFILE        T1090RAND
COMPILEGET     FORMULA        MICROCOMPUTE   OPTIONL        SETNAME        UC
COMPILESAVE    FUNCS          MINIMUM        OPTIONLIST     !SETPARAM      UNDERLINE
COMPRESS       FUNCTION       MIRR           OPTIONM        SIMULTANEOUS   UNIRAND
COMPUTE        GENDECBAL      MODEL          OPTIONN        SINGLE         UNLOAD
COMPUTEACROS   GENERATE       MODELNAMES     OPTIONNAME     SIZE           USING
!COND          GENRAND        MODIFIED       OPTIONO        !SKIP          VMATRIX
!CONDS         GENREPORT      MODS           OPTIONP        SKIPNONZERO    VS
CONSOLDB       GETDB          MONTE          ORDERBY        SKIPZERO       WHAT
CONSOLDF       GOAL           MOSTP          OUTPUTS        SOLVE          WHEREDB
CONSOLIDATE    !GOTO          MOVAVG         OVERLAY        SORT           WIDTH
CONSUC         GRID           MOVE           P              SOVER          XPOWERY
CONTENTS       GROUPBY        NA             PAGE           SPACE          ZEROPRINT
COPY           GROUPTITLES    NAIS           PAGELENGTH     SPECIAL        ZEROSUP
```

APPENDIX II
IFPS COMMANDS

This appendix reproduces the IFPS REFERENCE GUIDE RELEASE 10.0, which is copyright 1984 by EXECUCOM Systems Corporation and is used by permission.

Required words in the command are indicated by boldface, CAPITAL letters. Parameters that are optional are enclosed in brackets, (). Entries that you select (such as the names of models or files) are printed in small letters. If you have to choose one of several options, all the possible options are listed under one another ant they are shown in braces.

For a command having several parts, you separate the parts by spaces. You can use commas in place of spaces. You MUST use commas for separating lists of variable names or column names.

If your command requires more than one line, use an apostrophe (') at the end of the first line and continue the command on the next line.

1. Executive Commands

CATALOG
CMDFILE file
COMBINE [**SAVE**] model$_1$ model$_2$ model$_3$ . . .
[**AS** model]
COMMAND[S] file [startline [endline]]'
[parameters]
CONSOLDF file$_1$ [(c_1)] file$_2$ [(c_2)] . . . **NONE**
CONSOLIDATE model$_1$ [(c_1)] model$_2$ [(c_2)]'
. . . [**WITH** model [**USING** file]]
CONSOLIDATE model **USING**'
file$_1$[(C_1)] file$_2$[(C_2)] . . . [**WITH** model'
[**USING** file]]
COPY {entity | **FILE**} name [**TO**] [{**FILE** | entity}] newname
The "entity" may be a MODEL, REPORT, STRUCTURE, FORMULA, SUBTASK, or DIRECTIVE.

COPY MODEL name **TO FILE** newname'
TRANSLATE
CROSSREF modelname [[**APPEND**] [**ONLY**]'
ONTO {filename | **SPOOL**}]
DATAFILE file
DATASELECT
DELETE {**MODEL** | **REPORT** | **FILE** | **STRUCTURE** | **FORMULA** | **SUBTASK**} name [,name, ...]

DFNAME file
DIRECTORY
EDIT [editorname [entity name]]
The "entity" may be a MODEL, REPORT, STRUCTURE, FORMULA, SUBTASK, or DIRECTIVE.

EXECUTE subroutine

FILE [filename] {**b̸** | **YES** | **NO**}

FORMULA name [**USING** df1[, df2,...]]

HELP {**b̸** | ***** | **CONTENTS** | **HELP** | keyword | **WHERE**}

KEY File Encryption:
[command] filename {**/KEY = dddddd/** | **(KEY = dddddd)**}

LIST {**MODEL** | **REPORT** | **FILE** | **CMDFILE** | **DATAFILE** | **STRUCTURE** | **FORMULA** | **SUBTASK**} name[,name,...]'
[[**EXPAND**]'
[**GENERATE**]'
[[**APPEND**][**ONLY**]'
ONTO {file | **SPOOL**}]]

(The options EXPAND and GENERATE apply only with a MODEL, FORMULA, or SUBTASK.)

MERGE file$_1$ file$_2$ file$_3$ . . . **NONE**
MODEL name [**USING** file$_1$ [file$_2$ . . . file$_n$]]
NORECORD

OPTION Commands
Options control IFPS processing and output. The first entry in each brace is usually the default. When entering the command, replace the "•" with OPTION. The right and left columns offer alternative ways of entering the same options.

- • {A 1 | A 2} • {STATISTICS PRINT | STATISTICS SUPPRESS}
- • {B 1 | B 2 | B 3 | B 4} • {PERCENTILE 1 | PERCENTILE 2 | PERCENTILE 3 | PERCENTILE 4}
- • **C** linewidth [, namewidth]
  • **WIDTH** linewidth [, namewidth]
- • {D 1 | D 2} • {EXCESSCOLUMN ERROR | EXCESSCOLUMN ACCEPT}
- • {E 1 | E 2} • {ZERODIVIDE ERROR | ZERODIVIDE SUPPRESS}
- • {F 1 | F 2} • {PAGENUMBER RESET | PAGENUMBER CONTINUE}
- • {G 1 | G 2 | G 3} • {NA SUPPRESS | NA ACCEPT | NA ZEROCOMPUTE}
- • {H 1 | H 2} • {COEFFICIENTS SUPPRESS | COEFFICIENTS PRINT}
- • {I 1 | I 2} • {NEGATIVERATE SUPPRESS | NEGATIVERATE PRINT}
- • {J 1 | J 2} • {UNDEFINEDVAR ERROR | UNDEFINEDVAR SUPPRESS}
- • {K 1 | K 2} • {REDEFINITION ERROR | REDEFINITION SUPPRESS}
- • {L Ø | L n} • {ITERATIONVAL SUPPRESS | ITERATIONVAL colnumber}
- • {M 1 | M 2 | M 3} • {UCSCALE ALL | UCSCALE REGULAR | UCSCALE SCALEREG}
- • {N 1 | N 2} • {UCITERATION MAX | UCITERATION TEST}
- • {O 1 | O 2} • {TYPE IFPSDF | TYPE BINARY}
- • {P 1 | P 2} • {LOOKUP HASH | LOOKUP SEQUENTIAL}

OPTIONLIST

QUIT {b̸ | **YES** | **NO**}

RECORD {b̸ [filename] | **INPUT** [filename] | **OUTPUT** [filename] | **CLOSE**}

REPORT name

RESEQUENCE entity name [start [incr]]'
[**FROM** line-number [**TO** line-number]]'
[**ONLY**]
The "entity" may be a MODEL, REPORT CMDFILE, STRUCTURE, FORMULA, or SUBTASK.

SAVE

SCREENSIZE {n | Ø}

SETFILE [filename]

SETNAME {filename [,filename, . . .] | **ADD** filename [, filename, . . .] | **OFF**}

SPOOL {file | **CLOSE**}

STRUCTURE name

SUBTASK name [**USING** df1 [df2 . . .]]

SYSTEM [command]

2. Modeling Language Commands

ANALYZE variable-reference

AUTO [start [incr]] { b̸ / **S** / **SUPPRESS** }

BASE [**MODEL**]

COMMAND[**S**] file [startline [endline]]' [parameters]

COMPILEGET file

COMPILESAVE file

DFNAME file

END

GENREPORT name [[**APPEND**] [**ONLY**]' **ONTO** { file / **SPOOL** }]

GOAL [**SEEKING**]

IMPACT [**ON**] variable-reference [, **BY** pct]

LINK USER

LIST [**EXPAND**] [**GENERATE**]

MONTE CARLO n

NORECORD

OPTION { letter code / optionname code }

(All OPTIONS listed in Section 1 are valid in the MODEL subsystem.)

PLOT [variable-reference [/plot-character/], . . .]

RECOMPILE

RECORD { b̸ [filename] / **INPUT** [filename] / **OUTPUT** [filename] / **CLOSE** }

SAVE

SENSITIVITY [**TO**] variable-reference

SOLVE

SPOOL { file / **CLOSE** }

STORE file

(See Section 9B for valid STORE/STOREP options.)

STOREP file

STORENT file

(See Section 9B for valid STORENT options.)

USING $file_1$ [$file_2$ . . . $file_n$]

WHAT IF [**CONTINUE**]

3.
SOLVE/REPORT/PLOT Options

A. *Valid as SOLVE options and REPORT directives:*

CASELIST [BASESUP]
COLUMN[S] columnlist
COMDEC $\left\{\begin{array}{l}\text{A}\\\text{E1}\\\text{E2}\end{array}\right\}$
COMMAS
COMMENT[S]
CURRENCY symbol
DOUBLE
FORMAT specifications and replications
  Valid column descriptors are 9, B, D, and #. Periods are used for the name field, N's for the line number field.
FORMAT . . . n[(D,DDD)]
INDENT
INVERT [NOVAR]
LEFTMARGIN n
NAMEINDENT number
NAOUTPUT $\left\{\begin{array}{l}\text{b̸}\\\text{text}\\\text{NULL}\end{array}\right\}$
NAPRINT [NO]
NEGOPT $\left\{\begin{array}{l}\text{PAREN}\\-\\-\text{A}\\\text{DB}\\\text{CR}\end{array}\right\}$
NOCOMMAS
NOCOMMENT[S]
NOINDENT
NOPAGE
NORMAL
NOSCALE
OPT namewidth columnwidth [decimal-places]
OVERLAY [position] text
PAGE
PLOT [variable-reference [/plot-character/], . . .]
  (PLOT options are shown in Section 3C.)
POSOPT $\left\{\begin{array}{l}+\\\text{CR}\end{array}\right\}$
SCALE [MULTIPLY] $\left\{\begin{array}{l}\text{constant}\\\text{variable}\\\text{constant*variable}\end{array}\right\}$
SINGLE
SORT $\left\{\begin{array}{l}\text{b̸}\\\text{A}\\\text{D}\end{array}\right\}$ **ON** $\left\{\begin{array}{l}\text{col-refs}\\\text{NAME}\end{array}\right\}$ (var-refs)
SPACE [n]
WIDTH linewidth [namewidth columnwidth' [decimal places]]
ZEROPRINT
ZEROSUP

Print List
A print-list requesting only selected variables or lines of a model takes the forms:

Varname, varname, varname THRU varname, . . . L#, L# THRU L#, L#, L#, . . .

Line-number references must include "L". A sequence must be designated using THRU. All references must be entered on a single line. The items will print in the order specified.

SPACE [n] may be placed anywhere in the list.

Special Characters

$ The values of a variable will be printed with a dollar sign if the print request is followed with the dollar sign (in a report or SOLVE option).

% The values of a variable will be printed with a percent sign if the print request is followed with the percent sign (in a report or SOLVE option.)

Subscripted Variables
"Varname (n)" causes only column "n" of "Varname" to print.

B. *REPORT Directives Only:*

To test REPORT directives, use this command:

TESTREPORT [char] [[**APPEND**] [**ONLY**]'
ONTO $\left\{\begin{matrix}\text{filename}\\ \textbf{SPOOL}\end{matrix}\right\}$]

CENTER [**PROMPT**] text
CENTRE [**PROMPT**] text
COLUMN[**S**] **TITLE**[**S**] [title$_1$, title$_2$, . . .]

Date
The current date may be generated with **&DATE&** or **•DATE•** on a comment line.

NEWPAGE $\left[\begin{matrix}\textbf{1}\\ \textbf{FF}\end{matrix}\right]$

Page
The current page number may be generated with **•PAGE•** on a comment line or after the directive CENTER.

PAGELENGTH toplines bodylines bottomlines' [[newpage key] [repeatlines]]
PROMPT [text]
SKIPNONZERO variable-reference, reportline
SKIPZERO variable-reference, reportline

Tab
/text/**TAB** n, variable (column)'
[, **TAB** n2, variable (column), . . .]

Time
The current time may be generated with **&TIME&** or **•TIME•**.

UNDERLINE [character]

Special Characters

/ Slashes are used for variable name replacement (renaming a variable in the report at print time).

* Any report line starting with an asterisk will be printed verbatim in the report. (*PROMPT will prompt for the line's text before the report is generated.)

C. *Plot Options*

GRID vert-lines horiz-chars gridoption
INVERT
LEGEND
NOLEGEND

NORMAL
PLOT variable-reference [/plot-character/], . . .
RANGE y-minimum y-maximum x-minimum' x-maximum
SCALE scalefactor
SOVER {character | LAST}
TITLE number {TOP | LEFT | BOTTOM} {CENTER | CENTRE | MARGIN} /text
VS {variable | COLUMN}

D. *SOLVE Options for Probabilistic Value Control*

HIGH variable list
LOW variable list
MEAN variable list
MOSTP variable list
The preceding options may be reset to the default with a BASE [MODEL] command.

4. Special Modeling Language Statements & Identifiers

ACCESS {**FORMULA** / **SUBTASK**} name, filename

COLUMN[S] {1-n, [, name1 [, name2, . . .]] / 19nn [-19mm] / name1 [, name2, . . .]}

COMPILEFILE file

FUNCTION name, file

GENERATE [**NEST**] temp-list **AT** start-line'
  [**BY** incr]**FOR** symbol-list'
  [; symbol-list; . . .]

NA IS {text / **NULL**}

PERIODS number

PROTECT [**OFF**]

Relational Operators:

variable = **IF** relational-test'
      THEN true-expression'
      ELSE false-expression

for numerical operators:

.EQ.	**.LT.**	**.GT.**
.NE.	**.LE.**	**.GE.**

for textual operators:

.HAS. **.IS.**

SIMULTANEOUS {**AUTO** / variable-list / **ACROSS COLUMNS** list}

SUBROUTINE name, file

Variable-definition Matrix Identifiers:

FUTURE [n] variable-reference

PREVIOUS [n] variable-reference

5. IFPS Functions

Discounted Cash Flow Functions

BCRATIO (cash inflow, discount rate,' cash outflow)
CIRR (cash inflow, cash outflow)
IRR (cash inflow, cash outflow)
MDIRR (cash inflow, cash outflow)
MIRR (cash inflow, discount rate,' cash outflow)
NPV (cash inflow, discount rate, life, investment)
NPVC (cash inflow, discount rate, cash outflow)
NTV (cash inflow, compound rate, cash outflow)

Mathematical Functions

ABS (value)

DEFINITION { var-ref, expression | **PREVIOUS** n [var-ref] | **FUTURE** n var-ref }

The "expression" is a constant, variable, line-number reference, computational expression, or reference to another function.

GROWTHRATE (var-ref [, col-ref])
INTERPOLATION [ON] (variable reference, $x_1,y_1,\ x_2,y_2,\ldots$)
LOG10 (value)
MATRIX (var-ref, col-ref)
MAXIMUM (value_1, value_2, value_3,. . .)
MEAN (reference1, reference2)
MEDIAN (reference1, reference2)
MINIMUM (value_1, value_2, value_3,. . .)
NATEST (var-ref)
NATEXP (value)
NATLOG (value)
ROUND (value)
ROUNDUP (value)
STDDEV (reference1, reference2)
STEP (variable-reference, $x_1,y_1,\ x_2,y_2,\ldots$)

SUM ({ var-ref { **THRU** | , } var-ref | col-ref { **THRU** | , } col-ref })

TRUNCATE (value)
VMATRIX ([**FUTURE**] var-ref, col-ref)
XPOWERY (x, y)

Extrapolation Functions

MOVAVG (variable-reference, wt_1, wt_2, wt_3,. . .)
POLYFIT (k)
TREND (variable-reference)

Probability Distribution Functions

CUMRAND[R] (0%, 10%,. . .100%)
GENRAND[R] ($x_1,y_1,\ x_2,y_2,\ldots$)
NORRAND[R] (mean, std-deviation)
TRIRAND[R] (low, most-probable, high)
T1090RAND[R] (10%, most-probable, 90%)
UNIRAND[R] (low, high)

The R form of each distribution implies serial independence of columns. Without the R, the columns are completely correlated.

6. IFPS Subroutines

A subroutine differs from other variable definition statements in that several variables may be defined on one line of logic. The variables have no line number associated with their values. In the following descriptions, subroutine output variables will be underlined:

ACRS [**DEPR**] (category, start, cost, period-depreciation, book-value, cumulative depreciation)

AMORT (amortized loan, demand loan, interest rate, life, start column, payments per column, payment, interest, principal, balance)

DECBAL [**DEPR**] (asset value, salvage fraction, life, acceleration constant, switch key, period depreciation, book value, cumulative depreciation)

ERRORMSG (val1, val2, c, n)

GENDECBAL [**DEPR**] (asset value, salvage fraction, life, acceleration constant, switch key, allocation, period depreciation, book value, cumulative depreciation)

STLINE [**DEPR**] (asset value, salvage fraction, life, period depreciation, book value, cumulative depreciation)

SUM [**DEPR**] (asset value, salvage fraction, life, period depreciation, book value, cumulative depreciation)

7. User-Defined Operations

A. To activate the FORMULA or SUBTASK subsystem, enter one of the following:

FORMULA name [**USING** df1 [, df2, . . .]]

SUBTASK name [**USING** df1 [, df2, . . .]]

B. Before utilizing a user-defined operation, a model must contain the statement:

ACCESS {**FORMULA** | **SUBTASK**} name, filename

C. Statements required at the beginning of an operation (OUTPUTS valid in a SUBTASK only):

INPUTS input1 [, input2, . . .]

OUTPUTS output1 [, output2, . . .]

D. Commands used when building/solving operations:

LIST

PRESERVE filename

PROMPT

SAVE

SOLVE

Most modeling language commands of Section 2 and the SOLVE options of Section 3 are valid for user-defined operations. Executive level commands are also recognized.

8.
Command File Directives

To activate the CMDFILE subsystem and build/edit a command file:

CMDFILE filename

To execute a command file from the Executive level or MODEL subsystem:

COMMAND[S] filename [startline'
[stopline]] [param1 [, param2, . . .]]

!CALL filename [startline [endline]] [parameters]

!CLEARRC

!COMMENT [text]

!COND[S] statement [text]

!CPARAM[S] n prompt

!CSETPARAM number substitution

!END

!EXIT

!GOTO n

!IF ref1 operator ref2 **THEN** statement

!IFRC { .EQ. code / .NE. code } statement

!INPUT [text]

!INPUTC [text]

!MENU[S] number, . . ., number

!MESSAGE [text]

!ONERROR code statement

!PARAM[S] n prompt

!PARAMCOMPUTE number expression

!PAUSE [text]

!REPEAT [NEST] **WHILE PARAM** n **IS** text'
[,text, ...] [;**PARAM** n2 **IS** text [,text, ...]]

!RETURN [n]

!SETPARAM number substitution

!SKIP n

!SUPPRESS { b̸ / n [,n2, . . .] / ALL }

!SUPPRESS OFF

9. DATAFILE Commands and Options

To activate the DATAFILE subsystem and build/edit/execute a data file:
    DATAFILE filename

A. *Datafile Commands*

COLUMNS n
GENREPORT name [[**APPEND**] [**ONLY**]'
    ONTO { file | **SPOOL** }]
LIST
SAVE
SELECT { **TAG** tagname | **VARIABLE** var-name | **COLUMN** col-number }
SOLVE
    (The SOLVE options presented in Section 3 are also valid in the DATAFILE subsystem.)
    (OPTIONS D and G are valid in the DATAFILE subsystem—See Section 1.)
STORE file [**NEW**]
STOREP file [**NEW**]
STORENT file [**NEW**]
    (See Section 9B for STORE, STOREP, and STORENT options.)

B. *STORE/STORENT/STOREP Options*

COLUMN[**S**] columnspecs
INVERT
LINENUM[**NOL**]
    (Valid under STORENT only)
MICROSTORE
NAOUTPUT { text | **NULL** | ƀ }
NAPRINT { ƀ | **NO** }
NOAUTOST
NOSTORE
SCALE [**MULTIPLY**] { constant | variable | constant*variable }
STOREOPT sf dp
TAG tagname
    (Valid under STORE and STOREP)
ZEROSUP

Data Editing—See Section 12B

C. *BINARY File Creation*

dfname { **/TYPE = BINARY/** | **(TYPE = BINARY)** }

The binary designation may be included with a data file name entered for a STORE, STORENT, COPY, CONSOLDF, DATASELECT, or MERGE command. (It is *not* valid in a DATAFILE command.)

10. Universal Consolidation

To activate the STRUCTURE subsystem and build/edit/execute a structure:

STRUCTURE filename

A. *STRUCTURE Directives*

ALLOCATE dfname [**FROM** node1, . . .,'
noden]
list of distinct variable names

{**COMMENT** / * / **C**} text

DEFINE nodefile **AS** modname'
USING df1 [(fac1)] [, df2 [(fac2)], . . .]'
[**WITH** postmod [**USING** ppdf]]'
[[**ONLY**] **ONTO** rptfile]

DEFINESTATUS filename

GENREPORT rpt1 [, rpt2, . . .] **FROM**'
[**MODEL**] modname'
[**USING** df1 [, df2, . . .]]

GENREPORT rpt1 [, rpt2, . . .]'
FROM DATAFILE nodefile

SCALE [**MULTIPLY**] [**BY**] var-name'
[**EXCLUDE** variable-list]

STORE dfname [**COLUMNS** n1-nn]'
[**FROM** modname]'
variable-list

STORENT [**COLUMNS** n1-nn]'
FROM modname'
variable-list

B. *Universal Consolidation Commands*

ALTER {nodefile / **ALL**} [**FROM** dfname1]'
[, {nodefile / **ALL**} [**FROM** dfname2], . . .]

ALTERLIST

AUTO [start [incr]]

BASE

CONSOLIDATE [**THRU** nodefile]'
[**RECALCULATE**]

END

LIST

MODIFIED {dfname1 [, dfname2,...] / **ALL**}

RECALCULATE

RECOMPILE

SAVE

STATUSLIST

TRACE {b̸ / **ON** / **OFF**}

11. Micros

A micro reference takes the form:

&text&

It may appear anywhere in a model or report. A micro definition statement takes the form:

MICRO &text&definition&

In a datafile, it must appear before any variable definition statements.

The following form may be used to calculate new values based on previous MICRO definitions:

MICROCOMPUTE &name&expression&

12. Editing Commands

A. *Line Editing Commands*

APPEND Text

To append text to a line or lines, use one of the following commands. An S suppresses printing of the changed line. APPEND or "A" is valid:

10APPEND[S]
10,40APPEND[S]
10APPEND[S]/text/
10,40APPEND[S]/text/

AUTO [start [, increment]] **[SUPPRESS]**

COPY Lines

To copy line[s] to another place in the entity, enter one of these forms:

10COPYtarget-line
10,40COPYtarget-line
10,40COPYtarget-line, increment

END

Print

To print a line or lines, enter the number, optionally followed by the letter **P**:

10P
10
10,40
10,40P

Delete

To delete a line or lines, enter the number or the range immediately followed by the letter **D**:

10D
10,40D

Change**

To change the first occurrence of text on a line, any of the following forms may be used. The C form then prints the changed lines; the CS form does not:

10C/old text/new text
10,60C/old text/new text
10C"old text" new text"
10,60C"old text" new text"

10CS/old text/new text
10,60CS/old text/new text/
10CS"old text" new text"
10,60CS"old text" new text"

Global Change**

To change every occurrence of text on a line or lines, any of the forms below may be used. The G form then prints the changed lines; the GS form does not:

```
10G/old text/new text
10G"old text" new text"
10,60G/old text/new text/
10,60G"old text" new text"

10GS/old text/new text/
10GS"old text" new text"
10,60GS/old text/new text/
10,60GS"old text" new text"
```

**On some systems, the backslash character(\ ) may be used instead of the quote character (").

Insert or Replace

To insert or replace a line of text, enter the number of the line, followed by the text of the line:

```
10 text
```

MOVE Lines

To move line[s] from one place to another within an entity, use one of these commands:

```
10MOVEtarget-line
10,40MOVEtarget-line
10,40MOVEtarget-line, increment
```

Text Search

"text" or \text\

B. *Data Editing Commands*

CHANGE col-number'

[FOR variable-list [= { values / filename }]]

CHANGE variable'

[FOR column-list [= { values / filename }]]

INSERT col-number'

[FOR variable-list [= { values / filename }]]

REMOVE col-number **[FOR** variable-list]

The line editing commands shown in Section 12A are also valid with data entries.

APPENDIX III
RESERVED WORDS

IFPS imposes few limits on you when it comes to labeling or naming files, models, reports, and variables. There are , however, a few words which cannot be used to name files, models, or reports. These words are called "reserved" words. some words cannot form part of a compound (i.e., two or more word) variable name. Some words cannot be used by themselves as variable names. That is, IFPS assumes that these words have their specific meaning in the language rather than being a name you assigned. The reserved words and variable naming restrictions of IFPS are explained in detail in this appendix.

A3.1 MODEL , REPORT, and FILE NAMES

The names

END	NONE	USING
NO	STOP	WITH

cannot be used as names for models, reports, or files.

A3.2 VARIABLE NAMES

1. Variables in IFPS models cannot *begin* with the following words:

ACCESS	FUTURE	PERIODS
COLUMN	GENERATE	PREVIOUS
COLUMNS	IF	PROTECT
COMMENT	INPUTS	SIMULTANEOUS
COMPILEFILE	MATRIX	SPACE
DATA	NA IS	STOP
DEFINITION	NO	SUBROUTINE
END	NONE	USING
FUNCTION	OUTPUTS	

This restriction means, for example, that you *cannot* write:

```
30 FUTURE SAVINGS = 110
```

but you *can* write:

```
30 FUTURESAVINGS = 110.
```

That is, if any of the above words (e.g., FUTURE) appears as the first word of a multi-word variable name, IFPS will reject it and give you an error message. However, if the word is part of a longer word (e.g., FUTURESAVINGS) it is acceptable.

2. Several restrictions apply because of the need to distinguish comments and line numbers. Specifically,

- Variable names may not begin with C followed by a blank.
- Variable names may not begin with an L followed by a number.
- Variable names may not begin with LINE followed by a number.
- Variable names may not begin with RL followed by a number.

Thus,

```
C ALL   L3TWO   LINE2TWO   RL3
```

are all examples of names that *cannot* be used because of their confusion with comments, line numbers, and report line numbers.

Similarly, because the words THRU and FOR are used, respectively to indicate collections of variables and number of periods, they cannot be used by themselves in the middle of variable names. Thus,

```
A FOR B
PROFIT THRU INVESTEMENT
```

are invalid; however,

```
AFORB
PROFITTHRUINVESTMENT
```

are valid. The operating urle is that FOR and THRU cannot have a blank space on both sides of them in a variable name.

3. If you use a report with your model, you will run into trouble if a variable name is identical to a report directive. Since it is not unusual in practice to decide that you want to create a report format for presenting your results after you have developed a model, you will find it good practice to avoid using the following names for variables:

CASELIST	INDENT	NORMAL	SINGLE
CENTER	INVERT	NOSCALE	SKIPNONZERO
CENTRE	LEFTMARGIN	OPT	SKIPZERO
COLUMN	NAMEINDENT	OVERLAY	SORT
COLUMNS	NAOUTPUT	PAGE	SPACE
COMDEC	NAPRINT	PAGELENGTH	TAB
COMMAS	NEGOPT	PLOT	TESTREPORT
COMMENT	NEWPAGE	POSOPT	UNDERLINE
CURRENCY	NOCOMMAS	PROMPT	WIDTH
FORMAT	NOCOMMENT	SCALE	ZEROPRINT

4. Finally, although you can use the names of commands (e.g., LIST, MODEL, SOLVE) as variable names, or as the first words of variable names, you cannot change the value of these variables under WHAT IF. The reason is that IFPS treats these name as commands and does not recognize them as variables to be modified.

APPENDIX IV
20 MOST COMMON ERROR MESSAGES IN IFPS

This appendix lists the more common error messages that you may encounter in using IFPS. The list given is not complete. There are many more error messages than we have space for here. We have included those error messages that apply to commands described in this book. If you encounter an error message not listed in this appendix which you cannot figure out, consult the *IFPS USER'S MANUAL*.

UNDEFINED VARIABLE

The variable is not defined on the *left-hand* side of an equal sign. You either: (1) spelled the name of the variable differently on the right-hand side than on the left-hand side, or (2) you didn't define it al all. Look for the variable on the left-hand side. If it isn't there, add a line to your model defining the variable. If it is there, compare the spelling on the two sides.

VARIABLE NOT DEFINED

Similar to UNDEFINED VARIABLE. You referred to a variable on the right hand side of an equal sign, and IFPS did not find its definition anywhere on the left side of an equal sign.

UNRECOGNIZED COMMAND

This error typically occurs when you misspell a command such as writing KIST for LIST. To correct, retype the command. However, this error message also occurs if you forget to put an equal sign on a line. In this case, IFPS thinks your modeling instruction is a command and can't understand you. Retype the line.

This error message also occurs after a RESEQUENCE command if you do not specify the MODEL or REPORT that you want. When you give a RESEQUENCE command, your current model or report is no longer available to you. You therefore have to use the MODEL or REPORT command (Section 2.3) to go back to where you were.

FILE NAME MUST BE__OR FEWER CHARACTERS

You get this message whenever you try to give an IFPS file a name that is longer than the maximum allowed on your machine, IFPS is smart enought to tell you the maximum number allowed on your computer. Choose a different name which fits within the maximum allowed.

NUMBER OF EXPRESSIONS IS GREATER THAN NUMBER OF COLUMNS

If you define more columns of information than exist in your COLUMNS statement, IFPS asks you to correct the line. For example,

```
10 COLUMNS 1-3
20 X=1,2,3,4
```

leads to this message. Remember that if you define too few columns, you do not get an error message. IFPS simple assumes the last column value is true for all subsequent columns. For example,

```
10 COLUMNS 1-3
20 X=1,2
```

is OK. IFPS assumes the values of X are 1,2,and 2.

LINE__NEEDS CORRECTING

This message tells you where your error occurred. Look there first. However, in some cases, the mistake may be at a different place. For example, if you said:

```
10 PROFIT = REVENUE - COST
20 REVINU = 100
```

you may want to change the spelling of REVINU in Line 20 even though IFPS tells you that line 10 needs correcting since REVENUE is undefined.

IF LINE EXISTS, IT DOES NOT DEFINE A VARIABLE

You referenced a line in your model by a line number which is empty. For example,

```
10 X=3
20 Y= SUM(L10,L15)
```

would lead to this error.

MODEL NOT FOUND

This message results if you ask for a model in your file by the wrong name or you misspell the name of the file. It alsooccurs if you are ready to create a new model. IFPS will follow this message immediately with another message: NEW MODEL WILL BE CREATED. If you want to create a new model, ignore the message and begin entering your new model. If you thought you already had a model with that name, first check the spelling. If the spelling seems all right, use CATALOG in response to a question mark to obtain a list of the models in that file.

DIVISION BY ZERO IN COMPUTATION OF VARIABLE

Your model resulted in a zero in the denominator of a fraction. Division by zero does not stop the computation. Rather, IFPS prints a string of 9's in your output at the location where this division was attempted. Be sure to check your output to find out why you received this message. It usually means you made a modeling mistake. This error can propagate through your results if you refer to the location by PREVIOUS, FUTURE, or MATRIX.

ILLEGAL COLUMN NAME OR NUMBER

You referred to a column either by a name or by a number which does not exist in your model. This message often occurs when you are editing your model.

COLUMN NUMBER IS GREATER THAN THE NUMBER OF COLUMNS IN MODEL

You refered to a column number that is larger than the number of columns in your model. This error is typically encountered when using the special COLUMN commands.

COLUMN STATEMENT MUST PRECEDE ALL VARIABLE DEFINITIONS

You have to define the number or names of your columns as the first statement in your model. This means that, for example, if you write:

```
10 COLUMNS 1-12
```

you cannot have any lines numbered lower than 10. Your can also receive this message if you make a mistake in a special COLUMN command and IFPS thinks you are trying to define the number of columns in your model.

COLUMN NAME OR NUMBER MUST BE FOLLOWED BY FOR

If you use the special COLUMN commands to refer to specific variable, you have to use the word FOR right after the column name. For example,

```
20 COLUMN 5 OF PRICE = 3
```

is incorrect. You should write:

```
20 COLUMN 5 FOR PRICE = 3
```

THIS WHAT IF STATEMENT NOT ACCEPTED

If you make a mistake in writing a WHAT IF statement, such as a mistake in format, IFPS may reject the statement. If so, you have to start over. Retype WHAT IF and then follow it with the changes you want. If IFPS gives you this message again, review what you just typed and try to see what format error you made.

GOAL UNATTAINABLE - COLUMN__

IFPS tried to achieve your goal but could not. Usually thismeans that you have relations in your model that do not allow you to satisfy the goal criterion. You will find it useful to use the ANALYZE command for both the variable to be adjusted and the variable in your goal when you try to trace down the error.

NO CONVERGENCE FOR SIMULTANEOUS EQUATIONS IN COLUMN

If you have a set of simultaneous equations in your model, IFPS will try to solve them by an iterative method called Gauss-Seidel. This method terminates when all equations are satisfied simultaneously. If you define impossible relations, for example

```
10 X = Y + 3
20 Y = X - 6
```

then IFPS will tell you that your model is wrong. For complicated sets of simultaneous equations, IFPS may not be able to reach an answer in 50 iterations even through one exists. In this case, you also receive this message. Use the prompts for examining simultaneous equations and check the simultaneous equations by hand, if necessary.

MISSING (or OPERAND

Check for a different number of right-hand and left-hand parenthesies, or for missing arithmethic operator (+, –, *, /), or a missing THEN or ELSE in an IF statement.

RESEQUENCE NOT FOLLOWED BY MODEL, REPORT, OR CMDFILE

When you ask IFPS to resequence line numbers, you must specify whether a MODEL, REPORT, or command file is to be resequenced, and you must give the proper name. Repeate the resequence command giving the correct information.

STARTING NUMBER MUST BE LARGER THAN LAST LINE NUMBER

If you give an AUTO command when revising an existing model, you can only start after the last line of the existing model.

APPENDIX V
OPTIONS

IFPS provides a series of OPTIONS that are special commands which represent standard settings. To see what these OPTIONS are and what values they are set to currently, you type OPTIONLIST in response to a ?.

To call an option, you type OPTION followed by its shorthand abbreviation or its name and setting. For example,

```
?OPTION A 1
```

or

```
?OPTION STATISTICS PRINT
```

are equivalent. You can even mix abbreviations and names. Thus:

OPTION STATISTICS 1, and
OPTION A PRINT

are also equivalent to OPTION A 1.

When you ask for an OPTION it remains in effect until you change it. The following subsections list each option, then its abbreviation, its name, and its description.

OPTION A: MONTE CARLO SAMPLE STATISTICS

OPTION A 1	OPTION STATISTICS PRINT
OPTION A 2	OPTION STATISTICS SUPPRESS

DEFAULT: OPTION A1

If you specify OPTION A 2, the sample statistics normally printed out in Monte Carlo simulations (Sec. 5.8) are suppressed.

OPTION B: MONTE CARLO TABLES

		PERCENTILES PRINTED
OPTION B 1	OPTION PERCENTILE 1	90,80,70,.....,10
OPTION B 2	OPTION PERCENTILE 2	90,70,50,30,10
OPTION B 3	OPTION PERCENTILE 3	90,50,10
OPTION B 4	OPTION PERCENTILE 4	80,50,20

DEFAULT: OPTION B 1

This option allows you to select the percentiles shown in the frequency and normal approximation tables in Monte Carlo output (Sec. 5.8)

OPTION C: LINE WIDTH AND VARIABLE NAME LENGTH

OPTION C n   OPTION WIDTH n
OPTION C n m OPTION WIDTH n m
DEFAULT: OPTION C 78 24

This option allows you to set the length of the line (n) and the number of characters allocated to the name (m) of the variable in the output display. It is equivalent to the WIDTH command (Sec. 4.2).

OPTION D: EXCESS COLUMNS IN A DATAFILE

OPTION D 1   OPTION EXCESSCOLUMNS ERROR
OPTION D 2   OPTION EXCESSCOLUMNS ACCEPT
DEFAULT: OPTION D 1

If a data file has more columns of data than are called for in a model, an error message results. However, under some circumstances you may want to use the data even if they contain more columns than you need. For example, you may want to debug a model with only a few columns and then run it with the full data set. In that case, you ask for OPTION D 2.

OPTION E: DIVISION BY ZERO

OPTION E 1   OPTION ZERODIVIDE ERROR
OPTION E 2   OPTION ZERODIVIDE SUPPRESS
DEFAULT: OPTION E 1

Asking for Option E 2, overrides an error message (and avoids failure to complete the solution of a model) if division by zero occurs. The result is an undefined variable value and a blank in the output.

OPTION F: REPORT PAGINATION

OPTION F 1   OPTION PAGENUMBER RESET
OPTION F 2   OPTION PAGENUMBER CONTINUE
DEFAULT: OPTION F 1

Option F 2 numbers all reports generated to a single file in sequence starting with page 1. That is, there is only one page 1. Option F 1 restarts each report at page 1.

OPTION G: "NOT AVAILABLE"

OPTION G 1   OPTION NA SUPPRESS
OPTION G 2   OPTION NA ACCEPT
OPTION G 3   OPTION NA ZEROCOMPUTE
DEFAULT:OPTION NA

Option G 2 is equivalent to the NA IS NA statement (Sec. 4.6.10). Once issued, it is not needed in individual models or data files. Option G 3 asks IFPS to treat NA values as zeros when performing calculations.

OPTION H: PRINTING TREND AND POLYFIT COEFFICIENTS

OPTION H 1 OPTION COEFFICIENTS SUPPRESS
OPTION H 2 OPTION COEFFICIENTS PRINT
DEFAULT: OPTION H 1

Option H 2 results in printing out the values of the regression coefficients computed by IFPS whenever a TREND or POLYFIT function (Sec. 3.2.3) is used. In the case of TREND, the R-square value is also printed. The line number is also shown so that if there are several such functions, the outputs can be distinguished.

OPTION I: NEGATIVE RATES OF RETURN

OPTION I 1 OPTION NEGATIVERATE SUPPRESS
OPTION I 2 OPTION NEGATIVERATE PRINT
DEFAULT OPTION I 1

Because negative rates of return are difficult to interpret, IFPS normally leaves a blank (Option I 1) if the IRR function (Sec. 3.2.1) results in a negative value. Option I 2 prints the negative value if there is a solution or a -1 if there is no solution.

OPTION J: UNDEFINED VARIABLES

OPTION J 1 OPTION UNDEFINEDVAR ERROR
OPTION J 2 OPTION UNDEFINEDVAR SUPPRESS
DEFAULT OPTION J 1

IFPS generates an error message (UNDEFINED VARIABLE ...) if you try to solve a model that refers to a variable that has not been defined on the left-hand side of an equation. If you specify OPTION J 2 this error message is suppressed and computation can proceed. However, any undefined variables are given the value 0 and are printed out as blanks.

OPTION K: PROTECT

OPTION K 1 OPTION REDEFINITION ERROR
OPTION K 2 OPTION REDEFINITION SUPPRESS
DEFAULT OPTION K 1

This option deals with the PROTECT feature in data files. Consult the *IFPS USER'S MANUAL* , Chapter 7, before using it.

OPTION L: PRINT SIMULTANEOUS EQUATIONS

OPTION L 0 OPTION ITERATIONVAL SUPPRESS
OPTION L col-num OPTION ITERATIONVAL col-num
DEFAULT OPTION L 0

Option L can be used to obtain printout for each iteration when simultaneous equations are present. This is a tricky option and the *IFPS USER'S MANUAL* should be consulted before it is used.

OPTION M: SCALING UNDER UNIVERSAL CONSOLIDATION

OPTION M 1 OPTION UCSCALE ALL
OPTION M 2 OPTION UCSCALE REG
OPTION M 3 OPTION UCSCALE SCALEREG
DEFAULT: OPTION M 1

This option controls scaling during Universal Consolidation (Section 10). Option M 2 limits scaling to regular columns and is performed after the complete solution has been calculated. That is, special columns are not affected. In Option M 3, the SCALE directive is applied to regular columns before the special columns are calculated. As a result, under Option M 3, the special columns reflect the scaled values.

OPTION N: ITERATIONS UNDER UNIVERSAL CONSOLIDATION

OPTION N 1 OPTION UCITERATION MAX
OPTION N 2 OPTION UCITERATION TEST
DEFAULT: OPTION N 1

Under Universal Consolidation, up to five iterations are performed in an effort to obtain convergence. When testing, it is often useful to see results as they occur. With Option N 2, only a single iteration is performed and all reports are printed out.

OPTION O: BINARY DATA FILES

OPTION O 1 OPTION TYPE IFPSDF
OPTION O 2 OPTION TYPE BINARY
DEFAULT: OPTION O 1

IFPS datafiles are stored as characters unless TYPE = BINARY is specified when creating the file. Under Option O 2 all data files created with DATASELECT (Sec. 4.6.8),CONSOLDF (Sec 4.8.6), STORENT (Sec. 4.6.7), or STORE (Sec. 9.7.1) are binary.

OPTION P: HASH TABLES

OPTION P 1 OPTION LOOKUP HASH
OPTION P 2 OPTION LOOKUP SEQUENTIAL
DEFAULT: OPTION P 1

Option P 1 speeds up the solution of IFPS for models that have been compiled and saved (Sec. 4.5.6) and which contain over 250 variables. This feature can be disabled with OPTION P 2.

APPENDIX VI
TRANSLATING IFPS MODELS TO IFPS/PERSONAL

This book has been concerned with the mainframe version of IFPS. A version for personal computers, called IFPS/PERSONAL, is available for IBM/PC, IBM/PC compatibles, TI, and HP-150 computers. (A separate version, called MINDSIGHT, is available for the Apple Macintosh.)

The advantage of working with IFPS on a personal computer is that it makes you independent of the mainframe. Thus, if the mainframe is down for maintenance or other reasons, you can still work. If you (or your budget) are charged for mainframe connect time, working on a personal computer can be a great cost savings. A common way of working is to edit and test the model on the personal computer and then send the model up to the mainframe for number crunching. A second advantage is the full screen editor available in IFPS/PERSONAL which allows you to make changes more easily. On the other hand, IFPS/PERSONAL does not provide Monte Carlo (Chapter 5) for risk analysis or hierarchical consolidation (Chapter 10).

This appendix describes the procedures involved in translating IFPS models that reside on a mainframe to a form suitable for IFPS/PERSONAL. This translation is really quite automatic and takes place as you communicate. The Appendix concludes with a description of the differences between the mainframe and personal versions of IFPS.

A6.1 REQUIREMENTS

To accomplish translation requires the following software and hardware:

1. A version of IFPS/LINK has to be installed on your mainframe. You can determine if it is by looking at your screen when you call IFPS on your mainframe. A notation such as this appears:

```
IFPS/LINK 1.0 V3
```

2. A physical communications link must exist between your mainframe and your personal computer. Typically, this involves a modem or a local area network.

3. A version of IFPS/PERSONAL must be active in your personal computer.

A6.2 STEPS IN COPYING A MODEL FROM MAINFRAME TO PERSONAL

In the copy procedure, the personal computer acts as the terminal. The first thing you have to do is establish the parameters of the communications interface between the personal computer and the mainframe. This is done in the PROFILE subsystem on the personal computer through the use of the Interface menus. You need do this only once if you always work with the same mainframe.

The personal computer has to be connected to the mainframe. On an IBM/PC you can press ALT and F10 simultaneously or can enter the terminal command from the interface menus. Once connected, you log on to your mainframe operating system as you normally do and access IFPS. This part of the procedure is the same as described in Chapter 2.

Once you have connected your microcomputer to the mainframe, you can copy a mainframe model to IFPS/PERSONAL by following these steps:

1. In mainframe IFPS, ask for the Models-and-Reports file that contains the model you want to copy.

2. Make the mainframe active by using Alt-F10 and go to the top level of IFPS/PERSONAL either by pressing Alt-F5 or by hitting the escape key until the main menu appears. This main menu shows IFPS: at the left end of the command line. Select "IFPS". and you will see a new menu.

3. Choose "Interface" from the IFPS: menu. The Interface menu will appear.

4. Choose "Files" from the Interface: menu. The Files menu will appear.

5. Enter "Copy" from the Files: menu.

6. Enter "COM:name" as the source file specification where you use the name of the model you want to copy. Note that COM: must precede the model name to tell IFPS/Personal that you are copying a mainframe model.

7. Enter the destination file specification as `MODEL name` where name is the name you want the model to have in IFPS/PERSONAL. Note that this name does not have to be the same as the name you gave the model on the mainframe.

That's all there is to it. The translation is performed automatically for you and your mainframe model is transferred to your IFPS/PERSONAL disk. However, you should check to make sure that everything in the model was translated. Some features provided in IFPS mainframe models (e.g., probability distributions) are not available in IFPS/PERSONAL. When this is the case, the entire line on which they are referred to is translated as a comment. To check the translation, go to the Files menu and ask for a lisT. To lisT, you also have to specify the model name you gave to the IFPS/PERSONAL version.

A6.3 COPYING OTHER FILES

You can copy any type of file, not just models, from the mainframe to IFPS/PERSONAL. However, no translation is performed when you do so. You may have to edit the files after they are copied to remove things that work on the mainframe but are not available in IFPS/PERSONAL.

A6.4 IFPS MAINFRAME FEATURES NOT AVAILABLE IN IFPS/PERSONAL

Table A6-1 lists the features available in IFPS on mainframes that are not available in in IFPS/Personal. The principal section of this book in which each feature is discussed is shown in parenthesis.

TABLE A6-1

MAINFRAME IFPS FEATURES NOT AVAILABLE IN IFPS/PERSONAL

	Section
Not Available (NA) Data	4.6.10
Model-Based Consolidation with Postprocessing	4.8.4
Monte Carlo Modeling	5.1 to 5.14
Generate and Generate Nest	9.2
Set Files	9.3
User Defined Formulas	9.4.1
User Defined Subroutines	9.4.2
Tagged Data Files	9.7.1
Tagged Variables	9.7.2
Data Select	9.7.3
Universal Consolidation	10.1
IFPS/DIMENSION	10.2

A6.5 DIFFERENCES IN MODELING CONVENTIONS BETWEEN IFPS MAINFRAME AND IFPS/PERSONAL

IFPS/Personal and the mainframe version of IFPS differ in a number of conventions that are followed in modeling. The following is a list of some of the important differences. For many of the differences, we show you a sample of the way you write it in Mainframe and the way your write it in IFPS/Personal.

COLUMNS DEFINITION

Mainframe: **COLUMNS 1- 4**
Personal : **COLUMNS 1..4** or **COLUMNS 1 THRU 4**

LINE NUMBERS

Mainframe: each line requres a line number.
Personal: line numbers are not required. However, if you want to refer to a variable by line number, you can put a label in front of the variable. A label can be numeric, alphabetic, or a mix of numeric or alphabetic. You can substitute a label for a variable. For example:

```
CGS:COSTS OF GOODS SOLD =MATERIAL+LABOR+OVERHEAD
100:REVENUE = RETAIL SALES + WHOLESALE SALES
MARGIN = 100: - CGS:
```

COMMENTS

Mainframe: *** FOR ALL COMMENTS**
Personal: **\ FOR COMMENTS TO BE PRINTED AS TITLES IN THE OUTPUT**
\\ FOR COMMENTS NOT TO BE PRINTED OUT

RAISING TO A POWER

Mainframe: **OUTPUT = XPOWERY(INPUT, 3)**
Personal: **OUTPUT = INPUT **3**

MATRIX REFERENCES

Mainframe: **X = MATRIX(SALES,5)**
Personal: **X = SALES[5]** or **X=SALES{5}**

USE OF COLUMN OPERATIONS

Mainframe: **COLUMN VARIANCE = C1 – C3**
Personal: REDEFINE VARIANCE = [1] – [3]

Note: REDEFINE in IFPS/Personal is much more powerful than the COLUMNS statement in Mainframe. Consult your *IFPS/Personal User's Manual* for details.

COLUMN NUMBER REFERENCE

Mainframe: In Mainframe IFPS, you have to write a separate model line such as defining:

```
N = PREVIOUS + 1
```

to be able to refer to the number of the current column.

Personal: Use the function COLNUM. This function gives you the number of the current column.For example:

```
X=COLNUM
OVERHEAD = IF COLNUM .LT.3 THEN COST*.80 ELSE COST*.90
```

INTERPOLATION FUNCTION

Mainframe: SALES = INTERPOLATION ON (DISCOUNT,0,2000,.20, 4000)
Personal: SALES = INTERPOLATION (DISCOUNT, 0,2000,.20,4000)

PLOTTING GRAPHS

Mainframe: Use PLO T options to create graphs
Personal: Create graphs directly from the PLOT menu within REPORT. You must have a graphics card in your personal computer to see plots on the screen. You must have graphics capability on your printer to obtain hard copy of graphs.

EDITING

Mainframe: Use either the built-in editing commands (Sec. 2.5 and Sec. 4.10) or the full page edit system in your mainframe.(Sec. 4.11)
Personal: Move out of Report mode and into Edit mode. Use the full screen editor.

RECORD

Mainframe: Use the RECORD command to create a file that contains your work.
Personal: Use the FILE capabilities within the REPORT menu.

WHAT IF, GOAL SEEK,ANALYZE

Mainframe: Use the WHAT IF, GOAL SEEK, and ANALYZE commands
Personal: Use the VIEW mode to create WHAT IF, GOAL SEEK, and ANALYZE

CREATING NEW VARIABLES IN WHAT IF

Mainframe: If you create a new variable name in a WHAT IF statement, you receive a warning NEW VARIABLE CREATED. This is often (although not always) an indication to you that you have misspelled something.
Personal: No warning given. Variable is added to your model.

WHAT IF CONTINUE

Mainframe: Preserves previous What IF
Personal: Not available. Use the CASE option within the WHAT IF in VIEW.

CATALOG

Mainframe: CATALOG gives you a list of the models and reports in a file.
Personal: Use the FILE options to obtain access to the list of models and reports that you have on a disk.

USING THE SAME NAME FOR TWO VARIABLES

Mainframe: You can use the same name on the left-hand side for two variables. If you do, IFPS uses the name closes to the reference to it. Although legal, this is not good practice.

Personal: Not allowed. All names on the left-hand must be unique.

LIST ING YOUR MODEL

Mainframe: When you are working on a model, LIST gives you a listing of the model. .

Personal: You can obtain a listing by:

a. using the lisT command in the Model menu.
b. going into FILES and using the lisT command.
c. using the Include: Model__Logic Option in the Report Menu.

INDEX